Business Ethics

SEVENTH EDITION

Business Ethics

William H. Shaw

San Jose State University

WADSWORTH
CENGAGE Learning™

Australia • Brazil • Japan • Korea • Mexico • Singapore • Spain • United Kingdom • United States

WADSWORTH
CENGAGE Learning™

Business Ethics, Seventh Edition
William H. Shaw

Sr. Sponsoring Editor, Philosophy and Religion: Joann Kozyrev

Development Editor: Ian Lague

Assistant Editor: Nathan Gamache

Editorial Assistant: Michaela Henry

Media Editor: Diane Akerman

Marketing Manager: Mark T. Haynes

Marketing Communications Manager: Laura Localio

Content Project Management: PrePressPMG

Art Director: Faith Brosnan

Production Technology Analyst: Jeff Joubert

Print Buyer: Linda Hsu

Rights Acquisition Account Manager, Text: Roberta Broyer

Permissions Account Manager, Images/Media: Mandy Groszko

Production Service: PrePressPMG

Cover Designer: Althea Chen

Cover Image: © Sven Hagolani/Getty Images

Compositor: PrePressPMG

For product information and technology assistance, contact us at
Cengage Learning Customer & Sales Support, 1-800-354-9706

For permission to use material from this text or product, submit all requests online at **www.cengage.com/permissions.** Further permissions questions can be emailed to **permissionrequest@cengage.com.**

Library of Congress Control Number: 2009939799

Student Edition:

ISBN-13: 978-0-495-80876-3

ISBN-10: 0-495-80876-8

Wadsworth
20 Channel Center Street
Boston, MA 02210
USA

Cengage Learning is a leading provider of customized learning solutions with office locations around the globe, including Singapore, the United Kingdom, Australia, Mexico, Brazil and Japan. Locate your local office at **international.cengage.com/region**

Cengage Learning products are represented in Canada by Nelson Education, Ltd.

For your course and learning solutions, visit **www.cengage.com**

Purchase any of our products at your local college store or at our preferred online store **www.CengageBrain.com.**

Printed in the United States of America
2 3 4 5 6 7 14 13 12 11 10

CONTENTS

v

PART **3**   **Business and Society   207**

6   **Consumers**   209

7   **The Environment**   259

PART **4**   **The Organization and the People in It   299**

8   **The Workplace (1): Basic Issues**   301

PREFACE

It is difficult to imagine an area of study that has greater importance to society or greater relevance to students than business ethics. As this book enters its seventh edition, business ethics has become a well-established academic subject. Most colleges and universities offer courses in it, and scholarly interest continues to grow.

Yet some people still scoff at the idea of business ethics, jesting that the very concept is an oxymoron. To be sure, recent years have seen the newspapers filled with lurid stories of corporate misconduct and felonious behavior by individual businesspeople and many suspect that what the newspapers report represents only the proverbial tip of the iceberg. However, these reports should prompt a reflective person not to make fun of business ethics but rather to think more deeply about the nature and purpose of business in our society and about the ethical choices individuals must inevitably make in their business and professional lives.

Business ethics has various focal points and is concerned with a wide range of issues. It also has an interdisciplinary character. Questions of economic policy and business practice intertwine with issues in politics, sociology, and organizational theory. Although business ethics remains anchored in philosophy, even here abstract questions in normative ethics and political philosophy mingle with analysis of practical problems and concrete moral dilemmas. Furthermore, business ethics is not just an academic study but also an invitation to reflect on our own values and on our own responses to the hard moral choices that the world of business can pose.

GOALS AND ORGANIZATION OF THE BOOK

The purpose of this text is fourfold: to expose students to the important moral issues that arise in various business contexts; to provide students with an understanding of the moral, social, and economic environments within which those problems occur; to introduce students to the ethical concepts that are relevant for resolving those problems; and to assist students in developing the necessary reasoning and analytical skills for doing so. Although the book's primary emphasis is on business, its scope extends to related moral issues in other organizational and professional contexts.

Business Ethics has four parts. Part One, "Moral Philosophy and Business," discusses the nature of morality and presents the main theories of normative ethics and the leading approaches to questions of economic justice. Part Two, "American Business and Its Basis," examines the institutional foundations of business, focusing on capitalism as an economic system and the nature and role of corporations in our society. Part Three, "Business and Society," concerns moral problems involving business, consumers, and the natural environment. Part Four, "The Organization and the People in It," identifies a variety of ethical issues and moral challenges that arise out of the interplay of employers and employees within an organization, including the problem of discrimination.

CHANGES IN THIS EDITION

The four parts of the book have been reordered, but otherwise instructors who have used the previous edition will find the organization and general content of the book familiar. It retains the design and pedagogical features introduced in the previous edition and intended to improve student comprehension and enhance learning. Key passages in the text are summarized in the margin. Additional numbered summaries, also in the margin, provide readers with a continuous review of major ideas, and at the end of each chapter, important terms and concepts, as well as points for students to review, are listed in a "Study Corner" section. The text itself has been thoroughly revised. I have updated and reorganized material throughout the book and tried to enhance the clarity of its discussions and the accuracy of its treatment of both philosophical and empirical issues. At all times my goal has been to provide a textbook that students will find clear, understandable, and engaging.

Although I do not segregate them into a separate chapter, the moral challenges facing business in today's globalized world economy are well represented in *Business Ethics*. Chapter 1 discusses ethical relativism, Chapter 4 outsourcing and globalization, and Chapter 10 overseas bribery and the Foreign Corrupt Practices Act; and there are international examples or comparisons in other chapters. Moreover, almost all the basic issues discussed in the book (such as corporate responsibility, the nature of moral reasoning, and the value of the natural world—to name just three) remain as crucial as ever to moral decision making in business, whether it takes place at home or in an international context. In addition, cases 1.1, 2.3, 5.1, 5.2, 6.4, 7.2, and 10.4 deal explicitly with moral issues arising in today's global economic system.

Forty-two case studies now supplement the main text. Five of these are new to this edition; many of the others have been revised and updated. The case studies vary in kind and in length, but they are designed to enable instructors and students to pursue further some of the issues discussed in the text and to analyze them in more specific contexts. The case studies should provide a lively springboard for classroom discussions and the application of ethical concepts.

WAYS OF USING THE BOOK

A course in business ethics can be taught in a variety of ways. Some instructors prefer to treat the foundational questions of ethical theory thoroughly before moving on to particular moral problems; others reverse this priority. Still other instructors frame their courses around the question of economic justice, the analysis of capitalism, or the debate over corporate social responsibility. Some instructors stress individual moral decision making, others social and economic policy.

Business Ethics permits teachers great flexibility in how they organize their courses. A wide range of theoretical and applied issues are discussed; and the individual chapters, the major sections within them, and the case studies are to a surprising extent self-contained. Instructors can thus teach the book in whatever order they choose, and they can easily skip or touch lightly on some topics in order to concentrate on others without loss of coherence.

ACKNOWLEDGMENTS

I wish to acknowledge my great debt to the many people whose ideas and writing have influenced me over the years. Philosophy is widely recognized to involve a process of ongoing dialogue. This is nowhere more evident than in the writing to textbooks, whose authors can rarely claim that the ideas being synthesized, organized, and presented are theirs alone. Without my colleagues, without my students and without a larger philosophical community concerned with business and ethics, this book would not have been possible.

I particularly want to acknowledge my debt to Vincent Barry. Readers familiars with our textbook and reader *Moral Issues in Business** will realize the extent to which I have drawn on material from that work. *Business Ethics* is, in effect, a revised and updated version of the textbook portion of that collaborative work, and I am very grateful to Vince for permitting me to use our joint work here.

The Wadsworth/Cengage Learning team and I would like to thank the following individuals for their valuable input and contributions as members of the technology and media advisory board of this book

Barrie Peterson, Fairleigh Dickinson University

Krishna Mallick, Salem State College

Robert Barrett, University of La Verne

David Bauman, Washington University in St. Louis

Ralph Braithwaite, University of Hartford

Mike Campo, Regis University

Caleb Clanton, Pepperdine University

Daniel Collins-Cavanaugh, Prince George's Community College

Kevin Dunagan, College of DuPage

Margaret Garcia, Regis University

Robert Halliman, Austin Peay State University

Lisa Knowles, St. Thomas University

Dale Miller, Old Dominion University

---

* William H. Shaw and Vincent Barry, *Moral Issues in Business,* 11th ed. (Belmont, Calif.: Wadsworth, 2010).

PART 1

Moral Philosophy and Business

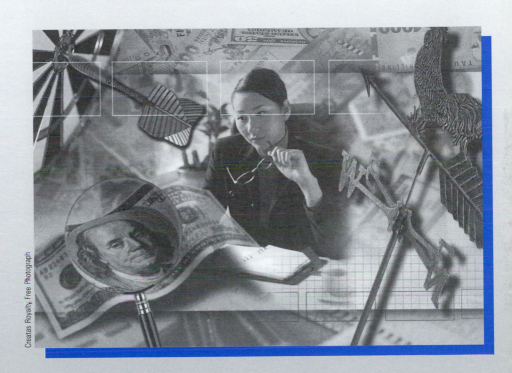

Creatas Royalty Free Photograph

CHAPTER 1

The Nature of Morality

Greg Smith/Corbis

1400 Smith Street

3

INTRODUCTION

Sometimes the rich and mighty fall. Take Kenneth Lay, for example. Convicted by a jury in 2006 of conspiracy and multiple counts of fraud, he had been chairman and CEO of Enron until that once mighty company nose-dived and crashed. Founded in the 1980s, Enron soon became a dominant player in the field of energy trading, growing rapidly to become America's seventh-biggest company. Wall Street loves growth, and Enron was its darling, admired as dynamic, innovative, and—of course—profitable. The fact that nobody could quite understand exactly how the company made its money didn't hurt either. In 1998 the value of Enron stock increased 40 percent. The next year it shot up 58 percent, and in 2000 it went up an unbelievable 89 percent.

After *Fortune* magazine voted it "the most innovative company of the year" in 2000, Enron proudly took to calling itself not just "the world's leading energy company" but also "the world's leading company." But when Enron was forced to declare bankruptcy in December 2001—at the time the largest Chapter 11 filing in U.S. history—the world learned that its legendary financial prowess was illusory and the company's success built on the sands of hype. And the hype continued to the end. Even with the company's financial demise fast approaching, Kenneth Lay was still recommending the company's stock to its employees—at the same time that he and other executives were cashing in their shares and bailing out.

Enron's crash cost the retirement accounts of its employees more than a billion dollars as the company's stock fell from the stratosphere to only a few pennies a share. Outside investors lost even more. The reason Enron's collapse caught investors by surprise—the company's market value was $28 billion just two months before its bankruptcy—was that Enron had always made its financial records and accounts as opaque as possible. It did this by creating a Byzantine financial structure of off-balance-sheet special-purpose entities—reportedly as many as 9,000—that were supposed to be separate and independent from the main company. Enron's board of directors condoned these and other dubious accounting practices and voted twice to permit executives to pursue personal interests that ran contrary to those of the company. When Enron was obliged to redo its financial statements for 1997–2000, its profits dropped $600 million and its debts increased $630 million.

Still, Enron's financial auditors should have spotted these and other problems. After all, the shell game Enron was playing is an old one, and months before the company ran aground, Enron Vice President Sherron Watkins had warned Lay that the company could soon "implode in a wave of accounting scandals." Yet both Arthur Andersen, Enron's longtime outside auditing firm, and Vinson & Elkins, the company's law firm, had routinely put together and signed off on various dubious financial deals, and in doing so made large profits for themselves. Arthur Andersen, in particular, was supposed to make sure that the company's public records reflected financial reality, but Andersen was more worried about its auditing and consulting fees than about its fiduciary responsibilities. Even worse, when the scandal began to break, a partner at Andersen organized the shredding of incriminating Enron documents before investigators could lay their hands on them. As a result, the eighty-nine-year-old accounting firm was convicted of obstructing justice. The Supreme Court later overturned that verdict on a technicality, but by then Arthur Andersen had already been driven out of business. (The year before Enron went under, by the way, the Securities and Exchange Commission fined Andersen $7 million for approving misleading accounts at Waste Management, and it also had to pay $110 million to settle a lawsuit for auditing work it did for Sunbeam before it, too, filed for bankruptcy. And when massive accounting fraud was later uncovered at WorldCom, it came out that the company's auditor was—you guessed it—Arthur Andersen.)

Enron's fall also revealed the conflicts of interest that threaten the credibility of Wall Street's analysts—analysts who are compensated according to their ability to bring in and support investment banking deals. Enron was known in the industry as the "deal machine" because it generated so much investment banking business—limited partnerships, loans, and derivatives. That may explain why, only days before Enron filed bankruptcy, just two of the sixteen Wall Street analysts who covered the company recommended that clients sell the stock. The large banks that

Enron did business with played a corrupt role, too, by helping manufacture its fraudulent financial statements. (Subsequent lawsuits have forced them to cough up some of their profits: Citibank, for example, had to pay Enron's victimized shareholders $2 billion.) But the rot didn't stop there. Enron and Andersen enjoyed extensive political connections, which had helped over the years to ensure the passage of a series of deregulatory measures favorable to the energy company. Of the 248 members of Congress sitting on the eleven House and Senate committees charged with investigating Enron's collapse, 212 had received money from Enron or its accounting firm.[1]

Stories of business corruption and of greed and wrongdoing in high places have always fascinated the popular press, and media interest in business ethics has never been higher. But one should not be misled by the headlines and news reports. Not all moral issues in business involve giant corporations and their well-heeled executives, and few cases of business ethics are widely publicized. The vast majority of them involve the mundane, uncelebrated moral challenges that working men and women meet daily.

Although the financial shenanigans at Enron were complicated, once their basic outline is sketched, the wrongdoing is pretty easy to see: deception, dishonesty, fraud, disregarding one's professional responsibilities, and unfairly injuring others for one's own gain. But many of the moral issues that arise in business are complex and difficult to answer. For example:

> Is passing a personality or honesty test a justifiable preemployment condition? Are drug tests? What rights do employees have on the job? How should business respond to employees who have AIDS? What, if anything, must it do to improve work conditions?

> Should manufacturers reveal all product defects? At what point does acceptable exaggeration become lying about a product or a service? When does aggressive marketing become consumer manipulation?

> What are businesses' environmental responsibilities? Is a corporation obliged to help combat social problems such as poverty, pollution, and urban decay? Must business fight sexism and racism? How far must it go to ensure equality of opportunity? How should organizations respond to the problem of sexual harassment?

> May employees ever use their positions inside an organization to advance their own interests? Is insider trading or the use of privileged information immoral? How much loyalty do workers owe their companies? What say should a business have over the off-the-job activities of its employees?

What obligations does a worker have to outside parties, such as customers, competitors, or society generally? When, if ever, is an employee morally required to blow the whistle?

These questions typify business issues with moral significance. The answers we give to them are determined, in large part, by our moral standards—that is, by the moral principles and values we accept. What moral standards are, where they come from, and how they can be assessed are some of the concerns of this opening chapter. In particular, you will encounter the following topics:

1. The nature, scope, and purpose of business ethics
2. The distinguishing features of morality and how it differs from etiquette, law, and professional codes of conduct
3. The relationship between morality and religion
4. The doctrine of ethical relativism and its difficulties
5. What it means to have moral principles, the nature of conscience, and the relationship between morality and self-interest
6. The place of values and ideals in a person's life
7. The social and psychological factors that sometimes jeopardize an individual's integrity
8. The characteristics of sound moral reasoning

ETHICS

Ethics (or moral philosophy) is a broad field of inquiry that addresses a fundamental query that all of us, at least from time to time, inevitably think about—namely, How should I live my life? That question, of course, leads to others, such as, What sort of person should I strive to be? What values are important? What standards or principles should I live by? Exploring these issues immerses one in the study of right and wrong. Among other things, moral philosophers and others who think seriously about ethics want to understand the nature of morality, the meaning of its basic concepts, the characteristics of good moral reasoning, how moral judgments can be justified, and, of course, the principles or properties that distinguish right actions from wrong actions. Thus, ethics deals with individual character and with the moral rules that govern and limit our conduct. It investigates questions of right and wrong, fairness and unfairness, good and bad, duty and obligation, and justice and injustice, as well as moral responsibility and the values that should guide our actions.

You sometimes hear it said that there's a difference between a person's ethics and his or her morals. This can be confusing because what some people mean by saying that something is a matter of ethics (as opposed to morals) is

Summary 1.1
Ethics deals with individual character and the moral rules that govern and limit our conduct. It investigates questions of right and wrong, duty and obligation, and moral responsibility.

often what other people mean by saying that it is a matter of morals (and not ethics). In fact, however, most people (and most philosophers) see no real distinction between a person's "morals" and a person's "ethics." And almost everyone uses "ethical" and "moral" interchangeably to describe people we consider good and actions we consider right, and "unethical" and "immoral" to designate bad people and wrong actions. This book follows that common usage.

Business and Organizational Ethics

The primary focus of this book is ethics as it applies to business. **Business ethics** is the study of what constitutes right and wrong, or good and bad, human conduct in a business context. For example, would it be right for a store manager to break a promise to a customer and sell some hard-to-find merchandise to someone else, whose need for it is greater? What, if anything, should a moral employee do when his or her superiors refuse to look into apparent wrongdoing in a branch office? If you innocently came across secret information about a competitor, would it be permissible for you to use it for your own advantage?

Recent business scandals have renewed the interest of business leaders, academics, and society at large in ethics. For example, the Association to Advance Collegiate Schools of Business, which comprises all the top business schools, has introduced new rules on including ethics in their curricula, and the Business Roundtable recently unveiled an initiative to train the nation's CEOs in the finer points of ethics. But an appreciation of the importance of ethics for a healthy society and a concern, in particular, for what constitutes ethical conduct in business go back to ancient times. The Roman philosopher Cicero (106–43 B.C.E.), for instance, discussed the example, much debated at the time, of an honest merchant from Alexandria who brings a large stock of wheat to Rhodes where there is a food shortage. On his way there, he has seen other traders setting sail for Rhodes with substantial cargos of grain. Should he tell the people of Rhodes that more wheat is on the way, or say nothing and sell at the best price he can? Some ancient ethicists argued that although the merchant must declare defects in his wares as required by law, as a vendor he is free—provided he tells no untruths—to sell his goods as profitably as he can. Others, including Cicero, argued to the contrary that all the facts must be revealed and that buyers must be as fully informed as sellers.[2]

"Business" and "businessperson" are broad terms. "Business" may denote a corner hot-dog stand or a multinational corporation that operates in several countries. A "businessperson" may be a gardener in business for herself or a company president responsible for thousands of workers and millions of shareholder dollars. Accordingly, the word **business** will be used here simply to mean any organization whose objective is to provide goods or services for profit. **Businesspeople** are those who participate in planning, organizing, or directing the work of business.

But this book takes a broader view as well because it is concerned with moral issues that arise anywhere that employers and employees come together.

Summary 1.2
Business ethics is the study of what constitutes right and wrong (or good and bad) human conduct in a business context. Closely related moral questions arise in other organizational contexts.

Thus, it addresses organizational ethics as well as business ethics. An *organization* is a group of people working together to achieve a common purpose. The purpose may be to offer a product or a service primarily for profit, as in business. But the purpose also could be health care, as in medical organizations; public safety and order, as in law-enforcement organizations; education, as in academic organizations; and so on. The cases and illustrations presented in this book deal with moral issues and dilemmas in both business and nonbusiness organizational settings.

People occasionally poke fun at the idea of business ethics, declaring that the term is a contradiction or that business has no ethics. Such people take themselves to be worldly and realistic. They think they have a down-to-earth idea of how things really work. In fact, despite its pretense of sophistication, their attitude is embarrassingly naive. It shows that they have little grasp of the nature of ethics and only a superficial understanding of the real world of business. After you read this book, you will perhaps see the truth of this judgment.

MORAL VERSUS NONMORAL STANDARDS

Moral questions differ from other kinds of questions. Whether your office computer can copy a pirated DVD is a factual question. By contrast, whether you should copy the DVD is a moral question. When we answer a moral question or make a moral judgment, we appeal to moral standards. These standards differ from other kinds of standards.

Wearing shorts and a T-shirt to a formal dinner party is boorish behavior. Murdering the King's English with double negatives violates the basic conventions of proper language usage. Photographing the finish of a horse race with low-speed film is poor photographic technique. In each case a standard is violated—fashion, grammatical, technical—but the violation does not pose a serious threat to human well-being.

Moral standards concern behavior that seriously affects human well-being.

Moral standards are different because they concern behavior that is of serious consequence to human welfare, that can profoundly injure or benefit people.[3] The conventional moral norms against lying, stealing, and killing deal with actions that can hurt people. And the moral principle that human beings should be treated with dignity and respect uplifts the human personality. Whether products are healthful or harmful, work conditions safe or dangerous, personnel procedures biased or fair, privacy respected or invaded are also matters that seriously affect human well-being. The standards that govern our conduct in these matters are moral standards.

Moral standards take priority over other standards.

A second characteristic follows from the first. Moral standards take priority over other standards, including self-interest. Something that morality condemns—for instance, the burglary of your neighbor's home—cannot be justified on the nonmoral grounds that it would be a thrill to do it or that it would pay off handsomely. We take moral standards to be more important than other considerations in guiding our actions.

The soundness of moral standards depends on the adequacy of the reasons that support them.

A third characteristic of moral standards is that their soundness depends on the adequacy of the reasons that support or justify them. For the most part, fashion standards are set by clothing designers, merchandisers, and consumers; grammatical standards by grammarians and students of language; technical standards by practitioners and experts in the field. Legislators make laws, boards of directors make organizational policy, and licensing boards establish standards for professionals. In those cases, some authoritative body is the ultimate validating source of the standards and thus can change the standards if it wishes. Moral standards are not made by such bodies. Their validity depends not on authoritative fiat but rather on the quality of the arguments or the reasoning that supports them. Exactly what constitutes adequate grounds or justification for a moral standard is a debated question, which, as we shall see in Chapter 2, underlies disagreement among philosophers over which specific moral principles are best.

Although these three characteristics set moral standards apart from other standards, it is useful to discuss more specifically how morality differs from three things with which it is sometimes confused: etiquette, law, and professional codes of ethics.

Morality and Etiquette

Summary 1.3
We appeal to moral standards when we answer a moral question or make a moral judgment. Three characteristics of moral standards distinguish them from other kinds of standards.

Etiquette refers to the norms of correct conduct in polite society or, more generally, to any special code of social behavior or courtesy. In our society, for example, it is considered bad etiquette to chew with your mouth open or to pick your nose when talking to someone; it is considered good etiquette to say "please" when requesting and "thank you" when receiving and to hold a door open for someone entering immediately behind you. Good business etiquette typically calls for writing follow-up letters after meetings, returning phone calls, and dressing appropriately. It is commonplace to judge people's manners as "good" or "bad" and the conduct that reflects them as "right" or "wrong." "Good," "bad," "right," and "wrong" here simply mean socially appropriate or socially inappropriate. In these contexts, such words express judgments about manners, not about ethics.

The rules of etiquette are prescriptions for socially acceptable behavior. If you violate them, you're likely to be considered ill-mannered, impolite, or even uncivilized, but not necessarily immoral. If you want to fit in, get along with others, and be thought well of by them, you should observe the common rules of politeness or etiquette. However, what's considered correct or polite conduct—for example, when greeting an elderly person, when using your knife and fork, or when determining how close to stand to someone you're conversing with—can change over time and vary from society to society.

Although rules of etiquette are generally nonmoral in character, violations of those rules can have moral implications. For example, the male boss who refers to female subordinates as "honey" or "doll" shows bad manners. If such epithets diminish the worth of female employees or perpetuate sexism, then they also raise moral issues concerning equal treatment and denial of dignity to human beings. More generally, rude or impolite conduct can be offensive, and it may sometimes fail to show the respect for other persons that morality requires of us. For this reason, it is important to exercise care, in business situations and elsewhere, when dealing with unfamiliar customs or people from a different culture.

Scrupulous observance of rules of etiquette, however, does not make a person moral. In fact, it can sometimes camouflage moral issues. In some parts of the United States fifty or so years ago, it was considered bad manners for blacks and whites to eat together. Those who obeyed this convention and were thus judged well-mannered certainly had no grounds for feeling moral. The only way to dramatize the injustice underlying this practice was to violate the rule and be judged bad-mannered. For those in the civil rights movement of the 1960s, being considered uncouth was a small price to pay for exposing the unequal treatment and human degradation that underlay this rule of etiquette.

Morality and Law

Before distinguishing between morality and law, let's examine the term *law*. Basically, there are four kinds of law: statutes, regulations, common law, and constitutional law.

Statutes are laws enacted by legislative bodies. The law that defines and prohibits theft is a statute. Congress and state legislatures enact statutes. (Laws enacted by local governing bodies such as city councils usually are termed *ordinances*.) Statutes make up a large part of the law and are what many of us mean when we speak of "laws."

Limited in their time and knowledge, legislatures often set up boards or agencies whose functions include issuing detailed regulations covering certain kinds of conduct—**administrative regulations**. For example, state legislatures establish licensing boards to formulate regulations for the licensing of physicians and nurses. As long as these regulations do not exceed the board's statutory powers and do not conflict with other kinds of law, they are legally binding.

Common law refers to the body of judge-made law that first developed in the English-speaking world centuries ago when there were few statutes. Courts frequently wrote opinions explaining the bases of their decisions in specific cases, including the legal principles those decisions rested on. Each of these opinions became a precedent for later decisions in similar cases. The massive body of precedents and legal principles that accumulated over the years is collectively referred to as "common law." Like administrative regulations, common law is valid if it harmonizes with statutory law and with still another kind: constitutional law.

Constitutional law refers to court rulings on the requirements of the Constitution and the constitutionality of legislation. The U.S. Constitution empowers the courts to decide whether laws are compatible with the Constitution. State courts may also rule on the constitutionality of state laws under state constitutions. Although the courts cannot make laws, they have far-reaching powers to rule on the constitutionality of laws and to declare them invalid. In the United States, the Supreme Court has the greatest judiciary power and rules on an array of cases, some of which bear directly on the study of business ethics.

Legality should not be
confused with morality.
Breaking the law isn't
always or necessarily
immoral, and the legality
of an action doesn't
guarantee its morality.

People sometimes confuse legality and morality, but they are different things. On one hand, breaking the law is not always or necessarily immoral. On the other hand, the legality of an action does not guarantee that it is morally right. Let's consider these points further.

1. **An action can be illegal but morally right.** For example, helping a Jewish family to hide from the Nazis was against German law in 1939, but it would have been a morally admirable thing to have done. Of course, the Nazi regime was vicious and evil. By contrast, in a democratic society with a basically just legal order, the fact that something is illegal provides a moral consideration against doing it. For example, one moral reason for not burning trash in your backyard is that it violates an ordinance that your community has voted in favor of. Some philosophers believe that sometimes the illegality of an action can make it morally wrong, even if the action would otherwise have been morally acceptable. But even if they are right about that, the fact that something is illegal does not trump all other moral considerations. Nonconformity to law is not always immoral, even in a democratic society. There can be circumstances where, all things considered, violating the law is morally permissible, perhaps even morally required.

    Probably no one in the modern era has expressed this point more eloquently than Dr. Martin Luther King, Jr. Confined in the Birmingham, Alabama, city jail on charges of parading without a permit, King penned his now famous "Letter from Birmingham Jail" to eight of his fellow clergymen who had published a statement attacking King's unauthorized protest of racial segregation as unwise and untimely. King wrote:

    > All segregation statutes are unjust because segregation distorts the soul and damages the personality. It gives the segregator a false sense of superiority and the segregated a false sense of inferiority. Segregation, to use the terminology of the Jewish philosopher Martin Buber, substitutes an "I-it" relationship for an "I-thou" relationship and ends up relegating persons to the status of things. Hence segregation is not only politically, economically, and sociologically unsound, it is morally wrong and sinful.... Thus it is that I can urge men to obey the 1954 decision of the Supreme Court,* for it is morally right; and I can urge them to disobey segregation ordinances, for they are morally wrong.[4]

2. **An action that is legal can be morally wrong.** For example, it may have been perfectly legal for the chairman of a profitable company to lay off 125 workers and use three-quarters of the money saved to boost his pay and that of the company's other top managers,[5] but the morality of his doing so is open to debate.

    Or, to take another example, suppose that you're driving to work one day and see an accident victim sitting on the side of the road, clearly in shock and needing medical assistance. Because you know first aid and

---

*In *Brown v. Board of Education of Topeka* (1954), the Supreme Court struck down the half-century-old "separate but equal doctrine," which permitted racially segregated schools as long as comparable quality was maintained.

are in no great hurry to get to your destination, you could easily stop and assist the person. Legally speaking, though, you are not obligated to stop and render aid. Under common law, the prudent thing would be to drive on, because by stopping you would bind yourself to use reasonable care and thus incur legal liability if you fail to do so and the victim thereby suffers injury. Many states have enacted so-called Good Samaritan laws to provide immunity from damages to those rendering aid (except for gross negligence or serious misconduct). But in most states the law does not oblige people to give such aid or even to call an ambulance. Moral theorists would agree, however, that if you sped away without rendering aid or even calling for help, your action might be perfectly legal but would be morally suspect. Regardless of the law, such conduct would almost certainly be wrong.

> **Summary 1.4**
> Morality must be distinguished from etiquette (rules for well-mannered behavior), from law (statutes, regulations, common law, and constitutional law), and from professional codes of ethics (the special rules governing the members of a profession).

What then may we say about the relationship between law and morality? To a significant extent, law codifies a society's customs, ideals, norms, and moral values. Changes in law tend to reflect changes in what a society takes to be right and wrong, but sometimes changes in the law can alter people's ideas about the rightness or wrongness of conduct. However, even if a society's laws are sensible and morally sound, it is a mistake to see them as sufficient to establish the moral standards that should guide us. The law cannot cover all possible human conduct, and in many situations it is too blunt an instrument to provide adequate moral guidance. The law generally prohibits egregious affronts to a society's moral standards and in that sense is the "floor" of moral conduct, but breaches of moral conduct can slip through cracks in that floor.

Professional Codes

Somewhere between etiquette and law lie **professional codes of ethics**. These are the rules that are supposed to govern the conduct of members of a given profession. Generally speaking, the members of a profession are understood to have agreed to abide by those rules as a condition of their engaging in that profession. Violation of a professional code may result in the disapproval of one's professional peers and, in serious cases, loss of one's license to practice that profession. Sometimes these codes are unwritten and are part of the common understanding of members of a particular profession—for example, that professors should not date their students. In other instances, these codes or portions of them may be written down by an authoritative body so they may be better taught and more efficiently enforced.

These written rules are sometimes so vague and general as to be of little value, and often they amount to little more than self-promotion by the professional organization. The same is frequently true when industries or corporations publish statements of their ethical standards. In other cases—for example, with attorneys—professional codes can be very specific and detailed. It is difficult to generalize about the content of professional codes of ethics, however, because they frequently involve a mix of purely moral rules (for example, client confidentiality), of professional etiquette (for example, the billing of services to other professionals), and of restrictions intended to benefit the group's economic interests (for example, limitations on price competition).

Given their nature, professional codes of ethics are neither a complete nor a completely reliable guide to one's moral obligations. Not all the rules of a professional code are purely moral in character, and even when they are, the fact that a rule is officially enshrined as part of the code of a profession does not guarantee that it is a sound moral principle. As a professional, you must take seriously the injunctions of your profession, but you still have the responsibility to critically assess those rules for yourself.

Regarding those parts of the code that concern etiquette or financial matters, bear in mind that by joining a profession you are probably agreeing, explicitly or implicitly, to abide by those standards. Assuming that those rules don't require morally impermissible conduct, then consenting to them gives you some moral obligation to follow them. In addition, for many, living up to the standards of one's chosen profession is an important source of personal satisfaction. Still, you must be alert to situations in which professional standards or customary professional practice conflicts with ordinary ethical requirements. Adherence to a professional code does not exempt your conduct from scrutiny from the broader perspective of morality.

Where Do Moral Standards Come From?

So far you have seen how moral standards are different from various non-moral standards, but you probably wonder about the source of those moral standards. Most, if not all, people have certain moral principles or a moral code that they explicitly or implicitly accept. Because the moral principles of different people in the same society overlap, at least in part, we can also talk about the moral code of a society, meaning the moral standards shared by its members. How do we come to have certain moral principles and not others? Obviously, many things influence what moral principles we accept: our early upbringing, the behavior of those around us, the explicit and implicit standards of our culture, our own experiences, and our critical reflections on those experiences.

For philosophers, though, the central question is not how we came to have the particular principles we have. The philosophical issue is whether the principles we have can be justified. Do we simply take for granted the values of those around us? Or, like Martin Luther King, Jr., are we able to think independently about moral matters? By analogy, we pick up our non-moral beliefs from all sorts of sources: books, conversations with friends, movies, various experiences we've had. What is important, however, is not how we actually got the beliefs we have, but whether or to what extent those beliefs—for example, that women are more emotional than men or that telekinesis is possible—can withstand critical scrutiny. Likewise, ethical theories attempt to justify moral standards and ethical beliefs. The next chapter examines some of the major theories of normative ethics. It looks at what some of the major thinkers in human history have argued are the best-justified standards of right and wrong.

But first we need to consider the relationship between morality and religion on the one hand and between morality and society on the other. Some people maintain that morality just boils down to religion. Others have argued for the doctrine of *ethical relativism,* which says that right and wrong are only a function of what a particular society takes to be right and wrong. Both those views are mistaken.

RELIGION AND MORALITY

Any religion provides its believers with a worldview, part of which involves certain moral instructions, values, and commitments. The Jewish and Christian traditions, to name just two, offer a view of humans as unique products of a divine intervention that has endowed them with consciousness and an ability to love. Both these traditions posit creatures who stand midway between nature and spirit. On one hand, we are finite and bound to earth, not only capable of wrongdoing but also born morally flawed (original sin). On the other, we can transcend nature and realize infinite possibilities.

Primarily because of the influence of Western religion, many Americans and others view themselves as beings with a supernatural destiny, as possessing a life after death, as being immortal. One's purpose in life is found in serving and loving God. For the Christian, the way to serve and love God is by emulating the life of Jesus of Nazareth. In the life of Jesus, Christians find an expression of the highest virtue—love. They love when they perform selfless acts, develop a keen social conscience, and realize that human beings are creatures of God and therefore intrinsically worthwhile. For the Jew, one serves and loves God chiefly through expressions of justice and righteousness. Jews also develop a sense of honor derived from a commitment to truth, humility, fidelity, and kindness. This commitment hones their sense of responsibility to family and community.

Religion, then, involves not only a formal system of worship but also prescriptions for social relationships. One example is the mandate "Do unto others as you would have them do unto you." Termed the "Golden Rule," this injunction represents one of humankind's highest moral ideals and can be found in essence in all the great religions of the world:

> Good people proceed while considering that what is best for others is best for themselves. (*Hitopadesa,* Hinduism)
>
> Thou shalt love thy neighbor as thyself. (*Leviticus* 19:18, Judaism)
>
> Therefore all things whatsoever ye would that men should do to you, do ye even so to them. (*Matthew* 7:12, Christianity)
>
> Hurt not others with that which pains yourself. (*Udanavarga* 5:18, Buddhism)
>
> What you do not want done to yourself, do not do to others. (*Analects* 15:23, Confucianism)
>
> No one of you is a believer until he loves for his brother what he loves for himself. (*Traditions,* Islam)

Although inspiring, such religious ideals are very general and can be difficult to translate into precise policy injunctions. Religious bodies, nevertheless, occasionally articulate positions on more specific political, educational, economic, and medical issues, which help mold public opinion on matters as diverse as abortion, the environment, national defense, and the ethics of scientific research. Roman Catholicism, in particular, has a rich history of formally applying its core values to the moral aspects of industrial relations and economic life. Pope John Paul II's encyclical *Centesimus Annus*, the National Conference of Catholic Bishops' pastoral letter *Economic Justice for All* on Catholic social teaching and the U.S. economy, and the Pontifical Council for Social Communication's reports on advertising and on ethics and the Internet stand in that tradition—as does Pope Benedict XVI's 2007 critique of the growing trend for companies to rely on short-term job contracts, which in his view undermine the stability of society and prevent young people from building families.[6]

Morality Needn't Rest on Religion

The idea that morality must be based on religion can be interpreted in three different ways, none of which is very plausible.

Many people believe that morality must be based on religion, either in the sense that without religion people would have no incentive to be moral or in the sense that only religion can provide moral guidance. Others contend that morality is based on the commands of God. None of these claims is convincing.

First, although a desire to avoid hell and to go to heaven may prompt some of us to act morally, this is not the only reason or even the most common reason that people behave morally. Often we act morally out of habit or just because that is the kind of person we are. It would simply not occur to most of us to swipe an elderly lady's purse, and if the idea did occur to us, we wouldn't do it because such an act simply doesn't fit with our personal standards or with our concept of ourselves. We are often motivated to do what is morally right out of concern for others or just because it is right. In addition, the approval of our peers, the need to appease our conscience, and the desire to avoid earthly punishment may all motivate us to act morally. Furthermore, atheists generally live lives as moral and upright as those of believers.

Second, the moral instructions of the world's great religions are general and imprecise: They do not relieve us of the necessity to engage in moral reasoning ourselves. For example, the Bible says, "Thou shall not kill." Yet Christians disagree among themselves over the morality of fighting in wars, of capital punishment, of killing in self-defense, of slaughtering animals, of abortion and euthanasia, and of allowing foreigners to die from famine because we have not provided them with as much food as we might have. The Bible does not provide unambiguous solutions to these moral problems, so even believers must engage in moral philosophy if they are to have intelligent answers. Nevertheless, there are lots of reasons for believing that, say, a cold-blooded murder motivated by greed is immoral. One need not believe in a religion to figure that out.

Third, although some theologians have advocated the **divine command theory**—that if something is wrong (like killing an innocent person for fun), then the only reason it is wrong is that God commands us not to do it—many theologians and certainly most philosophers would reject this view. They would contend that if God commands human beings not to do something, such as commit rape, it is because God sees that rape is wrong, but it is not God's forbidding rape that makes it wrong. The fact that rape is wrong is independent of God's decrees.

Most believers think not only that God gives us moral instructions or rules but also that God has moral reasons for giving them to us. According to the divine command theory, this would make no sense. In this view, there is no reason that something is right or wrong, other than the fact that it is God's will. All believers, of course, believe that God is good and that God commands us to do what is right and forbids us to do what is wrong. But this doesn't mean, say critics of the divine command theory, that it is God's saying so that makes a thing wrong, any more than it is your mother's telling you not to steal that makes it wrong to steal.

All this is simply to argue that morality is not necessarily based on religion in any of these three senses. That religion influences the moral standards and values of most of us is beyond doubt. But given that religions differ in their moral beliefs and that even members of the same faith often disagree on moral matters, you cannot justify a moral judgment simply by appealing to religion—for that will only persuade those who already agree with your particular interpretation of your particular religion. Besides, most religions hold that human reason is capable of understanding what is right and wrong, so it is human reason to which you will have to appeal in order to support your ethical principles and judgments.

Summary 1.5
Morality is not necessarily based on religion. Although we draw our moral beliefs from many sources, for philosophers the issue is whether those beliefs can be justified.

ETHICAL RELATIVISM

Some people do not believe that morality boils down to religion but rather that it is merely a function of what a particular society happens to believe. This view is called **ethical relativism**, the theory that what is right is determined by what a culture or society says is right. What is right in one place may be wrong in another, because the only criterion for distinguishing right from wrong—and so the only ethical standard for judging an action—is the moral system of the society in which the act occurs.

Abortion, for example, is condemned as immoral in Catholic Ireland but is practiced as a morally neutral form of birth control in Japan. According to the ethical relativist, then, abortion is wrong in Ireland but morally permissible in Japan. The relativist is not saying merely that the Irish believe abortion is abominable and the Japanese do not; that is acknowledged by everyone. Rather, the ethical relativist contends that abortion is immoral in Ireland because the Irish believe it to be immoral and that it is morally permissible in Japan because the Japanese believe it to be so. Thus, for the ethical relativist there is no absolute ethical standard independent of cultural context, no criterion of right and wrong by which to judge other than that of particular societies. In short, what morality requires is relative to society.

Those who endorse ethical relativism point to the apparent diversity of human values and the multiformity of moral codes to support their case. From our own cultural perspective, some seemingly immoral moralities have been adopted. Polygamy, pedophilia, stealing, slavery, infanticide, and cannibalism have all been tolerated or even encouraged by the moral system of one society or another. In light of this fact, the ethical relativist believes that there can be no non-ethnocentric standard by which to judge actions.

Some thinkers believe that the moral differences between societies are smaller and less significant than they appear. They contend that variations in moral standards reflect differing factual beliefs and differing circumstances rather than fundamental differences in values. But suppose they are wrong about this matter. The relativist's conclusion still does not follow. A difference of opinion among societies about right and wrong no more proves that none of the conflicting beliefs is true or superior to the others than the diversity of viewpoints expressed in a college seminar establishes that there is no truth. In short, disagreement in ethical matters does not imply that all opinions are equally correct.

Ethical disagreement does not imply that all opinions are equally correct.

Moreover, ethical relativism has some unsatisfactory implications. *First,* it undermines any moral criticism of the practices of other societies as long as their actions conform to their own standards. We cannot say that slavery in a slave society like that of the American South 150 years ago was immoral and unjust as long as that society held it to be morally permissible.

Second, and closely related, is the fact that for the relativist there is no such thing as ethical progress. Although moralities may change, they cannot get better or worse. Thus, we cannot say that our moral standards today are any more enlightened than moral standards were in the Middle Ages.

Third, from the relativist's point of view it makes no sense for people to criticize principles or practices accepted by their own society. People can be censured for not living up to their society's moral code, but that is all. The moral code itself cannot be criticized because whatever a society takes to be right really is right for it. Reformers who identify injustices in their society and campaign against them are only encouraging people to be immoral—that is, to depart from the moral standards of their society—unless or until the majority of the society agrees with the reformers. The minority can never be right in moral matters; to be right it must become the majority.

The ethical relativist is correct to emphasize that in viewing other cultures we should keep an open mind and not simply dismiss alien social practices on the basis of our own cultural prejudices. But the relativist's theory of morality doesn't hold up. The more carefully we examine it, the less plausible it becomes. There is no good reason for saying that the majority view on moral issues is automatically right, and the belief that it is automatically right has unacceptable consequences.

Relativism and the "Game" of Business

In his well-known and influential essay "Is Business Bluffing Ethical?" Albert Carr argues that business, as practiced by individuals as well as by corporations, has the impersonal character of a game—a game that demands both special strategy and an understanding of its special ethical standards.[7] Business has its own norms and rules that differ from those of the rest of society. Thus, according to Carr, a number of things that we normally think of as wrong are really permissible in a business context. His examples include conscious misstatement and concealment of pertinent facts in negotiation, lying about one's age on a résumé, deceptive packaging, automobile companies' neglect of car safety, and utility companies' manipulation of regulators and overcharging of electricity users. He draws an analogy with poker:

> Poker's own brand of ethics is different from the ethical ideals of civilized human relationships. The game calls for distrust of the other fellow. It ignores the claim of friendship. Cunning deception and concealment of one's strength and intentions, not kindness and openheartedness, are vital in poker. No one thinks any the worse of poker on that account. And no one should think any the worse of the game of business because its standards of right and wrong differ from the prevailing traditions of morality in our society.[8]

What Carr is defending here is a kind of ethical relativism: Business has its own moral standards, and business actions should be evaluated only by those standards.

One can argue whether Carr has accurately identified the implicit rules of the business world (for example, is misrepresentation on one's résumé really a permissible move in the business game?), but let's put that issue aside. The basic question is whether business is a separate world to which ordinary moral standards don't apply. Carr's thesis assumes that any special activity following its own rules is exempt from external moral evaluation, but as a general proposition this is unacceptable. The Mafia, for example, has an elaborate code of conduct, accepted by the members of the rival "families." For them, gunning down a competitor or terrorizing a local shopkeeper may be a strategic move in a competitive environment. Yet we rightly refuse to say that gangsters cannot be criticized for following their own standards. Normal business activity is a world away from gangsterism, but the point still holds. Any specialized activity or practice will have its own distinctive rules and procedures, but the morality of those rules and procedures can still be evaluated.

Moreover, Carr's poker analogy is itself weak. For one thing, business activity can affect others—such as consumers—who have not consciously and freely chosen to play the "game." Business is indeed an activity involving distinctive rules and customary ways of doing things, but it is not really a game. It is the economic basis of our society, and we all have an interest in the goals of business (in productivity and consumer satisfaction, for instance) and in the rules business follows. Why should these be exempt from public evaluation and assessment? Later chapters return to the question of what these goals and rules should be. But to take one simple point, note that a business/

Summary 1.6
Ethical relativism is the theory that right and wrong are determined by what one's society says is right and wrong. There are many problems with this theory. Also dubious is the notion that business has its own morality, divorced from ordinary ideas of right and wrong.

economic system that permits, encourages, or tolerates deception will be less efficient (that is, work less well) than one in which the participants have fuller knowledge of the goods and services being exchanged.

By divorcing business from morality, Carr misrepresents both.

In sum, by divorcing business from morality, Carr misrepresents both. He incorrectly treats the standards and rules of everyday business activity as if they had nothing to do with the standards and rules of ordinary morality, and he treats morality as something that we give lip service to on Sundays but that otherwise has no influence on our lives.

HAVING MORAL PRINCIPLES

At some time in their lives most people pause to reflect on their own moral principles and on the practical implications of those principles, and they sometimes think about what principles people should have or which moral standards can be best justified. (Moral philosophers themselves have defended different moral standards; Chapter 2 discusses these various theories.) When a person accepts a moral principle, when that principle is part of his or her personal moral code, then naturally the person believes the principle is important and well justified. But there is more to moral principles than that, as the philosopher Richard Brandt emphasized. When a principle is part of a person's moral code, that person is strongly motivated toward the conduct required by the principle, and against behavior that conflicts with that principle. The person will tend to feel guilty when his or her own conduct violates that principle and to disapprove of others whose behavior conflicts with it. Likewise, the person will tend to hold in esteem those whose conduct shows an abundance of the motivation required by the principle.[9]

Accepting a moral principle is not a purely intellectual act like accepting a scientific hypothesis or a mathematical theorem.

Other philosophers have, in different ways, reinforced Brandt's point. To accept a moral principle is not a purely intellectual act like accepting a scientific hypothesis or a mathematical theorem. Rather, it also involves a desire to follow that principle for its own sake, the likelihood of feeling guilty about not doing so, and a tendency to evaluate the conduct of others according to the principle in question. We would find it very strange, for example, if Sally claimed to be morally opposed to cruelty to animals yet abused her own pets and felt no inclination to protest when some ruffians down the street set a cat on fire.

Conscience

People can, and unfortunately sometimes do, go against their moral principles, but we would doubt that they sincerely held the principle in question if violating it did not bother their conscience. We have all felt the pangs of conscience, but what exactly is **conscience** and how reliable a guide is it? Our conscience, of course, is not literally a little voice inside us. To oversimplify a complex piece of developmental psychology, our conscience evolved as we internalized the moral instructions of the parents or other authority figures who raised us as children.

When you were very young, you were probably told to tell the truth and to return something you filched to its proper owner. If you were caught lying or being dishonest, you were probably punished—scolded, spanked, sent to bed without dinner, denied a privilege. In contrast, truth telling and kindness to your siblings were probably rewarded—with approval, praise, maybe even hugs or candy. Seeking reward and avoiding punishment motivate small children to do what is expected of them. Gradually, children come to internalize those parental commands. Thus, they feel vaguely that their parents know what they are doing even when the parents are not around. When children do something forbidden, they experience the same feelings as when scolded by their parents—the first stirrings of guilt. By the same token, even in the absence of explicit parental reward, children feel a sense of self-approval about having done what they were supposed to have done.

As we grow older, of course, our motivations are not so simple and our self-understanding is greater. We are able to reflect on and understand the moral lessons we were taught, as well as to refine and modify those principles. As adults we are morally independent agents. Yet however much our conscience has evolved and however much our adult moral code differs from the moral perspective of our childhood, those pangs of guilt we occasionally feel still stem from that early internalization of parental demands.

The Limits of Conscience

Telling someone to "follow your conscience" is not very helpful, and sometimes it can be bad advice.

How reliable a guide is conscience? People often say, "Follow your conscience" or "You should never go against your conscience." Such advice is not very helpful, however. Indeed, it can sometimes be bad advice. *First*, when we are genuinely perplexed about what we ought to do, we are trying to figure out what our conscience ought to be saying to us. When it is not possible to do both, should we keep our promise to a colleague or come to the aid of an old friend? To be told that we should follow our conscience is no help at all.

Second, it may not always be good for us to follow our conscience. It all depends on what our conscience says. On the one hand, sometimes people's consciences do not bother them when they should—perhaps because they didn't think through the implications of what they were doing or perhaps because they failed to internalize strongly enough the appropriate moral principles. On the other hand, a person's conscience might disturb the person about something that is perfectly all right.

Summary 1.7
Accepting a moral principle involves a motivation to conform one's conduct to that principle. Violating the principle will bother one's conscience, but conscience is not a perfectly reliable guide to right and wrong.

Consider an episode in Chapter 16 of Mark Twain's *The Adventures of Huckleberry Finn.* Huck has taken off down the Mississippi on a raft with his friend, the runaway slave Jim, but as they get nearer to the place where Jim will become legally free, Huck starts feeling guilty about helping him run away:

> It hadn't ever come home to me before, what this thing was that I was doing. But now it did; and it stayed with me, and scorched me more and more. I tried to make out to myself that I warn't to blame, because I didn't run Jim off from his rightful owner; but it warn't no use, conscience up and says, every time: "But you knowed he was running for his freedom, and you could a paddled ashore and told somebody." That was so—I couldn't get around that, no way. That was where it pinched. Conscience says to me: "What had poor Miss Watson done to you, that you could see her nigger go off right under your eyes and never say one

single word? What did that poor old woman do to you, that you could treat her so mean?..." I got to feeling so mean and miserable I most wished I was dead.

Here Huck is feeling guilty about doing what we would all agree is the morally right thing to do. But Huck is only a boy, and his pangs of conscience reflect the principles that he has picked up uncritically from the slave-owning society around him. Unable to think independently about matters of right and wrong, Huck in the end decides to disregard his conscience. He follows his instincts and sticks by his friend Jim.

The point here is not that you should ignore your conscience but that the voice of conscience is itself something that can be critically examined. A pang of conscience is like a warning. When you feel one, you should definitely stop and reflect on the rightness of what you are doing. But you cannot justify your actions simply by saying you were following your conscience. Terrible crimes have occasionally been committed in the name of conscience.

Moral Principles and Self-Interest

Sometimes doing what you believe would be morally right and doing what would best satisfy your own interests may be two different things. Imagine that you are in your car hurrying home along a quiet road, trying hard to get there in time to see the kickoff of an important football game. You pass an acquaintance who is having car trouble. He doesn't recognize you. As a dedicated fan, you would much prefer to keep on going than to stop and help him, thus missing at least part of the game. Although you might rationalize that someone else will eventually come along and help him out if you don't, deep down you know that you really ought to stop. **Self-interest**, however, seems to say, "Keep going."

Consider another example. You have applied for a new job, and if you land it, it will be an enormous break for you: It is exactly the kind of position you want and have been trying to get for some time. It pays well and will settle you into a desirable career for the rest of your life. The competition has come down to you and one other person, and you believe correctly that she has a slight edge on you. Now imagine that you could spread a nasty rumor about her that would guarantee that she wouldn't get the job, and that you could do this in a way that wouldn't come back to you. Presumably, circulating this lie would violate your moral code, but doing it would clearly benefit you.

Some people argue that moral action and self-interest can never really conflict. Although some philosophers have gone to great lengths to try to prove this, they are almost certainly mistaken. They maintain that if you do the wrong thing, then you will be caught, your conscience will bother you, or in some way "what goes around comes around," so that your misdeed will come back to haunt you. This is often correct. But unfortunate as it may be, sometimes—viewed just in terms of personal self-interest—it may pay off for you to do what you know to be wrong. People sometimes get away with their wrongdoings, and if their conscience bothers them at all, it may not bother them very much. To believe otherwise not only is wishful thinking but also shows a lack of understanding of morality.

Summary 1.8
Part of the point of morality is to make social existence possible by restraining self-interested behavior. Sometimes doing what is morally right can conflict with one's personal interests. In general, though, following your moral principles will enable you to live a more satisfying life.

Morality restrains our self-interested desires. A society's moral standards allow conflicts to be resolved by an appeal to shared principles of justification.

When morality and self-interest conflict, what you choose to do will depend on the kind of person you are.

Morality serves to restrain our purely self-interested desires so we can all live together. The moral standards of a society provide the basic guidelines for cooperative social existence and allow conflicts to be resolved by an appeal to shared principles of justification. If our interests never came into conflict—that is, if it were never advantageous for one person to deceive or cheat another—then there would be little need for morality. We would already be in heaven. Both a system of law that punishes people for hurting others and a system of morality that encourages people to refrain from pursuing their self-interest at great expense to others help make social existence possible.

Usually, following our moral principles is in our best interest. This idea is particularly worth noting in the business context. Recently, a number of business theorists have argued persuasively not only that moral behavior is consistent with profitability but also that the most morally responsible companies are among the most profitable.[10] Apparently, respecting the rights of employees, treating suppliers fairly, and being straightforward with customers pay off.

But notice one thing. If you do the right thing only because you think you will profit from it, you are not really motivated by moral concerns. Having a moral principle involves having a desire to follow the principle for its own sake—simply because it is the right thing to do. If you do the right thing only because you believe it will pay off, you might just as easily not do it if it looks as if it is not going to pay off.

In addition, there is no guarantee that moral behavior will always benefit a person in strictly selfish terms. As argued earlier, there will be exceptions. From the moral point of view, you ought to stop and help your acquaintance, and you shouldn't lie about competitors. From the selfish point of view, you should do exactly the opposite. Should you follow your self-interest or your moral principles? There's no final answer to this question. From the moral point of view, you should, of course, follow your moral principles. But from the selfish point of view, you should look out solely for "number one."

Which option you choose will depend on the strength of your self-interested or self-regarding desires in comparison with the strength of your other-regarding desires (that is, your moral motivations and your concern for others). In other words, your choice will depend on your character, on the kind of person you are, which depends in part on how you were raised. A person who is basically selfish will pass by the acquaintance in distress and will spread the rumor, whereas a person who has a stronger concern for others, or a stronger desire to do what is right just because it is right, will not.

Although it may be impossible to prove to selfish persons that they should not do the thing that best advances their self-interest (because if they are selfish, then that is all they care about), there are considerations that suggest it is not in a person's overall self-interest to be a selfish person. People who are exclusively concerned with their own interests tend to have less happy and less satisfying lives than those whose desires extend beyond themselves. This is usually called the **paradox of hedonism**, but it might equally well be dubbed the "paradox of selfishness." Individuals who care only about their own happiness will generally be less happy than those who care about others. Moreover, people often find greater satisfaction in a life lived according to moral principle, and in being the kind of person that entails, than in a life devoted solely to self-gratification. Thus, or so many philosophers have argued, people have self-interested reasons not to be so self-interested. How do selfish people make themselves less so? Not overnight, obviously, but by involving themselves in the concerns and cares of others, they can in time come to care sincerely about those persons.

MORALITY AND PERSONAL VALUES

Some philosophers distinguish between morality in a narrow sense and morality in a broad sense. In a narrow sense, morality is the moral code of an individual or a society (insofar as the moral codes of the individuals making up that society overlap). Although the principles that constitute our code may not be explicitly formulated, as laws are, they do guide us in our conduct. They function as internal monitors of our own behavior and as a basis for assessing the actions of others. **Morality in the narrow sense** concerns the principles that do or should regulate people's conduct and relations with others. These principles can be debated, however. (Take, for example, John Stuart Mill's contention that society ought not to interfere with people's liberty when their actions affect only themselves.) And a large part of moral philosophy involves assessing rival moral principles. This discussion is part of the ongoing development in our moral culture. What is at stake are the basic standards that ought to govern our behavior—that is, the fundamental framework or ground rules that make coexistence possible. If there were not already fairly widespread agreement about these principles, our social order would not be sustainable.

But in addition we can talk about our **morality in the broad sense,** meaning not just the principles of conduct that we embrace but also the values, ideals, and aspirations that shape our lives. Many different ways of living our lives would meet our basic moral obligations. The type of life each of us seeks to live reflects our individual values—whether following a profession, devoting ourselves to community service, raising a family, seeking solitude, pursuing scientific truth, striving for athletic excellence, amassing political power, cultivating glamorous people as friends, or some combination of these and many other possible ways of living. The life that each of us forges and the way we understand that life are part of our morality in the broad sense of the term.

It is important to bear this in mind throughout your study of business ethics. Although this book's main concern is with the principles that ought to govern conduct in certain business-type situations—for example, whether a hiring officer may take an applicant's race into account, whether employees may be forced to take an AIDS test, or whether corporate bribery is permissible in countries where people turn a blind eye to it—your choices in the business world will also reflect your other values and ideals or, in other words, the kind of person you are striving to be. What sort of ideal do you have of yourself as a businessperson? How much weight do you put on profitability, for instance, as against the quality of your product or the socially beneficial character of your service?

The decisions you make in your career and much of the way you shape your working life will depend not only on your moral code but also on the understanding you have of yourself in certain roles and relationships. Your morality—in the sense of your ideals, values, and aspirations—involves, among other things, your understanding of human nature, tradition, and society; of one's proper relationship to the natural environment; and of an individual's place in the cosmos. Professionals in various fields, for example, will invariably be guided not just by rules but also by their understanding of what being a professional involves, and a businessperson's conception of the ideal or model relationship to have with clients will greatly influence his or her day-to-day conduct.

Summary 1.9
Morality in the sense of the rules or principles that regulate one's conduct toward others can be distinguished from morality in the broader sense of the values, ideals, and aspirations that shape a person's life.

There is more to living a morally good life, of course, than being a good businessperson or being good at your job, as Aristotle (384–322 B.C.E.) argued long ago. He underscored the necessity of our trying to achieve virtue or excellence, not just in some particular field of endeavor, but also as human beings. Aristotle thought that things have functions. The function of a piano, for instance, is to make certain sounds, and a piano that performs this function well is a good or excellent piano. Likewise, we have an idea of what it is for a person to be an excellent athlete, an excellent manager, or an excellent professor—it is to do well the types of things that athletes, managers, or professors are supposed to do.

But Aristotle also thought that, just as there is an ideal of excellence for any particular craft or occupation, similarly there must be an excellence that we can achieve simply as human beings. He thought that we can live our lives as a whole in such a way that they can be judged not just as excellent in this respect or in that occupation but as excellent, period. Aristotle thought that only when we develop our truly human capacities sufficiently to achieve this human excellence will we have lives blessed with happiness. Philosophers since Aristotle's time have been skeptical of his apparent belief that this human excellence would come in just one form, but many would underscore the importance of developing our various potential capacities and striving to achieve a kind of excellence in our lives. How we understand this excellence is a function of our values, ideals, and worldview—our morality in a broad sense.

INDIVIDUAL INTEGRITY AND RESPONSIBILITY

Previous sections discussed what it is for a person to have a moral code, as well as the sometimes conflicting pulls of moral conscience and self-interest. In addition, we have seen that people have values and ideals above and beyond their moral principles, narrowly understood, that also influence the lives they lead. And we have seen the importance of reflecting critically on both moral principles and moral ideals and values as we seek to live morally good and worthwhile lives. None of us, however, lives in a vacuum, and social pressures of various sorts always affect us. Sometimes these pressures make it difficult to stick with our principles and to be the kind of person we wish to be. Corporations are a particularly relevant example of an environment that can potentially damage individual integrity and responsibility.

Organizational Norms

One of the major characteristics of an organization—indeed, of any group—is the shared acceptance of **organizational norms** and rules by its members. Acceptance can take different forms; it can be conscious or unconscious, overt or implicit, but it is almost always present, because an organization can survive only if it holds its members together. Group cohesiveness requires that individual members "commit" themselves—that is, relinquish some of their personal freedom in order to further organizational goals. One's degree of commitment—the extent to which one accepts group norms and subordinates self to organizational goals—is a measure of one's loyalty to the "team."

The corporation's overarching goal is profit. To achieve this goal, top management sets specific targets for sales, market share, return on equity, and so forth. For the most part the norms or rules that govern corporate existence are derived from these goals. But clearly there's nothing in either the norms or the goals that necessarily encourages moral behavior; indeed, they may discourage it.

According to a recent survey by the American Management Association, pressure to meet unrealistic business objectives and deadlines is the leading cause of unethical business conduct.[11] And mounting evidence suggests that most managers experience role conflicts between what is expected of them as efficient, profit-minded members of an organization and what is expected of them as ethical persons. In a series of in-depth interviews with recent graduates of the Harvard MBA program, researchers Joseph L. Badaracco, Jr., and Allen P. Webb found that these young managers frequently received explicit instructions or felt strong organizational pressure to do things they believed to be sleazy, unethical, or even illegal.[12] Another survey found that a majority of managers at all levels experience "pressure from the top" to meet corporate goals and comply with corporate norms. Of the managers interviewed, 50 percent of top managers, 65 percent of middle managers, and 84 percent of lower managers agreed that they felt pressure to "compromise personal standards to achieve company goals."[13]

The young managers interviewed by Badaracco and Webb identified four powerful organizational "commandments" as responsible for the pressure they felt to compromise their integrity:

> First, performance is what really counts, so make your numbers. Second, be loyal and show us that you're a team player. Third, don't break the law. Fourth, don't overinvest in ethical behavior.[14]

Pressure to meet corporate objectives, to be a team player, and to conform to organizational norms can lead people to act unethically.

Although most corporate goals and norms are not objectionable when viewed by themselves, they frequently put the people who must implement them into a moral pressure cooker. The need to meet corporate objectives, to be a team player, and to conform to organizational norms can lead otherwise honorable individuals to engage in unethical conduct.

Conformity

It is no secret that organizations exert pressure on their members to conform to norms and goals. What may not be so widely known is how easily individuals can be induced to behave as those around them do. A dramatic example is provided in the early conformity studies by social psychologist Solomon Asch.[15]

In a classic experiment, Asch asked groups of seven to nine college students to say which of three lines on a card matched the length of a single line on another card (see diagram below).

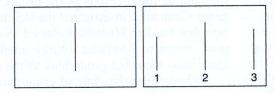

Only one of the subjects in each group was "naive," or unaware of the nature of the experiment. The others were shills or stooges of the experimenter, who had instructed them to make incorrect judgments in about two-thirds of the cases and in this way to pressure the naive subjects to alter their correct judgments.

The results were revealing. When the subjects were not exposed to pressure, they invariably judged correctly, but when the stooges gave false answers, the subjects changed their responses to conform with the unanimous majority judgments. When one shill differed from the majority and gave the correct answer, naive subjects maintained their position three-fourths of the time. However, when the honest shill switched to the majority view in later trials, the errors made by naive subjects rose to about the same level as that of subjects who stood alone against a unanimous majority.

Why did they yield? Some respondents said they didn't want to seem different, even though they continued to believe their judgments were correct. Others said that although their perceptions seemed correct, the majority couldn't be wrong. Still other subjects didn't even seem aware that they had caved in to group pressure. Even those who held their ground tended to be profoundly disturbed by being out of step with the majority and confessed to being sorely tempted to alter their judgments. Indeed, a subsequent study found that students who stood firm in their judgments suffered more anxiety than those who switched. One student with the strength of his correct convictions was literally dripping with perspiration by the end of the experiment.

In these experiments, which cumulatively included several hundred students, the subjects were not exposed to the authority symbols that people inside an organization face: bosses, boards, presidents, professional peers, established policy, and so on. Nor would correct responses have entailed the serious long-range impact that bucking the system can carry for members of an organization: being transferred, dismissed, frozen in a position, or made an organizational pariah. And, of course, the students did not bring to these experiments the financial and personal investments that individuals bring to their jobs. Men and women within an organization are under greater pressure to conform than were the students in Asch's studies.

Groupthink

Almost all groups require some conformity from their members, but in extreme cases the demand for conformity can lead to what social psychologists call "groupthink." **Groupthink** happens when pressure for unanimity within a highly cohesive group overwhelms its members' desire or ability to appraise the situation realistically and consider alternative courses of action. Members of the group close their eyes to negative information, ignore warnings that the group may be mistaken, and discount outside ideas that might contradict the thinking or the decisions of the group. For example, when the Senate Intelligence Committee investigated the U.S. intelligence community's false presumption that Saddam Hussein possessed weapons of mass destruction that posed a grave threat to American security interests, the committee's July 2004 report specifically identified groupthink as the problem.

When under the sway of groupthink, group members may have the illusion that the group is invulnerable or that because the group is good or right, whatever it does is permissible. Individuals in the group tend to self-censor thoughts that go against the group's ideas and rationalize away conflicting evidence, and the group as a whole may implicitly or explicitly pressure potential dissenters to conform. Groupthink thus leads to irrational, sometimes disastrous decisions, and it has enormous potential for doing moral damage.

Diffusion of Responsibility

Pressure to conform to the group and to adhere to its norms and beliefs can lead to the surrender of individual moral autonomy. This tendency is enhanced by the fact that group actions frequently involve the participation of many people. As a result, responsibility for what an organization does can become fragmented or diffused throughout the group, with no single individual seeing himself or herself as responsible for what happens. Indeed, it may be difficult to say exactly who should be held accountable. This **diffusion of responsibility** inside an organization leads individuals to have a diluted or diminished sense of their own personal moral responsibilities. They tend to see themselves simply as small players in a process or as cogs in a machine over which they have no control and for which they are unaccountable. They rationalize to themselves contributing to actions, policies, or events that they would refuse to perform or to authorize if they thought the decision were entirely up to them. "It's not my fault," they think. "This would happen anyway, with or without me." Diffusion of responsibility encourages the moral myopia of thinking "I'm just doing my job," instead of taking a 20/20 look at the bigger picture.

This sense of diminished individual moral responsibility for an outcome that many people bring about or allow to happen is something that social psychologists began studying more closely as a result of the sad case of Kitty Genovese, a young woman who was stabbed to death in the 1960s. Although the murder was not in itself so unusual, it made headlines and editorial pages across the nation because thirty-eight of her neighbors witnessed her brutal slaying. In answer to her pitiful screams of terror at 3 A.M., they came to their windows and remained there for the thirty or more minutes it took her assailant to brutalize her. (He evidently left for a while and then returned to finish

Summary 1.10
Several aspects of corporate structure and function work to undermine individual moral responsibility. Organizational norms, pressure to conform (sometimes leading to groupthink), and diffusion of responsibility inside large organizations can all make the exercise of individual integrity difficult.

Diffusion of responsibility inside an organization can weaken people's sense of moral responsibility.

the job.) Of the thirty-eight, not one attempted to intervene in any way; no one even phoned the police.

Why didn't Kitty Genovese's neighbors help her? Most social psychologists believe that an individual's sense of personal responsibility is inversely proportional to the number of people witnessing or involved in the episode. Thus, the more people who are observing an event, the less likely is any one of them to feel obliged to do anything. In emergencies, we seem naturally to let the behavior of those around us dictate our response—a phenomenon often called **bystander apathy**. But the point is more general. In any large group or organization, diffusion of responsibility for its actions can lead individuals to feel anonymous and not accountable for what happens. Submerged in the group, the individual may not even question the morality of his or her actions.[16]

Pressure to conform to organizational norms and a diminished sense of personal responsibility for group behavior undermine individual integrity and moral autonomy. Business corporations are not necessarily worse than many other groups in this respect, but certainly the pressure in business to help the company make a profit or achieve its other goals, to do what is expected of you, and generally to be a loyal and cooperative team player can foster, or at least do nothing to inhibit, these group propensities. Beyond that, many corporations fail to institutionalize ethics. They don't articulate or communicate ethical standards to their members; they don't actively enforce them; and they retain structures and policies that thwart individual integrity.

> Business corporations are no worse than other groups, but many of them do little to protect individual integrity and moral autonomy.

Although what is expected of members of a corporation sometimes clashes with their own moral values, they are rarely encouraged to deal with the conflict in an open, mature way. In fact, the more one suppresses individual moral urges in the cause of organizational interests, the more "mature," committed, and loyal one is considered to be; conversely, the less willing the individual, the less "mature" and the more suspect. For example, when a Beech-Nut employee expressed concerns about the fact that the concentrate the company was producing for its "100% pure" apple juice contained nothing more than sugar water and chemicals, his annual performance review described his judgment as "colored by naïveté and impractical ideals."[17] Or consider the reports of Wall Street analysts pressured by their firms to recommend to clients stocks or bonds the analysts knew to be "junk" or "dogs."[18] Employees frequently have to fight hard to maintain their moral integrity in a showdown with organizational priorities.

Often, however, the problem facing us is not that of doing what we know to be right but rather of deciding what the right thing to do is. In business and organizational contexts, many difficult and puzzling moral questions need to be answered. How do we go about doing that? Is there some reliable procedure or method for answering moral questions? In science, the scientific method tells us what steps to take if we seek to answer a scientific question, but there is no comparable moral method for engaging ethical questions. There is, however, general agreement about what constitutes good moral reasoning.

MORAL REASONING

It is useful to view moral reasoning at first in the context of argument. An **argument** is a group of statements, one of which (called the **conclusion**) is claimed to follow from the others (called the **premises**). Here's an example of an argument:

Argument 1

If a person is a mother, the person is a female.

Fran is a mother.

Therefore, Fran is a female.

The first two statements (the premises) of this argument happen to entail the third (the conclusion), which means that if I accept the first two as true, then I must accept the third as also true. Not to accept the conclusion while accepting the premises would result in a contradiction—holding two beliefs that cannot both be true at the same time. In other words, if I believe that all mothers are females and that Fran is a mother (the premises), then I cannot deny that Fran is a female (the conclusion) without contradicting myself. An argument like this one, whose premises logically entail its conclusion, is a **valid argument**.

An **invalid argument** is one whose premises do not entail its conclusion. In an invalid argument, I can accept the premises as true and reject the conclusion without any contradiction. Thus:

Argument 2

If a person is a mother, the person is a female.

Fran is a female.

Therefore, Fran is a mother.

The conclusion of this argument does not necessarily follow from the true premises. I can believe that every mother is a female and that Fran is a female but deny that Fran is a mother without contradicting myself.

One way to show this is by means of a **counterexample**, an example that is consistent with the premises but is inconsistent with the conclusion. Let's suppose Fran is a two-year-old, a premise that is perfectly consistent with the two stated premises. If she is, she can't possibly be a mother. Or let's suppose Fran is an adult female who happens to be childless, another premise that is perfectly consistent with the stated premises but obviously at odds with the conclusion. If an argument is valid (such as Argument 1), then no counterexamples are possible.

A valid argument can have untrue premises, as in the following:

Argument 3

If a person is a female, she must be a mother.

Fran is a female.

Therefore, Fran must be a mother.

Like Argument 1, this one is valid. If I accept its premises as true, I must accept its conclusion as true; otherwise I will contradict myself. Although valid, this argument is unsound because one of its premises is false—namely,

"If a person is a female, she must be a mother." Realizing the patent absurdity of one of its premises, no sensible person would accept this argument's conclusion. But notice why the argument is unsound—not because the reasoning procedure is invalid but because one of the premises is false. **Sound arguments**, such as Argument 1, have true premises and valid reasoning. **Unsound arguments** have at least one false premise, as in Argument 3, or invalid reasoning, as in Argument 2.

Now let's consider some **moral arguments**, which can be defined simply as arguments whose conclusions are moral judgments. Here are some examples that deal with affirmative action for women and minorities in the workplace:

Argument 4

If an action violates the law, it is morally wrong.

Affirmative action on behalf of women and minorities in personnel matters violates the law.

Therefore, affirmative action on behalf of women and minorities in personnel matters is morally wrong.

Argument 5

If an action violates the will of the majority, it is morally wrong.

Affirmative action on behalf of women and minorities in personnel matters violates the will of the majority.

Therefore, affirmative action on behalf of women and minorities in personnel matters is morally wrong.

Argument 6

If an action redresses past injuries that have disadvantaged a group, it is morally permissible.

Affirmative action on behalf of women and minorities in personnel matters redresses injuries that have disadvantaged these groups.

Therefore, affirmative action on behalf of women and minorities in personnel matters is morally permissible.

Argument 7

If an action is the only practical way to remedy a social problem, then it is morally permissible.

Affirmative action on behalf of women and minorities in personnel matters is the only practical way to remedy the social problem of unequal employment opportunity.

Therefore, affirmative action on behalf of women and minorities in personnel matters is morally permissible.

The first premise in each of these arguments is a moral standard, the second an alleged fact, and the conclusion a moral judgment. *Moral reasoning* or argument typically moves from a moral standard, through one or more factual judgments about some person, action, or policy related to that standard, to a moral judgment about that person, action, or policy. Good moral reasoning will frequently be more complicated than these examples; often it will involve an appeal to more than one standard as well as to various appropriate factual claims. Still, these examples illustrate its most basic form.

Defensible Moral Judgments

Moral judgments should be supported by moral standards and relevant facts.

If a moral judgment or conclusion is defensible, then it must be supportable by a defensible moral standard, together with relevant facts. A moral standard supports a moral judgment if the standard, taken together with the relevant facts, logically entails the moral judgment and if the moral standard itself is a sound standard. If someone argues that affirmative action for minorities and women is right (or wrong) but cannot produce a supporting principle when asked, then the person's position is considerably weakened. And if the person does not see any need to support the judgment by appeal to a moral standard, then he or she simply does not understand how moral concepts are used or is using moral words like "right" or "wrong" differently from the way they are commonly used.

Keeping this in mind—that moral judgments must be supportable by moral standards and facts—will aid your understanding of moral discourse, which can be highly complex and sophisticated. It will also sharpen your own critical faculties and improve your moral reasoning and ability to formulate relevant moral arguments.

Patterns of Defense and Challenge

In assessing arguments, one must be careful to clarify the meanings of their key terms and phrases. Often premises can be understood in more than one way, and this ambiguity may lead people to accept (or reject) arguments that they shouldn't. For example, "affirmative action" seems to mean different things to different people (see Chapter 11 on job discrimination). Before we can profitably assess Arguments 4 through 7, we have to agree on how we understand "affirmative action." Similarly, Argument 5 relies on the idea of "violating the will of the majority," but this notion has to be clarified before we can evaluate either the moral principle that it is wrong to violate the will of the majority or the factual claim that affirmative action does violate the majority's will.

Assuming that the arguments are logically valid in their form (as Arguments 4 through 7 are) and that their terms have been clarified and possible ambiguities eliminated, then we must turn our attention to assessing the premises of the arguments. Should we accept or reject their premises? Remember that if an argument is valid and you accept the premises, you must accept the conclusion.

Let's look at some further aspects of this assessment process:

1. **Evaluating the factual claims.** If the parties to an ethical discussion are willing to accept the moral standard (or standards) in question, then they can concentrate on the factual claims. Thus, for example, in

Argument 4 they will focus on whether affirmative action on behalf of women and minorities is in fact illegal. In Argument 7 they will need to determine whether affirmative action is really the only practical way to remedy the social problem of unequal employment opportunity. Analogous questions can be asked about the factual claims of Arguments 5 and 6. Answering them in the affirmative would require considerable supporting data.

2. **Challenging the moral standard.** Moral arguments generally involve more than factual disputes. The moral standards they appeal to may be controversial. One party might challenge the moral standard on which the argument relies, contending that it is not a plausible one and that we should not accept it. The critic might do this in several different ways— for example, by showing that there are exceptions to the standard, that the standard leads to unacceptable consequences, or that it is inconsistent with the arguer's other moral beliefs.

   In the following dialogue, for example, Lynn is attacking Sam's advocacy of the standard "If an action redresses past injuries that have disadvantaged a group, it is morally permissible."

Summary 1.11
Moral reasoning and argument typically appeal both to moral standards and to relevant facts. Moral judgments should be entailed by the relevant moral standards and the facts, and they should not contradict our other beliefs. Both standards and facts must be assessed when moral arguments are being evaluated.

Lynn: What would you think of affirmative action for Jews in the workplace?
Sam: I'd be against it.
Lynn: What about Catholics?
Sam: No.
Lynn: People of Irish extraction?
Sam: They should be treated the same as anybody else.
Lynn: But each of these groups and more I could mention were victimized in the past by unfair discrimination and probably in some cases continue to be.
Sam: So?
Lynn: So the standard you're defending leads to a judgment you reject: namely, that Jews, Catholics, and Irish should be compensated by affirmative action for having been disadvantaged. How do you account for this inconsistency?

At this point Sam, or any rational person in a similar position, has three alternatives: abandon or modify the standard, alter his moral judgment, or show how women and minorities fit the original principle even though the other groups do not.

3. **Defending the moral standard.** When the standard is criticized, then its advocate must defend it. Often this requires invoking an even more general principle. A defender of Argument 6, for example, might uphold the redress principle by appealing to some more general conception of social justice. Or defenders might try to show how the standard in question entails other moral judgments that both the critic and the defender accept, thereby enhancing the plausibility of the standard. In the following exchange, Lynn is defending the

standard of Argument 5: "If an action violates the will of the majority, it is morally wrong":

Lynn: Okay, do you think the government should impose a national religion on all Americans?

Sam: Of course not.

Lynn: What about requiring people to register their handguns?

Sam: I'm all for it.

Lynn: And using kids in pornography?

Sam: There rightly are laws against it.

Lynn: But the principle you're objecting to—that an action violating the will of the majority is wrong—leads to these judgments that you accept.

Of course, Lynn's argument is by no means a conclusive defense for her moral standard. Other moral standards could just as easily entail the judgments she cites, as Sam is quick to point out:

Sam: Now wait a minute. I oppose a state religion on constitutional grounds, not because it violates majority will. As for gun control, I'm for it because I think it will reduce violent crimes. And using kids in pornography is wrong because it exploits and endangers children.

Although Lynn's strategy for defending the standard about majority rule proved inconclusive, it does illustrate a common and often persuasive way of arguing for a moral principle.

4. **Revising and modifying the argument.** Arguments 4 through 7 are only illustrations, and all the moral principles they mention are very simple—too simple to accept without qualification. (The principle that it is immoral to break the law in all circumstances, for example, is implausible. Nazi Germany furnishes an obvious counterexample to it.) But once the standard has been effectively challenged, the defender of the argument, rather than abandoning the argument altogether, might try to reformulate it. For instance, the defender might replace the original, contested premise with a better and more plausible one that still supports the conclusion. For example, Premise 1 of Argument 4 might be replaced by: "If an action violates a law that is democratically decided and that is not morally unjust, then the action is immoral." Or the defender might revise the conclusion of his or her argument, perhaps by restricting its scope. A more modest, less sweeping conclusion will often be easier to defend.

In this way, the discussion continues, the arguments on both sides of an issue improve, and we make progress in the analysis and resolution of ethical issues. In general, in philosophy we study logic and criticize arguments not to be able to score quick debating points but rather to be able to think better and more deeply about moral and other problems. Our goal as moral philosophers is not to "win" arguments but to arrive at the truth—or, put less grandly, to find the most reasonable answers to various ethical questions.

Summary 1.12
Philosophical discussion generally involves the revision and modification of arguments; in this way progress is made in the analysis and resolution of moral and other issues.

Requirements for Moral Judgments

Moral discussion and the analysis of ethical issues can take different, often complicated, paths. Nevertheless, the preceding discussion implies certain minimum adequacy requirements for moral judgments. Although there is no complete list of adequacy criteria, moral judgments should be (1) logical, (2) based on facts, and (3) based on sound or defensible moral principles. A moral judgment that is weak on any of these grounds is open to criticism.

Moral Judgments Should Be Logical

Our moral judgments should follow logically from their premises.

To say that moral judgments should be logical implies several things. *First*, as indicated in the discussion of moral reasoning, our moral judgments should follow logically from their premises. The connection between (1) the standard, (2) the conduct or policy, and (3) the moral judgment should be such that 1 and 2 logically entail 3. Our goal is to be able to support our moral judgments with reasons and evidence, rather than basing them solely on emotion, sentiment, or social or personal preference.

Our moral judgments should be logically compatible with our other beliefs.

Second, our moral judgments should be logically compatible with our other moral and nonmoral beliefs. We must avoid inconsistency. Almost all philosophers agree that if we make a moral judgment—for example, that it was wrong of Smith to alter the figures she gave to the outside auditors—then we must be willing to make the same judgment in any similar set of circumstances—that is, if our friend Brown, our spouse, or our father had altered the figures. In particular, we cannot make an exception for ourselves, judging something permissible for us to do while condemning others for doing the very same thing.

Moral Judgments Should Be Based on Facts

Adequate moral judgments cannot be made in a vacuum. We must gather as much relevant information as possible before making them. For example, an intelligent assessment of the morality of insider trading would require an understanding of, among other things, the different circumstances in which it can occur and the effects it has on the market and on other traders. The information supporting a moral judgment, the facts, should be relevant—that is, the information should actually relate to the judgment; it should be complete, or inclusive of all significant data; and it should, of course, be accurate or true.

Moral Judgments Should Be Based on Acceptable Moral Principles

We know that moral judgments are based on moral standards. At the highest level of moral reasoning, these standards embody and express very general moral principles. Reliable moral judgments must be based on sound moral principles—principles that are unambiguous and can withstand critical scrutiny and rational criticism. What, precisely, makes a moral principle sound or acceptable is one of the most difficult questions that the study of ethics raises and is beyond the scope of this book. But one criterion is worth mentioning, what philosophers often call our **considered moral beliefs**.

These beliefs contrast with our gut responses, with beliefs based on ignorance or prejudice, and with beliefs we just happen to hold without having

Summary 1.13
Conformity with our considered moral beliefs is an important consideration in evaluating moral principles. A considered moral belief is one held only after we have made a conscientious effort to be conceptually clear, to acquire all relevant information, and to think rationally, impartially, and dispassionately about the belief and its implications. We should doubt any moral principle that clashes with many of our considered beliefs.

thought them through. As philosophy professor Tom Regan explains, our considered beliefs are those moral beliefs "we hold *after* we have made a conscientious effort … to think about our beliefs coolly, rationally, impartially, with conceptual clarity, and with as much relevant information as we can reasonably acquire."[19] We have grounds to doubt a moral principle when it clashes with such beliefs. Conversely, conformity with our considered moral judgments is good reason for regarding it as provisionally established.

This does not mean that conformity with our considered beliefs is the sole or even basic test of a moral principle, any more than conformity with well-established beliefs is the exclusive or even fundamental test of a scientific hypothesis. (Copernicus's heliocentric hypothesis, for example, did not conform with what passed in the medieval world as a well-considered belief, the Ptolemaic view that the earth was the center of the universe.) But conformity with our considered beliefs seemingly must play some part in evaluating the many alternative moral principles that are explored in the next chapter.

STUDY CORNER

Key Terms and Concepts

administrative regulations
argument
business
business ethics
businesspeople
bystander apathy
common law
conclusion
conscience
considered moral beliefs
constitutional law

counterexample
diffusion of responsibility
divine command theory
ethical relativism
ethics
etiquette
groupthink
invalid arguments
moral arguments
moral standards
morality in the broad sense

morality in the narrow sense
organizational norms
paradox of hedonism
premises
professional codes of ethics
self-interest
sound arguments
statutes
unsound arguments
valid arguments

Points to Review

- what happened at Enron
- three characteristics of moral standards
- four types of law
- what King's violation of the law shows
- the point of the example of not stopping to help an accident victim
- shortcomings of professional codes as an ethical guide
- where we get our moral standards
- three ways in which morality might be thought to be based on religion
- three unsatisfactory implications of ethical relativism
- what's wrong with Carr's idea that business is a game with its own moral rules

- what's involved in a person's accepting a moral principle
- why telling someone "Follow your conscience" isn't very helpful advice
- the point of the Huckleberry Finn example
- what determines what a person will do when morality and self-interest collide
- morality in the broad sense vs. morality in the narrow sense
- Aristotle and the ideal of achieving excellence
- what the experiments by Solomon Asch showed
- dangers of groupthink
- diffusion of responsibility and the Kitty Genovese example

- the difference between valid and invalid, sound and unsound, arguments
- moral judgments as resting on moral standards and facts

- what it means to say moral judgments should be logical
- role of "considered moral beliefs" in the evaluation of moral principles

CASE **1.1**

Made in the U.S.A.—Dumped in Brazil, Africa, Iraq...

When it comes to the safety of young children, fire is a parent's nightmare. Just the thought of their young ones trapped in their cribs and beds by a raging nocturnal blaze is enough to make most mothers and fathers take every precaution to ensure their children's safety. Little wonder that when fire-retardant children's pajamas first hit the market, they proved an overnight success. Within a few short years more than 200 million pairs were sold, and the sales of millions more were all but guaranteed. For their manufacturers, the future could not have been brighter. Then, like a bolt from the blue, came word that the pajamas were killers. The U.S. Consumer Product Safety Commission (CPSC) moved quickly to ban their sale and recall millions of pairs. Reason: The pajamas contained the flame-retardant chemical Tris (2,3-dibromoprophyl), which had been found to cause kidney cancer in children.

Because of its toxicity, the sleepwear couldn't even be thrown away, let alone sold. Indeed, the CPSC left no doubt about how the pajamas were to be disposed of—buried or burned or used as industrial wiping cloths. Whereas just months earlier the manufacturers of the Tris-impregnated pajamas couldn't fill orders fast enough, suddenly they were worrying about how to get rid of the millions of pairs now sitting in warehouses.

Soon, however, ads began appearing in the classified pages of *Women*'s *Wear Daily.*

"Tris-Tris-Tris ... We will buy any fabric containing Tris," read one. Another said, "Tris—we will purchase any large quantities of garments containing Tris." The ads had been placed by exporters, who began buying up the pajamas, usually at 10 to 30 percent of the normal wholesale price. Their intent was clear: to dump* the carcinogenic pajamas on overseas markets.[20]

Tris is not the only example of dumping. There were the 450,000 baby pacifiers, of the type known to have caused choking deaths, that were exported for sale overseas, and the 400 Iraqis who died and the 5,000 who were hospitalized after eating wheat and barley treated with a U.S.-banned organic mercury fungicide. Winstrol, a synthetic male hormone that had been found to stunt the growth of American children, was made available in Brazil as an appetite stimulant for children. DowElanco sold its weed killer Galant in Costa Rica, although the Environmental Protection Agency (EPA) forbade its sale to U.S. farmers because Galant may cause cancer. After the U.S. Food and Drug Administration (FDA) banned the painkiller dipyrone because it can cause a fatal blood disorder, Winthrop Products continued to sell dipyrone in Mexico City.

Dumping is a term apparently coined by *Mother Jones* magazine to refer to the practice of exporting to other countries products that have been banned or declared hazardous in the United States.

Manufacturers that dump products abroad clearly are motivated by profit, or at least by the hope of avoiding financial losses resulting from having to withdraw a product from the U.S. market. For government and health agencies that cooperate in the exporting of dangerous products, sometimes the motives are more complex.

For example, when researchers documented the dangers of the Dalkon Shield intrauterine device—among the adverse reactions were pelvic inflammation, blood poisoning, tubal pregnancies, and uterine perforations—its manufacturer, A. H. Robins Co., began losing its domestic market. As a result, the company worked out a deal with the Office of Population within the U.S. Agency for International Development (AID), whereby AID bought thousands of the devices at a reduced price for use in population-control programs in forty-two countries.

Why do governmental and population-control agencies approve for sale and use overseas a birth-control device proved dangerous in the United States? They say their motives are humanitarian. Because the death rate in childbirth is relatively high in third-world countries, almost any birth-control device is safer than pregnancy. Analogous arguments are used to defend the export of pesticides and other products judged too dangerous for use in the United States: Foreign countries should be free to decide for themselves whether the benefits of those products are worth their risks. In line with this, some third-world government officials insist that denying their countries access to these products is tantamount to violating their countries' national sovereignty.

This reasoning has found a sympathetic ear in Washington, for it turns up in the "notification" system that regulates the export of banned or dangerous products overseas. Based on the principles of national sovereignty, self-determination, and free trade, the notification system requires that foreign governments be notified whenever a product is banned, deregulated, suspended, or canceled by a U.S. regulatory agency. The State Department, which implements the system, has a policy statement on the subject that reads in part: "No country should establish itself as the arbiter of others' health and safety standards. Individual governments are generally in the best position to establish standards of public health and safety."

Critics of the system claim that notifying foreign health officials is virtually useless. For one thing, governments in poor countries can rarely establish health standards or even control imports into their countries. Indeed, most of the third-world countries where banned or dangerous products are dumped lack regulatory agencies, adequate testing facilities, and well-staffed customs departments.

Then there's the problem of getting the word out about hazardous products. In theory, when a government agency such as the EPA or the FDA finds a product hazardous, it is supposed to inform the State Department, which is to notify health officials in other nations. But agencies often fail to inform the State Department of the product they have banned or found harmful, and when it is notified, its communiqués typically go no further than U.S. embassies abroad. When foreign officials are notified by U.S. embassies, they sometimes find the communiqués vague or ambiguous or too technical to understand.

But even if communication procedures were improved or the export of dangerous products forbidden, there are ways that companies can circumvent these threats to their profits—for example, by simply changing the name of the product or by exporting the individual ingredients of a product to a plant in a foreign country. Once there, the ingredients can be reassembled and the product dumped. The United States does prohibit its pharmaceutical companies from exporting drugs banned in this country, but sidestepping the law is not difficult. "Unless the package bursts open on the dock," one drug company executive observes, "you have no chance of being caught."

Unfortunately for us, in the case of pesticides, the effects of overseas dumping are now coming home. In the United States, the EPA bans all crop uses of DDT and dieldrin, which kill fish, cause tumors in animals, and build up in the fatty tissue of humans. It also bans heptachlor, chlordane, leptophos, endrin, and many other pesticides, including 2,4,5-T (which contains the deadly poison dioxin, the active ingredient in Agent Orange, the notorious defoliant used in Vietnam) because they are dangerous to human beings. No law, however, prohibits the sale of DDT and these other U.S.-banned pesticides overseas, where thanks to corporate dumping they are routinely used in agriculture. In one three-month period, for example, U.S. chemical companies exported 3.9 million pounds of banned and withdrawn pesticides. The FDA now estimates, through spot checks, that 10 percent of our imported food is contaminated with residues of banned pesticides. And the FDA's most commonly used testing procedure does not even check for 70 percent of the pesticides known to cause cancer. With the doubling of exports of Mexican produce to the United States since the signing of the North American Free Trade Agreement (NAFTA), the problem of pesticide-laced food has only grown worse.[21]

Discussion Questions

1. Complete the following statements by filling in the blanks with either "moral" or "nonmoral" (e.g., factual, scientific, legal):
   a. Whether or not dumping should be permitted is a _____ question.
   b. "Are dangerous products of any use in the third world?" is a _____ question.
   c. "Is it proper for the U.S. government to sponsor the export of dangerous products overseas?" is a _____ question.
   d. Whether or not the notification system works as its supporters claim it works is a _____ question.
   e. "Is it legal to dump this product overseas?" is a _____ question.

2. Explain what dumping is, giving some examples. Does dumping raise any moral issues? What are they? What would an ethical relativist say about dumping?

3. Speculate on why dumpers dump. Do you think they believe that what they are doing is morally permissible? How would you look at the situation if you were one of the manufacturers of Tris-impregnated pajamas?

4. If no law is broken, is there anything wrong with dumping? If so, when is it wrong and why? Do any moral considerations support dumping products overseas when this violates U.S. law?

5. What moral difference, if any, does it make who is dumping, why they are doing it, where they are doing it, or what the product is?

6. Critically assess the present notification system. Is it the right approach, or is it fundamentally flawed?

7. Putting aside the question of legality, what moral arguments can be given for and against dumping? What is your position on dumping, and what principles and values do you base it on? Should we have laws prohibiting more types of dumping?

CASE 1.2

The A7D Affair

Kermit Vandivier could not have predicted the impact on his life of purchase order P-237138, issued by LTV Aerospace Corporation.[22] The order was for 202 brake assemblies for a new Air Force light attack plane, the A7D, and news of the LTV contract was cause for uncorking the champagne at the B. F. Goodrich plant in Troy, Ohio, where Vandivier worked. Although the LTV order was a small one, it signaled that Goodrich was back in LTV's good graces after living under a cloud of disrepute. Ten years earlier, Goodrich had built a brake for LTV that, to put it kindly, hadn't met expectations. As a result, LTV had written off Goodrich as a reliable source of brakes.

LTV's unexpected change of heart after ten years was easily explained. Goodrich made LTV an offer it couldn't refuse—a ridiculously low bid for making the four-disk brakes. Had Goodrich taken leave of its financial senses? Hardly. Because aircraft brakes are custom-made for a particular aircraft, only the brakes' manufacturer has replacement parts. Thus, even if it took a loss on the job, Goodrich figured it could more than make up for it in the sale of replacement parts. Of course, if Goodrich bungled the job, there wouldn't be a third chance.

John Warren, a seven-year veteran and one of Goodrich's most capable engineers, was made project engineer and lost no time in working up a preliminary design for the brake. Perhaps because the design was faultless or perhaps because Warren was given to temper tantrums when criticized, coworkers accepted the engineer's plan without question. So there was no reason to suspect that young Searle Lawson, one year out of college and six months with Goodrich, would come to think Warren's design was fundamentally flawed.

Lawson was assigned by Warren to create the final production design. He had to determine the best materials for brake linings and identify any needed adjustments in the brake design. This process called for extensive testing to meet military specifications. If the brakes passed the grueling tests, they would then be flight-tested by the Air Force. Lawson lost no time in getting down to work. What he particularly wanted to learn was whether the brake could withstand the extreme internal temperatures, in excess of 1,000 degrees F, when the aircraft landed.

When the brake linings disintegrated in the first test, Lawson thought the problem might be defective parts or an unsuitable lining. But after two more consecutive failures, he decided the problem lay in the design: The four-disk design was simply too small to stop the aircraft without generating so much heat that the brake linings melted. In Lawson's view, a larger, five-disk brake was needed.

Lawson knew well the implications of his conclusion. The four-disk brake assemblies that were arriving at the plant would have to be junked, and more tests would have to be conducted. The accompanying delays would preclude on-time delivery of the production brakes to LTV.

Lawson reported his findings and recommendations to John Warren. Going to a five-disk design was impossible, Warren told him. Officials at Goodrich, he said, were already boasting to LTV about how well the tests were going. Besides, Warren was confident that the problem lay not in the four-disk design but in the brake linings themselves.

Unconvinced, Lawson went to Robert Sink, who supervised engineers on projects. Sink was in a tight spot. If he agreed with Lawson, he would be indicting his own professional judgment: He was the man who had assigned Warren to the job. What's more, he had accepted Warren's design without reservation and had assured LTV more than once that there was little left to do but ship them the brakes. To recant now would mean explaining the reversal not only to LTV but also to the Goodrich hierarchy. In the end, Sink, who was not an engineer, deferred to the seasoned judgment of Warren and instructed Lawson to continue the tests.

His own professional judgment overridden, Lawson could do little but carry on. He built a production model of the brake with new linings and subjected it to the rigorous qualification tests. Thirteen more tests were conducted, and thirteen more failures resulted. It was at this point that data analyst and technical writer Kermit Vandivier entered the picture.

Vandivier was looking over the data of the latest A7D test when he noticed an irregularity: The instrument recording some of the stops had been deliberately miscalibrated to indicate that less pressure was required to stop the aircraft than actually was the case. Vandivier immediately showed the test logs to test lab supervisor Ralph Gretzinger. He learned from the technician who miscalibrated the instrument that Lawson had requested the miscalibration. Lawson later said he was simply following the orders of Sink and the manager of the design engineering section, who were intent on qualifying the brakes at whatever cost. For his part, Gretzinger vowed he would never permit deliberately falsified data or reports to leave his lab.

A month later, the brake was again tested, and again it failed. Nevertheless, Lawson asked Vandivier to start preparing the various graph and chart displays for qualification. Vandivier refused and told Gretzinger what he'd been asked to do. Gretzinger was livid. He again vowed that his lab would not be part of a conspiracy to defraud. Then, bent on getting to the bottom of the matter, Gretzinger rushed off to see Russell Line, manager of the Goodrich Technical Services Section.

An hour later, Gretzinger returned to his desk looking like a beaten man. He knew he had only two choices: defy his superiors or do their bidding.

"You know," he said to Vandivier, "I've been an engineer for a long time, and I've always believed that ethics and integrity were every bit as important as theorems and formulas, and never once has anything happened to change my beliefs. Now this…. Hell, I've got two sons I've got to put through school and I just …" When his voice trailed off, it was clear that he would in fact knuckle under. He and Vandivier would prepare the qualifying data; then someone "upstairs" would actually write the report. Their part, Gretzinger rationalized, wasn't really so bad. "After all," he said, "we're just drawing some curves, and what happens to them after they leave here—well, we're not responsible for that." Vandivier knew Gretzinger didn't believe what he was saying about not being responsible. Both of them knew that they were about to become principal characters in a plot to defraud.

Unwilling to play his part, Vandivier decided that he, too, would confer with Line. Line was sympathetic; he said he understood what Vandivier was going through. But in the end he said he would not refer the matter to chief engineer H. C. "Bud" Sunderman, as Vandivier had suggested. Why not? Vandivier wanted to know.

"Because it's none of my business, and it's none of yours," Line told him. "I learned a long time ago not to worry about things over which I had no control. I have no control over this."

Vandivier pressed the point. What about the test pilots who might get injured because of the faulty brakes? Didn't their uncertain fate prick Line's conscience?

"Look," said Line, growing impatient with Vandivier's moral needling, "I just told you I have no control over this thing. Why should my conscience bother me?" Then he added, "You're just getting all upset over this thing for nothing. I just do as I'm told, and I'd advise you to do the same."

Vandivier made his decision that night. He knew, of course, he was on the horns of a dilemma. If he wrote the report, he would save his job at the expense of his conscience. If he refused, he would honor his moral code and, he was convinced, lose his job—an ugly prospect for anyone, let alone a forty-two-year-old man with a wife and several children. The next day, Vandivier phoned Lawson and told him he was ready to begin on the qualification report.

Lawson shot over to Vandivier's office with all the speed of one who knows that, swallowed fast, a bitter pill doesn't taste so bad. Before they started on the report, though, Vandivier, still uneasy with his decision, asked Lawson if he fully understood what they were about to do.

"Yeah," Lawson said acidly, "we're going to screw LTV. And speaking of screwing," he continued, "I know now how a whore feels, because that's exactly what I've become, an engineering whore. I've sold myself. It's all I can do to look at myself in the mirror when I shave. I make me sick."

For someone like Vandivier, who had written dozens of them, the qualification report was a snap. It took about a month, during which time the brake failed still another final qualification test, and the two men talked almost exclusively about the enormity of what they were doing. In the Nuremberg trials they found a historical analogy to their own complicity and culpability in the A7D affair. More than once, Lawson opined that the brakes were downright dangerous, that anything could happen during the flight tests. His opinion proved prophetic.

When the report was finished, copies were sent to the Air Force and LTV. Within a week test flights were begun at Edwards Air Force Base in California. Goodrich dispatched Lawson to Edwards as its representative, but he wasn't there long. Several "unusual incidents" brought the flight tests literally to a screeching halt. Lawson returned to the Troy plant, full of talk about several near crashes caused by brake trouble during landings. That was

enough to send Vandivier to his attorney, to whom he told the whole sorry tale.

Although the attorney didn't think Vandivier was guilty of fraud, he was convinced that the analyst/writer was guilty of participating in a conspiracy to defraud. Vandivier's only hope, the attorney counseled, was to make a clean breast of the matter to the FBI. Vandivier did. At this point both he and Lawson decided to resign from Goodrich. In his letter of resignation, addressed to Russell Line, Vandivier cited the A7D report and stated: "As you are aware, this report contains numerous deliberate and willful misrepresentations which ... expose both myself and others to criminal charges of conspiracy to defraud."

Vandivier was soon summoned to the office of Bud Sunderman, who berated him mercilessly. Among other things, Sunderman accused Vandivier of making irresponsible charges and of arch disloyalty. It would be best, said Sunderman, if Vandivier cleared out immediately. Within minutes, Vandivier had cleaned out his desk and left the plant.

Two days later Goodrich announced it was recalling the qualification report and replacing the old brake with a new five-disk brake at no cost to LTV.

Aftermath

- A year later, a congressional committee reviewed the A7D affair. Vandivier and Lawson testified as government witnesses, together with Air Force officers and a General Accounting Office team. All testified that the brake was dangerous.
- Robert Sink, representing the Troy plant, depicted Vandivier as a mere high school graduate with no technical training, who preferred to follow his own lights rather than organizational guidance. R. G. Jeter, vice president and general counsel of Goodrich, dismissed as ludicrous even the possibility that some thirty engineers at the Troy plant would stand idly by and see reports changed and falsified.

- The congressional committee adjourned after four hours with no real conclusion. The following day the Department of Defense, citing the A7D episode, made major changes in its inspection, testing, and reporting procedures.
- The A7D eventually went into service with the Goodrich-made five-disk brake.
- Searle Lawson went to work as an engineer for LTV assigned to the A7D project.
- Russell Line was promoted to production superintendent.
- Robert Sink moved up into Line's old job.
- Kermit Vandivier became a newspaper reporter for the *Daily News* in Troy, Ohio.

Discussion Questions

1. Identify the main characters in this case, and explain what happened.
2. To what extent did Lawson, Vandivier, and Gretzinger consider the relevant moral issues before deciding to participate in the fraud? What was their reasoning? What would you have done if you were in their situation?
3. How did Sink and Line look at the matter? How would you evaluate their conduct?
4. Do you think Vandivier was wrong to work up the qualification report? Explain the moral principle or principles that underlie your judgment.
5. Was Vandivier right to "blow the whistle"? Was he morally required to so? Again, explain the moral principles on which your judgment is based.
6. Describe the different pressures to conform in this case and discuss the relevance of the concepts of groupthink and diffusion of responsibility. Do any of these factors excuse the conduct of particular individuals in this case? If so, who and why?
7. Should Goodrich be held morally responsible as a company for the A7D affair, or should just the individuals involved be held responsible?
8. What might Goodrich have done, and what steps should it take in the future, to ensure more moral behavior?

CHAPTER 2

Normative Theories
of Ethics

Orjan F. Ellingvag/Dagens Naringsliv/Corbis

INTRODUCTION

Head of a premier hedge fund and former president of the NASDAQ stock exchange, Bernard Madoff was a respected financier with a sterling reputation. So, when he stated in a speech that "in today's regulatory environment, it's virtually impossible [for fund managers] to violate the rules," his listeners were unlikely to have doubted the truth of what he was saying. They were even less likely to have foreseen how eerily prophetic his words would turn out to be when the FBI arrested him a year later for perpetrating what may have been the greatest scam of all times.

Madoff's celebrated hedge fund, it turns out, was a total fraud—in essence, a gigantic Ponzi scheme. In a Ponzi scheme, a con artist takes in money from investors but keeps it for himself rather than investing it as promised. On paper, the profits of the investors continue to grow. If they want to redeem some of their fund shares for cash, the fraudster uses money from new investors to pay them. This keeps investors happy and content but clueless about what really happened to their money.

The fact that Madoff's phony hedge fund reported consistently strong returns in both good markets and bad, with never a down quarter, made a few financial analysts suspicious. However, the law doesn't require hedge funds to operate as transparently as it does mutual funds, and Madoff was notoriously secretive about his investment strategy. The Securities and Exchange Commission, which is charged with policing the financial marketplace, never noticed anything amiss, and most business observers and investment advisors simply thought that Madoff had the Midas touch. And so it seemed he did—until, that is, the financial crisis of 2008 when the meltdown on Wall Street led more and more of his investors to seek to redeem fund shares for cash. With new investors now few and far between, Madoff simply had no money to pay those investors who wanted to cash in some or all of their chips. Unable to keep the game up, he confessed to his sons, who promptly turned him in to the authorities.

Madoff's victims included insurance companies, pension and investment funds, banks in Europe and Asia, and a number of prominent individuals such as, Hall of Fame baseball pitcher Sandy Koufax, filmmaker Steven Spielberg, and actors Kevin Bacon and John Malkovich. Many of them were bilked for millions and millions of dollars, in some cases losing nearly all their savings. Likewise, some of the charities that had invested with Madoff were completely ruined. Having lost their assets, they were forced to shut down. However, a few investors who had withdrawn money from their accounts on and off over the years ended up in an ethical quandary. The money that they thought was in their Madoff accounts was, of course, gone, but over the years they had actually taken more money out of the fund, sometimes substantially more money, than they had initially put into it. But what they thought at the time was legitimate profit was, they now realized, almost certainly money that Madoff had stolen from other clients. Should they keep quiet? Should they return the money to other investors, most of whom had ended up deep in the hole? Or should they insist that the money they received was legitimately theirs and push (along with all the other investors) to somehow get restitution of the balances that just a few weeks before they had assumed still remained in their Madoff accounts?

One's legal responsibilities in a situation like this are unclear, and it's anybody's guess whether investors who lost more could succeed in using the legal system to reclaim some of their losses from investors who came out ahead. For one thing, it's unclear where any individual investor's money actually went. But it's not just factual or legal complexities that make the question difficult. There are competing moral considerations. If you yourself were scammed, it might seem that you have no moral obligation to help those whose losses were greater—after all, you were a victim, too. On the other hand, although Madoff was ostensibly paying you money that you were entitled to, he was, in fact, paying you with purloined funds. Do those later investors have a right to get their money back from you? Would you act wrongly in hanging on to what you were lucky enough to get from Madoff before his scheme crashed? Or are the Madoff investors morally required to pool their gains and try to equalize their losses?

You don't need to study moral philosophy to see that Madoff acted immorally. Only a complete scoundrel steals from charities, pension funds, and friends and acquaintances who have entrusted him with their life savings. But determining what an investor should do who got back from Madoff more than other investors did—perhaps even more than his initial investment—is more difficult. Even if the person wants to do his or her duty, what exactly does morality require, and how are we to determine what that is? On what basis are we to judge what is right or wrong?

Chapter 1 explained that defensible moral judgments must be supportable by sound moral principles. That is because when we judge something wrong, we are not judging simply that it is wrong but also that it is wrong for some reason or by virtue of some general characteristic.[1] Moral principles thus provide the confirmatory standard for moral judgments. The use of these principles, however, is not a mechanical process in which one cranks in data and out pops an automatic moral judgment. Rather, the principles provide a conceptual framework that guides us in making moral decisions. Careful thought and open-minded reflection are always necessary to work from one's moral principles to a considered moral judgment.

But what are the appropriate principles to rely on when making moral judgments? The truth is that there is no consensus among people who have studied ethics and reflected on these matters. Different theories exist as to the proper standard of right and wrong. As the British philosopher Bernard Williams put it, we are heirs to a rich and complex ethical tradition, in which a variety of different moral principles and ethical considerations intertwine and sometimes compete.[2]

This chapter discusses the different normative perspectives and rival ethical principles that are our heritage. After distinguishing between what are called "consequentialist" and "nonconsequentialist" normative theories, it looks in detail at several ethical approaches, discussing their pros and cons and their relevance to moral decision making in an organizational context:

1. Egoism, both as an ethical theory and as a psychological theory
2. Utilitarianism, the theory that the morally right action is the one that achieves the most happiness for everyone concerned
3. Kant's ethics, with his categorical imperative and his emphasis on moral motivation and respect for persons

4. Other nonconsequentialist normative themes: duties, moral rights, and prima facie principles

The chapter concludes with an attempt to tie together the major concerns of the different normative theories and suggests a general way of approaching moral decision making.

_____

CONSEQUENTIALIST AND NONCONSEQUENTIALIST THEORIES

In ethics, **normative theories** propose some principle or principles for distinguishing right actions from wrong actions. These theories can, for convenience, be divided into two kinds: consequentialist and nonconsequentialist.

According to **consequentialist theories**, the moral rightness of an action is determined solely by its results. If its consequences are good, then the act is right; if they are bad, the act is wrong. Consequentialists (moral theorists who adopt this approach) determine what is right by weighing the ratio of good to bad that an action will produce. The right act is the one that produces (or will probably produce) at least as great a ratio of good to evil as any other course of action open to the agent.

One question that arises here is, Consequences for whom? Should one consider the consequences only for oneself? Or the consequences for everyone affected? The two most important consequentialist theories, *egoism* and *utilitarianism*, are distinguished by their different answers to this question. Egoism advocates individual self-interest as its guiding principle. Utilitarianism holds that one must take into account everyone affected by the action. But both theories agree that rightness and wrongness are solely a function of an action's results.

By contrast, **nonconsequentialist** (or *deontological*) **theories** contend that right and wrong are determined by more than the likely consequences of an action. Nonconsequentialists do not necessarily deny that consequences are morally significant, but they believe that other factors are also relevant to the moral assessment of an action. For example, a nonconsequentialist would hold that for Kevin to break his promise to Cindy is wrong not simply because it has bad results (Cindy's hurt feelings, Kevin's damaged reputation, and so on) but because of the inherent character of the act itself. Even if more good than bad were to come from Kevin's breaking the promise, a nonconsequentialist might still view it as wrong. What matters is the nature of the act in question, not just its results. This idea will become clearer later in the chapter as we examine some specific nonconsequentialist principles and theories.

Summary 2.1
Consequentialist moral theories see the moral rightness or wrongness of actions as a function of their results. If the consequences are good, the action is right; if they are bad, the action is wrong. Nonconsequentialist theories see other factors as also relevant to the determination of right and wrong.

EGOISM

In the late summer of 2000, a dismayed American public learned that the Firestone tires on Ford Explorers, one of the country's most popular vehicles, were dangerously prone to split apart on the road, causing the SUVs to roll over and crash. When officials began demanding a recall, the controversy was reminiscent of an earlier one involving Firestone's "500" steel-belted radials, which a House subcommittee had implicated in at least fifteen deaths. When Firestone announced that it was discontinuing the controversial "500," newspapers at the time interpreted this to mean that Firestone would immediately remove the tires from the market. In fact, Firestone intended only a "rolling phaseout" and continued to manufacture the tire. When a Firestone spokesperson was later asked why the company had not corrected the media's misinterpretation of its intent, the spokesperson said that Firestone's policy was to ask for corrections only when it was beneficial to the company to do so—in other words, only when it was in the company's self-interest.

The view that equates morality with self-interest is referred to as **egoism**. An egoist contends that an act is morally right if and only if it best promotes an agent's interests. (Here an "agent" can be a single person or, as in the Firestone example, an organization.) Egoists use personal advantage (both short term and long run) as the standard for measuring an action's rightness. If an action will produce more good for the agent than any alternative action would, then that action is the morally right one to perform.

Moral philosophers distinguish between two kinds of egoism: personal and impersonal. *Personal* egoists claim they should pursue their own best interests, but they do not say what others should do. *Impersonal* egoists claim that everyone should let self-interest guide his or her conduct.

Misconceptions about Egoism

Several misconceptions haunt both versions of egoism. One is that egoists do only what they like, that they believe in "eat, drink, and be merry." Not so. Undergoing unpleasant, even painful experience meshes with egoism, provided such temporary sacrifice is necessary for the advancement of one's long-term interests.

Another misconception is that all egoists endorse **hedonism**, the view that pleasure (or happiness) is the only thing that is good in itself, that it is the ultimate good, the one thing in life worth pursuing for its own sake. Although some egoists are hedonistic—as was the ancient Greek philosopher Epicurus (341–270 B.C.E.)—other egoists have a broader view of what constitutes self-interest. They identify the good with knowledge, power, or what some modern psychologists call "self-actualization." Egoists may, in fact, hold any theory of what is good.

A final but very important misconception is that egoists cannot act honestly, be gracious and helpful, or otherwise promote other people's interests. Egoism, however, requires us to do whatever will best further our own interests, and doing this sometimes requires us to advance the interests of others. In particular, egoism tells us to benefit others when we expect that our doing so will be reciprocated or when the act will bring us pleasure or in some way promote our own good. For example, egoism might discourage a shopkeeper from trying to cheat customers because it is likely to hurt business in the long run. Or egoism might recommend to the chair of the board that she hire as a vice president her nephew, who is not the best candidate for the job but of whom she is very fond. Hiring the nephew might bring her more satisfaction than any other course of action, even if the nephew doesn't perform his job as well as someone else might.

Psychological Egoism

According to egoism, we should assist others when doing so best promotes our own interests.

So egoism does not preach that we should never assist others but rather that we have no basic moral duty to do so. The only moral obligation we have is to ourselves. Although you and I are not required to act in the interests of others, we should if that is the best way to promote our own self-interest. In short: Always look out for "number one."

Proponents of the ethical theory of egoism generally attempt to derive their basic moral principle from the alleged fact that human beings are by nature selfish creatures. According to this doctrine, termed **psychological egoism**, people are, as a matter of fact, so constructed that they must behave selfishly. Psychological egoism asserts that all actions are selfishly motivated and that truly unselfish actions are therefore impossible. Even such apparently self-sacrificial acts as giving up one's own life to save the lives of one's children or blowing the whistle on one's organization's misdeeds at great personal expense are, according to psychological egoism, done to satisfy the person's own self-interested desires. For example, the parent may seek to perpetuate the family line or to avoid guilt, and the worker may be after fame or revenge.

Problems with Egoism

There are strong objections to egoism as an ethical doctrine.

Although egoism as an ethical doctrine has always had its adherents, the theory is open to very strong objections. It is safe to say that few, if any, philosophers today would advocate it as either a personal or an organizational morality. Consider these objections:

1. **Psychological egoism is not a sound theory.** Of course, self-interest motivates all of us to some extent, and we all know of situations in which someone pretended to be acting altruistically or morally but was really motivated only by self-interest. The theory of psychological egoism contends, however, that self-interest is the only thing that ever motivates anyone.

   Now this claim seems open to many counterexamples. Take the actual case of a man who, while driving a company truck, spotted smoke coming from inside a parked car and a child trying to escape from the vehicle. The man quickly made a U-turn, drove up to the burning vehicle, and found a little girl trapped in the backseat, restrained by a seat belt. Flames raged in the front seat as heavy smoke billowed from the car. Disregarding his own safety, the man entered the car and removed the child, who authorities said otherwise would have died from the poisonous fumes and the flames.

   Or take a more mundane example. It's Saturday, and you feel like having a beer with a couple of pals and watching the ball game. On the other hand, you believe you ought to take your two children to the zoo, as you earlier suggested to them you might. Going to the zoo would bring them a lot of pleasure—and besides, you haven't done much with them recently. Of course, you love your children and it will bring you some pleasure to go to the zoo with them, but—let's face it—they've been rather whiny lately and you'd prefer to watch the ball game. Nonetheless, you feel an obligation and so you go to the zoo.

These appear to be cases in which people are acting for reasons that are not self-interested. Of course, the reasons that lead you to take your children to the zoo—a sense of obligation, a desire to promote their happiness—are your reasons, but that by itself does not make them self-interested reasons. Still less does it show that you are selfish. Anything that you do is a result of your desires, but that fact doesn't establish what the believer in psychological egoism claims—namely, that the only desires you have, or the only desires that ultimately move you, are self-interested desires.

Psychological egoists (that is, advocates of the theory of psychological egoism) will claim that deep down both the heroic man who saved the girl and the unheroic parent who took the children to the zoo were really motivated by self-interest in some way or another. Maybe the hero was hoping to win praise or the parent to advance his or her own pleasure by enhancing the children's affection for the parent. Or maybe some other self-interested consideration motivated them. Psychological egoists can always claim that some yet-to-be-identified subconscious egoistic motivation is the main impulse behind any action.

At this point, though, the psychological egoists' claims sound a little far-fetched, and we may suspect them of trying to make their theory true by definition. Whatever example we come up with, they will simply claim that somehow or other the person is really motivated by self-interest. One may well wonder how scientific this theory is, or how much content it has, when the hero and the coward, the parent who goes to the zoo and the parent who stays home, are equally selfish in their motivations.

A defender of egoism as an ethical doctrine could concede that people are not fully egoistic by nature and yet continue to insist that people ought morally to pursue only their own interests. Yet without the doctrine of psychological egoism, the ethical thesis of egoism becomes less attractive. Other types of ethical principles are possible. We all care about ourselves, but how much sense does it make to see self-interest as the basis of right and wrong? Do we really want to say that someone acting altruistically is behaving immorally?

2. **Ethical egoism is not really a moral theory at all.** Many critics of egoism as an ethical standard contend that it misunderstands the nature and point of morality. As Chapter 1 explained, morality serves to restrain our purely self-interested desires so we can all live together. If our interests never came into conflict—that is, if it were never advantageous for one person to deceive or cheat another—then we would have no need for morality. The moral standards of a society provide the basic guidelines for cooperative social existence and allow us to resolve conflicts by appeal to shared principles of justification.

Summary 2.2
Egoism is the con-sequentialist theory that an action is right if and only if it pro-motes the indivi-dual's best interests. Proponents of this theory base their view on the alleged fact that human beings are, by na-ture, selfish (the doctrine of psycho-logical egoism). Critics of egoism ar-gue that (1) psycho-logical egoism is implausible, (2) ego-ism is not really a moral principle, and (3) egoism ignores blatant wrongs.

It is difficult to see how ethical egoism could perform this function. In a society of egoists, people might publicly agree to follow certain rules so their lives would run more smoothly. But it would be a very unstable world, because people would not hesitate to break the rules if they thought they could get away with it. Nor can egoism provide a means for settling conflicts and disputes, because it simply tells each party to do whatever is necessary to promote effectively his or her interests.

Many moral theorists maintain that moral principles apply equally to the conduct of all persons and that their application requires us to be objective and impartial. Moral agents are seen as those who, despite their own involvement in an issue, can be reasonably disinterested and objective—those who try to see all sides of an issue without being com-mitted to the interests of a particular individual or group, including themselves. If we accept this attitude of detachment and impartiality as at least part of what it means to take a moral point of view, then we must look for it in any proposed moral principle.

Those who make egoism their moral standard are anything but objective, for they seek to guide themselves by their own best interests, regardless of the issue or circumstances. They do not even attempt to be impartial, except insofar as impartiality furthers their own interests. And, according to their theory, any third party offering advice should simply represent his or her own interest.

3. **Ethical egoism ignores blatant wrongs**. The most common objection to egoism as an ethical doctrine is that by reducing everything to the stan-dard of best long-term self-interest, egoism takes no stand against such seemingly immoral acts as theft, murder, racial and sexual discrimination, deliberately false advertising, and wanton pollution. All such actions are morally neutral until the test of self-interest is applied.

Of course, the defender of egoism might argue that this objection begs the question by assuming that such acts are immoral and then repu-diating egoism on this basis when, in fact, their morality is the very issue that moral principles such as egoism are meant to resolve. Still, egoism must respond to the widely observed human desire to be fair or just, a desire that at least sometimes seems stronger than competing selfish de-sires. A moral principle that allows the possibility of murder in the cause of self-interest offends our basic intuitions about right and wrong; it clashes with one of our firmest moral convictions.

UTILITARIANISM

Utilitarianism tells us to bring about the most happiness for everyone affected by our actions. Jeremy Bentham and John Stuart Mill were impor-tant early utilitarians.

Utilitarianism is the moral doctrine that we should always act to produce the greatest possible balance of good over bad for everyone affected by our ac-tions. By "good," utilitarians understand happiness or pleasure. Thus, the greatest happiness of all constitutes the standard that determines whether an action is right or wrong. Although the basic theme of utilitarianism is present in the writings of many earlier thinkers, Jeremy Bentham (1748–1832) and John Stuart Mill (1806–1873) were the first to develop the theory explicitly and in detail. Both Bentham and Mill were philosophers with a strong interest in legal and social reform. They used the utilitarian standard to evaluate and criticize the social and political institutions of their day—for example, the prison system and the disenfranchisement of women. As a result, utilitarianism has long been associated with social improvement.

Bentham viewed a community as no more than the individual persons that it comprises. The interests of the community are simply the sum of the interests of its members. An action promotes the interests of an individual when it adds to the individual's pleasure or diminishes the person's pain. Correspondingly, an action augments the happiness of a community only insofar as it increases the total amount of individual happiness. In this way, Bentham argued for the utilitarian principle that actions are right if they promote the greatest human welfare, wrong if they do not.

For Bentham, pleasure and pain are merely types of sensations. He offered a "hedonic calculus" of six criteria for evaluating pleasure and pain exclusively by their quantitative differences—in particular, by their intensity and duration. This calculus, he believed, makes possible an objective determination of the morality of anyone's conduct, individual or collective, on any occasion.

Bentham rejected any distinctions based on the type of pleasure except insofar as they might indicate differences in quantity. Thus, if equal amounts of pleasure are involved, throwing darts is as good as writing poetry and baking a cake as good as composing a symphony; reading Stephen King is of no less value than reading Shakespeare. Although he himself was an intelligent, cultivated man, Bentham maintained that there is nothing intrinsically better about refined and intellectual pleasures than about crude or prosaic ones. The only issue is which yields the greater amount of enjoyment.

John Stuart Mill thought Bentham's concept of pleasure was too simple. He viewed human beings as having elevated faculties that allow them to pursue various higher kinds of pleasure. The pleasures of the intellect and imagination, in particular, have a higher value than those of mere physical sensation. Thus, for Mill the utility principle must take into consideration the relative quality of different pleasures and pains, not just their intensity and duration.

Bentham and Mill had different conceptions of pleasure, but they both equated it with happiness and believed that pleasure was the ultimate value.

Although Bentham and Mill had different conceptions of pleasure, both men equated pleasure and happiness and considered pleasure the ultimate value. In this sense they are hedonists: Pleasure, in their view, is the one thing that is intrinsically good or worthwhile. Anything that is good is good only because it brings about pleasure (or happiness), directly or indirectly. Take education, for example. The learning process itself might be pleasurable to us; reflecting on or working with what we have learned might bring us satisfaction at some later time; or by making possible a career and life that we could not have had otherwise, education might bring us happiness indirectly. In contrast, critics of Bentham and Mill contend that things other than happiness are also inherently good—for example, knowledge, friendship, and aesthetic satisfaction. The implication is that these things are valuable even if they do not lead to happiness.

Bentham and Mill cared about happiness because they implicitly identified it with well-being—that is, with what is good for people. In their view, our lives go well, we have well-being, just to the extent that our lives are pleasurable or happy. Some moral theorists have modified utilitarianism so that it aims at other consequences in addition to happiness. Other utilitarians, wary of trying to compare one person's happiness with another's, have interpreted their theory as requiring us not to maximize happiness but rather to maximize the satisfaction of people's desires or preferences. The focus here will be utilitarianism in its standard form, in which the good to be aimed at is human happiness or well-being, but what will be said about standard or classical utilitarianism applies, with the appropriate modifications, to other versions as well.

Although this chapter will later consider another form of utilitarianism, known as "rule utilitarianism," utilitarianism in its most basic version, often called **act utilitarianism**, states that we must ask ourselves what the consequences of a particular act in a particular situation will be for all those affected. If its consequences bring more total good than those of any alternative course of action, then this action is the right one and the one we should perform.

Six Points about Utilitarianism

Six important things to understand about utilitarianism.

Before evaluating utilitarianism, one should understand some points that might lead to confusion and misapplication. *First*, when deciding which action will produce the greatest happiness, we must consider unhappiness or pain as well as happiness. Suppose, for example, that an action produces eight units of happiness and four units of unhappiness. Its net worth is four units of happiness. Suppose also that an opposed action produces ten units of happiness and seven units of unhappiness; its net worth is three units. In this case we should choose the first action over the second. In the event that both lead not to happiness but to unhappiness, and there is no third option, we should choose the one that brings fewer units of unhappiness.

Second, actions affect people to different degrees. Your playing your radio loudly might enhance two persons' pleasure a little, cause significant discomfort to two others, and leave a fifth person indifferent. The utilitarian theory is not that each person votes on the basis of his or her pleasure or pain, with the majority ruling, but rather that we add up the various pleasures and pains, however large or small, and go with the action that brings about the greatest net amount of happiness.

Summary 2.3
Utilitarianism, another consequentialist theory, maintains that the morally right action is the one that provides the most happiness for all those affected. After assessing as best we can the likely results of each action, not just in the short term but in the long run as well, we are to choose the course of conduct that brings about the greatest net happiness.

Third, because utilitarians evaluate actions according to their consequences and because actions produce different results in different circumstances, almost anything might, in principle, be morally right in some particular situation. For example, whereas breaking a promise generally produces unhappiness, there can be circumstances in which, on balance, more happiness would be produced by breaking a promise than by keeping it. In those cases, utilitarianism would require us to break the promise.

Fourth, utilitarians wish to maximize happiness not simply immediately but in the long run as well. All the indirect ramifications of an act have to be taken into account. Lying might seem a good way out of a tough situation, but if and when the people we deceive find out, not only will they be unhappy, but also our reputations and our relationships with them will be damaged. This is a serious risk that a utilitarian cannot ignore.

Fifth, utilitarians acknowledge that we often do not know with certainty what the future consequences of our actions will be. Accordingly, we must act so that the expected or likely happiness is as great as possible. If I take my friend's money, unbeknownst to him, and buy lottery tickets with it, there is a chance that we will end up millionaires and that my action will have maximized happiness all around. But the odds are definitely against it; the most likely result is loss of money (and probably of a friendship, too). Therefore, no utilitarian could justify gambling with purloined funds on the grounds that it might maximize happiness.

Sometimes it is difficult to determine the likely results of alternative actions, and no modern utilitarian really believes that we can assign precise units of happiness and unhappiness to people. But as Mill reminds us, we actually do have quite a lot of experience as to what typically makes people happy or unhappy. In any case, as utilitarians our duty is to strive to maximize total happiness, even when it is difficult to know which action will produce the most good.

Finally, when choosing among possible actions, utilitarianism does not require us to disregard our own pleasure. Nor should we give it added weight. Rather, our own pleasure and pain enter into the calculus equally with the pleasures and pains of others. Even if we are sincere in our utilitarianism, we must guard against the possibility of being biased in our calculations when our own interests are at stake. For this reason, and because it would be time-consuming to do a utilitarian calculation before every action, utilitarians encourage us to rely on rules of thumb in ordinary moral circumstances. We can make it a rule of thumb, for example, to tell the truth and keep our promises, rather than to calculate possible pleasures and pains in every routine case, because we know that in general telling the truth and keeping promises result in more happiness than do lying and breaking promises.

Utilitarianism in an Organizational Context

Several features about utilitarianism make it appealing as a standard for moral decisions in business and nonbusiness organizations.

First, utilitarianism provides a clear and straightforward basis for formulating and testing policies. By utilitarian standards, an organizational policy, decision, or action is good if it promotes the general welfare more than any other alternative. A policy is considered wrong (or in need of modification) if it does not promote total utility as well as some alternative would. Utilitarians do not ask us to accept rules, policies, or principles blindly. Rather, they require us to test their worth against the standard of utility.

Second, utilitarianism provides an objective and attractive way of resolving conflicts of self-interest. This feature of utilitarianism dramatically contrasts with egoism, which seems incapable of resolving such conflicts. By proposing a standard outside self-interest, utilitarianism greatly minimizes and may actually eliminate such disputes. Thus, individuals within organizations make moral decisions and evaluate their actions by appealing to a uniform standard: the general good.

Third, utilitarianism provides a flexible, result-oriented approach to moral decision making. By recognizing no actions of a general kind as inherently right

Three features of utilitarianism make it appealing in an organizational context.

or wrong, utilitarianism encourages organizations to focus on the results of their actions and policies, and it allows them to tailor their decisions to suit the complexities of their situations. This facet of utilitarianism enables organizations to make realistic and workable moral decisions.

Critical Inquiries of Utilitarianism

1. **Is utilitarianism really workable?** Utilitarianism instructs us to maximize happiness, but in difficult cases we may be very uncertain about the likely results of the alternative courses of action open to us. Furthermore, comparing your level of happiness or unhappiness with mine is at best tricky, at worst impossible—and when many people are involved, the matter may get hopelessly complex. Even if we assume that it is possible to make comparisons and to calculate the various possible results of each course of action that a person might take (and the likelihood of each result), is it realistic to expect people to take the time to make those calculations and, if they do, to make them accurately? Some critics of act utilitarianism have contended that teaching people to follow the basic utilitarian principle would not in fact promote happiness because of the difficulties in applying utilitarianism accurately.

2. **Are some actions wrong, even if they produce good?** Like egoism, utilitarianism focuses on the results of an action, not on the character of the action itself. For utilitarians, no action is in itself objectionable. It is objectionable only when it leads to a lesser amount of total good than could otherwise have been brought about. Critics of utilitarianism, by contrast, contend that some actions can be immoral and thus things we must not do, even if doing them would maximize happiness.

    Suppose a dying woman has asked you to promise to send the $25,000 under her bed to her nephew in another part of the country. She dies without anyone else's knowing of the money or of the promise that you made. Now suppose, too, that, you know the nephew is a spendthrift and a drunkard and, were the money delivered to him, it would be wasted in a week of outrageous partying. On the other hand, a very fine orphanage in your town needs such a sum to improve and expand its recreational facilities, something that would provide happiness to many children for years to come. It seems clear that on utilitarian grounds you should give the money to the orphanage, because this action would result in more total happiness.

    Many people would balk at this conclusion, contending that it would be wrong to break your promise, even if doing so would bring about more good than keeping it. Having made a promise, you have an obligation to keep it, and a deathbed promise is particularly serious. Furthermore, the deceased woman had a right to do with her money as she wished; it is not for you to decide how to spend it. Likewise, having been bequeathed the money, the nephew has a right to it, regardless of how wisely or foolishly he might spend it. Defenders of utilitarianism, however, would insist that promoting happiness is all that really matters and warn you not to be blinded by moral prejudice.

Critics of utilitarianism respond that it is utilitarianism that is morally blind not just in permitting but also in requiring immoral actions in order to maximize happiness. Philosopher Richard Brandt states the case against act utilitarianism this way:

> Act-utilitarianism ... implies that if you have employed a boy to mow your lawn and he has finished the job and asks for his pay, you should pay him what you promised only if you cannot find a better use for your money.... It implies that if your father is ill and has no prospect of good in his life, and maintaining him is a drain on the energy and enjoyments of others, then, if you can end his life without provoking any public scandal or setting a bad example, it is your positive duty to take matters into your own hands and bring his life to a close.[3]

In the same vein, ethicist A. C. Ewing concludes that "[act] utilitarian principles, logically carried out, would result in far more cheating, lying and unfair action than any good man would tolerate."[4]

Defenders of act utilitarianism would reply that these charges are exaggerated. Although it is theoretically possible, for example, that not paying the boy for his work might maximize happiness, this is extremely unlikely. Utilitarians contend that only in very unusual circumstances will pursuit of the good conflict with our ordinary ideas of right and wrong, and in those cases—like the deathbed promise—we should put aside those ordinary ideas. The anti-utilitarian replies that the theoretical possibility that utilitarianism may require immoral conduct shows it to be an unsatisfactory moral theory.

3. **Is utilitarianism unjust?** Utilitarianism concerns itself with the sum total of happiness produced, not with how that happiness is distributed. If policy X brings two units of happiness to each of five people and policy Y brings nine units of happiness to one person, one unit each to two others, and none to the remaining two, then Y is to be preferred (eleven units of happiness versus ten), even though it distributes that happiness very unequally.

Worse still from the critic's point of view, utilitarianism may even require that some people's happiness be sacrificed in order to achieve the greatest overall amount of happiness. Sometimes the general utility may be served only at the expense of a single individual or group. For example, under the right of **eminent domain** (see Case 3.1), the government may appropriate private property for public use, usually with compensation to the owner. Thus, the government may legally purchase your house from you to widen a highway—even if you don't want to sell the house or want more money than the government is willing to pay. The public interest is served at your private expense. Is this just?

Or consider the Dan River experiment, part of the long-running controversy over the cause of brown lung disease. Claiming that the disease is caused by the inhalation of microscopic fibers in cotton dust, textile unions fought for years for tough regulations to protect their workers. The Occupational Safety and Health Administration (OSHA) responded by proposing cotton dust standards, which would require many firms to

Summary 2.4
In an organizational context, utilitarianism provides an objective way to resolve conflicts of self-interest and encourages a realistic and result-oriented approach to moral decision making. But critics contend that (1) utilitarianism is not really workable, (2) some actions are wrong even if they produce good results, and (3) utilitarianism incorrectly overlooks considerations of justice and the distribution of happiness.

install expensive new equipment. A few months before the deadline for installing the equipment, officials at Dan River textile plants in Virginia asked the state to waive the requirements for a time so the company could conduct an experiment to determine the precise cause of brown lung disease. Both the state and the Department of Labor allowed the extension. In response, the textile workers union contended, "It is simply unconscionable to allow hundreds of cotton mill workers to continue to face a high risk of developing brown lung disease."[5]

Suppose that the Dan River project did expose workers to a "high risk" of contracting lung disease. If so, then a small group of individuals—633 textile workers at ten locations in Danville, Virginia—were being compelled to carry the burden of isolating the cause of brown lung disease. Is that just?

Although their critics would say no, utilitarians would respond that it is, if the experiment maximizes the total good of society. Does it? In fact, the results of the experiment were inconclusive, but if the project had succeeded in identifying the exact cause of the disease, then thousands of textile workers across the country would have benefited. Researchers might also have discovered a more economical way to ensure worker safety than by installing expensive new equipment, which in turn would have profited both consumers and the textile industry. Certainly, utilitarians would consider the potentially negative impact on workers, but only as one factor among others. At the time of the decision, after the interests of all affected parties have been weighed, if extending the deadline is likely to yield the greatest net benefit or utility, then doing so is just—even though workers might be injured.

The Interplay between Self-Interest and Utility

Both self-interest and utility play important roles in organizational decisions, and the views of many businesspeople blend these two theories. To the extent that each business pursues its own interests and each businessperson tries to maximize personal success, business practice can be called egoistic. But business practice is also utilitarian in that pursuing self-interest is thought to maximize the total good, and playing by the established rules of the competitive game is seen as advancing the good of society as a whole. The classical capitalist economist Adam Smith (1723–1790) held such a view. He argued that if business is left to pursue its self-interest, the good of society will be served. Indeed, Smith believed that only through egoistic pursuits could the greatest economic good for the whole society be produced. The essence of Smith's position can be seen in the following passage from *The Wealth of Nations* (1776), in which Smith underscores the interplay between self-interest and the social good and between egoism and utilitarianism:

> Every individual is continually exerting himself to find out the most advantageous employment for whatever capital he can command. It is his own advantage, indeed, and not that of the society, which he has in view. But the study of his own advantage, naturally, or rather necessarily, leads him to prefer that employment which is most advantageous to the society....

Business practice is egoistic, but Adam Smith and others believe that it is also utilitarian because the pursuit of self-interest promotes the good of society.

As every individual, therefore, endeavours as much as he can … to employ his capital … [so] that its produce may be of the greatest value, every individual necessarily labors to render the annual revenue of the society as great as he can. He generally, indeed, neither intends to promote the public interest, nor knows how much he is promoting it…. He intends only his own security; and by directing that industry in such a manner as its product may be of the greatest value, he intends only his own gain, and he is in this, as in many other cases, led by an invisible hand to promote an end which was no part of his intention. Nor is it always the worse for the society that it was no part of it. By pursuing his own interest he frequently promotes that of the society more effectually than when he really intends to promote it. I have never known much good done by those who affected to trade for the public good. It is an affectation, indeed, not very common among merchants, and very few words need be employed in dissuading them from it.[6]

Many today would agree with Smith* that the pursuit of self-interest is central to our economic system because it provides the motivating force that turns the wheels of commerce and industry. Although acknowledging that business is part of a social system, that cooperation is necessary, and that certain ground rules are needed and should be followed, they would argue that the society is best served by the active pursuit of self-interest within the established rules of business practice. Thus what we might call **business egoism**— the view that it is morally acceptable (or even morally required) for individuals to pursue their economic interests when engaged in business—is defended on utilitarian grounds.

KANT'S ETHICS

Most of us find the ideal of promoting human happiness and well-being an attractive one and, as a result, admire greatly people like Mother Teresa (1910–1997), who devoted her life to working with the poor. Despite the attractiveness of this ideal, many moral philosophers are critical of utilitarianism— particularly because, like egoism, it reduces all morality to a concern with consequences. Although nonconsequentialist normative theories vary significantly, adopting different approaches and stressing different themes, the writings of the preeminent German philosopher Immanuel Kant (1724–1804) provide an excellent example of a thoroughly nonconsequentialist approach to ethics. Perhaps few thinkers today would endorse Kant's theory on every point, but his work has greatly influenced subsequent philosophers and has helped shape our general moral culture.

Kant sought moral principles that do not rest on contingencies and that define actions as inherently right or wrong apart from any particular circumstances. He believed that moral rules can, in principle, be known as a result of reason alone and are not based on observation (as are, for example, scientific judgments). In contrast to utilitarianism and other consequentialist doctrines,

Kant believed that moral reasoning is not based on factual knowledge and that the results of our actions do not determine whether they are right or wrong.

* Chapter 4 examines Smith's position in more detail.

Kant's ethical theory holds that we do not have to know anything about the likely results of, say, my telling a lie to my boss in order to know that it is immoral. "The basis of obligation," Kant wrote, "must not be sought in human nature, [nor] in the circumstances of the world." Rather it is *a priori*, by which he meant that moral reasoning is not based on factual knowledge and that reason by itself can reveal the basic principles of morality.

Good Will

Chapter 1 mentioned Good Samaritan laws, which shield from lawsuits those rendering emergency aid. Such laws, in effect, give legal protection to the humanitarian impulse behind emergency interventions. They formally recognize that the interventionist's heart was in the right place, that the person's intention was irreproachable. And because the person acted from right intention, he or she should not be held liable for any inadvertent harm except in cases of extreme negligence. The widely observable human tendency to introduce a person's intentions in assigning blame or praise is a good springboard for engaging Kant's ethics.

Nothing, said Kant, is good in itself except a **good will**. This does not mean that intelligence, courage, self-control, health, happiness, and other things are not good and desirable. But Kant believed that their goodness depends on the will that makes use of them. Intelligence, for instance, is not good when used by an evil person.

By *will* Kant meant the uniquely human capacity to act from principle. Contained in the notion of good will is the concept of duty: Only when we act from a sense of duty does our action have **moral worth**. When we act only out of feeling, inclination, or self-interest, our actions—although they may be otherwise identical with ones that spring from the sense of duty—have no true moral worth.

Suppose that you're a clerk in a small convenience store. Late one night a customer pays for his five-dollar purchase with a twenty-dollar bill, which you mistake for a ten. Only after the customer leaves do you realize you short-changed him. You race out the front door and find him lingering by a vending machine. You give him the ten dollars with your apologies, and he thanks you warmly.

Can we say with certainty that you acted from a good will? Not necessarily. You may have acted from a desire to promote business or to avoid legal entanglement. If so, you would have acted in accordance with, but not from, duty. Your apparently virtuous gesture just happened to coincide with what duty requires. According to Kant, if you do not will the action from a sense of your duty to be fair and honest, your action lacks moral worth. Actions have true moral worth only when they spring from a recognition of duty and a choice to discharge it.

What determines our duty? How do we know what morality requires of us? Kant answered these questions by formulating what he called the "categorical imperative." This extraordinarily significant moral concept is the linchpin of Kant's ethics.

Summary 2.5
Kant's theory is an important example of a purely nonconsequentialist approach to ethics. Kant held that only when we act from duty does our action have moral worth. Good will is the only thing that is good in itself.

The Categorical Imperative

We have seen that egoists and utilitarians allow factual circumstances or empirical data to determine moral judgments. In contrast, Kant believed that reason alone can yield a moral law. We need not rely on empirical evidence relating to consequences and to similar situations. Just as we know, seemingly through reason alone, such abstract truths as "Every change must have a cause," so we can arrive at absolute moral truth through nonempirical reasoning, and thereby discover our duty.

For Kant, an absolute moral truth must be logically consistent, free from internal contradiction. For example, it is a contradiction to say that an effect does not have a cause. Kant aimed to ensure that his absolute moral law would avoid such contradictions. If he could formulate such a rule, he maintained, everyone would be obliged to follow it without exception.

Kant believed that there is just one command (imperative) that is categorical—that is necessarily binding on all rational agents, regardless of any other considerations. From this one categorical imperative, this universal command, we can derive all the specific commands of duty. Kant's **categorical imperative** says that we should always act in such a way that we can will the maxim of our action to become a universal law. So Kant's answer to the question "What determines whether an act is right?" is that an act is morally right if and only if we can will it to become a universal law of conduct.

The obvious and crucial question that arises here is, "When are we justified in saying that the maxim of our action can become a universal law of conduct?"

By **maxim**, Kant meant the subjective principle of an action, the principle (or rule) that people in effect formulate in determining their conduct. For example, suppose building contractor Martin promises to install a sprinkler system in a project but is willing to break that promise to suit his purposes. His maxim can be expressed this way: "I'll make promises that I'll break whenever keeping them no longer suits my purposes." This is the subjective principle, the maxim, that directs his action.

Kant insisted that the morality of any maxim depends on whether we can logically will it to become a universal law. Could Martin's maxim be universally acted on? That depends on whether the maxim as law would involve a contradiction. The maxim "I'll make promises that I'll break whenever keeping them no longer suits my purposes" could not be universally acted on because it involves a contradiction of will. On the one hand, Martin is willing that it be possible to make promises and have them honored. On the other, if everyone intended to break promises whenever he or she wished to, then promises would not be honored in the first place, because it is in the nature of promises that they be believed. A law that allowed promise breaking would contradict the very nature of a promise. Similarly, a law that allowed lying would contradict the very nature of serious communication, for the activity of serious communication (as opposed to joking) requires that participants intend to speak the truth. I cannot, without contradiction, will both serious conversation and lying. By contrast, there is no problem, Kant thinks, in willing promise keeping or truth telling to be universal laws.

If you make a promise that you don't intend to keep, it is impossible to will the maxim governing your action as a universal law.

Consider, as another example, Kant's account of a man who, in despair after suffering a series of major setbacks, contemplates suicide. While still rational, the man asks whether it would be contrary to his duty to take his own life. Could the maxim of his action become a universal law of nature? Kant thinks not:

Summary 2.6
Kant's categorical imperative states that an action is morally right if and only if we can will that the maxim (or principle) represented by our action be a universal law. For example, a person making a promise with no intention of keeping it cannot universalize the maxim governing his action because if everyone followed this principle, promising would make no sense. Kant believed that the categorical imperative is binding on all rational creatures, regardless of their specific goals or desires and regardless of the consequences.

> His maxim is this: From self-love I make it my principle to shorten my life when its continued duration threatens more evil than it promises satisfaction. There only remains the question whether this principle of self-love can become a universal law of nature. One sees at once a contradiction in a system of nature whose law would destroy life by means of the very same feeling that acts so as to stimulate the furtherance of life…. Therefore, such a maxim cannot possibly hold as a universal law of nature and is, consequently, wholly inconsistent with the supreme principle of all duty.[7]

When Kant insists that a moral rule be consistently universalizable, he is saying that moral rules prescribe categorically, not hypothetically. A *hypothetical* prescription tells us what to do if we desire a particular outcome. Thus, "If I want people to like me, I should be nice to them" and "If you want to go to medical school, you must take biology" are **hypothetical imperatives**. They tell us what we must do on the assumption that we have some particular goal. If that is what we want, then this is what we must do; but if we don't want to go to medical school, then the command to take biology does not apply to us. In contrast, Kant's imperative is *categorical*: It commands unconditionally. It is necessarily binding on everyone, regardless of his or her specific goals or desires, regardless of consequences. A categorical imperative takes the form of "Do this" or "Don't do that"—no ifs, ands, or buts.

Universal Acceptability

There is another way of looking at the categorical imperative. Each person, through his or her own acts of will, legislates the moral law. The moral rules that we obey are not imposed on us from the outside. They are self-imposed and self-recognized, fully internalized principles. The sense of duty that we obey comes from within; it is an expression of our own higher selves.

Thus, moral beings give themselves the moral law and accept its demands on themselves. But that is not to say we can prescribe anything we want, for we are bound by reason and its demands. Because reason is the same for all rational beings, we all give ourselves the same moral law. In other words, when you answer the question "What should I do?" you must consider what all rational beings should do. You can embrace something as a moral law only if all other rational beings can also embrace it. It must have **universal acceptability**.

To see whether a rule or principle is a moral law, we can thus ask if what the rule commands would be acceptable to all rational beings. In considering lying, theft, or murder, for example, you must consider the act not only from your own viewpoint but also from the perspective of the person lied to, robbed, or murdered. Presumably, rational beings do not want to be lied to, robbed, or murdered. The test of the morality of a rule, then, is not whether people in fact accept it but whether all rational beings thinking impartially and rationally would accept it regardless of whether they are the doers or the receivers of the actions. This is an important moral insight, and most philosophers see it as implicit in Kant's discussion of the categorical imperative, even though Kant (whose writings are difficult to understand) did not make the point in this form.

The principle of universal acceptability has important applications. Suppose a man advocates a hiring policy that discriminates against women. For this rule to be universally acceptable, the man would have to be willing to accept it if he were a woman, something he would presumably be unwilling to do. Or suppose the manufacturer of a product decides to market it even though the manufacturer knows that the product is unsafe when used in a certain common way and that consumers are ignorant of this fact. Applying the universal-acceptability principle, the company's decision makers would have to be willing to advocate marketing the product even if they were themselves in the position of uninformed consumers. Presumably they would be unwilling to do this. So the rule that would allow the product to be marketed would fail the test of universal acceptability.

Humanity as an End, Never as Merely a Means

In addition to the principle of universal acceptability, Kant explicitly offered another, very famous way of formulating the core idea of his categorical imperative. According to this formulation, as rational creatures we should always treat other rational creatures as ends in themselves and never as only means to our ends. This formulation underscores Kant's belief that every human being has an inherent worth resulting from the sheer possession of rationality. We must always act in a way that respects this humanity in others and in ourselves.

As rational beings, humans would act inconsistently if they did not treat everyone else the way they themselves would want to be treated. Here we see shades of the Golden Rule. Indeed, Kant's moral philosophy can be viewed as a profound reconsideration of this basic nonconsequentialist principle. Because rational beings recognize their own inner worth, they would never wish to be used as entities possessing worth only as means to an end.

Thus, when brokers at the Dallas office of Prudential Securities encouraged unnecessary buying and selling of stocks in order to reap a commission (a practice called "churning"), they were treating their clients simply as a means and not respecting them as persons, as ends in themselves.[8] Likewise, Kant would object to using patients as subjects in a medical experiment without their consent. Even though great social benefit might result, the researchers would intentionally be using the patients solely as a means to the researchers' own goals and thus would be failing to respect the patients' basic humanity.

Kant maintained, as explained first, that an action is morally right if and only if we can will it to be a universal law. We now have two ways of reformulating his categorical imperative that may be easier to grasp and apply:

Two alternative formulations of the categorical imperative.

First reformulation: An action is right only if the agent would be willing to be so treated were the positions of the parties reversed.

Second reformulation: One must always act so as to treat other people as ends in themselves.

Kant in an Organizational Context

Like utilitarianism, Kant's moral theory has application for organizations.

First, the categorical imperative gives us firm rules to follow in moral decision making, rules that do not depend on circumstances or results and that do not permit individual exceptions. No matter what the consequences may be or who does it, some actions are always wrong. Lying is an example: No matter how much good may come from misrepresenting a product, such deliberate misrepresentation is always wrong. Similarly, it would be wrong to expose workers to some occupational health risk on the grounds that it advances medical knowledge.

Second, Kant introduces an important humanistic dimension into business decisions. One of the principal objections to egoism and utilitarianism is that they permit us to treat humans as means to ends. Kant's principles clearly forbid this. Many would say that respect for the inherent worth and dignity of human beings is much needed today in business, where encroaching technology and the pressure of globalization tend to dehumanize people under the guise of efficiency. Kant's theory puts the emphasis of organizational decision making where it belongs: on individuals. Organizations, after all, involve human beings working in concert to provide goods and services for other human beings. The primacy Kant gives the individual reflects this essential aspect of business.

Third, Kant stresses the importance of motivation and of acting on principle. According to Kant, it is not enough just to do the right thing; an action has moral worth only if it is done from a sense of duty—that is, from a desire to do the right thing for its own sake. The importance of this point is too often forgotten. Sometimes when individuals and organizations believe that an action promotes the interests of everyone, they are actually rationalizing—doing what is best for themselves and only imagining that somehow it will also benefit others. Worse still, they may defend their actions as morally praiseworthy when, in fact, they are only behaving egoistically. They wouldn't do the morally justifiable thing if they didn't think it would pay off for them. By stressing the importance of motivation, a Kantian approach serves as a corrective to this. Even an action that helps others has moral value for Kant only if the person doing it is morally motivated—that is, acting on principle or out of moral conviction.

Summary 2.7
There are two alternative formulations of the categorical imperative. The first is that an act is right only if the actor would be willing to be so treated if the positions of the parties were reversed. The second is that one must always act so as to treat other people as ends, never merely as means.

Critical Inquiries of Kant's Ethics

1. **What has moral worth?** According to Kant, the clerk who returns the ten dollars to the customer is doing the right thing. But if his action is motivated by self-interest (perhaps he wants to get a reputation for honesty), then it does not have moral worth. That seems plausible. But Kant also held that if the clerk does the right thing out of instinct, habit, or sympathy for the other person, then the act still does not have moral worth. Only if it is done out of a sense of duty does the clerk's action have moral value. Many moral theorists have felt that Kant was too severe on this point. Do we really want to say that giving money to famine relief efforts has no moral worth if one is emotionally moved to do so by

pictures of starving children rather than by a sense of duty? We might, to the contrary, find a person with strong human sympathies no less worthy or admirable than the person who gives solely out of an abstract sense of duty.

2. **Is the categorical imperative an adequate test of right?** Kant said that a moral rule must function without exception. Critics wonder why the prohibition against such actions as lying, promise breaking, and suicide must be exceptionless. They say that Kant failed to distinguish between saying that a person should not except himself or herself from a rule and that the rule itself cannot specify exceptions.

If stealing is wrong, it's wrong for me as well as for you. "Stealing is wrong, except if I do it" is not universalizable, for then stealing would be right for all to do, which contradicts the assertion that stealing is wrong. But just because no one may make of oneself an exception to a rule, it does not follow that the rule itself cannot specify exceptions.

Suppose, for example, that we decide that stealing is sometimes right, perhaps in the case of a person who is starving. Thus, the rule becomes "Never steal except when starving." This rule seems just as universalizable as "Never steal." The phrase "except …" can be viewed not as justifying a violation of the rule but as building a qualification into it. Critics in effect are asking why a qualified rule is not just as good as an unqualified one. If it is, then we no longer need to state rules in the simple, direct, unqualified manner that Kant did.

In fairness to Kant, it could be argued that his universalization formula can be interpreted flexibly enough to meet commonsense objections. For example, perhaps we could universalize the principle that individuals should steal rather than starve to death or that it is permissible to take one's own life to extinguish unspeakable pain. Yet to qualify the rules against stealing, lying, and taking one's life seems to invite a non-Kantian analysis to justify the exceptions. One could, it seems, universalize more than one moral rule in a given situation: "Do not lie unless a life is at stake" versus "Lying is wrong unless necessary to avoid the suffering of innocent people." If so, then the categorical imperative would supply at best a necessary, but not a sufficient, test of right. But once we start choosing among various alternative rules, then we are adopting an approach to ethics that Kant would have rejected.

3. **What does it mean to treat people as means?** Kant's mandate that individuals must always be considered as ends in themselves and never merely as means expresses our sense of the intrinsic value of the human spirit and has profound moral appeal. Yet it is not always clear when people are being treated as ends and when merely as means. For example, Kant believed that prostitution is immoral because, by selling their sexual services, prostitutes allow themselves to be treated as means. Prostitutes, however, are not the only ones to sell their services. Anyone who works for a wage does so. Does that mean that we are all being treated immorally, because our employers are presumably hiring us as a means to advance their own ends? Presumably not, because we freely agreed to do the work. But then the prostitute might have freely chosen that line of work, too.

Summary 2.8
Kant's ethics gives us firm standards that do not depend on results; it injects a humanistic element into moral decision making and stresses the importance of acting on principle and from a sense of duty. Critics, however, worry that (1) Kant's view of moral worth is too restrictive, (2) the categorical imperative is not a sufficient test of right and wrong, and (3) distinguishing between treating people as means and respecting them as ends in themselves may be difficult in practice.

OTHER NONCONSEQUENTIALIST PERSPECTIVES

For Kant, the categorical imperative provided the basic test of right and wrong, and he was resolutely nonconsequentialist in his application of it. You know now what he would say about the case of the deathbed promise: The maxim permitting you to break your promise cannot be universalized, and hence it would be immoral of you to give the money to the orphanage, despite the happiness that doing so would bring. But nonconsequentialists are not necessarily Kantians, and several different nonutilitarian moral concerns emerged in the discussion of the deathbed promise example.

Critics of act utilitarianism believe that it is faulty for maintaining that we have one and only one moral duty. A utilitarian might follow various principles as rules of thumb, but they are only calculation substitutes. All that matters morally to utilitarians is the maximization of happiness. Yet this idea, many philosophers think, fails to do justice to the richness and complexity of our moral lives.

Prima Facie Obligations

One influential philosopher who argued this way was the British scholar W. D. Ross (1877–1971).[9] Ross rejected utilitarianism as too simple and as untrue to the way we ordinarily think about morality and about our moral obligations. We see ourselves, Ross and like-minded thinkers contend, as being under various moral duties that cannot be reduced to the single obligation to maximize happiness. Often these obligations grow out of special relationships into which we enter or out of determinate roles that we undertake. Our lives are intertwined with other people's in particular ways, and we have, as a result, certain specific moral obligations.

Ross believed that we have various moral duties that cannot be reduced to one single obligation to maximize happiness.

For example, as a professor, Rodriguez is obligated to assist her students in the learning process and to evaluate their work in a fair and educationally productive way—obligations to the specific people in her classroom that she does not have to other people. As a spouse, Rodriguez must maintain a certain emotional and sexual fidelity to her partner. As a parent, she must provide for the individual human beings who are her children. As a friend to Smith, she may have a moral responsibility to help him out in a time of crisis. Having borrowed money from Chang, Rodriguez is morally obligated to pay it back. Thus, different relationships and different circumstances generate a variety of specific moral obligations.

In addition, we have moral duties that do not arise from our unique interactions and relationships with other people. For example, we ought to treat all people fairly, do what we can to remedy injustices, and make an effort to promote human welfare generally. The latter obligation is important, but for a nonconsequentialist like Ross it is only one among various obligations that people have.

At any given time, we are likely to be under more than one obligation, and sometimes these obligations can conflict—that is, we may have an obligation to do A and an obligation to do B, where it is not possible for us to do both A and B. For example, I promise to meet a friend on an urgent matter, and now, as I am hurrying there, I pass an injured person who is obviously in need of help. Stopping to aid the person will make it impossible for me to fulfill my promise. What should I do? For moral philosophers like Ross, there is no single answer for all cases. What I ought to do will depend on the circumstances and relative importance of the conflicting obligations. I have an obligation to keep my promise, and I have an obligation to assist someone in distress. What I must decide is which of these obligations is, in the given circumstance, the more important. I must weigh the moral significance of the promise against the comparative moral urgency of assisting the injured person.

Ross and many contemporary philosophers believe that all (or at least most) of our moral obligations are prima facie ones. A **prima facie obligation** is an obligation that can be overridden by a more important obligation. For instance, we take the keeping of promises seriously, but almost everyone would agree that in some circumstances—for example, when a life is at stake—it would be not only morally permissible, but morally required, to break a promise. Our obligation to keep a promise is a real one, and if there is no conflicting obligation, then we must keep the promise. But that obligation is not absolute or categorical; it could in principle be outweighed by a more stringent moral obligation. The idea that our obligations are prima facie is foreign to Kant's way of looking at things.

Consider an example that Kant himself discussed.[10] Imagine that a murderer comes to your door, wanting to know where your friend is so that he can kill her. Your friend is in fact hiding in your bedroom closet. Most people would probably agree that your obligation to your friend overrides your general obligation to tell the truth and that the right thing to do would be to lie to the murderer to throw him off your friend's trail. Although you have a genuine obligation to tell the truth, it is a prima facie obligation, one that other moral considerations can outweigh. Kant disagreed. He maintained that you must always tell the truth—that is, in all circumstances and without exception. For him, telling the truth is an absolute or categorical obligation, not a prima facie one.

Ross thought that our various prima facie obligations could be divided into seven basic types: duties of fidelity (that is, to respect explicit and implicit promises), duties of reparation (for previous wrongful acts), duties of gratitude, duties of justice, duties of beneficence (that is, to make the condition of others better), duties of self-improvement, and duties not to injure others.[11] Unlike utilitarianism, Ross's ethical perspective is pluralistic in recognizing a variety of genuine obligations. But contrary to Kant, Ross does not see these obligations as absolute and exceptionless. On both points, Ross contended that his view of morality more closely fits with our actual moral experience and the way we view our moral obligations.

Ross also saw himself as siding with commonsense morality in maintaining that our prima facie obligations are obvious. He believed that the basic principles of duty are as self-evident as the simplest rules of arithmetic and that any person who has reached the age of reason can discern that it is wrong to lie, to break promises, and to injure people needlessly. However, what we should do, all things considered, when two or more prima facie obligations conflict is often difficult to judge. In deciding what to do in any

Ross's pluralistic ethical perspective differs from utilitarianism. Ross also rejected Kant's belief that our moral obligations are absolute and exceptionless.

concrete situation, Ross thought, we are always "taking a moral risk."[12] Even after the fullest reflection, judgments about which of these self-evident rules should govern our conduct are only "more or less probable opinions which are not logically justified conclusions from the general principles that are recognised as self-evident."[13]

Assisting Others

Nonconsequentialists believe that utilitarianism presents too simple a picture of our moral world. In addition, they worry that utilitarianism risks making us all slaves to the maximization of total happiness. Stop and think about it: Isn't there something that you could be doing—for instance, volunteering at the local hospital or orphanage, collecting money for third-world development, helping the homeless—that would do more for the general good than what you are doing now or are planning to do tonight or tomorrow? Sure, working with the homeless might not bring you quite as much pleasure as what you would otherwise be doing, but if it would nonetheless maximize total happiness, then you are morally required to do it. However, by following this reasoning, you could end up working around the clock, sacrificing yourself for the greater good. This notion seems mistaken.

Most nonutilitarian philosophers, like Ross, believe that we have some obligation to promote the general welfare, but they typically view this obligation as less stringent than, for example, the obligation not to injure people. They see us as having a much stronger obligation to refrain from violating people's rights than to promote their happiness or well-being. From this perspective, a manufacturing company's obligation not to violate OSHA regulations and thereby endanger the safety of its employees is stronger than its obligation to open up day-care facilities for their children, even though the cost of the two is the same. The company, in other words, has a stronger duty to respect its legal and contractual employment-related obligations than to promote its employees' happiness in other ways. Likewise, for a company to violate people's rights by despoiling the environment through the discharge of pollutants would be morally worse than for it to decide not to expand a job training program in the inner city, even if expanding the program would bring about more total good.

Different nonutilitarian philosophers may weight these particular obligations differently, depending on their particular moral theory. But they typically believe that we have a stronger duty not to violate people's rights or in some other way injure them than we do to assist people or otherwise promote their well-being. A utilitarian, concerned solely with what will maximize happiness, is less inclined to draw such a distinction.

Many moral philosophers draw a related distinction between actions that are morally required and charitable or **supererogatory actions**—that is, actions that it would be good to do but not immoral not to do. Act utilitarianism does not make this distinction. Although we admire Mother Teresa and Albert Schweitzer for devoting their lives to doing good works among the poor, we see them as acting above and beyond the call of duty; we do not expect so much from ordinary people. Yet people who are not moral heroes or who fall short of sainthood may nonetheless be living morally satisfactory lives.

Nonutilitarian philosophers believe that we have a stronger obligation to respect people's rights and avoid injuring them than we do to promote their happiness.

Summary 2.9
Nonconsequentialists needn't be Kantians. W. D. Ross, for instance, rejects both Kantianism and utilitarianism, arguing that we are under a variety of distinct moral obligations. These are prima facie, meaning that any one of them may be outweighed in some circumstances by other, more important moral considerations. Nonconsequentialists believe that a duty to assist others and to promote total happiness is only one of a number of duties incumbent on us.

Nonutilitarian theorists see the distinction between morally obligatory actions and supererogatory actions not so much as a realistic concession to human weakness but as a necessary demarcation if we are to avoid becoming enslaved to the maximization of the general welfare. The idea here is that each of us should have a sphere in which to pursue our own plans and goals, to carve out a distinctive life plan. These plans and goals are limited by various moral obligations, in particular by other people's rights, but the demands of morality are not all-encompassing.

Moral Rights

What, then, are rights, and what rights do people have? Broadly defined, a *right* is an entitlement to act or have others act in a certain way. The connection between rights and duties is that, generally speaking, if you have a right to do something, then someone else has a correlative duty to act in a certain way. For example, if you claim a "right" to drive, you mean that you are entitled to drive or that others should—that is, have a duty to—permit you to drive. Your right to drive under certain conditions is derived from our legal system and is thus considered a **legal right**.

In addition to rights that are derived from some specific legal system, we also have **moral rights**. Some of these moral rights derive from special relationships, roles, or circumstances in which we happen to be. For example, if Tom has an obligation to return Bob's car to him on Saturday morning, then Bob has a right to have Tom return his car. If I have agreed to water your plants while you are on vacation, you have a right to expect me to look after them in your absence. As a student, you have a right to be graded fairly, and so on.

Even more important are rights that do not rest on special relationships, roles, or situations. For example, the rights to life, free speech, and unhampered religious affiliation are widely accepted, not just as the entitlements of some specific political or legal system but as fundamental moral rights. More controversial, but often championed as moral rights, are the rights to medical care, decent housing, education, and work. Moral rights that are not the result of particular roles, special relationships, or specific circumstances are called **human rights**. They have several important characteristics.

First, human rights are universal. For instance, if the right to life is a human right, as most of us believe it is, then everyone, everywhere, and at all times, has that right. By contrast, there is nothing universal about your right that I keep my promise to help you move or about my right to drive 65 miles per hour on certain roads.

Second, and closely related, human rights are equal rights. If the right to free speech is a human right, then everyone has this right equally. No one has a greater right to free speech than anyone else. In contrast, your daughter has a greater right than do the daughters of other people to your emotional and financial support.

Third, human rights are not transferable, nor can they be relinquished. If we have a fundamental human right, we cannot give, lend, or sell it to someone else. We cannot waive it, and no one can take it from us. That is what is meant in the Declaration of Independence when certain rights—namely, life,

Human rights have four important characteristics.

liberty, and the pursuit of happiness—are described as "unalienable." By comparison, legal rights can be renounced or transferred, as when one party sells another a house or a business.

Fourth, human rights are natural rights, not in the sense that they can be derived from a study of human nature, but in the sense that they do not depend on human institutions the way legal rights do. If people have human rights, they have these rights simply because they are human beings. They do not have them because they live under a certain legal system. Human rights rest on the assumption that people have certain basic moral entitlements merely because of their humanity. No authoritative body assigns them human rights. The law may attempt to protect human rights, to make them explicit and safe through codification, but the law is not their source.

Philosophers distinguish negative rights from positive rights.

Rights, and in particular human rights, can be divided into two broad categories: negative rights and positive rights. **Negative rights** reflect the vital interests that human beings have in being free from outside interference. The rights guaranteed in the Bill of Rights—freedom of speech, assembly, religion, and so on—fall within this category, as do the rights to freedom from injury and to privacy. Correlating with these are duties that we all have not to interfere with others' pursuit of these interests and activities. **Positive rights** reflect the vital interests that human beings have in receiving certain benefits. They are rights to have others provide us with certain goods, services, or opportunities. Today, positive rights often are taken to include the rights to education, medical care, a decent neighborhood, equal job opportunity, comparable pay, and so on. Correlating with these are positive duties for appropriate parties to assist individuals in their pursuit of these interests.

Thus a child's right to education implies not only that no one should interfere with the child's education but also that the necessary resources for that education ought to be provided. In the case of some positive rights—for example, the right to a decent standard of living, as proclaimed by the United Nations' 1948 Human Rights Charter—who exactly has the duty to provide the goods and services required to fulfill those rights is unclear. Also, interpreting a right as negative or positive is sometimes controversial. For example, is my right to liberty simply the right not to be interfered with as I live my own life, or does it also imply a duty on the part of others to provide me with the means to make the exercise of that liberty meaningful?

The significance of positing moral rights is that they provide grounds for making moral judgments that differ radically from utilitarianism's grounds. Once moral rights are asserted, the locus of moral judgment becomes the individual, not society. For example, if every potential human research subject has a moral right to be fully informed about the nature of a medical experiment and the moral right to decide freely for himself or herself whether to participate, then it is wrong to violate these rights—even if, by so doing, the common good would be served. Again, if workers have a right to compensation equal to what others receive for doing comparable work, then they cannot be paid less on the grounds that this will maximize total well-being. And if everyone has a right to equal consideration for a job regardless of color or sex, then sex and color cannot be introduced merely because so doing will result in greater net utility.

Summary 2.10
Nonconsequential-
ists typically empha-
size moral rights—
entitlements to act in
a certain way or to
have others act in a
certain way. These
rights can rest on
special relationships
and roles, or they
can be general hu-
man rights. Rights
can be negative,
protecting us from
outside interference,
or they can be posi-
tive, requiring others
to provide us with
certain benefits or
opportunities.

Utilitarianism, in effect, treats all such entitlements as subordinate to the general welfare. Thus, individuals are entitled to act in a certain way and entitled to have others allow or aid them to so act only insofar as acknowledging this right or entitlement achieves the greatest good. The assertion of moral rights, therefore, decisively sets nonconsequentialists apart from utilitarians.

Nonconsequentialism in an Organizational Context

We have already looked at Kant's ethics in an organizational context, but, as we have seen, many nonconsequentialists (like Ross) are not Kantians, and their ideas also have important implications for moral decision making in business and nonbusiness organizations.

First, in its non-Kantian forms nonconsequentialism stresses that moral decision making involves the weighing of different moral factors and considerations. Unlike utilitarianism, nonconsequentialism does not reduce morality solely to the calculation of consequences; rather, it recognizes that an organization must usually take into account other equally important moral concerns. Theorists like Ross emphasize that, contrary to what Kant believed, there can often be rival and even conflicting obligations on an organization. For example, obligations to employees, stockholders, and consumers may pull the corporation in different directions, and determining the organization's proper moral course may not be easy.

Second, nonconsequentialism acknowledges that the organization has its own legitimate goals to pursue. There are limits to the demands of morality, and an organization that fulfills its moral obligations and respects the relevant rights of individuals is morally free to advance whatever (morally permissible) ends it has—public service, profit, government administration, and so on. Contrary to utilitarianism, organizations and the people in them need not see themselves as under an overarching obligation to seek continually to enhance the general welfare.

Third, nonconsequentialism stresses the importance of moral rights. Moral rights, and in particular human rights, are a crucial factor in most moral deliberations, including those of organizations. Before it acts, any morally responsible business or nonbusiness organization must consider carefully how its actions will impinge on the rights of individuals—not just the rights of its members, such as stockholders and employees, but also the rights of others, such as consumers. Moral rights place distinct and firm constraints on what sorts of things an organization can do to fulfill its own ends.

Critical Inquiries of Nonconsequentialism

1. **How well justified are these nonconsequentialist principles and moral rights?** Ross maintained that we have immediate intuitive knowledge of the basic prima facie moral principles, and indeed it would seem absurd to try to deny that it is wrong to cause needless suffering or that making a promise imposes some obligation to keep it. Only someone the moral equivalent of colorblind could fail to see the truth of these statements; to reject them would seem as preposterous as denying some obvious fact

of arithmetic—for example, that $12 + 4 = 16$. Likewise, it appears obvious—indeed, as Thomas Jefferson wrote, "self-evident"—that human beings have certain basic and inalienable rights, unconditional rights that do not depend on the decrees of any particular government.

Yet we must be careful. What seems obvious, even self-evident, to one culture or at one time in human history may turn out to be not only not self-evident but actually false. That the earth is flat and that heavier objects fall faster than lighter ones were two "truths" taken as obvious in former centuries. Likewise, the inferiority of women and of various non-white races was long taken for granted; this supposed fact was so obvious that it was hardly even commented on. The idea that people have a right to practice a religion that the majority "knows" to be false—or, indeed, to practice no religion whatsoever—would have seemed morally scandalous to many of our forebears and is still not embraced in all countries today. Today, many vegetarians eschew meat eating on moral grounds and contend that future generations will consider our treatment of animals, factory farming in particular, to be as morally benighted as slavery. So what seems obvious, self-evident, or simple common sense may not be the most reliable guide to morally sound principles.

Summary 2.11
In an organizational context, nonconsequentialism (in its non-Kantian forms) stresses the plurality of moral considerations to be weighed. While emphasizing the importance of respecting moral rights, it acknowledges that morality has limits and that organizations have legitimate goals to pursue. Critics question whether (1) nonconsequentialist principles are adequately justified and whether (2) nonconsequentialism can satisfactorily handle conflicting rights and principles.

2. **Can nonconsequentialists satisfactorily handle conflicting rights and principles?** People today disagree among themselves about the correctness of certain moral principles. Claims of right, as we have seen, are often controversial. For example, do employees have a moral right to their jobs—an entitlement to be fired only with just cause? To some of us, it may seem obvious that they do; to others, perhaps not. And how are we to settle various conflicting claims of right? Jones, for instance, claims a right to her property, which she has acquired honestly through her labors—that is, she claims a right to do with it as she wishes. Smith is ill and claims adequate medical care as a human right. Because he cannot afford the care himself, acknowledging his right will probably involve taxing people like Jones and thus limiting their property rights.

To sum up these two points: First, even the deliverances of moral common sense have to be examined critically; and second, nonconsequentialists should not rest content until they find a way of resolving disputes among conflicting prima facie principles or rights. This is not to suggest that nonconsequentialists cannot find deeper and theoretically more satisfactory ways of grounding moral claims and of handling disputes between them. The point to be underscored here is simply the necessity of doing so.

UTILITARIANISM ONCE MORE

Until now, our discussion of utilitarianism has focused on the classic and most straightforward version of it, namely, "act utilitarianism." According to act utilitarianism, we have one and only one moral obligation, the maximization of happiness for everyone concerned, and every action is to be judged according to how well it lives up to this standard. But a different utilitarian approach, called "rule utilitarianism," is relevant to the discussion of the moral concerns characteristic of nonconsequentialism—in particular, relevant to the nonconsequentialist's criticisms of act utilitarianism. The rule utilitarian would, in fact, agree with many of these criticisms. (Rule utilitarianism has been formulated in different ways, but this discussion follows the version defended by Richard Brandt.)

Rule utilitarianism maintains that the utilitarian standard should be applied not to individual actions but to moral codes as a whole. The rule utilitarian asks what moral code (that is, what set of moral rules) a society should adopt to maximize happiness. The principles that make up that code would then be the basis for distinguishing right actions from wrong actions. As Brandt explains:

> A rule-utilitarian thinks that right actions are the kind permitted by the moral code optimal for the society of which the agent is a member. An optimal code is one designed to maximize welfare or what is good (thus, utility). This leaves open the possibility that a particular right act by itself may not maximize benefit....
> On the rule-utilitarian view, then, to find what is morally right or wrong we need to find which actions would be permitted by a moral system that is "optimal" for the agent's society.[14]

The notion of an optimal moral code takes into account the difficulty of getting people to follow a given set of rules.

The "optimal" moral code does not refer to the set of rules that would do the most good if everyone conformed to them all the time. The meaning is more complex. The **optimal moral code** must take into account what rules can reasonably be taught and obeyed, as well as the costs of inculcating those rules in people. Recall from Chapter 1 that if a principle or rule is part of a person's moral code, then it will influence the person's behavior. The person will tend to follow that principle, to feel guilty when he or she does not follow it, and to disapprove of others who fail to conform to it. Rule utilitarians must consider not just the benefits of having people motivated to act in certain ways but also the costs of instilling those motivations in them. As Brandt writes:

> The more intense and widespread an aversion to a certain sort of behavior, the less frequent the behavior is apt to be. But the more intense and widespread, the greater the cost of teaching the rule and keeping it alive, the greater the burden on the individual, and so on.[15]

Thus, the "optimality" of a moral code encompasses both the benefits of reduced objectionable behavior and the long-term costs. Perfect compliance is not a realistic goal. "Like the law," Brandt continues, "the optimal moral code normally will not produce 100 percent compliance with all its rules; that would be too costly."[16]

Some utilitarian thinkers in earlier centuries adopted or came close to adopting rule utilitarianism (although they did not use that term). For example, the nineteenth-century legal theorist John Austin wrote: "Utility [should] be the test of our conduct, ultimately, but not immediately.... Our rules [should] be fashioned on utility; our conduct, on our rules."[17] This accords well with the rule-utilitarian idea that we should apply the utilitarian standard only to the assessment of alternative moral codes; we should not try to apply it to individual actions. We should seek to determine the specific set of principles that would in fact best promote total happiness for society. Those are the rules we should promulgate, instill in ourselves, and teach to the next generation.

What Will the Optimal Code Look Like?

Rule utilitarians believe that the optimal moral code will not consist of just one rule—to maximize happiness.

Rule utilitarians such as Brandt argue strenuously that the ideal or optimal moral code for a society will not be the single act-utilitarian command to maximize happiness. They contend that teaching people that their only obligation is to maximize happiness would not in fact maximize happiness.

First, people will make mistakes if, before they act, they try to calculate the consequences of each and every thing they might possibly do. *Second*, if all of us were act utilitarians, such practices as keeping promises and telling the truth would be rather shaky, because we could expect others to keep promises or tell the truth only when they believed that doing so would maximize happiness. *Third*, the act-utilitarian principle is too demanding, because it seems to imply that each person should continually be striving to promote total well-being.

For these reasons, rule utilitarians believe that more happiness will come from instilling in people a pluralistic moral code, one with a number of different principles. By analogy, imagine a traffic system with just one rule: Drive your car in a way that maximizes happiness. Such a system would be counterproductive; we do much better in terms of total human well-being to have a variety of traffic regulations—for example, obey stop signs, yield to the right, and pass only on the left. In such a pluralistic system we cannot justify cruising through a red light with the argument that doing so maximizes total happiness by getting us home more quickly.

The principles of the optimal code would presumably be prima facie in Ross's sense—that is, capable of being overridden by other principles. Different principles would also have different moral weights. It would make sense, for example, to instill in people an aversion to killing that is stronger and deeper than the aversion to telling white lies. In addition, the ideal code would acknowledge moral rights. Teaching people to respect moral rights maximizes human welfare in the long run.

The rules of the optimal code provide the sole basis for determining right and wrong. An action is not necessarily wrong if it fails to maximize happiness; it is wrong only if it conflicts with the ideal moral code. Rule utilitarianism thus gets around many of the problems that plague act utilitarianism. At the same time, it provides a plausible basis for deciding which moral principles and rights we should acknowledge and how much weight we should attach to them. We try to determine those principles and rights that, generally adhered to, would best promote human happiness.

Critics of rule utilitarianism raise two objections.

Still, rule utilitarianism has its critics. There are two common objections. *First*, act utilitarians maintain that a utilitarian who cares about happiness should be willing to violate rules in order to maximize happiness. Why make a fetish out of the rules?

Summary 2.12
Rule utilitarianism is a hybrid theory. It maintains that the correct principles of right and wrong are those that would maximize happiness if society adopted them. Rule utilitarianism applies the utilitarian standard not directly to individual actions but rather to the choice of the moral principles that are to guide individual action. Rule utilitarianism avoids many of the standard criticisms of act utilitarianism.

Second, nonconsequentialists, while presumably viewing rule utilitarianism more favorably than act utilitarianism, still balk at seeing moral principles determined by their consequences. They contend, in particular, that rule utilitarians ultimately subordinate rights to utilitarian calculation and therefore fail to treat rights as fundamental and independent moral factors.

MORAL DECISION MAKING: TOWARD A SYNTHESIS

Theoretical controversies permeate the subject of ethics, and as we have seen, philosophers have proposed rival ways of understanding right and wrong. These philosophical differences of perspective, emphasis, and theory are significant and can have profound practical consequences. This chapter has surveyed some of these issues, but obviously it cannot settle all of the questions that divide moral philosophers. Fortunately, however, many problems of business and organizational ethics can be intelligently discussed and even resolved by people whose fundamental moral theories differ (or who have not yet worked out their own moral ideas in some systematic way). This section discusses some important points to keep in mind when analyzing and discussing business ethics and offers, as a kind of model, one possible procedure for making moral decisions.

In the abstract, it might seem impossible for people to reach agreement on controversial ethical issues, given that ethical theories differ so much and that people themselves place moral value on different things. Yet in practice moral problems are rarely so intractable that open-minded and thoughtful people cannot, by discussing matters calmly, rationally, and thoroughly, make significant progress toward resolving them. Chapter 1 stressed that moral judgments should be logical, should be based on facts, and should appeal to sound moral principles. Bearing this in mind can often help, especially when various people are discussing an issue and proposing rival answers.

First, in any moral discussion, make sure participants agree about the relevant facts. Often moral disputes hinge not on matters of moral principle but on differing assessments of what the facts of the situation are, what alternatives are open, and what the probable results of different courses of action will be. For instance, the directors of an international firm might acrimoniously dispute the moral permissibility of a new overseas investment. The conflict might appear to involve some fundamental clash of moral principles and perspectives when, in fact, it is the result of some underlying disagreement about the likely effects of the proposed investment on the lives of the local population. Until this factual disagreement is acknowledged and dealt with, little is apt to be resolved.

Second, once there is general agreement on factual matters, try to spell out the moral principles to which different people are, at least implicitly, appealing. Seeking to determine these principles will often help people clarify their own thinking enough to reach a solution. Sometimes they will agree on what moral principles are relevant yet disagree over how to balance them; identifying this discrepancy can itself be useful. Bear in mind, too, that skepticism is in order when someone's moral stance on an issue appears to rest simply on a hunch or an intuition and cannot be related to some more general moral principle. As moral decision makers, we are seeking not only an answer

Recall that moral judgments should be logical and based on facts and sound moral principles.

to a moral issue but an answer that can be publicly defended, and the public defense of a moral judgment usually requires an appeal to general principle. By analogy, judges do not hand down judgments based simply on what strikes them as fair in a particular case. They must relate their decisions to general legal principles or statutes.

A reluctance to defend our moral decisions in public is almost always a warning sign. If we are unwilling to account for our actions publicly, chances are that we are doing something we cannot really justify morally. In addition, Kant's point that we must be willing to universalize our moral judgments is relevant here. We cannot sincerely endorse a principle if we are not willing to see it applied generally. Unfortunately, we occasionally do make judgments—for example, that Alfred's being late to work is a satisfactory reason for firing him—that rest on a principle we would be unwilling to apply to our own situations; hence, the moral relevance of the familiar question: "How would you like it if ... ?" Looking at an issue from the other person's point of view can cure moral myopia.

Obligations, Ideals, Effects

As a practical basis for discussing moral issues in organizations, it is useful to try to approach those issues in a way that is acceptable to individuals of diverse moral viewpoints. We want to avoid as much as possible presupposing the truth of one particular theoretical perspective. By emphasizing factors that are relevant to various theories, both consequentialist and nonconsequentialist, we can find some common ground on which moral decision making can proceed. Moral dialogue can thus take place in an objective and analytical way, even if the participants do not fully agree on all philosophical issues.

What concerns, then, seem common to most ethical systems? Following Professor V. R. Ruggiero, three common concerns suggest themselves.[18] A first concern is with *obligations*. Every significant human action—personal and professional—arises in the context of human relationships. These relationships can be the source of specific duties and rights. In addition, we are obligated to respect people's human rights. Obligations bind us. In their presence, morality requires us, at least prima facie, to do certain things and to avoid doing others.

A second concern common to most ethical systems is the impact of our actions on important *ideals*. An **ideal** is some morally important goal, virtue, or notion of excellence worth striving for. Clearly, different cultures impart different ideals and, equally important, different ways of pursuing them. Our culture respects virtues such as tolerance, compassion, and loyalty, as well as more abstract ideals such as peace, justice, fairness, and respect for persons. In addition to these moral ideals, there are institutional or organizational ideals: efficiency, product quality, customer service, and so forth. Does a particular act serve or violate these ideals? Both consequentialists and nonconsequentialists can agree that this is an important concern in determining the moral quality of actions.

A third common consideration regards the *effects* of actions. When reflecting on a possible course of action, one needs to take into account its likely results. Although nonconsequentialists maintain that things other than

Summary 2.13
Despite disagreements on controversial theoretical issues, people can make significant progress in resolving practical moral problems through open-minded and reflective discussion. One useful approach is to identify the (possibly conflicting) obligations, ideals, and effects in a given situation and then to determine where the emphasis should lie among these different considerations.

consequences or results can affect the rightness or wrongness of actions, few if any of them would ignore consequences entirely. Almost all nonconsequentialist theories place some moral weight on the results of our actions. Practically speaking, this means that in making a moral decision, we must identify all the interested parties and how they would be affected by the different courses of action open to us.

In isolating these three concerns common to almost all ethical systems—obligations, ideals, and effects—Ruggiero provided a kind of practical synthesis of consequentialist and nonconsequentialist thought that seems appropriate for our purposes. A useful approach to moral questions in an organizational context will therefore reflect these considerations: the obligations that derive from organizational relationships or are affected by organizational conduct, the ideals at stake, and the effects or consequences of alternative courses of action. Any action that honors obligations while respecting ideals and benefiting people can be presumed to be moral. An action that does not pass scrutiny in these respects will be morally suspect.

This view leads to what is essentially a two-step procedure for evaluating actions and choices. The *first step* is to identify the important considerations involved: obligations, ideals, and effects. Accordingly, we should ask if any basic obligations are involved. If so, what are they and who has them? What ideals does the action respect or promote? What ideals does it neglect or thwart? Who is affected by the action and how? How do these effects compare with those of the alternatives open to us? The *second step* is to decide which of these considerations deserves emphasis. Sometimes the issue may be largely a matter of obligations; other times, some ideal may predominate; still other times, consideration of effects may be the overriding concern.

> A two-step approach to moral decision making is to identify the relevant obligations, ideals, and effects and then decide which consideration deserves the most emphasis.

Keep the following rough guidelines in mind when handling cases of conflicting obligations, ideals, and effects:

1. When two or more moral obligations conflict, choose the stronger one.
2. When two or more ideals conflict, or when ideals conflict with obligations, honor the more important one.
3. When rival actions will have different results, choose the action that produces the greater good or the lesser harm.

These guidelines imply that we know (1) which one of the conflicting obligations is greater, (2) which of the competing ideals is higher, and (3) which of the actions will achieve the greater good or the lesser harm. They also suggest that we have some definite way of balancing obligations, ideals, and effects when these considerations pull in different directions.

The fact is that we have no sure procedure for making such comparative determinations, which involve assessing worth and assigning relative priorities to our assessments. In large part, the chapters that follow attempt to sort out the values and principles embedded in the tangled web of frequently subtle, ill-defined problems we meet in business and organizational life. It is hoped that examining these issues will help you (1) identify the obligations, ideals, and effects involved in specific moral issues and (2) decide where the emphasis should lie among the competing considerations.

Key Terms and Concepts

act utilitarianism
business egoism
categorical imperative
consequentialist theories
egoism
eminent domain
good will
hedonism
human rights

hypothetical imperative
ideal
legal rights
maxim
moral rights
moral worth
negative rights
nonconsequentialist
   theories

normative theories
optimal moral code
positive rights
prima facie obligations
psychological egoism
rule utilitarianism
supererogatory actions
universal acceptability
utilitarianism

Points to Review

- consequentialist vs. nonconsequentialist normative theories
- personal vs. impersonal egoism
- the difference between egoism as an ethical theory and egoism as a psychological theory
- three problems with egoism
- Bentham's and Mill's differing views of pleasure
- six points about utilitarianism
- three features of utilitarianism in an organizational context
- three critical inquiries of utilitarianism
- the deathbed-promise example
- business as combining self-interest and social good (or egoism and utilitarianism)
- the convenience store clerk and acting from a sense of duty
- Martin's promise as an illustration of the categorical imperative
- hypothetical imperatives vs. the categorical imperative

- two alternative formulations of the categorical imperative
- three features of Kant's ethics in an organizational context
- three critical inquiries of Kant's ethics
- how Ross's theory differs from utilitarianism and from Kant's categorical imperative
- four important characteristics of human rights
- the difference between negative and positive rights
- how rule utilitarianism differs from act utilitarianism
- the optimal moral code and the analogy with traffic rules
- two objections to rule utilitarianism
- two points drawn from Chapter 1 that can help moral discussions
- two-step procedure for morally evaluating actions and choices

CASE 2.1

Hacking into Harvard

Everyone who has ever applied for admission to a selective college or who has been interviewed for a highly desired job knows the feeling of waiting impatiently to learn the result of one's application. So it's not hard to identify

with those applicants to some of the nation's most prestigious MBA programs who thought they had a chance to get an early glimpse at whether their ambition was to be fulfilled. While visiting a *Business Week Online* message board, they found instructions, posted by an anonymous hacker, explaining how to find out what admission decision the business schools had made in their case. Doing so wasn't hard. The universities in question—Harvard, Dartmouth, Duke, Carnegie Mellon, MIT, and Stanford—use the same application software from Apply Yourself, Inc. Essentially, all one had to do was change the very end of the applicant-specific URL to get to the supposedly restricted page containing the verdict on one's application. In the nine hours it took Apply Yourself programmers to patch the security flaw after it was posted, curiosity got the better of about two hundred applicants, who couldn't resist the temptation to discover whether they had been admitted.[19]

Many of them got only blank screens. But a few learned that they had been tentatively accepted or tentatively rejected. What they didn't count on, however, were two things: first, that it wouldn't take the business schools long to learn what had happened and who had done it and, second, that the schools in question were going to be very unhappy about it. Harvard was perhaps the most outspoken. Kim B. Clark, dean of the business school, said, "This behavior is unethical at best—a serious breach of trust that cannot be countered by rationalization." In a similar vein, Steve Nelson, the executive director of Harvard's MBA program, stated, "Hacking into a system in this manner is unethical and also contrary to the behavior we expect of leaders we aspire to develop."

It didn't take Harvard long to make up its mind what to do about it. It rejected all 119 applicants who had attempted to access the information. In an official statement, Dean Clark wrote that the mission of the Harvard Business School "is to educate principled leaders who make a difference in the world. To achieve that, a person must have many skills and qualities, including the highest standards of integrity, sound judgment and a strong moral compass—an intuitive sense of what is

right and wrong. Those who have hacked into this web site have failed to pass that test." Carnegie Mellon and MIT quickly followed suit. By rejecting the ethically challenged, said Richard L. Schmalensee, dean of MIT's Sloan School of Management, the schools are trying to "send a message to society as a whole that we are attempting to produce people that when they go out into the world, they will behave ethically."

Duke and Dartmouth, where only a handful of students gained access to their files, said they would take a case-by-case approach and didn't publicly announce their individualized determinations. But, given the competition for places in their MBA programs, it's a safe bet that few, if any, offending applicants were sitting in classrooms the following semester. Forty-two applicants attempted to learn their results early at Stanford, which took a different tack. It invited the accused hackers to explain themselves in writing. "In the best case, what has been demonstrated here is a lack of judgment; in the worst case, a lack of integrity," said Derrick Bolton, Stanford's director of MBA admissions. "One of the things we try to teach at business schools is making good decisions and taking responsibility for your actions." Six weeks later, however, the dean of Stanford Business School, Robert Joss, reported, "None of those who gained unauthorized access was able to explain his or her actions to our satisfaction." He added that he hoped the applicants "might learn from their experience."

Given the public's concern over the wave of corporate scandals in recent years and its growing interest in corporate social responsibility, business writers and other media commentators warmly welcomed Harvard's decisive response. But soon there was some sniping at the decision by those claiming that Harvard and the other business schools had overreacted. Although 70 percent of Harvard's MBA students approved the decision, the undergraduate student newspaper, *The Crimson*, was skeptical. "HBS [Harvard Business School] has scored a media victory with its hard-line stance," it said in an editorial. "Americans have been looking for a sign from the business community, particularly its leading educational institutions, that business ethics are a priority. HBS's false bravado has given them one, leaving 119 victims in angry hands."

As some critics pointed out, Harvard's stance overlooked the possibility that the hacker might have been a spouse or a parent who had access to the applicant's password and personal identification number. In fact, one applicant said that this had happened to him. His wife found the instructions at *Business Week Online* and tried to check on the success of his application. "I'm really distraught over this," he said. "My wife is tearing her hair out." To this, Harvard's Dean Clark responds, "We expect applicants to be personally responsible for the access to the website, and for the identification and passwords they receive."

Critics also reject the idea that the offending applicants were "hackers." After all, they used their own personal identification and passwords to log on legitimately; all they did was to modify the URL to go to a different page. They couldn't change anything in their files or view anyone else's information. In fact, some critics blamed the business schools and Apply Yourself more than they did the applicants. If those pages were supposed to be restricted, then it shouldn't have been so easy to find one's way to them.

In an interview, one of the Harvard applicants said that although he now sees that what he did was wrong, he wasn't thinking about that at the time—he just followed the hacker's posted instructions out of curiosity. He didn't consider what he did to be "hacking," because any novice could have done the same thing. "I'm not an IT person by any stretch of the imagination," he said. "I'm not even a great typist." He wrote the university a letter of apology. "I admitted that I got curious and had a lapse in judgment," he said. "I pointed out that I wasn't trying to harm anyone and wasn't trying to get an advantage over anyone." Another applicant said that he

knew he had made a poor judgment but he was offended by having his ethics called into question. "I had no idea that they would have considered this a big deal." And some of those posting messages at *Business Week Online* and other MBA-related sites believe the offending applicants should be applauded. "Exploiting weaknesses is what good business is all about. Why would they ding you?" wrote one anonymous poster.

Richard L. Schmalensee, dean of MIT's Sloan School of Management, however, defends Harvard and MIT's automatically rejecting everyone who peeked "because it wasn't an impulsive mistake." "The instructions are reasonably elaborate," he said. "You didn't need a degree in computer science, but this clearly involved effort. You couldn't do this casually without knowing that you were doing something wrong. We've always taken ethics seriously, and this is a serious matter." To those applicants who say that they didn't do any harm, Schmalensee replies, "Is there nothing wrong with going through files just because you can?"

To him and others, seeking unauthorized access to restricted pages is as wrong as snooping through your boss's desk to see whether you've been recommended for a raise. Some commentators, however, suggest there may be a generation gap here. Students who grew up with the Internet, they say, tend to see it as wide-open territory and don't view this level of web snooping as indicating a character flaw.

Discussion Questions

1. Suppose that you had been one of the MBA applicants who stumbled across an opportunity to learn your results early. What would you have done, and why? Would you have considered it a moral decision? If so, on what basis would you have made it?

2. Assess the morality of what the curious applicants did from the point of view of egoism, utilitarianism, Kant's ethics, Ross's pluralism, and rule utilitarianism.

3. In your view, was it wrong for the MBA applicants to take an unauthorized peek at their application files? Explain why you consider what they did morally permissible or impermissible. What obligations, ideals, and effects should the applicants have considered? Do you think, as some have suggested, that there is a generation gap on this issue?

4. Did Harvard and MIT overreact, or was it necessary for them to respond as they did in order to send a strong message about the importance of ethics? If you were a business-school admissions official, how would you have handled this situation?

5. Assess the argument that the applicants who snooped were just engaging in the type of bold and aggressive behavior that makes for business success. In your view,

are these applicants likely to make good business leaders? What about the argument that it's really the fault of the universities for not having more secure procedures, not the fault of the applicants who took advantage of that fact?

6. One of the applicants admits that he used poor judgment but believes that his ethics should not be questioned. What do you think he means? If he exercised poor judgment on a question of right and wrong, isn't that a matter of his ethics? Stanford's Derrick Bolton distinguishes between a lapse of judgment and a lack of integrity. What do you see as the difference? Based on this episode, what, if anything, can we say about the ethics and the character of the curious applicants?

CASE 2.2

The Ford Pinto

There was a time when the "made in Japan" label brought a predictable smirk of superiority to the face of most Americans. The quality of most Japanese products usually was as low as their price. In fact, few imports could match their domestic counterparts, the proud products of Yankee know-how. But by the late 1960s, an invasion of foreign-made goods chiseled a few worry lines into the countenance of U.S. industry. In Detroit, worry was fast fading to panic as the Japanese, not to mention the Germans, began to gobble up more and more of the subcompact auto market.

Never one to take a backseat to the competition, Ford Motor Company decided to meet the threat from abroad head-on. In 1968, Ford executives decided to produce the Pinto. Known inside the company as "Lee's car," after Ford president Lee Iacocca, the Pinto was to weigh no more than 2,000 pounds and cost no more than $2,000.[20]

Eager to have its subcompact ready for the 1971 model year, Ford decided to compress the normal drafting-board-to-showroom time of about three-and-a-half years into two. The compressed schedule meant that any design changes typically made before production-line tooling would have to be made during it.

Before producing the Pinto, Ford crash-tested various prototypes, in part to learn whether they met a safety standard proposed by the National Highway Traffic Safety Administration (NHTSA) to reduce fires from traffic collisions. This standard would have required that by 1972 all new autos be able to withstand a rear-end impact of 20 mph without fuel loss, and that by 1973 they be able to withstand an impact of 30 mph. The prototypes all failed the 20-mph test. In 1970 Ford crash-tested the Pinto itself, and the result was the same: ruptured gas tanks and dangerous leaks. The only Pintos to pass the test had been modified in some way—for example, with a rubber bladder in the gas tank or a piece of steel between the tank and the rear bumper.

Thus, Ford knew that the Pinto represented a serious fire hazard when struck from the rear, even in low-speed collisions. Ford officials faced a decision. Should they go ahead with the existing design, thereby meeting the production timetable but possibly jeopardizing consumer safety? Or should they delay production of the Pinto by redesigning the gas tank to make it safer and thus concede another year of subcompact dominance to foreign companies? Ford not only pushed ahead with the original design but also stuck to it for the next six years.

What explains Ford's decision? The evidence suggests that Ford relied, at least in part, on cost-benefit reasoning, which is an analysis in monetary terms of the expected costs and benefits of doing something. There were various ways of making the Pinto's gas tank safer. Although the estimated price of these safety improvements ranged from only $5 to $8 per vehicle, Ford evidently reasoned that the increased cost outweighed the benefits of a new tank design.

How exactly did Ford reach that conclusion? We don't know for sure, but an internal report, "Fatalities Associated with Crash-Induced Fuel Leakage and Fires," reveals the cost-benefit reasoning that the company used in cases like this. This report was not written with the Pinto in mind; rather, it concerns fuel leakage in rollover accidents (not rear-end collisions), and its computations applied to all Ford vehicles, not just the Pinto. Nevertheless, it illustrates the type of reasoning that was probably used in the Pinto case.

In the "Fatalities" report, Ford engineers estimated the cost of technical improvements that would prevent gas tanks from leaking in rollover accidents to be $11 per vehicle. The authors go on to discuss various estimates of the number of people killed by fires from car rollovers before settling on the relatively low figure of 180 deaths per year. But given that number, how can the value of those individuals' lives be gauged? Can a dollars-and-cents figure be assigned to a human being? NHTSA thought so. In 1972, it estimated that society loses $200,725 every time a person is killed in an auto accident (adjusted for inflation, today's figure would, of course, be considerably higher). It broke down the costs as follows:

Future productivity losses	
Direct	$132,000
Indirect	41,300
Medical costs	
Hospital	700
Other	425
Property damage	1,500
Insurance administration	4,700
Legal and court expenses	3,000
Employer losses	1,000
Victim's pain and suffering	10,000
Funeral	900
Assets (lost consumption)	5,000
Miscellaneous accident costs	200
Total per fatality	$200,725

Putting the NHTSA figures together with other statistical studies, the Ford report arrives at the following overall assessment of costs and benefits:

Benefits

Savings:	180 burn deaths, 180 serious burn injuries, 2,100 burned vehicles
Unit cost:	$200,000 per death, $67,000 per injury, $700 per vehicle
Total benefit:	(180 × $200,000) + (180 × $67,000) + (2,100 × $700) = $49.5 million

Costs

Sales:	11 million cars, 1.5 million light trucks
Unit cost:	$11 per car, $11 per truck
Total cost:	12.5 million × $11 = $137.5 million

Thus, the costs of the suggested safety improvements outweigh their benefits, and the "Fatalities" report accordingly recommends against any improvements—a recommendation that Ford followed.

Likewise in the Pinto case, Ford's management, whatever its exact reasoning, decided to stick with the original design and not upgrade the Pinto's fuel tank, despite the test results reported by its engineers. Here is the aftermath of Ford's decision:

- Between 1971 and 1978, the Pinto was responsible for a number of fire-related deaths. Ford puts the figure at 23; its critics say the figure is closer to 500. According to the sworn testimony of Ford engineers, 95 percent of the fatalities would have survived if Ford had located the fuel tank over the axle (as it had done on its Capri automobiles).

- NHTSA finally adopted a 30-mph collision standard in 1976. The Pinto then acquired a rupture-proof fuel tank. In 1978 Ford was obliged to recall all 1971–1976 Pintos for fuel-tank modifications.

- Between 1971 and 1978, approximately fifty lawsuits were brought against Ford in connection with rear-end accidents in the Pinto. In the Richard Grimshaw case, in addition to awarding over $3 million in compensatory damages to the victims of a Pinto crash, the jury awarded a landmark $125 million in punitive damages against Ford. The judge reduced punitive damages to $3.5 million.

- On August 10, 1978, the 1973 Ford Pinto that eighteen-year-old Judy Ulrich, her sixteen-year-old sister Lynn, and their eighteen-year-old cousin Donna were riding in was struck from the rear by a van near Elkhart, Indiana. The gas tank of the Pinto exploded on impact. In the fire that resulted, the three teenagers were burned to death. Ford was charged with criminal homicide. The judge in the case advised jurors that Ford should be convicted if it

had clearly disregarded the harm that might result from its actions, and that disregard represented a substantial deviation from acceptable standards of conduct. On March 13, 1980, the jury found Ford not guilty of criminal homicide.

For its part, Ford has always denied that the Pinto is unsafe compared with other cars of its type and era. The company also points out that in every model year the Pinto met or surpassed the government's own standards. But what the company doesn't say is that successful lobbying by it and its industry associates was responsible for delaying for seven years the adoption of any NHTSA crash standard. Furthermore, Ford's critics claim that there were more than forty European and Japanese models in the Pinto price and weight range with safer gas-tank position. "Ford made an extremely irresponsible decision," concludes auto safety expert Byron Bloch, "when they placed such a weak tank in such a ridiculous location in such a soft rear end."

Has the automobile industry learned a lesson from Ford's experience with the Pinto? Some observers thought not when twenty years later an Atlanta jury held the General Motors Corporation responsible for the death of a Georgia teenager in the fiery crash of one of its pickup trucks. Finding that the company had known that its "side-saddle" gas tanks, which are mounted outside the rails of the truck's frame, are dangerously prone to rupture, the jury awarded $4.2 million in actual damages and $101 million in punitive damages to the parents of the seventeen-year-old victim, Shannon Moseley.

After the verdict, General Motors said that it still stood behind the safety of its trucks and contended "that a full examination by the National Highway Traffic Safety Administration of the technical issues in this matter will bear out our contention that the ... pickup trucks do not have a safety related defect." Subsequently, however, the Department of Transportation determined that GM pickups of the style Shannon Moseley drove do pose a fire hazard and that they are more prone than competitors' pickups to catch fire when struck from the side. Still, GM rejected requests to recall the pickups and repair them, and later the Georgia Court of Appeals threw out the jury's verdict on a legal technicality—despite ruling that the evidence submitted in the case showed that GM was aware that the gas tanks were hazardous but, to save the expense involved, did not try to make them safer.

Expense seems to be the issue, too, when it comes to SUV rollovers. After nearly three hundred rollover deaths in Ford Explorers equipped with Firestone tires in the late 1990s, Congress mandated NHTSA to conduct roll-over road tests on all SUVs. (Previously, the agency had relied on mathematical formulas based on accident statistics to evaluate rollover resistance, rather than doing real-world tests.) In August 2004 NHTSA released its results, and they weren't pretty—at least not for several of Detroit's most popular models. The Chevrolet Tahoe and the Ford Explorer, in particular, have between a 26 and a 29 percent chance of rolling over in a single-vehicle crash, almost twice that of models from Honda, Nissan, and Chrysler. The Saturn Vue couldn't even finish the test because its left-rear suspension broke, leading General Motors to recall all 250,000 Vues.

Ford and General Motors have the anti-rollover technology necessary to make their SUVs safer. The problem is that rollover sensors and electronic stability systems add about $800 to the price of a vehicle, so the companies have offered them only as options. The same is true of side-curtain airbags to protect occupants when a vehicle rolls over. They cost about $500. Improved design—wider wheel tracks, lower center of gravity, and reinforced roofs to protect passengers in a rollover—would also help. Embarrassed by the test results, the companies promised to make more safety features standard equipment on new SUVs. Lawsuits by rollover victims are also prodding the companies to enhance their

commitment to safety. Two months before NHTSA released its results, Ford had to pay $369 million in damages—one of the largest personal-injury awards ever against an automaker—to a San Diego couple whose Explorer flipped over four-and-a-half times when they swerved to avoid a metal object on the highway.

Discussion Questions

1. What moral issues does the Pinto case raise?
2. Suppose Ford officials were asked to justify their decision. What moral principles do you think they would invoke? Assess Ford's handling of the Pinto from the perspective of each of the moral theories discussed in this chapter.
3. Utilitarians would say that jeopardizing motorists does not by itself make Ford's action morally objectionable. The only morally relevant matter is whether Ford gave equal consideration to the interests of each affected party. Do you think Ford did this?
4. Is cost-benefit analysis a legitimate tool? What role, if any, should it play in moral deliberation? Critically assess the example of cost-benefit analysis given in the case study. Is there anything unsatisfactory about it? Could it have been improved upon in some way?
5. Speculate about Kant's response to the idea of placing a monetary value on a human life. Is doing so ever morally legitimate?
6. What responsibilities to its customers do you think Ford had? What are the most important moral rights, if any, operating in the Pinto case?
7. Would it have made a moral difference if the savings resulting from not improving the Pinto gas tank had been passed on to Ford's customers? Could a rational customer have chosen to save a few dollars and risk having the more dangerous gas

tank? What if Ford had told potential customers about its decision?

8. The maxim of Ford's action might be stated thus: "When it would cost more to make a safety improvement than not, it's all right not to make it." Can this maxim be universalized? Does it treat humans as ends in themselves? Would manufacturers be willing to abide by it if the positions were reversed and they were in the role of consumers?

9. Should Ford have been found guilty of criminal homicide in the Ulrich case?

10. Was GM responsible for Shannon Moseley's death? Compare that case with the case of Ford and the Pinto.

11. Assess Ford's and GM's actions with respect to SUV rollovers. Have the auto-makers met their moral obligation to consumers, or have they acted wrongly by not doing more to increase SUV safety? Should they be held either morally or legally responsible for deaths from roll-overs that would not have occurred in other vehicles? What should automakers do to increase SUV safety?

12. Is it wrong for business to sell a product that is not as safe as it could be, given current technology? Is it wrong to sell a vehicle that is less safe than competing products on the market? Are there limits to how far automakers must go in the name of safety?

CASE 2.3

Blood for Sale

Sol Levin was a successful stockbroker in Tampa, Florida, when he recognized the potentially profitable market for safe and uncontaminated blood and, with some colleagues, founded Plasma International. Not everybody is willing to make money by selling his or her own blood, and in the beginning Plasma International bought blood from people addicted to drugs and alcohol. Although innovative marketing increased Plasma International's sales dramatically, several cases of hepatitis were reported in recipients. The company then began looking for new sources of blood.[21]

Plasma International searched worldwide and, with the advice of a qualified team of medical consultants, did extensive testing. Eventually they found that the blood profiles of several rural West African tribes made them ideal prospective donors. After negotiations with the local government, Plasma International signed an agreement with several tribal chieftains to purchase blood.

Business went smoothly and profitably for Plasma International until a Tampa paper charged that Plasma was purchasing blood for as little as fifteen cents a pint and then reselling it to hospitals in the United States and South America for $25 per pint. In one recent disaster, the newspaper alleged, Plasma International had sold 10,000 pints, netting nearly a quarter of a million dollars.

The newspaper story stirred up controversy in Tampa, but the existence of commercialized blood marketing systems in the United States is nothing new. Approximately half the blood and plasma obtained in the United States is bought and sold like any other commodity. By contrast, the National Health Service in Great Britain relies entirely on a voluntary system of blood donation. Blood is neither bought nor sold. It is available to anyone who needs it without charge or obligation, and donors gain no preference over nondonors.

In an important study, economist Richard Titmuss showed that the British system works better than the American one in terms of economic and administrative efficiency, price, and blood quality. The commercialized blood market, Titmuss argued, is wasteful of blood and plagued by shortages. In the United States, bureaucratization, paperwork, and administrative overhead result in a cost per unit of blood that is five to fifteen times higher than in Great Britain. Hemophiliacs, in particular, are disadvantaged by the U.S. system and have enormous bills to pay. In addition, commercial markets are much more likely to distribute contaminated blood.

Titmuss also argued that the existence of a commercialized system discourages voluntary donors. People are less apt to give blood if they know that others are selling it. Philosopher Peter Singer has elaborated on this point:

> If blood is a commodity with a price, to give blood means merely to save someone money. Blood has a cash value of a certain number of dollars, and the importance of the gift will vary with the wealth of the recipient. If blood cannot be bought, however, the gift's value depends upon the need of the recipient. Often, it will be worth life itself. Under these circumstances blood becomes a very special kind of gift, and giving it means providing for strangers, without hope of reward, something they cannot buy and without which they may die. The gift relates strangers in a manner that is not possible when blood is a commodity.

This may sound like a philosopher's abstraction, far removed from the thoughts of ordinary people. On the contrary, it is an idea spontaneously expressed by British donors in response to Titmuss's questionnaire. As one woman, a machine operator, wrote in reply to the question why she first decided to become a blood donor: "You can't get blood from supermarkets and chain stores. People themselves must come forward; sick people can't get out of bed to ask you for a pint to save their life, so I came forward in hopes to help somebody who needs blood."

The implication of this answer, and others like it, is that even if the formal right to give blood can coexist with commercialized blood banks, the respondent's action would have lost much of its significance to her, and the blood would probably not have been given at all. When blood is a commodity, and can be purchased if it is not given, altruism becomes unnecessary, and so loosens the bonds that can otherwise exist between strangers in a community. The existence of a market in blood does not threaten the formal right to give blood, but it does away with the right to give blood which cannot be bought, has no cash value, and must be given freely if it is to be obtained at all. If there is such a right, it is incompatible with the right to sell blood, and we cannot avoid violating one of these rights when we grant the other.[22]

Both Titmuss and Singer believe that the weakening of the spirit of altruism in this sphere has important repercussions. It marks, they think, the increasing commercialization of our lives and makes similar changes in attitude, motive, and relationships more likely in other fields.

Update   Dr. Arthur Matas, a prominent kidney-transplant surgeon, is pushing for one change that it's doubtful either Titmuss or Singer would like. Lately, he's been traveling the United States making the case for lifting the legal ban on kidney sales. That ban was imposed in 1984 by an outraged Congress after a Virginia physician had proposed buying kidneys from poor people and selling them to the highest bidder. By contrast, Dr. Matas isn't trying to make money. He would like the government to handle kidney sales, and the kidneys to go to whoever is at the top of the current waiting list, whether the patient is rich or poor. And that list grows longer every year as the gap continues to widen—it's now nearly five to one—between patients in need and the number of kidneys available from either living or deceased donors.

With eligible patients often waiting for five or six years, more and more people are taking Dr. Matas seriously, but many experts still balk at the idea of organ sales. One of them is Dr. Francis Delmonico, a professor at Harvard University and president of the network that runs the nation's organ-distribution system. He worries that Dr. Matas' plan would exploit the poor and vulnerable, that it would cause altruistic kidney donations to wither, and that wealthy patients would manage to find a way around a regulated market to get a kidney faster.[23]

Discussion Questions

1. Is Sol Levin running a business "just like any other business," or is his company open to moral criticism? Defend your answer by appeal to moral principle.

2. Did Plasma International strike a fair bargain with the West Africans who supplied their blood to the company? Or is Plasma guilty of exploiting them in some way? Explain your answer.

3. What are the contrasting ideals of the British and U.S. blood systems? Which system, in your opinion, better promotes human freedom and respect for people? Which system better promotes the supply of blood?

4. Examine the pros and cons of commercial transactions in blood from the egoistic, the utilitarian, and the Kantian perspectives.

5. Are Titmuss and Singer correct to suggest that the buying and selling of blood reduces altruism? Does knowing that you can sell your blood (and that others are selling theirs) make you less inclined to donate your blood?

6. Singer suggests that although the right to sell blood does not threaten the formal right to give blood, it is incompatible with "the right to give blood, which cannot be bought, which has no cash value, and must be given freely if it is to be obtained at all." Assess that idea. Is there such a right?

7. Many believe that commercialization is increasing in all areas of modern life. If so, is it something to be applauded or condemned? Is it wrong to treat certain things—such as human organs—as commodities?

8. Do you believe that we have a moral duty to donate blood? If so, why and under what circumstances? If not, why not?

CHAPTER 3

Justice and Economic Distribution

Joel Stettenheim/CORBIS

The Nature of Justice
Rival Principles of Distribution

The Utilitarian View
Utilitarianism and Economic Distribution

The Libertarian Approach
Nozick's Theory of Justice
Nozick's Wilt Chamberlain Example
The Libertarian View of Liberty
Markets and Free Exchange
Property Rights

Rawls's Theory of Justice
The Original Position
Choosing the Principles
Rawls's Two Principles
Fairness and the Basic Structure
Benefits and Burdens

CASES
Eminent Domain
Battling over Bottled Water
Poverty in America

It seems strange to recall that until the early years of the twentieth century, there was no federal tax on personal income. Only when the Sixteenth Amendment to the U.S. Constitution was adopted in 1913 did Congress gain the right to tax people's income. Since then, the income tax laws have grown enormously complex. At over 67,000 pages, the federal tax code is two-and-a-half-times longer than it was in 1985.[1] Lawyers study for years to master the intricacies of the system, and most people with middle incomes or better require professional assistance to file their annual tax forms.

Because the tax rules do so much to shape the character of our economy and the distribution of income and wealth across the country, their fairness is frequently a political issue—take, for example, President Barack Obama's campaign-trail criticism of the tax cuts that George W. Bush pushed through during his term in office. Those tax cuts favored the well-to-do.[2] By contrast, Bush's predecessor, Bill Clinton, had raised the federal income tax on individuals with taxable incomes over $115,000. They saw their income tax rate increase from 31 percent to 36 percent. Clinton also slapped a 10 percent surcharge on those with incomes above $240,000. However, until Ronald Reagan lowered it, the tax rate for the wealthiest individuals had been 63 percent (indeed, until 1960 it had been 91 percent).

When President Reagan reduced taxes on the wealthy, he also eliminated some important tax loopholes. But the most significant feature of his personal tax philosophy was its rejection of the principle of "progressivity"— namely, that the wealthy ought to pay taxes at a higher rate than the poor. Today's income tax system, with six different tax brackets, remains progressive, but some complain that in reality those who are less well-off often end up paying more. One of the people making this charge is— surprisingly enough—Warren Buffett, the nation's second richest man. In 2006, he says, he earned $46 million but paid only 18 percent of it in federal tax, whereas the average tax rate paid by his employees, whose salaries range from $60,000 to $750,000, was 33 percent. Buffett is convinced that this is no statistical fluke. In fact, he is willing to bet anyone $1 million (to be paid to a charity selected by the winner) that the average tax rate (income and payroll) paid by the four hundred wealthiest people in the country is lower than that paid by their secretaries and receptionists.[3]

TABLE **3.1**
Share of Aggregate Household Income

	1970	1980	1990	2000	2006
Best-off fifth	43.3%	44.1%	46.6%	49.8%	50.5%
Second fifth	24.5	24.7	24.0	23.0	22.9
Middle fifth	17.4	16.8	15.9	14.8	14.5
Fourth fifth	10.8	10.2	9.6	8.9	8.6
Poorest fifth	4.1	4.2	3.8	3.6	3.4
Top 5 percent	16.6	16.5	18.5	22.1	22.3

Still, it remains true that America's wealthier citizens pay the bulk of the nation's income tax—for the simple reason that most of the nation's income goes to them. The top one million households now take home more than do the 56 million households at the bottom.[4] And the top 0.1 percent of Americans earns 77 times the income of the bottom 90 percent. In 1979 they earned only 20 times as much.[5] This is part of a trend since 1980 toward an increasingly unequal distribution of national income in the United States, with those who are already very well-off—the top fifth of the country—now getting a larger slice of the pie than before, as Table 3.1 shows.[6]

The flip side, of course, is that the bottom 80 percent now receives less. From World War II through 1980, the inflation-adjusted income of the median family more than doubled, but since then it has been relatively flat despite the fact that people work longer hours and more wives have entered the workforce.[7] In fact, adjusted for inflation, wages for men remain below their 1973 peak,[8] with young men in their thirties now earning 12 percent less than they did thirty years ago.[9] By contrast, middle-level managers have fared much better, and top executives have done spectacularly well. A *Business Week* survey of the two highest-paid executives at America's largest companies shows their average total pay (salary, bonuses, and long-term compensation) to be $9.6 million a year, while a *Wall Street Journal* study puts the median direct compensation of CEOs at 350 major U.S. corporations at only a little over $6 million.[10] Either way, that dwarfs the pay of the average worker, who makes $36,140 per year.[11]

The United States leads the world in executive pay.[12] Japan's CEOs, for example, earn a salary of only $300,000 to $500,000 a year, with far fewer bonuses and stock options than their American counterparts.[13] Recently, average pay for American CEOs has declined slightly because stock prices are lower. Nevertheless, since 1980 the compensation of the top CEOs has grown from 42 times that of the average person working under them to more than 300 times greater.[14] The median weekly salary for all workers is less than $700. If the average CEO works 60 hours a week, 52 weeks a year, then he or she earns that much every twenty or thirty minutes. Since 1990, CEO pay has gone up 571 percent. In comparison, corporate profits have grown by a relatively modest 114 percent, and the average worker's pay by a mere 37 percent (which is just above inflation at 32 percent).[15] A schoolteacher who made $31,000 in 1990 would now make $177,000 if teachers' salaries had grown at the same rate as CEO pay.

While those on top do better than ever, life continues to be a struggle for people in the middle and lower echelons. Indeed, according to economist Larry Summers, head of President Obama's National Economic Council, the lack of middle-class income growth is "the defining issue of our time."[16] Although our economy has created millions of new jobs in the last two decades, most of them pay relatively low wages.[17] Productivity gains have gone predominantly to investors, not to wage earners, with capitalists grabbing a larger share of the national income at the expense of workers.[18] Whereas output per hour and real hourly compensation rose hand in hand from 1950 to 1980, U.S. Department of Labor statistics show that since then compensation has lagged behind.[19] In fact, between 1995 and 2006 the growth of employee productivity exceeded the growth of employee real wages by 340 percent.[20] Although the average American works hard—two weeks more each year than thirty years ago[21]—many families have trouble coping. Most American jobs do not pay enough to support a full household or to provide what most people feel are necessities,[22] and the number of people who define themselves as "have-nots" has increased.[23] Many Americans struggle to pay for health care or simply do without, which is not surprising when one in five jobs pays only a poverty-level wage.[24] For a variety of reasons, moreover, people's incomes are more volatile, and their lives less economically secure, these days. For example, the chance that a person or family will experience a year-to-year drop in income of more than 50 percent has almost doubled since the 1970s (from one in twenty to about one in eleven).[25]

These trends are even more alarming when set against the background of the extremely unequal distribution of wealth in this country. The top 1 percent (about one and a half million families) not only receives a dispro-portionate share of the national income but also owns nearly 40 percent of the nation's total net worth. That's double the share of total national wealth owned by the top 1 percent in 1976 and is more than is owned by the en-tire bottom 90 percent of U.S. households. This economic elite owns half of all stocks, mutual funds, financial securities, and trusts, two-thirds of all business equity, and 36 percent of nonresidential real estate.[26] In contrast, the bottom 60 percent of Americans owns only 5 percent of the nation's wealth, and the lowest 40 percent less than 1 percent.[27]

Although the United States has always prided itself on being a land of opportunity and upward mobility, recent evidence suggests that the econ-omy is becoming more rigid and class-bound. Nowadays, mobility is no greater in the United States than in Britain or France, and it is lower than in Canada and some Scandinavian countries.[28] More and more Americans are ending up stuck on the bottom rung, with less chance of getting ahead than their counterparts in Europe have.[29] "You can't take solace anymore in the American dream of working hard and migrating up through society," says William J. McDonough, president of the Federal Reserve Bank of New York.[30] Or as one Federal Reserve Bank economist puts it, "The apple falls even closer to the tree than we thought."[31]

One reason, of course, is that parents work very hard to transmit their advantages to their children, especially with respect to education, a crucial determinant of future income. These days, social class increasingly deter-mines access to college. Three-quarters of the students at the nation's top 146 universities hail from the richest fourth of the nation. Only 3 percent of them come from the bottom income quartile, and only 10 percent from the bottom half of the income scale. This means that at an elite university you are twenty-five times more likely to run into a rich student than a poor one.[32] Even at the better state universities, the number of students from families making more than $100,000 has increased to 40 percent. In general, qualified high school graduates from low-income families are only one-third as likely to complete a bachelor's degree as are students from families earning $75,000 or more.[33]

There is nothing inevitable about declining social mobility or about large inequalities in income and wealth. They are not brute facts of nature, even in market-oriented societies. For example, the distribution of income in Germany and Japan is far more equal than in the United States, even though both are just as thoroughly capitalist, and an American is three times more likely to be poor than is someone in Italy.[34] Rather, political choices determine how income and wealth are distributed and what sort of assistance is given to those who are struggling to get by. The United States simply chooses to spend a smaller percentage of its GDP than European countries do combating inequality and pursuing policies intended to assist the bottom half of society to advance.[35] That is why, for example, 17 percent of America's children live in poverty but only 3 percent of Norway's do,[36] and why, more generally, the gap between the wealthiest 10 percent and the poorest 10 percent is greater in the United States than in any industrialized country except Russia.[37] How much inequality and what sort of socioeconomic disparities a society is willing to accept reflect both its moral values and the relative strength of its contending social and political forces.

This chapter focuses on the subject of economic justice, which concerns the constellation of moral issues raised by a society's distribution of wealth, income, status, and power. Ethical questions arise daily about these matters. Is it just, for example, that CEOs pull in astronomical salaries and help themselves to enormous benefits when this reduces the profits of stockholders, who own the company? Or, to take another issue, thanks to modern technology today's hospitals are able to perform life-prolonging feats of medicine that were undreamed of only a couple of decades ago, but these services are often extraordinarily costly. Who, then, should have access to them? Those who can afford them? Any who need them? Those who are most likely to benefit?

Chapter 2 discussed several basic moral theories and the general principles of right and wrong associated with them. This chapter focuses on the more specific topic of justice and economic distribution—that is, on the principles that are relevant to the moral assessment of society's distribution of economic goods and services. Although the topic is an abstract one, it is particularly relevant to the study of business ethics, because it concerns the moral standards to be used in evaluating the institutional frameworks within which both business and nonbusiness organizations operate. Specifically, this chapter will examine these topics:

1. The concept of justice, its relation to fairness, equality, rights, and what people deserve, and some rival principles of economic distribution
2. The utilitarian approach to justice in general and economic justice in particular
3. The libertarian theory, which places a moral priority on liberty and free exchange
4. The contractualist and egalitarian theory of John Rawls

THE NATURE OF JUSTICE

Justice is an old concept with a rich history, a concept that is fundamental to any discussion of how society ought to be organized. Philosophical concern with justice goes back at least to ancient Greece. For Plato and some of his contemporaries, justice seems to have been the paramount virtue or, more precisely, the sum of virtue with regard to our relations with others. Philosophers today, however, generally distinguish justice from the whole of morality. The complaint that something is "unjust" is more specific than that something is "bad" or "immoral." What, then, makes an act, policy, or institution unjust? Unfortunately, the terms *just* and *unjust* are vague, and different people use them in different ways. Still, talk of justice or injustice typically focuses on at least one of several related ideas: fairness, equality, desert, and rights.

Questions of justice typically focus on fairness, equality, desert, or rights.

First, **justice** is often used to mean *fairness*. Justice frequently concerns the fair treatment of members of groups of people or else looks backward to the fair compensation of prior injuries. Exactly what fairness requires is difficult to say, and different standards may be pertinent in different cases. If corporate manager Smith commits bribery, he is justly punished under our laws. If other managers commit equally serious crimes but are allowed to escape punishment, then Smith suffers a comparative injustice because he was unfairly singled out. But Smith and other white-collar criminals are treated unfairly and thus unjustly, although this time for the opposite reason, if stiffer sentences are meted out to common criminals for less grave offenses.

One way unfairness creates injustice occurs when like cases are not treated in the same fashion. Following Aristotle, most philosophers believe that we are required, as a formal principle of justice, to treat similar cases alike except where there is some relevant difference. This principle emphasizes the role of impartiality and consistency in justice, but it is a purely formal principle because it is silent about which differences are relevant and which are not. Furthermore, satisfying this formal requirement does not guarantee that

Summary 3.1

Justice is one important aspect of morality. Talk of justice and injustice generally involves appeals to the related notions of fairness, equality, desert, and rights. Economic or distributive justice concerns the principles appropriate for assessing society's distribution of social benefits and burdens, particularly wealth, income, status, and power.

justice is done. For example, a judge who treats similar cases alike can succeed in administering fairly and nonarbitrarily a law that is itself unjust (like a statute requiring racial segregation).

Related to Aristotle's fairness requirement is a second idea commonly bound up with the concept of justice: *equality*. Justice is frequently held to require that our treatment of people reflect their fundamental moral equality. While Aristotle's formal principle of justice does not say whether we are to assume equality of treatment until some difference between cases is shown or to assume the opposite until some relevant similarities are demonstrated, a claim of injustice based on equality is meant to place the burden of proof on those who would endorse unequal treatment. Still, the premise that all persons are equal does not establish a direct relationship between justice and economic distribution. We all believe that some differences in the treatment of persons are consistent with equality (punishment, for example), and neither respect for equality nor a commitment to equal treatment necessarily implies an equal distribution of economic goods.

Despite equality, then, individual circumstances—in particular, what a person has done—make a difference. We think it is unjust, for example, when a guilty person goes free or an innocent person hangs, regardless of how others have been treated. This suggests that in addition to equal or impartial treatment justice has a third aspect, the idea of *desert*. Justice requires that people get what they deserve or, as a number of ancient moralists put it, that each receive his or her due.

This is closely related to a fourth and final idea—namely, that one is treated unjustly when one's moral *rights* are violated. John Stuart Mill, in fact, made this the defining characteristic of injustice. In his view, what distinguishes injustice from other types of wrongful behavior is that it involves a violation of the rights of some identifiable person:

> Whether the injustice consists in depriving a person of a possession, or in breaking faith with him, or in treating him worse than he deserves, or worse than other people who have no greater claims—in each case the supposition implies two things: a wrong done, and some assignable person who is wronged.... It seems to me that this feature in the case—a right in some person, correlative to the moral obligation—constitutes the specific difference between justice and generosity or beneficence. Justice implies something which it is not only right to do, and wrong not to do, but which some individual person can claim from us as a moral right.[38]

Rival Principles of Distribution

Justice, then, is an important subclass of morality in general, a subclass that generally involves appeals to the overlapping notions of fairness, equality, desert, and rights. Turning to the topic of **distributive justice**—that is, to the proper distribution of social benefits and burdens (in particular, economic benefits and burdens)—we see that a number of rival principles have been proposed. Among the principles most frequently recommended as a basis of distribution are these: to each an equal share, to each according to individual need, to each according to personal effort, to each according to social contribution, and to each according to merit. Every one of these principles has its advocates, and each seems plausible in some circumstances. But only in some. There are problems with each. For example, if equality of income were guaranteed, then the lazy would receive as much as the industrious; however, effort is hard to measure and compare, and what one is able to contribute to society may depend on one's luck in being at the right place at the right time. And so on. No single principle seems to work in enough circumstances to be defended successfully as the sole principle of justice in distribution.

It often seems that we simply employ different principles of distributive justice in different circumstances. For example, corporations in certain industries may be granted tax breaks because of their social contribution, welfare programs operate on the basis of need, and business firms award promotions for meritorious performance. Moreover, multiple principles may often be relevant to a single situation. Sometimes they may pull in the same direction, as when wealthy professionals such as doctors defend their high incomes simultaneously on grounds of superior effort, merit, social contribution, and even (because of the high cost of malpractice insurance) need. Or the principles may pull in different directions, as when a teacher must balance effort against performance in assigning grades to pupils. Some philosophers are content to leave the situation here. As they see it, there are various equally valid, prima facie principles of just distribution—equality, need, effort, and so on—and one must try to find the principle that best applies in the given circumstances. If several principles seem to apply, then one must simply weigh them the best one can.

In his book *Spheres of Justice*, Michael Walzer pursues a more sophisticated version of this pluralistic approach.[39] Skeptical of the assumption that justice requires us to implement (in different contexts) some basic principle or set of principles, Walzer argues

> that different goods ought to be distributed for different reasons, in accordance with different procedures, by different agents; and that all these differences derive from different understandings of the social goods themselves—the inevitable product of historical and cultural particularism.[40]

Different norms and principles govern different distributive spheres, and these norms and principles are shaped by the implicit social meanings of the goods in question. He continues:

> Every social good or set of goods constitutes, as it were, a distributive sphere within which only certain criteria and arrangements are appropriate. Money is inappropriate in the sphere of ecclesiastical office.... There is no single standard [against which all distributions are to be measured]. But there are standards (roughly knowable even when they are also controversial) for every social good and every distributive sphere in every particular society.[41]

As Walzer sees it, distributive criteria are determined by the particular, historically shaped social meanings of the goods in question. The philosophical task is to tease out the inner logic of each type of good, thus revealing the tacit, socially shared values that govern (or should govern) its distribution.

Summary 3.2
Economic distribution might be based on pure equality, need, effort, social contribution, or merit. Each of these principles is plausible in some circumstances but not in others. In some situations, the principles pull us in different directions. Dissatisfied with a pluralistic approach, some moral philosophers have sought to develop more general theories of justice.

Some philosophers believe that there are a number of equally valid principles of just distribution. We must determine which one best applies in a given situation.

Walzer's historically informed discussion of topics like medical care or dirty and degrading work are rich and intriguing, but his view implies that when it comes to issues of distributive justice, the best philosophers can do is to try to unravel the implicit, socially specific norms that govern the distribution of different goods in a particular society. Many contemporary philosophers disagree. They believe that we should step farther back than Walzer does from existing norms and social arrangements and seek some general theory of justice in economic distribution, on the basis of which we can assess current social practices. Three such theories are the utilitarian, the libertarian, and the Rawlsian (egalitarian).

Other philosophers seek a general theory of economic justice. The utilitarian, libertarian, and Rawlsian theories are important examples.

THE UTILITARIAN VIEW

For utilitarians, as Chapter 2 explained, happiness is the overarching value. Whether one assesses the rightness and wrongness of actions in terms of how much happiness they produce, as an act utilitarian does, or uses happiness as the standard for deciding what moral principles a society should accept as the basis for determining right and wrong, as a rule utilitarian does, happiness is the only thing that is good in and of itself. On that utilitarians are agreed.

Earlier we considered John Stuart Mill's idea that injustice involves the violation of the rights of some identifiable person. This is what distinguishes it from other types of immoral behavior. But if injustice involves the violation of moral rights, the question arises of how a utilitarian like Mill understands talk of rights. Mill's position was that saying I have a right to something is saying I have a valid claim on society to protect me in the possession of that thing, either by the force of law or through education and opinion. And I have that valid claim in the first place because society's protection of my possession of that thing is warranted on utilitarian grounds. "To have a right, then, is … to have something which society ought to defend me in the possession of. If the objector goes on to ask why it ought, I can give him no other reason than general utility."[42] What utilitarianism identifies as rights are certain moral rules, the observance of which is of the utmost importance for the long-run, overall maximization of happiness.

Accordingly, Mill summed up his view of justice as follows:

> Justice is a name for certain classes of moral rules which concern the essentials of human well-being more nearly, and are therefore of more absolute obligation, than any other rules for the guidance of life; and the notion which we have found to be of the essence of the idea of justice—that of a right residing in an individual—implies and testifies to this more binding obligation.
>
> The moral rules which forbid mankind to hurt one another (in which we must never forget to include wrongful interference with each other's freedom) are more vital to human well-being than any maxims, however important, which only point out the best mode of managing some department of human affairs.[43]

Mill believed that justice concerns certain rules or rights that are vitally important for human well-being.

Although justice for Mill was ultimately a matter of promoting social well-being, not every issue of social utility was a matter of justice. The concept of justice identifies certain important social utilities—that is, certain rules or rights, the upholding of which is crucial for social well-being.

For utilitarians, then, justice is not an independent moral standard, distinct from their general principle. Rather, the maximization of happiness ultimately determines what is just and unjust. Critics of utilitarianism contend that knowing what will promote happiness is always difficult. People are bound to estimate consequences differently, thus making the standard of utility an inexact and unreliable principle for determining what is just. Mill, however, did not see much merit in this criticism. For one thing, it presupposes that we all agree about what the principles of justice are and how to apply them. This is far from the case, Mill argued. Indeed, without utilitarianism to provide a determinate standard of justice, one is always left with a plethora of competing principles, all of which seem to have some plausibility but are mutually incompatible.

As an example, Mill pointed to the conflict between two principles of justice that occurs in the realm of economic distribution. Is it just or not, he asked, that more talented workers should receive a greater remuneration? There are two possible answers to this question:

> On the negative side of the question it is argued that whoever does the best he can deserves equally well, and ought not in justice to be put in a position of inferiority for no fault of his own; that superior abilities have already advantages more than enough ... without adding to these a superior share of the world's goods; and that society is bound in justice rather to make compensation to the less favored for this unmerited inequality of advantages than to aggravate it.

This argument sounds plausible, but then so does the alternative answer:

> On the contrary side it is contended that society receives more from the more efficient laborer; that, his services being more useful, society owes him a larger return for them; that a greater share of the joint result is actually his work, and not to allow his claim to it is a kind of robbery; that, if he is only to receive as much as others, he can only be justly required to produce as much.

Here we have two conflicting principles of justice. How are we to decide between them? The problem, Mill said, is that both principles seem plausible:

> Justice has in this case two sides to it, which it is impossible to bring into harmony, and the two disputants have chosen opposite sides; the one looks to what it is just that the individual should receive, the other to what it is just that the community should give.[44]

Each disputant is, from his or her own point of view, unanswerable. "Any choice between them, on grounds of justice," Mill continued, "must be perfectly arbitrary." What, then, is the solution? For Mill, the utilitarian, it was straightforward: "Social utility alone can decide the preference."[45] The utilitarian standard must be the ultimate court of appeal in such cases. Only the utilitarian standard can provide an intelligent and satisfactory way of handling controversial questions of justice and of resolving conflicts between competing principles of justice.

Utilitarianism and Economic Distribution

The utilitarian theory of justice ties the question of economic distribution to the promotion of social well-being or happiness. Utilitarians want an economic system that will bring more good to society than any other system.

Summary 3.3
Utilitarianism holds that the maximization of happiness ultimately determines what is just and unjust. Mill contended, more specifically, that the concept of justice identifies certain rules or rights—the upholding of which is crucial for promoting well-being—and that injustice always involves violating the rights of some identifiable individual.

Utilitarianism doesn't tell us which economic system will produce the most happiness. That question hangs on the social, economic, and political facts.

But what system is that? Utilitarianism itself, as a normative theory, provides no answer. The answer depends on the relevant social, economic, and political facts. A utilitarian must understand the various possibilities, determine their consequences, and assess the available options. Obviously, this is not a simple task. Deciding what sort of economic arrangements would best promote human happiness requires the utilitarian to consider many things, including (1) the type of economic ownership (private, public, mixed); (2) the way of organizing production and distribution in general (pure laissez faire, markets with government planning and regulation, fully centralized planning); (3) the type of authority arrangements within the units of production (worker control versus managerial prerogative); (4) the range and character of material incentives; and (5) the nature and extent of social security and welfare provisions.

As a matter of historical fact, utilitarians in the early nineteenth century tended to favor free trade and the laissez-faire view of Adam Smith that unregulated market relations and free competition best promote the total social good.[46] Today it is probably fair to say that few, if any, utilitarians believe happiness would be maximized by a pure nineteenth-century-style capitalism, without any welfare arrangements. However, they are not in agreement on the question of what economic arrangements would in fact maximize happiness. Nonetheless, many utilitarians would favorably view increased **worker participation** in industrial life and more equal distribution of income.

Worker Participation

In his *Principles of Political Economy,* originally published in 1848, Mill argued for the desirability of breaking down the sharp and hostile division between the producers, or workers, on the one hand, and the capitalists, or owners, on the other. Not only would this be a good thing, it was also something that the advance of civilization was tending naturally to bring about: "The relation of masters and workpeople will be gradually superseded by partnership, in one or two forms: in some cases, association of the labourers with the capitalist; in others, and perhaps finally in all, association of labourers among themselves."[47] These developments would not only enhance productivity but also—and more important—promote the fuller development and well-being of the people involved. The aim, Mill thought, should be to enable people "to work with or for one another in relations not involving dependence."[48]

By the association of labor and capital, Mill had in mind different schemes of profit sharing. For example, "in the American ships trading to China, it has long been the custom for every sailor to have an interest in the profits of the voyage; and to this has been ascribed the general good conduct of those seamen."[49] This sort of association, however, would eventually give way to a more complete system of worker cooperatives:

> The form of association, however, which if mankind continue to improve, must be expected in the end to predominate, is not that which can exist between a capitalist as chief, and workpeople without a voice in the management, but the

association of the labourers themselves on terms of equality, collectively owning the capital with which they carry on their operations, and working under managers elected and removable by themselves.[50]

In *Principles* Mill discussed several examples of successful cooperative associations and viewed optimistically the future of the cooperative movement:

> Eventually, and in perhaps a less remote future than may be supposed, we may, through the cooperative principle, see our way to a change in society, which would combine the freedom and independence of the individual, with the moral, intellectual, and economical advantages of aggregate production; and which … would realize, at least in the industrial department, the best aspirations of the democratic spirit.[51]

What that transformation implied for Mill was nothing less than "the nearest approach to social justice, and the most beneficial ordering of industrial affairs for the universal good, which it is possible at present to foresee."[52]

Greater Equality of Income

Summary 3.4
Utilitarians must examine a number of factual issues in order to determine for themselves which economic system and principles will best promote social well-being or happiness. Many utilitarians favor increased worker participation and a more equal distribution of income.

Utilitarians are likely to be sympathetic to the argument that steps should be taken to reduce the great disparities in income that characterize our society. They are likely to believe that making the distribution of income more equal is a good strategy for maximizing happiness. The reason for this goes back to what economists would call the **declining marginal utility of money**. This phrase simply means that successive additions to one's income produce, on average, less happiness or welfare than did earlier additions.

The declining utility of money follows from the fact, as Professor Richard Brandt explains it, that the outcomes we want are preferentially ordered, some being more strongly wanted than others:

> So a person, when deciding how to spend his resources, picks a basket of groceries which is at least as appealing as any other he can purchase with the money he has. The things he does not buy are omitted because other things are wanted more. If we double a person's income, he will spend the extra money on items he wants less (some special cases aside), and which will give less enjoyment than will the original income. The more one's income, the fewer preferred items one buys and the more preferred items one already has. On the whole, then, when the necessities of life have been purchased and the individual is spending on luxury items, he is buying items which will give less enjoyment.… This conclusion corresponds well with common-sense reflection and practice.[53]

The obvious implication is that a more egalitarian allocation of income—that is, an allocation that increases the income of those who now earn less—would boost total happiness. Brandt, for one, therefore defends equality of after-tax income on utilitarian grounds, subject to the following exceptions: supplements to meet special needs, supplements necessary for incentives or to allocate resources efficiently, and variations to achieve other socially desirable ends, such as population control.[54] Brandt states that this guiding principle of distribution is of only prima facie force and may have to be balanced against other principles and considerations. Still, it illustrates the point that utilitarians today are likely to advocate increased economic equality.

THE LIBERTARIAN APPROACH

Whereas utilitarians associate justice with social utility, philosophers who endorse what is called **libertarianism** identify justice with an ideal of liberty. For them, liberty is the prime value, and justice consists in permitting each person to live as he or she pleases, free from the interference of others. Accordingly, one libertarian asserts: "We are concerned with the condition of men in which coercion of some by others is reduced as much as possible in society."[55] Another maintains that libertarianism is "a philosophy of personal liberty—the liberty of each person to live according to his own choices, provided he does not attempt to coerce others and thus prevent them from living according to their choices."[56] Such views show clearly the libertarian's association of justice with liberty and of liberty itself with the absence of interference by other persons.

Libertarians firmly reject utilitarianism's concern for total social well-being. Utilitarians are willing to restrict the liberty of some, to interfere with their choices, if doing so will promote greater net happiness than not doing so. Libertarians cannot stomach that approach. As long as you are not doing something that interferes with anyone else's liberty, then no person, group, or government should disturb you in living the life you choose—not even if its doing so would maximize social happiness.

Although individual liberty is something that all of us value, it may not be the only thing we value. For the libertarian, however, liberty takes priority over other moral concerns. In particular, justice consists solely of respect for individual liberty. A libertarian world, with a complete commitment to individual liberty, would be a very different world from the one we now live in. Consider the following: Until 2003 the U.S. Supreme Court upheld laws forbidding sodomy between consenting male homosexuals; the government registers young men for military service and can, if it chooses, draft them; laws prevent adults from ingesting substances that the legislature deems harmful or immoral (such as marijuana and cocaine); and the state imposes taxes on our income to—among many other things—support needy citizens, provide loans to college students, and fund various projects for the common good. From a libertarian perspective, none of these policies is just.

Given the assumption that *liberty* means "noninterference," libertarians generally agree that liberty allows only a minimal or "night-watchman" state. Such a state is limited to the narrow functions of protecting its citizens against force, theft, and fraud; enforcing contracts; and performing other such basic maintenance functions. In this view, a more extensive state—in particular, one that taxes its better-off citizens to support the less fortunate ones—violates the liberty of individuals by forcing them to support projects, policies, or persons they have not freely chosen to support.

Libertarians refuse to restrict individual liberty even if doing so would increase overall happiness.

Nozick's Theory of Justice

Although libertarians differ in how they formulate their theory, the late Harvard professor Robert Nozick's *Anarchy, State, and Utopia* is a very influential statement of the libertarian case.[57] Nozick's challenging and powerful advocacy of libertarianism has stimulated much debate, obliging philosophers of all political

Summary 3.5
The libertarian theory identifies justice with liberty, which libertarians understand as living according to our own choices, free from the interference of others. They reject utilitarianism's concern for total social well-being.

persuasions to take the libertarian theory seriously. His views are thus worth presenting in detail.

Nozick begins from the premise that people have certain basic moral rights, which he calls **Lockean rights.** By alluding to the political philosophy of John Locke (1632–1704), Nozick wishes to underscore that these rights are both negative and natural. They are negative because they require only that people forbear from acting in certain ways—in particular, that we refrain from interfering with others. Beyond this, we are not obliged to do anything positive for anyone else, nor is anyone required to do anything positive for us. We have no right, for example, to be provided with satisfying work or with any material goods that we might need. These negative rights, according to Nozick, are natural in the sense that we possess them independently of any social or political institutions.

These individual rights impose firm, nearly absolute restrictions (or, in Nozick's phrase, "side constraints") on how we may act. We cannot morally infringe on someone's rights for any purpose. Not only are we forbidden to interfere with a person's liberty in order to promote the general good, we are prohibited from doing so even if violating that individual's rights would somehow prevent other individuals' rights from being violated. Each individual is autonomous and responsible, and should be left to fashion his or her own life free from the interference of others—as long as doing so is compatible with the rights of others to do the same. Only an acknowledgment of this almost absolute right to be free from coercion, Nozick argues, fully respects the distinctiveness of individuals, each with a unique life to lead.

A belief in these rights shapes Nozick's theory of economic justice, which he calls the **entitlement theory.** Essentially, Nozick maintains that people are entitled to their holdings (that is, goods, money, and property) as long as they have acquired them fairly. Stated another way, if you have obtained your possessions without violating other people's Lockean rights, then you are entitled to them and may dispose of them as you choose. No one else has a legitimate claim on them. If you have secured a vast fortune without injuring other people, defrauding them, or otherwise violating their rights, then you are morally permitted to do with your fortune whatever you wish— bequeath it to a relative, endow a university, or squander it in riotous living. Even though other people may be going hungry, justice imposes no obligation on you to help them.

The *first principle of Nozick's entitlement theory* concerns the original acquisition of holdings—that is, the appropriation of unheld goods or the creation of new goods. If a person acquires a holding in accordance with this principle, then he or she is entitled to it. If, for example, you discover and remove minerals from the wilderness or make something out of materials you already legitimately possess, then you have justly acquired this new holding. Nozick does not spell out this principle or specify fully what constitutes a just original acquisition, but the basic idea is clear and reflects the thinking of John Locke.

Property is a moral right, said Locke, because individuals are morally entitled to the products of their labor. When they mix their labor with the

According to Nozick's theory, you are entitled to your holdings if you have acquired them without violating other people's rights.

natural world, they are entitled to the resulting product. Thus, if a man works the land, then he is entitled to the land and its products because through his labor he has put something of himself into them. This investment of self through labor is the moral basis of ownership, Locke wrote, but he acknowledged limits to this right:

> In the beginning ... men had a right to appropriate, by their labour, each one of himself, as much of the things of nature, as he could use.... Whatsoever he tilled and reaped, laid up and made use of, before it spoiled, that was his peculiar right; whatsoever he enclosed, and could feed, and make use of, the cattle and product was also his. But if either the grass of his inclosure rotted on the ground, or the fruit of his planting perished without gathering, and laying up, this part of the earth ... was still to be looked on as waste, and might be the possession of any other.[58]

Summary 3.6
The libertarian philosopher Robert Nozick defends the entitlement theory. This theory holds that the distribution of goods, money, and property is just if people are entitled to what they have—that is, if they have acquired their possessions without violating the rights of anyone else.

In this early **state of nature** (the phrase is Locke's) prior to the formation of government, property rights were limited not only by the requirement that one not waste what one claimed, but also by the restriction that "enough and as good" be left for others—that is, that one's appropriation not make others worse off. Later, however, with the introduction of money, Locke thought that both these restrictions were overcome. You can pile up money beyond your needs without its spoiling; and if your property is used productively and the proceeds are offered for sale, then your appropriation leaves others no worse off than before.

Nozick's second principle concerns transfers of already-owned goods from one person to another: how people may legitimately transfer holdings to others and how they may legitimately get holdings from others. If a person possesses a holding because of a legitimate transfer, then he or she is entitled to it. Again, Nozick does not work out the details, but it is clear that acquiring something by purchase, as a gift, or through exchange would constitute a legitimate acquisition. Gaining something through theft, force, or fraud would violate the principle of justice in transfer.

Nozick's third and final principle states that one can justly acquire a holding only in accord with the two principles previously discussed. If you come by a holding in some other way, you are not entitled to it.

Nozick sums up his theory this way:

1. A person who acquires a holding in accordance with the principle of justice in acquisition is entitled to that holding.

2. A person who acquires a holding in accordance with the principle of justice in transfer, from someone else entitled to the holding, is entitled to the holding.

3. No one is entitled to a holding except by (repeated) applications of 1 and 2.

All that matters for Nozick is how people came to have what they have, not the pattern or results of the distribution of goods.

In short, the distribution of goods in a society is just if and only if all are entitled to the holdings they possess. Nozick calls his entitlement theory "historical" because what matters is how people come to have what they have. If people are entitled to their possessions, then the distribution of economic holdings is just, regardless of what the actual distribution happens to look like (for instance, how far people are above or below the average income) or what its consequences are.

Nozick's Wilt Chamberlain Example

Nozick argues that respect for liberty inescapably leads one to repudiate other conceptions of economic justice in favor of his entitlement approach. One of his most ingenious examples features Wilt Chamberlain, the late basketball star.

Suppose, Nozick says, that things are distributed according to your favorite non-entitlement theory, whatever it is. (He calls this distribution D_1.) Now imagine that Wilt Chamberlain signs a contract with a team that guarantees him $5 from the price of each ticket. Whenever people buy a ticket to a game, they drop $5 into a special box with Chamberlain's name on it. To them, seeing him play is worth $5. Imagine then that in the course of a season 1 million people attend his games and Chamberlain ends up with far more than the average income—far more, indeed, than anyone else in the society earns. This result (D_2) upsets the initial distributional pattern (D_1). Can the proponent of D_1 complain? Nozick thinks not:

> Is [Chamberlain] entitled to this income? Is this new distribution, D_2, unjust? If so, why? There is *no* question about whether each of the people was entitled to the control over the resources they held in D_1; because that was the distribution (your favorite) that (for the purposes of the argument) we assumed was acceptable. Each of these persons *chose* to give [$5] of their money to Chamberlain.... If D_1 was a just distribution, and people voluntarily moved from it to D_2, transferring parts of their shares they were given under D_1 ... isn't D_2 also just? If the people were entitled to dispose of the resources to which they were entitled (under D_1), didn't this include their being entitled to give it to, or exchange it with, Wilt Chamberlain? Can anyone else complain on grounds of justice?[59]

Having defended the legitimacy of Chamberlain's new wealth, Nozick pushes his case further, arguing that any effort to maintain some initial distributional arrangement like D_1 will interfere with people's liberty to use their resources as they wish. To preserve this original distribution, he writes, society would have to "forbid capitalist acts between consenting adults":

Summary 3.7
In the Wilt Chamberlain example, Nozick argues that other theories of economic justice inevitably fail to respect people's liberty.

> The general point illustrated by the Wilt Chamberlain example ... is that no [non-entitlement] principle of justice can be continuously realized without continuous interference with people's lives. Any favored pattern would be transformed into one unfavored by the principle, by people choosing to act in various ways; for example, by people exchanging goods and services with other people, or giving things to other people.... To maintain a pattern one must either continually interfere to stop people from transferring resources as they wish to, or continually (or periodically) interfere to take from some persons resources that others for some reason chose to transfer to them.[60]

The Libertarian View of Liberty

Libertarianism clearly involves a commitment to leaving market relations—buying, selling, and other exchanges—totally unrestricted.* Force and fraud are forbidden, of course, but there should be no meddling with the uncoerced

---

* Chapter 4 examines the nature of market economies in general and capitalism in particular.

exchanges of consenting individuals. Not only is the market morally legitimate, but any attempt to interfere with voluntary and nonfraudulent transactions between adults will be unacceptable, even unjust. Thus, libertarians are for economic laissez faire and against any governmental economic activity that interferes with the marketplace, even if the point of the interference is to enhance the performance of the economy.

It is important to emphasize that libertarianism's enthusiasm for the market rests on this commitment to liberty. By contrast, utilitarians who defend an unregulated market do so on the ground that it works better than either a planned, socialist economy or the sort of regulated capitalism with some welfare benefits that we in fact have in the United States. If a utilitarian defends laissez faire, he or she does so because of its consequences. If we convinced a utilitarian that some other form of economic organization would better promote human well-being, the utilitarian would advocate that instead. With libertarians this is definitely not the case. As a matter of fact, libertarians typically agree with Adam Smith that unregulated capitalist behavior best promotes everyone's interests. But even if, hypothetically, someone like Nozick were convinced that some sort of socialism or welfare capitalism would outperform laissez-faire capitalism economically—greater productivity, shorter workday, higher standard of living—he or she would still reject this alternative as morally unacceptable. To tinker with the market, however beneficial it might be, would involve violating someone's liberty.

Libertarians say that their commitment to an unrestricted **free market** reflects the priority of liberty over other values. However, libertarians do not value liberty in the mundane sense of people's freedom to do what they want to do. Rather, libertarians understand freedom in terms of their theory of rights, thus building a commitment to private property into their concept of liberty. According to them, being able to do what you want does not automatically represent an increase in your liberty. It does so only if you remain within the boundaries set by the Lockean rights of others. Likewise, one is unfree or coerced only when one's rights are infringed.

Imagine, for example, that having purchased the forest in which I occasionally stroll, the new owner bars my access to it. It would seem that my freedom has been reduced because I can no longer ramble where I wish. But libertarians deny that this is a restriction of my liberty. My liberty is restricted if and only if someone violates my Lockean rights, which no one has done. Suppose that I go for a hike in the forest anyway. If the sheriff's deputies arrest me, they prevent me from doing what I want to do. But according to libertarianism, they do not restrict my liberty, nor do they coerce me. Why not? Because my hiking in the forest violates the landowner's rights.

Here libertarians seem driven to an unusual use of familiar terminology, but they have no choice. They cannot admit that abridging the landowner's freedom to do as he wants with his property would expand my freedom. If they did, then their theory would be in jeopardy. They would have to acknowledge that restricting the liberty or property rights of some could enhance the liberty of others. In other words, if their theory committed them simply to promoting as much as possible the goal of people doing what they want to do, then libertarians would be in the position of balancing the freedom of some against the freedom of others. But this sort of balancing and trading off is exactly what libertarians dislike about utilitarianism.

If liberty means being free to do what you want, it's not true that libertarians value it above everything else. What they value are Lockean property rights, which then set the parameters of liberty. Libertarians frequently contend that (1) private property is necessary for freedom and (2) any society that doesn't respect private property rights is coercive. But libertarianism makes 1 true by definition, and 2 is incorrect. Any system of property (whether Lockean, socialist, or something in between) necessarily puts restrictions on people's conduct; its rules are coercive. What one system of property permits, another forbids. Society X prevents me from hiking in your woods, whereas society Y prevents you from stopping me. Both systems of rules are coercive. Both grant some freedoms and withhold others.

Markets and Free Exchange

Libertarians defend market relations, then, as necessary to respect human liberty (as their theory understands liberty). However, in doing so, libertarians do not assert that, morally speaking, people deserve what they receive from others through gift or exchange, only that they are entitled to whatever they receive. The market tends generally, libertarians believe, to reward people for skill, diligence, and successful performance. Yet luck plays a role, too. Jack makes a fortune from having been in the right place at the right time with his Beanie Babies, while Jill loses her investment because the market for bottled water collapses. The libertarian position is not that Jack deserves to be wealthy and Jill does not; rather, it is that Jack is entitled to his holdings if he has acquired them in accordance with the principles of justice.

> Libertarians don't contend that people morally deserve what they get in a free market, but only that they are entitled to it.

The same point comes up with regard to gifts and inheritance. Inheritance strikes many people as patently unfair. How can it be just, they ask, that one child inherits a vast fortune, the best schooling, and social, political, and business connections that will ensure his or her future, while another child inherits indigence, inferior schooling, and connections with crime? At birth neither youngster deserves anything—a fact suggesting, perhaps, that an equal division of holdings and opportunities would be the only fair allocation. For his part, Nozick contends that deserving has no bearing on the justice of inherited wealth; people are simply entitled to it as long as it is not ill gotten. Or looking at it the other way, if one is entitled to one's holdings, then one has a right to do with them as one wishes, including using them to benefit one's children.

> Unregulated market transactions can sometimes lead to disastrous results as Amartya Sen has shown.

According to libertarians, a totally free market is necessary for people to exercise their fundamental rights. Sometimes, however, unregulated market transactions can lead to disastrous results. Unfortunately, this is more than just a theoretical possibility. Amartya Sen, the Nobel Prize–winning economist, has shown how in certain circumstances changing market entitlements have led to mass starvation. Although the average person thinks of famine as caused simply by a shortage of food, Sen and other experts have established that famines are frequently accompanied by no shortfall of food in absolute terms. Indeed, even more food may be available during a famine than in nonfamine years—if one has the money to buy it. Famine occurs because large numbers of people lack the financial wherewithal to obtain the necessary food.[61]

For example, drought may cause food output in one area to decline and the peasants in that area to starve because they lack the means to buy food from elsewhere, even though there is no dearth of food in the country as a whole (Ethiopia in 1973). Or famine may result when the purchasing power of one occupational group shoots up, ruining the chances of other groups, whose nominal incomes have not changed, to buy food (Bengal in 1943). A reduction of food output because of potato blight triggered the great Irish famine of the 1840s, which killed a higher proportion of the population than any other famine in recorded history. But if one looks at the United Kingdom as a whole, there was no shortage of food. Food could certainly have moved from Britain to Ireland if the Irish could have afforded to purchase it. As it was, at the height of the famine, food was exported from Ireland to England because the prosperous English could pay a higher price for it.[62]

Libertarians would find it immoral and unjust to force people to aid the starving or to tax the affluent in order to set up programs to relieve hunger or prevent famines in the first place. Nor does justice require that a wealthy merchant assist the hungry children in his community to stay alive. And it would certainly violate the merchant's property rights for the children to help themselves to his excess food. Nevertheless, although justice does not require that one assist those in need, libertarians would generally acknowledge that we have some humanitarian obligations toward others. Accordingly, they would not only permit but also presumably encourage people to voluntarily assist others. Justice does not require the merchant to donate, and it forbids us from forcing him to do so, but charity on his part would be a good thing. This reflects the libertarian's firm commitment to **property rights**: What you have legitimately acquired is yours to do with as you will.

Property Rights

Nozick's theory makes property rights nearly sacrosanct. From the perspective of libertarianism, property rights grow out of one's basic moral rights, reflecting one's initial creation or appropriation of the product, some sort of exchange or transfer between consenting persons, or a combination of these. Property rights exist prior to any social arrangements and are morally antecedent to any legislative decisions that a society might make. However, Nozick's critics argue that it is a mistake to think of property as a simple, pre-social relation between a person and a physical thing.

First, property is not restricted to material objects like cars, watches, or houses. In developed societies, it may include abstract goods, interests, and claims. For instance, property may include the right to pay debts with the balance in a bank account, the right to dividends from a corporate investment, and the right to collect from a pension plan one has joined. In fact, the courts have counted as property a wide range of items such as new life forms, an original idea, pension payments, the news, or a place on the welfare rolls.[63]

Summary 3.8
Libertarians operate with a distinctive concept of liberty, defend free exchange and laissez-faire markets without regard to results, put a priority on freedom over all other values, and see property rights as existing prior to any social arrangements. Critics contest each of these features of libertarianism.

It is mistake to think of property as a simple presocial relation between a person and a thing.

Second, property ownership involves a bundle of different rights—for instance, to possess, use, manage, dispose of, or restrict others' access to something in certain specified ways. The nature of this bundle differs among societies, as do the types of things that can be owned. In any society, property ownership is structured by the various implicit or explicit rules and regulations governing the legitimate acquisition and transfer of various types of goods, interests, and claims. Not only do property rights differ between societies, but the nature of ownership can also change over time in any given society. As a general trend, the social restrictions on property ownership in the United States have increased dramatically during our history (much to the displeasure of libertarians).

Most nonlibertarian theorists believe that property rights are determined by social institutions.

For these reasons, most nonlibertarian social and political theorists view property rights as a function of the particular institutions of a given society. This is not to say that a society's property arrangements cannot be criticized. On the contrary, their morality can be assessed just as the morality of any other institution can.

RAWLS'S THEORY OF JUSTICE

A Theory of Justice by John Rawls (1921–2002) is generally thought to be the most influential work of the post–World War II period in social and political philosophy, at least in the English language.[64] Not only has Rawls's elegant theory touched a responsive chord in many readers, but also his book helped rejuvenate serious work in normative theory. Even those who are not persuaded by Rawls find themselves obliged to come to terms with his thinking. Although Rawls's basic approach is not difficult to explain (and Rawls himself had sketched out his key concepts in earlier articles), *A Theory of Justice* elaborates his ideas with such painstaking care and philosophical thoroughness that even vigorous critics of the book (such as his colleague Robert Nozick) pay sincere tribute to its many virtues.

By his own account, Rawls presents his theory as a modern alternative to utilitarianism, one that he hopes will be compatible with the belief that justice must be associated with fairness and the moral equality of persons. Rawls firmly wishes to avoid reducing justice to a matter of society utility. At the same time, his approach differs fundamentally from Nozick's. Rawls conceives of society as a cooperative venture among its members, and he elaborates a conception of justice that is thoroughly social. He does not base his theory, as Nozick does, on the postulate that individuals possess certain natural rights prior to any political or social organization.

Rawls's strategy is to ask what principles people would choose to govern their society if they were in the "original position."

Two features of Rawls's theory are particularly important: his hypothetical-contract approach and the principles of justice that he derives with it. Rawls's strategy is to ask what we would choose as the fundamental principles to govern society if, hypothetically, we were to meet for this purpose in what he calls the **original position.** He then elaborates the nature of this original position, the constraints on the choice facing us, and the reasoning that he thinks people in the original position would follow. In this way, Rawls offers a modern variant of social contract theory, in the tradition of Hobbes,

Locke, Rousseau, and other earlier philosophers. Rawls argues that people in the original position would agree on two principles as the basic governing principles of their society, and that these principles are, accordingly, the principles of justice. The first is a guarantee of certain familiar and fundamental liberties to each person. The second—more controversial—holds in part that social and economic inequalities are justified only if those inequalities benefit the least advantaged members of society. These principles are examined at some length in this chapter.

The Original Position

Various principles of economic justice have been proposed, but an important question for philosophers is whether, and how, any such principles can be justified. Thinking of possible principles of economic distribution is not very difficult, but proving the soundness of such a principle, or at least showing it to be more plausible than its rivals, is a challenging task. After all, people seem to differ in their intuitions about what is just and unjust, and their sentiments are bound to be influenced by their social position. Nozick's entitlement theory, for example, with its priority on property rights, is bound to seem more plausible to a corporate executive than to a migrant farmworker. The justice of a world in which some children are born into wealth while other children struggle by on welfare is unlikely to seem as obvious to the poor as it may to the well-to-do.

The strategy Rawls employs to identify and justify the basic principles of justice is to imagine that people come together for the purpose of deciding on the ground rules for their society, in particular on the rules governing economic distribution. Although in the past groups of people have written down constitutions and similar political documents, never have the members of a society decided from scratch on the basic principles of justice that should govern them. Nor is it even remotely likely that people will do this in the future. What Rawls imagines is a thought experiment. The question is hypothetical: What principles would people choose in this sort of original position? If we can identify these principles, Rawls contends, then we will have identified the principles of justice precisely because they are the principles that we would all have agreed to.

The Nature of the Choice

On what basis are we to choose these principles? The most obvious answer is that we should select principles that strike us as just. But this won't work. Even if we all agreed about what is just and unjust, we would be relying on our already-existing ideas about justice as a basis for choosing the principles to govern our society. Philosophically, this approach doesn't accomplish anything. We would simply be going in a circle, using our existing conception of justice to prove the principles of justice.

Rawls suggests instead that we imagine people in the original position choosing solely on the basis of self-interest: Each individual chooses the set of principles for governing society that will be best for himself or herself (and loved ones). We don't have to imagine that people are antagonistic or that outside of the original position they are selfish; we simply imagine that they hope to get the group to choose those principles that will, more than any other possible principles, benefit them. If people in the original position can agree on some governing principles on the basis of mutual self-interest, then these principles will be, Rawls thinks, the principles of justice. Why? Because the principles are agreed to under conditions of equality and free choice. By analogy, if we make up a game and all agree ahead of time, freely and equally, on how the game is to be played, nobody can later complain that the rules are unfair.

The Veil of Ignorance

If people in the original position are supposed to choose principles on the basis of self-interest, agreement seems unlikely. If Carolyn has vast real estate holdings, she will certainly want rules that guarantee her extensive property rights, whereas her tenants are likely to support rules that permit rent control. Likewise, the wealthy will tend to advocate rules rather like Nozick's entitlement theory, whereas the poor will, on the basis of their self-interest, desire a redistribution of property. Conflicts of self-interest seem bound to create totally irreconcilable demands. For instance, artists may contend that they should be rewarded more than professional people, men that they should earn more than women, and laborers that they merit more than people with desk jobs.

Given that some rules would benefit one group while other rules would benefit another, it seems improbable that people in the original position would concur. As a way around this problem, Rawls asks us to imagine that people in the original position do not know what social position or status they hold in society. They do not know whether they are rich or poor, and they do not know their personal talents and characteristics—whether, for example, they are athletic or sedentary, artistic or tone deaf, intelligent or not very bright, physically sound or handicapped in some way. They do not know their race or even their sex. Behind what Rawls calls the **veil of ignorance**, people in the original position know nothing about themselves personally or about what their individual situation will be once the rules are chosen and the veil is lifted. They do, however, have a general knowledge of history, sociology, and psychology—although no specific information about the society they will be in once the veil is lifted.

Under the veil of ignorance, the people in Rawls's original position have no knowledge about themselves or their situation that would lead them to argue from a partial or biased point of view. No individual is likely to argue that some particular group—such as white men, property owners, star athletes, philosophers—should receive special social and economic privileges when, for all that individual knows, he or she will be nonwhite, propertyless, unathletic, and bored by philosophy when the veil is lifted. Because individuals in the original position are all equally ignorant of their personal predicaments and they are all trying to advance their self-interest, agreement is possible. The reasoning of any one person will be the same as the reasoning of each of the others, for each is in identical circumstances and each has the same motivation. As a result, no actual group has to perform Rawls's thought experiment. People who read Rawls's book can imagine that they are in the original position and then decide whether they would choose the principles Rawls thinks they would.

The veil of ignorance, in effect, forces people in the original position to be objective and impartial and makes agreement possible. Also, according to Rawls, the fact that people have no special knowledge that would allow them to argue in a biased way accords with our sense of fairness. The circumstances of the original position are genuinely equal and fair, and because of this, the principles agreed to under these conditions have a good claim to be considered the principles of justice.

> The veil of ignorance eliminates bias and makes the original position a fair way of choosing principles.

Choosing the Principles

Although people in the original position are ignorant of their individual circumstances, they know that whatever their particular goals, interests, and talents turn out to be, they will want more, rather than less, of what Rawls calls **primary social goods**. These include not only income and wealth but also rights, liberties, opportunities, status, and self-respect. Of course, once the veil of ignorance is lifted, people will have more specific ideas about what is good for them. For example, they may choose a life built around religion, one spent in commerce and industry, or one devoted to academic study. But whatever these particular individual goals, interests, and plans turn out to be, they will almost certainly be furthered, and definitely never limited, by the fact that people in the original position secured for themselves more rather than less in the way of primary goods.

How, then, will people in the original position choose their principles? *A Theory of Justice* explores in depth the reasoning that Rawls thinks would guide their choice. At the heart of Rawls's argument is the contention that people in the original position will be conservative, in the sense that they will not wish to gamble with their futures. In setting up the ground rules for their society, they are determining their own fates and those of their children. This exercise is not something to be taken lightly, a game to be played and replayed. Rather, with so much at stake, people will reason cautiously.

Consider, for example, the possibility that people in the original position will set up a feudal society: 10 percent of the population will be nobles, living a life of incredible wealth, privilege, and leisure; the other 90 percent will be serfs, toiling away long hours to support the extravagant lifestyles of the aristocracy. Perhaps some people would consider the joy of being a pampered noble so great that they would vote for such an arrangement behind the veil of ignorance, but they would be banking on a long shot. When the veil of ignorance is lifted, the odds are nine to one that they will be poor and miserable serfs, not lords. Rawls thinks that people in the original position will not, in fact, gamble with their futures. They will not agree to rules that make it overwhelmingly likely that they will have to face a grim life of hardship.

Rawls argues that for similar reasons people in the original position will not adopt the utilitarian standard to govern their society, because the utilitarian principle might sacrifice the well-being of some to enhance society's total

Summary 3.9

John Rawls's theory of justice lies within the social-contract tradition. He asks us to imagine people meeting in the original position to choose the basic principles that are to govern their society. Although in this original position people choose on the basis of self-interest, we are to imagine that they are behind a veil of ignorance, with no personal information about themselves. Rawls contends that any principles agreed to under these circumstances have a strong claim to be considered the principles of justice.

happiness. People in the original position, Rawls argues, will not be willing to risk sacrificing their own happiness, once the veil of ignorance is lifted, for the greater good.

What people in the original position would actually do, Rawls believes, is follow what game strategists call the **maximin rule** for making decisions. According to this rule, you should select the alternative under which the worst that could happen to you is better than the worst that could happen to you under any other alternative—that is, you should try to *maximize* the *minimum* that you will receive. This rule makes sense when you care much more about avoiding an unacceptable or disastrous result (such as being a serf) than about getting the best possible result (being a noble) and when you have no real idea what odds you are facing. It is a conservative decision principle, but Rawls thinks that people in the original position will find it a rational and appropriate guideline for their deliberations.

Rawls's Two Principles

Rawls argues that people in the original position considering various alternatives will eventually endorse two principles as the fundamental governing principles of their society:

1. Each person is to have an equal right to the most extensive total system of equal basic liberties compatible with a similar system of liberty for all.[65]

2. Social and economic inequalities are to satisfy two conditions: First, they are to be attached to positions and offices open to all under conditions of fair equality of opportunity; and second, they are to be to the greatest expected benefit of the least-advantaged members of society.[66]

These principles, because they are agreed to in an initial situation of equality and fairness, will be the principles of justice. Once these two principles of justice have been endorsed, people in the original position can gradually be given more information about their specific society. They can then go on to design their basic social and political institutions in more detail.

According to Rawls, the first principle takes priority over the second, at least for societies that have attained a moderate level of affluence. The liberties Rawls has in mind are the traditional democratic ones of freedom of thought, conscience, and religious worship, as well as freedom of the person and political liberty. Explicitly absent are "the right to own certain kinds of property (e.g., means of production), and freedom of contract as understood by the doctrine of laissez-faire." The first principle guarantees not only equal liberty to individuals but also as much liberty to individuals as possible, compatible with others having the same amount of liberty. There is no reason why people in the original position would settle for anything less.

All regulations could be seen as infringing on personal liberty, because they limit what a person may do. The law that requires you to drive on the right-hand side of the road denies you the freedom to drive on either side whenever you wish. Some would argue that justice requires only an equal liberty. For example, as long as every motorist is required to drive on the

Rawls believes that people in the original position would endorse his two principles.

These are the principles of justice because they would be agreed to in an initial situation of equality and fairness.

right-hand side of the road, justice is being served; or if everyone in a dictatorial society is forbidden to criticize the leader's decisions, then all are equal in their liberty. But Rawls argues that if a more extensive liberty were possible, without inhibiting the liberty of others, then it would be irrational to settle for a lesser degree of liberty. In the case of driving, permitting me to drive on either side of the road would only interfere with the liberty of others to drive efficiently to their various destinations, but introducing right-turn-on-red laws enhances everyone's liberty. In the dictatorship example, free speech could be more extensive without limiting anyone's liberty.

The second principle concerns social and economic inequalities. Regarding inequalities, Rawls writes:

> It is best to understand not *any* differences between offices and positions, but differences in the benefits and burdens attached to them either directly or indirectly, such as prestige and wealth, or liability to taxation and compulsory services. Players in a game do not protest against there being different positions, such as batter, pitcher, catcher, and the like, nor to there being various privileges and powers as specified by the rules; nor do the citizens of a country object to there being the different offices of government such as president, senator, governor, judge, and so on, each with their special rights and duties.[67]

Rather, at issue are differences in wealth and power, honors and rewards, privileges and salaries that attach to different roles in society.

Rawls's second principle states that insofar as inequalities are permitted—that is, insofar as it is compatible with justice for some jobs or positions to bring greater rewards than others—these positions must be open to all. In other words, there must be meaningful equality of opportunity in the competition among individuals for those positions in society that bring greater economic and social rewards. This, of course, is a familiar ideal, but what exactly a society must do to achieve not just legal but full and fair equality of opportunity will be a matter of debate.

The other part of the second principle is less familiar and more controversial. Called the **difference principle**, it is the distinctive core of Rawls's theory. It states that inequalities are justified only if they work to the benefit of the least-advantaged group in society. By "least-advantaged," Rawls simply means those who are least well-off. But what does it mean to require that inequalities work to the benefit of this group?

Imagine that we are back in the original position. We wish to make sure that under the principles we choose, the worst that can happen to us once the veil of ignorance is lifted is still better than the worst that might have happened under some other arrangement. We might, therefore, choose strict social and economic equality. With an equal division of goods, there's no risk of doing worse than anyone else, no danger of being sacrificed to increase the total happiness of society. In the case of liberty, people in the original position do insist on full equality, but with social and economic inequality, the matter is a little different.

Suppose, for instance, that as a result of dividing things up equally, people lack an incentive to undertake some of the more difficult work that society needs done. It might then be the case that allowing certain inequalities—for

Summary 3.10
Rawls argues that people in the original position would follow the maximin rule for making decisions. They would choose principles guaranteeing that the worst that could happen to them is better than the worst that could happen to them under any rival principles. Rawls argues that they would agree on two principles: (1) Each person has a right to the most extensive scheme of liberties compatible with others having the same amount of liberty. (2) To be justified, any inequalities must be to the greatest expected benefit of the least advantaged and open to all under conditions of fair equality of opportunity.

People in the original position do not want equality at all costs. They will permit inequality only if it improves the lot of the least advantaged.

example, paying people more for being particularly productive or for undertaking the necessary training to perform some socially useful task—would work to everyone's benefit, including those who would be earning less. If so, then why not permit those inequalities?

Compare theses two diagrams:

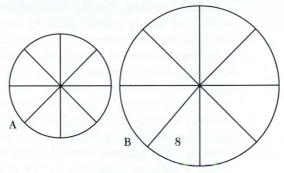

Each pie represents a possible social and economic distribution among eight basic groups (the number eight is arbitrary) in society. In Figure A, things are divided equally; in Figure B, unequally. Suppose, then, that because a society permits inequalities as an incentive to get people to work harder or to do work that they otherwise would not have wanted to do, the overall amount to be distributed among society's members increases—that is, the economic pie grows in size from A to B, and the people with the thinnest slice of B are better-off than they would have been with an equal slice of A.

Which society will people in the original position prefer? Obviously the one represented by Figure B, because the least they could receive in B (the slice labeled 8) is bigger than any of the eight equal slices in A. People in the original position do not care about equality of distribution as a value in and of itself; they want the social and economic arrangement that will provide them with the highest minimum.

Rawls is not trying to prove that the benefits received by the better-off will always, or even usually, trickle down to the least advantaged (although, of course, some people believe that). Rather, his point is simply that people in the original position would not insist on social and economic equality at all costs. If permitting some people to be better-off than the average resulted in the least-well-off segment of society being better-off than it would have been under a strictly equal division, then this is what people in the original position will want. Rawls's difference principle is intended to capture this idea. Rawls's principles permit economic inequalities only if they do in fact benefit the least advantaged.

Consider the recurrent proposal to further lower or even eliminate the income tax on capital gains (that is, on personal income from the sale of assets like stocks, bonds, and real estate). Proponents claim that the tax break will spur trading in financial assets, which in turn will lead to growth in tax revenues, and that the cut will trigger more long-term investment, helping revitalize the economy. Critics of the proposal contest both claims. Still, everyone agrees that the tax break would certainly increase the income of the rich because the wealthiest 1.4 percent of households receives 73.2 percent of all capital-gains income.[68] Will lowering taxes on the rich benefit the least-advantaged members of society more in the long run than any alternative tax policy?

This question illustrates the application of Rawls's difference principle in a practical context, but we must remember that Rawls intends his principles to be used not as a direct guide to day-to-day policy decisions but rather as the basis for determining what form society's primary social, political, and economic institutions should take in the first place. What will these institutions look like? More specifically, what sort of economic system will best satisfy Rawls's difference principle? Rawls does not answer this question. He sees it as primarily a question for economists and other social scientists, whereas the task of philosophers like himself is the preliminary one of working out a satisfactory conception of justice. Rawls does appear to believe, however, that a liberal form of capitalism, with sufficient welfare provisions, would satisfy his principles, but he does not rule out the possibility that a democratic socialist system could as well.

Fairness and the Basic Structure

Rawls rejects utilitarianism because it could permit an unfair distribution of benefits and burdens.

Rawls intends his theory as a fundamental alternative to utilitarianism, which he rejects on the grounds that maximizing the total well-being of society could permit an unfair distribution of burdens and benefits. Utilitarianism, in Rawls's view, treats people's pleasures and pains as completely interchangeable: A decrease of happiness here is justified by greater happiness there. Within a person's own life, such trade-offs are sensible. An increase of pain now (as the dentist fills a cavity in my tooth) is justified in terms of greater happiness later (no painful, rotted tooth). But between individuals, as when Jack's happiness is decreased to provide Jill with a more-than-compensating gain, such trade-offs are morally problematic.

Thus Rawls stresses that, in his view,

> each person possesses an inviolability founded on justice that even the welfare of society as a whole cannot override.... Therefore ... the rights secured by justice are not subject to political bargaining or to the calculus of social interests.[69]

And he emphasizes that the difference principle

> excludes, therefore, the justification of inequalities on the grounds that the disadvantages of those in one position are outweighed by the greater advantages of those in another position. This rather simple restriction is the main modification I wish to make in the utilitarian principle as usually understood.[70]

Contrary to Nozick, Rawls believes that social justice concerns the basic structure of society, not transactions between individuals.

Rawls, however, is equally unsympathetic to the libertarian approach adopted by Nozick. Contrary to the entitlement theory, he argues that the primary subject of justice is not, in the first instance, transactions between individuals but rather "the **basic structure**, the fundamental social institutions and their arrangement into one scheme." Why? As Rawls explains:

> Suppose we begin with the initially attractive idea that the social circumstances and people's relationships to one another should develop over time in accordance with free agreements fairly arrived at and fully honored. Straightaway we need an

account of when agreements are free and the social circumstances under which they are reached are fair. In addition, while these conditions may be fair at an earlier time, the accumulated results of many separate and ostensibly fair agreements ... are likely in the course of time to alter citizens' relationships and opportunities so that the conditions for free and fair agreements no longer hold. The role of the institutions that belong to the basic structure is to secure just background conditions against which the actions of the individuals and associations take place. Unless this structure is appropriately regulated and adjusted, an initially just social process will eventually cease to be just, however free and fair particular transactions may look when viewed by themselves.[71]

Additional considerations support taking the basic structure of society as the primary subject of justice—in particular, the fact that the basic structure shapes the wants, desires, hopes, and ambitions of individuals. Thus, Rawls continues:

Everyone recognizes that the institutional form of society affects its members and determines in large part the kind of person they want to be as well as the kind of person they are. The social structure also limits people's ambitions and hopes in different ways.... So an economic regime, say, is not only an institutional scheme for satisfying existing wants but a way of fashioning desires and aspirations in the future.[72]

Rawls stresses that because the basic structure is the proper focus of a theory of justice, we cannot expect the principles that apply to it to be simply an extension of the principles that govern everyday individual transactions:

The justice of the basic structure is, then, of predominant importance. The first problem of justice is to determine the principles to regulate inequalities and to adjust the profound and long-lasting effects of social, natural, and historical contingencies, particularly since these contingencies combined with inequalities generate tendencies that, when left to themselves, are sharply at odds with the freedom and equality appropriate for a well-ordered society. In view of the special role of the basic structure, we cannot assume that the principles suitable to it are natural applications, or even extensions, of the familiar principles governing the actions of individuals and associations in everyday life which take place within its framework. Most likely we shall have to loosen ourselves from our ordinary perspective and take a more comprehensive viewpoint.[73]

Benefits and Burdens

The passages quoted here touch on a theme that is central to Rawls's theory. Inevitably, there will be natural differences among human beings—in physical prowess, mental agility, and so on—but there is nothing natural or inevitable about the weight attached by society to those differences. For Rawls, a desirable feature of any account of justice is that it strives to minimize the social consequences of purely arbitrary, natural differences. He stresses that no one deserves his or her particular natural characteristics. We cannot say that Angelina Jolie deserves to be beautiful or that Albert Einstein deserved to be blessed with an excellent mind any more than we can say that Fred merits his shortness or Pamela her nearsightedness. Their attributes are simply the result of a genetic lottery. But Rawls goes beyond this to argue that even

Rawls believes that justice tries to minimize the social consequences of purely arbitrary, natural differences. People do not deserve the attributes they were born with or that reflect their environment and upbringing.

personal characteristics like diligence and perseverance reflect the environment in which one was raised:

> We do not deserve our place in the distribution of native endowments, any more than we deserve our initial starting place in society. That we deserve the superior character that enables us to make the effort to cultivate our abilities is also problematic; for such character depends in good part upon fortunate family and social circumstances in early life for which we can claim no credit. The notion of desert does not apply here.[74]

Summary 3.11
Rawls rejects utilitarianism because it might permit an unfair distribution of burdens and benefits. Contrary to the entitlement theory, he argues that the primary focus of justice should be the basic social structure, not transactions between individuals. He contends that society is a cooperative project for mutual benefit and that justice requires us to reduce the social and economic consequences of arbitrary natural differences among people.

Accordingly, Rawls thinks we cannot really claim moral credit for our special talents or even our virtuous character. In Rawls's view, then, if our personal characteristics are not something that we deserve, we have no strong claim to the economic rewards they might bring. On the contrary, justice requires that the social and economic consequences of these arbitrarily distributed assets be minimized.

The difference principle represents, in effect, an agreement to regard the distribution of natural talents as in some respects a common asset and to share in the greater social and economic benefits made possible by the complementarities of this distribution. Those who have been favored by nature, whoever they are, may gain from their good fortune only on terms that improve the situation of those who have lost out. The naturally advantaged are not to gain merely because they are more gifted, but only to cover the costs of training and education and for using their endowments in ways that help the less fortunate as well. No one deserves his greater natural capacity nor merits a more favorable starting place in society. But, of course, this is no reason to ignore, much less to eliminate these distinctions. Instead, the basic structure can be arranged so that these contingencies work for the good of the least fortunate. Thus we are led to the difference principle if we wish to set up the social system so that no one gains or loses from his arbitrary place in the distribution of natural assets or his initial position in society without giving or receiving compensating advantages in return.[75]

This important passage from *A Theory of Justice* reflects well Rawls's vision of society as a cooperative project for mutual benefit.

STUDY CORNER

Key Terms and Concepts

basic structure	free market	primary social goods
declining marginal utility of money	justice	property rights
	libertarianism	state of nature
difference principle	Lockean rights	veil of ignorance
distributive justice	maximin rule	worker participation
entitlement theory	original position	

Points to Review

- distribution of income and wealth in the United States
- four related ideas bound up with the concept of justice
- Aristotle's formal principle of justice
- John Stuart Mill's definition of injustice
- some different principles often used as a basis of distribution
- Walzer's pluralistic approach to distributive justice
- how a utilitarian like Mill looks at justice
- Mill's discussion of whether more talented workers should receive greater pay
- Mill's view of worker participation
- utilitarianism and the declining utility of money

- Locke's account of property rights
- three principles of Nozick's entitlement theory
- the point of the Wilt Chamberlain example
- how libertarians understand freedom in terms of rights
- Amartya Sen's analysis of famines
- how libertarians and nonlibertarians differ in their view of property rights
- the nature of the choice and the reasoning people would use in the original position
- Rawls's two principles of justice
- the point illustrated by the diagram on p. 121
- how Rawls's theory differs from utilitarianism and libertarianism
- why Rawls thinks we should minimize the social consequences of natural differences

CASE 3.1

Eminent Domain

Susette Kelo's nondescript, pink clapboard house sits above the Thames River in the Fort Trumbull area of New London, Connecticut. It's surrounded by vacant lots, where neighbors once lived. One by one, these neighbors have left, and their homes have been razed. Their property has been taken over by the City of New London, which has used its power of eminent domain to clear the land where dozens of homes once stood in order to prepare the way for new development.[76]

Eminent domain is the ancient right of government to take property from an individual without consent for the common good—for example, to build a highway, an airport, a dam, or a hospital. The U.S. Constitution recognizes that right, permitting private property to be taken for "public use" as long as "just compensation" is paid. In this case, however, New London is taking land from one private party and giving it to another. By tearing down Susette Kelo's old neighborhood, the city hopes to attract new development, which,

in turn, will help revitalize the community and bring in more tax revenue. "This isn't for the public good," says Kelo, a nurse who works three jobs. "The public good is a firehouse or a school, not a hotel and a sports club."

Connecticut officially designates New London a blighted area. When the Navy moved its Undersea Warfare Center away from New London in 1996, taking 1,400 jobs with it, the city's already high rate of unemployment only got worse. Much of its housing stock is old and second-rate. The Fort Trumbull area, in particular, is—or was, anyway—a rather gritty neighborhood, where earlier generations of immigrants struggled to get a start. But New London saw a chance to turn things around when the pharmaceutical company Pfizer built a $350 million research center along the river below historic Fort Trumbull. Since then, city and state governments have created a park around the fort, cleaned up the Navy's old asbestos-laden site, and opened the riverfront to public access. Now the city wants to build a hotel, office buildings, and new homes to fill the riverfront blocks around Fort Trumbull. And it's not talking about new homes for people like Susette Kelo.

"We need to get housing at the upper end, for people like the Pfizer employees," says Ed O'Connell, the lawyer for the New London Development Corporation, which is in charge of the city's redevelopment efforts. "They are the professionals, they are the ones with the expertise and the leadership qualities to re-make the city—the young urban professionals who will invest in New London, put their kids in school, and think of this as a place to stay for 20 or 30 years." And housing developers want open space to work with; they don't want to build around a few old properties like Ms. Kelo's and that of her neighbors, Wilhelmina and Charles Dery.

Age 87 and 85, respectively, they live in the house Wilhelmina was born in. The city is willing to pay a fair price for their home, but it's not an issue of money. "We get this all the time," says their son Matt. "'How much did they offer? What will it take?' My parents don't want to wake up rich tomorrow. They just want to wake up in their own home."

Unfortunately for the Derys, the U.S. Supreme Court in 2005 upheld the city's condemnation rights. In a close, 5-to-4 decision, it ruled that compulsory purchase to foster economic development falls under "public use" and is thus constitutionally permissible. "Promoting economic development is a traditional and long accepted function of government," Justice John Paul Stevens wrote for the majority. Intended to increase jobs and tax revenues, New London's plan "unquestionably serves a public purpose." In her dissenting opinion, however, Justice Sandra Day O'Connor objected: "Under the banner of economic development, all private property is now vulnerable to being taken and transferred to another private owner, so long as it might be upgraded.... Nothing is to prevent the state from replacing any Motel 6 with a

Ritz-Carlton, any home with a shopping mall, or any farm with a factory."

The Supreme Court's decision pushes the debate over eminent domain back to the states and local communities. Although many cities have successfully used eminent domain to re-build decayed urban areas or spark economic growth,[77] resistance to it is now intensifying, with political and legal battles being fought far beyond Susette Kelo's home in New London. For example, in Highland Park, New Jersey, the owners of a photography studio worry that a plan to redevelop their street will force them out of the location they've occupied for twenty-five years. In Port Chester, New York, a state development agency wants the site of a small furniture plant for a parking lot for Home Depot, and its owners are resisting. And in Salina, New York, twenty-nine little businesses—with names like Butch's Automotive and Transmission, Syracuse Crank and Machine, Gianelli's Sausage, and Petersen Plumbing—are battling local government's use of eminent domain to pave the way for DestiNY's proposed 325-acre, $2.67 billion research-and-development park.

Like New London, Salina desperately needs big ideas and big development, and it may not get another chance soon. But is tearing down these businesses fair? "We're here," says Philip Jakes-Johnson, who owns Solvents & Petroleum Service, one of the twenty-nine businesses in question. "We pay our taxes. We build companies and run them without tax breaks." Brian Osborne, another owner, adds: "Everything I and my family have worked for over the past 25 years is at stake because of the way eminent domain is being used in this state and across the country."

Discussion Questions

1. Is New London treating Susette Kelo and her neighbors fairly? Assuming that the proposed development will help to revitalize New London, is it just for the city to

appropriate private property around Fort Trumbull?

2. Are towns such as New London and Salina pursuing wise, beneficial, and progressive social policies, or are their actions socially harmful and biased against ordinary working people and small-business owners?

3. Do you believe that eminent domain is a morally legitimate right of government? Explain why or why not.

4. "If 'just compensation' is paid, then by definition those who lose their property cannot claim that they have been treated unjustly." Assess this argument. Can compensation be just if one of the parties is unwilling to accept it?

5. Is it fair to the community if an individual refuses payment and blocks a socially useful project? Putting legal issues aside, are there situations in which it would be morally permissible for government to seize private property for the public good with less than full compensation or even with no compensation at all?

6. Assess the concept of eminent domain, in general, and the plight of Susette Kelo and her neighbors, in particular, from the point of view of the different theories of justice discussed in this chapter. Is it possible to square the government's exercise of eminent domain with a libertarian approach to justice?

CASE 3.2

Battling over Bottled Water

Water is the lifeblood of the earth, but by 2025, according to the U.N., two-thirds of the world's population could face chronic shortages of water. In fact, some countries are already importing huge supertankers of freshwater from other countries. But one place that's definitely not short of water is the state of Michigan, which has 11,000 lakes and is surrounded by Lakes Michigan, Huron, Superior, and Erie. So it came as a surprise to some that the Nestlé company's new Ice Mountain bottled-water plant in Mecosta County, Michigan, dredged up so much controversy when it began pumping water from a local spring.[78]

Nestlé's willingness to invest $100 million to build a new 410,000-square-foot bottling plant in Mecosta reflects the fact that bottled water is big business, with annual sales of $6 billion (up 35 percent since 1997). Many county residents, in fact, are thrilled about Nestlé's being there. The Ice Mountain plant employs about a hundred people at $12 to $23

per hour, significantly more than many local jobs pay. And the company shells out hundreds of thousands of dollars in local taxes. Township supervisor Maxine McClellan says, "This is probably the best project we've ever brought into Mecosta County." She adds that she wants "a diversified economy where our kids don't have to move away to find jobs."

The problem, as some local residents see it, is that Nestlé has also built a 12-mile stainless steel pipeline from the plant to Sanctuary Spring, which sits on an 850-acre private deer-hunting ranch and is part of the headwaters of the Little Muskegon River, which flows into the Muskegon and then into Lake Michigan. The company started pumping 130 gallons of water every minute from the spring, with plans to increase that to 400 gallons per minute, or about 262 million gallons a year. But whose water is Nestlé pumping? That's the question being asked by Michigan Citizens for Water Conservation (MCWC), a local Mecosta group that has filed suit contesting Nestlé's right to the spring's waters. Although the company has a ninety-nine-year lease on the land, MCWC contends that the water itself is a public resource. As Jim Olson, MCWC's lawyer, explains it, under the doctrine of "reasonable use" the owners of a stream can use its water for drinking, boating, swimming, or anything else "as long as it's in connection with their land." But, he argues, "this does not include the right to transport water to some distant land for [some other] use. We're arguing that the same is true with groundwater—you can't sever it from the estate."

Michigan State Senator Ken Sikkema, who chaired a task force on Michigan water issues, rejects that argument: "A farmer pumps water out of the ground, waters potatoes, and sends the potatoes to Illinois—there's no real difference. The water in those potatoes is gone." This reasoning hasn't assuaged the fears of three American Indian tribes who have joined the fray. Citing an 1836 treaty that protects their fishing and hunting rights in the Great Lakes region, they have brought a federal lawsuit against Nestlé and the state of Michigan to stop what they see as a massive water grab. "Our fear," says a spokesperson for the Little Traverse Bay Bands of Odawa Indians, "is that the export could significantly and permanently damage the fishery."

However, David K. Ladd, head of the Office of Great Lakes, argues that bottled water is a special case. Legally, he contends, it's a "food," regulated by the Food and Drug Administration. "There's no difference between Perrier bottling water, Gerber making baby food, or Miller brewing beer. When you incorporate water from the basin into a product, it's no longer water per se." And Brendan O'Rourke, an Ice Mountain plant manager, adds that the 262 million gallons it wants to pump are less than 1 percent of the annual recharge rate of the local watershed, equivalent to just 14 minutes of evaporation from the surface of Lake Michigan.

For their part, scientists opposed to the project argue that Nestlé's pumping has already lowered the local water table and that northern pike are having trouble spawning in a stream fed by Sanctuary Spring. Jim Olson argues that the Ice Mountain plant should reduce its water consumption to 100 gallons per minute or less, not increase it to 400 gallons. "Every gallon removed is needed for the stream to sustain itself," he states. "The right to withdraw groundwater does not include the right to diminish … existing or future uses."

In 2003, to the surprise of many, Michigan state court judge Lawrence Root bought that argument and upheld the MCWC's lawsuit. Ruling that the environment is at risk no matter how much water Nestlé draws out, he ordered the pumps turned off. Two years later, an appellate court reversed Judge Root's decision, and MCWC and Nestlé subsequently entered an agreement limiting Nestlé's withdrawals from Sanctuary Spring to 250 gallons per minute—although there has been some legal skirmishing between the two antagonists since then. In the meantime, however, the political tide has turned against Nestlé. Small towns in Maine and California have opposed its building new bottled water plants in their jurisdictions; Congress has held hearings into the diversion of groundwater by bottled water companies and other businesses; and in 2008 Michigan's governor, Jennifer M. Granholm, signed into law legislation that, among other things, makes it virtually impossible for operations such as the Ice Mountain plant to remove more than 100,000 gallons of groundwater per day.

Discussion Questions

1. Should people in Michigan be concerned about how, and by whom, the state's ground water is used? In your view, what issues of justice does this case raise?
2. Does Nestlé's pumping 262 million gallons of water per year from Sanctuary Spring constitute "reasonable use"? Is the company treating either local residents or the Native American tribes unfairly, or

would it be unfair to restrict Nestlé's use of water from the spring?

3. Is groundwater a public resource, the use of which is appropriate for society to regulate? Or is it the property of those who own the land to use as they see fit? Who has the strongest claim on groundwater—the owners of the land from which it is pumped, the original inhabitants of the area (that is, the local Indian tribes), local residents, citizens of the whole Great Lakes region, or all Americans?

4. Assess this case from the perspective of the utilitarian, libertarian, and Rawlsian theories of justice. How would each address the case? Which theory's approach do you find the most helpful or illuminating?

CASE **3.3**

Poverty in America

More than forty-five years after President Lyndon Johnson declared "war on poverty," 38.7 million Americans continue to live in penury, a third of them children. True, the number of families with incomes below the poverty line—defined as $21,200 for a family of four—declined appreciably during the long economic boom of the 1990s, with the poverty rate in 2000 reaching its lowest level since 1973. Since then, however, the poverty rate has crept up steadily to 13.3 percent. That's more than one out of every eight people.[79] And that figure will almost certainly get worse once the effects of the economic crisis and recession of 2008–9—the most serious economic meltdown since the Great Depression of the 1930s—come to be included in the Census Bureau's data. Even before that economic disaster, however, the average American adult had a 60 percent chance of living at least one year below the poverty line and a 33 percent chance of experiencing dire poverty.[80]

Poverty is particularly hard on children. Among other things, it mars their brain development. This is not just a result of poor nutrition or exposure to environmental toxins, as one might expect. Rather, researchers have found that children growing up in very poor families experience unhealthy levels of stress hormones that impair memory and language acquisition.[81] Still, many people think that those described as "poor" in the United States are pretty well-off by world standards. The truth is, in life expectancy, twenty-year-old U.S. males rank thirty-sixth among the world's nations, and twenty-year-old U.S. females rank twenty-first. Our infant mortality rate is worse than that in twenty-one other Western nations. Even Beijing's infant mortality rate is lower than New York City's. In fact, if our infant mortality rate were as good as Cuba's, we would save an additional 2,212 babies each year. If it were as good as Singapore's, we'd save 18,900 babies.[82]

Furthermore, millions of Americans endure hunger. According to the U.S. Department of Agriculture, 11.1 percent of U.S. households lack "food security," and in 4.7 million American households one or more persons go hungry during the year.[83] In addition, one out of every four Americans lives in substandard housing, and in most cities a visitor is likely to see people roaming the streets in tattered clothing, picking their food out of garbage cans, and sleeping in doorways or in makeshift shacks and abandoned cars. Contrary to the popular perception that the homeless consist mostly of young men with drug, alcohol, or mental-health problems, the majority are simply jobless individuals or families who cannot afford housing. Reliable figures are hard to come by, but probably between 700,000 and 800,000 Americans are homeless on any given night and between 2.5 and 3.5 million people are homeless sometime during the year.[84]

People in different walks of life and in different circumstances experience poverty. Many others live on the edge of poverty and are in continual danger of falling into it through illness, job loss, or other misfortune. In the United States today, the "working poor"—those who work full-time but do not earn enough to pull themselves and their families out of poverty—number 28 million.[85] They represent a higher percentage of the workforce than in the 1970s as well-paid unionized manufacturing jobs have been replaced by non-union service jobs.[86] At $7.25 per hour, the minimum wage is less in real terms than it was in the 1960s and 70s. Someone working 40 hours a week, every week, for that wage cannot raise his or her family out of poverty. In fact, according to an advocacy group, a minimum-wage earner can afford to pay rent and utilities on a one-bedroom apartment in only four counties in the whole country.[87]

Many poor people are unable to work and depend on outside assistance, but living decently on welfare has always been difficult, if not impossible. The old system of AFDC (Aid to Families with Dependent Children) was popular when it was created in 1935 and most AFDC recipients were widows. But by the 1990s, fewer than 2 percent of recipients were widows and most had never been married to their child's other parent.[88] Public support for the program ebbed as many Americans came to believe that AFDC discouraged its recipients from marrying and from working. As a result, benefits grew even stingier. By the time AFDC came to an end in 1996, welfare benefits had fallen, in real terms, to 51 percent of what they had been in 1971.[89] With annual cash allowances for a family on AFDC ranging from $1,416 in Mississippi to $6,780 in New York, even in the most

generous states stipends were never enough to allow a family to escape from poverty.[90]

In 1996 Congress replaced AFDC with TANF (Temporary Assistance to Needy Families). Under the new system, the entitlement of poor people to support has been replaced by block grants to the states to run their own welfare programs. The grants are limited to a certain amount of money; if they run out, the states are not required to make additional expenditures. Welfare recipients are required to work for pay or to enroll in training programs, and financial support is limited to a lifetime maximum of five years. This shift in policy has been controversial. Since the TANF system began, the number of people receiving welfare benefits has declined, but experts disagree about the reasons: Was it a growing economy offering more opportunities, the success of the new approach in encouraging welfare recipients to make themselves employable, or simply people who are not able to take care of themselves being denied support?[91] Even now, with soaring unemployment and the worst economic crisis in decades, the number of people receiving assistance remains at or near a forty-year low.[92]

One thing that is clear is the large number of women living in poverty. This includes women with inadequate income following divorce, widowhood, or retirement, as well as women raising children alone. Wage discrimination against women is one factor. Women who work full-time, year-round earn only about two-thirds of what men earn. And millions of women hold full-time jobs that pay wages near or below the poverty line.

Women's responsibilities for child rearing are another important factor. Despite many changes in recent years, women continue to have primary responsibility in this area. When marriages break up, mothers typically take custody and bear the major financial burden. Fewer than half the women raising children alone are awarded child support, and fewer than half of those entitled to it receive the full amount. Of family households headed by women, 43.4 percent have incomes below $25,000 and 25.6 percent have incomes below $15,000.[93] Not only do households headed by women earn only half the median income of all households, but also their overall net worth is two-thirds less.[94]

Most poor people in our nation—about two-thirds of them—are white, but blacks are about two and a half times more likely to be poor. Whereas one out of every ten white Americans is poor, one of every four African Americans and one out of every five Hispanics live below the poverty line. Many members of these minority communities have succeeded in moving up the economic ladder, but the overall picture is disheartening. African-American family income, to pick just one statistic, is only 62 percent that of white family income.[95]

Although it is doubtful that there is more social mobility in the United States than in Europe, what is certainly clear is that Americans believe that they have plenty of it. In line with that belief, 71 percent of them, but only 40 percent of Europeans, think that the poor have a good chance to escape their plight.[96] Americans figure that the poor can push their way out of poverty on their own because they typically assume that one's success or failure is largely determined by factors within one's own control.[97] Americans, even poor Americans, favor individualistic explanations of poverty (such as lack of effort or ability, deficient morals, poor work habits) over structural explanations (such as inadequate schooling, low wages, lack of jobs), whereas Europeans favor structural explanations of poverty over individualistic explanations.[98] They tend to see the poor as unfortunate rather than as personally responsible for their condition. Seventy percent of West Germans, for example, express the belief that people are poor because of imperfections in society, not

their own laziness, whereas 70 percent of Americans hold the opposite view.[99] Because of that belief and because the majority of Americans believe that redistribution favors racial minorities (an idea which they tend to dislike), they support the present political system, which assists those at the socioeconomic bottom far less than European governments do.[100] As a result, you are twice as likely to be poor if you live in the United States than if you live in Western Europe.[101]

Discussion Questions

1. Does the existence of poverty imply that our socioeconomic system is unjust? Does the concentration of poverty in certain groups make it more unjust than it would be otherwise?
2. What are the causes of poverty? Are they structural or individual? How is one's answer to this question likely to affect one's view of the justice or injustice of poverty?
3. What moral obligation, if any, do we have individually and as a society to reduce poverty? What steps could be taken? What role should business play?
4. How would a utilitarian view the facts about poverty? What are the implications for our society of the concept of the declining utility of money?
5. How would a libertarian like Nozick view poverty in the United States? How plausible do you find the libertarian's preference for private charity over public assistance?
6. How would our economy be assessed from the point of view of Rawls's difference principle? Can it be plausibly maintained that, despite poverty, our system works to "the greatest expected benefit of the least advantaged"? Is this an appropriate standard?

American Business and Its Basis

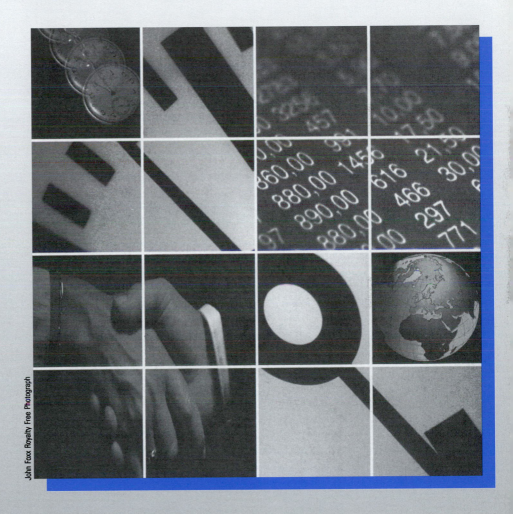

John Foxx Royalty Free Photograph

127

PART

2

American Business
and Its Basis

The Nature of Capitalism

Pictor/Imagestate/Photolibrary

INTRODUCTION

October is often said to be a bad month for stocks. This was certainly true in 2008. On Friday, October 10, 2008, the Dow Jones Industrial Average capped the worst week in its 112-year history with its most volatile day ever as the index swung 1,019 points in one trading session. In the weeks that followed, the gyrating stock market calmed down. As the dust settled, however, stockholders and mutual fund investors—many of them employees diligently saving for retirement—were forced to come to terms with the cold reality that their portfolios were worth only about half of what they had been a year before, with little prospect of stock prices bouncing back any time soon. And that was true not just on Wall Street but also in Hong Kong, Mumbai, Tokyo, Johannesburg, Frankfurt, and London as stock markets around the world crashed. That's not too surprising: Capitalism is a worldwide system, and what happens on Wall Street reverberates around the globe, and vice versa, because the economies of all capitalist nations are intricately interconnected and their markets tightly intertwined.

In this case, it was the United States that pushed the world economic system into crisis. The collapse of the U.S. subprime mortgage market, following the bursting of the real estate bubble, had been causing financial jitters since early in 2008. But only that autumn did it become clear that a number of once rich and haughty U.S. financial institutions were floating perilously on an ocean of debt. In an effort to maximize profit, they had underwritten loans that left them with potential liabilities thirty to forty times greater than their underlying assets. With that kind of exposure, it doesn't take much to bring the whole house of cards down. And that's what began happening. When AIG, the world's biggest insurer, began tottering, the U.S. government rushed to its assistance, fearing that its collapse would wreak havoc throughout the financial system. Earlier the government had facilitated the sale, first, of Bear Sterns, the investment bank and brokerage firm, and then of Washington Mutual Bank, to JPMorgan Chase because both institutions were about to fail. The government had also effectively nationalized the mortgage giants Fannie Mae and Freddie Mac in order to keep them afloat. Now, after rescuing AIG, the U.S. Treasury Department and Federal Reserve Board were worried that they were sending the wrong message to the business world, namely, that they were prepared to rescue any financial firm that needed help. So, a few days after bailing out AIG, they decided to let Lehman Brothers, a global financial services firm that was in deep trouble, go under. The rapid demise of Lehman Brothers and the government's willingness to let it happen, however, immediately caused credit markets to panic, the movement of capital to freeze, investors to flee, the stock market to plunge—and the world economy to begin sliding inexorably into recession.

Governments around the world moved quickly to try to stabilize financial markets and free up credit by lowering interest rates and propping up their banks and other financial institutions. The United States pumped money into its financial system on an unprecedented scale—taking over bad assets, guaranteeing debts, and pouring new capital into private capitalist firms. Anyone predicting even a few months earlier that liberals and conservatives in Congress would rapidly unite to approve a bank bailout of over $700 billion—that's more than $2,000 for every man, woman, and child in the country—would have been dismissed as a lunatic. But that's what happened. Although government economic intervention couldn't stave off the worse economic slump that most Americans had ever seen, it probably prevented the financial meltdown of 2008 from turning into a 1930s-style depression. In doing so, however, it may also have changed the face of capitalism forever.

But what exactly is the nature of the economic system called capitalism? What are its underlying values, principles, and economic philosophy? What has it accomplished, and what are its prospects for the future? This chapter examines these and related questions.

Looking back in history, one must credit capitalism with helping break the constraints of medieval feudalism, which had severely limited individual possibilities for improvement. In place of a stifling economic system, capitalism offered opportunities for those blessed with imagination, an ability to plan, and a willingness to work. Capitalism must also be credited with enhancing the abundance and diversity of consumer goods beyond Adam Smith's wildest dreams. It has increased material wealth and standards of living and has converted cities from modest bazaars into treasure troves of dazzling merchandise.

In the light of such accomplishments and the acculturation process that tends to glorify them, it is possible to overlook capitalism's theoretical and operational problems. This chapter attempts to identify some of these problems and their moral ramifications. It provides some basic historical and conceptual categories for understanding the socioeconomic framework within which business transactions occur and moral issues arise. In particular, this chapter addresses the following topics:

1. The definition of capitalism and its major historical stages
2. Four of the key features of capitalism: companies, profit motive, competition, and private property
3. Two classical moral justifications of capitalism—one based on the right to property, the other on Adam Smith's concept of the invisible hand
4. Fundamental criticisms of capitalism—in particular, the persistence of inequality and poverty, capitalism's implicit view of human nature, the rise of economic oligarchies, the shortcomings of competition, and employees' experience of alienation and exploitation on the job
5. The problems facing capitalism in the United States today—in particular, the decline of manufacturing, along with job outsourcing and the trade deficit; an excessive focus on the short term; and changing attitudes toward work

CAPITALISM

Capitalism can be defined ideally as an economic system in which the major portion of production and distribution is in private hands, operating under what is termed a "profit" or "market" system. The United States is the world's leading capitalistic economy. All manufacturing firms are privately owned, including those that produce military hardware for the government. The same applies to most banks, insurance companies, and transportation companies. Almost all other businesses—small, medium, and large—are also privately owned, as are power companies. With the exception of government expenditures for such things as health, education, welfare, highways, and military equipment, no central governing body dictates to these private owners what or how much of anything will be produced. For example, officials at Ford Motor Company, Chrysler, and General Motors design their products and set their own production goals in anticipation of consumer demand.

The private ownership and market aspects of capitalism contrast with its polar opposite, socialism. Ideally, **socialism** is an economic system characterized by public ownership of property and a planned economy. Under socialism, a society's productive equipment is owned not by individuals (capitalists) but by public bodies. Socialism depends primarily on centralized planning rather than on a market system for both its overall allocation of resources and its distribution of income; crucial economic decisions are made not by individuals but by government. In the former Soviet Union, for example, government

Summary 4.1
Capitalism is an economic system in which the major portion of production and distribution is in private hands, operating under a profit or market system. Socialism is an economic system characterized by public ownership of property and a planned economy. Worker control socialism is a hybrid, market-oriented form of socialism.

agencies decided the number of automobiles—including models, styles, and colors—to be produced each year. Top levels of the Soviet government formulated production and cost objectives, which were then converted to specific production quotas and budgets that individual plant managers had to follow.

A hybrid economic system advocated by some socialists (and once approximated by Yugoslavia) is **worker control socialism**. Individual firms respond to a market when acquiring the necessary factors of production and when deciding what to produce. The workforce of each enterprise controls the enterprise (although it may elect or hire managers to oversee day-to-day operations), and profits accrue to the workers as a group to divide in whatever manner they agree on. The workers manage their factories, but the capital assets of each enterprise are owned by society as a whole and not by private individuals.

Historical Background of Capitalism

What we know as "capitalism" did not fully emerge until the Renaissance in Europe during the fifteenth and sixteenth centuries. Before the Renaissance, business exchanges in medieval Europe were organized through guilds, which were associations of individuals involved in the same trade.

Today if you want a pair of shoes, you head for a shoe store, where you find an array of shoes. If nothing strikes your fancy, you set out for another shop, and perhaps another, until at last you find what you want. Or, if still disappointed, you might ask the store clerk to order a pair in your size from the manufacturer or its distributor. You certainly wouldn't ask the clerk to have someone make you a pair of shoes. Under the guild organization, shoemakers were also shoe sellers and made shoes only to fill orders. If they had no orders, they made no shoes. The shoemaker's sole economic function was to make shoes for people when they wanted them. His labor allowed him to maintain himself, not advance his station in life. When the shoemaker died, his business went with him—unless he had a son to inherit and carry on the enterprise. As for shoe quality and cost, the medieval shopper could generally count on getting a good pair of shoes at a fair price because the cobblers' guild strictly controlled quality and price.

Weaving was another big medieval trade. In fact, in the fourteenth century weaving was the leading industry in the German town of Augsburg. Little wonder, then, that an enterprising young man named Hans Fugger became a weaver when he settled there in 1357. But young Hans had ambitions that stretched far beyond the limits of the weaving trade and the handicraft guild system. And they were grandly realized, for within three short generations a family of simple weavers was transformed into a great German banking dynasty.[1]

Not content with being a weaver, Hans Fugger began collecting and selling the products of other weavers. Soon he was directly employing the other weavers, paying them for their labor and selling their products as his own. His sons continued the business and expanded it in new directions, as did his grandsons, especially Jacob Fugger, the foremost capitalist of the Renaissance.

Among other things, Jacob Fugger lent large sums of money to the Hapsburg emperors to finance their wars. In return, he obtained monopoly rights on silver and copper ores, which he then traded. When Fugger bought the mines themselves, he acquired all the components necessary to erect an extraordinary financial dynasty and to make himself one of the richest persons of all times.

Like latter-day titans of American industry, Fugger employed thousands of workers and paid them wages, controlled all his products from raw material to final market, set his own quality standards, and charged whatever the traffic would bear. In one brief century, what was once a handicraft inseparable from the craftsperson had become a company that existed outside any family members. What had once motivated Hans Fugger—namely, maintenance of his station in life—had given way to gain for gain's sake, the so-called profit motive. Under Jacob Fugger, the company amassed profits—a novel concept—that well exceeded the needs of the Fugger family. And the profits were measured not in goods or land but in money.

Capitalism has undergone changes since then. The kind of capitalism that emerged in the Fuggers' time is often termed **mercantile capitalism**, which is capitalism that is based on mutual dependence between state and commercial interests. Central to mercantile capitalism is the belief that the economic health of a nation is determined by the bullion (precious metals, gold, and silver) it possesses and that therefore government should regulate production and trade with the goal of encouraging exports while keeping out imports, thus building up the nation's bullion reserves. A prudent nation should strive to be economically self-sufficient while using sea power, if it can, to control foreign markets and establish colonies for the benefit of the mother country.

During the eighteenth and nineteenth centuries, however, new economic ideas spread. These emphasized the importance of competition and open markets and of freeing trade and production from government oversight. Trade between nations was now seen as mutually beneficial, and national wealth and prosperity was no longer identified with bullion. With the Industrial Revolution, industrialists replaced merchants as the dominant power in a capitalist economy, and the period of **industrial capitalism** emerged, which is associated with large-scale industry. In the United States, the confluence of many factors after the Civil War—including a sound financial base, the technology for mass production, expanding markets for cheaply manufactured goods, and a large and willing labor force—produced industrial expansion. Exploiting these fortuitous conditions was a group of hard-driving, visionary entrepreneurs called "robber barons" by their critics and "captains of industry" by their supporters: Cornelius Vanderbilt, Cyrus McCormick, Andrew Carnegie, John D. Rockefeller, Jay Gould, and others.

As industrialization increased, so did the size and power of business. The private fortunes of a few individuals could no longer underwrite the accelerated growth of business activity. The large sums of capital necessary could be raised only through a corporate form of business, in which risk and potential profit were distributed among numerous investors.

As competition intensified, an industry's survival came to depend on its financial strength to reduce prices and either eliminate or absorb competition. To shore up their assets, industries engaged in **financial capitalism,** characterized by pools, trusts, holding companies, and the interpenetration of banking, insurance, and industrial interests. Hand in hand with this development, the trend continued toward larger and larger corporations, controlling more and more of the country's economic capacity.

The economic and political challenges of the Great Depression of the 1930s helped usher in still another phase of capitalism, often called **state welfare capitalism,** in which government plays an active role in regulating economic activities in an effort to smooth out the boom-and-bust pattern of the business cycle. In addition, government programs like Social Security and unemployment insurance seek to enhance the welfare of the workforce, and legislation legitimizes the existence of trade unions. Conservative politicians sometimes advocate less government control of business, but in reality the governments of all capitalist countries are deeply involved in the management of their economies.

> **Summary 4.2**
> Capitalism has gone through several stages: mercantile, industrial, financial, and state welfare. Many believe we are now at a new stage, globalized capitalism.

These days, the increasingly worldwide scale of capitalism leads many contemporary commentators to see **globalized capitalism** as a new stage or level of capitalist development. Although capitalism has always involved international trade, today—thanks to the computer, the Internet, satellites, cell phones, and other technological advances—the economies of most countries are becoming more and more integrated, a process labeled *globalization.* Although the world is still far from constituting a single global economy, investment capital is more mobile than ever, and the currencies, stock exchanges, and economic fortunes of all capitalist countries are bound together in a single financial system. The business operations of a growing number of companies take place on a world stage. Capitalist enterprises are more likely than ever before to utilize foreign components and draw on foreign labor or services, to export products or provide services abroad, and to acquire or start foreign subsidiaries or engage in joint ventures with overseas companies. Many apparently national companies produce one component in one country and another component in a different country, assemble them in a third country, and market them throughout the world.

> Although capitalism will continue to evolve, it has four characteristic features.

Although the study of capitalism's evolution is best left to economic historians, it is important to keep in mind capitalism's dynamic nature. There is nothing fixed and immutable about this or any other economic system; it is as susceptible to the social forces of change as any other institution. Nevertheless, the capitalism we know does have some prominent features that were evident in the earliest capitalistic businesses.

KEY FEATURES OF CAPITALISM

Complete coverage of capitalism's central features and defining characteristics has filled many a book. Four features of particular significance—the existence of companies, profit motive, competition, and private property—will be discussed briefly here.

Companies

Chapter 2 mentioned the Firestone case, in which a media misrepresentation was left uncorrected. When asked why Firestone officials had not corrected the error, a Firestone spokesperson said that Firestone's policy was to ask for corrections only when it was beneficial to the company to do so. Expressions like "Firestone's policy" and "beneficial to the company" reflect one key feature of capitalism: the existence of companies or business firms separate from the human beings who work for and within them.

"It's not in the company's interests," "The company thinks that," "From the company's viewpoint," "As far as the company is concerned"—all of us have heard, perhaps even used, expressions that treat a business organization like a person or at least like a separate and distinct entity. Such personifications are not mere lapses into the figurative but bespeak a basic characteristic of capitalism: Capitalism permits the creation of companies or business organizations that exist separately from the people associated with them. We take the existence of companies for granted, but some experts believe that it is not church or state but the company that is "the most important organization in the world."[2]

Today the big companies we're familiar with—General Electric, Microsoft, Ford, Verizon—are, in fact, incorporated businesses, or corporations. Chapter 5 discusses the nature of the modern corporation, including its historical evolution and its social responsibilities. Here it's enough to observe that, in the nineteenth century, Chief Justice John Marshall defined a *corporation* as "an artificial being, invisible, intangible, and existing only in the contemplation of law." Although a corporation is not something that can be seen or touched, it does have prescribed rights and legal obligations within the community. Like you or me, a corporation may enter into contracts and may sue or be sued in courts of law. It may even do things that the corporation's members disapprove of. The corporations that loom large on our economic landscape harken back to a feature of capitalism evident as early as the Fugger dynasty: the existence of the company.

Profit Motive

A second characteristic of capitalism lies in the motive of the company: to make profit. As dollar-directed and gain-motivated as our society is, most of us take for granted that the human being is by nature an acquisitive creature who, left to his or her own devices, will pursue profit with all the instinctual vigor of a cat chasing a mouse. However, as economist Robert Heilbroner points out, the "profit motive, as we understand it, is a very recent phenomenon. It was foreign to the lower and middle classes of Egyptian, Greek, Roman, and medieval cultures, only scattered throughout the Renaissance times, and largely absent in most Eastern civilizations." The medieval church taught that no Christian ought to be a merchant. "Even to our Pilgrim forefathers," Heilbroner writes, "the idea that gain ought to be a tolerable—even a useful—goal in life would have appeared as nothing short of a doctrine of the devil." Heilbroner concludes: "As a ubiquitous characteristic of society, the profit motive is as modern an invention as printing."[3]

The profit motive is central to capitalism. It assumes that economic self-interest motivates human beings.

Modern or not, profit in the form of money is the lifeblood of the capitalist system. Companies and capitalists alike are motivated by a robust appetite for money profit. Indeed, the **profit motive** implies and reflects a critical assumption about human nature: that human beings are basically economic creatures, who recognize and are motivated by their own economic interests.

Competition

If self-interest and an appetite for money profit drive individuals and companies, then what stops them short of holding up society for exorbitant ransom? What stops capitalists from bleeding society dry?

Adam Smith provided an answer in his famous treatise on political economy, *An Inquiry into the Nature and Causes of the Wealth of Nations* (1776). Free **competition**, said Smith, is the regulator that keeps a community activated only by self-interest from degenerating into a mob of ruthless profiteers. When traditional restraints are removed from the sale of goods and from wages and when all individuals have equal access to raw materials and markets (the doctrine of **laissez faire**, from the French meaning "to let [people] do [as they choose]"), we are all free to pursue our own interests. In pursuing our own interests, however, we come smack up against others similarly motivated. If any of us allow blind self-interest to dictate our actions—for example, by price gouging or employee exploitation—we will quickly find ourselves beaten out by a competitor who, let's say, charges less and pays a better wage. Competition thus regulates individual economic activity.

To sample the flavor of Smith's argument, imagine an acquisitive young woman in a faraway place who wants to pile up as much wealth as possible. She looks about her and sees that people need and want strong twilled cotton trousers, so she takes her investment capital and sets up a jeans factory. She charges $45 for a pair of jeans and soon realizes handsome profits. The woman's success is not lost on other business minds, especially manufacturers of formal slacks and dresses, who observe a sharp decline in those markets. Wanting a piece of the jeans action, numerous enterprises start up jeans factories. Many of these start selling jeans for $40 a pair. No longer alone in the market, our hypothetical businesswoman must check her appetite for profit by lowering her price or risk folding. As the number of jeans on the market increases, their supply eventually overtakes demand, and the price of jeans declines further and further. Inefficient manufacturers start dropping like flies. As the competition thins out, the demand for jeans slowly balances with the supply, and the price regulates itself. Ultimately, an equilibrium is reached between supply and demand, and the price of jeans stabilizes, yielding a normal profit to the efficient producer.

Competition makes individual pursuit of self-interest socially beneficial.

In much this way, Adam Smith tried to explain how economic competition steers the individual pursuit of self-interest in a socially beneficial direction. By appealing to their self-interest, society can induce producers to provide it with what it wants—just as manufacturers of formal slacks and dresses were enticed into jeans production. But competition keeps prices for desired goods from escalating; high prices are self-correcting because they call forth an increased supply.

Private Property

In its discussion of the libertarian theory of justice, Chapter 3 emphasized that property should not be identified only with physical objects like houses, cars, and DVD players. Nor should ownership be thought of as a simple relationship between the owner and the thing owned. One can have property rights over things that are not simple physical objects, as when one owns stock in a company. Also, property ownership involves a complex bundle of rights and rules governing how, under what circumstances, and in what ways both the owner and others can use, possess, dispose of, and have access to the thing in question.

Private property is central to capitalism. To put it another way, capitalism as a socioeconomic system is a specific form of private property. What matters for capitalism is not private property simply in the sense of personal possessions, because a socialist society can permit people to own cars, television sets, and jogging shoes. Rather, capitalism requires private ownership of the major *means of production* and distribution. The means of production and distribution include factories, warehouses, offices, machines, computer systems, trucking fleets, agricultural land, and whatever else makes up the economic resources of a nation. Under capitalism, private hands control these basic economic assets and productive resources. Thus, the major economic decisions are made by individuals or groups acting on their own in pursuit of profit. These decisions are not directly coordinated with those of other producers, nor are they the result of some overall plan. Any profits (or losses) that result from these decisions about production are those of the owners.

Capital, as an economic concept, is closely related to private property. Putting it simply, capital is money that is invested for the purpose of making more money. Individuals or corporations purchase various means of production or other related assets and use them to produce goods or provide services, which are then sold. They do this not for the purpose of being nice or of helping people out but rather to make money—more money, they hope, than they spent to make the goods or provide the services in the first place. Using money to make money is at the heart of the definition of capitalism.

Summary 4.3
Four key features of capitalism are the existence of companies, profit motive, competition, and private property.

Capitalism requires private ownership of the means of production.

MORAL JUSTIFICATIONS OF CAPITALISM

People tend to take for granted the desirability and moral legitimacy of the political and economic system within which they live. Americans are no exception. We are raised in a society that encourages individual competition, praises capitalism, promotes the acquisition of material goods, and worships economic wealth. Newspapers, television, recordings, movies, and other forms of popular culture celebrate these values, and rarely are we presented with fundamental criticisms of or possible alternatives to our socioeconomic order. Small wonder, then, that most of us blithely assume, without ever bothering to question, that our capitalist economic system is a morally justifiable one.

Yet as thinking people and moral agents, we need to reflect on the nature and justifiability of our social institutions. The proposition that capitalism is a morally acceptable system is open to debate. Whether we decide that capitalism is morally justified will depend, at least in part, on which general theory of justice turns out to be soundest. Chapter 3 explored in detail the utilitarian approach, the libertarian alternative, and the theory of John Rawls. Now, against that background, this chapter looks at two basic ways defenders of capitalism have sought to justify their system: (1) the argument that the moral right to property guarantees the legitimacy of capitalism and (2) the utilitarian-based economic argument of Adam Smith. The chapter then considers some criticisms of capitalism.

The Natural Right to Property

As Americans, we live in a socioeconomic system that guarantees us certain property rights. Although we are no longer permitted to own other people, we are certainly free to own a variety of other things, from livestock to stock certificates, from our own homes to whole blocks of apartment buildings. A common defense of capitalism is the argument that people have a fundamental, **natural right to property** and that our capitalist system is simply the outcome of this right.

> One argument for capitalism is that it reflects people's natural right to property.

In Chapter 3, we saw how Locke attempted to base the right to property in human labor. According to Locke, when individuals mix their labor with the natural world, they are entitled to the results. This idea seems plausible in many cases. For example, if Carl diligently harvests coconuts on the island he shares with Adam, while Adam himself idles away his days, then most of us would agree that Carl has an entitlement to those coconuts that Adam lacks. But property ownership as it actually exists in the real world today is a complex, socially shaped phenomenon. This is especially true in the case of sophisticated forms of corporate and financial property—for example, bonds and stock options.

One could, of course, reject the whole idea of a natural right to property as a fiction, as, for example, utilitarians do. In their view, although various property systems exist, there is no natural right that things be owned privately, or collectively, or in any particular way whatsoever. The moral task, according to utilitarians, is to find the property system, the way of organizing production and distribution, that has the greatest utility.

Even if one believes that there is a natural right to property at least under some circumstances, one need not believe that this right leads to capitalism or that there is a right to have a system of property rules and regulations exactly like the one we now have in the United States. In other words, even if Carl has a natural right to his coconuts, there may still be moral limits on how many coconuts he can rightfully amass and what he can use them for. When he takes his coconuts to the coconut bank and receives more coconuts as interest, his newly acquired coconuts are not the result of any new labor on his part. When we look at capitalistic property—that is, at socioeconomic environments in which people profit from ownership alone—then we have left Locke's world far behind.

A defender of capitalism may reply, "Certainly, there's nothing unfair about Carl's accruing these extra coconuts through his investment; after all,

Summary 4.4
One basic defense of capitalism rests on a supposed natural moral right to property. Utilitarians deny the existence of such rights; other critics doubt that this right entitles one to have a system of property rules and regulations identical to the one we now have in the United States.

he could have eaten his original coconuts instead." And, indeed, within our system this reasoning seems perfectly correct. It is the way things work in our society. But this fact doesn't prove that Carl has some natural right to use his coconuts to earn more coconuts—that is, that it would be unfair or unjust to set up a different economic system (for example, one in which he had a right to consume coconuts but no right to use them to accrue more coconuts). The argument here is simply that the issue is not an all-or-nothing one. There may be certain fundamental moral rights to property, without those rights being unlimited or guaranteeing capitalism as we know it.

Adam Smith's Concept of the Invisible Hand

Relying on the idea of a natural right to property is not the only way and probably not the best way to defend capitalism. Another, very important argument defends capitalism in terms of the many economic benefits the system brings, claiming that the free and unrestrained market system that exists under capitalism is more efficient and more productive than any other possible system and is thus to be preferred on moral grounds. Essentially, this is a utilitarian argument, but one doesn't have to be a utilitarian to take it seriously. As mentioned in Chapter 2, almost every normative theory puts some moral weight on the consequences of actions. Thus if capitalism does indeed work better than other ways of organizing economic life, then this outcome will be a relevant moral fact—one that will be important, for instance, for Rawlsians.

> A second argument for capitalism is that it is the most efficient and productive economic system. This is basically a utilitarian consideration.

This section sketches Adam Smith's economic case for capitalism, as presented in *The Wealth of Nations*. Smith argues that when people are left to pursue their own interests, they will, without intending it, produce the greatest good for all. Each person's individual and private pursuit of wealth results—as if guided (in Smith's famous words) by an **invisible hand**—in the most beneficial overall organization and distribution of economic resources. Although the academic study of economics has developed greatly since Smith's times, his classic arguments remain extraordinarily influential.

Smith took it for granted that human beings are acquisitive creatures. Self-interest and personal advantage, specifically in an economic sense, may not be all that motivate people, but they do seem to motivate most people much of the time. At any rate, they are powerful enough forces that any successful economic system must strive to harness them. We are, Smith thought, strongly inclined to act so as to acquire more and more wealth.

In addition, humans have a natural propensity for trading—"to truck, barter, and exchange." Unlike other species, we have an almost constant need for the assistance of others. Yet because people are creatures of self-interest, it is folly for us to expect others to act altruistically toward us. We can secure what we need from others only by offering them something they need from us:

> Whoever offers to another a bargain of any kind, proposes to do this. Give me that which I want, and you shall have this which you want, is the meaning of every such offer; and it is in this manner that we obtain from one another the far greater part of those good offices which we stand in need of. It is not from the benevolence of the butcher, the brewer, or the baker that we expect our dinner, but from their regard to their own interest. We address ourselves, not to their

humanity but to their self love, and never talk to them of our own necessities but of their advantages.[4]

This disposition to trade, said Smith, leads to the division of labor—dividing the labor and production process into areas of specialization, which is the prime means of increasing economic productivity.

Thus, Smith reasoned that the greatest utility will result from unfettered pursuit of self-interest. Individuals should be allowed unrestricted access to raw materials, markets, and labor. Government interference in private enterprise should be eliminated, free competition encouraged, and economic self-interest made the rule of the day. Because human beings are acquisitive creatures, we will, if left free, engage in labor and exchange goods in a way that results in the greatest benefit to society. In our efforts to advance our own economic interests, we inevitably act to promote the economic well-being of society generally:

> Every individual is continually exerting himself to find the most advantageous employment for whatever capital he can command. It is his own advantage, indeed, and not that of the society, which he has in view.... [But] by directing that industry in such a manner as its produce may be of the greatest value, he [is] ... led by an invisible hand to promote an end that was no part of his intention.... By pursuing his own interest he frequently promotes that of society more effectually than when he really intends to promote it.[5]

To explain why pursuit of self-interest necessarily leads to the greatest social benefit, Smith invoked the law of supply and demand, which was alluded to in our discussion of competition. The law of supply and demand tempers the pursuit of self-interest exactly as competition keeps the enterprising capitalist from becoming a ruthless profiteer. The law of supply and demand similarly solves the problems of adequate goods and fair prices.

Some think the law of supply and demand even solves the problem of fair wages, for labor is another commodity up for sale like shoes or jeans. Just as the price of a new product at first is high, like the jeans in our earlier hypothetical example, so, too, are the wages of labor in a new field. But as labor becomes more plentiful, wages decline. Eventually they fall to a point at which inefficient laborers are eliminated and forced to seek other work, just as the inefficient manufacturers of jeans were forced out of that business and into others. And like the price of jeans, the price of labor then stabilizes at a fair level. As for the inefficient laborers, they find work and a living wage elsewhere. In seeking new fields of labor, they help maximize the majority's opportunities to enjoy the necessities, conveniences, and trifles of human life.

Some modern defenders of capitalism claim that it operates as Smith envisioned and can be justified on the same utilitarian grounds. But not everyone agrees.

Summary 4.5
Utilitarian defense of capitalism is associated with the classical economic arguments of Adam Smith. Smith believed that human beings are acquisitive and that they have a natural propensity for trading, and he insisted that when people are left free to pursue their own economic interests, they will, without intending it, produce the greatest good for all.

CRITICISMS OF CAPITALISM

The two major defenses of capitalism have not persuaded critics that it is a morally justifiable system. Their objections to capitalism are both theoretical and operational. *Theoretical* criticisms challenge capitalism's fundamental values, basic assumptions, or inherent economic tendencies. *Operational* criticisms focus more on capitalism's alleged deficiencies in actual practice (as opposed to theory)—in particular, on its failure to live up to its own economic ideals.

The following criticisms are a mix of both theoretical and operational concerns. They raise political, economic, and philosophical issues that cannot be fully assessed here. The debate over capitalism is a large and important one; the presentation that follows should be viewed as a stimulus to further discussion and not as the last word on the pros and cons of capitalism.

Inequality

Chapter 3 and Case 3.3 documented the profound economic inequality that exists in our capitalist society. The disparity in personal incomes is enormous; a tiny minority of the population owns the vast majority of the country's productive assets; and our society continues to be marred by poverty and homelessness. With divisions of social and economic class comes inequality of opportunity. A child born to a working-class family, let alone to an unwed teenager in an inner-city ghetto, has life prospects and possibilities that pale beside those of children born to wealthy, stock-owning parents. This reality challenges capitalism's claim of fairness, and the persistence of poverty and economic misfortune provides the basis for a utilitarian objection to it.

Critics argue that poverty and inequality challenge the fairness of capitalism and its claim to advance the interests of all. Defenders of capitalism respond to this in different ways.

Few doubt that poverty and inequality are bad things, but defenders of capitalism make several responses to those who criticize it on these grounds:

1. A few extreme supporters of capitalism simply deny that it is responsible for poverty and inequality. Rather, they say, government interference with the market causes these problems. Left to itself, the market would eliminate unemployment and poverty while ultimately lessening inequality. But neither theoretical economics nor the study of history supports this reply. Most economists and social theorists would agree that in the past seventy-five years or so activist government policies have done much, in all the Western capitalist countries, to reduce poverty and (to a lesser extent) inequality.

2. More moderate defenders of capitalism concede that in its pure laissez-faire form, capitalism does nothing to prevent and may even foster inequality and poverty. However, they argue that the system can be modified or its inherent tendencies corrected by political action, so that inequality and poverty are reduced or even eliminated. Critics of capitalism reply that the policies necessary to seriously reduce inequality and poverty are either impossible within a basically capitalist economic framework or unlikely to be carried out in any political system based on capitalism.

3. Finally, defenders of capitalism argue that the benefits of the system outweigh this weak point. Inequality is not so important if living standards are rising and if even the poor have better lives than they did in previous times. This contention rests on an implicit comparison with what things would be like if society were organized differently and is, accordingly,

difficult to assess. Naturally, it seems more plausible to those who are relatively favored by, and content with, the present economic system than it does to those who feel disadvantaged by it.

Some critics of capitalism go on to maintain that, aside from inequalities of income and ownership, the inequality inherent in the worker–capitalist relationship is itself morally undesirable. John Stuart Mill found capitalism inferior in this respect to more cooperative and egalitarian economic arrangements. "To work at the bidding and for the profit of another," he wrote, "is not ... a satisfactory state to human beings of educated intelligence, who have ceased to think themselves inferior to those whom they serve."[6] The ideal of escaping from a system of "superiors" and "subordinates" was well expressed by the great German playwright and poet Bertolt Brecht when he wrote that "He wants no servants under him / And no boss over his head."[7]

Human Nature and Capitalism

The theory of capitalism rests on a view of human beings as rational economic creatures, individuals who recognize and are motivated largely by their own economic self-interest. Adam Smith's defense of capitalism, for instance, assumes that consumers have full knowledge of the diverse choices available to them in the marketplace. They are supposed to know the price structures of similar products, to be fully aware of product differences, and to be able to make the optimal choice regarding price and quality.

But the key choices facing today's consumers are rarely simple. From foods to drugs, automobiles to appliances, fertilizers to computers, the modern marketplace is a cornucopia of products whose nature and nuances require a high level of consumer literacy. Even with government agencies and public interest groups to aid them, today's consumers are rarely an equal match for powerful industries that can influence prices, control product quality, and create and shape markets. The effectiveness of advertising, in particular, is difficult to reconcile with the picture of consumers as the autonomous, rational, and perfectly informed economic maximizers that economics textbooks presuppose when they attempt to demonstrate the benefits of capitalism. Consumers frequently seem to be pawns of social and economic forces beyond their control.

According to some critics of capitalism, however, what is objectionable about capitalism's view of human beings as essentially economic creatures is not this gap between theory and reality but rather the fact that it presents little in the way of an ideal to which either individuals or societies may aspire. As George Soros puts it, "Humans are capable of transcending the pursuit of narrow self-interest. Indeed, they cannot live without some sense of morality. It is market fundamentalism, which holds that the social good is best served by allowing people to pursue their self-interest without any thought for the social good ... that is a perversion of human nature."[8] Not only does capitalism rest on the premise that people are basically acquisitive, individualistic, and materialistic, but in practice capitalism strongly reinforces those human tendencies. Capitalism, its critics charge, presents no higher sense of human mission or purpose, whereas other views of society and human nature do.

Summary 4.6
Critics question the basic assumptions of capitalism (theoretical challenges) and whether it has delivered on its promises (operational challenges). One criticism is that capitalism produces severe inequality and is unable to eliminate poverty. Another is that capitalism wrongly assumes that human beings are rational economic maximizers and that well-being comes from ever greater material consumption. It is also alleged that capitalism offers us no higher sense of human purpose.

Critics charge that capitalism reinforces materialism and offers no higher sense of human purpose.

Christianity, for example, has long aspired to the ideal of a truly religious community united in *agape*, selfless love. And socialism, because it views human nature as malleable, hopes to see people transformed from the "competitive, acquisitive beings that they are (and that they are *encouraged* to be) under all property-dominated, market-oriented systems." In the more "benign environment of a propertyless, non-market social system," socialists believe that more cooperative and less selfish human beings will emerge.[9] Such positive ideals and aspirations are lacking in capitalism—or so its critics charge.

Capitalism operates on the debatable assumption that human beings find increased well-being through ever greater material consumption.

Finally, an implicit assumption of capitalism is that human beings find increased well-being through ever greater material consumption. That's why the avid pursuit of economic gain, as mediated through the invisible hand of the market, is supposed to make us all better-off. Moreover, contemporary capitalism needs people to keep on buying and consuming goods for the system to continue running. Consumer demand makes the economic wheels turn. And that, in turn, requires people in general to choose working more so they can consume more rather than working less, having more leisure, and buying fewer things. However, this bias in favor of material consumption runs up against the fact, according to social psychologists, that people today—in America, Europe, and Japan—are no more pleased with their lives than people were in the 1950s, despite the very substantial increase in standard of living that all these societies have enjoyed.[10]

Competition Isn't What It's Cracked Up to Be

Critics contend that capitalism's supposed commitment to competition is belied by oligopoly and corporate welfare. Some also challenge the belief that competition is desirable and beneficial.

As we have seen, one of the key features of capitalism is competition. Unfettered competition supposedly serves the collective interest while offering rich opportunities for the individual. But competition is one of the targets of capitalism's critics. They contend that capitalism breeds oligopolies that eliminate competition and concentrate economic power, that a system of corporate welfare protects many businesses from true marketplace competition, and finally that competition is neither generally beneficial nor desirable in itself.

Capitalism Breeds Oligopolies

As early as the middle of the nineteenth century, the German philosopher and political economist Karl Marx (1818–1883) argued that capitalism leads to **oligopolies**—a concentration of property and resources, and thus economic power, in the hands of a few. High costs, complex and expensive machinery, intense competition, and the advantages of large-scale production all work against the survival of small firms, said Marx. Many see proof of Marx's argument in today's economy.

Before the Industrial Revolution, capitalism was characterized by comparatively free and open competition among a large number of small firms. As late as 1832, for instance, hardly any private firms in the United States had ten or more employees.[11] Since then, the economy has come to be dominated by a relatively small number of enormous companies that, to a distressing extent, can conspire to set prices, eliminate competition, and monopolize an industry. The oil industry is a perfect example: The five biggest refiners in the United States control 56 percent of the market (up from 35 percent in 1993).[12]

Today, the five hundred largest U.S. firms constitute at least three-quarters of the American economy. They frequently have revenues that exceed the revenues of state governments and the gross domestic product (GDP) of many countries: The annual revenue of General Motors, for instance, is greater than the GDP of more than 148 countries, and that of Wal-Mart outweighs the combined GDP of all of sub-Saharan Africa.[13] Increasingly multinational in character, these giant corporations do business around the globe, disavowing allegiance to any particular nation. In fact, more than a quarter of the world's economic activity comes from the two hundred largest corporations.[14] Since the 1980s, wave after wave of corporate takeovers and mergers has further accelerated the trend toward oligopoly and ever greater economic concentration. The latest wave crested in 2007 with a record-setting $4.74 trillion worth of merger and acquisition deals worldwide, surpassing the previous year's record of $3.9 trillion.[15]

True, antitrust laws have sometimes fostered competition and broken up monopolies, as in the cases of such corporate behemoths as Standard Oil and AT&T. More recently, the government went after Microsoft for "exclusionary and predatory" businesses practices. On the whole, however, such actions have proved ineffectual in halting the concentration of economic power. Because of their sway over the market and their political clout, the gigantic corporations that we know today have so altered the face of capitalism that Adam Smith would have trouble recognizing it. As a result, in terms of competition our present-day economic system differs significantly from the textbook model of capitalism. One expert puts it this way:

> In surveying the American business system it is obvious that competition still exists; however, it is not a perfect competition. Often it is not price competition at all. With the possible exception of some farm markets where there are still large numbers of producers of similar and undifferentiated products (wheat, for instance), virtually every producer of goods and services has some control over price. The degree of control varies from industry to industry and between firms within an industry. Nevertheless, it does exist and it amounts to an important modification in our model of a free-enterprise economy.[16]

These days, in fact, some of the most vigorous corporate competition occurs not in the marketplace but in Washington, D.C., where companies jockey for competitive advantage by getting Congress to pass laws that help them and hold back their rivals.[17] More than five hundred American companies now maintain permanent offices there, employing sixty-one thousand lobbyists.[18] And that doesn't include corporate-sponsored foundations, centers, and institutes that also try to steer public policy in profitable, industry-friendly directions. In this respect, the pharmaceutical industry is a leader. In a recent six-year period, it spent $759 million to influence fourteen hundred congressional bills.[19]

Corporate Welfare Programs Protect Businesses

When the United States slapped tariffs ranging from 8 to 30 percent on imported steel in 2001, it was continuing a thirty-year tradition of cosseting the steel industry with various subsidies and protections that have cost the country a small fortune. The 2001 tariffs were held to be necessary because of a surge of imported steel, even though foreign steel imports had declined 27.5 percent in the preceding four years.[20] Since then, the U.S. steel industry has also received $17 billion in subsidies and continues to win favorable trade decisions that limit foreign imports—even as the demand for steel exceeds domestic supply and the steel companies ring up strong profits.[21] Unfortunately, what's good for one industry can be bad for the rest of the country. Businesses that use steel, for example, employ roughly forty times more people than do steel producers. According to the Institute for International Economics, until a ruling by the World Trade Organization led to the 2001 tariffs being canceled, between 45,000 and 75,000 jobs were lost because higher steel prices made U.S. steel-using industries less competitive.[22] Similarly, U.S. quotas on sugar imports in recent years have resulted in the domestic price of sugar being three-and-a-half times the world market price. As a result, to survive, American candy makers have been forced to move production to countries where sugar is cheaper, at the cost of 7,500 to 10,000 jobs.[23]

From 1995 to 2002, U.S. taxpayers spent more than $114 billion on subsidies to farmers. Congress then increased agricultural subsidies in 2002 to an estimated $180 billion to $190 billion over the next ten years. In a single year, U.S. spending on farm subsidies exceeds the gross domestic product of more than seventy nations.[24] Most of that money goes to the largest and wealthiest farmers; 10 percent of the recipients receive 65 percent of the loot.[25] When it comes to cotton, the disparity is even greater. Of the $19.1 billion that cotton growers received in a recent ten-year period, more than 80 percent went to only 10 percent of the recipients.[26] Meanwhile, more than two hundred different kinds of subsidies support America's ethanol program. The oil industry itself receives a 51-cent federal subsidy for each gallon of ethanol it mixes with gasoline, and there is a 54-cent tariff on each gallon of imported ethanol.[27] Subsidies for farmers and tariffs on steel, sugar, and ethanol are only the most blatant examples of the way **corporate welfare** assists business and protects it from competition. Thanks to duties, fees, and restrictions on imported products, American consumers pay far more for goods than they otherwise would—quotas imposed in 2004 on Chinese clothing are a case in point. And that, of course, is in addition to what corporate subsidies cost consumers as taxpayers.

Every year the federal government doles out billions of dollars to private business in direct subsidy programs. For example, the U.S. Agriculture Department's Market Access Program spends millions funding both generic and brand-name advertising abroad for American agricultural products,[28] and the U.S. Forest Service builds roads and subsidizes logging in national forests for the benefit of private timber companies.[29] The Foreign Military Financing Program assists foreign countries to purchase U.S. military products—to the tune of around $3.3 billion a year. The U.S. Department of Commerce's Advanced Technology Program supports high-tech research. In practice, this has meant payments of $14.5 million to General Electric, $34 million to AT&T, and a whopping $50.9 million to Boeing.[30] Other government-sponsored corporate welfare programs include the Export Enhancement Program, the

Export-Import Bank, and the Overseas Private Investment Corporation. The latter two agencies provide loans and financial guarantees for corporate energy projects. Among the beneficiaries are Unocal, which was loaned $350 million to develop an oil and gas field in Indonesia, and ExxonMobil, which received $500 million in financing to build a pipeline in Cameroon.[31]

The list goes on and on.[32] Some put total federal spending for corporate welfare at over $167 billion a year, which is far more than combined state and federal spending on social welfare programs for the poor.[33] This figure doesn't take into account the tax breaks that corporations receive. The costs of these are difficult to calculate, but a 2008 government report revealed that during a seven-year period of soaring profits, 55 percent of large U.S. corporations had at least one year of paying no tax at all.[34] It's not surprising, then, that some American companies pay more in taxes to foreign governments than they do to their own government—in Exxon Mobil's case five times as much.[35]

State governments also pamper business with subsidies and protectionist restrictions on competition. It's impossible to put a price tag on these, but looking at the Internet alone, experts calculate that state impediments to buying and selling cost consumers $15 billion a year. For example, Georgia forbids the online sale of contact lenses, and Oklahoma the online sale of caskets. And all fifty states shield their car dealers from competition by prohibiting manufacturers from selling directly to consumers over the Internet.[36] In addition, cities and states frequently provide tax breaks to corporations to lure them to, or prevent them from leaving, the local area. These subsidies cost taxpayers $50 billion a year, but for many reasons, they rarely pay off in jobs or higher overall tax revenues.[37]

As staggering as corporate welfare already is, it was taken to a whole new level in 2008 by the federal government's $700 billion Troubled Assets Relief Program (TARP). Put together in response to the financial meltdown, TARP enabled the government to purchase nonliquid, difficult-to-value assets from banks and other financial institutions, in particular, so-called collaterized debt obligations, which had been hit hard by foreclosures caused by the real estate slump. The theory was that by authorizing the Treasury Department to buy these "troubled assets"—assets, that is, that the banks couldn't sell on the open market for the simple reason that no one was willing to buy them—TARP would increase the banks' liquidity and improve their balance sheets, thus stabilizing the financial system. In addition to "cash for trash," TARP provided funds for the government to purchase loans from and make direct equity investments in the banks themselves, and the Treasury Department was creative in finding ways to assist the banks outside the TARP framework at a potential cost to tax payers that is greater than TARP itself. Few doubt the necessity of something like TARP or of the Treasury Department's taking bold measures. Nevertheless, with few strings attached, and with most banks choosing to shore up their bottom line by sitting on the money (or using it for executive bonuses) rather than to help stimulate the economy by lending it out, the bailout represents an unprecedented expenditure of taxpayer money—for example, a $120 billion (not million) package of capital investment and financial guarantees to

Summary 4.7
Critics of capitalism also charge that competition is not what it's cracked up be to because (1) capitalism breeds oligopolies, (2) corporate welfare often shelters business from competition, and (3) competition is not a good thing.

Bank of America, and a $300 billion (not million) package to Citigroup—to save what had been some of the largest and wealthiest firms in the country, and their well-heeled managers, from the consequences of own greed, recklessness, and mismanagement.

Competition Is Not a Good

Because the profit motive governs capitalism, it should not be surprising that even those companies that preach the doctrine of free competition are willing to shelve it when collusion with other firms, or government tariffs and subsidies, make higher profits possible. How else to explain the fact that the United States forbids foreign companies from owning airlines in America and prevents foreign airlines from picking up passengers at more than one American city? In these ways, capitalism fails to live up to its own ideal. This was something that worried Adam Smith, who once wrote, "People of the same trade seldom meet together, even for merriment or diversion, but the conversation ends in a conspiracy against the public, or in some contrivance to raise prices."[38]

Unlike Adam Smith, however, some critics of capitalism repudiate competition as an ideal, arguing that it is neither beneficial in general nor desirable in itself. They point to empirical studies establishing that in business there is frequently a negative correlation between performance and individual competitiveness.[39] In other words, it is often cooperation, rather than competitiveness, that best enhances both individual and group achievement. According to Alfie Kohn, the reason is simple: "Trying to do well and trying to beat others are two different things."[40] Competition is an extrinsic motivator; not only does it not produce the kinds of results that flow from enjoying the activity itself, but also the use of extrinsic motivators can undermine intrinsic motivation and thus adversely affect performance in the long run. The unpleasantness of competition can also diminish people's performance.

The critics also contend that competition often precludes the more efficient use of resources that cooperation allows. When people work together, coordination of effort and an efficient division of labor are possible. By contrast, competition can inhibit economic coordination, cause needless duplication of services, retard the exchange of information, foster copious litigation, and lead to socially detrimental or counterproductive results such as business failures, mediocre products, unsafe working conditions, and environmental neglect. When presented with examples of the beneficial results of competition, the critics argue that on closer inspection the supposed advantages turn out to be short-lived, illusory, or isolated instances.

Critics of competition contend that cooperation leads to better individual and group performance.

Critics also content that cooperation is more efficient than competition.

Exploitation and Alienation

Karl Marx argued that as the means of production become concentrated in the hands of the few, the balance of power between capitalists (bourgeoisie) and laborers (proletariat) tips further in favor of the bourgeoisie. Because workers have nothing to sell but their labor, said Marx, the bourgeoisie is able to exploit them by paying them less than the true value created by their labor. In fact, Marx thought, it is only through such **exploitation** that capitalists are able to make a profit and increase their capital. And the more capital they accumulate, the more they can exploit workers. Marx predicted that eventually workers would revolt. Unwilling to be exploited further, they would rise and overthrow their oppressors and set up an economic system that would truly benefit all.

The development of capitalist systems since Marx's time belies his forecast. Legal, political, and economic changes have tempered many of the greedy, exploitative dispositions of early capitalism. The twentieth century witnessed legislation curbing egregious worker abuse, guaranteeing a minimum wage, and ensuring a safer and more healthful work environment. The emergence of labor unions and their subsequent victories significantly enlarged the worker's share of the economic pie. Indeed, many of the specific measures proposed by Marx and his collaborator Friedrich Engels in the *Communist Manifesto* (1848) have been implemented in capitalist countries: a program of graduated income tax, free education for all children in public schools, investiture of significant economic control in the state, and so on.

Still, many would say that although democratic institutions may have curbed the excesses of capitalism, they can do nothing to prevent the alienation of workers that results from having to do unfulfilling work. Again, because of the unequal positions of capitalist and worker, laborers must work for someone else—they must do work imposed on them as a means of satisfying the needs of others. As a result, they inevitably come to feel exploited and debased. And this is true, critics of capitalism claim, not just of manual laborers but also of white-collar workers, many of whom identify with the cubicle dwellers of the cartoon strip *Dilbert*.

But what about workers who are paid handsomely for their efforts? They, too, said Marx, remain alienated, for as the fruits of their labor are enjoyed by someone else, their work ultimately proves meaningless to them. The following selection from Marx's "Economic and Philosophic Manuscripts" (1844) summarizes his notion of **alienation** as the separation of individuals from the objects they create, which in turn results in one's separation from other people, from oneself, and ultimately from one's human nature:

> The worker is related to the *product of his labor* as to an *alien* object. For it is clear … that the more the worker expends himself in work the more powerful becomes the world of objects which he creates in face of himself, the poorer he becomes in his inner life, and the less he belongs to himself…. The worker puts his life into the object, and his life then belongs no longer to himself but to the object…. What is embodied in the product of his labor is no longer his own. The greater this product is, therefore, the more he is diminished. The *alienation* of the worker in his product means not only that his labor becomes an object, assumes an *external* existence, but that it exists independently, *outside himself*, and alien to him, and that it stands opposed to him as an autonomous power….
>
> What constitutes the alienation of labor? First, that the work is *external* to the worker, that it is not part of his nature; and that, consequently, he does not fulfill himself in his work but denies himself…. His work is not voluntary but imposed, *forced labor*. It is not the satisfaction of a need, but only a *means* for satisfying other needs. Its alien character is clearly shown by the fact that as soon as there is no physical or other compulsion it is avoided like the plague. External labor, labor in which man alienates himself, is a labor of self-sacrifice…. Finally,

Marx argued that under capitalism workers are alienated in several different ways.

Summary 4.8
Karl Marx was an important nineteenth-century critic of capitalism. He argued that workers are exploited by capitalism and inevitably experience alienation.

the external character of work for the worker is shown by the fact that it is not his own work but work for someone else, that in work he does not belong to himself but to another person....

We have now considered the act of alienation of practical human activity, labor, from two aspects: (1) the relationship of the worker to the *product of labor* as an alien object which dominates him ... [and] (2) the relationship of labor to the *act of production* within *labor*. This is the relationship of the worker to his own activity as something alien and not belonging to him.... This is *self-alienation* as against the above-mentioned alienation of the *thing*.[41]

In Marx's view, when workers are alienated they cannot be truly free. They may have the political and social freedoms of speech, religion, and governance, but even with these rights, individuals still are not fully free. Freedom from government interference and persecution does not necessarily guarantee freedom from economic exploitation and alienation, and it is for this kind of freedom that Marx and Engels felt such passion.

Some would say that one need not wade through Marxist philosophy to get a feel for what Marx and others mean by worker alienation. Just talk to workers themselves, as writer Studs Terkel did. In different ways the hundreds of workers from diverse occupations whom Terkel interviewed speak of the same thing: dehumanization.

Mike Fitzgerald ... is a laborer in a steel mill. "I feel like the guys who built the pyramids. Somebody built 'em. Somebody built the Empire State Building, too. There's hard work behind it. I would like to see a building, say the Empire State, with a footwide strip from top to bottom and the name of every bricklayer on it, the name of every electrician. So when a guy walked by, he could take his son and say, 'See, that's me over there on the 45th floor. I put that steel beam in.' ... Everybody should have something to point to."

Sharon Atkins is 24 years old. She's been to college and acidly observes, "The first myth that blew up in my face is that a college education will get you a worthwhile job." For the last two years she's been a receptionist at an advertising agency. "I didn't look at myself as 'just a dumb broad' at the front desk, who took phone calls and messages. I thought I was something else. The office taught me differently."

... Harry Stallings, 27, is a spot welder on the assembly line at an auto plant. "They'll give better care to that machine than they will to you. If it breaks down, there's somebody out there to fix it right away. If I break down, I'm just pushed over to the other side till another man takes my place. The only thing the company has in mind is to keep that machine running. A man would be more eager to do a better job if he were given proper respect and the time to do it."[42]

TODAY'S ECONOMIC CHALLENGES

Capitalism faces a number of important critical questions, both theoretical and operational. These criticisms are a powerful challenge, especially to capitalism in its pure laissez-faire form. But, as we have seen, today's capitalism is a long way from the laissez-faire model. Corporate behemoths able to control markets and sway governments have replaced the small-scale entrepreneurs and free-wheeling competition of an earlier day. And governments in all capitalist countries actively intervene in the economic realm; they endeavor to assist or modify the so-called invisible hand; and over the years they have reformed or supplemented capitalism with programs intended to enhance the security of the workforce and increase the welfare of their citizens.

This reality complicates the debate over capitalism. Its defenders may be advocating either the pure laissez-faire ideal or the modified state welfare capitalism that we in fact have. Likewise, those who attack the laissez-faire ideal may do so on behalf of a modified, welfarist capitalism, or they may criticize both forms of capitalism and defend some kind of socialism, in which private property and the pursuit of profit are no longer governing economic principles. We thus have a three-way debate over the respective strengths and weaknesses of laissez-faire capitalism, state welfare capitalism, and socialism.

The rest of this chapter leaves this fundamental debate behind. Instead of looking at criticisms of capitalism in general and at issues relevant to any capitalist society, it examines some of the more specific socioeconomic challenges facing the United States today. These include (1) the decline of American manufacturing and the related problems posed by the outsourcing of jobs and the growing U.S. trade deficit; (2) business's obsession with short-term results; (3) and changing attitudes toward work.

The Decline of American Manufacturing

Historically, capitalists have made money by producing goods. Manufacturing was the backbone of the American economy and the basis of our prosperity. In industry after industry, however, U.S. companies have conceded manufacturing dominance to foreign competitors. Today, for example, one can't buy a television made in the United States, Wal-Mart employs more people than the Big Three automakers do, and more Americans work in government than in manufacturing. Whereas manufacturing accounted for 27 percent of GDP in the mid-1960s, it has fallen to about half that,[43] and for the first time since the Industrial Revolution, manufacturing employs less than 10 percent of the American workforce.[44]

Since the 1980s, many U.S. manufacturers have been closing up shop or curtailing their operations and becoming marketing organizations for other producers, usually foreign. The result is the evolution of a new kind of company: manufacturers that do little or no manufacturing. They may perform a host of profit-making functions—from design to distribution—but they lack their own production base. Instead, they **outsource**, buying parts or whole products from other producers, both at home and abroad.[45] The traditional vertical structure of manufacturing, in which the manufacturer makes nearly all crucial parts, is thereby replaced by a network of small operators. Companies that in years past were identified with making goods of all sorts now are likely to produce only the package and the label. In contrast to traditional manufacturers, they have become, in current business jargon, **hollow corporations**.

Proponents of the new system describe it as flexible and efficient, a logical outcome of the drive to lower the costs of doing business. But critics worry whether the United States can prosper without a strong manufacturing base. As Tsutomu Ohshima, a senior manufacturing director of Toyota

Manufacturing has declined in the United States as American companies have conceded manufacturing dominance to foreign competitors.

Motor Corporation, puts it: "You can't survive with just a service industry."[46] In wages, productivity, and innovation, the service sector fails to compare with basic industry. Manufacturing jobs generate significantly more goods and services from other industries than do service jobs, and three times as many additional employment opportunities.[47] Because the rate of technical change is higher in manufacturing than in other sectors, it's hard to imagine the United States sustaining its technological leadership with a withered manufacturing sector.[48]

Outsourcing Jobs

As America's manufacturing base dwindles and American firms outsource more and more of their operations, over 1.3 million manufacturing jobs have moved abroad since 1992.[49] That's not surprising when a Barbie doll that retails in America for $9.99 costs only 35 cents for a Chinese factory to make, including the price of labor.[50] But it's no longer just blue-collar jobs that are disappearing. Many upscale, nonmanufacturing jobs also are migrating overseas. Engineers, financial analysts, computer technicians, and other white-collar workers living in countries such as Russia, India, and the Philippines now handle airline reservations, design chips, edit books, draw architectural blueprints, provide accounting services, process loans and insurance claims, and engage in research and development for American corporations.[51] With 54 percent of the 1,000 largest U.S. companies outsourcing or planning to outsource white-collar jobs, some experts predict that at least 300,000 white-collar jobs will flow overseas every year through 2015, for a total loss of 3.4 million jobs.[52] Because skilled, highly educated foreigners work for far less than do their American counterparts, outsourcing these jobs overseas makes U.S. firms leaner and more profitable. But can America lose these jobs and still prosper? That's the question that is worrying more and more people.

Most mainstream economists are upbeat. They believe that outsourcing jobs increases shareholder wealth and benefits consumers by keeping prices down and that as old jobs move overseas, the economy will create new ones at home—higher-level jobs that add greater product value than the lost jobs did. Although they can't predict the new industries and occupations that will emerge to replace the old ones, these economists are confident that it will happen. Even in this optimistic scenario, however, there are genuine human costs. Sometimes economists refer to this downside as "short-term friction," but of course that's not how it feels to those workers whose relatively high-paying jobs are outsourced. They still have bills and mortgages to pay. And there's no reason to suppose that they will be the ones who eventually fill the "replacement" positions that the economy will supposedly create. Moreover, if they remain unemployed, settle for lower-paid work, or retire early, their lowered incomes affect their families, communities, and local businesses. In this way, then, the welfare of some is being sacrificed for the greater good of society.

A minority of economists, however, are challenging the rosy assumption that, despite the costs, outsourcing benefits America overall.[53] Going back to the nineteenth-century economist David Ricardo, conventional economic theory has taught that a country should focus on producing for the world market those goods in which it has a **comparative advantage**—the goods that it can produce at a lower opportunity cost than other countries can (that is, that it can produce more cheaply relative to other goods than is the case in other countries).* If countries sell what they are comparatively better at producing and buy from other countries what those countries are comparatively better at producing, then free trade benefits everyone. But the situation changes, or so some economists are now arguing, if a country's competitive edge comes solely from cheaper labor, especially in a world in which advanced telecommunication makes it possible for brainpower to zip around the world. In this case, there's no identifiable point at which the outsourcing process should stop: Even the so-called replacement jobs will move overseas. In theory, of course, wages in countries such as China and India should eventually rise to the point where outsourcing provides no benefit to American firms. But it will be decades and decades before that happens, if it ever does, and in the meantime white-collar wages in the United States have a long way to fall. In addition, if cheaper white-collar labor slashes the prices of those exports in which the United States has a comparative advantage, that could hurt the economy overall. For these reasons, even Paul Samuelson, the dean of American economists, has acknowledged that "comparative advantage cannot be counted on to create ... net gains greater than net losses from trade."[54]

Summary 4.8
Our capitalist socio-economic system is facing a number of challenges. These include the decline of American manufacturing and the related problems of job outsourcing and a growing trade deficit. Economists disagree about whether outsourcing benefits America overall and about the risks posed by our foreign indebtedness.

As the United States continues to run an enormous trade deficit, its foreign borrowing keeps increasing—with risky consequences, according to some economists.

The U.S. Trade Deficit

For thirty-five years, the United States has been steadily losing its share of both foreign and domestic markets. The nation's huge balance-of-trade deficit is the most visible sign of this. After decades and decades of trade surpluses, the United States has posted a trade deficit every year since 1975. America today imports twice as much merchandise as it exports. Our relentlessly growing trade deficit is now over $700 billion annually, equivalent to almost 6 percent of GDP. With this deficit the country's reliance on foreign borrowing has increased, and foreign creditors now provide two-thirds of America's net domestic investment. Today we owe the rest of the world around $3 trillion (one-third of it to the Chinese)—twice what we owed in 2000.[55]

Some, economists believe that it is irrelevant that the United States buys more than it sells. Although we are now the world's largest debtor nation, they reason, we are still the world's largest and most important economy, so foreigners don't mind lending us money. Other economists, however, are worried by the country's consumption-happy ways. They fear that the United States is creating unsustainable global imbalances—imbalances which they see as the root cause of the global economic crisis.[56] In their view, unless both domestic savings and the production of tradable goods increase dramatically, these imbalances will go on causing economic pain at home and serious dislocations abroad.[57] Many economists also worry that its growing trade deficit makes the United States vulnerable to economic extortion. What happens,

---

* *Comparative* advantage does not mean *absolute* advantage. What Ricardo showed was that two countries can benefit from trade even if one is better (or more efficient) than the other at producing everything.

they ask, if foreigners choose to stop financing our debt? Finally, the trade deficit and our growing international debt have meant an enormous transfer of American assets into foreign hands. The rest of the world now owns significantly more of the United States than it owns of other countries—equivalent to more than 10 percent of the total combined value of the stock market and all residential real estate in the United States. And this gap expands every year as assets, dividends, and interest flow to foreign owners.[58]

Exclusive Focus on the Short Term

Many observers believe that American corporations are too focused on short-term performance.

Observers of the business scene have long charged that U.S. companies are preoccupied with short-term performance at the expense of long-term strategies. According to the critics, this **short-term focus** tends to make U.S. corporations unimaginative, inflexible, and ultimately uncompetitive. These business strategists urge U.S. companies to become more visionary—to define long-term goals and to be willing to stick to them even at the expense of short-term profit. Some businesspeople have accepted that advice, as evidenced by the willingness of Amazon and other dot-com companies to lose money for years as they attempt to build market share. Yet many American companies appear less willing than foreign rivals to gamble on long-term research and development or to sacrifice current profits for benefits ten or fifteen years into the future. By comparison with countries such as Germany and Japan, established U.S. corporations continue to be obsessed with their stock market performance and to govern themselves far more by short-term indicators such as share value and quarterly profits. As a result, they often sacrifice capital improvements or fail to make strategic investments.[59] And some worry that America may lose its technological edge.[60]

An exclusive focus on the short term can also encourage dubious business practices. As management consultants Adrian Slywotsky and Richard Wise write, "Many [American] companies with apparently strong growth records in recent years have achieved them through relatively short-term, unsustainable tactics—acquisitions, international expansion, price increases, or accounting gimmicks."[61] Indeed, many theorists blame the financial meltdown of 2008–9 on a short-term focus on profits that ignored long-term risks.[62]

An obsession with short-term performance can lead to fraudulent behavior.

Moreover, there's no question that corporate America's obsession with short-term performance—when coupled with what former Federal Reserve chairman Alan Greenspan famously called "infectious greed"[63]—has created a high-pressure economic environment conducive to fraudulent behavior. Since the exposure of criminal conduct at Enron in late 2001, a long list of companies—including Adelphia Communications, Computer Associates, Dynegy, Global Crossing, Qwest, Rite Aid, Tyco International, WorldCom, Xerox, and Fannie Mae, to name the best-known cases—have been found to have manipulated financial data or committed outright fraud so as to appear to meet their short-term financial goals. These and other revelations of unethical conduct, in turn, have weakened the trust necessary for the efficient functioning of our economic system. That is why President George W. Bush stated in 2002 that "America's greatest economic need is higher ethical standards." Although it's true, as he also said, that "in the long run, there's no capitalism without conscience; there is no wealth without character," Bush may have neglected the extent to which a relentless emphasis on short-term results pressures some of the nation's most prominent business leaders to do things they normally wouldn't do.[64] As one business ethicist writes:

> Managing a corporation with the single measure of share price is like flying a 747 for maximum speed. You can shake the thing apart in the process. It's like a farmer forcing more and more of a crop to grow, until the soil is depleted and nothing will grow. Or like an athlete using steroids to develop muscle mass, until the body's health is damaged.
>
> Enron's problem was not a lack of focus on shareholder value. The problem was a lack of accountability to anything except share value. This contributed to a mania, a detachment from reality. And it led to a culture of getting the numbers by any means necessary.[65]

Changing Attitudes toward Work

Some commentators believe that the socioeconomic problems facing us today include not only a shrunken manufacturing sector, outsourced jobs, a trade deficit, and a short-term performance mentality but also the challenge of coming to grips with people's changing attitudes toward government, social institutions, business, and work. And with regard to work in particular, there's little question that, in recent decades, people's ideas about its value and the role it should play in their lives have been evolving. The fabled American work ethic seems to be fading away. Or is it?

At first glance the answer would seem to be no. After all, Americans work a lot. In fact, per person they now work 20 percent more than they did in 1970, more than workers in any other highly industrialized country. By contrast, the Japanese work 17 percent less and the French 24 percent less than they used to.[66] But appearances can be deceptive.

The so-called **work ethic** values work for its own sake, seeing it as something necessary for every person. It also emphasizes the belief that hard work pays off in the end and is thus part and parcel of the American Dream. "If you work hard enough," the expression goes, "you'll make it." Today, however, only one in three people believes this, down from 60 percent in a 1960 survey.[67] In addition, some experts believe that as people become less optimistic about the future and begin to doubt that their efforts will pay off, they become less interested in work than in looking out for themselves. Paul Kostek, a career development expert, contends that "people more so than ever are looking out for themselves and focus on what they want out of their career as the old social contract is broken." "I see more of a 'me-first' attitude," adds management professor Abigail Hubbard.[68]

In addition, with increased education, people are rearranging their ideas about what's important and about what they want from life. The evidence can be seen in the workplace itself. For example, it is not uncommon for operative workers to balk at doing the monotonous tasks their ancestors once accepted, albeit grudgingly. Loyalty to employers seems on the decline, and loyalty to fellow workers seems on the rise. Turnover rates in many industries are enough to make discontinuity an expensive problem. Organizational

People's attitudes about work are changing, and some worry that the famous American work ethic is disappearing.

plans, schedules, and demands no longer carry the authoritative clout they once did; workers today often subordinate them to personal needs. Moreover, employee sabotage and violence, once unheard-of, occur frequently enough today to worry management.

According to an international survey about what matters most to different cultures, Americans place work eighth in importance behind values such as their children's education and a satisfactory love life. (In Japan, by contrast, work ranks second only to good health.)[69] Another survey reveals that more and more Americans—both men and women—are shelving job success to be with their families.[70] Although it is impossible to pin down workers' attitudes toward work today, basically they seem willing to work hard at tasks they find interesting and rewarding as long as they have the freedom to influence the nature of their jobs and pursue their own lifestyles. They have a growing expectation that work should provide self-respect, nonmaterial rewards, and substantial opportunities for personal growth. And they have a growing willingness to demand individual rights, justice, and equality on the job.

If industry is to improve productive capacity and be competitive, it must seriously confront these changing social attitudes. As Paul Bernstein argues, it is counterproductive to compare today's worker with an idealized worker of yesteryear. Rather, we must acknowledge that we have a new work ethic, which in Bernstein's words

is part and parcel of the individual desire for meaningful and challenging labor in which some autonomy is an integral feature. An increasingly professionalized work force will not accept a golden embrace unless it is accompanied by fulfilling jobs that have been designed for a labor force that sees work in relation to family, friends, leisure and self-development. Work, for most of us, continues as an important part of our lives, but only in relation to our total experience.[71]

Summary 4.10
An exclusive focus on short-term performance can prevent business from pursuing long-term goals and strategies, and it can encourage dubious, even fraudulent, business practices. People's changing attitudes toward work represent another challenge facing our socioeconomic system, according to some experts.

STUDY CORNER

Key Terms and Concepts

alienation	globalized capitalism	profit motive
capital	hollow corporations	short-term focus
capitalism	industrial capitalism	socialism
comparative advantage	invisible hand	state welfare capitalism
competition	laissez faire	work ethic
corporate welfare	mercantile capitalism	worker control socialism
exploitation	natural right to property	
financial capitalism	oligopolies	
	outsource	

Points to Review

- how capitalism, socialism, and worker control socialism differ
- the story of the Fugger dynasty
- five historical stages of capitalism and their characteristics
- four key features of capitalism

- criticisms of the natural-right-to-property argument for capitalism
- how the invisible hand guides self-interest in a socially beneficial direction
- responses to criticisms of capitalism because of inequality and poverty
- capitalism's questionable assumptions about human nature
- oligopolies and corporate welfare under capitalism
- why some critics reject competition as an ideal

- different ways workers are alienated, according to Marx
- the decline of American manufacturing, its manifestations and implications
- conflicting views of outsourcing
- why the trade deficit causes some economists to worry
- negative consequences of an exclusive focus on the short term
- changes in the work ethic

CASE **4.1**

Licensing and Laissez Faire

The United States is a capitalist country, and our system of medical care is, to a significant extent, organized for profit. True, many hospitals are nonprofit, but the same cannot be said of doctors, who, judged as a whole, form an extremely affluent and privileged occupational group.

Sometimes physicians themselves seem a little uncomfortable about the business aspect of their professional lives or worry that outsiders will misinterpret their attention to economic matters. For example, the professional journal *Medical Economics*, which discusses such pocketbook issues as malpractice insurance, taxes, fees, and money management ("Are You Overpaying Your Staff?" is a typical cover story), works hard at not being available to the general public. When a subscriber left his copy on a commercial airliner, another reader found it and sent the mailing label to the magazine; the magazine's editor sent a cautionary note to the subscriber. The editor advises readers to "do your part by restricting access to your personal copies of the magazine. Don't put them in the waiting room, don't leave them lying about in the examination rooms, and don't abandon them in public places."[72]

Medical Economics probably suspects that even in our capitalist society many people,

including probably most doctors, would not like to think of physicians simply as medical entrepreneurs who are in it for the money. And, indeed, many people here and many more in other countries criticize our medical system for being profit oriented. They think medical care should be based on need and that ability to pay should not affect the quality of medical treatment one receives. Interestingly, though, some people criticize medical practice in the United States as being insufficiently market oriented; prominent among them was the late Milton Friedman, a Nobel Prize–winning economist at the University of Chicago.

Friedman was a long-standing critic of occupational licensure in all fields. His reasoning is straightforward: Licensure—the requirement that one obtain a license from a recognized authority in order to engage in an occupation—restricts entry into the field. Licensure thus permits the occupational or professional group to enjoy a monopoly in the provision of services. In Friedman's view, this contravenes the principles of a free market to the disadvantage of us all.

Friedman had no objection to certification—that is, to public or private agencies certifying that an individual has certain skills. But he rejected the policy of preventing people who do not have such a certificate from practicing the occupation of their choice. Such a policy restricts freedom and keeps the price of the services in question artificially high. When one reads the long lists of occupations for which some states require a license—librarians, tree surgeons, pest controllers, well diggers, barbers, carpet installers, movie projectionists, florists, upholsterers, makeup artists, even potato growers, among many others[73]—Friedman's case gains plausibility. But Friedman pushed his argument to include all occupations and professions.

Does this mean we should let incompetent physicians practice? Friedman would say yes.[74] In his view the American Medical Association (AMA) is simply a trade union, though probably the strongest one in the United States. It keeps the wages of its members high by restricting the number of those who can practice medicine.

The AMA does this not only through licensure but also, even more effectively, through controlling the number of medical schools and the number of students admitted to them. Today, for instance, over 42,000 applicants vie every year for roughly 18,000 medical school vacancies. The medical profession, Friedman charged, limits entry into the field both by turning down applicants to medical school and by making standards for admission and licensure so difficult as to discourage many young people from ever trying to gain admission. And, in fact, fewer students apply to medical school these days than in the 1990s.

Viewed as a trade union, the AMA has been singularly effective. As recently as the 1920s, physicians were far down the list of professionals in terms of income; the average doctor made less than the average accountant. Today physicians constitute the profession that arguably has the highest status and the best pay in the country. The median income for primary-care physicians is $157,000. For general surgeons it is $265,000. And in certain specialties, it is a great deal higher. Cardiologists, pain specialists, radiologists, hand surgeons, and others often earn over half a million dollars a year.[75] American doctors earn far more than their foreign counterparts do, even in countries where average wages are similar to those in the United States. Still, the medical establishment remains worried. It believes that there are too many doctors in the United States, and that "this surplus breeds inefficiency and drives up costs."[76]

The economic logic behind this proposition is murky. An increase in the supply of barbers, plumbers, or taxi drivers does not drive up the cost of getting a haircut, having your pipes fixed, or taking a cab. Why should it be different with doctors? Critics of the medical profession believe that its real worry is the prospect of stabilizing or even declining incomes. In any case, the doctors have written two prescriptions.

The first is to reduce the number of medical students by closing some medical schools; the second is to make it more difficult for foreign doctors to practice in the United States. Although the medical establishment has often expressed concern about the quality of foreign medical training, today the worry is strictly a matter of quantity. "We've got to stop the pipeline of foreign medical graduates," says Dr. Ed O'Neil of the Center for the Health Professions at the University of California, San Francisco. "They are a big chunk of physician oversupply.... We're just trying to be rational."[77] As for homegrown doctors, Congress is following medical advice. To stem the supposed glut, it decided to pay hospitals around the country hundreds of millions of dollars to decrease the number of physicians they train. It turns out, however, that the United States has fewer doctors per 1,000 than do almost all European countries.[78] In fact, the United States is now predicted to have a shortage of between 85,000 and 200,000 physicians by 2020.[79]

Medical licensure restricts the freedom of people to practice medicine and prevents the public from buying the medical care it wants. Nonetheless, most people would probably defend the principle of licensure on the grounds that it raises the standards of competence and the quality of care. Friedman would contest this. By reducing the amount of care available, he contended, licensure also reduces the average quality of care people receive. (By analogy, suppose that automobile manufacturers were forbidden to sell any car that did not have the quality of a Mercedes-Benz. As a result, people who owned cars would have cars of higher average quality than they do now. But because fewer people could afford cars and more of them would, therefore, have to walk or ride bicycles, such a regulation would not raise the quality of transportation enjoyed by the average person.) Friedman charged, furthermore, that the monopoly created by the licensing of physicians has reduced the incentive for research, development, and experimentation, both in medicine and in the organization and provision of services.

Since Friedman initially presented his argument over forty years ago, some of the alternatives to traditional practice that he proposed have come to pass; prepaid services have emerged, and group and clinic-based practices are on the increase. But what about his main contention that instead of licensure we should allow the marketplace to sort out the competent from the incompetent providers of medical services?

Friedman's critics contend that even if the licensing of professionals "involves violating a moral rule" against restricting individuals' "freedom of opportunity," it is still immoral to allow an unqualified person to engage in potentially harmful activities without having subjected the person to adequate tests of competence.[80] Despite the appeal of Friedman's arguments on behalf of free choice, the danger still remains, they say, that people will be victimized by the incompetent.

Consider, for example, the quack remedies and treatments peddled to AIDS patients here and abroad. Bottles of processed pond scum and concoctions of herbs, injections of hydrogen peroxide or of cells from the glands of unborn calves, the eating of bee pollen and garlic, $800 pills containing substances from mice inoculated with the AIDS virus, and even whacking the thymus gland of patients to stimulate the body's immune system—all these are among the treatments that have been offered to desperate people by the unscrupulous and eccentric. Deregulation of the medical field seems most unlikely to diminish such exploitation.

Discussion Questions

1. What explains the fact that licenses are required for so many occupations? What do you see as the pros and cons of occupational licensure in general? Does it have benefits that Friedman overlooked?
2. Do you believe that licensure in medicine or any other field is desirable? In which fields and under what circumstances? What standards would you use to determine where licensure is needed?
3. Is occupational licensure consistent with the basic principles and values of capitalism? Is it a violation of the free-market ideal? How would you respond to the argument that licensure illegitimately restricts individual freedom to pursue a career or a trade?
4. Does licensure make the market work more or less effectively? Would you agree that as long as consumers are provided accurate information, they should be permitted to make their own choices with regard to the services and products they purchase—even when it comes to medical care? Or is licensing necessary to protect them from making incorrect choices?
5. Friedman and others view the AMA as a trade union, and they believe that the high incomes of doctors are due more to artificial restrictions on the free market than to

the inherent value of their services. Is this an accurate or fair picture of the medical profession?

6. Is licensing an all-or-nothing issue? Or is it possible that although only licensed professionals should be permitted to perform certain services, paraprofessionals and lay-persons could perform less expensively but equally competently other services now monopolized by licensed professionals?

CASE 4.2

An Internet Parasite

When you're cruising the web, do those little pop-up ads bother you? If so, one of the companies you have to thank is Gator Corp., an Internet advertising firm. It makes software that monitors what you do online and then displays those ads when you visit certain websites. Gator has cut deals with various software makers to have them include its software on their programs. As a result, millions of computer owners have Gator's software on their PCs. Gator also gives away software like "e-wallet," which helps you fill out forms on websites, but this free software comes with Gator's "adware" or "spyware" built in.[81]

Gator sells those pop-up ads to advertisers who want to reach people who visit certain websites but without paying the fees that the owners of those websites would charge. For example, with Gator adware on their computers, people visiting the Hertz website may be greeted by pop-up ads for rival car-rental companies. In an ad campaign for an automaker, Gator recently searched its database and found 1.3 million computers whose users had clicked through automotive websites to look at certain types of vehicles. It then sent ads to those computers, varying the message depending on whether the pattern of web visits suggested the person was close to making a purchase or was looking at competitors' cars.

Gator argues that its ads provide useful information for shoppers who want to compare prices and products. It labels what it does "behavioral marketing." Critics, however, call the company a "parasite" because it siphons ad money from websites that others have constructed. Not only does Gator need other people's websites to exist, but also its program threatens the existence of those sites by taking away some of the income they need to keep running. Critics accuse Gator of unfair competition, and several large American publishing companies with websites have filed suit against Gator to protect their online business interests. Ironically, one of the companies joining the lawsuit is the *New York Times*, which once used Gator's services to sell subscriptions to people who visited the websites of its competitors.

Although his employer is one of the companies suing Gator, *Wall Street Journal* columnist Lee Gomes worries that the publishers' lawsuit may impinge on your right to control what you do with your computer and to use it to interact with the Internet in the way you choose. "The publishers," he says, "seem to be saying that you should look at their websites only the way they say you should. They say you can't have someone else's pop-up ad on top of their sites." If the publishers win, he reasons, this will be another setback for the concept of "fair use"—the idea that people who use copyrighted material have certain rights, too (for example, to record a copyrighted television program for their own use later).

Instead, Gomes thinks the publishers should try persuasion instead of litigation, free speech instead of legal coercion. In particular, the publishers claim that most Gator users don't realize that they have it on their computers or, at least, don't understand how it tracks their web-surfing habits. Gator denies this, but in any case the publishers could, Gomes says, inform their website visitors that there are programs like Ad-Aware that allow PC owners to check whether their computers have Gator or other sorts of adware on them and then, if they want, to delete those programs. The publishers could also point out that Microsoft, Yahoo, and others provide the software that Gator gives away, but without any Gator-like tracking built in. This, Gomes argues, is the right way to respond to the challenge of Gator—by giving computer users more choice, not less.

Fred von Lohman, spokesperson for the online advocacy group Electronic Frontiers Foundation, agrees. He supports Gator because, as he sees it, the issue is who controls your computer. "Is it you, or is it the company whose website you happen to be using?" Not everyone is persuaded, however. They see what Gator does as a clear violation of private property rights. It's analogous, they think, to sticking your message on a roadside sign or a billboard that someone else has paid for.

Update The publishers' lawsuit against Gator was settled out of court, although the terms of the settlement weren't disclosed to the public. But whatever its terms are, the settlement affects only the specific websites that were party to the suit. Since then, however, Gator has been trying to present a more respectable face to the world. It changed its name to Claria Corporation and is suing anyone who refers to its adware programs as spyware. Claria has helped Yahoo to develop new search vehicles, and Microsoft has considered taking over the company to utilize its technology for tracking the movements of people online as well as the consumer behavior data that Claria has accumulated. Meanwhile, Claria is not the only company with technology that messes with companies' websites. Google has added to its popular toolbar a new feature that inserts links right into the body of any web page. These links lead you to Google's own map site or to other sites Google selects. For example, if you look up a book on eCampus, a book-selling site, Google's "autolink" feature converts the ISBN numbers on the page into a link to Amazon, which wants you to buy the book from it instead of eCampus.

Discussion Questions

1. Is Gator a threat to the business interests of the publishers and other website owners? If so, do they have a legitimate complaint against Gator? Or is this a case of big companies' ganging up to thwart a smaller business rival?

2. Is Gator guilty of unfair competition? Has it violated the implicit rules of a free-market, capitalistic system? Is it a parasite that should be put out of business or a legitimate business operation?

3. What, if anything, should the publishers do about Gator? Is Gomes's "free-speech" strategy likely to work? How would you deal with Gator if you owned a popular, expensive-to-run website?

4. Does Gator's software violate the right to privacy of PC owners? Would outlawing Gator-like adware be a setback for the idea of "fair use"? Would it violate the rights of PC owners?

5. Is your view of this case affected by whether you personally find pop-up ads annoying?

CASE **4.3**

One Nation Under Wal-Mart

The huge corporations that produce our cars, appliances, computers, and other products—many of them household names like Nike, Coca-Cola, and Johnson & Johnson—are a familiar feature of contemporary capitalism. But Wal-Mart represents something new on the economic landscape. Now the world's largest company, Wal-Mart has achieved its corporate preeminence not in production but in retail. No other retailer, at any time or in any place, has ever come close to being as large and influential as Wal-Mart has become. After years of nonstop growth, there are now more than 4,750 Wal-Mart stores, visited every week by 138 million shoppers. And the company is opening more stores all the time as it moves beyond its stronghold in the rural South and Midwest and into urban America. In fact, 82 percent of American households purchase at least one item from Wal-Mart every year. As a result, the company's marketplace clout is enormous: It controls about 30 percent of the market in household staples; it sells 15 percent of all magazines and 15–20 percent of all CDs, videos, and DVDs; and it is expected to control soon over 35 percent of U.S. food sales. For most companies selling consumer products, sales from Wal-Mart represent a big hunk of their total business: 28 percent for Dial, 24 percent for Del Monte, and 23 for Revlon. Wal-Mart is also responsible for 10 percent of all goods imported to the United States from China.[82]

The good news for consumers is that Wal-Mart has risen to retail supremacy through the bargain prices it offers them. The retail giant can afford its low prices because of the cost efficiencies it has achieved and the pressure it puts on suppliers to lower their prices. And the larger the store gets, the more market clout it has and the further it can push down prices for its customers.

Everyone, of course, loves low prices, but not everyone, it seems, loves Wal-Mart. Why

not? Here are some of the charges that critics level against the retail behemoth:

- Wal-Mart's buying power and cost-saving efficiencies force local rivals out of business, thus costing jobs, disrupting local communities, and injuring established business districts. Typically, for example, within five years after a Wal-Mart supercenter opens, two other supermarkets close. Further, Wal-Mart often insists on tax breaks when it moves into a community, so its presence does little or nothing to increase local tax revenues.

- Wal-Mart is staunchly anti-union and pays low wages. Its labor costs are 20 percent lower than those of unionized supermarkets; its average sales clerk earns only $8.23 an hour, and most of its 1.4 million employees must survive without company health insurance. Small wonder that employee turnover is 44 percent per year. Moreover, because of its size, Wal-Mart exerts a downward pressure on retail wages and benefits throughout the country. Critics also charge that Wal-Mart's hard line on costs has forced many factories to move overseas, which sacrifices American jobs and holds wages down.

- Government welfare programs subsidize Wal-Mart's poverty-level wages. According to one congressional report, a two-hundred-employee store costs the government $42,000 a year in housing assistance, $108,000 in children's health care, and $125,000 in tax credits and deductions for low-income families. And internal Wal-Mart documents, leaked to the press, confirm that 46 percent of the children of Wal-Mart's 1.33 million workers are uninsured or on Medicaid. The document also discusses strategies for holding down spending on health care and other benefits—for example, by hiring more part-time workers and discouraging unhealthy people from working at the store by requiring all jobs to include some physical labor.

• As Wal-Mart grows and grows, and as its competitors fall by the wayside, consumer choices narrow, and the retail giant exerts ever greater power as a cultural censor. Wal-Mart, for example, won't carry music or computer games with mature ratings. As a result, the big music companies now supply the chain with sanitized versions of the explicit CDs that they provide to radio stations and that are sold elsewhere. The retailer has removed racy magazines such as *Maxim* and *FHM* from its racks, and it obscures the covers of *Glamour*, *Redbook*, and *Cosmopolitan* with binders. Although most locations offer inexpensive firearms, Wal-Mart won't sell Preven, a morning-after pill—the only one of the top ten drug chains to decline to do so.

For these reasons, Wal-Mart's expansion is frequently meeting determined local resistance, as concerned residents try to preserve their communities and their local stores and downtown shopping areas from disruption by Wal-Mart through petitions, political pressure, and zoning restrictions. As one economist remarks, for Wal-Mart "the biggest barrier to growth" is not competition from rivals like Target or Winn-Dixie stores but "opposition at the local level." As a result, Wal-Mart has begun responding to the criticism that it is a poor corporate citizen and miserly employer by improving employee health insurance coverage and adopting greener business practices. And even its usual critics applauded when the company responded rapidly to Hurricane Katrina, sending truckloads of water and food, much of it reaching residents before federal supplies did.

When it comes to Wal-Mart, Professor John E. Hoopes of Babson College encourages people to take a long-term view: "The history of the last 150 years in retailing would say that if you don't like Wal-Mart, be patient. There will be new models eventually that will do Wal-Mart in, and Wal-Mart won't see it coming." And, indeed, since 2005 the company's sales growth has slipped as the Internet has changed people's shopping habits and as other discounters have done a better job of attracting affluent consumers and providing higher quality and better service.

In the meantime, where you stand on Wal-Mart probably depends on where you sit, as Jeffrey Useem writes in *Fortune* magazine: "If you're a consumer, Wal-Mart is good for you. If you're a wage-earner, there's a good chance it's bad for you. If you're a Wal-Mart shareholder, you want the company to grow. If you're a citizen, you probably don't want it growing in your backyard. So, which one are you?"

Discussion Questions

1. Do you like Wal-Mart? Do you shop there? If so, how frequently? If not, why not?

2. Is there a Wal-Mart store in your area? If so, has it had any impact on your community or on the behavior of local consumers? If there's no store in your area, would you be in favor of Wal-Mart opening one? Explain why or why not.

3. Is Wal-Mart's rapid rise to retail dominance a positive or a negative development for our society? What does it tell us about capitalism, globalization, and the plight of workers?

4. Can a retailer ever become too large and too powerful?

5. Is opposition to Wal-Mart's expansion a legitimate part of the political process or is it unfair interference with our market system and a violation of the company's rights? Do opponents of Wal-Mart have any valid concerns?

CASE **4.4**

A New Work Ethic?

You would think that employees would do something if they discovered that a customer had died on the premises. But that's not necessarily so, according to the Associated Press, which reported that police discovered the body of a trucker in a tractor trailer rig that had sat—with its engine running—in the parking lot of a fast-food restaurant for nine days. Employees swept the parking lot around the truck but ignored the situation for over a week until the stench got so bad that someone finally called the police.

That lack of response doesn't surprise James Sheehy, a human resources manager in Houston, who spent his summer vacation working undercover at a fast-food restaurant owned by a relative.[83] Introduced to coworkers as a management trainee from another franchise location who was being brought in to learn the ropes, Sheehy was initially viewed with some suspicion, but by the third day the group had accepted him as just another employee. Sheehy started out as a maintenance person and gradually rotated through various cooking and cleaning assignments before ending up as a cashier behind the front counter.

Most of Sheehy's fellow employees were teenagers and college students who were home for the summer and earning additional spending money. Almost half came from upper-income families and the rest from middle-income neighborhoods. More than half were women, and a third were minorities. What Sheehy reports is a whole generation of workers with a frightening new work ethic: contempt for customers, indifference to quality and service, unrealistic expectations about the world of work, and a get-away-with-what-you-can attitude.

A recent survey shows that employee theft accounts for 50 percent more revenue loss for retailers than shoplifting.[84] Sheehy's experience was in line with this. He writes that the basic work ethic at his place of employment was a type of gamesmanship that focused on milking the place dry. Theft was rampant, and younger employees were subject to peer pressure to steal as a way of becoming part of the group. "It don't mean nothing," he says, was the basic rationale for dishonesty. "Getting on with getting mine" was another common phrase, as coworkers carefully avoided hard work or dragged out tasks like sweeping to avoid additional assignments.

All that customer service meant was getting rid of people as fast as possible and with the least possible effort. Sometimes, however, service was deliberately slowed or drive-through orders intentionally switched in order to cause customers to demand to see a manager. This was called "baiting the man," or purposely trying to provoke a response from management. In fact, the general attitude toward managers was one of disdain and contempt. In the eyes of the employees, supervisors were only paper-pushing functionaries who got in the way.

Sheehy's coworkers rejected the very idea of hard work and long hours. "Scamming" was their ideal. Treated as a kind of art form and as an accepted way of doing business, scamming meant taking shortcuts or getting something done without much effort, usually by having someone else do it. "You only put in the time and effort for the big score" is how one fellow worker characterized the work ethic he shared with his peers. "You got to just cruise through the job stuff and wait to make the big score," said another. "Then you can hustle. The office stuff is for buying time or paying for the groceries."

By contrast, they looked forward to working "at a real job where you don't have to put up with hassles." "Get out of school and you can leave this to the real dummies." "Get an office and a computer and a secretary and you can scam your way through anything." On the other hand, these young employees believed that most jobs were like the fast-food industry: automated, boring, undemanding and unsatisfying, and dominated by difficult people. Still, they dreamed of an action-packed business world, an image shaped by a culture of video games and action movies. The college students in particular, reports Sheehy, believed that a no-holds-barred, trample-over-anybody, get-what-you-want approach is the necessary and glamorous road to success.

Discussion Questions

1. How typical are the attitudes that Sheehy reports? Does his description of a new work ethic tally with your own experiences?

2. What are the implications for the future of American business of the work ethic Sheehy describes?

3. Some might discount Sheehy's experiences either as being the product of one particular industry or as simply reflecting the immaturity of young employees. Would you agree?

4. Is it reasonable to expect workers, especially in a capitalist society, to be more devoted to their jobs, more concerned with quality and customer service, than Sheehy's coworkers were? What explains employee theft?

5. In what ways does the culture of our capitalist society encourage attitudes like those Sheehy describes?

Corporations

Glowimages/Getty Images

Fifty years ago the vice president of Ford Motor Company described the modern business corporation as the dominant institution of American society. Today few observers would disagree. As one of them puts it, "The modern corporation is *the* central institution of contemporary society."[1] As an aggregate, corporations wield awesome economic clout, and the five hundred largest U.S. companies constitute at least three-quarters of the American economy. But the dominant role of corporations in our society extends well beyond that. Not only do they produce almost all the goods and services we buy, but also they and their ethos permeate everything from politics and communications to athletics and religion. And their influence is growing relentlessly around the world.

By any measure, the biggest corporations are colossi that dominate the earth. Many of them employ tens of thousands of people, and the largest have hundreds of thousands in their ranks. PepsiCo, for example, has about 116,000 employees worldwide, a figure that pales beside General Electric's approximately 316,000 and General Motors's 327,000—not to mention the 1.9 million people who work for Wal-Mart, the world's largest private-sector employer. And their revenues are dazzling. For example, Dell Computer takes in more than $61 billion a year, Procter & Gamble $76 billion, IBM $98 billion, AT&T $118 billion, and Ford $172 billion. Recently, Wal-Mart topped the list with an annual revenue of $378.9 billion. ExxonMobil came in second at $372 billion but earned $45.2 billion in profit—the most money ever earned by any company at any time anywhere. By comparison, Austria's gross domestic product (GDP) is approximately $323 billion, Chile's $145 billion, and New Zealand's $104 billion. The state of California, which has far and away the largest annual revenue of any U.S. state, makes less than half of what General Motors does. Kansas takes in only about $4.5 billion, and Vermont about a fifth of that.

And corporations are growing larger and wealthier every year. For example, in 1989 Time Inc. merged with Warner Communications to form Time Warner. Seven years later Time Warner combined with Turner Broadcasting. Then in January 2001, in a move that shook up Wall Street, Time Warner and America Online merged. At a stroke, the new company they created, initially called AOL Time Warner, then simply Time Warner, was valued at $350 billion. What does $350 billion mean? It is equivalent to the GDP of Saudi Arabia and is more than the combined GDPs of Hungary, the Czech Republic, Bulgaria, Serbia, Bolivia, and Kenya. And it is more than the industrial output of the United Kingdom or the manufacturing output of China.

Like any other modern corporation, in principle Time Warner is a three-part organization, made up of (1) **stockholders**, who provide the capital, own the corporation, and enjoy liability limited to the amount of their investments; (2) managers, who run the business operations; and (3) employees, who produce the goods and services. However, a corporate giant such as Time Warner, ExxonMobil, or Citigroup is less like a single company and more like "a fabulously wealthy investment club with a limited portfolio." Such companies invest in subsidiaries, whose heads, writes business analyst Anthony J. Parisi, "oversee their territories like provincial governors, sovereigns in their own lands but with an authority stemming from the power center.... The management committee exacts its tribute (the affiliate's profits from current operations) and issues doles (the money needed to sustain and expand those operations)."[2] In the best-run organizations the management system is highly structured and impersonal. It provides the corporation's overall framework, the formal chain of command, which ensures that the company's profit objectives are pursued.

The emergence of corporate behemoths like ChevronTexaco or Bank of America is one of the more intriguing chapters in the evolution of capitalism. Certainly the political theory of John Locke and the economic theory of Adam Smith admitted no such conglomerates of capital as those that originated in the nineteenth century—in their day hardly any private firms had more than a handful of or employees—and that today dominate America's, even the world's, economic, political, and social life. This book isn't the place to analyze why a people committed to an individualistic social philosophy and a free-competition market economy allowed vast oligopolistic organizations to develop. Rather, the concern here is with the problem of applying moral standards to corporate organizations and with understanding their social responsibilities. After a brief review of the history of the corporation, this chapter looks at the following specific topics:

1. The debate over whether corporations are moral agents and can be meaningfully said to have moral responsibilities
2. The controversy between the narrow view and the broader view of corporate responsibility

3. Three key arguments in this debate: the invisible-hand argument, the let-government-do-it argument, and the business-can't-handle-it argument

4. The importance of institutionalizing ethics within corporations and how this may be done

---

THE LIMITED-LIABILITY COMPANY

If you ask a lawyer for a definition of **corporation**, you will probably get something like the following: A corporation is a thing that can endure beyond the natural lives of its members and that has incorporators who may sue and be sued as a unit and who are able to consign part of their property to the corporation for ventures of limited liability. **Limited liability** is a key feature of the modern corporation. The members of the corporation—unlike the members of a partnership or the proprietors of a business—are financially liable for the debts of the organization only up to the extent of their investments.

In addition to the limited liability of their members, corporations differ from partnerships in two ways.

Limited-liability companies—corporations—differ from partnerships and other forms of business association in two other ways as well. *First,* a corporation is not formed simply by an agreement entered into among its first members. An organization becomes incorporated by being publicly registered or in some other way having its existence officially acknowledged by the law. *Second,* unlike a partner, who is automatically entitled to his or her share of the profits of a partnership as soon as they are ascertained, the shareholder in a corporation is entitled to a dividend from the company's profits only when it has been "declared." Under U.S. law, dividends are usually declared by the directors of a corporation.

When we think of corporations, we naturally think of giants such as General Motors, ExxonMobil, Microsoft, and Wal-Mart, which exert enormous influence over our economy and society. But the local independently owned convenience store may be a corporation, and historically the concept of a corporation has been broad enough to encompass churches, trade guilds, and local governments. Corporations may be either *for-profit* or *nonprofit* organizations. Princeton University, for example, is a nonprofit corporation. Safeway, Lockheed Martin, McDonald's, and other companies, by contrast, aim to make money for shareholders. Corporations may be privately owned or owned (wholly or in part) by the government. Almost all U.S. corporations are privately owned; but Renault of France, for example, was once a publicly owned, for-profit corporation. A small group of investors may own all the outstanding shares of a privately owned, profit-making corporation (a **privately held company**). Mars, Bechtel, Chrysler, and Enterprise Rent-A-Car are examples. Or stock may be traded among the general public (a **publicly held company**). All companies whose stocks are listed on the New York and other stock exchanges are publicly held corporations.

In 1911 Nicholas Murray Butler, president of Columbia University, declared that "the limited liability corporation is the single greatest discovery

Summary 5.1
Corporations are legal entities, with legal rights and responsibilities similar but not identical to those enjoyed by individuals. Business corporations are limited-liability companies—that is, their owners or stock-holders are liable for corporate debts only up to the extent of their investments.

of modern times.... Even steam and electricity are far less important ... and ... would be reduced to comparative impotence without it."[3] Many business theorists and historians still agree with that assessment. But several stages mark the evolution of the corporation. The corporate form itself developed during the early Middle Ages, and the first corporations were towns, universities, and ecclesiastical orders. They were chartered by government and regulated by public statute. As corporate bodies, they existed independently of the particular individuals who constituted their membership at any given time. By the fifteenth century, the courts of England had evolved the principle of limited liability—thus setting limits, for example, on how much an alderman of the Liverpool Corporation might be required to pay if the city went bankrupt. During the medieval period, however, the law did not grant corporate status to purely profit-making associations. In those days, something besides economic self-interest had to be seen as uniting the members of the corporation: religion, a trade, shared political responsibilities.

This state of affairs changed during the Elizabethan era, as the incorporation of business enterprises began. European entrepreneurs were busy organizing trading voyages to the East and to North America. The East India Company, which epitomizes the great trading companies of this period, was formed in 1600, when Queen Elizabeth I granted to a group of merchants the right to be "one body corporate" and bestowed on it a trading monopoly to the East Indies. In the following decades, numerous other incorporated firms were granted trading monopolies and colonial charters. Much of North America's settlement, in fact, was initially underwritten as a business venture.

Although the earliest corporations typically held special trading rights from the government, their members did not pool capital. Rather, they individually financed voyages using the corporate name and absorbed the loss individually if a vessel sank or was robbed by pirates. But as ships became larger and more expensive, no single buyer could afford to purchase and outfit one, and the loss of a ship would have been ruinous to any one individual. The solution was to pool capital and share liability. Thus emerged the prototype of today's corporations.[4]

The first instance of the corporate organization of a manufacturing enterprise in the United States occurred in 1813, but only after the Civil War did the movement toward the corporate organization of business gain steam.[5] The loosening of government restrictions on corporate chartering procedures in the nineteenth century marks this final stage of corporate evolution. Until the mid-1800s, prospective corporations had to apply for charters—in England to the Crown, and in the United States to state government. Charters were custom-crafted; each one was an individual act of legislation. Charters were often burdened with precise terms or limited to specific business objectives, all in the name of promoting the public good. (For example, a corporation might be chartered for the sole purpose of shipping freight between two cities, or a charter might designate where the new corporation could begin and end its proposed railroad line.) Critics of the

In the nineteenth century, government loosened restrictions on corporate charters.

incorporation system charged that it fostered favoritism, corruption, and unfair monopolies. Gradually, the old system of incorporation was replaced by the system we know today, in which corporate status is granted essentially to any organization that fills out the forms and pays the fees.

Lurking behind this change were two important theoretical shifts. *First,* underlying the old system was the mercantilist idea that a corporation's activities should advance some specific public purpose. But Adam Smith and, following him, Alexander Hamilton, the first U.S. secretary of the treasury, challenged the desirability of a direct tie between business enterprise and public policy. They believed that businesspeople should be encouraged to explore their own avenues of enterprise, and that the "invisible hand" of the market would direct their activities in a socially beneficial direction more effectively than any public official could.

Second, when nineteenth-century reformers argued for changes in incorporation procedures, they talked not only about government favoritism and the advantages of a laissez-faire approach but also about the principle of a corporation's right to exist.[6] Any petitioning body with the minimal qualifications, they asserted, has the right to receive a corporate charter. By contrast, the early Crown-chartered corporations were clearly creations of the state, in accordance with the legal-political doctrine that corporate status was a privilege bestowed by the state as it saw fit. The reformers, however, argued that incorporation is a by-product of the people's right of association, not a gift from the state.

Even though the right of association supports relaxed incorporation procedures, the state must still incorporate companies and guarantee their legal status. Corporations must be recognized by the law as a single agent in order to enjoy their rights and privileges. To a large extent, then, the corporation remains, as Chief Justice John Marshall put it in 1819, "an artificial being, invisible, intangible, and existing only in the contemplation of the law."[7]

Summary 5.2
What we know as the modern business corporation has evolved over several centuries, and incorporation is no longer the special privilege it once was.

Corporations are clearly legal agents. They can enter into contracts, own property, and sue and be sued. But are they also moral agents? And whereas corporations have definite legal responsibilities, what, if any, social and moral responsibilities do they have?

CORPORATE MORAL AGENCY

Some time ago, the citizens of Massachusetts were asked in a referendum whether they wanted to amend the state constitution to allow the legislature to enact a graduated personal income tax. Predictably enough, they said no.

What made this otherwise unremarkable exercise of the initiative process noteworthy was that the First National Bank of Boston and four other businesses in the state wanted to spend money to express opposition to the referendum. The Massachusetts Supreme Judicial Court said they could not, that banks and business corporations were prohibited by law from spending corporate funds to publicize political views that did not materially affect their property, business, or assets. However, the U.S. Supreme Court in a 5-to-4 decision (*First National Bank of Boston v. Bellotti*)[8] struck down the Massachusetts court's decision and thereby defined the free-speech rights of corporations for the first time.

Writing for the majority, Justice Lewis Powell said: "If the speakers here were not corporations, no one would suggest that the state could silence their proposed speech. It is the type of speech indispensable to decision making in a democracy, and this is no less true because the speech comes from a corporation rather than from an individual." In a dissenting opinion, however, Justice Byron R. White said that states should be permitted to distinguish between individuals and corporations. "Ideas which were not a product of individual choice," said White, "are entitled to less First Amendment protection."

Some view the *Bellotti* decision as a blow to consumers and citizens, but there was legal precedent for the ruling because prior Supreme Court decisions had extended other constitutional rights to corporations—for example, to due process (Fourteenth Amendment), against unreasonable searches and seizures (Fourth Amendment), to a jury trial (Seventh Amendment), to freedom from double jeopardy (Fifth Amendment), and to compensation for government takings (Fifth Amendment). Still, in holding that the First Amendment applies not just to individual citizens but also to business corporations, the Court further blurred the distinction between real persons and artificial or legal persons. However, in doing so, it has laid a basis for claiming not only that corporations enjoy the same moral and political rights as citizens but also that, because of this, corporations bear the same responsibilities that individual human beings do. In other words, if corporations have the same rights that moral agents have, then, like individuals, they can and should be held morally responsible for their actions.

The problem, of course, is that they are not human beings. Or, to quote Lord Thurlow, an eighteenth-century lawyer, how can you "expect a corporation to have a conscience, when it has no soul to be damned and no body to be kicked?"[9] But although corporations are not people, they are collective entities that in some sense really exist, and they have an identity above and beyond the people whom they comprise at any given time. And the law recognizes them as "persons." Do they have moral obligations just as individual human beings do? Can they be held morally responsible, not just legally liable, for the things they do? The answer to these questions hangs on another question, namely: Does it make sense to view corporations as moral agents—that is, as entities capable of making moral decisions? If so, then corporations can be held morally responsible for their actions. They—and not just the individual human beings who make them up—can be seen as having moral obligations and as being blameworthy for failing to meet those obligations. They can, accordingly, be praised or blamed, even punished, for the decisions they make and the actions and policies they undertake.

The task of determining whether corporations can make moral decisions is anything but simple. Immediately, we must ponder whether it makes sense to say that any entity other than an individual person can make decisions in the first place, moral or otherwise.

*Cases like *Bellotti* have blurred the distinction between individuals and corporations.*

If corporations are moral agents, then they can be seen as having obligations and as being morally responsible for their actions, just as individuals are.

Can Corporations Make Moral Decisions?

Corporate internal decision (CID) structures amount to established procedures for accomplishing specific goals. For example, consider ExxonMobil's system, as depicted by Anthony J. Parisi:

> All through the Exxon system, checks and balances are built in. Each fall, the presidents of the 13 affiliates take their plan for the coming year and beyond to New York for review at a meeting with the management committee and the staff vice presidents. The goal is to get a perfect corporate fit. Some imaginary examples: The committee might decide that Exxon is becoming too concentrated in Australia and recommend that Esso Eastern move more slowly on that continent. Or it might conclude that if the affiliates were to build all the refineries they are proposing, they would create more capacity than the company could profitably use. One of the affiliates would be asked to hold off, even though, from its particular point of view, a new refinery was needed to serve its market.[10]

The implication here is that any decisions coming out of ExxonMobil's annual sessions are formed and shaped to effect corporate goals, "to get a perfect corporate fit." Metaphorically, all data pass through the filter of corporate procedures and objectives. The remaining distillation constitutes the decision. Certainly the participants actively engage in decision making. But in addition to individual persons, the other major component of corporate decision making consists of the framework in which policies and activities are determined.

The CID structure lays out lines of authority and stipulates under what conditions personal actions become official corporate actions. Some philosophers have compared the corporation to a machine or have argued that because of its structure it is bound to pursue its profit goals single-mindedly. As a result, they claim, it is a mistake to see a corporation as being morally responsible or to expect it to display such moral characteristics as honesty, considerateness, and sympathy. Only the individuals within a corporation can act morally or immorally; only they can be held responsible for what it does.

Others have argued in support of **corporate moral agency**. The CID structure, like an individual person, collects data about the impact of its actions. It monitors work conditions, employee efficiency and productivity, and environmental impacts. Professors Kenneth E. Goodpaster and John B. Matthews argue that as a result, there is no reason a corporation cannot show the same kind of rationality and respect for persons that individual human beings can. By analogy, they contend, it makes just as much sense to speak of corporate moral responsibility as it does to speak of individual moral responsibility.[11] Thomas Donaldson agrees. He argues that a corporation can be a moral agent if moral reasons enter into its decision making and if its decision-making process controls not only the company's actions but also its structure of policies and rules.[12]

Philosopher Peter French arrives at the same conclusion in a slightly different way.[13] The CID structure, says French, in effect absorbs the intentions and acts of individual persons into a "corporate decision." Perhaps no corporate official intended the course or objective charted by the CID structure,

Summary 5.3
The question of corporate moral agency is whether a corporation is the kind of entity that can make moral decisions and bear moral responsibility for its actions. Philosophers disagree about whether corporate internal decision (CID) structures make it reasonable to see corporations as morally responsible agents.

but, French contends, the corporation did. And he believes that these corporate intentions are enough to make corporate acts "intentional" and thus make corporations "morally responsible." Professor of philosophy Manuel Velasquez demurs. An act is intentional, says Velasquez, only if the entity that formed the intention brings about the act through its bodily movements. But it is only the people who make up the corporation who carry out the acts attributed to it. Velasquez concludes that only corporate members, not the corporation itself, can be held morally responsible.[14]

The debate over corporate moral agency bears on the question of **corporate punishment.** Whether or not corporations are moral actors, the law can fine them, monitor and regulate their activities, and require the people who run them to do one thing or another. But one can talk in a literal sense about "punishing" corporations only if they are entities or "persons" capable of making moral decisions. And even if they are, not all the usual goals and methods of punishment make sense when applied to corporations. If corporations are moral agents, then the law can deter them with the threat of punishment, and it can force them to make restitution. Punishment can, perhaps, even rehabilitate a corporation, viewed as a moral agent. Retribution, as a goal of punishment, however, seems to have little application to corporations. And obviously corporations cannot be jailed for breaking the law. Even imposing fines on them can be problematic. Financial penalties stiff enough to have an impact can easily injure innocent parties, for example, if they lead to layoffs, plant closures, or higher prices for consumers.

Vanishing Individual Responsibility

Some might argue that regardless of whether corporations as artificial entities can properly be held morally responsible, the nature and structure of a modern corporate organization allows nearly everyone in it to share moral accountability for what it does. In practice, however, this **diffusion of responsibility** can mean that no particular person or persons are held morally responsible. For example, does responsibility for an injury caused by a defective product fall on the shoulders of the worker who last handled the product, the foreman overseeing the running of the assembly line, the factory supervisor, the quality control team, the engineers who designed and tested the equipment, the regional managers who decided to produce the item, or the company's CEO, whose office is in another city? Indeed, each of these individuals may have been only following established procedures and decision-making guidelines. Inside a corporation it may often be difficult, even impossible, to assign responsibility for a particular outcome to any single individual because so many different people, acting within a given CID framework, contributed to it in small ways.

Assigning individual responsibility for corporate outcomes is difficult.

This masking of moral accountability may not seem so surprising. After all, in situations that don't involve corporations, assigning praise and blame can also be problematic. But it raises the troubling possibility that the size and impersonal bureaucratic structure of the corporation may so envelop its members that it becomes vacuous to speak of individual moral agency. This, in turn, raises the specter of actions without actors in any moral sense—of defective products, broken laws, or flouted contracts, without any morally responsible parties.

This raises the possibility of actions for which no one is responsible. There are two ways to escape this conclusion.

There are two ways to escape this uncomfortable conclusion. *One* is to attribute moral agency to corporations just as we do to individual persons. *The other,* not necessarily incompatible with the first, is to realize that these days too many people are willing, even eager, to duck personal responsibility—"it's not my job," "there's nothing I can do about it," "I was just following procedure"—by submerging it in the protoplasmic CID structures of the modern corporation. Perhaps until CID structures are reconstituted to deal explicitly with non-economic matters, we can expect more of the same evasion of personal responsibility.

The issue of corporate moral agency undoubtedly will continue to exercise scholars. Meanwhile, the inescapable fact is that corporations are increasingly being accorded the status of biological persons, with all the rights and responsibilities implied by that status. Before it was gobbled up by another corporation, Continental Oil Company expressed in an in-house booklet the public perception and its implications as follows:

Summary 5.4
Individual responsibility can tend to vanish inside large, impersonal corporations. One response is to attribute moral agency to the corporation itself. Another is to refuse to let individuals duck their personal responsibility.

> No one can deny that in the public's mind a corporation can break the law and be guilty of unethical and amoral conduct. Events … such as corporate violation of federal laws and failure of full disclosure [have] confirmed that both our government and our citizenry expect *corporations* to act lawfully, ethically, and responsibly.
>
> Perhaps it is then appropriate in today's context to think of Conoco as a *living corporation*; a sentient being whose conduct and personality are the collective effort and responsibility of its employees, officers, directors, and shareholders.[15]

Today many companies and many of the people inside them accept without hesitation the idea that corporations are moral agents with genuinely moral, not just legal, responsibilities.

This point was illustrated when Colonial Pipeline of Atlanta published full-page advertisements in several newspapers headlined "We Apologize." The company used the ads to take responsibility for having spilled oil into the Reedy River of South Carolina three years before. True, the ads were part of a plea agreement with the U.S. Justice Department for having violated the Clean Water Act (the company also agreed to pay a $7 million fine). Yet the company's words had ethical overtones. As Laura Nash of Harvard Divinity School comments, they put "moral emotion into what is essentially a legal statement" because "the word 'apologize' … admits a sense of shame and humility."[16] Shame and humility were evident, too, when in 2004 the world saw photographs of Charles Prince, the chief executive of Citigroup, and Douglas Petersen, Citibank Japan CEO, bowing their heads at a press conference in Tokyo in a public act of remorse for Citigroup's illegal actions in Japan.

Assuming it makes sense to talk of the moral responsibilities of corporations, what are they?

If, then, it makes sense to talk about the social and moral responsibilities of corporations, either in a literal sense or as a shorthand way of referring to the obligations of the individuals that make up the corporation, what are these responsibilities?

RIVAL VIEWS OF CORPORATE RESPONSIBILITY

Summary 5.5
Despite continuing controversy over the concept of corporate moral agency, the courts and the general public find the notion of corporate responsibility useful and intelligible— either in a literal sense or as short-hand for the moral obligations of individuals in the corporation.

In 1963 Tennessee Iron & Steel, a subsidiary of United States Steel, was by far the largest employer, purchaser, and taxpayer in Birmingham, Alabama. In the same city at the same time, racial tensions exploded in the bombing of an African American church, killing four black children. The ugly incident led some to blame U.S. Steel for not doing more to improve race relations, but Roger Blough, chairman of U.S. Steel, defended his company:

> I do not either believe that it would be a wise thing for United States Steel to be other than a good citizen in a community, or to attempt to have its ideas of what is right for the community enforced upon the community by some sort of economic means....
>
> When we as individuals are citizens in a community we can exercise what small influence we may have as citizens, but for a corporation to attempt to exert any kind of economic compulsion to achieve a particular end in the racial area seems to me quite beyond what a corporation can do.[17]

Not long afterward, Sol M. Linowitz, chairman of the board of Xerox Corporation, declared in an address to the National Industrial Conference Board: "To realize its full promise in the world of tomorrow, American business and industry—or, at least, the vast portion of it—will have to make social goals as central to its decisions as economic goals; and leadership in our corporations will increasingly recognize this responsibility and accept it."[18] Thus, the issue of business's corporate responsibility was joined. Just what responsibilities does a corporation have? Is its responsibility to be construed narrowly as merely profit making? Or more broadly to include refraining from harming society and even contributing actively and directly to the public good?

The Narrow View: Profit Maximization

Summary 5.6
The debate over corporate responsibility is whether it should be construed narrowly to cover only profit maximization or more broadly to include acting morally, re-fraining from social-ly undesirable behavior, and contributing actively and directly to the public good.

As it happened, the year preceding the Birmingham incident had seen the publication of *Capitalism and Freedom,* in which economist Milton Friedman (1912–2006) forcefully argued the **narrow view of corporate responsibility**: that business has no social responsibilities other than to maximize profits:

> The view has been gaining widespread acceptance that corporate officials ... have a social responsibility that goes beyond serving the interest of their stock-holders.... This view shows a fundamental misconception of the character and nature of a free economy. In such an economy, there is one and only one social responsibility of business—to use its resources and engage in activities designed to increase its profits so long as it stays within the rules of the game, which is to say, engages in open and free competition, without deception or fraud.... Few trends could so thoroughly undermine the very foundations of our free society as the acceptance by corporate officials of a social responsibility other than to make as much money for their stockholders as possible.[19]

Although from Friedman's perspective the only responsibility of business is to make money for its owners, obviously a business may not do literally anything whatsoever to increase its profits. Gangsters pursue profit maximization when they ruthlessly rub out their rivals, but such activity falls outside what Friedman referred to as "the rules of the game." Harvard professor Theodore Levitt echoed this point when he wrote, "In the end business has only two responsibilities—to obey the elementary canons of face-to-face civility (honesty, good faith, and so on) and to seek material gain."[20]

What, then, are the rules of the game? Obviously, elementary morality rules out deception, force, and fraud, and the rules of the game are intended to promote open and free competition. The system of rules in which business is to pursue profit is, in Friedman's view, one that is conducive to the laissez-faire operation of Adam Smith's "invisible hand" (discussed in Chapter 4). Friedman, a conservative economist, believed that if the market is allowed to operate with only the minimal restrictions necessary to prevent fraud and force, society will maximize its overall economic well-being. Pursuit of profit, he insisted, is what makes our system go. Anything that dampens this incentive or inhibits its operation will weaken the ability of the "invisible hand" to deliver the economic goods.

Because the function of a business organization is to make money, the owners of corporations employ executives to accomplish that goal, thereby obligating these managers always to act in the interests of the owners. According to Friedman, to say that executives have *social* responsibilities beyond the pursuit of profit means that at least sometimes they must subordinate owner interests to some social objective, such as controlling pollution or fighting inflation. They are then spending stockholder money for general social interests—in effect, taxing the owners and spending those taxes on social causes. But taxation is a function of government, not private enterprise; executives are not public employees but employees of private enterprise. The doctrine that corporations have social responsibilities beyond profit making thus transforms executives into civil servants and business corporations into government agencies, thereby diverting business from its proper function in the social system.

Summary 5.7
Proponents of the narrow view, such as Milton Friedman, contend that diverting corporations from the pursuit of profit makes our economic system less efficient. Business's only social responsibility is to make money within the rules of the game. Private enterprise should not be forced to undertake public responsibilities that properly belong to government.

Friedman was critical of those who would impose on business any duty other than that of making money, and he was particularly harsh with business leaders who take a broader view of their social responsibilities: They may believe that they are defending the free-enterprise system when they give speeches proclaiming that profit isn't the only goal of business or affirming that business has a social conscience and takes seriously its responsibility to provide employment, refrain from polluting, eliminate discrimination, and so on. But these business leaders are shortsighted; they are helping to undermine capitalism by implicitly reinforcing the view that the pursuit of profit is wicked and must be regulated by external forces.[21]

Friedman acknowledged that corporate activities often are described as an exercise of "social responsibility" when, in fact, they are intended simply to advance the company's self-interest. For example, it might be in the long-term self-interest of a corporation that is a major employer in a small town to spend money to enhance the local community by helping to improve its schools, parks, roads, or social services, thereby attracting good employees to the area, reducing the company's wage bill, or improving worker morale and productivity. By portraying its actions as dictated by a sense of social responsibility, the corporation can generate goodwill as a by-product of expenditures that are entirely justified by self-interest. Friedman had no problem with a company pursuing its self-interest by these means, but he rued the fact that "the attitudes of the public make it in the self-interest [of corporations] to cloak their actions in this way."[22] Friedman's bottom line was that the bottom line is all that counts, and he firmly rejected any notion of corporate *social* responsibility that would hinder a corporation's profit maximization.

The Broader View: Corporate Social Responsibility

Critics of the narrow view believe that businesses have other obligations besides making a profit.

The rival position to that of Friedman and Levitt is simply that business has obligations in addition to pursuing profits. The phrase "in addition to" is important. Advocates of the **broader view of corporate responsibility** do not as a rule believe there is anything wrong with corporate profit. They maintain, rather, that corporations have other responsibilities as well—to consumers, to employees, to suppliers and contractors, to the surrounding community, and to society at large. They see the modern corporation as a social institution that should consider the interests of all the groups it has an impact on. Sometimes called the **social entity model** or the **stakeholder model**, this broader view maintains that a corporation has obligations not only to its stockholders but also to other constituencies that affect or are affected by its behavior—that is, to all parties that have a legitimate interest (a "stake") in what the corporation does or doesn't do. Years ago, the chairman of Standard Oil of New Jersey expressed the basic idea this way: "The job of management is to maintain an equitable and working balance among the claims of the various directly affected interest groups ... stockholders, employees, customers, and the public at large."[23]

If the adherents of the broader view share one belief, it is that corporations have responsibilities beyond simply enhancing their profits because, as a matter of fact, they wield such great social and economic power in our society and with that power must come social responsibility. As professor of business administration Keith Davis put it:

> One basic proposition is that *social responsibility arises from social power.* Modern business has immense social power in such areas as minority employment and environmental pollution. If business has the power, then a just relationship demands that business also bear responsibility for its actions in these areas. Social responsibility arises from concern about the consequences of business's acts as they affect the interests of others. Business decisions do have social consequences. Businessmen cannot make decisions that are solely economic decisions, because they are interrelated with the whole social system. This situation requires that businessmen's thinking be broadened beyond the company gate to the whole social system. Systems thinking is required.
>
> Social responsibility implies that a business decision maker in the process of serving his own business interests is obliged to take actions that also protect and enhance society's interests. The net effect is to improve the quality of life in the broadest possible way, however quality of life is defined by society. In this manner, harmony is achieved between business's actions and the larger social system. The businessman becomes concerned with social as well as economic outputs and with the total effect of his institutional actions on society.[24]

Proponents of the broader view, such as Davis, stress that modern business is intimately integrated with the rest of society. Business is not some self-enclosed world, like a private poker party. Rather, business activities have profound ramifications throughout society, and their influence on our lives is hard to escape. Business writer John Kay makes this point with reference to General Electric: "The company's activities are so extensive that you necessarily encounter them daily, often without knowing you are doing so. GE's business is our business even if we do not want it to be."[25]

As a result, although society permits and expects corporations to pursue their economic interests, they have other responsibilities as well. Thus, for example, it is wrong for corporations to raid the pension funds of their employees, as many have done,[26] or to evade taxes through creative accounting or by re-incorporating in tax havens such as Bermuda,[27] even if doing so is legal and enhances the bottom line. "We reasonably expect that GE should care that its engines are safe," writes John Kay, "not just that they comply with FAA procedures; that if there is a problem with its medical equipment the company will try to put it right, not cover it up; that GE financial statements are true and fair and not just compliant with accounting standards."[28]

Melvin Anshen has cast the case for the broader view of corporate responsibility in a historical perspective.[29] He maintains that there is always a kind of "social contract" between business and society. This contract is, of course, only implicit, but it represents a tacit understanding within society about the proper goals and responsibilities of business. In effect, in Anshen's view, society always structures the guidelines within which business is permitted to operate in order to derive certain benefits from business activity. For instance, in the nineteenth century, society's prime interest was rapid economic growth, which was viewed as the source of all progress, and the engine of economic growth was identified as the drive for profits by unfettered, competitive, private enterprise. That attitude was reflected in the then-existing social contract. Today, however, society has concerns and interests other than rapid economic growth—in particular, a concern for the quality of life and for the preservation of the environment. Accordingly, the social contract is in the process of being modified. In particular, Anshen writes, "it will no longer be acceptable for corporations to manage their affairs solely in terms of the traditional internal costs of doing business, while thrusting external costs on the public."[30]

In recent years we have grown more aware of the possible deleterious side effects of business activity, or what economists call **externalities**: the unintended negative (or in some cases positive) consequences that an economic transaction between two parties can have on some third party. Industrial pollution provides the clearest illustration. Suppose a factory makes widgets and sells them to your firm. A by-product of this economic transaction is the waste that the rains wash from the factory yard into the local river, waste that damages recreational and commercial fishing interests downstream. This damage to third parties is an unintended side effect of the economic transaction between the seller and the buyer of widgets.

Summary 5.8
Defenders of the broader view maintain that corporations have responsibilities that go beyond making money because of their great social and economic power. Business is governed by an implicit social contract that requires it to operate in ways that benefit society. In particular, corporations must take responsibility for the unintended side effects of their business transactions (externalities) and weigh the full social costs of their activities.

Defenders of the new social contract, like Anshen, maintain that externalities should no longer be overlooked. In the jargon of economists, externalities must be "internalized"—that is, the factory should be made to absorb the cost, either by disposing of its waste in an environmentally safe (and presumably more expensive) way or by paying for the damage the waste does downstream. On the one hand, basic fairness requires that the factory's waste no longer be dumped onto third parties. On the other hand, from the economic point of view, requiring the factory to internalize the externalities makes sense, for only when it does so will the price of the widgets it sells reflect their true social cost. The real production cost of the widgets includes not only labor, raw materials, machinery, and so on, but also the damage done to the fisheries downstream. Unless the price of widgets is raised sufficiently to reimburse the fisheries for their losses or to dispose of the waste in some other way, then the buyer of widgets is paying less than their true cost. Part of the cost is being paid by the fishing interests downstream.

Advocates of the broader view believe that business must internalize its externalities and consider the social costs of its activities.

Advocates of the broader view go beyond requiring business to internalize its externalities in a narrow economic sense. Keith Davis, for example, maintains that in addition to considering potential profitability, a business must weigh the long-range social costs of its activities as well. Only if the overall benefit to society is positive should business act:

> The expectation of the social responsibility model is that a detailed cost/benefit analysis will be made prior to determining whether to proceed with an activity and that social costs will be given significant weight in the decision-making process. Almost any business action will entail some social costs. The basic question is whether the benefits outweigh the costs so that there is a net social benefit. Many questions of judgment arise, and there are no precise mathematical measures in the social field, but rational and wise judgments can be made if the issues are first thoroughly explored.[31]

Stockholders and the Corporation

When asked, most Americans say that a corporation's top obligation is to its employees; others say it is to the community or the nation, but only 17 percent think stockholders deserve the highest priority.[32] In fact, even a majority of managers rejects a profit-only philosophy of corporate management.[33] Advocates of the narrow view, however, believe that those attitudes reflect a misunderstanding of the proper relationship between management and stockholders. Stockholders own the company. They entrust management with their funds, and in return management undertakes to make as much money for them as it can. As a result, according to proponents of the narrow view, management has a fiduciary duty to maximize shareholder wealth, a duty that is inconsistent with any social responsibility other than the relentless pursuit of profit.

The narrow view holds that management's responsibility to maximize shareholder wealth outweighs any other obligations.

The managers of a corporation do indeed have a **fiduciary responsibility** to look after the interests of shareholders, a duty that is clearly violated by corporate executives who take advantage of their position to enrich themselves at company expense with extravagant bonuses, stock options, and retirement packages or to waste corporate money on jets, apartments, private parties, and various personal services that lack any plausible business rationale. But it doesn't follow from this, as proponents of the narrow view maintain, that the corporation should be run entirely for the benefit of stockholders, that their interests always take priority over the interests of everyone else. To the contrary, argue critics of the narrow view, management has fiduciary responsibilities to other constituencies as well—for example, to employees, bondholders, and consumers. The duty to make money for shareholders is real, but it doesn't trump all of a company's other responsibilities. Indeed, it's debatable whether most shareholders believe that it does. Many of them may want the company they "own" to act in a morally responsible manner—say, by not contributing to environmental pollution or by treating employees with respect—even if that means less profit.

Against that point of view, however, Milton Friedman argued, "The whole justification for permitting the corporate executives to be selected by the shareholders is that the executive is an agent serving the interests of his principal."[34] This justification disappears, he believed, when executives expend corporate resources in ways that don't necessarily enhance the bottom line. They are then acting more like public servants than like employees of a private enterprise. But even if one agrees with Friedman that stockholders select corporate managers to act as their agents and advance their interests, this doesn't prove that those executives are bound to act solely to increase shareholder wealth, ignoring all other moral considerations. Undertaking to look after other people's interests or promising to try to make money for them creates a genuine obligation, but that obligation is not absolute. It doesn't eliminate all other moral responsibilities. By analogy, promising to meet someone at a certain time and place for lunch creates an obligation, but that obligation doesn't override one's duty to assist someone having a heart attack. And something that it would be immoral for you to do (such as making a dangerous product) doesn't become right just because you're acting on behalf of someone else or promised him that you would do it.

Friedman believed that if executives "impose taxes on stockholders and spend the proceeds for 'social' purposes, they become 'civil servants,' and thus should be selected through a political process."[35] He considered such a proposal absurd or, at best, socialistic. Yet others contend that corporations are too focused on profits, and they fear the damage to society when firms are willing to sacrifice all other values on the altar of the bottom line. They don't think it absurd at all that corporations should take a broader view of their social role and responsibilities. They see nothing in the management-stockholder relationship that would morally forbid corporations from doing so.

Who Controls the Corporation?

According to the narrow view of corporate responsibility, stockholders own the corporation and select managers to run it for them. That model may make sense for some small firms or when venture capitalists invest in a start-up company, but it doesn't accurately reflect modern corporate reality. To begin with, most stockholders purchase shares in a company from current stockholders, who acquired their shares the same way. Very few investors put their money directly

Summary 5.9
Advocates of the narrow view stress that management's fiduciary duty to the owners (stockholders) of a corporation takes priority over any other responsibilities and obligates management to focus on profit maximization alone. Critics challenge this argument. They also point out that the assumption that stockholders own or control the corporation is dubious.

into a corporation; rather, they buy secondhand shares that were initially issued years before. They pick companies that look profitable or seem likely to grow or whose products or policies appeal to them, or they may simply be following the advice of their broker. And they are generally prepared to resell their shares, perhaps even the same day they bought them, if it is profitable to do so. Stockholders have no legal obligation to the company. They are a far-flung, diverse, and ever-changing group. They come and go, and rarely, if ever, have direct contact with the managers of the company or even know or care who they are.

For those reasons, then, it's implausible to see stockholders in, say, Home Depot or Procter & Gamble as being genuine owners or proprietors of the company. "A share of stock," write two legal experts, "does not confer ownership of the underlying assets owned by the corporation. Instead, it provides the holder with a right to share in the financial returns produced by the corporations' business." A share of stock is a financial instrument, more akin to a bond, than to a car or building.[36]

Few economists or business theorists believe that stockholders are really in charge of the companies whose shares they hold or that they select the managers who run them. As long ago as 1932, Adolf Berle and Gardiner Means showed that because stock ownership in large corporations is so dispersed, actual control of the corporation has passed to management.[37] Today, as most business observers acknowledge, management handpicks the board of directors, thus controlling the body that is supposed to police it. "The CEO puts up the candidates; no one runs against them, and management counts the votes," says Nell Minow of Corporate Library, a corporate watchdog website. "We wouldn't deign to call this an election in a third-world country."[38] Even in those rare cases when shareholders put up their own candidates, such proxy fights are expensive and the incumbent management has the corporate coffers at its disposal to fight them.

As a result, the board of directors typically rubber-stamps the policies and recommendations of management. That's why it's not too surprising that the directors of Enron ignored shareholder interests and approved paying out $750 million in executive compensation—$140 million of it to its chairman—in a year when the company's entire net income was only $975 million. The Enron example is extreme, but since the 1990s the share of corporate net income going to top management has doubled; that's money that otherwise would have ended up in shareholders' pockets.[39] And how else to explain the fat payouts to CEOs when their companies do poorly or are acquired by other corporations[40] or the lavish retirement packages that boards bestow on former CEOs. These often include a million-dollar annual pension, an expensive apartment, a car and driver, and free use of the company aircraft.[41] True, in the past couple of decades, institutional investors like pension funds and large mutual funds have increased their sway over corporate policies, but it's still exceedingly difficult for shareholders to change policies they don't like, because the voting rules are rigged in management's favor.[42] The upshot is simple, according to Michael Jensen, professor emeritus at Harvard Business School: "The CEO has no boss." That, he says, is "the major thing wrong with large public corporations in the United States."[43]

Stockholders do not really own or control the companies whose shares they hold.

DEBATING CORPORATE RESPONSIBILITY

We can pursue the debate over corporate responsibility further by examining three arguments in support of the narrow view: the invisible-hand argument, the let-government-do-it argument, and the business-can't-handle-it argument. Advocates of the broader view of corporate responsibility reject all three.

The Invisible-Hand Argument

Adam Smith claimed that when each of us acts in a free-market environment to promote our own economic interests we are led by an invisible hand to promote the general good. Like-minded contemporary thinkers such as Friedman advance the same **invisible-hand argument**. They point out that corporations, in fact, were chartered by states precisely with utility in mind. If businesses are permitted to seek self-interest, their activities will inevitably yield the greatest good for society as a whole. To invite corporations to base their policies and activities on anything other than profit making is to politicize business's unique economic function and to hamper its ability to satisfy our material needs. As Roberto C. Goizueta, former CEO of Coca-Cola, argues, "businesses are created to meet economic needs." When they "try to become all things to all people, they fail.... We have one job: to generate a fair return for our owners."[44] Accordingly, corporations should not be invited to fight racial prejudice or global warming, to contribute to the local community, or to improve working conditions or enhance the lives of employees, except insofar as these activities increase profits.

Yet this argument allows that corporations may still be held accountable for their actions. To the degree that they fulfill or fail to fulfill their economic role, they can be praised or blamed. And they can rightly be criticized for breaking the law or violating the rules of the game—for example, by shady accounting practices that mislead investors about company assets. But corporations should not be held morally responsible for non-economic matters; to do so would distort the economic mission of business in society and undermine the foundations of the free-enterprise system.

The invisible-hand argument, however, runs up against the fact that modern corporations bear about as much resemblance to Smith's self-sufficient farmers and craftspersons as today's military bears to the Continental militia. Given the sway they have over our economy and society, the enormous impact they have on our lives, our communities, and our environment, today's gigantic corporations are more like public enterprises than private ones. They constitute powerful economic fiefdoms, far removed from the small, competitive producers of classical economics. Perhaps within a restricted area of economic activity, when the parties to the exchange are roughly equal, then each pursuing self-interest can result in the greatest net good. But in the real world of large corporations, the concept of an invisible hand orchestrating the common good often stretches credulity. For example, California deregulated its electricity market to promote competition and give the invisible hand room to operate. But the result was a disaster. Instead of cheaper energy, the state got power blackouts and soaring prices as energy companies adroitly and greedily manipulated the market. Each time the state tried to make the market

The invisible-hand argument seems economically unrealistic. In addition, corporations today find it in their interest to acknowledge values other than profit.

work better, energy sellers devised new ways to exploit the system. The state government only stanched the crisis by a costly intervention that has basically put it in the power business.[45]

The invisible-hand argument in favor of the narrow view of corporate responsibility is thus open to criticism as theoretically unsound and economically unrealistic. Moreover, in practice the argument is complicated by the fact that corporations today find themselves in a social and political environment in which they are pressured by public opinion, politicians, the media, and various activist groups to act—or at least be perceived to be acting—as responsible corporate citizens, as socially conscious enterprises that acknowledge other values besides profit and that seek to make a positive contribution to our society. Few if any corporations can afford to be seen as exploiters of foreign labor, as polluters of the environment, or as indifferent to consumer welfare or the prosperity of our communities. Companies today religiously guard their name and their brands against the slander that they care only about profits. And the larger the corporation, the more susceptible it is to the demand that it behave with a developed sense of moral responsibility, and the more it needs to guard its image and to take steps to assure the public that it is striving to make the world a better place.

Admittedly, this is in part a matter of public relations, but it's also true that business success in today's world requires companies to respond to society's demand that they act as morally responsible agents. For purely self-interested reasons, even corporations that take a very narrow view of their responsibilities may have to behave as if they held a broader view. For example, in a world in which 88 percent of young people believe that companies have a responsibility to support social causes and 86 percent of them say that they switch brands based on social issues, a world in which 72 percent of job seekers prefer to work for a company that supports social causes,[46] corporate philanthropy promotes the bottom line. Moreover, almost all studies indicate that socially responsible corporate behavior is positively correlated with financial success and that the most profitable companies treat their consumers, employees, and business partners ethically.[47] Ironically, then, this gives companies a self-interested reason not merely to pretend to have a broad sense of social responsibility but, rather, to become the kind of company that really does want to make a positive mark in the world. Of course, whether we are talking about individuals or about corporations, there's no guarantee that acting morally will always pay off, and indeed if that is one's only motivation for doing the right thing, then one can hardly be said to be acting morally. Even so, there's little reason for either individuals or companies to believe that acting selfishly or sacrificing moral values to profits will pay off for them in the long run.

The Let-Government-Do-It Argument

According to the narrow view of corporate responsibility, business's role is purely economic, and corporations should not be considered moral agents. Some adherents of this view, however, such as economist and social critic John Kenneth Galbraith (1908–2006), reject the assumption that Smith's invisible hand will solve all social and economic problems or that market forces will moralize corporate activities. Left to their own self-serving devices, Galbraith and others warn, modern corporations will enrich themselves while impoverishing society. If they can get away with it, they will pollute, exploit workers, deceive customers, and strive to eliminate competition and keep prices high through oligopolistic practices. They will do those things, the argument continues, because as economic institutions they are naturally and quite properly profit motivated.

What is profitable for corporations, however, is not necessarily useful or desirable for society. How is the corporation's natural and insatiable appetite for profit to be controlled? Through government regulation. Proponents of the **let-government-do-it argument** believe that the strong hand of government, through a system of laws and incentives, can and should bring corporations to heel. "I believe in corporations," Teddy Roosevelt once proclaimed. "They are indispensable instruments of our modern civilization; but I believe that they should be so supervised and so regulated that they shall act for the interests of the community as a whole."[48]

"Do not blame corporations and their top executives" for things like layoffs or urge them to acknowledge obligations beyond the bottom line, writes the economist Robert Reich, secretary of labor under President Clinton. "They are behaving exactly as they are organized to behave." He poohpoohs moral appeals and rejects the idea that CEOs should seek to balance the interests of shareholders against those of employees and their communities. Rather, Reich says, "if we want corporations to take more responsibility" for the economic well-being of Americans, then government "will have to provide the proper incentives."[49]

The let-government-do-it argument rejects broadening corporate responsibility just as much as the invisible-hand argument does.

This advice sounds realistic and is intended to be practical, but the let-government-do-it argument rejects the notion of broadening corporate responsibility just as firmly as the invisible-hand argument does. The latter puts the focus on the market. Galbraith's and Reich's argument puts it on the *visible* hand of government. The two positions agree, however, in thinking it misguided to expect or demand that business firms do anything other than pursue profit.

Critics of the let-government-do-it argument contend that it is a blueprint for big, intrusive government. Moreover, they doubt that government can control any but the most egregious corporate immorality. They fear that many questionable activities will be overlooked, safely hidden within the labyrinth of the corporate structure. Lacking intimate knowledge of the goals and sub-goals of specific corporations, as well as of their daily operations, government simply can't anticipate a specific corporation's moral challenges. Rather, it can prescribe behavior only for broad, cross-sectional issues, such as bribery, price fixing, and unfair competition.

Finally, is government a credible custodian of morality? If recent experience has taught anything, it is that government officials are not always paragons of virtue. Looked at as another organization, government manifests many of the same structural characteristics that test moral behavior inside the corporation. Furthermore, given the awesome clout of corporate lobbyists, one wonders whether, as moral police, government officials will do anything more than impose the values and interests of their most generous financiers. Can we seriously expect politicians to bite the hand that feeds them?

The Business-Can't-Handle-It Argument

Some argue that business is the wrong group on which to place broad social responsibilities for two reasons.

In support of the narrow view of corporate responsibility, some maintain that it is misguided to encourage corporations to address nonbusiness matters. According to the **business-can't-handle-it argument**, corporations are the wrong group to be entrusted with broad responsibility for promoting the well-being of society. They are not up to the job for two reasons: (1) They lack the necessary expertise. (2) In addressing non-economic matters, they inevitably impose their own materialistic values on the rest of society.

Corporations Lack the Expertise

Those who develop the first point contend that business can't handle the job—that it is the wrong group to rely on to promote the well-being of society—because corporate executives lack the moral and social expertise to make other-than-economic decisions. To assign them non-economic responsibilities would be to put social welfare in the hands of inept custodians. For example, Robert Reich argues that corporate executives lack the moral authority to "balance profits against the public good" or "undertake any ethical balancing." They have no "expertise in making such moral calculations."[50] In his view, corporate leaders lack the moral insight or social know-how that a broader view of corporate responsibility would seem to require of them.

Against that, however, one can argue that we don't normally restrict the moral responsibilities of individuals, professional bodies, or other organizations to matters that fall within the narrow confines of their business or other expertise. We see nothing wrong, for example, with physicians advocating AIDS awareness or trying to promote the use of seat belts in automobiles, or with a teachers union involving itself in a campaign to combat the use of illegal drugs. And ordinary citizens may sometimes have a duty to educate themselves about, and do what they can to address, social issues that fall outside their usual sphere of knowledge and activity. What, if anything, asks the critic, makes the social role of the corporation unique, so that its responsibilities and those of its employees should be confined solely to profit making?

The argument that corporations aren't up to addressing social issues because they lack the necessary expertise runs up against the fact that, often, it is only business that has the know-how, talent, experience, and organizational resources to tackle certain problems. If society, for example, wants to eradicate malaria in Africa or increase longevity at home, to reduce diesel engine emissions or retard global warming, to improve agricultural productivity while lowering the risks from pesticides, or to see that inner-city youth learn entrepreneurship or that community groups have the business skills necessary for success, then society will need the assistance of business. To take a specific illustration, Citibank supports microfinance programs in Mexico and India, intended to give poor rural women the tiny loans they need, say, to buy a sewing machine and start their own business. True, as a Citigroup executive says, "there is not going to be a huge short-term profit" for the company.[51] But who is better able to help these women than a company like Citigroup?

Corporations Will Impose Their Values on Us

Others argue that corporations are the wrong group to address social issues, that business can't handle the assignment, for a different reason. They fear that if permitted to stray from strictly economic matters, corporate officials will impose their materialistic values on all of society. Broadening corporate responsibility will thus "materialize" society instead of "moralizing" corporate activity. More than fifty years ago, Harvard professor Theodore Levitt expressed this concern:

> The danger is that all these things [resulting from having business pursue social goals other than profit making] will turn the corporation into a twentieth-century equivalent of the medieval church. ... For while the corporation also transforms itself in the process, at bottom its outlook will always remain materialistic. What we have then is the frightening spectacle of a powerful economic functional group whose future and perception are shaped in a tight materialistic context of money and things but which imposes its narrow ideas about a broad spectrum of unrelated noneconomic subjects on the mass of man and society. Even if its outlook were the purest kind of good will, that would not recommend the corporation as an arbiter of our lives.[52]

Summary 5.10
Three arguments in favor of the narrow view are the invisible-hand argument, the let-government-do-it argument, and the business-can't-handle-it argument. Finding flaws in each of these arguments, critics claim there is no solid basis for restricting corporate responsibility to profit making.

This argument seems to assume that corporations do not already exercise enormous discretionary power over us. But as Keith Davis points out, business already has immense social power. "Society has entrusted to business large amounts of society's resources," says Davis, "and business is expected to manage these resources as a wise trustee for society. In addition to the traditional role of economic entrepreneurship, business now has a new social role of trusteeship. As trustee for society's resources, it serves the interests of all claimants on the organization, rather than only those of owners, or consumers, or labor."[53]

As Paul Camenisch notes, business is already using its privileged position to propagate, consciously or unconsciously, a view of humanity and the good life.[54] Implicit in the barrage of advertisements to which we are subjected daily are assumptions about happiness, success, and human fulfillment. In addition, corporations or industry groups sometimes speak out in unvarnished terms about social and economic issues. For example, ExxonMobil disputes the notion that fossil fuels are the main cause of global warming and lobbies against the Kyoto Protocol capping global-warming emissions, while drug companies such as Eli Lilly, Procter & Gamble, and Bristol-Myers Squibb contribute to conservative think tanks that seek to reduce the regulatory powers of the U.S. Food and Drug Administration.

The point here is that business already promotes consumerism and materialistic values. It doesn't hesitate to use its resources to express its views and influence our political system on issues that affect its economic interests. If corporations take a broader view of their responsibilities, are they really likely to have a more materialistic effect on society, as Levitt suggests, than they do now? It's hard to believe they could. Levitt's view implies that there is some threat to society's values when corporations engage in philanthropy or use their economic and political muscle for other than purely self-interested ends. But society's values are not endangered when Sara Lee donates 2 percent of its pretax profits (nearly $13 million) to charitable causes, mostly cultural institutions and organizations serving disadvantaged people,[55] or when General Mills gives away 3 percent of its domestic pretax earnings ($45 million) to community organizations, donates food to people in need, and helps inner-city companies to get up and running.[56] And where is the "materialization of society" if, instead of advertising on a silly situation comedy that reaches a large audience, a corporation spends the same amount underwriting a science program with fewer viewers solely out of a sense of social responsibility?

INSTITUTIONALIZING ETHICS WITHIN CORPORATIONS

Society permits corporations to exist and, in turn, expects them to act in a socially responsible way.

The criticisms of these three arguments in support of the narrow view of corporate responsibility have led many people inside and outside business to adopt the broader view—that the obligations of the modern business corporation extend beyond simply making money for itself. Society grants corporations the right to exist and gives them legal status as separate entities. It does this not to indulge the profit appetites of owners and managers but, as Camenisch says, as a way of securing the necessary "goods and services to sustain and enhance human existence."[57] In return for its sufferance of corporations, society has the right to expect corporations not to cause harm, to take into account the external effects of their activities, and whenever possible to act for the betterment of society.

The list of corporate responsibilities goes beyond such negative injunctions as "Don't pollute," "Don't misrepresent products," and "Don't bribe." Included also are affirmative duties like "See that your product or service makes a positive contribution to society," "Improve the skills of your employees," "Seek to hire the disabled," "Give special consideration to the needs of historically disadvantaged groups," "Contribute to the arts and education," "Locate plants in economically depressed areas," and "Improve working conditions." This class of affirmative responsibilities includes activities that are not intrinsically related to the operations of the corporation—responsibilities that each of us, whether individuals or institutions, has simply by virtue of our being members of society. Precisely how far each of us must go to meet these responsibilities depends largely on our capacity to fulfill them, which, of course, varies from person to person, institution to institution. But given their considerable power and resources, large corporations seem better able to promote the common good than most individuals or small businesses.

To make ethics a priority, corporations should do four things.

How corporations are to promote the common good cannot be answered very specifically; methods will depend on the type of firm and its particular circumstances. Proponents of broadening corporate responsibility probably would agree that the first step is for corporations to expand their moral horizons and make ethical conduct a priority. How to do this? At least four actions seem called for:

1. Corporations should acknowledge the importance, even necessity, of conducting business morally. Their commitment to ethical behavior should be unequivocal and highly visible, from top management down.

Summary 5.11
To become more socially responsible, companies need to expand their moral horizons and make ethical conduct a priority. Doing so will require them to acknowledge the critical importance of ethics, to encourage morally responsible conduct by their employees, to recognize the pluralistic nature of our social system, and to be open to public discussion and review.

2. Corporations should make a real effort to encourage their members to take moral responsibilities seriously. This commitment would mean ending all forms of retaliation against those who buck the system and rewarding employees for evaluating corporate decisions in their broader social and moral contexts.

3. Corporations should end their defensiveness in the face of public discussion and criticism. Instead, they should actively solicit the views of stockholders, managers, employees, suppliers, customers, local communities, and even society as a whole. Corporations should invite outside opinions and conduct a candid ethical audit of their organizational policies, priorities, and practices.

4. Corporations must recognize the pluralistic nature of the social system of which they are a part. Society consists of diverse, interlinked individuals and groups, all vying to maintain their autonomy and advance their interests. The actions of any one group invariably affect the interests of others. As part of society, corporations affect many groups, and these groups and the individuals they comprise affect corporations. Failing to realize this, corporations can lose sight of the social framework that governs their relationship with the external environment.

Undoubtedly, other general directives could be added to this list. Still, if corporate responsibility is to be expanded, then something like the preceding approach seems basic.

Limits to What the Law Can Do

Critics of the let-government-do-it argument question Galbraith's and Reich's view that society should not expect business to behave morally but rather should simply use government to direct business's pursuit of profit in socially acceptable directions. This issue is worth returning to in the present context. All defenders of the broader view of corporate responsibility believe that more than laissez faire is necessary to ensure that business behavior is socially and morally acceptable. Yet there is a tendency to believe that law is a fully adequate vehicle for this purpose.

Stone gives three reasons why there are limits to what we can achieve through law.

Law professor Christopher Stone has argued, however, that there are limits on what the law can be expected to achieve.[58] Three of his points are particularly important. *First,* many laws, such as controls on the disposal of toxic waste, are passed only after there is general awareness of the problem; in the meantime, damage has already been done. The proverbial barn door has been shut only after the horse has left.

Second, formulating appropriate laws and designing effective regulations are difficult. It is hard to achieve consensus on the relevant facts, to determine what remedies will work, and to decide how to weigh conflicting values. In addition, our political system gives corporations and their lobbyists significant input into the writing of laws. Not only that, but the specific working regulations and day-to-day interpretation of the law require the continual input of industry experts. This is not a conspiracy but a fact of life. Government bureaus generally have limited time, staffing, and expertise, so they must rely on the cooperation and assistance of those they regulate.

Third, enforcing the law is often cumbersome. Legal actions against corporations are expensive and can drag on for years, and the judicial process is often too blunt an instrument to use as a way of managing complex social and business issues. In fact, recourse to the courts can be counterproductive, and Stone argues that sometimes the benefits of doing so may not be worth the costs. Legal action may simply make corporations more furtive, breeding distrust, destruction of documents, and an attitude that "I won't do anything more than I am absolutely required to do."

What conclusion should be drawn? Stone's argument is not intended to show that regulation of business is hopeless. Rather, what he wants to stress is that the law cannot do it alone. We do not want a system in which businesspeople believe that their only obligation is to obey the law and that it is morally permissible for them to do anything not (yet) illegal. With that attitude, disaster is just around the corner. More socially responsible business behavior requires, instead, that corporations and the people within them not simply respond to the requirements of the law but also hold high moral standards—and that they themselves monitor their own behavior.

Ethical Codes and Economic Efficiency

It is, therefore, important that corporations examine their own implicit and explicit codes of conduct and the moral standards that are being propagated to their employees. As mentioned earlier in this chapter and in Chapter 1,[59] there is no necessary trade-off between profitability and ethical corporate behavior. Indeed, the contrary appears to be true: The most morally responsible companies are consistently among the most profitable companies. Yet ethical behavior in the business world is often assumed to come at the expense of economic efficiency. Defenders of the broader view, such as Anshen, as well as defenders of the narrow view, such as Friedman, seem to make this assumption. Anshen believes that other values should take priority over economic efficiency, whereas Friedman contends business should concern itself only with profit and, in this way, maximize economic well-being. In his important essay "Social Responsibility and Economic Efficiency," Nobel Prize–winning economist Kenneth Arrow has challenged this assumption.[60]

To begin with, says Arrow, any kind of settled economic life requires a certain degree of ethical behavior, some element of trust and confidence. Much business, for instance, is conducted on the basis of oral agreements. In addition, Arrow points out, "there are two types of situation in which the simple rule of maximizing profits is socially inefficient: the case in which costs are not paid for, as in pollution, and the case in which the seller has considerably more knowledge about his product than the buyer."

The first type of situation relates to the demand that corporations "internalize their externalities." In the second situation, in which the buyer lacks the expertise and knowledge of the seller, an effective moral code, either requiring full disclosure or setting minimal standards of performance (for example, the braking ability of a new automobile), enhances rather than diminishes economic efficiency. Without such a code, buyers may purchase products or services they don't need. Or because they don't trust the seller, they may

---

People in business need to acknowledge that obeying the law is not their only obligation because the law alone cannot guarantee responsible business behavior.

Summary 5.12 Corporations and the people who make them up must have high moral standards and monitor their own conduct because there are limits to what the law can do to ensure that business behavior is socially and morally acceptable.

Ethics and efficiency aren't necessarily in opposition. Normal business activity requires some degree of ethics, and focusing only on profit maximization is socially inefficient in two situations.

refrain from purchasing products and services they do need. Either way, from the economist's point of view the situation is inefficient.

An effective professional or business moral code—as well as the public's awareness of this code—is good for business. Most of us, for example, have little medical knowledge and are thus at the mercy of doctors. Over hundreds of years, however, a firm code of ethical conduct has developed in the medical profession. As a result, people generally presume that their physician will perform with their welfare in mind. They rarely worry that their doctor might be taking advantage of them or exploiting them with unnecessary treatment. By contrast, used-car dealers have historically suffered from a lack of public trust.

For a code to be effective it must be realistic, Arrow argues, in the sense of connecting with the collective self-interest of business. And it must become part of the corporate culture, "accepted by the significant operating institutions and transmitted from one generation of executives to the next through standard operating procedures [and] through education in business schools."

For both Arrow and Stone, then, the development of feasible and effective business and professional codes of ethics must be a central focus of any effort to enhance or expand corporate responsibility. The question is how to create a corporate atmosphere conducive to moral decision making.

Summary 5.13
All settled economic life requires trust and confidence. The adoption of realistic and workable codes of ethics in the business world can actually enhance business efficiency. This is particularly true when there is an imbalance of knowledge between the buyer and the seller.

Corporate Moral Codes

What can be done to improve the organizational climate so individual members can reasonably be expected to act ethically? If those inside the corporation are to behave morally, they need clearly stated and communicated ethical standards that are equitable and enforced. This development seems possible only if the standards of expected behavior are institutionalized—that is, only if they become a fixture in the corporate organization. To institutionalize ethics within corporations, Professor Milton Snoeyenbos suggests that top management should (1) articulate the firm's values and goals, (2) adopt a moral code applicable to all members of the company, (3) set up a high-ranking ethics committee to oversee, develop, and enforce the code, and (4) incorporate ethics training into all employee-development programs.[61]

There are several steps companies should take to institutionalize ethics.

The company's code of ethics should not be window dressing or so general as to be useless. A **corporate moral code** should set reasonable goals and subgoals, with an eye on blunting unethical pressures on subordinates. In formulating the code, the top-level ethics committee should solicit the views of corporate members at all levels regarding goals and subgoals, so that the final product articulates "a fine-grained ethical code that addresses ethical issues likely to arise at the level of subgoals."[62] Moreover, the committee should have full authority and responsibility to communicate the code and decisions based on it to all corporate members, clarify and interpret the code when the need arises, facilitate the code's use, investigate grievances and violations of the code, discipline violators and reward compliance, and review, update, and upgrade the code.

To help employees in ethically difficult situations, a good corporate ethics program must be user friendly. It should provide a support system with a variety of entry points, one that employees feel confident about using.[63] In addition, part of all employee-training programs should be devoted to ethics.

Summary 5.14
To improve organizational climate so we can reasonably expect individuals to act morally, corporations need to institutionalize ethics. Among other things, this involves articulating their values and goals, adopting a moral code, setting up an ethics committee, and including ethics training in their employee-development programs. Attention to corporate culture is also crucial to the successful institutionalization of ethics inside an organization.

Management must pay attention to the values and behavior reinforced by its corporate culture.

At a minimum, this should include study of the code, review of the company's procedures for handling ethical problems, and discussion of employer and employee responsibilities and expectations. Snoeyenbos and others believe that institutionalizing ethics within the corporation in these ways, when supplemented by the development of industry-wide codes of ethics to address issues beyond a particular firm, will go far toward establishing a corporate climate conducive to individual moral decision making.

Corporate Culture

During the past two decades, organizational theorists and writers on business management have increasingly emphasized "corporate culture" as the factor that makes one company succeed while another languishes. Although intangible in comparison with things like sales revenue and profit margin, corporate culture is often the key to a firm's success. According to one study, 30 percent of the difference in performance between companies can be attributed to differences in culture, but only 5 percent to differences in strategy.[64]

What is **corporate culture**? One writer puts it this way: "Culture is the pattern of shared values and beliefs that gives members of an institution meaning and provides them with rules for behavior in their organization."[65] A fuller definition is given by another writer, who describes corporate culture as "a general constellation of beliefs, mores, customs, value systems and behavioral norms, and ways of doing business that are unique to each corporation, that set a pattern for corporate activities and actions, and that describe the implicit and emergent patterns of behavior and emotions characterizing life in the organization."[66] Corporate culture may be both overt and implicit. The formal culture of a corporation, as expressed in idealized statements of values and norms, should also be distinguished from the informal culture that shapes beliefs, values, and behavior. In addition, there may be multiple and overlapping cultures within an organization because employees have different backgrounds, work in different divisions of the organization and even in different countries, and may be subject to different systems of rewards and sanctions.

Organizational theorists emphasize the importance of monitoring and managing corporate culture—beginning with an attempt to understand each corporation's distinctive culture—to prevent dysfunctional behavior and processes. As one consultant puts it, "A corporation's culture is what determines how people behave when they are not being watched."[67] If management does not make explicit the values and behavior it desires, the culture will typically develop its own norms, usually based on the types of behavior that lead to success within the organization. Thus, the desired values must be communicated and transmitted throughout the organization. Conduct congruent with them must be rewarded and conduct inconsistent with them sanctioned. Overlooking behavior that contradicts the desired norms can have the effect of encouraging and even rewarding it.

William Donaldson, former chairman of the U.S. Securities and Exchange Commission, emphasizes the importance of ethical leadership, of the example set by upper management. "The tone is set at the top," he says. "You must have an internal code that goes beyond the letter of the law to encompass the spirit of the company. Does that concept exist in all companies? No. All you have to do is look at executive compensation to recognize that we still have a long way to go."[68]

These points are crucial when it comes to corporate social responsibility. Management needs to understand the real dynamics of its own organization. At Sears, for example, new minimum work quotas and productivity incentives at its auto centers created a high-pressure environment that led employees to mislead customers and sell them unnecessary parts and services, from brake jobs to front-end alignments.[69] At Fannie Mae, an "earnings-at-any-cost culture" led to accounting fraud.[70] Thus, it is necessary for socially responsible executives to ask: How do people get ahead in the company? What conduct is actually rewarded, what values are really being instilled in employees? Andrew C. Sigler, chairman of Champion International, stresses this point: "Sitting up here in Stamford, there's no way I can affect what an employee is doing today in Texas, Montana, or Maine. Making speeches and sending letters just doesn't do it. You need a culture and peer pressure that spells out what is acceptable and isn't and why. It involves training, education, and follow-up."[71]

Internal or external corporate responsibility audits can help close the gap between stated values, goals, and mission, on the one hand, and reality on the other.[72] Another aspect of follow-up is strict enforcement. Chemical Bank, for instance, fired employees for violations of the company's code of ethics even when nothing illegal was done. Xerox dismissed people for minor manipulation of records and the padding of expense accounts. (By contrast, some of the nation's most prestigious stock brokerage firms have employed salespeople with long records of violating securities laws).[73] In a recent but typical year, General Electric investigated 1,338 cases in which concerns had been raised internally about employee integrity. It dismissed 125 employees and took disciplinary action against 243 others for legal or ethical violations.[74] Executives at both Xerox and General Mills also emphasize that civic involvement is a crucial part of corporate ethics. As one General Mills executive puts it: "It's hard to imagine that a person who reads to the blind at night would cheat...."[75]

Johnson & Johnson is widely seen as a model of corporate responsibility, especially because of its decisive handling of the Tylenol crisis of 1982, when seven people in the Chicago area died from cyanide-laced Extra-Strength Tylenol capsules. The company immediately recalled 31 million bottles of Tylenol from store shelves across the nation and notified 500,000 doctors and hospitals about the contaminated capsules. A toll-free consumer hotline was set up the first week of the crisis, and consumers were offered the opportunity to replace Tylenol capsules with a free bottle of Tylenol tablets. Johnson & Johnson was also open with the public instead of being defensive about the deaths. Accurate information was promptly released, and domestic employees and retirees were kept updated on developments. The chairman of the company appeared on the talk show *Donahue* and on *60 Minutes* to answer questions about the crisis, and other executives were interviewed by *Fortune* and the *Wall Street Journal*.

Despite the setback—the recall alone cost Johnson & Johnson $50 million after taxes—Tylenol rebounded within a year, in large part because the public never lost faith in Johnson & Johnson. Despite this happy ending, many companies fail to emulate Johnson & Johnson's example. A case in point is the RC2 Corporation, which makes Thomas the Tank Engine and other toy trains. In 2007 the public learned that many of the company's trains were made with lead paint, which can cause brain damage if a child ingests it. RC2, however, declined to issue refunds to unhappy parents but asked them to return the affected toys—at their own expense—in order to receive replacement trains and a free bonus gift. Unbelievable as it may seem, one of the toy trains that RC2 mailed out as a gift (a gray boxcar called Toad) was also made with lead paint. Even worse, RC2 executives hid from public view throughout this whole sorry episode, never explaining why their safety checks had failed or why they deserved to be trusted in the future.[76]

In the case of Johnson & Johnson, the company credits its sixty-year-old, one-page statement of values, known as the Credo, with enabling it to build the employee trust necessary for maintaining a firm corporate value system. The Credo acknowledges the company's need to make a sound profit while addressing its obligations to provide a quality product, to treat its employees fairly and with respect, and to be a good corporate citizen, supporting the community of which it is a member. The Credo is "the most important thing we have in this company," says chairman Ralph Larsen.

Creating and maintaining a morally sound corporate culture is an ongoing task, and even Johnson & Johnson hasn't always been able to live up to its own values. For instance, the company had to pay $7.5 million in fines and costs after admitting that wayward employees had shredded papers to hinder a federal probe into the marketing of an acne cream. "There was no excuse," admits Larsen. "But it is a huge undertaking to spread our values around the world."[77]

STUDY CORNER

Key Terms and Concepts

broader view of corporate responsibility
business-can't-handle-it argument
CID structures
corporate culture
corporate moral agency
corporate moral code

corporate punishment
corporation
diffusion of responsibility
externalities
fiduciary responsibility
invisible-hand argument
let-government-do-it argument

limited liability
narrow view of corporate responsibility
privately held company
publicly held company
social entity (stakeholder) model
stockholders

Points to Review

- three ways corporations differ from partnerships
- privately held vs. publicly held companies

- historical evolution of the corporation
- two theoretical shifts that led to the relaxing of incorporation procedures

- significance of the Supreme Court's *Bellotti* decision
- whether the CID structure is compatible with, or rules out, corporate moral responsibility
- the concept of corporate punishment
- problem of vanishing individual responsibility and two responses to it
- Milton Friedman's view of corporate responsibility
- Melvin Anshen's idea of a social contract between business and society
- how both fairness and economics support the internalizing of externalities
- criticisms of the invisible-hand argument

- difference between the let-government-do-it and the invisible-hand arguments
- two versions of the business-can't-handle-it argument
- four things companies can do to become more socially responsible
- three limits to what we can expect the law to do
- two situations in which the rule of maximizing profits is socially inefficient
- what top management should do to institutionalize ethics inside the company
- the importance of creating a morally oriented corporate culture

CASE 5.1
Yahoo in China

Shi Tao is a thirty-seven-year-old Chinese journalist and democracy advocate. Arrested for leaking state secrets in 2005, he was sentenced to ten years in prison. His crime? Mr. Shi had disclosed that the Communist Party's propaganda department had ordered tight controls for handling the anniversary of the infamous June 4, 1989, crackdown on demonstrators in Beijing's Tiananmen Square. A sad story, for sure, but it's an all too familiar one, given China's notoriously poor record on human rights. What makes Mr. Shi's case stand out, however, is the fact that he was arrested and convicted only because the American company Yahoo revealed his identity to Chinese authorities.[78]

You see, Mr. Shi had posted his information anonymously on a Chinese-language website called Democracy Forum, which is based in New York. Chinese journalists say that Shi's information, which revealed only routine instructions on how officials were to dampen possible protests, was already widely circulated. Still, the Chinese government's elite State Security Bureau wanted to put its hands on the culprit behind the anonymous posting.

And for that it needed Yahoo's help in tracking down the Internet address from which huoyan1989@yahoo.com.cn had accessed his e-mail. This turned out to be a computer in Mr. Shi's workplace, Contemporary Business News in Changsha, China.

A few months after Shi's conviction, the watchdog group Reporters Without Borders revealed the story of Yahoo's involvement and embroiled the company in a squall of controversy. After initially declining to comment on the allegation, Yahoo eventually admitted that it had helped Chinese authorities catch Mr. Shi and that it had supplied information on other customers as well. But the company claimed that it had no choice, that the information was provided as part of a "legal process," and that the company is obliged to obey the laws of any country in which it operates. Yahoo cofounder, Jerry Yang, said: "I do not like the outcome of what happens with these things ... but we have to comply with the law. That's what you need to do in business."

Some critics immediately spied a technical flaw in that argument: The information on Mr. Shi was provided by Yahoo's subsidiary in Hong Kong, which has an independent judiciary and a legal process separate from that of mainland China. Hong Kong legislation does not spell out what e-mail service providers must do when presented with a court order by mainland authorities. Commentators pointed out, however, that even if Yahoo was legally obliged to reveal the information, there was a deeper question of principle involved. As the *Financial Times* put it in an editorial: "As a general principle, companies choosing to operate in a country should be prepared to obey its laws. When those laws are so reprehensible that conforming to them would be unethical, they should be ready to withdraw from that market." Congressional representative Christopher H. Smith, a New Jersey Republican and chair of a House subcommittee on human rights, was even blunter: "This is about accommodating a dictatorship. It's outrageous to be complicit in cracking down on dissenters." And in an open letter to Jerry Yang, the Chinese dissident Liu Xiabo, who has himself suffered censorship, imprisonment, and other indignities, wrote: "I must tell you that my indignation at and contempt for you and your company are not a bit less than my indignation and contempt for the Communist regime.... Profit makes you dull in morality. Did it ever occur to you that it is a shame for you to be considered a traitor to your customer Shi Tao?"

Whether profit is dulling their morality is an issue that must be confronted not just by Yahoo but also by other Internet-related companies doing business in China. Microsoft, for example, recently shut down the MSN Spaces website of a popular Beijing blogger whose postings had run afoul of censors. Google has agreed to apply the Chinese censors' blacklist to its new Chinese search engine. And a congressional investigative committee has accused Google, Yahoo, and Cisco of helping to maintain in China "the most sophisticated Internet control system in the world." In their defense, the companies ask what good it would do for them to pull out of the Chinese market. They

contend that if they resist the Chinese government and their operations are closed down or if they choose to leave the country for moral reasons, they would only deny to ordinary Chinese whatever fresh air the Internet, even filtered and censored, can provide in a closed society. It's more important for them to stay there, play ball with the government, and do what they can to push for Internet freedom. As Yahoo chairman Terry S. Semel puts it: "Part of our role in any form of media is to get whatever we can into those countries and to show and to enable people, slowly, to see the Western way and what our culture is like, and to learn." But critics wonder what these companies, when they are complicit in political repression, are teaching the Chinese about American values.

Some tech companies are turning to the U.S. government for help. Bill Gates, for example, thinks that legislation making it illegal for American companies to assist in the violation of human rights overseas would help. A carefully crafted American anti-repression law would give Yahoo an answer the next time Chinese officials demand evidence against cyber-dissidents. We want to obey your laws, Yahoo officials could say, but our hands are tied; we can't break American law. The assumption is that China would have no choice but to accept this because it does not want to forgo the advantages of having U.S. tech companies operating there.

Still, this doesn't answer the underlying moral questions. At a November 2007 congressional hearing, however, a number of lawmakers made their own moral views perfectly clear. They lambasted Yahoo, describing the company as "spineless and irresponsible" and "moral pygmies." In response, Jerry Yang apologized to the mother of Shi Tao, who attended the hearing. Still, Yahoo has its defenders. Robert Reich, for instance, argues that "Yahoo is not a moral entity" and "its executives have only one responsibility ... to make money for their shareholders and, along the way, satisfy their consumers." And in this case, he thinks, the key "consumer" is the Chinese government.

Discussion Questions

1. What moral issues does this controversy raise? What obligations should Yahoo have weighed in this situation? Was the company a "traitor" to its customer, as Liu Xiabo says?

2. In your view, was Yahoo right or wrong to assist Chinese authorities? What would you have done if you were in charge of Yahoo?

3. Is Jerry Yang correct that the company had "no choice"? Assuming that Yahoo was legally required to do what it did, does that justify its conduct morally?

4. Assess the actions of Yahoo and of Microsoft, Google, and Cisco from the point of view of both the narrow and the broader views of corporate responsibility. What view of corporate responsibility do you think these companies hold? Do you think they see themselves as acting in a morally legitimate and socially responsible way?

5. In light of this case, do you think it makes sense to talk of a corporation like Yahoo as a moral agent, or is it only the people in it who can be properly described as having moral responsibility?

6. Would American companies do more good by refusing to cooperate with Chinese authorities (and risk not being able to do business in China) or by cooperating and working gradually to spread Internet freedom? In general, under what circumstances is it permissible for a company to operate in a repressive country or do business with a dictatorial regime?

7. Assess the pros and cons of a law forbidding American high-tech companies from assisting repressive foreign governments.

CASE **5.2**

Levi Strauss at Home and Abroad

Juvenile Manufacturing of San Antonio, Texas, began making infants' and children's garments in a plant on South Zarzamora Street in 1923; in the 1930s, the company switched to boys' and men's clothing and changed its name to Santone Industries. During the 1970s, Santone manufactured sports jackets for Levi Strauss & Co., which eventually decided to buy out the company. In 1981, Levi Strauss paid $10 million and took over operations on South Zarzamora Street.[79]

Although the garment industry had been struggling in some parts of the country, it had prospered in San Antonio—not least on South Zarzamora Street. One of three Levi's plants in the city, the plant was slowly converted in the late 1980s from making sports jackets to manufacturing the company's popular Dockers trousers, which had surpassed Levi's 501 jeans as the firm's top-selling line. And despite the sweatshop image that the industry brings to people's minds, many of San Antonio's semiskilled workers were happy to be employed at Levi Strauss. They thought that pay at the plant was good. Benefits were respectable, too: paid maternity leave for qualified employees, health insurance, and ten days of paid vacation at Christmas and ten during the summer.

Then in 1990, Levi Strauss decided to close the plant—the largest layoff in San Antonio's history—and move its operations to Costa Rica and the Dominican Republic. This was the course of action that had been recommended the previous year by Bruce Stallworth, the firm's operations controller. Closing the plant would cost $13.5 million, Stallworth calculated, but transferring its production abroad would "achieve significant cost savings," enabling the company to recover its closing costs within two years. In 1989, it cost $6.70 to make a pair of Dockers at the South Zarzamora plant. Plant management had hoped to reduce that to $6.39 per unit in 1990, but even that would be significantly higher than the per unit cost of $5.88 at the Dockers plant in Powell, Tennessee—not to mention the $3.76 per unit cost Levi Strauss could get by using third-world contractors.

Stallworth attributed the San Antonio plant's high costs to workers' compensation expenses, to less-than-full-capacity plant operation, and to the fact that "conversion from sports coats to Dockers has not been totally successful." Retraining workers who have spent years sewing jackets to sew trousers, it seems, is not very easy. Furthermore, running the San Antonio plant efficiently would mean running it at full capacity, but operating at full capacity on South Zarzamora Street with 1,115 workers—compared with 366 and 746 employees, respectively, at the company's other two U.S. Dockers plants—meant too many pairs of trousers produced by high-priced American labor. Workers at San Antonio averaged $6 an hour, which was about a day's pay in the Caribbean and Central America for workers with the same level of skill.

Bob Dunn, Levi Strauss vice president of community affairs and corporate communications, denies that the company did anything it shouldn't have done with regard to closing the plant. "We didn't see any way to bring costs in line." And he adds: "As much as people like Dockers, our research shows people are not willing to pay $5 or $10 more for a pair of pants just because the label says 'Made in the U.S.A.'"

Closing plants is nothing new for Levi Strauss. Before closing South Zarzamora Street, it had already closed twenty-five plants and shifted the work overseas, either to its foreign production plants or to overseas contractors. Using overseas contractors saves the firm even more money, because in addition to paying lower wages, the company avoids paying directly for benefits like health insurance and workers' compensation. This time, though, the company's decision to close a domestic plant and move its production abroad prompted local labor activists to fight back. They filed a class-action lawsuit and organized a boycott of Levi's products.

The boycott, however, gained little publicity outside San Antonio, and the lawsuit fizzled out. Neither seems to have dampened sales, but they embarrassed the company, which donated nearly $100,000 to help local agencies retrain its former employees and gave San Antonio an additional $340,000 to provide them with extra job counseling and training services.

Most politicians kept a low profile on the issue, praising Levi Strauss for offering its workers more than was legally required and promising to try to recruit a new company to use the empty factory. U.S. Representative Henry B. Gonzales, however, spoke out harshly: "When a company is so irresponsible—a company that has been making money and then willy-nilly removes a plant to get further profit based on greed and cheaper labor costs in the Caribbean—I say you have a bad citizen for a company."

To this, Bob Dunn responded, "Our sense is we do more than anyone in our industry and more than almost anyone in American industry." He was proud of the way Levi Strauss treated people when it closed plants. "We try to stress the right values," he said. "It's not easy. There isn't always one right answer."

Levi Strauss in China

Dunn's emphasis on values reflects the thinking of Levi Strauss's Robert D. Haas, CEO until 1999, now chairman of its board. Ever since he organized a successful leveraged buyout of the company, Haas has tried to create a more values-centered management at Levi Strauss by emphasizing social responsibility and employee rights. A year after the closure on South Zarzamora Street, the company's values-centered management received a second blow when a contractor in the U.S. territory of Saipan was accused of virtually enslaving some of its Chinese workers. When the company learned the contractor was not paying the island's legal minimum wage, it fired him and formed a top-management committee to monitor its overseas contractors. Levi Strauss then went on to become the first multinational to adopt guidelines for its hired factories. The first part of its "Global Sourcing Guidelines" covers the treatment of workers and the environmental impact of production; the second part sets out the company's standards for choosing the countries in which it will do business.

As a result of its guidelines, Levi Strauss stopped all production in China because of human rights abuses and systemic mistreatment of labor. For instance, in a factory in Shenzhen, women sew for twelve hours a day plus overtime and receive only two days off a month. They have no health care and no compensation for injury (although Chinese legislation requires this). Their pay is often below the legal minimum of 12 cents an hour. Back home in San Francisco, the decision to pull out of China caused a fiery debate within the company. Because Chinese labor is so cheap, a committee had recommended that the company stay in China and work to make things better, but Haas decided to withdraw from China altogether. With an annual revenue of $6.5 billion, Levi Strauss is the largest clothing company in the world, and because it has no direct investment in China, it could afford to pull out. But some business analysts worried that in the long run the company would be sacrificing a great deal by leaving China. China is the world's fastest-growing economy, and some predict that it will be the world's largest economy in twenty years.

Many people praised Levi Strauss's decision, but it dumbfounded some companies. At Nike, one executive said, "I can't figure it out.

I have no idea what Levi's is doing." Nike was still having trouble figuring it out when the cartoon strip *Doonesbury* began pummeling the athletic footwear company for having its products made in sweatshops in Vietnam. Cheap Asian labor is a high priority for Nike's top executive Philip Knight, and his company has long favored places like Indonesia and China, where pay is poor and labor unions are suppressed. In Indonesia, the women who work at the sweatshops of Nike contractors make $2.20 a day, and it took four years of violent struggle to get the minimum wage raised that high. Now Nike has moved into Vietnam, where labor costs are cheaper yet. At one Nike plant in Vietnam, investigators found that employees worked sixty-five hours a week—more than Vietnamese law allows—for a weekly wage of $10 and that 77 percent of them suffered respiratory problems from breathing chemical fumes at work.

By contrast, Levi Strauss believes that a growing number of its customers shun products made in sweatshops. Consumers "don't want to buy a shirt made by children in Bangladesh or forced labor in China," says one industry observer. The firm's top management also believes that Levi Strauss is emblematic of American culture and that its mildly anti-establishment image must be guarded. "Anyone seeking to protect their brand and company reputation will realize these policies make sense," says Bob Dunn, who helped design the company's overseas guidelines. For this reason, some critics do not charge that Levi Strauss was foolish to leave China, but rather that its decision was dictated only by bottom-line profitability—that it was a publicity stunt aimed at attracting more customers.

But the team of inspectors that Levi Strauss has monitoring its contractors is a reality, not a publicity stunt. They regularly visit factories and are prepared to fire violators of the company's guidelines—such as the factory operator who was strip-searching female workers to determine whether they were, as they claimed, menstruating and thus, according to local Muslim law, entitled to a day off with pay. The firm has also pulled out of Myanmar because of human rights abuses in that country. The company is sensitive to local mores, however, and its first goal is not to boycott countries or cancel contracts. In Bangladesh, its inspectors discovered that a contractor was employing children under the age of fourteen—something that is legal there but contrary to Levi Strauss guidelines. The company didn't want the children discharged, which would have hurt the families who were dependent on their income, but it didn't want the children working, either. So Levi Strauss devised a solution: Younger children would be paid while attending school and would be offered full-time jobs when they turned fourteen.

Six Years Later

Six years after withdrawing from China because of human rights violations, Levi Strauss reported in April 1998 that it would resume manufacturing its clothing there. The company denied that its decision was related to its having just closed several U.S. plants, but the reversal of its China policy provoked an outcry among human rights groups, who accused Levi Strauss of putting profits before its self-proclaimed concern for workers. The company's critics pointed to a National Labor Committee report that found gross labor violations in twenty-one Chinese factories. These include forced overtime (sometimes amounting to a workweek of ninety-six hours), wages as low as 13 cents per hour, and restrictions on workers' freedom to assemble. And the U.S. State Department declared that it had not detected any "appreciable" improvement in China's human rights record during that period. Executives at Levi Strauss responded, however, that it is now possible for the company to operate in China while adhering to its corporate code of conduct. Unlike before, it now has contracting partners who are willing

and able to adhere to its code, and improvements in the company's monitoring system enable it to prevent abuses at its own factories.

For its part, Nike has begun to see the light of social responsibility. Bowing to pressure from its critics, the company has now pledged to root out underage workers and to require overseas manufacturers of its wares to meet strict U.S. health and safety standards. It also agreed to allow outsiders from labor and human rights groups to join the auditors who inspect Nike's Asian factories—a demand the company had long resisted. Nike CEO Knight acknowledged the public-relations problem facing his company, which stood accused, he said, of having "single-handedly lowered the human rights standard for the sole purpose of maximizing profits." Nike had "become synonymous with slave wages, forced overtime and arbitrary abuse." But, Knight continued, "I believe that the American consumer does not want to buy products made in abusive conditions." He did not, however, pledge to increase wages.

Meanwhile, Back Home...

Levi Strauss, which in the early 1980s had fifty U.S. plants, has now abandoned all American production. In 2003, it shut the historic ninety-six-year-old San Francisco factory that made its 501 jeans, and in 2004 it stopped production at its only remaining North American operations: three manufacturing plants in Canada and two sewing and finishing plants in San Antonio. The company still owns eight manufacturing plants outside the United States, but it is expected to close those eventually as well. "The closures are an absolutely necessary part of ensuring the long-term competitiveness of our business," said Julie Klee, a Levi Strauss general manager. "Moving away from owned-and-operated manufacturing to a broader sourcing base will strengthen our business by giving us much more flexibility." Levi's Robert Haas added that the closures were inevitable. The company had invested tens of millions of dollars in automated equipment, training, and incentives to keep domestic plants competitive enough to offset the overseas wage differential, but it was not enough, he said. "We've resisted all of the pressures that have been on us to close plants. As you know, we are one of the very last major companies that has any kind of manufacturing presence in North America anymore. ... Belatedly and reluctantly, we're having to follow in the footsteps of other apparel manufacturers" and shift work overseas.

However, to help its displaced workers, Levi Strauss gave them eight months' notice of the layoff, instead of the two months required by law, and provided them with three weeks' severance pay per year of service. Levi Strauss also offered displaced workers up to $6,000 each to help them make the transition into new fields. The money was to be used for job training, community college education, English-language lessons, moving expenses, or setting up a small business. "We can't ignore the fact that certain jobs are not ... sustainable in North America," said Haas. "They're done better in other countries. But companies ... must be sensitive to [the workers'] circumstances and help move [them] into the next stage of their lives."

Discussion Questions

1. Evaluate the pros and cons of Levi Strauss's decision to close its South Zarzamora Street plant. Was it a sound business decision? Was it a socially responsible decision? Could the company have reasonably been expected to keep the plant running?

2. Having decided to close the plant, was there more that Levi Strauss could and should have done for its laid-off workers?

3. How, if at all, is your assessment of Levi Strauss's responsibilities affected by the fact that the company bought the plant and then closed it nine years later?

4. Should consumers avoid products that are made by sweatshops? Should they shun companies that lay workers off needlessly? Are consumer boycotts ever justified? When are such boycotts likely to be effective? Under what circumstances would you participate in a consumer boycott?

5. How would you feel if you had been an employee at the plant? Bob Dunn said, "My hope is that as time passes and people have a chance to reflect on what we've done, [people who have lost jobs] will judge us to have been responsible and fair." Do you think Levi Strauss's former employees will judge the company that way?

6. With regard to Levi Strauss's conduct both at home and abroad, does it make sense to talk about the company as a morally responsible agent whose actions can be critically assessed, or can we assess only the actions and decisions of individual human beings inside the company?

7. Do corporations have a responsibility to monitor the conduct of the companies they do business with—in particular, their contractors and suppliers? Do they have a responsibility to avoid doing business in countries that are undemocratic, violate human rights, or permit exploitative work conditions? Compare and critically assess the conduct of Levi Strauss and Nike in this respect.

8. Should Levi Strauss have resumed its manufacturing operations in China? Should it have pulled out in the first place?

9. Is Levi Strauss sincere in its professed concern for foreign workers? Is Nike?

10. American consumers say that they don't like having their clothes made by exploited workers in foreign sweatshops. Is consumer pressure sufficient to get American companies to improve the pay and working conditions of foreign factory workers?

11. Some pessimists say that because most companies don't make social welfare a priority, competition will ultimately undermine the efforts of companies like Levi Strauss to establish standards. Assess this argument.

CASE **5.3**

Free Speech or False Advertising?

With annual sales of over $16.3 billion and annual profits of around $1.5 billion, Nike is one of the giants in the sports apparel business, and its trademark "Swoosh" logo is recognized around the world. However, for a company its size, Nike directly employs surprisingly few workers—only about 22,000. That is because overseas contractors manufacture all Nike's products. These independent contractors employ approximately 600,000 workers at 910 factories, mostly in China, Indonesia, Vietnam, and Thailand.

Like many other firms, Nike outsources its manufacturing to take advantage of cheap overseas labor. But the price of doing so began getting higher for Nike in the late 1990s, when anti-sweatshop activists started campaigning against the company, charging that the third-world workers making its products were exploited and abused. Activists on many college campuses, for instance, encouraged their peers to boycott Nike shoes and clothing and tried to pressure their universities' athletic departments not to sign deals with Nike for team sports apparel.

Instead of ducking the issue, as other companies might have, Nike responded vigorously to the criticisms. At the University of North Carolina, for example, Nike ran full-page ads in the student newspaper, asserting that it was a good corporate citizen and upheld humane labor standards. It sent representatives to meet with student activists, and company CEO Philip Knight took the unusual step of showing up at an undergraduate seminar on corporate globalization to defend his company. Nike issued press releases and sent letters to many college presidents and athletic departments, asserting, among other things, that Nike paid "on average, double the minimum wage as defined in countries where its products are produced" and that its workers "are protected from physical and sexual abuse."

Enter Marc Kasky, a fifty-nine-year-old San Francisco activist. He thought Nike's campaign was misleading the public about working conditions inside its factories, so he sued the company for false advertising under California's consumer protection law. In Kasky's view, the case was simply a matter of protecting consumers from corporate deceit. In response, Nike argued that the statements in question were protected by the First Amendment because they were made in news releases, letters to the editor, and op-ed essays and because they related to the company's labor practices—which are a matter of public concern—and not the products it sold. Two lower courts agreed with Nike, but then the California Supreme Court overturned their verdict, ruling in a 4–3 decision that the company's campaign was essentially commercial speech (which generally receives less First Amendment protection than political or personal speech) even though Nike was not specifically talking about shoes. In the court's view, Nike's speech was directed at customers and dealt with its business operations; the form in which the information was released was irrelevant. The judges, however, didn't determine whether Nike really did abuse workers or mislead consumers; it left those factual questions for a trial court to decide.

Nike then appealed the case to the U.S. Supreme Court. California Attorney General Bill Lockyer filed a brief in support of Kasky, which seventeen other states joined. The brief contended that the case was not about free speech but rather about "Nike's ability to exploit false facts to promote commercial ends." Harvard law professor Laurence Tribe, however, defended the company, arguing that treating Nike's letters and press releases as equivalent to advertising would undercut the ability of companies to speak out on political issues. He urged that the California decision would have a "chilling effect on freedom of speech." To this, however, the chief author of the California brief, deputy attorney general Roland Reiter, responded: "I believe the concerns expressed are really overblown. We have a company talking about itself. It's difficult to see why holding them to the truth would cause any kind of calamity." USC law professor Erwin Chemerinsky agreed. He argued that it didn't matter whether Nike issued the information in the form of a press release: "If a company makes false statements about its product or practices with the intent of increasing profits, that's commercial speech."

After having heard the case, however, the Supreme Court declined to decide the substantive legal issues at stake. Instead, it dismissed the case on a technicality and sent it back to California for trial. Before the trial began, however, Nike settled out of court with Kasky. As part of the deal, Nike agreed to donate $ 1.5 million to the Fair Labor Association, a sweatshop-monitoring group, and in a joint statement, Kasky and Nike "mutually agreed that investments designed to strengthen workplace monitoring and factory worker programs are more desirable than prolonged litigation." A happy ending? Not in everyone's eyes. Friends of Nike argued that because the Supreme Court did not act forthrightly to protect corporate speech, companies will be reluctant to discuss public issues involving their products. Those on the other side, however, responded that when disclosing information about wages and working conditions, companies should be held to the same standards of truth and accuracy as when they disclose financial data.[80]

Discussion Questions

1. In this case, was Nike engaged in commercial speech, or were its statements political or social speech? What determines whether speech is commercial or not?

2. Was the out-of-court settlement a reasonable resolution of this case? What would have been the good or bad consequences of the Supreme Court's deciding in Nike's favor? Of its deciding in Kasky's favor?

3. Should commercial speech receive less First Amendment protection than other types of speech, or does this violate the rights of corporations? Explain your answer.

4. Do corporations have the same moral rights as individual human beings? Should they have the same political rights? Is it morally permissible to limit the speech of corporations in ways that would be wrong if applied to the speech of individual citizens? If it is permissible, is it good public policy?

5. Does Nike have a social responsibility to address matters of public concern such as the working conditions in its overseas operation? If it chooses to do so, does it have an obligation to make its statements as truthful and accurate as it can? Under what circumstances should corporations be held liable for the truth of their public statements?

CASE **5.4**

Charity to Scouts?

"I don't care what Bank of America does," fumed Lynn Martin at a meeting of the board of directors of Baytown Company, a San Francisco Bay Area firm that runs four different family-oriented restaurants and owns a string of six popular fast-food take-out establishments (called "Tip-Top"). "We took a principled stand at the time," she continued, "and I don't think there's enough evidence to justify changing our minds now."

Like a lot of local companies, Baytown supports various charitable causes in the Bay Area. The company has always figured that it had an obligation to give more back to the community than good food; besides, people in the Bay Area expect local companies to display a sense of social responsibility. Among the groups that Baytown has always helped support is the regional Boy Scouts district. Not only did Baytown think the Scouts worthy of its corporate help but giving to the organization seemed to fit well with Tip-Top's all-American theme and with the family character of Baytown's other restaurants.

A simple thing suddenly got complicated, however, when the San Francisco Bay Area United Way decided to pull $1 million in annual funding for the Scouts because of the group's refusal to admit gays. Soon after that, Bank of America, Wells Fargo Bank, and Levi Strauss & Co. also decided to stop funding the Boy Scouts. A month later, Baytown's directors resolved to follow suit.

"We were pretty clear at the time," continued Martin, "that we didn't have any business supporting an organization that was perceived as discriminatory."

"Not me," said Tom Boyd. "I always thought that since the Boy Scouts are a private group, they can do whatever they want."

"Well, maybe they have a right to discriminate if they want, but that's not the point," said Ed Framers. "The rest of us agreed with Lynn that as a company we shouldn't be helping a group that discriminates. Of course, that was before everybody around the country started making such a fuss about companies' stopping their funding of the Scouts. We all know about those anti-gay groups demonstrating against the United Way and threatening to boycott the bank."

"Those groups hardly represent thinking in the Bay Area," Lynn Martin shot back.

"That's true," agreed Scott Arming, "but still we run a family-oriented business."

"What's that supposed to mean? Do you think gays and lesbians don't come to our restaurants? Do you think they don't have families? Do you think—"

"O.K., O.K.," Arming interjected.

"Lynn's right about that," Ed Framers said. "In fact, as far as I know, our customers never said much about it, one way or the other."

Executive Director Susan Lee then spoke up: "Well, I got a few phone calls about it, but there weren't really complaints. It was more people wanting to get more information about the situation. Of course, you always get a few cranks...."

"Ain't that the truth," murmured Boyd to Framers.

"Anyway," Lee continued, "things are different now. Bank of America has reversed its decision and is resuming funding to the Boy Scouts because the Scouts have lifted their ban on gays."

"That's what the bank says," said Lynn Martin. "But the whole thing is pretty murky if you ask me. Here, look at the newspaper story. The article reports company spokesman Peter Magnani as explaining that

> the bank had first interpreted the Scouts membership policy as banning gay members. But after consulting with Boy Scouts national President John Clendenin, the organization clarified its policy and 'made it clear' that membership is open to all boys who subscribe to Scouting oaths and laws. 'We take that to mean all boys, regardless of their sexual orientation,' said Magnani.[81]

"But then," Martin continued, "the newspaper goes on to quote a spokesperson for the Boy Scouts of America as saying that there has been 'absolutely no change in our policy. We do not believe that homosexuals provide positive role models.' What are we supposed to make of that? It looks as if the bank is trying to wriggle out of a stand that turned out not to be as popular as it thought it would be."

"That sounds pretty cynical," Ed Framers said. "The bank says here that its decision 'was based solely on the Scouts' clarification of its policy,' and the Scouts' national president is quoted as saying that the organization is 'open to all boys as long as they subscribe to the Boy Scouts Oath and Law.' You weren't a Scout, Lynn, but I was, and the oath and law are only basic stuff about trustworthiness and honesty; there's nothing about sexuality. Besides we're talking about boys, not adults. I think the whole thing has been blown out of proportion."

Martin quickly responded, "Don't you think boys have sexual feelings? Come on, Ed, give me a break. And besides, if there is nothing in the Scout oath or whatever it is about sexuality, why does the organization have to take a stand one way or the other?"

"Maybe the Scouts shouldn't have taken a stand," Susan Lee inserted, "but at this point it looks as if we have to. When we stopped giving to the Scouts, that sent one message; if we reverse our decision now, that sends another. Frankly, I don't like being in the position of having to impose our values, one way or the other."

"Yes, but you yourself said that there's no way to avoid it," Lynn Martin shot back. "So we should at least stand behind the right values."

"And what are those?" asked Lee.

"I don't have the slightest idea myself," Tom Boyd whispered to Scott Arming.

Arming ignored him as he turned to the group: "You know, I think we are and should continue to be a socially responsible company. But maybe we should reconsider whether being socially responsible means giving to charitable causes in the first place. Is that something we are truly obligated to do, or are we just following a fad? I mean, I hate to bring up the bottom line, but every dollar we give to the Boy Scouts or anybody else is one less dollar for the company and its stockholders."

"Come on, Scott, you know it's not as simple as that," responded Susan Lee. "Charitable contributions bring us good will, and it's the kind of thing the community expects an enlightened company to do."

"You may not be persuaded, Scott," Ed Framers added, "but I think what Susan says is right. In any case, we don't need a debate about general principles. We need to figure out what we are going to do about the Boy Scouts."

The meeting continued....

Discussion Questions

1. What do you think Baytown should do? Explain your reasoning. What business factors are relevant to your decision? What moral factors?

2. Are Baytown's directors operating with a broad or a narrow conception of corporate responsibility?

3. Were Baytown and the other companies right to have withdrawn their support from the Boy Scouts? Is there anything wrong with companies' attempting to influence the policies of an organization like the Scouts?

4. What do you think explains Bank of America's policy reversal? Is Lynn Martin's cynicism warranted?

5. Scott Arming doubts that businesses have an obligation to support charitable organizations. Do they?

PART3

Business and Society

Laurence Mouton/PhotoAlto/Corbis

207

CHAPTER **6**

Consumers

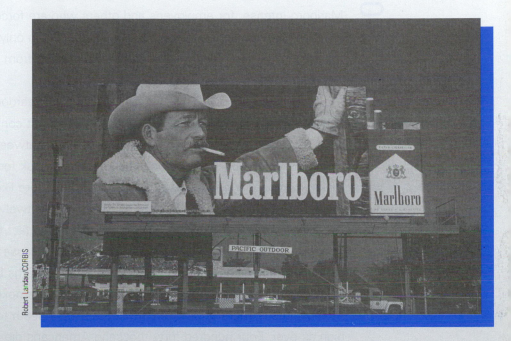

Robert Landau/CORBIS

Product Safety
The Legal Liability of Manufacturers
Government Safety Regulation
How Effective Is Regulation?
The Responsibilities of Business

Other Areas of Business Responsibility
Product Quality
Pricing
Labeling and Packaging

Deception and Unfairness in Advertising
Deceptive Techniques
The Federal Trade Commission's Role
Ads Directed at Children

The Debate over Advertising
Consumer Needs
Market Economics
Free Speech and the Media

CASES
Breast Implants
Hot Coffee at McDonald's
Sniffing Glue Could Snuff Profits
Drug Dilemmas

The "Marlboro Man" has long mesmerized people around the world, and few can deny the glamour of the ruggedly good-looking Marlboro cowboy, with boots, hat, chaps—and, of course, a cigarette in his mouth. Product of one of the most successful advertising campaigns in history, the Marlboro Man revolutionized the image of Marlboro cigarettes, making it the best-selling brand in the United States. Always a leader in its field, Marlboro has now begun test marketing a short, "snack-size" cigarette, the Marlboro Intense, for employees and others who are forced to take quick outdoor cigarette breaks. Smokers can consume it in only seven puffs yet receive the same amount of nicotine as they would from a regular-size cigarette.

Everybody, of course, knows that smoking is hazardous to one's health—everyone, that is, but the tobacco industry. It continues, publicly at least, to deny any cause-and-effect relationship between smoking and disease, even though smoking doubles a person's risk for stroke and makes coronary artery disease two to four times more likely. Furthermore, male smokers are twenty-two, and female smokers twelve, times more likely than nonsmokers to die from lung cancer. The fact that "about half of all Americans who continue to smoke will die because of the habit"[1] makes smoking the leading cause of preventable deaths in the United States. Although the percentage of Americans who smoke is dropping, the absolute number of smokers—and smoking's death toll—remains as high as ever. Four hundred forty thousand Americans die each year of tobacco-related causes (up from 400,000 in 1990), at an annual price tag of $75 billion in medical expenditures and another $80 billion in indirect costs.[2]

Virtually no other consumer good compares to cigarettes in terms of individual injury and social cost. Because of this, in the mid-1990s forty-six state governments came together to sue the big tobacco companies, demanding compensation for the money that they spend on health problems caused by smoking. The suit was settled in 1998 for $206 billion. Among other things, the agreement required tobacco firms to accept a tax hike on their products, to finance anti-smoking commercials, to cease tobacco-product placement in films and television shows, and to end outdoor tobacco advertisements. As a result, cigarette billboards came down across the country, including a famous 64-foot-high Marlboro Man that loomed for years over Sunset Strip in Los Angeles.

Not long afterward, the federal government also filed suit against the large tobacco companies. Based on anti-racketeering legislation, the suit contended that cigarette manufacturers "have engaged in and executed … a massive 50-year scheme to defraud the public" by suppressing evidence that cigarette smoke contains carcinogens and that nicotine is addictive. In addition, the suit accused tobacco companies of marketing cigarettes to teenagers, agreeing among themselves not to develop safer cigarettes, and manipulating nicotine levels in cigarettes to create and sustain addiction. (Even so-called low-tar and low-nicotine cigarettes, marketed as "light" or "ultra-light," have been designed so that addicted smokers inhale as much nicotine as they always have.)[3] After a nine-month trial, the government won its lawsuit in 2006—although not the $280 billion in damages it had sought. But U.S. District Court Judge Gladys Kessler did require cigarette manufacturers to correct their falsehoods, to desist from making incorrect, misleading, or deceptive statements about the health risks of cigarettes, and to disclose their marketing practices annually to government officials.

In 2009 Congress took things a step further by empowering the Federal Drug Administration to regulate cigarettes—although not to outlaw smoking or ban nicotine altogether. Among other things, the FDA now has the legal authority to reduce nicotine content and regulate the chemicals in cigarettes and to bar tobacco flavorings (which are thought to be a lure to first-time smokers). It can also further restrict the advertising and promotion of tobacco products and prohibit terms like "light," "mild," and "low tar." Meanwhile, smokers continue to sue cigarette manufacturers for injuries allegedly caused by their deadly habit. Despite the warnings that have been required on cigarette packs and ads since 1966, many smokers—or their estates—contend that they were addicted and couldn't stop. Many of these lawsuits are large class-action suits involving dozens of law firms with the collective resources to take on the big tobacco companies. As a result, the smokers have been winning. In cases around the country, juries have been penalizing the tobacco companies with compensatory and punitive damage verdicts for millions, even billions, of dollars (although the companies often succeed in getting the largest of these judgments, such as that of a Miami jury for $144.8 billion, reduced or overturned on appeal). In response to this and to declining cigarette consumption in the United States and parts of Europe, the tobacco companies are marketing their wares more aggressively than ever in Asia and the developing world.[4]

Cigarettes are an especially dangerous product, and their manufacture, marketing, advertising, and sale raise a number of acute questions relevant to the consumer issues discussed in this chapter. For instance, what are the responsibilities to consumers of companies that sell potentially or (in the case of cigarettes) inherently harmful products? To what extent do manufacturers abuse advertising? When is advertising deceptive? Can advertisers create or at least stimulate desires for products that consumers would not otherwise want or would not otherwise want as much? How, if at all, should advertising be restricted?

Are consumers sufficiently well informed about the products they buy? Are they misled by deceptive labeling and packaging? In general, how far should society go in controlling the claims of advertisers, in regulating product packaging and labels, in monitoring product quality and price, and in upholding explicit standards of reliability and safety? What are the moral responsibilities of businesses in these matters? In a market-oriented economic system, how do we balance the interests of business with the rights of consumers? How do we promote social well-being while still respecting the choices of individuals?

These are among the issues probed in this chapter—in particular:

1. Product safety—the legal and moral responsibilities of manufacturers and the pros and cons of government regulations designed to protect consumers

2. The responsibilities of business to consumers concerning product quality, prices, labeling, and packaging

3. Deceptive and morally questionable techniques used in advertising

4. The choice between the "reasonable" consumer and "ignorant" consumer standards as the basis for identifying deceptive advertisements

5. Advertising and children

6. The social desirability of advertising in general: Is it a positive feature of our economic system? Does it manipulate, or merely respond to, consumer needs?

_____

PRODUCT SAFETY

Business's responsibility for understanding, providing for, and protecting the interests of consumers derives from the fact that citizen-consumers depend on business to satisfy their many and varied material needs and wants. This dependence is particularly true in our highly technological society, characterized as it is by a complex economy, intense specialization, and urban concentration. These conditions contrast with those prevailing in the United States when the country was primarily agrarian, composed of people who could satisfy most of their own needs. Today we rely on others to provide the wherewithal for our survival and prosperity. We rarely make our own clothing, supply our own fuel, manufacture our own tools, or construct our own homes, and our food is more likely to come from thousands of miles away than from our own gardens.

The increasing complexity of today's economy and the multifaceted dependence of consumers on business for their survival and enrichment have heightened business's responsibilities to consumers—particularly in the area of product safety. From toys to tools, cars to baby cribs, consumers use countless products every day believing that neither they nor their loved ones will be harmed or injured by them. Consumers, however, lack the expertise to judge many of the sophisticated products they utilize. Being human, they also make mistakes in handling the things they buy—mistakes that the manufacturers of those products can often anticipate and make less likely. For these reasons, society must rely on the conscientious efforts of business to promote consumer safety.

Statistics suggest that faith in the conscientiousness of business is sometimes misplaced. Every year millions of Americans require medical treatment from product-related accidents. For example, in a typical year, lawn mowers send 78,000 consumers to hospital emergency rooms, and home workshop equipment causes 130,000 people to seek emergency care, packaging and containers for household products injure 215,000 people, and sports and recreational equipment over 860,000.[5] Consumer products also electrocute approximately 200 people a year.[6]

The Legal Liability of Manufacturers

If any of us is injured by a defective product, we can sue the manufacturer of that product. We take this legal right for granted, but it didn't always exist. Before the landmark case of **MacPherson v. Buick Motor Car** in 1916, injured consumers could recover damages only from the retailer of the defective product—that is, from the party with whom they had actually done business. That made sense in a bygone day of small-scale, local capitalism. If your buggy crashed because the harness you bought from the local harnessmaker

Summary 6.1
The complexity of an advanced economy and the necessary dependence of consumers on business to satisfy their many wants increase business's responsibility for product safety.

The 1916 *MacPherson* case expanded the liability of manufacturers for injuries caused by defective products.

was defective, then your complaint was against him. By contrast, when a wheel fell off Donald MacPherson's Buick, the firm he had bought the Buick from hadn't actually made it.

Legal policy before *MacPherson* based a manufacturer's liability for damage caused by a defective product on the contractual relationship between the manufacturer and the purchaser (the "privity doctrine"). Their contractual relationship is simply the sale—that is, the exchange of money for a commodity of a certain description. But that contractual relationship is an important source of moral and legal responsibilities for the producer. It obligates business firms to provide customers with a product that lives up to the claims the firm makes about the product. Those claims shape customers' expectations about what they are buying and lead them to enter into the contract in the first place. The question in *MacPherson,* however, was whether a manufacturer's liability for defective products was limited to consumers with whom it had a direct contractual relationship.

The New York Court of Appeals's *MacPherson* decision recognized the twentieth-century economic reality of large manufacturing concerns and national systems of product distribution. Among other things, local retailers are not as likely as large manufacturers to be able to bear financial responsibility for defective products that injure others. One can also see the court moving in *MacPherson* to a "due-care" theory of the manufacturer's duties to consumers. **Due care** is the idea that consumers and sellers do not meet as equals and that the consumer's interests are particularly vulnerable to being harmed by the manufacturer, who has knowledge and expertise the consumer does not have. MacPherson, for instance, was in no position to have discovered the defective wheel before he purchased the Buick. According to the due-care view, then, manufacturers have an obligation, above and beyond any contract, to exercise due care to prevent the consumer from being injured by defective products.

As the concept of due care spread, legal policy moved decisively beyond the old doctrine of **caveat emptor**—literally "let the buyer beware"—which was seldom the guiding principle by the time of *MacPherson* anyway. Today we associate caveat emptor with an era of patent medicines and outrageously false product claims. Although legally the doctrine of "let the buyer beware" was never upheld across the board, there was a time when consumer's legal responsibility to accept the consequences of their product choices was greater than it is today. Consumers were held to the ideal of being knowledgeable, shrewd, and skeptical. Because they freely chose whether to buy a certain product, they were expected to take the claims of manufacturers and salespeople with a grain of salt, to inspect any potential purchase carefully, to rely on their own judgment, and to accept any ill results of their decision to use a given product. In the first part of the twentieth century, however, the courts repudiated this doctrine, largely on grounds of its unrealistic assumptions about consumer knowledge, competence, and behavior.

Strict Product Liability

Despite its support for the due-care theory and for a broader view of manufacturer's liability, the *MacPherson* case still left the injured consumer with

Summary 6.2
The legal liability of manufacturers for injuries caused by defective products has evolved over the years. Today the courts have moved to the doctrine of strict liability, which holds the manufacturer of a product responsible for injuries suffered as a result of defects in the product, regardless of whether the manufacturer was negligent.

Two broadly utilitarian considerations support strict product liability.

the burden of proving that the manufacturer had been negligent. Not only might such an assertion be difficult to prove, but also a product might be dangerously defective despite the manufacturer's having taken reasonable steps to avoid such a defect.

Two important cases changed this situation. In the 1960 New Jersey case *Henningsen v. Bloomfield Motors* and in the 1963 California case *Greenman v. Yuba Power Products,* injured consumers were awarded damages without having to prove that the manufacturers of the defective products were negligent. Consumers, the courts ruled, have a right to expect that the products they purchase are reasonably safe when used in the intended way. On the basis of these and hundreds of subsequent cases, the "strict liability" approach to product safety has come to dominate legal thinking.

The doctrine of **strict product liability** holds that the manufacturer of a product has legal responsibilities to compensate the user of that product for injuries suffered because the product's defective condition made it unreasonably dangerous, even though the manufacturer has not been negligent in permitting that defect to occur. Under this doctrine a judgment for the recovery of damages could conceivably be won even if the manufacturer adhered to strict quality-control procedures. Strict liability, however, is not absolute liability. The product must be defective, and the consumer always has the responsibility to exercise care.

Critics of strict product liability contend that the doctrine is unfair. A firm that has exercised due care and taken reasonable precautions to avoid or eliminate foreseeable dangerous defects, they insist, should not be held liable for defects that are not its fault—that is, for defects that happen despite its best efforts to guard against them. To hold such a firm liable seems unjust.

The argument for strict liability is basically utilitarian. *First,* its advocates contend that only such a policy will induce firms to bend over backward to guarantee product safety. Because they know they will be held liable for injurious defects no matter what, they will make every effort to enhance safety. *Second,* proponents of strict liability contend that the manufacturer is best able to bear the cost of injuries due to defects. Naturally, firms raise the price of their products to cover their legal costs (or pay for liability insurance). But defenders of strict liability do not disapprove of this. They see it as a perfectly reasonable way to spread the cost of injuries among all consumers of the product, rather than letting the cost fall on a single individual—a kind of insurance scheme.

Government Safety Regulation

These developments in product liability law set the general framework within which manufacturers must operate today. In addition, a number of government agencies have become involved in regulating product safety. Congress created one of the most important of these agencies in 1972 when it passed the Consumer Product Safety Act. This act empowers the **Consumer Product Safety Commission (CPSC)** to protect the public "against unreasonable risks of injury associated with consumer products." The five-member commission sets standards for products, bans products presenting undue risk of injury, and in general polices the entire consumer-product marketing process from manufacture to final sale.

In undertaking its policing function, the CPSC aids consumers in evaluating product safety, develops uniform standards, gathers data, conducts research, and coordinates local, state, and federal product safety laws and enforcement. The commission's jurisdiction extends to more than fifteen thousand products, and it has the power to require recalls, public warnings, and refunds. Exceptionally risky products can be banned or seized. Rather than stressing punitive action, however, the commission emphasizes developing new standards and redesigning products to accommodate possible consumer misuse. It is less concerned with assigning liability than with avoiding injuries in the first place.

Aside from drugs and motor vehicles, however, most products—such as toys, tools, and appliances—go to the market without regulation.[7] Compared with many other developed countries, the United States regulates fewer products on grounds of safety, implicitly relying more on the tort system and the threat of private lawsuits to protect consumers and keep corporations in line. By contrast, the European Union follows a "better safe than sorry" approach and regulates products that haven't been definitively proved dangerous but that might cause harm. Europe bans some products (such as cheap Chinese cigarette lighters that can flare up and explode) that are readily available in the United States and regulates other products (such as decorative oil lamps) more closely than the United States does. Moreover, American safety regulators, unlike their European counterparts, frequently find themselves entangled in red tape, which retards or prevents their defending consumers from unsafe products. A *Wall Street Journal* report on comparative approaches to product safety remarks, "As Europe increasingly gives regulators more clout and flexibility, their American counterparts remain hamstrung by a bureaucratic thicket that prolongs efforts to remedy all but the most egregious product defects."[8]

Economic Costs

Safety regulations benefit consumers but raise the price of products. Is the expense always worth it?

Although most product safety regulations bring obvious benefits, critics worry about the economic costs. New safety standards add millions of dollars to the cumulative price tag of various goods. Often economists can estimate how many lives a regulation saves and then compare that number with the cost of implementing the rule. For example, the cost of requiring labels showing the trans fat content of foods is only $3,000 per life saved, whereas the cost of insulation to protect against fire in airplane cabins is $300,000. For other regulations, the cost to save one life is considerably higher: stronger automobile doors $500,000; flame-retardant children's sleepwear $2.2 million; and reducing the asbestos exposure of factory workers $5.5 million.[9] Is the expense always worth it?

And what about recalls? The number of automobile recalls per year has doubled since 1993; today, one in twelve cars is recalled.[10] And recalls are expensive. BMW's recall of seventeen thousand 7 Series sedans to check problematic electronic fuel pumps set the company back $3 million—a large sum, one might think, but only a tiny fraction of the $200–$300 million Ford spent a few years earlier to recall 8.7 million vehicles with fire-prone ignition switches. And the estimated cost of Firestone's recall of 6.5 million tires it had made for Ford Explorers—the largest recall in the United States since the Tylenol scare of 1982—surpasses that.

Consumer Choice

In addition to cost is the issue of consumer choice. Sometimes consumers dislike mandated safety technology. In 1974, for example, Congress legislated an interlock system that would require drivers to fasten their seat belts before their cars could move. No doubt the law would have saved lives, but a public outcry forced lawmakers to rescind it. Apparently, many drivers saw interlock systems as a nuisance and believed their inconvenience outweighed any gain in safety.

In other cases, safety regulations may prevent individuals from choosing to purchase a riskier, though less expensive, product. Take, for example, the notorious Ford Pinto with its unsafe gas tank. In 1978, after all the negative publicity, scores of lawsuits, and the trial of Ford Motor Company for reckless homicide, the sale of Pintos fell dramatically. Consumers evidently preferred a safer car for comparable money. But when the state of Oregon took all the Pintos out of its fleet because of safety concerns and sold them, at least one dealer reported brisk sales of the turned-in Pintos at their low, secondhand price. Some consumers were willing to accept the risks of a Pinto if the price was right.

Economists worry about the inefficiencies of preventing individuals from balancing safety against price. Philosophers worry about interfering with people's freedom of choice. Take automobile safety again. Because smaller cars provide less protection than larger ones, people in small cars are less likely to survive accidents. Bigger, safer cars are more expensive, however, and many would prefer to spend less on their cars despite the increased risk. If only those cars that were as safe as, say, a Mercedes-Benz were allowed on the market, then there would be fewer deaths on the highways. But then fewer people could afford cars.

Preventing consumers from being able to choose a cheaper but riskier product can have both economic and ethical drawbacks.

Legal Paternalism

That example touches on the larger controversy over legal paternalism: the idea that the law may justifiably be used to restrict the freedom of individuals for their own good. No one doubts that laws justifiably restrain people from harming or endangering other people, but a sizable number of moral theorists deny that laws should attempt to prevent people from running risks that affect only themselves. There is nothing paternalistic about requiring you to have working brakes in your car. This protects other people; without brakes, you are more likely to run over a pedestrian. But requiring you to wear a seat belt when you drive affects only you. Anti-paternalists would protest that forcing you to wear a seat belt violates your moral autonomy. Nonetheless, in the past hundred years growing numbers of paternalistic laws have been enacted. In 2008, for example, California basically outlawed retail sales of raw, unpasteurized milk because of potential health risks, even though a number of consumers prefer it to pasteurized milk.[11]

Three points about
paternalism and safety
regulations.

Paternalism is a large issue that can't be done justice here, but in regard to safety regulations, three comments are in order. *First,* the safety of some products or some features of products (such as a car's tires) affects not only the consumer who purchases the product but third parties as well. Regulating these products or product features can be defended on nonpaternalistic grounds. *Second,* anti-paternalism gains plausibility from the view that individuals know their own interests better than anyone else does and that they are fully informed and able to advance those interests. But in the increasingly complex consumer world, that assumption is often doubtful. Whenever citizens lack knowledge and are unable to make intelligent comparisons and safety judgments, they may find it in their collective self-interest to set minimal safety standards. Such standards are particularly justifiable when few, if any, reasonable persons would want a product that did not satisfy those standards.

Finally, the controversy over legal paternalism pits the values of individual freedom and autonomy against social welfare. Requiring people to wear seat belts may infringe the former but saves thousands of lives each year. We may simply have to acknowledge that clash of values and be willing to make trade-offs. This doesn't imply a defense of paternalism across the board. Arguably, some paternalistic regulations infringe autonomy more than laws about seat belts do but bring less gain in social welfare. In the end, one may have to examine paternalistic product safety legislation case by case and weigh the conflicting values and likely results.

How Effective Is Regulation?

Consumers usually assume that if a product is on the market, especially if it is something they ingest, then it has been certified as safe. That assumption can be mistaken. For example, compared with Canada, Japan, and the European Union, the United States takes an approach to testing for mad cow disease that can only be called lackadaisical,[12] and there are serious gaps in its effort to keep beef free from contamination by E. coli.[13] Unapproved drugs, to take another example, can linger on the market for years while the **Food and Drug Administration** (FDA) studies them. For instance, since the hormone replacement Estratest became available in 1964, millions and millions of women have taken it, but the drug is still under FDA review and has yet to be approved.[14] Unfortunately, however, even FDA approval is no guarantee of safety as the scandal a few years ago over the high risk of heart attack from Vioxx and related painkillers revealed.

No government agency vouches for the safety of cosmetics and personal-care products such as shampoos, even though many of them are alleged to contain ingredients that are untested or known to be harmful.[15] Herbal remedies and dietary supplements are another source of concern. Although they represent an enormous—and enormously profitable—industry, they are exempt from the regulatory scrutiny applied to drugs.[16] There are few studies of the effectiveness of folk medicines such as kava, ginseng, and ginko biloba. Ephedra, for example, is supposed to help people lose weight, but it contains a potent chemical that can mimic the effects of amphetamines, causing heart attack, stroke, and arrhythmia. After Baltimore Orioles pitcher Steve Bechler died

Summary 6.3
Government agencies, such as the Consumer Product Safety Commission, have broad powers to regulate product safety, although the United States is less aggressive than the European Union about doing so. Critics contend that these regulations are costly and prevent individuals from choosing to purchase a riskier but less expensive product. This argument touches on the controversy over legal paternalism, the doctrine that the law may justifiably be used to restrict the freedom of individuals for their own good.

while taking it, the FDA proposed rules to give consumers more information about the contents of herbal supplements and to standardize their manufacture to ensure purity and uniformity. But merely informing consumers about what's inside the bottle doesn't tell them what risks they run in taking it.

In some cases, public opinion and political considerations can interfere with regulatory efforts to protect consumers. For example, pressure from gun enthusiasts caused the Consumer Product Safety Commission to drop its effort to get Daisy Manufacturing to recall BB guns with a defective magazine that had contributed to the accidental shooting death of a teenage boy.[17] The same year, political pressure appears also to have led the FDA to override the recommendation of its panel of medical experts and to refuse to lift the ban on over-the-counter sales of the "morning after" pill.[18] This decision stirred so much controversy that two years later the FDA relented and approved selling the pill to women over eighteen (and then in 2009 to women over seventeen). One thing the FDA has not changed its mind about, however, is medical marijuana. In 2006 the FDA ignored a report by the National Academy of Science's Institute of Medicine as well as other medical and scientific evidence and once again ruled that the use of marijuana has no medical benefits for any patients.[19]

Political pressure aside, the FDA, the CPSC, and other regulatory agencies frequently have difficulty fulfilling their many responsibilities. The FDA, for example, receives nearly half a million reports each year of adverse reactions to popular medicines (most of them false alarms).[20] Nor can it keep up with legal requirements to inspect manufacturers of medical devices (ranging from contact lenses to defibrillators).[21] And at its current rate of inspection, it would take the FDA 1,900 years to check all the plants around the world that process our food.[22] The 2004 shortage of flu vaccine, the massive 2007 recall of children's toys made in China with lead paint, and the salmonella outbreak of 2008 only underscored the difficulty that federal agencies have ensuring that products entering the country are safe.[23] Even when a regulatory agency recalls a product, it often ends up lingering on the shelves for years. Ask Walter Friedel: He spent four days in intensive care after breathing fumes from a do-it-yourself product to waterproof tile floors that he found at his local Home Depot, even though the CPSC had banned it a year earlier.[24]

Part of the reason for these regulatory lapses is underfunding. The CPSC, for instance, has only half the employees it did in 1980,[25] and the FDA has lost nearly one-third of its inspectors since 2004.[26] Still, regulatory agencies do generally succeed in protecting the interests of consumers and prodding business to act responsibly. In addition to government regulation, of course, public opinion, media attention, pressure from consumer advocacy groups, and the prospect of class-action lawsuits often goad companies to take product safety seriously.

Self-Regulation

Businesspeople tend to be hostile both to regulation and to consumer lawsuits or other pressure. When it comes to safety, they generally prefer self-regulation, competition, and voluntary, industry-determined safety standards.

Business dislikes regulation and consumer lawsuits or other pressure. But self-regulation sometimes falls short.

Their point of view is certainly in keeping with the tenets of classical capitalism, and self-regulation is arguably an attractive ideal on both moral and economic grounds. However, self-regulation can easily become an instrument for subordinating consumer interests to profit making when the two goals clash. Under the guise of self-regulation, businesses can end up ignoring or minimizing their responsibilities to consumers.

For example, nothing enrages airplane passengers more than being stuck on a runway because of bad weather and congested terminals, waiting for hours to take off, with little to eat or drink, overflowing toilets, and poor ventilation. (One passenger, made desperate after several hours trapped in a parked plane, made national news when he used his cell phone to call 911 to report that he and his fellow travelers were being held against their will. That call got authorities to empty the plane, but it also brought him a jail sentence.) The airlines, however, have avoided threatened regulation by successfully lobbying Congress to be allowed to solve the problem themselves. The result? Although a few airlines have committed themselves to release passengers after two or three hours, most have no rules at all.[27]

Recently, however, some industries have reversed their usual stance and sought out federal regulation. Why the change of attitude? In the case of children's toys, retailers and manufacturers have sought regulation in the hope of reassuring customers, scared off by massive recalls, that their products are safe.[28] Other companies figure that they can use federal safety regulations to thwart competition from cheap foreign imports or as a way of heading off liability lawsuits and legal action by individual states.[29]

Automobile Safety

Summary 6.4
Regulations help ensure that business meets its responsibilities to consumers, although many products are not as closely regulated as people think and political considerations sometimes interfere with the regulatory process. Business people tend to favor self-regulation and government deregulation, but—as the auto industry shows—this sometimes provides insufficient consumer protection.

The auto industry, however, has a long and consistent history of fighting against safety regulations. For example, it successfully lobbied the federal government to delay the requirement that new cars be equipped with air bags or automatic seat belts. Each year of the delay saved the industry millions of dollars. But the price paid by consumers was high: According to the National Highway Traffic Safety Administration (NHTSA), driving with your seat belt on in a car with air bags cuts in half your chance of dying in a crash.

When the law finally required passive restraint systems in new vehicles, Chrysler became (in 1989) the first U.S. auto manufacturer to install driver-side air bags in all its new models. Only five years earlier, Chrysler chairman Lee Iacocca had boasted in his autobiography of fighting against air bags since their invention in the mid-1960s. In 1971, he and Henry Ford II (then the top executives at Ford) met secretly with President Richard Nixon to persuade him to kill a pending Department of Transportation regulation requiring air bags in every new car sold in the United States.[30] Had air bags been made standard equipment in 1974, more than seventy thousand deaths and many times that number of severe injuries would have been avoided.

Decades earlier, Alfred Sloan decided not to fit Chevrolets with safety glass, one of the most important safety protections ever, in order to save money. Even after Ford began doing so, Sloan insisted, "It's not my responsibility to sell safety glass."[31] More recently, design changes that automakers initially resisted and then only reluctantly adopted have significantly reduced the number of people killed when their automobiles are struck by SUVs or pickups. In the late 1990s the auto industry denied that car passengers were at greater risk from pickups or SUVS than from automobiles despite the fact that those larger vehicles can easily slide over the doorsills and bumpers of autos and pierce deep into their passenger compartments. However, the National Highway Safety Administration threatened to impose mandatory regulations if the industry did not act. In a landmark pact, fifteen automakers from four nations agreed that by 2009 all SUVs and pickups would be built either lower to the ground or with an energy-absorbing beam that fits under the front and rear bumpers. A study released by the Insurance Institute for Highway Safety shows that an SUV that complies with these standards is 18 to 21 percent less likely to kill the driver of a passenger car in a front-to-front collision and 47 to 48 percent less likely to do so in a front-to-side collision. "To cut somebody's risk of death in half, that's huge," says one auto safety expert. "That's almost as good as seat belts. You're lucky if a new regulation gets you a 5 to 10 percent reduction in the death rate."[32]

As car buyers have become better informed, automobile manufacturers are rethinking Iacocca's old bromide "Safety doesn't sell." But even if safety does sometimes sell, for an industry to wait for marketplace demand before increasing safety standards can be irresponsible. Anti-lock brakes, for instance, save lives because they greatly improve a car's ability to stop short without skidding. Although the technology has been around for years, anti-lock brakes are still not required on new vehicles. The same point holds for side-curtain air bags and for microchip-based tire-pressure monitoring systems. Or, to take another example, hardly any cars built in the United States have electronic stability control (ESC), although a majority of new vehicles in Germany and northern Europe come with it. ESC prevents the kind of skids that often lead to rollovers, but it will remain a rare and expensive option until regulation requires it, thus bringing down the cost through manufacturing economies of scale. If society always waited for marketplace demand before insisting on public health and safety regulations, then pasteurization of milk and sprinkler systems to suppress fires in public places would still be "options."

The Responsibilities of Business

When it comes to consumer safety, the moral responsibilities of business go beyond merely obeying the law.

Simply obeying laws and regulations does not exhaust the moral responsibilities of business in the area of consumer safety. The Consumer Product Safety Commission, for example, has long required toy manufacturers to analyze their products for choking hazards, and it has banned toys that small children can easily choke on. By contrast, until 2003 no agency conducted safety testing of, or otherwise regulated or monitored, candy for its potential to choke children—even though in recent years many more children have choked to death on candy, particularly little gel candies, than on toys.[33] However, this regulatory asymmetry between toy manufacturers and candy manufacturers marked no significant difference in their moral obligations. Regardless of what the law does or doesn't require, candy manufacturers have as great a responsibility as toy manufacturers do to minimize choking deaths.

When it comes to product safety, the exact nature of business's moral responsibilities is difficult to specify in general, because much depends on the particular product or service being provided. But attending to the following points would go a long way in helping business behave morally with respect to consumer safety:

1. **Business should give safety the priority warranted by the product.** This injunction is important because businesses often base safety considerations strictly on cost. If the margin of safety can be increased without significantly insulting budgetary considerations, fine; if not, then safety questions are shelved.

   Cost cannot be ignored, of course, but neither can two other factors. One is the seriousness of the injury the product can cause. A police officer may seldom have to rely on a bulletproof vest, but the potential harm from a defective one is obvious. Yet Second Chance Body Armor suppressed evidence of a defect in its product because company executives feared that it would hurt plans for an initial stock offering.[34] The second factor to consider is the frequency of occurrence. Is a design flaw on a lawn mower, for example, likely to result in one customer out of a thousand—or one out of two million—cutting off a finger? The higher a product scores on either the seriousness or the frequency test (or both), the greater is the priority that needs to be placed on safety issues.

2. **Business should abandon the misconception that accidents occur exclusively as a result of product misuse and that it is thereby absolved of all responsibility.** At one time such a belief may have been valid, but in using today's highly sophisticated products, even people who follow product instructions explicitly sometimes still suffer injuries. In any case, the point is that the company shares responsibility for product safety with the consumer. Rather than insisting that consumers' abuse of product leads to most accidents and injuries, firms would probably accomplish more by carefully pointing out how their products can be used safely.

   A Pennsylvania court has endorsed this perspective. It awarded $11.3 million in damages to a twenty-year-old Philadelphia woman who was shot in the head when a handgun owned by her neighbor accidentally went off. The court decided the shop that had sold the weapon should pay 30 percent of the damages because it had provided the buyer with no demonstration or written instructions for safe use of the gun.[35]

   Both manufacturers and retailers have an obligation to try to anticipate and minimize the ways their products can cause harm, whether or not those products are misused. For example, a four-year-old girl was seriously injured when she stood on an oven door to peek into a pot on top of the stove and her weight caused the stove to tip over. A manufacturer can reasonably foresee that a cook might place a heavy roasting pan on the oven door. If doing so caused the stove to tip over, a court would almost certainly find the stove's design defective. But should the manufacturer have foreseen the use of the door not as a shelf but as a step stool? The courts ruled that it should have. In the case of guns, manufacturers could make their product safer with trigger locks or internal safety locks, and they could work with wholesalers to crack down on dealers who repeatedly sell weapons that end up in the hands of criminals (the police give gun makers the serial numbers of any of their guns used in crimes).

3. **Business must monitor the manufacturing process itself.** This holds true as well for large companies that outsource all or part of a product's production to independent contractors. Frequently firms' failure to control key variables during the manufacturing process results in product defects. Companies should periodically review working conditions and the competence of key personnel. At the design stage of the process, they need to predict ways the product might fail and the consequences of such failure. For production, companies ordinarily can select materials that have been pretested or certified as flawless. If a company fails to do this, then we must question its commitment to safety. Similar questions arise when companies do not make use of available research about product safety. To answer some questions a company may have to generate its own research. However, independent research groups ensure impartial and disinterested analysis and are usually more reliable than in-house studies.

   Testing should be rigorous and simulate the toughest conditions. Tests shouldn't assume that the product will be used in exactly the way the manufacturer intends it to be used. Even established products should be tested. Neither a trouble-free history nor governmental approval of a product guarantees that it is free of defects.[36]

   When a product moves into production, it is often changed in various ways. These changes should be documented and referred to some appropriate party, such as a safety engineer, for analysis. The firm must be scrupulous about coordinating department activities so manufacturing specifications are not changed without determining any potential dangers related to these changes.

4. **When a product is ready to be marketed, companies should have their product safety staff review their market strategy and advertising for potential safety problems.** This step is necessary because both product positioning and advertising influence how a product is used, which in turn affects the likelihood of safety problems. For example, ATVs (all-terrain vehicles) are marketed in a way that appeals to young people, who have comparatively little driving experience and a propensity to take risks. Yet ATVs result in more injuries per vehicle than cars do, and they cause more deaths and injuries than snowmobiles or personal watercraft. Every year, around 44,000 children are injured, and 150 killed, riding ATVs.[37] Or consider the feeder auger manufacturer whose promotional brochure stated that "even a child can do your feeding." The brochure had a photograph of the auger with its safety cover removed to show the auger's inner workings. When a young boy was injured while using the feeder auger with the safety cover removed, a jury found the promotional brochure misleading with respect to operating conditions and product safety.[38]

5. **When a product reaches the marketplace, firms should make available to consumers written information about the product's performance.** This

Summary 6.5
To increase product safety, companies need to (1) give safety the priority necessitated by the product, (2) abandon the misconception that accidents are solely the result of consumer misuse, (3) monitor closely the manufacturing process, (4) review the safety implications of their marketing and advertising strategies, (5) provide consumers with full information about product performance, and (6) promptly investigate consumer complaints. Some successful companies already put a premium on safety.

information should include operating instructions, the product's safety features, conditions that will cause the product to fail, a complete list of the ways the product can be used, and a cautionary list of the ways it should not be used. Warnings must be specific. But no matter how specific they are, warnings are of little value if a consumer cannot read them. St. Joseph Aspirin for Children is marketed in Spanish-speaking areas and is advertised in Spanish-language media. But you have to know English to read the crucial warning: "Children and teenagers should not use this medicine for chicken pox or flu symptoms before a doctor is consulted about Reye's Syndrome, a rare but serious illness reported to be associated with aspirin." Because his mother spoke only Spanish and couldn't read the label on the St. Joseph's box, little Jorge Ramirez of Modesto, California, contracted Reye's Syndrome. Today, he is blind, quadriplegic, and mentally impaired.[39]

6. **Companies should investigate consumer complaints and do so quickly.** Federal law requires that manufacturers report all claims of potentially hazardous defects within 24 hours, even if it is unclear whether a recall is warranted. However, in at least three major cases, Mattel took months to gather information on reports of potentially hazardous problems with certain of its toys, collecting scores of consumer complaints in the meantime, before disclosing the problems to the CPSC. Despite having been fined twice for "knowingly" withholding information regarding safety defects that "created an unreasonable risk of serious injury or death," the company contends that it is right for it to proceed at its own pace regardless of what the law says.[40]

Even if firms seriously attended to these safety considerations, they couldn't guarantee an absolutely safe product. Some hazards invariably attach to certain products, heroic efforts notwithstanding. But business must acknowledge and discharge its responsibilities in this area. Morally speaking, no one's asking for an accident- and injury-proof product, only that a manufacturer do everything reasonable to approach that ideal.

Cigarette fires illustrate the shortcomings of the tobacco industry in this respect. According to government estimates, about 1,500 Americans are killed each year in cigarette fires, making cigarettes the country's leading cause of fatal fires. Cigarette fires are responsible for 7,000 serious injuries per year and for property damage of $400 million annually. For years, however, research has shown that small design changes in cigarettes would make them less likely to ignite furniture and bedding—not to mention forest fires. Lawmakers in a number of states have called for legislation to set a fire-resistance standard for cigarettes, but the tobacco industry remains staunchly opposed to this.[41]

The tire industry offers another example. On a Montana road, the tread on the left rear tire of Joseph Cartus's classic sports car separated, causing the car to flip and leaving his girlfriend disfigured and with brain damage. The tire had only 4,000 miles on it, but it was eleven years old, and as the NHTSA has now documented, even pristine tires deteriorate with age and become prone to sudden failure. "The age issue is the tire industry's dirty little secret," says one safety expert. Tire makers are reluctant to address the age problem because it would create havoc with their distribution systems. New tires often sit around for two years or more before being sold, and if they had "use by" dates on them, consumers would do what they do when buying milk or meat, namely, refuse to buy anything other than the freshest item.[42]

Unfortunately, there are numerous other examples of companies and entire industries that play fast and loose with safety, resisting product improvements and dodging responsibility for consumer injury. But many companies do respond quickly to perceived or suspected hazards. Consider two examples of successful companies that place a premium on product safety.[43]

JCPenney and Burning Radios

Back in the early 1960s, a few of the radios sold by JCPenney were reported to have caught fire in customers' homes. JCPenney tested the radios and discovered a defective resistor in a few of them—less than 1 percent. Nonetheless, JCPenney informed the manufacturer, withdrew the entire line of radios, ran national ads informing the public of the danger, and offered immediate refunds. "This was before the Consumer Product Safety Commission even existed," said JCPenney vice chairman Robert Gill. "I guess some people might have thought we were crazy, and said that liability insurance was specifically designed to take care of such problems. But we felt we just could not sell that kind of product."

Johnson Wax and Fluorocarbons

In the mid-1970s, environmentalists became seriously alarmed at the possibility that fluorocarbons released from aerosol cans were depleting the earth's thin and fragile ozone layer. The media rapidly picked up the story, but nearly all manufacturers of aerosol cans denounced the scientific findings and stood by their products. The exception was Johnson Wax. The company acknowledged that the scientific questions were difficult to resolve, but it took seriously consumer concern about ozone depletion. Years before the FDA ban, Johnson Wax withdrew all its fluorocarbon products worldwide. "We picked up a lot of flak from other manufacturers," recalled company chairman Samuel Johnson, "and we lost business in some areas, but I don't have any question we were right.... Our belief is that as long as you can make do without a potentially hazardous material, why not do without it?"

OTHER AREAS OF BUSINESS RESPONSIBILITY

Product safety is naturally a dominant concern of consumers. No one wants to be injured by the products he or she uses. But safety is far from the only interest of consumers. The past forty years have seen a general increase in consumer awareness and an ever stronger consumer advocacy movement. One chief consumer issue has been advertising and its possible abuse, which is discussed in subsequent sections of this chapter. Three other areas of business responsibility—product quality, pricing, and labeling and packaging—are equally important and are taken equally seriously by the consumer movement.

Product Quality

The demand for high-quality products is closely related to a number of themes mentioned in the discussion of safety. Most people would agree that business bears a general responsibility to ensure that the quality of a product measures up to the claims made about it and to reasonable consumer expectations. They would undoubtedly see this responsibility as deriving primarily from the consumer's basic right to get what he or she pays for.

Although high product quality can also be in a company's interest, sometimes business shirks this responsibility. For example, in 1973 new car bumpers had to withstand a 5-mile-per-hour collision with no damage. Ten years later, the auto industry succeeded in getting this quality standard lowered: The speed was cut in half, and damage to the bumpers themselves was no longer taken into account. Or consider the bottled-water industry. Most people who buy bottled water do so because they believe that it is purer and safer than tap water. Not so, reports the Natural Resources Defense Council, which tested 103 brands and found that one-third of them, including some of the best-known brands, contained contaminants that exceeded state or federal standards. These results do not mean that bottled water is dangerous, but they do suggest that consumers are not getting the product quality they're paying for.[44]

One way that business assumes responsibilities to consumers for product quality and reliability is through *warranties,* which are obligations to purchasers that sellers assume. People generally speak of two kinds of warranties: express and implied. **Express warranties** are the claims that sellers explicitly state—for example, that a product is "shrinkproof" or will require no maintenance for two years. The moral concern, of course, is whether a product lives up to its billing. Express warranties include assertions about the product's character, assurances of product durability, and other statements on warranty cards, labels, wrappers, and packages or in the advertising of the product. Many companies offer detailed warranties that are very specific about what defects they cover. Few go as far as L. L. Bean does with its "100% guarantee," which allows customers to return any purchase at any time for a full refund if it proves unsatisfactory.

Implied warranties include the claim, implicit in any sale, that a product is fit for its ordinary, intended use. The law calls this the implied warranty of **merchantability**. It's not a promise that the product will be perfect; rather, it's a guarantee that it will be of passable quality or suitable for the ordinary purpose for which it is used. Implied warranties can also be more specific—for example, when the seller knows that a buyer has a particular purpose in mind and is relying on the seller's superior skill or judgment to furnish goods adequate for that purpose.

The concept of an implied warranty is relevant to the case of Kodak's instant cameras. When Polaroid won a patent violation judgment against Kodak, Kodak was forced not only to stop selling its instant cameras but also to compensate previous purchasers, who could no longer obtain film for their cameras. Those purchasers had relied on the implicit claim that Kodak would not suddenly make its products obsolete.[45]

With or without warranties, however, consumers today are more militant than ever in their insistence on product quality and on getting exactly what they paid for. For example, when Ira Gore learned that his new car had been damaged and repainted before he took delivery, he sued BMW for having reduced his car's value by $4,000 and sought punitive damages based on the fact that BMW had sold 983 such "refinished" cars over a ten-year period. An Alabama jury agreed with Gore. It viewed the practice as consumer fraud and awarded him $4 million in punitive damages—not bad recompense for an injury to his car that it had cost BMW only $601.78 to fix. The Alabama Supreme Court subsequently cut the award in half, and later the U.S. Supreme Court ordered Alabama to lower it still further, holding that $2 million is "grossly excessive" punishment for the minor economic injury Gore had suffered.[46] Although the Court's precedent-setting ruling cheered many corporations, it left no doubt that punitive damages are appropriate in product-quality cases like this. The only question is whether they are excessive.

Pricing

Have you ever wondered why a product sells at three for a dollar or is priced at $6.99 rather than simply $7.00? Or why a product that retails for $9.80 on Monday is selling for $11.10 on Friday? The answer may have little to do with the conventional determinants of product price such as overhead, operating expenses, and the costs of materials and labor. More and more frequently, purely psychological factors enter into the price-setting equation.

For example, why would a retailer price T-shirts at $9.88 instead of $9.99? "When people see $9.99, they say, 'That's $10,'" explains the general sales manager of one company. "But $9.88 isn't $10. It's just psychological."[47] Similar psychological considerations are at work when airlines advertise one-way fares that are available only with the purchase of a round-trip ticket for twice the price.

For many consumers, higher prices mean better products, so manufacturers arbitrarily raise the price of a product to give the impression of superior quality or exclusivity. But as often as not, the price is higher than the product's extra quality. For example, a few years ago Proctor-Silex's most expensive fabric iron sold for $54.95, a price $5 higher than the company's next most expensive. Its wholesale price was $26.98 against $24.20, a difference of only $2.78. Moreover, the extra cost of producing the top model was less than $1 for a light that signaled when the iron was ready.[48]

Manufacturers trade on human psychology when they sell substantially identical products at different prices. For example, Heublein raised the price of its Popov brand vodka about 10 percent. Why the price increase? Heublein sales representatives believed that consumers wanted a variety of vodka prices to choose from. Apparently they were right: Even though Popov lost 1 percent of its market share, it increased its profits by 30 percent. Applying its theory further, Heublein offers vodka-drinkers an even more expensive vodka: Smirnoff. Yet analysts insist that there is no qualitative difference among vodkas made in the United States.[49] In this case, the use of psychological pricing is closely related to the problem of pricing branded products higher than generic products that are otherwise indistinguishable. Consumers pay more assuming that the brand name or the higher price implies a better product.

Manipulative Pricing

Sometimes consumers are misled by prices that conceal a product's true cost. Hidden charges, surcharges, and other stealth fees can boost the consumer's actual cost significantly above announced price: for example, charges for mounting and balancing when you buy tires; multiple taxes and services fees on cell-phone plans; "visitor" taxes and collision insurance on rental cars; "convenience" charges, processing fees, and shipping charges on concert tickets. In addition, manufacturers often disguise price increases by reducing the quality or the quantity of the product—downsizing a "pound" of coffee to 13 ounces, for example, or shrinking a candy bar but not its price.

Promotional pricing can also be manipulative. Discount cards and "card specials" lure consumers into grocery stores like Dominick's, Kroger, and Safeway, where customers typically pay more for their food overall than they would at rival stores.[50] Sale-priced items have ballooned from 8 percent of U.S. retail sales in 1971 to as high as 78 percent in some sectors today.[51] But the initial markup also has increased. A survey of San Francisco area furniture stores illustrates how misleading sale prices can be. While one retailer was advertising a Henredon sofa, model no. 8670, at an "original price" of $2,320, on sale for $2,170, and another small retailer had it on sale for $2,476, or 20 percent off an original price of $3,095, a major department store was offering the same sofa, with the same "E-grade" upholstery, for $2,500, "35 percent off" the "original price" of $4,000.[52]

Rebates, too, are a type of manipulative pricing. Most consumers dislike them. Satisfying the redemption rules and mailing them in are hassles. Sometimes the rebates are arbitrarily denied, and, even when they're not, it usually takes weeks and weeks to receive the check. When a long-forgotten check does arrive, consumers sometimes toss it in the trash because it looks like junk mail. Companies love them, though. Rebates get consumers to focus on the discounted price of a product and then buy it at full price. And then, as one consultant explains, "anything less than 100 percent redemption is free money" for the company. With millions of rebates offered every year, that translates into more than $2 billion of extra revenue for retailers and their suppliers. Small wonder then that many consumers—and some state and federal authorities—suspect that companies design the rules to keep redemption rates down.[53]

Some cases of manipulative pricing are not so obvious. For example, the pharmaceutical company Cephalon repeatedly raised the price of its popular narcolepsy drug Provigil to get patients and insurance companies to switch to a longer-acting version of it, called Nuvigil. That's because Cephalon's patent on Provigil was set to expire, after which the drug would face stiff competition from generic equivalents. Before that happened, the company wanted to make sure that Provigil users were taking Nuvigil instead because its patent—and the high profits that go with it—was still good for years to come.[54]

Tricky or manipulative pricing is not just a nuisance; it also raises moral questions.

Many practical consumers think of these pricing practices and gimmicks as a nuisance or irritant that they must live with, not as something morally objectionable. But tricky or manipulative pricing does raise moral questions—not least about business's view of itself and its role in the community—that businesspeople and ethical theorists are now beginning to take seriously.

Price Fixing

Much more attention has been devoted to price fixing, which despite its prevalence is widely recognized as a violation of the rules of the game in a market system whose ideal is open and fair price competition. **Horizontal price fixing** occurs when competitors agree to adhere to a set price schedule, not to cut prices below a certain minimum, or to restrict price advertising or the terms of sales, discounts, or rebates. A recent example is furnished by the two dozen Mercedes-Benz dealers in New York, New Jersey, and Connecticut who conspired not to undercut one another with discounts.[55] There is nothing illegal about businesses consciously charging the same prices as their competitors. It is the agreement to do so that violates the law.

Vertical price fixing takes place when manufactures and retailers—as opposed to direct competitors—agree to set prices. For example, a federal judge found Toys "R" Us guilty of conspiring to keep prices for Barbie, Mr. Potato Head, and other popular toys artificially high. The retail giant used its market clout to force Mattel, Hasbro, and other major toymakers not to sell their toys to warehouse clubs like Sam's Club and Costco.[56] Sometimes, it is the manufacturer, not the retailer, that engages in vertical price fixing. For example, Panasonic was found guilty of pressuring retailers such as Circuit City, Kmart, and Montgomery Ward into selling its products at the company's suggested retail price and not at a discount. Although manufacturers often suggest prices to their retailers, the retailers are supposed to be free to set their own prices, depending on the profit they foresee in the market.

Until 2007 any agreement between a manufacturer and a retailer to fix prices was illegal. That's when the U.S. Supreme Court reversed a 100-year-old precedent and held that minimum-retail-price agreements do not automatically violate the Sherman Antitrust Act.[57] In fact, some "resale price maintenance" agreements, the Court held, might even promote competition. It therefore instructed lower courts to adopt a case-by-case approach, forcing them to specify when such agreements unfairly disadvantage consumers and, more generally, when and why such price fixing is wrong. In response to the Court's decision, in 2009 Maryland passed a law that prohibits manufacturers from requiring retailers to charge minimum prices for their goods. Some other states are likely to do the same. In the meantime, small companies have sprung up that scour the web on behalf of clients such as Sony, Samsung, and Black & Decker, looking for retailers who are offering bargains below the minimum price set by the manufacturer. If the discounter is an authorized dealer, it is contractually bound to raise its price. If the seller is not an authorized dealer, other tactics are used, such as threatening people selling the product on eBay with trademark or copyright infringement.[58]

Summary 6.6
Business has obligations to consumers that go beyond safety: Product quality must live up to express and implied warranties, and prices should be fair. In particular, business should refrain from price fixing, price gouging, and manipulative pricing, which raise issues of honesty and consumer exploitation. In assessing a particular pricing practice, we should ask whether it would be good for our socioeconomic system as a whole if it were widespread or generally followed.

Horizontal price fixing, however, remains unambiguously outside the law. And it's easy to see why. When a handful of companies dominates a given market and conspires to charge artificially high prices, this clearly disadvantages consumers and subverts the principles of a market system. To take a notorious example, in 1960 General Electric, Westinghouse, and twenty-seven other companies producing electrical equipment were found guilty of fixing prices in that billion-dollar industry. Given the oligopolistic nature of the electrical equipment market, consumers could not reasonably be said to have had the option to take their business elsewhere and thus drive down prices. (In fact, until it was exposed, they had no reason to believe they were being victimized by price fixing.) More recently, federal and state investigators established that executives at the nation's largest national and regional dairy companies conspired—sometimes for decades—to rig bids on milk products sold to schools and military bases. Forty-three companies, among them Borden, Pet, Dean, and Flav-O-Rich, were convicted of price fixing and bid rigging.[59]

Of course, controlling prices need not be done so blatantly. Firms in an oligopoly can tacitly agree to remain uncompetitive with one another, thereby avoiding losses that might result from price-cutting competition. They can then play "follow the leader": Let the lead firm in the market raise its prices, and then the rest follow suit. The result is a laundered form of price fixing. Even when there is no tacit price fixing, the firms that dominate a field are often reluctant to compete on the basic of price. Nobody, they say to themselves, wants a price war, as if price competition were a threat to the market system rather than its lifeblood. Thus, familiar rivals such as Pepsi and Coca-Cola or McDonald's and Burger King usually prefer to compete by means of image and jingles rather than price.

Price Gouging

From the moral point of view, prices, like wages, should be just or fair. Merchants cannot morally charge whatever they want or whatever the market will bear any more than employers can pay workers whatever they (the employers) wish or can get away with. In particular, price gouging is widely viewed as unethical, although what exactly constitutes price gouging is often debated. Some define it as charging what the market will bear regardless of production costs. But that definition doesn't take into account supply and demand. Because they are in short supply, tickets for the World Series or houses in a popular neighborhood may command an extremely high price relative to their production costs, yet this does not constitute price gouging. **Price gouging** is better understood as a seller's exploiting a short-term situation in which buyers have few purchase options for a much-needed product by raising prices substantially. New York hotels that doubled or tripled their prices in the aftermath of the September 11, 2001, attacks were guilty of this, as were oil companies, innkeepers, and merchants who took advantage of Hurricane Katrina to jack up their prices. Some jurisdictions make it illegal for retailers to raise their prices during a natural disaster or some other emergency. However, the morality or immorality of some instances of possible gouging seems open to debate. Is it unethical for a hardware store to boost the price of snow shovels from

Although price gouging is generally viewed as unethical, there is disagreement about what it is and whether all instances of it are wrong.

$15 to $20 after a large snowstorm or for a car dealer to mark up the price of a popular car model that is temporarily in short supply?

When a gas station raises the price of its current stock of gasoline because the wholesale price is scheduled to go up or when the big oil companies set the wholesale price of gasoline 10 to 19 cents a gallon higher in San Francisco than in Los Angeles because average household income is greater there,[60] that may not fit the definition of price gouging, but it strikes many people as unfair. So does the fact that Americans have to pay substantially more for medicines than do Canadians or Europeans. This is not a matter of cheap generics or illegal knockoffs. Brand-name drugs such as Lipitor, Zoloft, and Nexium cost 30 to 100 percent more in the United States than in Canada or Europe.[61]

Apple's decision to cut the price of its iPhone by $200 might have sounded like good news for consumers, but it ignited loud protests from some of Apple's most devoted fans. That's because Apple had introduced the iPhone only seventy-five days before. Early customers who had stood in long lines to purchase theirs felt like chumps. Maybe they weren't victims of price gouging in the traditional sense, but they believed they'd been exploited and they quickly let Steve Jobs hear about it. As a result, he apologized and issued early buyers a store credit for $100. That move was unprecedented, but it still left some of them unhappy. After all, a store credit is not the same as cash, and given the new, reduced price, Apple was still coming out $100 ahead.

In the end, the question "What is a fair price?" probably defies a precise answer. Still, one can approach an answer by assessing the factors on which the price is based and the process used to determine it. Certainly factors such as the costs of material and production, operating and marketing expenses, and profit margin are relevant to price setting. One can also ask whether a seller's pricing practices try to exploit buyers by taking advantage of a lack of competition or some other buyer vulnerability or in some other way treat people as means rather than respecting them as ends in themselves. Also relevant is whether it would be good for our socioeconomic system as a whole if a particular pricing practice were widespread or generally followed.

Product price, of course, reflects in part the consuming public's judgment of the relative value of the article. Ideally, this judgment is formed in the open market in a free interplay between sellers and buyers. However, for this process to function satisfactorily, buyers must be in a position to exercise informed consent. As will be discussed further in Chapter 9, informed consent calls for deliberation and free choice, which require in turn that buyers understand all significant relevant facts about the goods and services they are purchasing. But consumers do not always receive the clear, accurate, and complete information about product quality and price that they need to make prudent choices.

Labeling and Packaging

Business's general responsibility to provide clear, accurate, and adequate information undoubtedly applies to product labeling and packaging. The reason is that, despite the billions of dollars spent annually on advertising, a product's label and package remain the consumer's primary source of product

Product labels and packages often fail to tell consumers what they need to know or even exactly what they are getting.

information. Often, however, labels and packages do not tell consumers what they need to know, or even what exactly they are getting. For example, many high-energy drinks do not list their caffeine content, and few cigarette cartons tell consumers which of the nearly six hundred additives that manufacturers sometimes use have been added to their cigarettes.

Even when product labels provide pertinent information, they are often difficult to understand or even misleading, and what they omit may be more important than what they say. For example, organic milk often comes from cows that are not on pasture, and products that bear the label "organic" or "USDA organic" are not necessarily 100 percent organic but may contain the same kind of synthetics that conventional food processors use.[62] One-third of the fresh chicken sold in the United States is "plumped" with water, salt, and sometimes a seaweed extract called carrageenan that helps it retain the added water. Although chickens processed this way contain up to eight times as much sodium per serving, they are still labeled "all natural" or "100% natural." That's because water, salt, and carrageenan are natural ingredients, even though they are not naturally found in chicken.[63] Equally confusing is environmental labeling. Manufacturers label products "biodegradable," "environmentally safe," or "recyclable" without defining those terms or providing any scientific evidence to back them up. As environmental awareness has grown, so has the prevalence of "greenwashing"—the making of false or misleading environmental claims—by marketers.[64] And even the most socially and environmentally conscious consumers have difficulty distinguishing among "fair trade certified," "fairly traded," "Rainforest Alliance certified," "sustainable," and "certified sustainable."

The FDA's labeling requirements now oblige manufacturers of packaged foods to provide nutritional information that is clear, specific, and of benefit to health-conscious consumers, and the FDA has cracked down on grain and vegetable cooking oils that label themselves "cholesterol free." (Although it is true that only animal products or by-products contain cholesterol, cooking oils are often replete with saturated vegetable fats and hydrogenated oils, which the body converts into cholesterol.) The FDA also went after Procter & Gamble for labeling as "pure, squeezed, 100% orange juice" processed orange juice that is made from water, concentrated orange juice, pulp, and "orange essence." But Atkins-brand packaged foods continue to label items as "low-carb" because they are low in what Atkins calls "net carbs," even though their total carbohydrate count may be much higher. (The company's plain bagels, for example, contain only 7 grams worth of "net carbs" but 18 grams of "total carbs" while its blueberry muffins weigh in at 4 grams of "net" but 21 grams of "total" carbohydrates.)[65] In addition, companies frequently put serving sizes on their labels that are misleading because they are far smaller than the amount a typical consumer would eat or drink.

Labels can beguile consumers in various ways. For example, the label on Aquafina, the bottled water, creates the false impression that its water comes from a mountain stream, and Gerber's Fruit Juice Snacks is packaged with images of a various fruits that the product does not contain. A particularly blatant example of label abuse was Sebastiani Vineyards' wine product, Domaine

Chardonnay. "Chardonnay" has a high level of name recognition and a positive reputation among wine consumers. Unfortunately for them, however, there wasn't a drop of chardonnay in Domaine Chardonnay, which was a blend of chenin blanc, sauvignon blanc, French colombard, riesling, and other grapes. After a public outcry when the wine was introduced, the Bureau of Alcohol, Tobacco, and Firearms required the company to redesign its label so that "Domaine Chardonnay" was in smaller letters at the bottom. Many people, however, felt that letting Sebastiani use the name of a grape varietal as a brand name was a travesty of labeling law—even if in the future Sebastiani were to include a little chardonnay in the wine mixture.

The question of misleading labels takes an interesting twist in the case of companies that choose to omit their corporate logo from products. For example, a brand called Cascadian Farm sells organic breakfast cereal, but from looking at the box you can't tell that it's actually made by General Mills. That's because General Mills is aiming the cereal at buyers who tend to eschew the brands of the big conglomerates. Similarly, you can't guess from reading the label of Blue Moon beer that it comes from Adolph Coors Company, and the label of Red Dog beer identifies its maker as Plank Road Brewery although it is really produced by Miller Brewing Company. This practice is spreading as big food and drink makers buy up the little brands that populate organic food stores or create their own "natural" products and boutique brands.[66]

Food that doesn't come in packages can be labeled in misleading or confusing ways, too. For example, restaurants and steakhouses frequently describe their steaks as "prime" even though they are not "USDA prime beef," a label that designates the gold standard in beef and that inspectors award to only 3 percent of cattle carcasses (55 percent are graded "choice" and 42 percent "select" or below). As Wayne Schick, executive corporate chef for Columbus Mitchell Restaurants, which owns steakhouses in Michigan and Ohio, explains, "Prime is not the same as saying USDA prime. We're using it to mean superb, great, prime, premium, all of those things." He adds, "I agree it is confusing."[67]

In addition to misleading labels, package shape can trick consumers by exploiting certain optical illusions. Tall and narrow cereal boxes look larger than short, squat ones that actually contain more cereal; shampoo bottles often have pinched waists to give the illusion of quantity; fruits are packed in large quantities of syrup; and dry foods often come in tins or cartons stuffed with cardboard. Package terms such as *large, extra large, jumbo, economy size,* and *value pack* frequently confuse or mislead shoppers about what they are buying and how good a deal they are getting. Even when unit pricing allows shoppers to compare the relative prices of items, time-pressed buyers often err anyway.

This is part of the explanation of why many retailers are able to sell "economy size" items for a higher per unit price than their smaller counterparts. These **quantity surcharges** are a much more widespread phenomenon than most people realize. For example, at 3.7 ounces the candy bar that Snickers calls "The Big One" is nearly twice the size of the familiar 2.07-ounce bar,

Summary 6.7
Business also has a responsibility to provide product information that is accurate, clear, and understandable and that suffices to meet the needs of consumers. Product labels frequently fail to do this. Package shape, package terms, and quantity surcharges also sometimes mislead shoppers.

which runs about 50 cents. But when priced at 99 cents—which it was at a store visited by the *Wall Street Journal*—The Big One costs 11 percent more per ounce. At another store the gallon jug of Ocean Spray cranberry juice—so big it had a special handle on it—cost 41 cents more than two half-gallon bottles. Although consumers frequently compare prices between brands, they generally neglect to make intra-brand comparisons because they take it for granted that the larger the volume, the better the deal. "You assume 'bigger' is a better deal," says Tom Pirko, president of a beverage and food consulting company, "and that gives marketers an open door to take advantage of people."[68] Because quantity surcharges exploit a common consumer error, the practice raises at least two moral questions: Can it be justified as a conscious pricing policy, and can retailers ethically remain silent about its existence?[69]

In general, the moral issues involved in packaging and labeling, as in marketing as a whole, relate primarily to truth telling and consumer exploitation. Sound moral conduct in this matter must rest on a strong desire to provide consumers with clear and usable information about the price, quality, and quantity of a product so they can make intelligent comparisons and choices. In this regard, the French perfume company L'Occitane is a model: It labels its products in Braille.[70] When marketers are interested primarily in selling a product and only secondarily in providing relevant information, then morally questionable practices are bound to follow. Those responsible for labeling and packaging would be well advised to consider at least the following questions, a negative answer to any of which could signal a moral problem: Is there anything about the packaging that is likely to mislead consumers? Have we clearly and specifically identified the exact nature of the product in an appropriate part of the label? Is the net quantity prominently displayed? Is it readily understandable to those wishing to compare prices? Are ingredients listed so they can be readily recognized and understood? Have we indicated and represented the percentage of the contents that is filler, such as the bone in a piece of meat?

These questions represent only some that a morally responsible businessperson might ask. In addition, we must not forget people whose health necessitates certain dietary restrictions. They often have great difficulty determining what products they can safely purchase.

Moral conduct in this area begins with a determination to provide consumers with what they need to know to make informed product choices.

DECEPTION AND UNFAIRNESS IN ADVERTISING

We tend to take advertising for granted, yet its social and economic significance is difficult to exaggerate. Ads dominate our environment. Famous ones become part of our culture; their jingles dance in our heads, and their images haunt our dreams and shape our tastes. Advertising is also big business. Sprint and McDonald's, for example, each shell out $1.7 billion a year on advertising, Ford spends $2.5 billion, and General Motors and Procter & Gamble a whopping $3.2 and $4.9 billion, respectively. As a whole, advertisers in the United States spend around $285 billion annually on all forms of media advertising.[71] That works out to over $900 for every person in the country. And that doesn't include what companies are paying for product placement in movies, television shows, and even songs and books.

When people are asked what advertising does, their first thought is often that it provides consumers with information about goods and services. In fact, advertising conveys very little information. Nor are most ads intended to do so. Except for classified ads (by amateurs!) and newspaper ads reporting supermarket prices, very few advertisements offer any information of genuine use to the consumer. (Those wanting useful product information must go to a magazine like *Consumer Reports,* which publishes objective and comparative studies of various products.) Instead, advertisements offer us jingles, rhymes, and attractive images.

The goal of advertising, of course, is to persuade us to buy the products that are being touted. Providing objective and comparative product information may be one way to do that, but it is not the only way, and judging from ads these days—which frequently say nothing at all about the product's qualities—it is not a very common way. The similarity among many competing products may be the explanation. One writer identifies the effort to distinguish among basically identical products as the "ethical, as well as economic, crux of the [advertising] industry"; another refers to it as the "persistent, underlying bad faith" of much American advertising.[72]

Deceptive Techniques

Because advertisers are trying to persuade people to buy their products and because straight product information is not necessarily the best way to do that, there is a natural temptation to obfuscate, misrepresent, or even lie. In an attempt to persuade, advertisers are prone to exploit ambiguity, conceal facts, exaggerate, and use psychological appeals.

Because providing frank product information is not always the most effective way to sell something, advertisers are tempted to misrepresent and deceive.

Ambiguity

Ads that are ambiguous—that can be understood in two or more ways—can be deceiving. Continental Baking Company was charged with such **ambiguity** by the Federal Trade Commission (FTC). In ads for its Profile bread, Continental *implied* that eating the bread would lead to weight loss, and a large number of people interpreted the ad to mean that eating Profile bread really would lead to weight loss. The fact was that Profile had about the same number of calories per ounce as other breads. Each slice of Profile contained seven fewer calories—but only because it was thinner than slices of most other breads.

Likewise, for years consumers inferred from advertisements that Listerine mouthwash effectively fought bacteria and sore throats. Not so. Accordingly, the FTC ordered Listerine to run a multimillion-dollar disclaimer. And when Sara Lee began promoting its Light Classics desserts, the implicit message was that "light" meant the products contained fewer calories than other Sara Lee desserts. When pressed by investigators to support this implied claim, Sara Lee contended that "light" referred only to the texture of the product. In such cases, advertisers and manufacturers invariably deny that they intended consumers to draw false inferences, but sometimes the ambiguity is such that a reasonable person wouldn't infer anything else.

Aiding and abetting ambiguity is the use of **weasel words**, words used to evade or retreat from a direct or forthright statement. Consider the weasel word *help*. Help means "aid" or "assist" and nothing else. Yet as one author has observed, "'help' is the one single word which, in all the annals of advertising, has done the most to say something that couldn't be said."[73] Because the word *help* is used to qualify, almost anything can be said after it. Thus we're exposed to ads for products that "help keep us young," "help prevent cavities," "help keep our houses germ-free." Consider for a moment how many times a day you hear or read phrases like these: helps stop, helps prevent, helps fight, helps overcome, helps you feel, helps you look. And, of course, *help* is hardly the only weasel word. *Like, virtual* or *virtually, can be, up to* (as in "provides relief up to eight hours"), *as much as* (as in "saves as much as one gallon of gas"), and numerous other weasel words are used to imply what can't be said. Sometimes weasel words deprive the message of any meaning whatsoever, as when *up to* and *more* come together in "save up to 40 to 50 percent and more."

The fact that ads are open to interpretation doesn't exonerate advertisers from the obligation to provide clear information. Indeed, this fact intensifies their responsibility, because the danger of misleading through ambiguity increases as the ad is subject to interpretation. Misleading ads exploit consumers, damaging their interests and costing them money, and they display a cavalier disregard for the truth. For these reasons ambiguity in ads is of serious moral concern.

> Misleading ads exploit consumers and play fast and loose with the truth.

Concealment of Facts

Advertisers that conceal facts suppress information that is unflattering to their products. They neglect to mention or they distract consumers' attention away from information, knowledge of which would probably make their products less desirable.

Shell resorted to **concealment of facts** when it advertised that its gasoline had "platformate" but neglected to mention that all other brands did too. Similarly, subway ads for the Bowery Bank in New York touted the fact that it is "federally insured," but so is almost every bank in the country. And Kraft advertised its Philadelphia Cream Cheese as having "half the calories of butter" but didn't tell consumers that it is also high in fat. When peanut butter makers advertise their products as cholesterol free, they omit the fact that only animal products contain cholesterol and that peanut butter is rich in fat. Weight Watchers tells consumers that its frozen meals are without butter, chicken fat, or tropical oils but not that they are high in salt. Caverject promotes itself as an alternative to Viagra as a treatment for male impotence. Its ads say that "Caverject can help you and your partner enjoy renewed spontaneity and sexual satisfaction." But they don't say that Caverject is a prescription medicine that must be injected with a needle inserted directly into the penis.

Ads for prepaid telephone calling cards often promise more minutes than they deliver, or they fail disclose fees, such as a 99-cent change to use a pay phone. Likewise, ads that promise savings for dialing long distance with a 10-10 number rarely mention the hidden costs that often make these services more expensive than the discount plan offered by one's regular long-distance carrier. Indeed, many of the most popular dial-around numbers are subsidiaries of the large carriers. For example, AT&T owns Lucky Dog (10-10-343), although you won't find that information on any Lucky Dog ads. As a result, some customers who dial a 10-10 number end up using their own long-distance carrier—and paying a higher rate to boot.

Likewise, advertisements for painkillers routinely conceal relevant information. For years, Bayer aspirin advertised that it contained "the ingredient that doctors recommend most." What is that ingredient? Aspirin. The advertising claim that "last year hospitals dispensed ten times as much Tylenol as the next four brands combined" does not disclose the fact that Johnson & Johnson supplies hospitals with Tylenol at a cost well below what consumers pay. Interestingly, American Home Products sued Johnson & Johnson on the grounds that the Tylenol ad falsely implies that it is more effective than competing products. But at the same time, American Home Products was advertising its Anacin-3 by claiming that "hospitals recommended acetaminophen, the aspirin-free pain reliever in Anacin-3, more than any other pain reliever"—without telling consumers that the acetaminophen hospitals recommend is, in fact, Tylenol.

Concealment of relevant facts and information can exploit people by misleading them; it also undermines truth telling. Unfortunately, truth rarely seems foremost in the minds of advertisers. For example, Coors continued to advertise its beer as brewed from "Rocky Mountain spring water" even after it opened plants outside Colorado that use local water. And Perrier advertised its bottled water as having bubbled up from underground springs decades after it had begun pumping the water up from the ground through a pipe and combining it with processed gas.

As one advertising-industry insider writes: "Inside the agency the basic approach is hardly conducive to truth telling. The usual thinking in forming a campaign is first what can we say, true or not, that will sell the product best? The second consideration is, how can we say it effectively and get away with it so that (1) people who buy won't feel let down by too big a promise that doesn't come true, and (2) the ads will avoid quick and certain censure by the FTC."[74] This observation shows the common tendency to equate what's legal with what's moral. It's precisely this outlook that leads to advertising behavior of dubious morality.

Examples of ads that conceal important facts are legion. An old Colgate-Palmolive ad for Rapid Shave Cream used sandpaper to demonstrate the cream's effect on tough beards. Colgate concealed the fact that the "sandpaper" in the ad was actually Plexiglas and that actual sandpaper had to be soaked in Rapid Shave for about eighty minutes before the "beard" would come off in one stroke. A few years ago, ads for Campbell's vegetable soup showed pictures of a thick, rich brew calculated to whet even a gourmet's appetite. What the ads didn't show were clear glass marbles deposited in that bowl to give the soup the appearance of solidity. Similarly, a television ad for Volvo showed a row of cars being crushed by a bigwheel truck, with only a Volvo remaining intact. What the ad neglected to say was that the

Volvo had been reinforced and the other cars weakened. More recently, ads run in travel magazines to encourage Americans to vacation in Bermuda have pictured people swimming or diving or sunning themselves on the beach—in Hawaii!

If business has an obligation to provide clear, accurate, and adequate information, we must wonder if it meets that charge when it hides facts germane to the consumer's purchase of a product. Concealing information raises serious moral concerns relative to truth telling and consumer exploitation. When consumers are deprived of relevant knowledge about a product, their choices are constricted and distorted.

If pushed further, the moral demand for full information challenges almost all advertising. Even the best advertisements never point out the negative features of their products or concede that there is no substantive difference between the product being advertised and its competitors, as is often the case. In this sense, they could be accused of concealing relevant information. Most advertisers would be shocked at the suggestion that honesty requires an objective presentation of the pros and cons of their products, and in fact consumers don't expect advertisers or salespeople to be impartial. Nevertheless, it is not clear why this moral value should not be relevant to assessing advertising. And it can be noted that retail salespeople, despite a sometimes negative reputation, often do approach this level of candor—at least when they are fortunate enough to sell a genuinely good and competitive product or when they do not work on commission.

> In a broad sense, almost all advertising is vulnerable to the moral complaint that it conceals relevant information.

Exaggeration

Advertisers can mislead through **exaggeration**—that is, by making claims unsupported by evidence. For example, claims that a pain reliever provides "extra pain relief," is "50 percent stronger than aspirin," or is "superior to any other nonprescription painkiller on the market" contradict evidence that all analgesics are effective to the same degree. Manufacturers of vitamins and other dietary supplements, such as Airborne, are notorious for exaggerating the possible benefits of their products. Some drug companies do the same. Ads for Propecia tell men, "Starting today, you need not face the fear of more hair loss." But while Propecia can slow hair loss, it doesn't necessarily stop it. Similarly, the FDA recently found General Mills guilty of exaggerating the health benefits of eating Cheerios, which the company claimed "can lower your cholesterol by 4 percent."

Nabisco's advertising of its 100 percent bran cereal as being "flavored with two naturally sweet fruit juices" is typical of exaggerated product claims. Although fig juice and prune juice have indeed been added to the product, they are its least significant ingredients in terms of weight; the primary sweetener is sugar. As in this case, exaggeration often goes hand in hand with concealed information. Until stopped by legal action, General Electric advertised its 90-watt Energy Choice bulb as an energy-saving replacement for a conventional 100-watt bulb. But there is nothing special about the GE bulb; it simply produces fewer lumens than a 100-watt bulb. Trident chewing gum, to take another example, has long advertised that it helps fight cavities, but its ads (which describe Trident as a "dental instrument") clearly exaggerate the benefits of chewing Trident. Chewing gum can indeed help dislodge debris on dental enamel, but so can eating an apple or rinsing one's mouth with water. And the sugar substitute used by Trident (sorbitol) can indirectly promote tooth decay: It nurtures the normally harmless bacteria that sugar activates into decay-producing microorganisms.

"Anti-aging" skin-care products are one of the fastest-growing segments of the cosmetics industry, partly because the baby boom generation is getting older. Here exaggeration is rampant, as advertisers make claims for their products that are, to put it as gently as possible, scientifically unfounded. For example, Face Lift asserts that it boosts collagen production and "reduces deep wrinkles up to 70%"; L'Oréal brags that its "dermo-smoothing complex" called "d-contraxol" significantly reduces wrinkles, and Procter & Gamble touts Regenerist, an "amino peptide complex" that supposedly provides "revolutionary cell care" to "regenerate" skin.[75] When it comes to exaggeration, though, few products surpass weight-loss pills, powders, and patches. Starch Away, Slimspadiet, UltraLipoLean, Femina, Body Trim, and many other similar products take advantage of gullible, often desperate consumers by promising them that they can shed unwanted pounds and excess inches without reducing their caloric intake or exercising more.

The line between such deliberate deception and puffery is not always clear.[76] **Puffery** is the supposedly harmless use of superlatives and subjective praise in advertisements. Thus advertisers frequently boast of the merits of their products by using words such as *best, finest*, or *most*, or phrases and slogans like *king of beers, breakfast of champions*, or *the ultimate driving machine*. In most instances, puffery appears innocuous, but sometimes it's downright misleading, as in the Dial soap ad that claimed Dial was "the most effective deodorant soap you can buy." When asked to substantiate that claim, the Armour-Dial company insisted that it was not claiming product superiority; all it meant was that Dial soap was as effective as any other soap.

Although people are often taken in by puffery, the law permits it.

The law permits puffery on the grounds that it doesn't deceive people. University of Wisconsin professor Ivan L. Preston, however, argues that puffery shouldn't be immune from regulation. Why? Because the public is often taken in by it. Consider the following pieces of puffery: "State Farm is all you need to know about life insurance," "Ford has a better idea," and "It's the real thing [Coca-Cola]." Although these statements may seem like meaningless verbal posturing, in one survey 22 percent of those sampled thought the first claim was "completely true" while 36 percent considered it "partly true." The second claim was judged "completely true" by 26 percent and "partly true" by 42 percent while 35 percent believed the third claim was "completely true" and 29 percent "partly true."[77] Moreover, argues Preston, if puffery didn't work, salespeople and advertisers wouldn't use it.[78]

Psychological Appeals

A **psychological appeal** is a persuasive effort aimed primarily at emotion, not reason. This is potentially the advertising technique of greatest moral concern. An automobile ad that presents the product surrounded by people who look wealthy and successful taps into our need and desire for status. A life insurance ad that portrays a destitute family struggling in the aftermath of a provider's death tries to persuade through pity and fear. Reliance on such appeals is not automatically unethical, but it raises moral concerns because rarely do the products fully deliver what the ads promise.

Ads that rely extensively on pitches to power, prestige, sex, masculinity, femininity, acceptance, approval, and the like aim to sell more than a product. They are peddling psychological satisfaction. Perhaps the best example is the increasingly explicit and pervasive use of sexual pitches in ads:

> *Scene:* An artist's skylit studio.
> A young man lies nude, the bedsheets in disarray.
> He awakens to find a tender note on his pillow.
> The phone rings and he gets up to answer it.
>
> *Woman's voice:* You snore.
>
> *Artist (smiling):* And you always steal the covers.

More cozy patter between the two. Then a husky-voiced announcer intones: "Paco Rabanne. A cologne for men. What is remembered is up to you."

Summary 6.8
Advertising tries to persuade people to buy products. Because straight product information is not always the most effective way to do this, there is a temptation to misrepresent. Ambiguity, concealment of relevant facts, exaggeration, and psychological appeals are among the morally dubious techniques that advertisers use.

Although sex has always been used to sell products, it has never before been used as explicitly in advertising as it is today—as the nudes in the ads for Calvin Klein products demonstrate. And the sexual pitches are by no means confined to products like cologne or clothes. The California Avocado Commission supplemented its "Love Food from California" recipe ads with a campaign featuring a leggy actress sprawled across two pages of some eighteen national magazines to promote the avocado's nutritional value. The copy line reads: "Would this body lie to you?" Similarly, Dannon yogurt ran ads featuring a bikini-clad beauty and this message: "More nonsense is written on dieting than any other subject—except possibly sex."

Some students of marketing claim that ads like these appeal to the subconscious mind of both marketer and consumer. Purdue University psychologist and marketing consultant Jacob Jacoby contends that marketers, like everyone else, carry around in their subconscious sexual symbols that, intentionally or not, they use in ads. A case in point: the Newport cigarette "Alive with Pleasure" campaign. One campaign ad featured a woman riding the handlebars of a bicycle driven by a man. The main strut of the bike wheel stands vertically beneath her body. In Jacoby's view, such symbolism needs no interpretation.

Author Wilson Bryan Key, who has extensively researched the topic of subconscious marketing appeals, claims that many ads take a subliminal form. **Subliminal advertising** is advertising that communicates at a level beneath conscious awareness, where, some psychologists claim, the vast reservoir of human motivation primarily resides. Most marketing experts deny that such advertising occurs or that ads with hidden messages can work. Key disagrees. Indeed, he goes so far as to claim: "It is virtually impossible to pick up a newspaper or magazine, turn on a radio or television set, read a promotional pamphlet or the telephone book, or shop through a supermarket without having your subconscious purposely massaged by some monstrously clever artist, photographer, writer, or technician."[79]

Concern with the serious nature of psychological appeals appears to have motivated the California Wine Institute to adopt an advertising code of standards. The following restrictions are included:

> No wine ad shall present persons engaged in activities with appeal particularly to minors. Among those excluded: amateur or professional sports figures, celebrities, or cowboys; rock stars, race car drivers.
>
> No wine ad shall exploit the human form or "feature provocative or enticing poses or be demeaning to any individual."
>
> No wine ad shall portray wine in a setting where food is not presented.
>
> No wine ad shall present wine in "quantities inappropriate to the situation."
>
> No wine ad shall portray wine as similar to another type of beverage or product such as milk, soda, or candy.
>
> No wine ad shall associate wine with personal performance, social attainment, achievement, wealth, or the attainment of adulthood.
>
> No wine ad shall show automobiles in a way that one could construe their conjunction.

In adopting such a rigorous code of advertising ethics, the California Wine Institute rightly acknowledged the subtle implications and psychological nuances that affect the message that an ad communicates.

The Federal Trade Commission's Role

The **Federal Trade Commission (FTC)** was originally created in 1914 as an antitrust weapon, but its mandate was expanded to include protecting consumers against deceptive advertising and fraudulent commercial practices. Although the FTC is not the only regulatory body monitoring advertisements, it is mainly thanks to the FTC that today we are spared the most blatant abuses of advertising.

One important question running through the FTC's history is relevant to all efforts to prohibit deceptive advertising: Is the FTC (or any other regulatory body) obligated to protect only reasonable, intelligent consumers who conduct themselves sensibly in the marketplace, or should it also protect ignorant consumers who are careless or gullible in their purchases?[80] If the FTC uses the **reasonable-consumer standard**, it would prohibit only advertising claims that would deceive reasonable people. People who are taken in because they are more gullible or less bright than average would be unprotected. If the FTC uses the **ignorant-consumer standard** and prohibits an advertisement that might mislead someone who is ill informed and naive, it would handle a lot more cases and greatly restrict advertising; but in spending its time and resources on such cases, it is not clear that the FTC would be proceeding in response to a substantial public interest, as it is legally charged with doing.

The reasonable-person standard was traditional in a variety of areas of the law long before the FTC was established. If you are sued for negligence, you can successfully defend yourself if you can establish that you behaved as a hypothetical reasonable person would have behaved under like circumstances. And, according to the law of misrepresentation, when you as a deceived consumer sue a seller on grounds that you were misled, then—assuming the deception is not proved to be intentional—you must establish that you were acting reasonably in relying on the false representation. If a reasonable person would not have been misled in like circumstances, you will not win your case. Ads that make physically impossible or obviously exaggerated claims would thus escape legal liability under the reasonable-person standard.

The 1937 *Standard Education* case moved the law away from the reasonable-person standard.

One decisive case in the legal transition away from the reasonable-person standard in matters of advertising, sales, and marketing was ***FTC v. Standard Education*** in 1937.[81] In this case an encyclopedia company was charged by the FTC with a number of deceptive and misleading practices. The company's agents told potential customers that their names had been specially selected and that the encyclopedia they were being offered was being given away free as part of an advertising plan in return for use of their names for advertising purposes and in testimonials. The customer was only required to pay $69.50 for a series of looseleaf update volumes. Potential buyers were not told that both books and supplements regularly sold for $69.50.

In deciding the case, the U.S. Supreme Court considered the view of the appellate court, which had earlier dismissed the FTC's case. Writing for the appellate court, Judge Learned Hand had declared that the FTC was occupying itself with "trivial niceties" that only "divert attention from substantial evils." "We cannot take seriously the suggestion," he wrote, "that a man who is buying a set of books and a ten years' 'extension service' will be fatuous enough to be misled by the mere statement that the first are given away, and that he is paying only for the second." The Supreme Court itself, however, looked at the matter in a different light and held for the FTC and against Standard Education.

First, the Court noted that the practice had successfully deceived numerous victims, apparently including teachers, doctors, and college professors. But instead of resting its decision on the claim that a reasonable person might have been deceived, it advocated a change of standard to something like the ignorant-consumer standard:

> The fact that a false statement may be obviously false to those who are trained and experienced does not change its character, nor take away its power to deceive others less experienced. There is no duty resting upon a citizen to suspect the honesty of those with whom he transacts business. Laws are made to protect the trusting as well as the suspicious. The best element of business has long since decided that honesty should govern competitive enterprises, and that the rule of *caveat emptor* should not be relied upon to reward fraud and deception.

The decision in *FTC v. Standard Education,* as Ivan L. Preston notes, led the FTC to apply the ignorant-person standard liberally, even in cases in which there was no intent to deceive. In the 1940s the FTC challenged ads in some cases in which it is difficult to believe that anyone could possibly have been deceived. For example, it issued a complaint against Clairol for advertising that its product would "color hair permanently" because some people might not know that new hair growth would still have its natural color, and it went after

Bristol-Myers's Ipana toothpaste on the grounds that its "smile of beauty" slogan would lead some to believe that Ipana toothpaste would straighten their teeth. Eventually, however, the FTC abandoned the ignorant-consumer standard in its extreme form and stopped trying to protect everybody from everything that might possibly deceive them. It now follows the "modified" ignorant-consumer standard and protects consumers from ads that mislead significant numbers of people, whether those people acted reasonably or not.[82]

These days the FTC follows what might be called the "modified" ignorant-consumer standard.

Still, deciding what is likely to be misleading to a significant number of consumers is not necessarily easy. Consider these advertising claims, which are contested by some as deceptive: that Kraft Cheez Whiz is real cheese; that Chicken McNuggets are made from "whole breasts and thighs" (when they allegedly contain processed chicken skin as well and are fried in highly saturated beef fat); that ibuprofen causes stomach irritation (as Tylenol's ads seem to imply). Was Sprint's "dime-a-minute" ad campaign deceptive when a minute-and-a-half telephone call was rounded up to 20 cents? Was it deceptive of Diet Coke to proclaim that it was sweetened "now with NutraSweet," even though the product also contained saccharin? Under legal pressure, Diet Coke changed its ads to read "NutraSweet blend." Is that phrase free of any misleading implications?

Ads Directed at Children

The FTC has always looked after one special group of consumers without regard to how reasonable they are: children. Still, several consumer groups think the FTC has not done enough, and they advocate even stricter controls over advertisements that reach children.

Summary 6.9
The Federal Trade Commission protects us from blatantly deceptive advertising. But it is debatable whether the FTC should ban only advertising that is likely to deceive reasonable people or whether it should protect careless or gullible consumers as well. The FTC now seeks to prohibit advertising that misleads a significant number of consumers, regardless of whether a reasonable person would have been taken in.

Advertising to children is big business. Every year children under twelve spend $40 billion and teenagers a whopping $172 billion.[83] And these figures don't begin to take into account the billions of adult purchases for gifts, clothes, and groceries that are influenced by children. In recent years advertising aimed specifically at children has grown exponentially. Advertisers spend billions a year on ads for children, and there are more and more venues for such ads—with news magazines, websites, and entire television channels aimed at children.[84]

Furthermore, it's no longer just cereal, candy, and toys that are being advertised. Advertisers of other products are wooing children in an effort to create customers for the future. As Jackie Pate of Delta Air Lines puts it, "By building brand loyalty in children today, they'll be the adult passengers of the future." Ann Moore, chairman and CEO of Time Inc., which publishes *Sports Illustrated for Kids,* adds, "We believe children make brand decisions that will carry into their adult lives."[85] Although the magazine attracts mostly eight- to fourteen-year-old boys as readers, it sometimes features two-page spreads for Chevy minivans.

Of course, advertisers admit that it's not just future consumers they want. "We're relying on the kid to pester the mom to buy the product, rather than going straight to the mom," says Barbara A. Martino of Grey Advertising. Pursuing this strategy, marketing consultants study different ways that children nag and how effective their nagging styles are on different types of parents.[86] No one doubts the influence children have on what their parents buy, and that influence extends beyond children's products to high-end adult items. Karen Francis, a brand manager for Chevy, reports that even she was surprised how often parents tell her that their kids played a tie-breaking role in deciding which car to buy.[87] Naturally, advertisers argue that parents still have ultimate control over what gets purchased and what doesn't. But is the strategy of selling to parents by convincing the children a fair one? As one parent complains, "Brand awareness has been an incredibly abusive experience—the relentless requests to go to McDonald's [or] to see movies that are inappropriate for six-year-olds [but] that are advertised on kids' shows."

Television and advertising play a large role in most children's lives. At age seven a typical child sees twenty thousand television commercials a year, and children remember what they see. For example, in the 1990s researchers found that the frogs in the Budweiser beer commercials were more widely recognized among children than any cartoon characters other than Bugs Bunny. The problem is that children, particularly young children, are naive and gullible and thus particularly vulnerable to advertisers' enticements. Consider, for example, ads in which children are shown, after eating a certain cereal, to have enough power to lift large playhouses. No adult would be misled by that ad, but children lack experience and independent judgment. This provides at least a prima facie case for protecting them.

"Kids are the most pure consumers you could have," says one advertising expert. "They tend to interpret your ad literally. They are infinitely open." This problem is growing greater because the line between children's shows and the commercials that come with them is fading away. Children's entertainment features characters whose licensed images are stamped on toys, sheets, clothes, and food. Moreover, at the same time that movies and television shows are ever more tightly linked to the selling of toys and other items, commercials are becoming more like entertainment. Is it any wonder that many children perceive little difference between ads and television shows? As one nine-year-old sees it, the only distinction is that "commercials are shorter."

Some writers contend that it is "ethical to advertise toys, sugar-loaded cereal or non-violent games to children ... as long as it is *truthful* and as long as children understand the message."[88] But that overlooks children's special susceptibilities and the need to protect them from manipulation and endless commercial enticement. After all, the ads directed at them for cereals, snacks, and soft drinks say nothing untrue, and children understand their message all too well. But few youngsters understand much about nutrition or are aware that obesity among children has reached epidemic proportions in the United States.

Because of their susceptibility, children need special protection from being enticed and manipulated by advertising.

Childhood Obesity

In 2005 the Institute of Medicine released a report reviewing 123 scientific research studies spanning a thirty-year period. It concluded what most Americans probably already suspected: namely, that "statistically, there is strong evidence" that exposure to television ads is "associated" with obesity in children under twelve.[89] Meanwhile, legal and political pressure has been building on food companies, which spend $11 billion a year marketing to kids, to change

Summary 6.10
Advertising to children is big business, but children are particularly susceptible to the blandishments of advertising. Advertisers contend that parents still control what gets purchased and what doesn't. Critics, however, doubt the fairness of selling to parents by appealing to children.

their ways and rein in their advertising of nutritionally empty calories to children. At the very least, many parents and consumer advocates want cartoon characters like Shrek, Scooby-Doo, and SpongeBob SquarePants to stop hawking junk food.[90] In response, Kraft Foods broke ranks with its competitors and said that it will quit advertising certain products to youngsters under twelve, although the company will continue to market "healthier" food to kids between six and twelve. An advantage for Kraft in taking the initiative is that it, not government regulators, gets to decide which products are "healthier." Even so, Kraft's policy challenges the food industry's long-held tenet that there are no "bad" foods. Kraft shies away from discussing the causes of obesity or the legal risks to food companies. "This is not about complying with our legal obligations or disputing the science," says Kraft vice president Mark Berlind. "We're formulating our response based on what our consumers are telling us, and parents are most concerned about ads directed at younger children."[91]

The ethical issues raised by advertising to children lead to the larger and more general question of the nature and desirability of advertising's role in today's media-dominated society, which is our next topic.

THE DEBATE OVER ADVERTISING

The controversy over advertising does not end with the issue of deceptive techniques and unfair advertising practices. Advertising provides little usable information to consumers. Advertisements almost always conceal relevant negative facts about their products, and they are frequently based on subtle appeals to psychological needs, which the products they peddle are unlikely to satisfy. These realities are the basis for some critics' wholesale repudiation of advertising on moral grounds. They also desire a less commercially polluted environment, one that does not continually reinforce materialistic values.

Consumer Needs

Some defenders of advertising take these points in stride. They concede that images of glamour, sex, or adventure sell products, but they argue that these images are what we, the consumers, want. We don't want just blue jeans; we want romance or sophistication or status with our blue jeans. By connecting products with important emotions and feelings, advertisements can also satisfy our deeper needs and wants. As one advertising executive puts it:

> Advertising can show a consumer how a baby powder helps affirm her role as a nurturing mother—Johnson & Johnson's "The Language of Love." Or it can show a teenager how a soft drink helps assert his or her emerging independence—Pepsi's "The Choice of a New Generation."[92]

Harvard business professor Theodore Levitt has drawn an analogy between advertising and art. Both take liberties with reality, both deal in symbolic communication, and neither is interested in literal truth or in pure functionality. Rather, both art and advertising help us repackage the otherwise crude, drab, and generally oppressive reality that surrounds us. They create "illusions, symbols, and implications that promise more." They help us modify, transform, embellish, enrich, and reconstruct the world around us.

"Without distortion, embellishment, and elaboration," Levitt writes, "life would be drab, dull, anguished, and at its existential worst." Advertising helps satisfy this legitimate human need. Its handsome packages and imaginative promises produce that "elevation of the spirit" that we want and need. Embellishment and distortion are therefore among advertising's socially desirable purposes. To criticize advertising on these counts, Levitt argues, is to overlook the real needs and values of human beings.[93]

Levitt's critics contend that even if advertising appeals to the same deep needs that art does, advertising promises satisfaction of those needs in the products it sells, and that promise is rarely kept. At the end of the day, blue jeans are still just blue jeans, and your love life will be unaffected by which soap you shower with. The imaginative, symbolic, and artistic content of advertising, which Levitt sees as answering real human needs, is viewed by critics as manipulating, distorting, and even creating those needs.

In his influential books *The Affluent Society* and *The New Industrial State*, the late John Kenneth Galbraith criticized advertising on exactly this point. Galbraith argued that the process of production today, with its expensive marketing campaigns, subtle advertising techniques, and sophisticated sales strategies, creates the very wants it then satisfies. In other words, producers create both the goods and the demand for those goods. If a new breakfast cereal or detergent were really wanted, Galbraith reasoned, why must so much money be spent trying to get the consumer to buy it? He thought it is obvious that "wants can be synthesized by advertising, catalyzed by salesmanship, and shaped by" discreet manipulations.

Galbraith believed that nowadays, instead of shaping the production process, consumer demand tends to be shaped by it.

Accordingly, Galbraith rejected the economist's traditional faith in **consumer sovereignty**: the idea that consumers should and do control the market through their purchases. Rather than independent consumer demand shaping production, as classical economic theory says it does, nowadays it is the other way around. Galbraith dubbed this the **dependence effect**: "As a society becomes increasingly affluent, wants are increasingly created by the process by which they are satisfied."[94]

One consequence, Galbraith thought, is that our system of production cannot be defended on the ground that it is satisfying urgent or important wants. We can't defend production as satisfying wants if the production process itself creates those wants. "In the absence of the massive and artful persuasion that accompanies the management of demand," Galbraith argued,

> increasing abundance might well have reduced the interest of people in acquiring more goods. They would not have felt the need for multiplying the artifacts—autos, appliances, detergents, cosmetics—by which they were surrounded.[95]

Another consequence is our general preoccupation with material consumption. In particular, Galbraith claimed, our pursuit of private goods, continually reinforced by advertising, leads us to neglect important public goods and services. We need better schools, parks, artistic and recreational facilities; safer and cleaner cities and air; more efficient, less crowded transportation systems. We are rich in the private production and use of goods, Galbraith thought, and starved in public services. In 2004 Galbraith summarized his long-held views this way:

Belief in a market economy in which the consumer is sovereign is one of our most pervasive forms of fraud. Let no one try to sell without consumer management, control. As power over the innovation, manufacture, and sale of goods and services has passed to the producer and away from the consumer, the aggregate of this production has been the prime test of social achievement.... Not education or literature or the arts but the production of automobiles, including SUVs: Here is the modern measure of economic and therefore social achievement.[96]

Summary 6.11
Defenders of advertising view its imaginative, symbolic, and artistic content as answering real human needs. Critics maintain that advertising manipulates those needs or even creates artificial ones. John Kenneth Galbraith contended that today the same process that produces products also produces the demand for those products (the dependence effect). Galbraith argued, controversially, that advertising encourages a preoccupation with material goods and leads us to favor private consumption at the expense of important public goods and services.

Galbraith's critics have concentrated their fire on a couple of points. *First,* Galbraith never shows that advertising has the power he attributed to it. Advertising campaigns like that for Listerine in the 1920s, which successfully created the problem of "halitosis" in order to sell the new idea of "mouthwash," are rare.* And even though in recent years pharmaceutical countries have found large profits in promoting new or exaggerated medical conditions with serious-sounding names—for example, "premenstrual dysphoric disorder" (premenstrual tension), "gastro-esophageal reflux disease" (heartburn), or "social anxiety disorder" (sadness)—and selling drugs to treat them,[97] most new products fail to win a permanent place in the hearts of consumers, despite heavy advertising. We are inundated with ads everyday, but experiments suggest we no longer care much about them. Each of us sees an average of 1,600 advertisements a day, notices around 1,200 of them, and responds favorably or unfavorably to only about 12. We also appear to pay more attention to ads for products that we already have.

Second, critics have attacked Galbraith's assumption that the needs supposedly created by advertisers and producers are, as a result, "false" or "artificial" needs and therefore less worthy of satisfaction. Human needs, they stress, are always socially influenced and are never static. How are we to distinguish between "genuine" and "artificial" wants, and why should the latter be thought less important? Ads might produce a want that we would not otherwise have had without that want being in any way objectionable.

Although conclusive evidence is unavailable, critics of advertising continue to worry about its power to influence our lives and shape our culture and civilization. Even if producers cannot create wants out of whole cloth, many worry that advertising can manipulate our existing desires—that it can stimulate certain desires, both at the expense of other, less materialistic desires and out of proportion to the likely satisfaction that fulfillment of those desires will bring.

Market Economics

Defenders of advertising are largely untroubled by these worries. They see advertising as an aspect of free competition in a competitive market, which ultimately works to the benefit of all. But this simple free-market defense of advertising has weaknesses. First, advertising doesn't fit too well into the economist's model of the free market. Economists can prove, if we grant them enough assumptions, that free-market buying and selling lead to optimal

---

* Given that the saliva in one's mouth is completely replenished every fifteen minutes or so anyway, no mouthwash can have an effect longer than that.

results.* One of those assumptions is that everyone has full and complete information, on the basis of which they then buy and sell. But if that were so, advertising would be pointless.

One might argue that advertising moves us closer to the ideal of full information, but there is good reason to doubt this. Even if we put aside the question of whether ads can create, shape, or manipulate wants, they do seem to enhance brand loyalty, which generally works to thwart price competition. A true brand-name consumer is willing to pay more for a product that is otherwise indistinguishable from its competitors. He or she buys a certain beer despite being unable to taste the difference between it and other beers.

Critics charge that because advertising's only goal is to persuade consumers to buy, there is no reason to think it enhances well-being.

More generally, critics of advertising stand the invisible-hand argument on its head. The goal of advertisers is to sell you products and to make money, not to promote your well-being. Rational demonstration of how a product will in fact enhance your well-being is not the only way advertisers can successfully persuade you to buy their products. Indeed, it is far from the most common technique. Critics charge, accordingly, that there is no reason to think that advertising even tends to maximize the well-being of consumers.

Defenders of advertising may claim that, nonetheless, advertising is necessary for economic growth, which benefits us all. The truth of this claim, however, is open to debate. Critics maintain that advertising is a waste of resources and serves only to raise the price of advertised goods. Like Galbraith, they may also contend that advertising in general reinforces mindless consumerism. It corrupts our civilization and misdirects our society's economic effort toward private consumption and away from the public realm. The never-ending pursuit of material goods may also divert us as a society from the pursuit of a substantially shorter workday.[98]

Free Speech and the Media

Summary 6.12
Defenders of advertising see it as a necessary and desirable aspect of competition in a free-market system, a protected form of free speech, and a useful sponsor of the media, in particular, television. Critics challenge all three claims.

Two final issues should be briefly noted. Defenders of advertising claim that, despite criticisms, advertising enjoys protection under the First Amendment as a form of speech. Legally this claim probably requires qualification, especially in regard to radio and television, for which one must have a license to broadcast. Banning cigarette advertisements from television, for instance, did not run contrary to the Constitution. More important, even if we concede advertisers the legal right to free speech, not every exercise of that legal right is morally justifiable. If advertisements in general or of a certain type or for certain products were shown to have undesirable social consequences, or if certain sorts of ads relied on objectionable or nonrational persuasive techniques, then there would be a strong moral argument against such advertisements regardless of their legal status.

Advertising subsidizes the media, and that is a positive but far from conclusive consideration in its favor. This is not the place to launch a discussion of the defects of American television. But the very fact that it is free results in far more consumption than would otherwise be the case and probably, as

---

* Technically, they lead to *Pareto optimality,* which means that no one person can be made better-off without making someone else worse-off.

many think, far more than is good for us. Although satellite and cable television have improved things, the mediocrity of much American television fare is hardly accidental. The networks need large audiences. Obviously they can't run every-one's favorite type of program, because people's tastes differ, so they seek to reach a common denominator. If viewers instead of advertisers paid for each show they watched, things would be different.

STUDY CORNER

Key Terms and Concepts

ambiguity (in advertising)
caveat emptor
concealment of facts (in advertising)
Consumer Product Safety Commission
consumer sovereignty
dependence effect
due care
exaggeration (in advertising)
Federal Trade Commission

Food and Drug Administration
FTC v. Standard Education
ignorant-consumer standard
legal paternalism
MacPherson v. Buick Motor Car
merchantability
price fixing, horizontal and vertical
price gouging

psychological appeal (in advertising)
puffery
quantity surcharges
reasonable-consumer standard
strict product liability
subliminal advertising
warranties, express and implied
weasel words

Points to Review

- issues raised by the manufacture, marketing, and advertising of cigarettes
- importance of *MacPherson v. Buick Motor Car*
- why critics of strict product liability believe it is unfair
- two arguments in favor of strict product liability
- comparing lives saved vs. costs of different regulations
- economic and philosophical worries about safety restrictions on consumer choice
- three points to bear in mind about paternalism
- examples of shortfalls in, and political interference with, safety regulations
- what the auto industry's safety record illustrates
- six things business should do to increase product safety
- cigarette fires and old tires vs. burning radios and fluorocarbons as examples of irresponsible and responsible business conduct
- difference between express and implied warranties

- examples of manipulative pricing
- types of price fixing
- difficulty of defining price gouging and assessing its morality
- examples of misleading labeling and packaging
- examples of ambiguity, concealment of facts, exaggeration, and psychological appeals
- how almost all advertising fails to provide full information.
- the case against puffery
- importance of *FTC v. Standard Education*
- reasonable-consumer standard vs. ignorant-consumer standard
- why companies spend so much on advertising to children
- issues raised by ads directed at children, including problem of childhood obesity
- Levitt's defense of advertising
- Galbraith's "dependence effect" and his critique of advertising
- two criticisms of Galbraith
- why advertising doesn't fit well with economists' model of the free market

CASE **6.1**

Breast Implants

In the last few decades, silicone has become a crucial industrial product, playing a role in the manufacture of thousands of products, from lubricants to adhesive labels to Silly Putty. One of its medical uses, however, has been controversial—namely, as the gel used for breast implants. Dow Corning, which was founded in 1943 to produce silicones for commercial purposes, invented mammary prostheses in the 1960s. Since then a million American women have had bags of silicone gel implanted in their breasts. For many of them, silicone implants are part of reconstructive surgery after breast cancer or other operations. However, by 1990 four out of five implants were for the cosmetic augmentation of normal, healthy breasts—a procedure that became increasingly popular in the 1980s as celebrities such as Cher and Jenny Jones spoke openly of their surgically enhanced breasts.

Today, however, what used to be a common elective operation is rarely performed.[99] The reason dates from the 1980s, when women with silicone breast implants first began reporting certain patterns of illness. There were stories of ruptured or leaky bags, although the estimates of the proportion of women affected ranged from 1–5 percent to 32 percent. And there were allegations that the silicone implants were responsible for various autoimmune disorders—such as rheumatoid arthritis, lupus erythematosus, and scleroderma—in which the body's immune system attacks its own connective tissue. Then, in 1991, a jury heard the case of Mariann Hopkins, who claimed that her implants had ruptured and released silicone gel, causing severe joint and muscle pain, weight loss, and fatigue. On the basis of documents suggesting that Dow Corning knew of the dangers of leaky bags, a San Francisco jury found the company guilty of negligence and fraud and awarded Hopkins $ 7.3 million.

When Dow Corning first sold breast implants in 1965, they were subject to no specific government regulations. In 1978 the Food and Drug Administration classified them as "Class II" devices, meaning that they did not need testing to remain on the market. In 1989, however, as worries about the dangers of silicone implants increased, the FDA reclassified them as "Class III" devices and in 1991 required all manufacturers to submit safety and effectiveness data. Although some FDA staff members were scathingly critical of the poor and inconclusive documentation submitted by the manufacturers, the FDA's advisory panel ruled that the implants were not a major threat to health. Based on public need, it voted to keep them on the market.

After the Hopkins case, however, David A. Kessler, the FDA's new chairman, called for a moratorium on breast implants. He asked doctors to stop performing the operation, but he told women who had already had the operation not to have the bags removed. Still, the moratorium terrified the women who had had breast implants, a few of whom tried in desperation to carve them out themselves, and it galvanized a political movement led by women who were upset about having been used, yet again, as guinea pigs for an unsafe medical procedure. For them, it was just one more episode in a long history of the mistreatment of women by a medical, scientific, and industrial establishment that refused to treat them as persons and take their needs seriously. The FDA moratorium also galvanized the legal forces marshaled against the manufacturers of silicone bags. By 1994, some twenty thousand lawsuits had been filed against Dow Corning alone. Entrepreneurial lawyers organized most of these actions into a few large class-action suits so that their pooled legal resources would be more than a match for the manufacturers.

Meanwhile, Kessler instructed the FDA's advisory panel to restudy the breast implant question. Presented with a series of anecdotal reports about diseases that are not rare, the panel complained about the lack of hard scientific data. From the scientific point of view, the problem was how to distinguish coincidence from causation. For example, if connective-tissue disease strikes 1 percent of all women and if 1 million women have implants, then statistically one should expect that ten thousand women will have both implants and connective-tissue disease. So if a woman develops the disease, can it correctly be said that it was caused by her breast implants? Moreover, not only does silicone appear to be chemically inert, but silicone from a ruptured breast implant will remain trapped inside a fibrous capsule of scar tissue. Nevertheless, on the basis of the panel's recommendation, the FDA ruled that silicone may be used only for reconstruction and that cosmetic breast augmentation must be done only with saline packs.

At that point the gulf between science, on the one hand, and the FDA and public opinion, on the other, began to widen further. A Mayo Clinic study published in the prestigious *New England Journal of Medicine* in June 1994 showed that there was no difference between women with breast implants and other women with respect to incidence of connective-tissue disease; by the summer of 1995 two larger studies had confirmed the Mayo Clinic's report. On top of that, the FBI and other investigators exposed several labs that were selling to lawyers and victims fraudulent test results purporting to show the presence of silicone in the blood of women with breast implants.

Lawyers and other advocates for the women with implants repudiate those studies, contending that the women have a new disease. To this contention scientists respond that the description of the symptoms of this supposed disease keeps changing. Some say it looks like fibromyalgia, which is included in their studies. Many feminist activist groups distrust science; they believe that we should pay less attention to statistics and medical studies and greater attention to the women who have suffered. These women know what their bodies have been through, and they are convinced that their implants are responsible.

This reasoning, and the skepticism toward science and statistics that it represents, has swayed jurors. After Dow Corning filed bankruptcy in 1995, which brought to a halt the lawsuits against it, new lawsuits were filed against its parent company, Dow Chemical. The first of these resulted in a $14.1 million verdict against the company, despite the lack of scientific evidence. Disregarding the studies in the *New England Journal of Medicine,* the jurors were convinced that this particular plaintiff's suffering somehow stemmed from her Dow-manufactured breast implant. A few years later, the women who said their silicone breast implants made them ill agreed to settle their claims against Dow Corning for $3.2 billion. The settlement is part of its bankruptcy reorganization plan and is similar to a settlement entered into earlier by 3M, Bristol-Myers Squibb, and other manufacturers of breast implants.

Update By now, more than twenty reputable scientific studies have been conducted on implant safety. Three European governments have convened scientific panels. The American College of Rheumatology, the American Academy of Neurology, the Institute of Medicine, and the American Medical Association have all published reviews of the evidence, as has an independent scientific panel appointed by a federal court. The conclusion is unanimous and unequivocal: There is no evidence that breast implants cause disease of any kind.[100]

In light of these findings and the recommendations of a federal advisory panel, in July 2005 the FDA gave conditional approval to Mentor Corporation's application to produce silicone breast implants, thus effectively ending a thirteen-year ban on the use of silicone for cosmetic breast enhancements.

Discussion Questions

1. What does the breast implant controversy reveal about society's attitudes toward product safety, about the legal liability of manufacturers, and about the role of regulatory agencies like the FDA in protecting consumers? Is our society too cautious about product safety or not cautious enough?

2. Was the FDA justified in placing a moratorium on silicone breast implants and then halting them altogether for cosmetic purposes?

3. Is the agency too concerned with public opinion? Should it pay greater attention to scientific evidence or to the individual women who have suffered?

4. Was it irresponsible of the manufacturers of breast implants to have marketed them without first conclusively proving they were safe? If you were on the jury, would you have found Dow Corning or its parent company liable for the illnesses suffered by women who have had breast implants?

5. On safety matters, should the FDA or any regulatory agency err on the side of overprotection or underprotection? Has the FDA's stance on breast implants been fair to women who would like breast augmentation but cannot get it? Some people disapprove of cosmetic augmentation or believe it to be a frivolous operation. Do you think that attitudes like this played a role in the controversy over the safety of breast implants?

6. Some argue that in the case of new drugs or medical procedures in which the dangers are uncertain, consumers should be free to decide for themselves whether they wish to run the health risks associated with these products or services. Assess this argument.

CASE **6.2**

Hot Coffee at McDonald's

To aficionados of the bean, there's nothing like a piping-hot cup of java to get the day off to a good start, and nothing more insipid than luke-warm coffee. That's what McDonald's thought, anyway—until it learned differently, the hard and expensive way, when seventy-nine-year-old Stella Liebeck successfully sued the company after she was burned by a spilled cup of hot coffee that she'd bought at the drive-through window of her local McDonald's. The jury awarded her $160,000 in compensatory damages and a whopping $2.7 million in punitive damages. After the trial judge reduced the punitive damages to $480,000, she and McDonald's settled out of court for an undisclosed sum.[101]

Unlike the outcome of most other lawsuits, the hot-coffee verdict received nationwide attention, most of it unfavorable. To many ordinary people, the case epitomized the excesses of a legal system out of control. If hot coffee is dangerous, what's next: soft drinks that are too cold? To conservatives, the case represented the all-too-familiar failure of consumers to take responsibility for their own conduct, to blame business rather than themselves for their injuries. More policy-oriented pundits used the case as an occasion to call for reform of product liability law—in particular, to make winning frivolous suits more difficult and to restrict the punitive awards that juries can hand down.

However, those who examined the facts more closely learned that the Liebeck case was more complicated than it first appeared. For one thing, Liebeck suffered third-degree burns on her thighs and buttocks that were serious enough to require skin grafting and leave permanent scars. After her injury, she initially requested $10,000 for medical expenses and an additional amount for pain and suffering. When McDonald's refused, she went to court, asking for $300,000. Lawyers for the company argued in response that McDonald's coffee was not unreasonably hot and that Liebeck was responsible for her own injuries.

The jury saw it differently, however. First, McDonald's served its coffee at 185 degrees Fahrenheit, significantly hotter than home-brewed coffee. The jury was persuaded that coffee at that temperature is both undrinkable and more dangerous than a reasonable consumer would expect. Second, before Liebeck's accident, the company had received over seven hundred complaints about burns from its coffee. In response to the complaints, McDonald's had in fact put a warning label on its cups and designed a tighter-fitting lid for them. Ironically, the new lid was part of the problem in the Liebeck case because she had held the coffee cup between her legs in an effort to pry it open.

Although the jury found that Liebeck was 20 percent responsible for her injuries, it also concluded that McDonald's had not done enough to warn consumers. The jury's $2.7 million punitive-damage award was intended,

jurors later said, to send a message to fast-food chains. Although the judge reduced the award—equivalent to only about two days' worth of coffee sales for McDonald's—he called McDonald's conduct "willful, wanton, reckless, and callous."

Discussion Questions

1. Is hot coffee so dangerous, as the jury thought? Should a reasonable consumer be expected to know that coffee can burn and to have assumed this risk? Is a warning label sufficient? Is our society too protective of consumers these days, or not protective enough?

2. In serving hot coffee, did McDonald's act in a morally responsible way? What ideals, obligations, and effects should it have taken into consideration?

3. McDonald's claims that most consumers would prefer to have their coffee too hot than not hot enough. After all, if it's too hot, they can always wait a minute before drinking it. Suppose this is true. How does it affect McDonald's responsibilities? Given that McDonald's serves millions of cups of coffee every week, how important are a few hundred complaints about its coffee being too hot?

4. Was Liebeck only 20 percent responsible for her injuries? Do you agree with the amount of compensatory and punitive damages that the jury awarded her? If not, what would have been a fairer monetary award?

5. Should juries be permitted to award punitive damages in product liability cases? If so, should there be a limit to what they can award? Is it right for a jury to award punitive damages against one company in order to send a message to a whole industry?

CASE **6.3**

Sniffing Glue Could Snuff Profits

Harvey Benjamin Fuller founded the H. B. Fuller Company in 1887. Originally a one-man wallpaper-paste shop, H. B. Fuller is now a leading manufacturer of industrial glues, coatings, and paints, with operations worldwide. The company's 10,000 varieties of glue hold together everything from cars to cigarettes to disposable diapers. However, some of its customers don't use Fuller's glues in the way they are intended to be used.

That's particularly the case in Central America, where Fuller derives 27 percent of its profits and where tens of thousands of homeless children sniff some sort of glue. Addicted to glue's intoxicating but dangerous fumes, these unfortunate children are called *resistoleros* after Fuller's Resistol brand. Child-welfare advocates have urged the company to add a noxious oil to its glue to discourage abusers, but the company has resisted, either because it might reduce the glue's effectiveness or because it will irritate legitimate users.[102]

Either way, the issue is irritating H. B. Fuller, which has been recognized by various awards, honors, and socially conscious mutual funds as a company with a conscience. Fuller's mission statement says that it "will conduct business legally and ethically, support the activities of its employees in their communities and be a responsible corporate citizen." The St. Paul–based company gives 5 percent of its profits to charity; it has committed itself to safe environmental practices worldwide (practices that are "often more stringent than local government standards," the company says); and it has even endowed a chair in business ethics at the University of Minnesota. Now Fuller must contend with dissident stockholders inside, and demonstrators outside, its annual meetings.

The glue-sniffing issue is not a new one. In 1969 the Testor Corporation added a noxious ingredient to its hobby glue to discourage abuse, and in 1994 Henkel, a German chemical company that competes with Fuller, stopped making certain toxic glues in Central America. However, Fuller seems to have been singled out for criticism not only because its brand dominates Central America but also because—in the eyes of its critics, anyway—the company has not lived up to its own good-citizen image. Timothy Smith, executive director of the Interfaith Center for Corporate Responsibility, believes that companies with a reputation as good corporate citizens are more vulnerable to attack. "But as I see it," he says, "the hazard is not in acting in a socially responsible way. The hazard is in over-marketing yourself as a saint."

Saintly or not, the company has made matters worse for itself by its handling of the issue. H. B. Fuller's board of directors acknowledged that "illegal distribution was continuing" and that "a suitable replacement product would not be available in the near future." Accordingly, it voted to stop selling Resistol adhesives in Central America. "We simply don't believe it is the right decision to keep our solvent product on the market," a company spokesman said.

The Coalition on Resistoleros and other corporate gadflies were ecstatic, but their jubilation turned to anger when they learned a few months later that Fuller had not in fact stopped selling Resistol in Central America, and did not intend to. True, Fuller no longer sold glue to retailers and small-scale users in Honduras and Guatemala, but it continued to sell large tubs and barrels of it to industrial customers in those countries and to a broader list of commercial and industrial users in neighboring countries.

The company says that it has not only restricted distribution but also taken other steps to stop the abuse of its product. It has altered Resistol's formula, replacing the sweet-smelling but highly toxic solvent toluene with the slightly less toxic chemical cyclohexane. In addition, the company has tried—without success, it says—to develop a nonintoxicating water-based glue, and it contributes to community programs for homeless children in Central America. But the company's critics disparage these actions as mere image polishing. Bruce Harris, director of Latin American programs for Covenant House, a nonprofit child-welfare advocate, asserts that Resistol is still readily available to children in Nicaragua and El Salvador and, to a lesser extent, in Costa Rica. "If they are genuinely concerned about the children," he asks, "why haven't they pulled out of all the countries—as their board mandated?"

Discussion Questions

1. What are H. B. Fuller's moral obligations in this case? What ideas, effects, and consequences are at stake? Have any moral rights been violated? What would a utilitarian recommend? A Kantian?

2. What specifically should H. B. Fuller do about Resistol? Are the critics right that the steps the company has taken so far are mere image polishing? Is the company's only moral option to withdraw from the Central American market altogether?

3. When, if ever, is a company morally responsible for harm done by the blatant misuse of a perfectly legitimate and socially useful product? Does it make a difference whether the abusers are adults or children? Is it relevant that other companies market similar products?

4. Tobacco companies have a strong financial interest in cultivating future smokers, and although they deny doing so, they consciously market their product to make it attractive to young people. Contrast their conduct with that of H. B. Fuller.

5. Given H. B. Fuller's conduct in other matters, would you judge it to be a morally responsible company, all things considered? Are companies that pride themselves on being morally responsible likely to be held to a higher standard than other companies? If so, is this fair?

CASE **6.4**

Drug Dilemmas

Everyone knows how high the cost of prescription medicines is these days, and many Americans dislike having to pay significantly more than Canadians or Europeans do for the very same drugs. Many of them also resent the huge profit margins that drug companies enjoy in comparison with other U.S. corporations. Year after year, for over two decades the drug industry has been far and away the most profitable sector of our economy. However, many people are also inclined to accept high prices as the cost we must bear for drug

research and the development of new medicines. But, in fact, the prices drug companies charge bear little relationship to the cost of making or developing them, and those prices could be cut dramatically without coming close to threatening their R&D budgets. Less than 15 percent of the sales revenue of the large pharmaceutical companies goes into R&D, half what they spend on "marketing and administration."[103]

Moreover, the pharmaceutical industry is nowhere near as innovative as most people think. According to Marcia Angell, former editor in chief of the *New England Journal of Medicine,* only a handful of important drugs have been brought to the market in recent years, and they were based mostly on taxpayer-funded research. She writes, "The great majority of 'new drugs' are not new at all but merely variations on older drugs already on the market. These are called 'me-too' drugs. The idea is to grab a share of an established, lucrative market by producing something very similar to a top-selling drug." This is made possible by the fact that the FDA will generally approve a drug if it is better than a placebo. "It needn't be better than an older drug," Angell says. "In fact it may be worse. There is no way of knowing, since companies do not test their drugs against older ones for the same conditions at equivalent doses." Of the seventy-eight drugs approved by the FDA in a recent year, only seventeen contained new active ingredients, and the FDA classified only seven of those as improvements over older drugs. And none of those seven came from a major U.S. drug company.

When it comes to research and innovation, the record of the big, profitable pharmaceutical corporations contrasts poorly with that of the small biotechnology companies that are responsible for most of today's medical advances. CV Therapeutics of Palo Alto, California, is one such company. Founded by cardiologist Louis G. Lange, it has developed a new drug, ranolazine, which promises to be the first new treatment for angina in over twenty-five years. The *Journal of the American Medical Association* has praised ranolazine as helping patients whom standard therapies have failed. But this medical breakthrough has brought an ethical dilemma with it. Patients in Russia and Eastern Europe constituted 60 percent of the one thousand or so test subjects involved in the studies that enabled CV Therapeutics to develop the drug. Now that the drug is ready, does the company have a moral obligation to make its drug available to them?

Other drug companies today are struggling with the same dilemma. They frequently test experimental drugs overseas, where there is less red tape and both doctors and patients are keen to participate in the tests. In Russia, for example, doctors are eager for the money they can get as study monitors, traveling to medical offices to make sure protocols are being followed. They also receive medical equipment such as treadmills for exercise testing. For their part, patients see it as a chance to get medications that they cannot afford to buy and that their government doesn't pay for. Moreover, says Richard Leach, the American business manager of a company called Russian Clinical Trials, "Eastern European and Russian people tend to be very compliant. … They will follow the trial and they will do whatever is asked. If they have to keep a diary, they do it. If they have to make office visits, they do it."

With at least 40 percent of drug testing now done offshore, critics worry that drug companies are exploiting their human subjects. In the United States and other well-to-do countries, experimental subjects must be given full information about the nature of the research, and they have a right to refuse to participate without penalty or consequence for their usual health care. Not so in Africa and many poor regions, where doctors profit from enrolling their patients, and local officials sometimes encourage whole villages or provinces to enroll in research programs. Conducting research overseas not only saves drug companies money, but it also circumvents FDA restrictions, which require companies to gain its approval before human testing in the United States can begin. The FDA obliges companies to describe their proposed research in detail and to file plans for guaranteeing informed consent and for monitoring the progress of the study. They must set up a review board to monitor each clinical trial and to ensure that risks to human subjects are "reasonable in relation to anticipated benefits, if any, to subjects, and the importance of the knowledge that may reasonably be expected to result." In addition, all risk must be "minimized."

Requirements for foreign research are much looser, and there is very little oversight. "Companies can conduct preliminary studies of drugs in poorer countries before formal testing even begins," writes Marcia Angell. "Quite literally, the participants are used as guinea pigs, subjects of research that really should be done on experimental animals." And when it comes to formal testing, the FDA may not learn about it until the company applies for final approval of its new drug.

These moral issues, however, are not the concern of companies like Russian Clinical Trials. Nor do they see it as their business to ask what happens when the studies end. Dr. Alan Wood, general manager of Covance, another American firm that conducts medical trials in Eastern Europe, says quite plainly, "What our clients do is not our affair."

But what about the drug companies themselves? What, if anything, do they owe overseas test subjects when their new drugs pan out? Some companies never even sell their drugs in the poor countries where they were developed. Others do, but often there are few patients who can afford them. "This is something that the biotech industry, as it develops more and more drugs, will have to come to grips with," says Carl B. Feldbaum, president of the Biotechnology Industry Organization. "It's not that we are lacking compassion, but the economics are tough."

"Do we have an obligation to everyone in the trial or to everyone in the community, the province, the nation, the region, or the world?" asks Dr. Ruth Faden, director of the Berman Bioethics Institute at Johns Hopkins University. "We really haven't figured this out." She acknowledges, though, that "many physician investigators feel uncomfortable with the idea of using patients in studies and then not being able to continue to help them when the trial ends." We seem "to have hit a wall of moral unease," she says. "I'm not sure exactly where we ought to end up."

Dr. Lawrence O. Goskin, director of the Center for Law and the Public's Health at Georgetown and Johns Hopkins Universities, is also troubled. Drug companies, he says, should not be seen as "the deep pocket that helps everyone," yet there is something disturbing about "parachute research," in which a company drops into a country, conducts its drug research, and then leaves. "It raises the question of what ethical obligation, if any, there might be to give back and make sure there is access to the drug after the trials are over."

Drug companies are businesses, of course, and they have to decide whether they can earn enough money in a foreign country to justify applying for approval to market a new drug there, then setting up a business office, and hiring a sales force. Even if they decide to provide the drug to patients free of charge—so-called compassionate use—things are not so simple. They still have to set up a distribution system, train doctors to administer the drug, and monitor the patients who take it. In the case of life-saving drugs, such as those for combating AIDS, many companies do, in fact, provide them for free or at low cost in poor countries, especially to patients who were involved in their development. But with a drug like ranolazine it's more complicated. Angina can cause terrible, crushing chest pains, and it can make the lives of chronic suffers miserable. Ranolazine can cut in half the number of angina attacks a patients suffers, but it's not a life-saving drug. It improves the quality of patients' lives, but it doesn't extend them.

Dr. Lange, meanwhile, is torn. His company is not a charity, and because CV Therapeutics is small, it can't afford to market ranolazine in countries where few people have enough money to buy it or to set up the distribution systems necessary to give it away. "We're not Merck," he says. "But we're concerned."

Discussion Questions

1. What explains the high price of prescription medicines in the United States? What if anything should be done about it? Do you believe that in the United States drug prices reflect the operation of a fair and competitive market?

2. Given the nature of their product, do pharmaceutical companies have ethical responsibilities that other corporations don't have? In your view, are the large U.S. drug companies good corporate citizens?

3. Are the large drug companies guilty of price gouging or of charging an unfair or exploitative price for their products? In general, what factors should determine the price of drugs? Should Americans be permitted to import drugs from Canada or other countries?

4. Assess the motivations of drug companies that do their testing overseas. Do you think test subjects are being exploited or taken advantage of? Under what circumstances, if any, are companies morally justified in testing overseas?

5. Do drug companies have an obligation to make new drugs available to patients who were involved in their development, either here or overseas? Does the size of the company make a difference? What would you do if you were Dr. Lange? What obligations, ideals, and consequences should he take into account?

6. Is it ethical for companies to decline to sell a useful drug like ranolazine in a poor country because they can make more money marketing it elsewhere?

7. When it comes to life-saving drugs, do pharmaceutical companies have a moral obligation to make them available in poor countries at little or no cost? Explain why or why not. What about effective but non-life-saving drugs like ranolazine?

CHAPTER 7

The Environment

D. Falconer/PhotoLink/PhotoDisc/Getty Images

INTRODUCTION

In December 2008, a coal-ash pond ruptured and disgorged a billion gallons of toxic sludge across three hundred acres of east Tennessee, destroying homes, killing fish, and threatening the local water supply. The sludge, which contains heavy metals such as arsenic, lead, mercury, and selenium, is a by-product of the coal that the Tennessee Valley Authority burns to produce electricity at its Kingston Fossil Plant. With the ever-expanding demand for electricity in the United States, the amount of coal ash produced has swelled in the past twenty years from 90 million tons to 131 million tons a year. But most of the 1,300 coal-ash dumps around the country go unregulated and unmonitored.[1]

Coal production destroys mountains and abrades the countryside, and burning it for energy damages the environment. Coal is the least efficient fossil fuel in terms of energy generated per unit of carbon released.[2] If it relies on coal-generated electricity, the average U.S. household consumes 1,140 lbs. of coal per month and emits 3,369 lbs. of carbon dioxide (CO_2).[3] The coal-ash spill at Kingston Fossil thus encapsulates many of the environmental problems we face as the ill effects of our environmental recklessness come home to roost.

Our rivers and lakes are dirty, and our air is unclean. The planet is warming, its protective ozone fraying. Lush forests are disappearing, and with them countless species of plants and animals. Half the world's wetlands have disappeared; 80 percent of its grasslands now suffer from soil degradation; and 20 percent of its drylands are in danger of turning into deserts. Groundwater is seriously depleted. As a result, the earth is losing its capacity to continue to provide the goods we need, threatening our economic well-being and ultimately our survival—so concludes a mammoth U.N.-sponsored assessment of global ecosystems.[4] Humankind is even making a mess of outer space. Of the 18,000 tracked objects now orbiting our planet only 900 are active satellites; the rest is rubbish—fragments of old rockets, smashed bits of equipment, and other debris, all of which pose hazards to working satellites.[5]

The environment is thus a huge topic, but as one expert remarks, "the concerns of environmental ethics might begin with the food on our plate."[6] Fertilizers, herbicides, and pesticides: Agriculture uses hundreds of chemicals in crop production. Although chemically intensive agriculture has yielded many benefits, it is hard on the environment—because of what it consumes and because of its impact on the surrounding ecosystem. In addition to the ecological price we pay for what we eat, there is the risk of chemical residues left in food.

In the United States, pesticide use has doubled in recent decades and presents a greater danger than most people realize.[7] Because of exposure to pesticides, many fish and birds in the Great Lakes region have lost their ability to reproduce. After a pesticide spilled into Florida's Lake Apopka, alligators were born with half-sized penises. When laboratory rats were fed DDT, they developed genital abnormalities. Now researchers believe that by mimicking estrogen and testosterone, the chemicals in pesticides may threaten human reproduction by disrupting the endocrine system that regulates it.[8] The pesticide problem is even more alarming when we consider children. Because they have smaller bodies and different eating patterns than adults, children's exposure to carcinogens and neurotoxins can be hundreds of times what is safe for them.[9] Yet until recently, the **Environmental Protection Agency (EPA)** set the legal limits on the amount of pesticide residues allowed to remain on food with adults in mind.

Pesticides, of course, are not the only problem. Thanks to environmentally insensitive industrial, agricultural, and waste management practices, our bodies now contain measurable quantities of a wide range of unnatural metals and potentially hazardous chemicals, including PCBs, furans, dioxin, mercury, lead, benzene, and other nasty items.[10] Perfluorochemicals, for example, were introduced in 1956, primarily in Teflon and other nonstick products. Now 96 percent of American children have one of these non-biodegradable chemicals in their bloodstream.[11]

One way these materials enter our bodies is through our water as various contaminants used in farming, manufacturing, and transportation run off into rivers, lakes, and underground reservoirs. In 1972 Congress passed the **Clean Water Act,** which proclaimed the goal of eliminating all water pollution by 1985. Since Congress acted, billions have been spent on pollution control. Some streams and lakes have improved; others have gotten worse. On average, though, according to government figures, water quality hasn't changed much. Two-thirds of all U.S. waters still fail to meet the goal set nearly forty years ago of being safe for fishing and swimming.[12]

Pollutants also contaminate the air we breathe, despoiling vegetation and crops, corroding construction materials, and threatening our lives and health. Each year, over 2 billion pounds of hazardous materials, including tons of toxic chemicals, are emitted into the air.[13] In addition to that is the emission of nontoxic substances such as sulfur and nitrogen oxide, which are a major source of acid rain and of the smog that blankets so many cities, and of the dust, soot, smoke, and tiny drops of acid that create the fine-particle pollution known to be so dangerous to human health.

Although precise figures are impossible to obtain, there is little doubt that air pollution is responsible for thousands of deaths and millions of sick days every year because of air-related ailments such as asthma, emphysema, and lung cancer.[14] Air pollution is especially harmful to young people, whose lungs are still developing.[15] It also contributes to heart disease, and pregnant women residing in regions with significant air pollution are up to three times more likely to give birth to children with serious birth defects.[16] Unfortunately, one in six Americans lives in areas where particle pollution poses a year-round health risk, and even more live in areas where it is an occasional but significant danger. Furthermore, 92.5 million people, almost a third of the U.S. population, reside in areas with harmful levels of ozone.[17]

Thanks to the groundbreaking **Clean Air Act** of 1970, our air is better than it would otherwise have been, and by most measures it is better than it was forty years ago. In particular, by banning lead as a fuel additive in gasoline, the act has reduced its presence in the air by nearly 90 percent. And the **Clean Air Act Amendments of 1990** require further measures be taken to fight smog, acid rain, and toxic emissions. But the fact remains: More than three-and-a-half decades after Congress first set a strict deadline for reducing air pollution to safe levels, the air in more than twenty-one major metropolitan areas remains a health risk.[18]

Related to the problem of atmospheric pollution is the issue of global warming. After years of study and debate, there is now a firm scientific consensus that human activity is indeed heating up the planet.[19] As we burn coal, oil, and gasoline for heat, electricity, and transportation, carbon dioxide (CO_2) is released into the atmosphere—now at higher rates than

ever[20]—trapping excess energy from the sun and warming the globe—
the so-called greenhouse effect. The evidence of global warming is all
around us. The past decade has been the hottest on record; in the
Northern Hemisphere, spring now comes, on average, a week earlier
than it used to. Storms have become more intense and weather patterns
more erratic. The Arctic ice sheet is melting, the world's glaciers are
shrinking fast, and sea levels are rising. Global warming also favors the
spread of disease and threatens countless plant and animal species with
extinction.[21] Only by drastically reducing the consumption of fossil fuels
can we hope to slow this trend and stabilize the climate at current levels
of disruption.

Surprisingly, one of the largest sources of pollution is not at all exotic—
namely, the animals we raise for food. In fact, the ecological costs of
producing beef, poultry, and pork are second only to the manufacture and
use of cars and light trucks. In addition to the electrical energy, fuel,
fertilizer, and pesticides consumed by the meat industry is the manure
problem. Megafarms with tens or hundreds of thousands of animals have
replaced factories as the biggest polluters of America's waterways. The
United States generates 1.4 billion tons of animal manure every year—
130 times more than the annual production of human waste. This waste
wasn't a problem when small farms crisscrossed the nation and farmers
used the manure as fertilizer. But giant farms with 100,000 hogs or a
million chickens all defecating in the same place seriously damage the
environment.[22] Heretofore, runoff and water pollution were the major
concern, but now scientists are also worried about air pollution and the
emission of noxious fumes from the disposal of animal waste.[23]

Nuclear wastes, of course, are in a class by themselves. Significant
danger arises from even the small amounts that are released into the
atmosphere during normal operation of a nuclear power plant or in mining,
processing, or transporting nuclear fuels. A nuclear-plant accident would, of
course, have frightening consequences, as the 1986 disaster at Chernobyl,
Ukraine, brought vividly home to the world. Illnesses caused by the fallout
from Chernobyl are still emerging, over twenty years later.[24] In addition, the
disposal of nuclear wastes has to worry anyone who is sensitive to the
legacy we leave future generations. Will the nuclear wastes we bury today
return to haunt them tomorrow?

It is little wonder, then, that considerable attention has focused on business's and industry's responsibility for preserving the integrity of our natural environment. This chapter explores some of the moral dilemmas posed for business by our environmental relationships—not just the problem of pollution but also the ethical issues posed by the depletion of natural resources and by our treatment of animals. The chapter's purpose is not to argue that the environmental problems facing us are serious and that industry has greatly contributed to them. Few people doubt this. Rather, this chapter is largely concerned with a more practical question: Given the problems of environmental degradation, of resource depletion, and of the abuse of animals for commercial purposes, what are business's responsibilities? Specifically, this chapter examines the following topics:

1. The meaning and significance of *ecology*
2. The traditional business attitudes toward the environment that have encouraged environmental degradation and resource depletion
3. The moral problems underlying business's abuse of the environment—in particular, the question of externalities, the problem of free riders, and the right to a livable environment
4. The costs of environmental protection and the question of who should pay them
5. Different methods for pursuing our environmental goals—regulations, incentives, pricing mechanisms, and pollution permits
6. Some of the deeper and not fully resolved questions of environmental ethics: What environmental responsibilities do we have to the rest of the world? What obligations do we have to future generations? Does nature have value in itself? Is our commercial exploitation of animals immoral?

———————

BUSINESS AND ECOLOGY

To deal intelligently with the question of business's responsibilities for the environment, one must realize that as business uses energy and materials, discharges waste, and generates products and services, it is functioning within an ecological system. **Ecology** refers to the science of the interrelationships among organisms and their environments. The operative term is "interrelationships," implying that an interdependence exists among all entities in the environment. In particular, we must not forget that human beings are part of nature and thus intricately connected with and interrelated to the natural environment.

Ecosystems

In speaking about ecological matters, ecologists frequently use the term **eco-system**, which refers to a total ecological community, both living and nonliv-ing. Webs of interdependency structure ecosystems. Predators and prey, producers and consumers, hosts and parasites are linked together, creating interlocking mechanisms—checks and balances—that stabilize the system. A change in any one element can have ripple effects throughout the system.

For example, a decade after wolves were reintroduced into Yellowstone Park in the mid-1990s, their presence was discovered to have changed the be-havior of elk.[25] Skittish of wolves, the elk now spend more time than they used to in places that afford a 360-degree view, and they shy away from rises or bluffs that conceal wolves. In those places, aspen, cottonwoods, and wil-low thickets have bounced back as a result. The trees, in turn, have stabilized the banks of streams, and by lowering the water temperature, their shade has improved the habitat for trout, resulting in more and bigger fish. Beavers, which eat willow and aspen, have also returned to the streams. So have yel-low warblers, Lincoln sparrows, and other songbirds. When wolves kill an elk, they don't eat the whole carcass, so scavengers like magpies and ravens prosper. Coyotes, in contrast, have declined. The creatures they used to prey on—voles, mice, and other rodents—are flourishing and their increased num-bers have boosted the population of raptors and red foxes. The wolves them-selves, however, are under threat from the dogs that visitors bring into the park. Dogs can carry parvovirus, which is now killing 60 to 70 percent of wolf pups and is largely responsible for the recent decline in the wolf popula-tion from 170 to 130.

Every living organism affects its environment, yet *Homo sapiens* pos-sesses the power to upset dramatically the stability of natural ecosystems. In particular, many human commercial activities (for example, using pesticides and establishing oil fields) have unpredictable and disruptive consequences for ecosystems. For example, farmers in the Midwest use nitrogen fertilizer liberally. Excess nitrogen runs off their fields and finds its way into the Mississippi River and eventually into the Gulf of Mexico. There, in what has historically been the nation's best shrimping grounds, it has created what is known as the dead zone, where the water is devoid of life to about 10 feet be-low the surface. This dead zone has now grown to about 8,500 square miles, an area the size of New Jersey.[26]

Nevertheless, tampering with ecosystems does not always have injurious effects. Sometimes unforeseen benefits result, as was true years ago when oil and gas drilling expanded into the Gulf. Much to everyone's surprise, the op-erational docks, pipes, and platforms provided a better place for lower forms of life to attach themselves than the silt-laden sea ever did. This in turn in-creased the fish catch in the area. But even in fortuitous instances like this, en-vironmental intrusions affect the integrity of ecosystems. And that's the point. Because an ecosystem represents a delicate balance of interrelated entities, the introduction of any new element, whether biotic or abiotic, can disrupt it. And we are not usually so lucky in the results. Dr. Paul Ehrlich, one of the best-known exponents of ecological awareness, put the matter succinctly.

Many commercial activi-ties have unpredictable and often disruptive envi-ronmental consequences.

Summary 7.1
Ecology studies the interrelationships among organisms and their environments. Because of the interdependence of an ecosystem's elements and because intrusion into an ecosystem frequently creates unfavorable effects, business must be sensitive to its impacts on the physical environment.

"There are a number of ecological rules it would be wise for people to remember," Ehrlich said. "One of them is that there is no such thing as a free lunch. Another is that when we change something into something else, the new thing is usually more dangerous than what we had originally."[27]

As it produces the goods and services we need or want, business inevitably intrudes into ecosystems, but not all intrusions or all kinds of intrusions are justifiable. In fact, precisely because of the interrelated nature of ecosystems and because intrusions generally produce serious unfavorable effects, business must scrupulously avoid actions, practices, and policies that have an undue impact on the environment. There's ample documentation to show that business traditionally has been remiss in both recognizing and adequately discharging its obligations in this regard. We needn't spend time retelling the sorry tale, but it does seem worthwhile to isolate some business attitudes that have been responsible for this indifference.

Business's Traditional Attitudes toward the Environment

Several related attitudes, prevalent in our society in general and in business in particular, have led to or increased our environmental problems. One of these is the tendency to view the natural world as a "free and unlimited good"—that is, as something we can exploit, even squander, without regard to the future. Writer John Steinbeck once reflected on this attitude:

> I have often wondered at the savagery and thoughtlessness with which our early settlers approached this rich continent. They came at it as though it were an enemy, which of course it was. They burned the forests and changed the rainfall; they swept the buffalo from the plains, blasted the streams, set fire to the grass, and ran a reckless scythe through the virgin and noble timber. Perhaps they felt that it was limitless and could never be exhausted and that a man could move on to new wonders endlessly....
>
> This tendency toward irresponsibility persists in very many of us today; our rivers are poisoned by reckless dumping of sewage and toxic industrial wastes, the air of our cities is filthy and dangerous to breathe from the belching of uncontrolled products from combustion of coal, coke, oil, and gasoline. Our towns are girdled with wreckage and debris of our toys—our automobiles and our packaged pleasures. Through uninhibited spraying against one enemy we have destroyed the natural balances our survival requires. All these evils can and must be overcome if America and Americans are to survive; but many of us conduct ourselves as our ancestors did, stealing from the future for our clear and present profit.[28]

Traditionally, business has considered the environment to be a free, nearly limitless good. In other words, air, water, land, and other natural resources from coal to beavers (trapped almost to extinction for their pelts in the nineteenth century) were seen as available for business to use as it saw fit. In this context, pollution and the depletion of natural resources are two aspects of the same problem: Both involve using up natural resources that are limited. Pollution uses up clean air and water, just as extraction uses up the minerals or oil in the ground. The belief that both sorts of resources are unlimited and free promotes wasteful consumption of them.

Both pollution and the depletion of natural resources involve using up something that is in limited supply.

Garrett Hardin describes the consequences of this attitude in his well-known parable, the **tragedy of the commons.** Hardin asks us to imagine villagers who allow their animals to graze in the commons, the collectively shared village pasture. Even though it is in the interest of each person to permit his or her animals to graze without limit on the public land, the result of doing so is that the commons is soon overgrazed, making it of no further grazing value to anyone.[29]

Today the international fishing industry exemplifies Hardin's point: Over-fishing by ships armed with advanced technology is dramatically reducing the world's stock of fish, threatening to undermine the whole industry.[30] But the moral of Hardin's story is perfectly general: When it comes to "the commons"—that is, to public or communal goods like air, water, and wilderness—problems arise as the result of individuals' and companies' following their own self-interest. Each believes that his or her own use of the commons has only a negligible effect, but the cumulative result can be the gradual destruction of the public domain, which is bad for everyone. In the tragedy of the commons we have the reverse of Adam Smith's invisible hand: Each person's pursuit of self-interest makes everyone worse-off.

The tragedy of the commons also illustrates the more general point that there can be a difference between the private costs and the social costs of a business activity. Chapter 5 discussed this issue when it described what economists call "externalities," but it is worth reviewing the point in the present context.

Suppose a paper mill only partially treats the chemical wastes it releases into a lake that's used for fishing and recreational activities, thus saving on production costs. If the amount of effluent is great enough to reduce the fishing productivity of the lake, then while the mill's customers pay a lower price for its paper than they otherwise would, other people end up paying a higher price for fish. Moreover, the pollution may make the lake unfit for recreational activities such as swimming or for use as a source of potable water. The result is that other people and the public generally pay the cost of the mill's inadequate water-treatment system. Economists term this disparity between private industrial costs and public social costs an **externality,** or **spillover.** In viewing things strictly in terms of private industrial costs, business overlooks spillover. This is an economic problem because the price of the paper does not reflect the true cost of producing it. Paper is underpriced and overproduced, thus leading to a misallocation of resources. This is also a moral problem because the purchasers of paper are not paying its full cost. Instead, part of the cost of producing paper is being unfairly imposed on other people.

The same sort of disparity between the private costs and the social costs of business activity also arises in the context of resource depletion, rather than pollution. For example, it takes 100,000 gallons of water to make one automobile, but no manufacturer considers, let alone pays for, the damage done to the water table. Yet America is in the environmentally unsustainable position of sucking up 75 gallons of groundwater for every 60 that nature puts back in.[31]

Summary 7.2
Traditionally, business has regarded the natural world as a free and unlimited good. Pollution and resource depletion are examples of situations in which each person's pursuit of self-interest can make everyone worse-off (the "tragedy of the commons"). Business must be sensitive to possible disparities between its private economic costs and the social costs of its activities (the problem of externalities, or spillovers).

Several factors have combined to create the serious environmental problems facing us today.

In sum, then, externalities or spillover effects, pursuit of private interest at the expense of the commons, and a view of the environment as a free good that can be consumed without limit have combined with an ignorance of ecology and of the often fragile interconnections and interdependencies of the natural world to create the serious environmental problems facing us today.

THE ETHICS OF ENVIRONMENTAL PROTECTION

Much of what we do to reduce, eliminate, or avoid pollution and the depletion of scarce natural resources is in our collective self-interest. Many measures that we take—for example, recycling our cans or installing catalytic converters in our cars—are steps that benefit all of us, collectively and individually: Our air is more breathable and our landscapes less cluttered with garbage. But even if such measures benefit each and every one of us, there is still a **free-rider problem** because of the temptation to shirk individual responsibilities. The individual person or company may rationalize that the little bit it adds to the total pollution problem doesn't make any difference. It benefits from the efforts of others to prevent pollution but "rides for free" by not making the same effort itself.

The unfairness here is obvious. Likewise, as explained in the previous section, the failure of companies to "internalize" their environmental "externalities" spells unfairness. Others are forced to pick up the tab when companies do not pay all the environmental costs involved in producing their own products. As mentioned in Chapter 5, those who adopt the broader view of corporate responsibility emphasize that business and the rest of society have an implicit social contract. This contract reflects what society hopes to achieve by allowing business to operate; it sets the "rules of the game" governing business activity. Companies that try to be free riders in environmental matters or that refuse to address the spillover or external costs of their business activity violate this contract.

So far this chapter has emphasized that we need to view the environment differently if we are to improve our quality of life and even to continue to exist. And it has just stressed how the failure of an individual or business to play its part is unfair. Some moral theorists, like William T. Blackstone, have gone further to argue that each of us has a **right to a livable environment.** In Blackstone's view, this is a human right. "Each person," he argues, "has this right *qua* being human and because a livable environment is essential for one to fulfill his human capacities."[32] This right has emerged, he contends, as a result of changing environmental conditions, which affect the very possibility of human life as well as the possibility of realizing other human rights.

Recognition of a right to a livable environment would strengthen further the ethical reasons for business to respect the integrity of the natural world. In addition, recognition of this moral right could, Blackstone suggests, form a sound basis for establishing a legal right to a livable environment through legislation and even, perhaps, through a constitutional amendment or an environmental bill of rights. An official recognition of such rights would enhance our ability to go after polluters and other abusers of the natural environment.

Summary 7.3
Companies that attempt to be free riders in environmental matters or that refuse to address the external costs of their business activities behave unfairly. Some philosophers maintain, further, that every human being has a right to a livable environment.

Acknowledging a human right to a livable environment, however, does not solve many of the difficult problems facing us. In the effort to conserve irreplaceable resources, to protect the environment from further degradation, and to restore it to its former quality, we are still faced with difficult choices, each with its economic and moral costs. The next section focuses on pollution-control, but most of the points apply equally to other problems of environmental protection, as well as to the conservation of scarce resources.

The Costs of Pollution Control

It is easy to say that we should do whatever it takes to improve the environment. Before this answer has any operational worth, however, we must consider a number of things. One is the quality of environment that we want. This can vary from an environment restored to its pristine state to one minimally improved over its current condition. Then there's the question of precisely what is necessary to bring about the kind of environment we want. In some cases we may lack the technological capacity to restore the environment. Finally, an important concern in any determination of what should be done to improve the environment is a calculation of what it will cost.

To draw out this point, we must consider a major technique for determining the total costs of environmental improvement. **Cost-benefit analysis** is a device used to determine whether it's worthwhile to incur a particular cost—for instance, the cost of employing a particular pollution-control device. The general approach is to evaluate a project's direct and indirect costs and benefits, the difference being the net result for society. Suppose that the estimated environmental damage of operating a particular plant is $1 million per year, that closing the plant would have dire economic consequences for the community, and that the only technique that would permit the plant to operate in an environmentally nondamaging way would cost $6 million per year. In this case, cost-benefit analysis would rule against requiring the plant to introduce the new technique.* If the cost of the technique had been only $800,000, however, cost-benefit analysis would have favored it.

Cost-benefit analysis can quickly get complicated. For example, to determine whether it would be worthwhile to initiate more stringent air-pollution standards for a particular industry, a multitude of factors must be considered. Possible costs might include lower corporate profits, higher prices for consumers, unfavorable effects on employment, and adverse consequences for the nation's balance of payments. On the side of anticipated benefits, a reduction in airborne particulates over urban areas would reduce illness and premature death from bronchitis, lung cancer, and other respiratory diseases by some determinate percentage. The increase in life expectancy would have to be estimated along with projected savings in medical costs and increases in productivity. In addition, diminished industrial discharges would mean reduced

---

* Cost-benefit analysis would not, however, prevent other strategies for getting the plant to internalize this externality. It could be taxed $1 million or be required to reimburse those who suffer the $1 million loss.

property and crop damage from air pollution, and that would save more money.

This example suggests the extreme difficulty of making reliable estimates of actual costs and benefits, of putting price tags on the different effects of the policy being considered. Any empirical prediction in a case like this is bound to be controversial. This problem is compounded by the fact that decision makers are unlikely to know for certain all future results of the policy being studied. Not only is estimating the likelihood of its various possible effects difficult, but also some future effects may be entirely unanticipated.

The new discipline of **ecological economics** is attempting to expand further the boundaries of environmental cost-benefit analysis by calculating the value of an ecosystem in terms of what it would cost to provide the benefits and services it now furnishes us—for example, the worth of a wetland in terms of the cost of constructing structures that provide the same flood control and storm protection that natural wetlands do.[33] Although conventional economists dismiss the idea of equating the value of something with its replacement cost rather than with what people are willing to pay for it, ecological economists respond that traditional market pricing fails to capture the nonmarketed externalities that nature provides, such as the nutrients that a forest recycles. In one study, for example, ecological economists established that a mangrove swamp in Thailand was worth 72 percent more when left intact to provide timber, charcoal, fish, and storm protection than when converted to a fish farm. "In every case we looked at," states Cambridge University biologist Andrew Balmford, "the loss of nature's services outweighed the benefits of development, often by large amounts."[34]

Even putting aside the debate over ecological economics, cost-benefit analyses of rival environmental policies will frequently prove controversial because they inevitably involve making value judgments about nonmonetary costs and benefits. Costs relative to time, effort, and discomfort can and must be introduced. Benefits can take even more numerous forms: health, convenience, comfort, enjoyment, leisure, self-fulfillment, freedom from odor, enhanced beauty, and so on. Benefits are especially difficult to calculate in environmental matters because they often take an aesthetic form. Some environmentalists, for example, may campaign for the preservation of a remote forest visited annually by only a handful of stalwart backpackers, whereas developers wish to convert it into a more accessible and frequented ski resort. Should the forest be preserved or should it be converted into a ski resort? Conflicting value judgments are at stake.

With the assistance of an economics consulting firm, the U.S. Department of the Interior asked Americans how much they are willing to shell out for environmental restoration. For instance, what would each consent to pay to restore the ecological balance of the Grand Canyon, even if few of them will actually see or truly understand the improvements: ten cents a month? a dollar a month? ten dollars a month? The Interior Department used this technique to justify reintroducing wolves into parts of Montana, Wyoming, and Idaho—a controversial move opposed by some taxpayers, ranchers, and consumers of beef. Some environmentalists applaud this attempt to calculate

Summary 7.4
Pollution control has a price, and trade-offs must be made. Weighing environmental costs and benefits is often difficult, though. The new discipline of ecological economics and recent attempts to measure "non-use value" try to offer a wider perspective on environmental issues, but any kind of cost-benefit analysis inevitably involves controversial factual assessments and value judgments.

what economists call "non-use value," but others fear that the attempt to put a monetary price tag on ecosystems belittles the values they champion.[35]

An assessment of costs and benefits inevitably involves value judgments and factual uncertainties.

An evaluation of costs and benefits is unavoidably wed to value judgments—to assessments of worth and the ranking of values. Although a cost-effectiveness analysis may be necessary for determining the soundness of an environmental-preservation measure or a pollution-control project, it seems inevitable that any assessment of costs and benefits will be subject to various factual uncertainties and significantly influenced by the values one holds. This is especially true in situations where environmental concerns clash. Windmills, for example, offer a clean, endlessly renewable source of energy, but they blemish the natural landscape and can chop up migratory birds. Likewise, plans to harvesting solar power on a large scale would sacrifice hundreds of thousands of acres of wilderness and threaten some endangered species.[36] Technology that replaces wood fiber with calcium carbonate in the production of paper saves trees, but mining it sometimes despoils bucolic areas.[37] Natural gas burns more cleanly than other fossil fuels, but the new offshore terminals that process it kill sea life and put pressure on an already fragile marine ecosystem.[38]

Who Should Pay the Costs?

The most comprehensive federal study of air-pollution rules shows the cost of compliance to be outweighed five to seven times by the economic benefits from reductions in hospitalization, emergency room visits, premature deaths, and lost workdays.[39] Indeed, over recent decades cleaner air has added nearly five months to average life expectancy in the United States.[40] In addition, of course, money spent to minimize pollution also benefits those paid to clean up or prevent the pollution. Indeed, restoring the environment could become the biggest economic enterprise of our times, a huge source of jobs, profits, and poverty alleviation.[41] Still, environmental protection and restoration do not come cheap, and determining who should pay the necessary costs raises a tough question of social justice. Two popular answers to this question currently circulate: (1) Those responsible for causing the pollution ought to pay. (2) Those who stand to benefit from protection and restoration should pick up the tab.

Those Responsible

The claim that those responsible for causing the pollution ought to pay the costs of pollution control and environmental restoration seems eminently fair until one asks a simple question: Who, exactly, is responsible for the pollution? Who are the polluters?

Many people argue that big business is the chief polluter and therefore ought to bear the lion's share of the costs of environmental protection and restoration. Business probably has profited more than any other group from treating the environment as a free good, but consumers themselves have benefited enormously by not having to pay higher costs for products. In fact, some would argue that consumers are primarily to blame for pollution because they create the demand for the products whose production impairs the environment. As Milton Friedman put it, "the people who use electricity are responsible for the smoke that comes out of the stacks of generating plants."[42] Therefore, the argument goes, it is consumers, not business, who should pay to protect and restore the environment. This argument can be extended globally. International agreements like the Kyoto Protocol, which became effective in 2005, look at greenhouse emissions on a country-by-country basis, requiring every participating nation to reduce the carbon dioxide produced within its borders. As the main producer of MP3 players, China contributes significantly to global warming because manufacturing a single player releases about 17 pounds of CO_2 into the atmosphere. But if a Chinese factory makes something only so that it can be exported to consumers in America, don't they bear the ultimate responsibility for the pollution that results?[43]

Actually, both versions of the polluter-should-pay-the-bill thesis—one attributing primary responsibility for pollution to big business, the other to consumers—largely ignore the manifold, deep-rooted causes of environmental-degradation. Population growth and the increasing concentration of population in urban areas are two of them. In 1900 Americans numbered 76.2 million; by the beginning of the twenty-first century the U.S. population had quadrupled, to more than 300 million. An increasingly urbanized nation, the United States is a long way from the rural, agriculturally oriented society it once was. Today, for example, the number of college students is more than three times the entire U.S. farm population, which has fallen from over 40 percent in 1900 to less than 2 percent today. More than 70 million Americans live in our ten largest metropolitan areas, and nearly half the population resides in metropolitan areas with populations of a million or more. Accompanying this tremendous growth and equally staggering level of urbanization is an ever-increasing demand for goods and services, natural resources, energy, and industrial production. Viewing the matter globally only underscores the point. The world's population has more than doubled since 1960 and is increasingly urbanized. Half the world's population lives in cities, and sixteen of the world's twenty largest cities are in developing countries.

Another root cause of environmental problems is rising affluence. As people get more money to spend, they buy and consume more tangible goods, discard them more quickly, and produce more waste, all of which put pressure on the environment, hastening its degradation. Americans today produce 60 percent more garbage per person than Americans thirty years ago, almost 1,600 pounds per person per year.[44] We own more than 241 million motor vehicles—that's about a quarter of the world total—and are only making matters worse by our preference for big, gas-guzzling pickups, minivans, and sport-utility vehicles, which emit significantly more carbon dioxide (a principle cause of global warming) and nitrogen oxides (the main source of smog) than ordinary passenger cars do.* Naturally enough, people in less-developed countries aspire to the material lifestyle that Americans enjoy, and their rapidly growing economies are beginning to make this possible. But the

---

* The average passenger vehicle now weighs more and has greater horsepower than ever before. It also gets fewer miles per gallon than in 1987.[45]

environmental consequences of even a third of the world's population consuming as much and as wastefully as Americans do would be catastrophic.[46]

Thus, the enemy in the war against environmental abuse turns out, in a sense, to be all of us. No solution to the question of who should pay the costs of pollution control can ignore this fact.

Those Who Would Benefit

The other popular reply to the payment question is that those who will benefit from environmental improvement should pay the costs.

Workers in certain industries and people living in certain neighborhoods or regions benefit more than other people from environmental controls. The residents of the Los Angeles basin, for instance, gain more from stringently enforced auto-emission standards than do people living in a remote corner of Wyoming. The trouble with this argument, though, is that every individual, rich or poor, and every institution, large or small, stands to benefit in some way from environmental protection and restoration, albeit not necessarily to the same degree. As a result, the claim that those who will benefit should pay the costs is problematic because pollution touches everyone. This point holds true internationally. Improved environmental controls in China would undoubtedly benefit the Chinese people first and foremost; but the global warming to which this pollution contributes is a worldwide problem, and addressing it will benefit us all.

If, however, this position means that individuals and groups should pay to the degree that they will benefit, then one must wonder how this could possibly be determined. For example, changing the operation of the Glen Canyon Dam has raised electricity bills in the West, but it has reduced ecological damage to the Grand Canyon. Who benefits the most—local residents, visitors to the Grand Canyon, everyone who values this national resource—and how much should they pay?[47] But perhaps the most serious objection to this thesis is that it seems to leave out responsibility as a legitimate criterion. Pollution restrictions on American power plants in the Midwest benefit Canadians by reducing acid rain, but to make them pay the costs wouldn't seem fair.

Any equitable solution to the problem of who should pay the bill for environmental cleanup should take into account responsibility as well as benefit. The preceding analysis suggests that, to a certain extent, we all share the blame for pollution and all stand to benefit from environmental improvement. This doesn't mean, however, that we can't pinpoint certain areas of industry as chronic polluters. Electric-power plants, for example, are one of the major sources of greenhouse gases, but not all plants are equally dirty. Old coal-burning plants that have resisted modernization produce a disproportionate share of the pollution. Likewise, some companies can be singled out as having particularly distressing environmental records. One business magazine recently named ten of them.[48] They include Alcoa, whose aluminum smelters release 6.1 million pounds of air pollution annually; American Electric Power, one of the biggest mercury polluters in the United States; Chevron, which has contributed to more than 90 Superfund toxic waste sites; and Cargill, whose various facilities are responsible for inordinate air

Summary 7.5
Any equitable solution to the problem of who should bear the costs of environmental protection and restoration must recognize that all of us in some way contribute to the problem and benefit from environmental safeguards and improvements. Among the deep-rooted causes of environmental degradation are population growth, increasing urbanization, and rising affluence.

Although we all share some responsibility for pollution, certain companies and industries stand out as excessive polluters.

pollution, groundwater contamination, and toxic discharges into Virginia's North Folk Shenandoah River. Or consider Massey Energy Company, the nation's fourth-largest coal producer. A repeat violator of the Clean Water Act, it has clogged and polluted hundreds of streams and rivers in Kentucky and West Virginia.[49]

Still, the point is that a fair and just program for assigning costs begins with a recognition that we all bear responsibility for environmental problems and that we all stand to benefit from correcting them. But even if we agree that it is only fair that everyone share the cost of environmental improvement, we can still wonder about how the bill ought to be paid. What would be the fairest and most effective way of handling those costs?

ACHIEVING OUR ENVIRONMENTAL GOALS

Without an environmentally informed citizenry making conscientious political, business, and consumer choices, it will prove impossible to reverse the degradation of our environment by halting pollution, stemming global warming, and reducing the utilization of natural resources to sustainable levels. Just as obviously, business and government must work together if we are to achieve our shared environmental goals. Government, in particular, has a crucial role to play by initiating programs that prod business into behaving in more environmentally responsible ways. That's easy to see. The more challenging moral and economic task is to determine fair and effective methods for doing so.

Three distinct approaches to environmental protection are the use of regulations, the use of incentives, and the use of pricing mechanisms and pollution permits. Though similar in some respects, they carry different assumptions about the roles of government and business, as well as about what's fair and just. Each approach has distinct advantages and weaknesses; each raises some questions of social justice.

Regulations

The **regulatory approach** makes use of direct public regulation and control in determining how the pollution bill is paid. State and federal legislation and regulations formulated by agencies such as the EPA set environmental standards, which are then applied and enforced by those agencies, other regulatory bodies, and the courts. An emissions standard that, for example, prohibits industrial smokestacks from releasing more than a certain percentage of particulate matter would require plants exceeding that standard to comply with it by installing an appropriate pollution-control device.

A clear advantage to such a regulatory approach is that standards would be legally enforceable. Firms not meeting them could be fined or even shut down. Also, from the view of morality, such standards are fair in that they apply to all industries in the same way. There are, however, distinct disadvantages in this approach.

First, pollution statutes and regulations generally require polluters to use the strongest feasible means of pollution control. But that requires the EPA

Although a regulatory approach is fair in the sense of setting legally enforced standards that apply equally to all, it has four drawbacks.

or some other regulatory body to investigate pollution-control technologies and economic conditions in each industry to find the best technology that companies can afford. Such studies may require tens of thousands of pages of documentation, and legal proceedings may be necessary before the courts give final approval to the regulation. Moreover, expecting the EPA to master the economics and technology of dozens of industries, from petrochemicals to steel to electric utilities, may be unreasonable. It is bound to make mistakes, asking more from some companies than they can ultimately achieve while letting others off too lightly.[50]

Second, although universal environmental standards are fair in the sense that they apply to all equally, this very fact raises questions about their effectiveness. In attempting to legislate realistic and reliable standards for all, will government so dilute the standards that they become ineffectual? Or consider areas where the environment is cleaner than government standards. In such cases, should an industry be allowed to pollute up to the maximum of the standard? The Supreme Court thinks not. In a case brought before it by the Sierra Club, the Court ruled that states with relatively clean air must prohibit industries from producing significant air pollution even when EPA standards are not violated. In this case a firm was being forced to pay the costs of meeting an environmental standard that, in one sense, was sterner than what competitors were required to meet elsewhere. One can also question both the equity and the economic sense of requiring compliance with universal standards, without regard for the idiosyncratic nature of each industry or the particular circumstances of individual firms. Is it reasonable to force companies that cause different amounts of environmental damage to spend the same amount on pollution abatement? In one case, the courts required two paper mills on the West Coast to install expensive pollution-control equipment, even though their emissions were diluted effectively by the Pacific Ocean. It took a special act of Congress to rescue the mills.[51]

Third, regulation can also take away an industry's incentive to do more than the minimum required by law. No polluter has an incentive to discharge less muck than regulations allow. No entrepreneur has an incentive to devise technology that will bring pollution levels below the registered maximum. Moreover, firms have an incentive not to let the EPA know they can pollute less. Under the regulatory approach, a government agency may have the desire to regulate pollution but lack the information to do it efficiently. The position of industry is reversed: It may have the information and the technology but no desire to use it.[52]

Finally, there's the problem of displacement costs resulting from industrial relocation or shutdown due to environmental regulations. For example, Youngstown Sheet and Tube Company moved its corporate headquarters and some production lines to the Chicago area, thus eliminating five hundred jobs in Youngstown, Ohio, and causing serious economic problems in nearby communities. One of the reasons for the transfer was the need to implement water-pollution controls, which depleted vital capital. Consider also the marginal firms that would fail while attempting to meet the costs of such standards. When air-pollution regulations were applied to a sixty-year-old

Summary 7.6
Regulation is the most familiar way of pursuing environmental goals, but requiring firms to use the strongest feasible means of pollution control is problematic. Although regulations treat all parties equally, this often comes at the cost of ignoring the special circumstances of particular industries and individual firms. Regulations also remove a company's incentive to do more than the law requires and can cause plants to shut down or relocate.

cement plant in San Juan Bautista, California, the plant had to close because it was too obsolete to meet the standard economically. The shutdown seriously injured the economy of the little town, which had been supported primarily by the cement plant.

But if regulations are tougher for new entrants to an industry than for existing firms, as they often are, then new investment may be discouraged—even if newer plants would be cleaner than older ones. For example, a clause in the Clean Air Act exempts old coal-fired plants from complying with current emissions rules. As a result, much of America's electricity is produced by plants that are over forty years old and far dirtier than newer plants would be.[53] Perhaps in 1970 it was fair not to force existing plants into compliance with new rules. But is it still fair? Clearly, a regulatory approach to environmental improvement, though having advantages, raises serious questions.

Incentives

A widely supported approach to the problem of cost allocation for environmental improvement is government investment, subsidy, and general economic incentive. For instance, government might give firms a tax break for purchasing (and using) pollution-control equipment, or it might offer matching grants to companies that install such devices. A different example is the "Future-Gen" project, launched in 2003. It commits the federal government to underwriting 80 percent of the $1 billion or so cost of industry's developing a cost-effective new generation of coal-fired plants that emit no greenhouse gases into the atmosphere.

In its "33/50 Program," the EPA tried a new approach. It asked six hundred industrial facilities to reduce voluntarily their discharges of seventeen toxic contaminants, first by 33 percent, then by 50 percent. The incentive for firms to commit to the reductions was simply the public relations opportunities afforded by EPA press releases and outstanding performance awards—along with, perhaps, the firms' desire to stave off future regulatory action.[54]

The advantage of an **incentive approach** is that it minimizes government interference in business and encourages voluntary action rather than coercing compliance, as in the case of regulation. By allowing firms to move at their own pace, it avoids the evident unfairness to firms that cannot meet regulatory standards and must either relocate or fail. In addition, whereas regulated standards can encourage minimum legal compliance, an incentive approach provides an economic reason for going beyond minimal compliance. Firms have a financial inducement to do more than just meet EPA standards.

An incentives-based approach is likely to be slow and sometimes amounts to paying polluters not to pollute.

But incentives are not without disadvantages that bear moral overtones. *First* as an essentially voluntary device, an incentive program is likely to be slow. Environmental problems that cry out for a solution may continue to fester. Incentive programs may allow urgently needed action to be postponed. *Second*, government incentive programs often amount to a subsidy for polluters, with polluting firms being paid not to pollute. Although this approach may sometimes address the economics of pollution more effectively than the regulatory approach, it nonetheless raises questions about the justice of benefiting not the victims of pollution but some of the egregious polluters.

Special interests can distort incentive programs.

Third, incentive programs can be abused, and determining their cost-effectiveness can be problematic. Indeed, when promoted by business lobbyists and sectional political interests, the environmental gain they bring may not be worth the cost. For example, the United States spends billions upon billions to subsidize the conversion of corn to ethanol. The subsidy benefits agribusiness and other corporate interests, but its positive environmental impact is slight. Worse, by reducing the amount of food produced, the subsidy has helped drive up world food prices, with painful consequences for the poor.[55]

Pricing Mechanisms and Pollution Permits

A third approach to the cost-allocation problem involves programs designed to charge firms for the amount of pollution they produce. **Pricing mechanisms,** or effluent charges, spell out the cost for a specific kind of pollution in a specific area at a specific time. Prices are tied to the amount of damage caused and thus vary from place to place and from time to time. For example, during the summer months in the Los Angeles basin, a firm might pay much higher charges for fly ash emitted into the environment than it would pay during the winter months. Whatever the set of prices, they would apply equally to every producer of a given type of pollution at the same time and place. The more a firm pollutes, the more it pays.

One advantage of this approach is that it places the cost of pollution control squarely on the polluters. Pricing mechanisms penalize, rather than compensate, industrial polluters. For many persons this is inherently fairer than incentive programs that subsidize companies that pollute. Also, because costs are internalized, firms are encouraged to do more than meet the minimal requirements established under a strict regulatory policy. Under this approach a firm, in theory, could be charged for any amount of pollution and not just incur legal penalties whenever it exceeded an EPA standard. In effect, pollution costs would become production costs.

Instead of imposing a tax or a fee on the pollutants released into the environment, the government could charge companies for **pollution permits,** or it could auction off a limited number of permits. An even more market-oriented strategy is to give companies permits to discharge a limited amount of pollution and then to allow them to buy and sell the right to emit pollutants. With pollution permits, companies with low pollution levels can make money by selling their pollution rights to companies with poorer controls. Thus, each firm can estimate the relative costs of continuing to pollute as opposed to investing in cleaner procedures. The government can also set the precise amount of pollution it is prepared to allow and, by lowering the amount permitted over time, can reduce or even eliminate it.

The EPA successfully experimented with this strategy in the 1970s when it gave oil refineries two years to reduce the allowable lead content in gasoline. Refineries received quotas on lead, which they could trade with one another. Later, the 1990 Clean Air Act Amendments adopted this approach with respect to the sulfur dioxide (SO_2) emissions of electric utilities. Though controversial at the time—the power industry insisted the SO_2 cuts were prohibitively costly and environmental groups derided the measure as a

Summary 7.7
Two other methods for protecting the environment are incentives and charges or permits for pollution. Each has advantages and disadvantages. Incentives can be slow to work and may amount to subsidizing polluters. Economists favor pricing mechanisms and pollution permits, but critics dislike the idea of turning pollution into a commodity to be bought and sold.

sham—the scheme has surpassed its initial objective and at a far lower cost than expected.[56] In 2008 ten northeastern states joined together to limit emissions from power plants within their borders by auctioning a limited number of permits to emit carbon dioxide.[57] Meanwhile, a global market has emerged for trading carbon-emission credits because of the Kyoto Protocol on greenhouse gases.[58]

For both economic and scientific reasons, however, pricing mechanisms and pollution permits do not work well in all situations and for all environmental problems; dealing with mercury pollution is one example.[59] Still, economists generally favor using them wherever possible. However, they trouble many environmentalists. For one thing, the price tag for polluting seems arbitrary. How will effluent charges or permit prices be set? What is a fair price? Any decision seems bound to reflect debatable economic and value judgments. Moreover, environmentalists dislike the underlying principle of pricing mechanisms and pollution permits and view with suspicion anything that sounds like a license to pollute. They resent the implication that companies have a right to pollute, and they reject the notion that companies should be able to make money by selling that right to other firms. In fact, Michael J. Sandel, professor of government at Harvard, argues that it's immoral to buy the right to pollute. "Turning pollution into a commodity to be bought and sold removes the moral stigma that is properly associated with it," he says.[60]

In sum, although each of these approaches—regulations, incentives, pricing mechanisms, pollution permits—has its advantages, none is without its weak points. Because there appears to be no single, ideal approach to all our environmental problems, a combination of regulations, incentives, effluent charges, and permits is probably called for. Any such combination must take into account not only effectiveness but also fairness to those who will have to foot the bill. Fairness in turn calls for input from all sectors of society, a deliberate commitment by all parties to work in concert, a sizable measure of good faith, and perhaps above all else a heightened sense of social justice. This is no mean challenge.

Measures to protect the environmental often force firms to become more efficient.

Still, environmental protection is not always a static or zero-sum trade-off, with a fixed economic price to be paid for the gains we want. One reason is that higher environmental standards and properly designed regulatory programs can pressure corporations to invest capital in newer, state-of-the-art manufacturing technology; this both reduces pollution and enhances productive efficiency. In addition, international data in a range of industrial sectors show that innovation can minimize or even eliminate the costs of conforming to tougher environmental standards by increasing productivity, lowering total costs, and improving product quality.[61] The reason is that pollution is evidence of economic waste. The discharge of scrap, chemical wastes, toxic substances, or energy in the form of pollution is a sign that resources have been used inefficiently.

Consider some examples.[62] Environmental regulations forced Dow Chemical to redesign the production process at its complex in California to avoid storing chemical waste in evaporation ponds. Not only did the new

Summary 7.8
Environmental protection isn't a static or zero-sum trade-off. Higher environmental standards can pressure companies to invest in new technology, thus enhancing efficiency as well as reducing pollution. Many economists believe that measures to reduce greenhouse gas emissions may improve U.S. productivity in the long run.

process reduce waste, but the company also found that it could reuse part of it as raw material in other parts of the plant. For a cost of $250,000 Dow is now saving $2.4 million each year. Likewise, when new environmental standards forced 3M to reduce the volume of solvents to be disposed of, the company found a way to avoid the use of solvents altogether, which yielded it an annual savings of more than $200,000. Most distillers of coal tar opposed regulations requiring them to reduce benzene emissions; they thought the only solution was to cover tar storage tanks with costly gas blankets. But Aristech Chemical Corporation found a way to remove benzene from tar in the first processing step. Instead of a cost increase, the company saved itself $3.3 million.

Many other companies are finding that going green not only is environmentally responsible but also improves efficiency and saves them money, thus benefiting the bottom line.[63] And a broad array of economists, led by Nobel laureates Kenneth J. Arrow and Robert M. Solow, have urged that with regard to global warming, measures to reduce greenhouse gas emissions need not harm the economy and "may in fact improve U.S. productivity in the long run." This is because many innovative, energy-efficient technologies are just waiting for the right financial incentives to enter the market. And in many of these fields, U.S. industry is the leader.[64]

DELVING DEEPER INTO ENVIRONMENTAL ETHICS

So far, our discussion of environmental ethics has focused on business's obligation to understand its environmental responsibilities, to acknowledge and internalize its externalities (or spillovers), and to avoid free riding. It has stressed the extent to which environmental protection is in our collective self-interest, and it has looked at the operational and moral dilemmas involved in dealing with the costs of pollution. The subject of environmental ethics can be pursued more deeply than this, however.

Global Environmental Fairness

For one thing, we need to consider our obligations to those who live outside our society. For example, the United States represents only 4.6 percent of the world's population but uses 30 percent of the world's refined oil. And every day our demand for oil increases, leaving us more and more dependent on foreign nations to supply our needs.[65] In fact, if the United States were forced to rely entirely on its own resources, it would run out of oil in four years and three months.[66] The situation is similar, although less dramatic, for many other nonrenewable resources.

The average amount of energy consumed per year by a person in the United States is 3 times that of the average Hungarian, 4.3 times that of a Chilean, 6.6 times that of a Chinese, and 23 times that of someone in India.[67] Americans also contribute far more than their proportional share to global warming, emitting close to 25 percent of all greenhouse gasses. Wyoming, with a population of only half a million people, emits more carbon dioxide than do seventy-four developing countries with a combined population of nearly 400 million. The 22 million residents of Texas are responsible for emissions exceeding those of 120 developing nations combined, with over 1.1 billion people.[68] It's not surprising, then, that the birth of a baby in the United States imposes a hundred times more stress on the world's resources than does a birth in, say, Bangladesh. Babies from Bangladesh do not grow up to own automobiles and air conditioners or to eat huge quantities of grain-fed beef. Their lifestyles do not require large inputs of minerals and energy, and they do not undermine the planet's life-support capacity. To add insult to unfairness, the United States exports much of its garbage (which it produces more of than any other nation) overseas, including the old, "recycled" computers and other electronic equipment that now litter many poor nations.[69]

Tropical rain forests are of special concern. They are the earth's richest, oldest, and most complex ecosystems. Tropical forests are major reservoirs of biodiversity, home to 40 to 50 percent of all types of living things—as many as 5 million species of plants, animals, and insects. An estimated 49 million acres of tropical rain forest are destroyed each year, or nearly 100 acres every minute. And already half the globe's original rain forest has disappeared. Tropical forests are often cleared in an attempt to provide farms for growing third-world populations, but the affluence of people in rich nations like the United States is responsible for much forest destruction. Central American forests are cleared in part for pasture land to make pet food and convenience food slightly cheaper in the United States. In response to the demand for beef and leather in the developed world, cattle ranches are carving into the Amazon rainforest. In Papua New Guinea, forests are destroyed to supply cardboard packaging for Japanese electronic products. Thus, an affluent American living thousands of miles away can cause more tropical forest destruction than a poor person living within the forest itself.

To satisfy its dispropor- *(marginal note)* Our bloated levels of consumption, our dependence on foreign resources to satisfy our needs, and the impact of both on the economies and environments of other nations raise a variety of moral and political issues. Two of those issues are particularly pressing.

First is the question of how the continued availability of foreign resources is to be secured. Will our need for resources outside our territory lead us to try to control other countries, politically and economically, particularly in the Middle East and the developing world? To do so is morally risky, because political and economic domination almost always involves violations of the rights and interests of the dominated population, as well as of our own moral ideals and values.

Second is the question of whether any nation has a right to consume the world's irreplaceable resources at a rate so grossly out of proportion to the size of its population. Of course, we pay to consume oil and other resources that other nations own, but in the view of many the fact that these nations acquiesce in our disproportionate consumption of resources does not resolve the moral problem of our doing so. Are we respecting the needs and interests of both our present co-inhabitants on this planet and the future generations who will live on Earth? This question is particularly burning now that

(Marginal note, left column, in blue:) To satisfy its disproportionate consumption of nonrenewable resources, America turns to foreign lands. This raises two moral questions.

scientists believe that human demand for natural resources has outstripped the biosphere's regenerative capacity.[70]

Obligations to Future Generations

Almost everybody feels intuitively that it would be wrong to empty the globe of resources and to irreparably contaminate the environment that we pass on to future generations. Certainly there is a danger that we will do both of these things. But the question of what moral obligations we have to future generations is surprisingly difficult, and discussion among philosophers has not resolved all the important theoretical issues.

Even though most of us agree that it would be immoral to make the world uninhabitable for future people, can we talk meaningfully of those **future generations** having a right that we not do this? After all, our remote descendants are not yet alive and thus cannot claim a right to a livable environment. In fact, since these generations do not yet exist, they cannot at present, it seems, be said to have any interests at all. How can they then have rights?

Professor of philosophy Joel Feinberg argues, however, that whatever future human beings turn out to be like, they will have interests that we can affect, for better or worse, right now. Even though we do not know who the future people will be, we do know that they will have interests and what the general nature of those interests will be. This is enough, he contends, both to talk coherently about their having rights and to impose a duty on us not to leave ecological time bombs for them.

Feinberg concedes that it doesn't make sense to talk about future people having a right to be born. The child that you could conceive tonight, if you felt like it, cannot intelligibly be said to have a right to be born. Thus, the rights of future generations are "contingent," says Feinberg, on those future people coming into existence. But this qualification does not affect his main contention: "The interests that [future people] are sure to have when they come into being ... cry out for protection from invasions that can take place now."[71]

Even if we are persuaded that future generations have rights, we still do not know exactly what those rights are or how they are to be balanced against the interests and rights of present people. If we substantially injure future generations to gain some small benefit for ourselves, we are being as selfish and shortsighted as we would be by hurting other people today for some slight advantage for ourselves. Normally, however, if the benefits of some environmental policy outweigh the costs, then a strong case can be made for adopting the policy. But what if it is the present generation that receives the benefits and future generations that pay the costs? Would it be unfair of us to adopt such a policy? Would doing so violate the rights of future people?

An additional puzzle is raised by the fact that policies we adopt will affect who is born in the future. Imagine that we must choose between two environmental policies, one of which would cause a slightly higher standard of living over the next century. Given the effects of those policies on the details of our lives, over time it would increasingly be true that people would marry

Can we talk meaningfully of future generations having a right that we not despoil the world they inherit?

different people under one policy than they would under the other. And even within the same marriages, children would increasingly be conceived at different times:

> Some of the people who are later born would owe their existence to our choice of one of the two policies. If we had chosen the other policy, these particular people would never have existed. And the proportion of those later born who owe their existence to our choice would, like ripples in a pool, steadily grow. We can plausibly assume that, after three centuries, there would be no one living in our community who would have been born whichever policy we chose.*

Summary 7.9
America's bloated level of consumption puts a disproportionate strain on the world's resources. A broader view of environmental ethics considers our obligations to those in other societies as well as to future generations. Some philosophers argue that we must respect the right of future generations to inherit an environment that is not seriously damaged, but talk of the rights of future people raises puzzles. Other ways of thinking about this issue are suggested by utilitarianism and the social contract theory of John Rawls.

This reasoning suggests that subsequent generations cannot complain about an environmental policy choice we make today that causes them to have fewer opportunities and a lower standard of living. If we had made a different choice, then those people would not have existed at all. It might be claimed, however, that we act immorally in causing people to exist whose rights to equal opportunity and to a standard of living at least on a par with ours cannot be fulfilled. But if those future people knew the facts, would they regret that we acted as we did?[72]

Perhaps it is mistaken to focus on the rights and interests of future people as individuals. Annette Baier argues that the important thing is to "recognize our obligations to consider the good of the continuing human community."[73] This stance suggests adopting a utilitarian perspective and seeking to maximize total human happiness through time. But a utilitarian approach is also not without problems. If our concern is with total happiness, we may be required to increase greatly the earth's population. Even if individuals on an overcrowded earth do not have much happiness, there may still be more total happiness than there would be if we followed a population-control policy that resulted in fewer but better-off people. This distasteful conclusion has led some utilitarians to modify their theory and maintain that with regard to population policy we should aim for the highest average happiness rather than the highest total happiness. But this, too, is problematic because in theory one could, it seems, increase average happiness by eliminating unhappy people.

John Rawls has suggested another approach to the question of our obligations to future generations, an approach that reflects his general theory of justice (discussed in Chapter 3). He suggests that the members of each generation put themselves in the "original position." Then, without knowing what generation they belong to, they could decide what would be a just way of distributing resources between consecutive generations. They would have to balance how much they are willing to sacrifice for their descendants against how much they wish to inherit from their predecessors. In other words, the original position and the veil of ignorance might be used to determine our

---

* Derek Parfit, *Reasons and persons* (New York: Oxford University Press, 1986), 361. Parfit adds: "It may help to think about this question: How many of us could truly claim, 'Even if railways and motor cars had never been invented, I would still have been born'?"

obligations to future generations—in particular, how much each generation should save for use by those who inherit the earth from it.[74]

The Value of Nature

A radical approach to environmental ethics challenges the human-centered assumption that preserving the environment is good only because it is good for us.

A more radical approach to environmental ethics goes beyond the question of our obligations to future generations. It challenges the human-centered approach adopted so far. Implicit in the discussion has been the assumption that preservation of the environment is good solely because it is good for human beings. This reflects a characteristic human attitude that nature has no intrinsic value, that it has value only because people value it. If human nature were different and none of us cared about the beauty of, say, the Grand Canyon, then the Grand Canyon would be without value.

Many writers on environmental issues do not recognize their anthropocentric, or human-oriented, bias. One who does is William F. Baxter. In discussing his approach to the pollution problem, Baxter mentions the fact that the use of DDT in food production is causing damage to the penguin population. He writes:

> My criteria are oriented to people, not penguins. Damage to penguins, or sugar pines, or geological marvels is, without more, simply irrelevant.... Penguins are important because people enjoy seeing them walk about rocks.... In short, my observations about environmental problems will be people-oriented.... I have no interest in preserving penguins for their own sake....
>
> I reject the proposition that we *ought* to respect the "balance of nature" or to "preserve the environment" unless the reason for doing so, express or implied, is the benefit of man.[75]

Contrast Baxter's position with what Holmes Rolston III calls the **naturalistic ethic.** Advocates of a naturalistic ethic contend, contrary to Baxter's view, "that some natural objects, such as whooping cranes, are morally considerable in their own right, apart from human interests, or that some ecosystems, perhaps the Great Smokies, have intrinsic values, such as aesthetic beauty, from which we derive a duty to respect these landscapes."[76] Human beings may value a mountain for a variety of reasons—because they can hike it, build ski lifts on it, mine the ore deep inside it, or simply because they like looking at it. According to a naturalistic ethic, however, the value of the mountain is more than a simple function of these human interests: Nature can have value in and of itself, apart from human beings.*

Proponents of a naturalistic ethic contend that we have a particularly strong obligation to preserve species from extinction. Many environmentalists share this moral conviction, and it's easy to see why. Every year three thousand animal and plant species disappear, and the rate of extinction is accelerating so rapidly that over the next hundred years or so the earth could lose

---

* The people of Ecuador recently endorsed this idea by changing their constitution to recognize the ecosystem as having rights enforceable in court.[77]

half its species.[78] But do species really have value above and beyond the individuals that make them up? Scientists have formally identified 1.8 million species (including, for example, 6,700 kinds of starfish, 12,000 species of earthworm, and 400,000 types of beetle), and recent studies suggest that the number of species inhabiting the planet may be much, much higher—perhaps as many as 30 million kinds of insects alone. Species are always coming into and going out of existence.[79] How valuable is this diversity of species, and how far are we morally required to go in maintaining it?

Adopting a naturalistic ethic would definitely alter our way of looking at nature and our understanding of our moral obligations to preserve and respect the natural environment. Many philosophers, however, doubt that nature has intrinsic value or that we can be said to have moral duties to nature. Having interests is a precondition, they contend, of something's having rights or of our having moral duties to that thing. Natural objects, however, have no interests. Can a rock meaningfully be said to have an interest in not being eroded or in not being smashed into smaller pieces?

Of course, plants and trees are different from rocks and streams: They are alive; we can talk intelligibly about what is good or bad for a tree, plant, or vegetable; and they can flourish or do poorly. Even so, philosophers who discuss moral rights generally hold that this is not enough for plants to be said to have rights. To have rights, a thing must have genuine interests, and to have interests, most theorists contend, a thing must have beliefs and desires. Vegetative life, however, lacks any cognitive awareness. Claims to the contrary are biologically unsupportable.

Even if the plant world lacks rights, can it still have intrinsic value? Can we still have a moral obligation to respect that world and not abuse it? Or are the only morally relevant values the various interests of human beings and other sentient creatures? These are difficult questions. Among philosophers there is no consensus on how to answer them.

Our Treatment of Animals

Above a certain level of complexity, animals do have at least rudimentary cognitive awareness. No owner of a cat or dog doubts that his or her pet has beliefs and desires. Accordingly, a number of philosophers have recently defended the claim that animals can have rights. Because they have genuine interests, animals can have genuine moral rights—despite the fact that they cannot claim their rights, that they cannot speak, that we cannot reason with them, and that they themselves lack a moral sense. Animals, it is more and more widely contended, do not have to be equal to human beings to have certain moral rights that we must respect.

Rather than talking about animals' rights, utilitarians would stress that higher animals are sentient—that is, that they are capable of feeling pain. Accordingly, there can be no justifiable reason for excluding their pleasures and pains from the overall utilitarian calculus. As Jeremy Bentham, one of the founders of utilitarianism, put it: "The question is not, Can they *reason*? nor, Can they *talk*? but, Can they *suffer*?"[80] Our actions have effects on animals, and these consequences cannot be ignored. When one is deciding, then,

---

Adopting a naturalistic ethic would change our way of looking at nature, but many philosophers are skeptical of the idea that nature has intrinsic value.

Summary 7.10
Philosophers disagree about whether nature has intrinsic value. Adopting a human-oriented point of view, some theorists contend that the environment is valuable only because human beings value it. However, those adopting a naturalistic ethic believe that the value of nature is not simply a function of human interests.

Many philosophers urge that animals have moral rights. Utilitarians, for their part, stress the moral necessity of taking into account animal pain and suffering.

what the morally right course of action is, the pleasures and pains of animals must be taken into account too.

Business affects the welfare of animals very substantially. One way is through experimentation and the testing of products on animals. Critics such as Peter Singer contend that the vast majority of experiments and tests cannot be justified on moral grounds. Consider the "LD 50" test, which used to be the standard method of testing new foodstuffs. The object of the test was to find the dosage level at which 50 percent of the test animals would die. Nearly all test animals became very sick before finally succumbing or surviving. When the substance was harmless, huge doses had to be forced into the animals, until in some cases the sheer volume killed them.[81]

In principle, utilitarians are willing to permit testing and experimentation on animals, provided the overall results justify their pain and suffering. Not only is this proviso frequently ignored, but human beings typically disregard altogether the price the animals must pay. Consider the actions of the pharmaceutical firm Merck Sharp and Dohme, which sought to import chimpanzees to test a vaccine for hepatitis B. Chimps are an endangered species and highly intelligent. Capturing juvenile chimps requires shooting the mother. One analyst assessed the situation this way:

> The world has a growing population of 4 billion people and a dwindling population of some 50,000 chimpanzees. Since the vaccine seems unusually innocuous, and since the disease is only rarely fatal, it would perhaps be more just if the larger population could find some way of solving its problem that was not to the detriment of the smaller.[82]

Factory Farming

Business's largest and most devastating impact on animals, however, is through the production of animal-related products—in particular, meat. Many of us still think of our chicken and beef as coming from something like the idyllic farms pictured in storybooks, where the animals roam contentedly and play with the farmer's children. But meat and egg production is big business: Every year in the United States 10 billion birds and mammals are raised and killed for food.[83] Today most of the animal products we eat are from factory farms. In 1921 the largest commercial egg farm had a flock of 2,000 hens that ran loose in a large pasture; today the largest commercial flock contains 2.5 million birds, and 80 percent of the 440 million laying hens are housed in 3 percent of the known chicken farms. These birds live in small multi-tier wire cages.[84]

Laying hens that are stuffed into tiny cages with several other chickens now produce over 95 percent of our eggs. In these cages, hens are unable to satisfy such fundamental behavioral needs as stretching their wings, perching, walking, scratching, and nest building. Unsuited for wire cages, they suffer foot damage, feather loss, and other injuries. Birds are "debeaked" to prevent pecking injuries and cannibalism from overcrowding.[85]

Of the 95 million hogs born each year in the United States, 80 percent spend their lives in intensive confinement. Piglets are weaned after only three weeks and placed in wire cages or tiny cement pens. Once they reach 50 pounds, they are moved into bare 6-foot stalls with concrete-slatted floors.

Veal calves have even worse lives. To produce gourmet "milk-fed" veal, new-born calves are taken from their mothers and chained in crates measuring only 22 inches by 54 inches. Here they spend their entire lives. To prevent muscle development and speed weight gain, the calves are allowed absolutely no exercise; they are unable even to turn around or lie down. Their special diet of growth stimulators and antibiotics causes chronic diarrhea, and the withholding of iron to make their meat light-colored makes them anemic. The calves are kept in total darkness to reduce restlessness.[86]

The desire of the meat and animal-products industries to economize leads to their treating animals in ways that many reject as cruel and immoral.

The individuals involved in the meat and animal-products industries are not brutal, but the desire to cut business costs and to economize routinely leads to treatment of animals that can only be described as cruel. Philosopher and animal rights advocate Tom Regan describes their treatment this way:

> In increasing numbers, animals are being brought in off the land and raised in-doors, in unnatural, crowded conditions—raised "intensively," to use the jargon of the animal industry.... The inhabitants of these "farms" are kept in cages, or stalls, or pens...living out their abbreviated lives in a technologically created and sustained environment: automated feeding, automated watering, automated light cycles, automated waste removal, automated what-not. And the crowding: as many as 9 hens in cages that measure 18 by 24 inches; veal calves confined to 22 inch wide stalls; hogs similarly confined, sometimes in tiers of cages, two, three, four rows high. Could any impartial, morally sensitive person view what goes on in a factory farm with benign approval?[87]

Is It Wrong to Eat Meat?

Moral vegetarians are people who reject the eating of meat on moral grounds. Their argument is simple and powerful: The raising of animals for meat, especially with modern factory farming, sacrifices the most important and basic interests of animals simply to satisfy human tastes. Americans eat, per capita, a phenomenal amount of meat, by some estimates more than twice as much as we ate in the 1950s. Chicken production alone is now five times what it was in 1960. Many people eat meat three times a day. Our preference for a Big Mac over a soybean burger is only a matter of taste and culture, but it accounts for many of the 100,000 cows we slaughter every day.[88] The extra pleasure we believe we get from eating the hamburger cannot justify the price the animals must pay, insist the moral vegetarians.

Would it be wrong to eat animals that were raised humanely, like those that run around freely and happily in children's picture books of farms? Unlike the lives of animals that we do in fact eat, the lives of such humanely raised animals, before being abruptly terminated, are not painful ones. Some philosophers would contend that it is permissible to raise animals for food if their lives are, on balance, positive. Other moral theorists challenge this view, contending that at least higher animals have a right to life and should not be killed.

This debate raises important philosophical issues, but it is also rather hypothetical. Given economic reality, mass production of meat at affordable prices currently dictates factory farming, although increased consumer concern for animal welfare could conceivably change this economic logic. The important moral issue, in any case, is the real suffering and unhappy lives

Summary 7.11
Through experimentation, testing, and the production of animal products, business has an enormous impact on the welfare of animals. The meat and animal-products industries rely on factory-farming techniques, which many describe as cruel and horrible. Because of these conditions, moral vegetarians argue that eating meat is wrong. There are signs that human indifference toward animal suffering and factory farming is changing.

that billions of creatures experience on the way to our dinner tables. This often overlooked aspect of environmental ethics raises profound and challenging questions for business and consumers alike.

There are hopeful signs that human attitudes toward animal suffering, in general, and factory farming, in particular, are changing. Recently, Florida, Arizona, Oregon, and California passed laws or constitutional amendments prohibiting the confinement of pregnant pigs or calves raised for veal. California has also begun requiring larger cages for egg-laying hens. Likewise, McDonald's insists that its egg suppliers provide their hens with a minimum of 72 square inches of living space.[89] Other fast-food chains are following suit. For most American hens this is a 50 percent increase, but it falls well short of the European requirement that by 2012 all hens have at least 120 square inches as well as access to a perch and a nesting box to lay their eggs. Some companies such as Google have gone a step further. Their cafeterias now serve eggs only from "cage-free" hens. And in 2005 Whole Foods Markets (180 stores) and Wild Oats Markets (80 stores) became the first national grocery chains to sell only cage-free eggs and egg products.

In general, however, other countries are ahead of the United States with respect to their treatment of animals. In Europe it is illegal to treat pregnant sows or veal calves the way most American companies do.[90] In New Zealand, one cannot experiment on great apes unless the research actually benefits the apes and this benefit outweighs their discomfort or suffering. And in 2002 the German constitution was changed to include the right of animals to be treated decently.[91]

STUDY CORNER

Key Terms and Concepts

Clean Air Act (1970)
Clean Air Act Amendments of 1990
Clean Water Act (1972)
cost-benefit analysis
ecological economics
ecology
ecosystem
Environmental Protection Agency
externalities (spillovers)
free-rider problem
future generations
incentive approach
moral vegetarianism
naturalistic ethic
pollution permits
pricing mechanisms
regulatory approach
right to a livable environment
tragedy of the commons

Points to Review

- progress against pollution since the Clean Air and Clean Water Acts
- ecological costs of producing beef, poultry, and pork
- what the reintroduction of wolves into Yellowstone illustrates about ecosystems
- Ehrlich's two ecological rules
- pollution and resource depletion as two aspects of the same problem
- meaning and implications of the tragedy of the commons
- pollution as an externality
- why free riding and failing to internalize externalities are unfair
- difficulties of cost-benefit analysis
- what's new and different about ecological economics and estimates of "non-use value"

- deep-rooted causes of environmental degradation
- problems with the idea that those who benefit from environmental improvements should pay for them
- four problems with regulations
- the pros and cons of requiring old plants to meet new standards
- disadvantages of an incentive approach
- what many environmentalists find troubling about pollution permits
- why higher environmental standards may increase efficiency and productivity
- disproportionate environmental impact of the United States

- puzzles raised by the idea that future people have rights
- implications of the fact that our policies affect who is born in the future
- utilitarian and Rawlsian approaches to future generations
- contrasting environmental ethics of William Baxter and Holmes Rolston
- Bentham on animal suffering
- why many consider factory farming cruel
- moral vegetarianism and the question of the morality of killing animals
- signs that attitudes toward animal suffering and factory farming are changing

CASE **7.1**

Hazardous Homes in Herculaneum

Twenty-five miles or so outside of St. Louis, Missouri, lies little Herculaneum, a town of only 2,800 people. Looming over the town's economy and the local environment is the Doe Run Company's lead smelter, which dates back to 1892 and is the largest in the United States. For over twenty years now federal and state regulators have been after the company for polluting. In 1991 they required Doe Run to replace the contaminated topsoil in the gardens of about ninety houses in the vicinity of its smelter. In 2001 a study found that 24 percent of the children under six living within a mile of the company's plant had dangerously high levels of lead in their blood.

Doe Run now has agreed to clean up the site and has started installing new pollution-control devices to prevent further contamination.[92] In the meantime, however, environmental investigators have found lead levels as high as 300,000 parts per million on a road used by the plant's trucks. Because of the health hazard that lead contamination poses,

the state has put up signs warning residents of Herculaneum not to let children play outside, and the federal government is helping out by advising people to alter their diets to resist lead poisoning (the gist: Don't drink tea but eat more liver, eggs, whole-grain bread, and ice cream). Not so surprisingly, many residents of Herculaneum find this sort of assistance insulting. Instead, they want the federal government to step in, declare Herculaneum a Superfund cleanup site, and use federal funds to buy up the whole town. The Environmental Protection Agency (EPA), however, believes that adding Herculaneum to the long list of places seeking a Superfund buyout will only delay a solution.

The EPA is right not to exaggerate the speed with which Superfund projects move. When Congress created Superfund in 1980, sponsors of the legislation believed that the program could mop up the nation's worst toxic dumps and other dangerously polluted sites within five years and do so for a relatively modest $1.6 billion, to be covered by sales taxes on chemical and petroleum-based products. Superfund was authorized to recover its costs from the polluters themselves and to use this money to pay for future cleanup efforts. In this way, Superfund would become self-financing, with industry, not the taxpayers, picking up the tab. But the hopes of Superfund's sponsors have yet to be realized. Congress has repeatedly had to pour money into the program to keep it going; there are continual complaints about inefficient, top-heavy administration, and to date only a portion of the country's most environmentally damaged sites have been restored.

Moreover, Superfund has grown increasingly and staggeringly expensive. Its cleanup efforts have become mired in lawsuits, with the resulting litigation costs climbing to the stars. The problem, many observers believe, goes back to the initial Superfund legislation, which permits the EPA to penalize companies for dumping and polluting that was not illegal at the time it occurred. In addition, it makes individual polluters liable for the entire cleanup costs of toxic sites that may have been used by many other firms. Corporations dislike these liability principles, and they find it less expensive to resist the EPA in court than to pay up. "From the individual corporation's perspective," says David Morell, a toxic removal consultant and an expert on Superfund's history, "lawyers' bills are still cheaper than paying for an entire cleanup." And he adds: "The longer you can stall—and convince yourself that you may never have to pay at all—the more the legal fees seem like a bargain."

As a result, a flood of lawsuits has slowed Superfund's cleanup efforts to a crawl while the costs of those efforts have ballooned. "The idea [behind Superfund]," Morell says, "was supposed to be 'shovels first and litigation later.' Instead, it has become 'litigation first and shovels never.'" Many experts agree that Superfund has become a financial black hole. Legal fees, transaction costs, and administrative overhead associated with its cleanup projects are projected to exceed $200 billion. Others put the bill as high as $2,000 per person—paid in price increases on countless everyday chemical and petroleum-based products. And this sum doesn't pay for the removal of hazardous wastes; it covers only litigation-related costs.

According to critics, Congress has done little to solve the problems with Superfund, except to keep digging deeper into the national coffers to keep it going. However, in 2001 Congress did exempt small businesses from Superfund liability if they contributed only a relatively small amount of hazardous waste to a targeted site, and it required the EPA to consider a company's ability to pay when negotiating a settlement. For its part, the EPA contends that it is making good progress. It reports that 1,306 or close to three-quarters of the toxic waste sites designated as National Priorities List Sites have been cleaned up. Still, every day of delay increases the cleanup costs as waste from untreated sites seeps into the groundwater and increases the size of the polluted area. "These sites are not like fine wine," John O'Connor, director of the National Campaign Against Toxic Hazards, has explained. "They get worse with age, and they get more difficult and costly to clean up."

Meanwhile, back in Herculaneum, Doe Run has—in accord with a plan drawn up with the state of Missouri—purchased more than 130 local homes. Some of these it has torn down; others stand vacant. The buyouts have removed many young children from harm's way, but they have given many blocks of Herculaneum an eerie ghost-town quality. Doe Run continues to operate its lead smelter, but despite advice and prodding from the Missouri Department of Natural Resources, the plant still regularly exceeds legally permissible limits on lead emissions, and Herculaneum remains one of only two places in the nation that fail to meet federal air standards for lead. Although it may be too late to help poor Herculaneum, those standards are getting tougher. In response to a lawsuit by an environmental group and a couple from Herculaneum, in 2008 the EPA significantly tightened air-pollution standards for lead—the first update in over thirty years.

Discussion Questions

1. Identify the values and describe the attitudes that have contributed to pollution problems like those at Herculaneum. How would you feel if you lived in Herculaneum?

2. Do individuals inside the company, now or in the past, bear responsibility for causing the environmental damage at Herculaneum, or is it only the company as a whole? Is that responsibility shared by anyone outside the company? Should families who moved to Herculaneum have known better?

3. Who should pay the costs of cleaning up Herculaneum—the company? the town? the state of Missouri? the federal government? What if the cost of restoring Herculaneum exceeds Doe Run's resources? In general, whose responsibility is it to clean up the country's hazardous pollution sites and waste dumps?

4. Was either the government or Doe Run morally required to buy the most contaminated homes? Should anything else be done for those families? What about the rest of the town—should Superfund purchase all of it?

5. Is it fair for Superfund to fine polluters for dumping or polluting that was legal at the time it occurred? Is it fair that each individual polluter have full liability for cleaning up environmental damage to which others also may have contributed? How might Superfund be made to work better?

6. With regard to pollution in general and the disposal of toxic wastes in particular, what are the obligations of individual manufacturers and of society as a whole to future generations?

CASE **7.2**

Poverty and Pollution

It is called Brazil's "valley of death," and it may be the most polluted place on Earth. It lies about an hour's drive south of São Paulo, where the land suddenly drops 2,000 feet to a coastal plain. More than 100,000 people live in the valley, along with a variety of industrial plants that discharge thousands of tons of pollutants into the air every day. A reporter for *National Geographic* recalls that within an hour of his arrival in the valley, his chest began aching as the polluted air inflamed his bronchial tubes and restricted his breathing.[93]

The air in the valley is loaded with toxins—among them benzene, a known carcinogen. One in ten of the area's factory workers has a low white-blood-cell count, a possible precursor to leukemia. Infant mortality is 10 percent higher here than in the region as a whole. Of the 40,000 urban residents in the valley municipality of Cubatão, nearly 13,000 suffer from respiratory disease.

Few of the local inhabitants complain, however. For them, the fumes smell of jobs. They also distrust bids to buy their property by local industry, which wants to expand, as well as government efforts to relocate them to free homesites on a landfill. One young mother says, "Yes, the children are often ill and sometimes can barely breathe. We want to live in another place, but we cannot afford to."

A university professor of public health, Dr. Oswaldo Campos, views the dirty air in Cubatão simply as the result of economic priorities. "Some say it is the price of progress," Campos comments, "but is it? Look who pays the price—the poor."[94]

Maybe the poor do pay the price of pollution, but there are those who believe that they should have more of it. One of them is Lawrence Summers, director of the National Economic Council and formerly president of Harvard University. He has argued that the bank should encourage the migration of dirty, polluting industries to the poorer, less-developed countries.[95] Why? First, Summers reasons, the costs of health-impairing pollution depend on the earnings forgone from increased injury and death. So polluting should be done in the countries with the lowest costs—that is, with the lowest wages. "The economic logic behind dumping a load of toxic waste in the lowest-wage country," he writes, "is impeccable."

Second, because pollution costs rise disproportionately as pollution increases, it makes sense to shift pollution from already dirty places such as Los Angeles to clean ones like the relatively underpopulated countries in Africa, whose air Summers describes as "vastly *under*-polluted." Third, people value a clean environment more as their incomes rise. If other things are equal, costs fall if pollution moves from affluent places to less affluent places.

Critics charge that Summers views the world through "the distorting prism of market economics" and that his ideas are "a recipe for ruin." Not only do the critics want "greener" development in the third world, but also they are outraged by Summers's assumption that the value of a life—or of increases or decreases in life expectancy—can be measured in terms of per capita income. This premise implies that an American's life is worth that of a hundred Kenyans and that society should value an extra year of life for a middle-level manager more than it values an extra year for a blue-collar, production-line worker.

Some economists, however, believe that Summers's ideas are basically on the right track. They emphasize that environmental policy always involves trade-offs and that therefore we should seek a balance between costs and benefits. As a matter of fact, the greatest cause of misery in the third world is poverty. If environmental controls slow growth, then fewer people will be lifted out of poverty by economic development. For this reason, they argue, the richer countries should not impose their standards of environmental protection on poorer nations.

But even if economic growth is the cure for poverty, other economists now believe that sound environmental policy is necessary for durable growth, or at least that growth and environmental protection may not be incompatible. First, environmental damage can undermine economic productivity, and the health effects of pollution on a country's workforce reduce output. Second, poverty itself is an important cause of environmental damage because people living at subsistence levels are unable to invest in environmental protection. Finally, if economic growth and development are defined broadly enough, then enhanced environmental quality is part and parcel of the improvement in welfare that development must bring. For example, 1 billion people in developing countries lack access to clean water while 1.7 billion suffer from inadequate sanitation. Economic development for them means improving their environment.

Still, rich and poor countries tend to have different environmental concerns: Environmentalists in affluent nations worry about protecting endangered species, preserving biological diversity, saving the ozone layer, and preventing climate change, whereas their counterparts in poorer countries are more concerned with dirty air, dirty water, soil erosion, and deforestation. However, global warming—heretofore of concern mostly to people in the developed world—threatens to reverse the progress that the world's poorest nations are gradually making toward prosperity. Or so concludes a 2007 U.N. study.[96] It offers a detailed view of how poor areas, especially near the equator, are extremely vulnerable to the water shortages, droughts, flooding rains, and severe storms that increasing concentrations of greenhouse gases are projected to make more frequent, and the authors call on rich countries to do more to curb emissions linked to global warming and to help poorer nations leapfrog to energy sources that pollute less than coal and oil.

Update According to a World Bank report, environmental conditions have improved in Cubatão, where, thanks to state action and an aroused population, pollution is no worse today than in other medium-size industrial cities in Brazil. True, it's no paradise, but some days you can see the sun, children are healthier, and fish are returning to the river (though their tissues are laced with toxic metals).[97]

Discussion Questions

1. What attitudes and values on the part of business and others lead to the creation of areas like the "valley of death"?

2. Should the third world have more pollution, as Lawrence Summers argues? Assess his argument that dirty industries should move to poorer and less-polluted areas.

3. Some say, "Pollution is the price of progress." Is this assertion correct? What is meant by "progress"? Who in fact pays the price? Explain the moral and the economic issues raised by the assertion. What are the connections between economic progress and development, on the one hand, and pollution controls and environmental protection, on the other?

4. Do human beings have a moral right to a livable environment? To a nonpolluted environment? It might be argued that if people in the "valley of death" don't complain and don't wish to move, then they accept the risks of living there and the polluters are not violating their rights. Assess this argument.

5. Assess the argument that people in the third world should learn from the errors of the West and seek development without pollution. Should there be uniform, global environmental standards, or should pollution-control standards be lower for less-developed countries?

6. Even though they will probably be hit hardest by it, poor nations are less able than are rich countries to deal with the consequences of global warming. As a result, do rich nations owe to it to poorer nations to curb their own emissions more than they otherwise would be inclined to do? Do they have an obligation to provide poorer nations with, or help them develop, greener industries and sources of energy? Explain why or why not.

CASE 7.3

The Fordasaurus

Before Ford publicly unveiled the biggest sport-utility vehicle ever, the Sierra Club ran a contest for the best name and marketing slogan for it. Among the entries were "Fordasaurus, powerful enough to pass anything on the highway except a gas station" and "Ford Saddam, the truck that will put America between Iraq and a hard place." But the winner was "Ford Valdez: Have you driven a tanker lately?"[98]

Ford, which decided to name the nine-passenger vehicle the Excursion, was not amused.

Sales of sport-utility vehicles (SUVs) exploded in the 1990s, going up nearly sixfold, and the company saw itself as simply responding to consumer demand for ever larger models. Although most SUVs never leave the pavement, their drivers like knowing their vehicles can go anywhere and do anything. They also like their SUVs to be big. Before the Hummer passed it, the Excursion was the largest passenger vehicle on the road, putting Ford well ahead of its rivals in the competition to build the biggest and baddest SUV. The Excursion weighs 8,500 pounds, equivalent to two midsize sedans or three Honda Civics. It is more than 6½ feet wide, nearly 7 feet high, and almost 19 feet long—too big to fit comfortably into some garages or into a single parking space.

Although the Excursion is expensive ($40,000 to $50,000 when loaded with options), it is, like other SUVs, profitable to build. Because Ford based the Excursion on the chassis of its Super Duty truck, the company was able to develop the vehicle for a relatively modest investment of about $500 million. With sales of 50,000 to 60,000 per year, Ford earns about $20,000 per vehicle.

Classified as a medium-duty truck, the Excursion is allowed to emit more smog-causing gases that do passenger cars. However, Ford says that the Excursion, with its 44-gallon gas tank, gets 10 to 15 miles per gallon and that its emission of pollutants is 43 percent below the maximum for its class. By weight, about 85 percent of the vehicle is recyclable, and 20 percent of it comes from recycled metals and plastics. The company thus believes that the Excursion is in keeping with the philosophy of William Clay Ford, Jr. When he became chairman in September 1998, he vowed to make Ford "the world's most environmentally friendly auto maker." He added, however, that "what we do to help the environment must succeed as a business proposition. A zero-emission vehicle that sits unsold on a dealer's lot is not reducing pollution."

The company, however, has failed to win environmentalists to its side. They believe that with the Excursion, the Ford Company is a long way from producing an environmentally friendly product. Daniel Becker of the Sierra Club points out that in the course of an average lifetime of 120,000 miles, each Excursion will emit 130 tons of carbon dioxide, the principal cause of global warming. "It's just bad for the environment any way you look at it," he says. John DeCicco of the American Council for an Energy-Efficient Economy agrees. He worries further that the Excursion is clearing the way for bigger and bigger vehicles. "This is the antithesis of green leadership."

Stung by criticism of the Excursion, Bill Ford vowed to make the company a more responsible environmental citizen. Worried that if automobile producers didn't clean up their act, they would become as vilified as cigarette companies, in August 2000 Ford promised it would improve the fuel economy of its SUVs by 25 percent over the next five years, smugly inviting other automakers to follow its green leadership. To this GM responded that it was the real green leader and "will still be in five years, or 10 years, or for that matter 20 years. End of story." When they aren't bragging about their greenness, however, both companies continue to lobby Congress, and battle in the courts, against new mandates on emissions and fuel efficiency.[99]

Update   Ford Motor Company failed to keep its promise to improve fuel economy by 25 percent by 2005, but it has phased out the Excursion. After a five-year stint as president and CEO of Ford, Bill Ford remains chairman of its board of directors and is still hoping to push the company toward a greener future. Recently, the company introduced the Escape, an SUV that is a gas-electric hybrid, and Ford's research-and-development people are working hard on developing a hydrogen engine. Still, Ford is filling the void left by the Excursion with an extra-long version of its Expedition.

Not only do gas guzzlers continue to roll out of Detroit's assembly plants, but some of the auto makers' supposedly environmentally conscious efforts—consider the new Cadillac Escalade Hybrid—seem to be a sham. Perhaps that is not so surprising when one finds Bob Lutz, vice president of GM, stating in 2008 that hybrids like the Toyota Prius "make no economic sense" and that global warming "is a total crock of [expletive]." However, with higher gas prices and the average fuel economy of new vehicles sold in the United States no better than it was twenty years ago, the backlash against SUVs is growing. Environmentalists have now been joined by conservatives, who in the aftermath of September 11, 2001, are worried about supporting Middle Eastern oil producers who fund terrorism, and by evangelical groups, whose bumpers stickers ask, "What would Jesus drive?"[100]

Discussion Questions

1. Are environmentalists right to be concerned about the environmental impact of SUVs? How do you explain the demand for ever larger passenger vehicles? Will higher gas prices change that?

2. In developing and producing the Excursion, was the Ford Motor Company sacrificing the environment to profits, or was it acting in a socially responsible way by making the Excursion relatively energy efficient for its vehicle class? If you had been on the board of directors, would you have voted for the project? Why or why not? Do Ford's stockholders have a right to insist that it produce the most profitable vehicles it legally can, regardless of their environmental impact?

3. Assess William Clay Ford's promise to make his company the "world's most environmentally friendly automaker." What are the environmental responsibilities of automakers?

4. Is Ford Motor Company simply responding to consumer demand for large vehicles, or is it helping to shape and encourage that demand?

5. Should there be tighter pollution restrictions on SUVs? Should the government try to discourage the production and use of SUVs?

6. Is it moral or environmentally responsible to drive an SUV? What *would* Jesus drive?

CASE **7.4**

The Fight over the Redwoods

Dense forests of coastal redwood trees once covered 2.2 million acres of southern Oregon and northern California. Today, only about 86,000 acres of virgin redwood forest remain. Most of this is in public parks and preserves, but about 6,000 acres of old-growth forest are privately owned—nearly all of it by the Pacific Lumber Company, headquartered in San Francisco.

Founded in 1869, Pacific Lumber owns 220,000 acres of the world's most productive timberland, including the old-growth redwoods. For years the family-run company was a model of social responsibility and environmental awareness. Pacific Lumber paid its employees well, supported them in bad times, funded their pensions, and provided college scholarships for their children. It sold or donated nearly 20,000 acres of forest to the public, and instead of indiscriminate clearcutting, the company logged its forests carefully and selectively. Throughout its history, the company harvested only about 2 percent of its trees annually, roughly equivalent to their growth rate. After other timber firms had logged all their old-growth stands, Pacific Lumber had a virtual monopoly on the highly durable lumber that comes from the heart of centuries-old redwood trees.[101]

Because Pacific Lumber was debt free and resource rich, its potential value drew attention on Wall Street, where the firm of Drexel Burnham Lambert suspected that the company was undervalued—and thus ripe for raiding. In 1985 Drexel hired a timber consultant to fly over Pacific Lumber's timberland to estimate its worth. With junk-bond financing arranged by its in-house expert, Michael Milken, Drexel assisted Charles Hurwitz, a Texas tycoon, and his firm, Maxxam, Inc., to take over Pacific Lumber for $900 million. After initially resisting the leveraged buyout, the timber company's directors eventually acquiesced, and by the end of the year Hurwitz and Maxxam had control of Pacific Lumber. At the time, Hurwitz was primary owner of United Financial Group, the parent company of United Savings Association of Texas. In exchange for Milken's raising the money for the takeover of Pacific Lumber, Hurwitz had United Savings purchase huge amounts of risky junk bonds from Drexel. Three years later, the savings and loan failed, and taxpayers were stuck with a bill for $1.6 billion.

The takeover of Pacific Lumber left Maxxam with nearly $900 million in high-interest debt. To meet the interest payments, Maxxam terminated Pacific Lumber's pension plan and replaced it with annuities purchased from an insurance company owned by Hurwitz. Worse still, Maxxam tripled the rate of logging on Pacific Lumber's lands, and it was soon clear that Hurwitz intended to log the now-famous Headwaters forest, a 3,000-acre grove of virgin redwoods—the largest single stand of redwoods still in private hands "It was the reason we were interested in Pacific Lumber," Hurwitz says. And one can see why. The value of the grove is astronomical: Milled into lumber, some of the trees are worth $100,000 each.

The potential lumber may be worth a fortune to Hurwitz, but environmentalists consider the Headwaters grove to be priceless as it is, and they have stepped in to do battle with Hurwitz. They see the Headwaters forest with its 500- to 2,000-year-old trees as an intricate ecosystem that took millions of years to evolve, a web of animals and plants that depend not just on living trees but also on dead, fallen redwoods that provide wildlife habitat and reduce soil erosion. Some of these activists—including Darryl Cherney, a member of the environmental group Earth First!—have devoted their lives to stopping Hurwitz. Earth First! is not a mainstream conservation organization; it has a reputation for destroying billboards, sabotaging bulldozers and lumber trucks, and spiking trees with nails that chew up the blades of saws. "Hurwitz is a latter-day robber baron," says Cherney. "The only thing that's negotiable … is the length of his jail sentence."

Other environmental organizations opposed Hurwitz in court. The Sierra Club Legal Defense Fund and the Environmental Protection Information Center filed sixteen lawsuits against Pacific Lumber, giving the company's legal experts a run for their money. One of these suits bore fruit when a judge blocked the company's plan to harvest timber in a smaller old-growth forest known as Owl Creek Grove. The legal reason was protection of the marbled murrelet, a bird about the size of a thrush, which breeds in the forest and is close to extinction. The judge also noted that "after the logging of an old-growth forest, the original cathedral-like columns of trees do not regenerate for a period of 200 years." Pacific Lumber appealed the Owl Creek decision, but the ruling was upheld a year later. However, at the same time, the company won the right to appeal to another court to be allowed to harvest timber in the larger Headwaters forest. Meanwhile, both conservationists and a number of public officials were making strenuous efforts to acquire Headwaters and some surrounding redwood groves from Hurwitz.

Some environmentalists, however, worried that too much attention was being directed toward saving the 3,000-acre Headwaters grove while leaving Pacific Lumber free to log the rest of its land with abandon. They were less concerned about the murrelets in particular or even the redwoods themselves; rather, what disturbed them was the dismantling of an ancient and intricate ecosystem—an irreplaceable temperate rain forest, home to some 160 species of plants and animals. Their aim was to build a new style of forestry based on values other than board feet of lumber and dollars of profit. They sought sustainable forest management and a new resource ethic devoted to rebuilding and maintaining habitats for coho salmon, the murrelet, the weasel-like fisher, and the northern spotted owl. As a first step, these conservationists called for protection, not just of the 3,000 Headwaters acres, but also for an area nearly twenty times that amount, called the Headwaters Forest Complex. This tract included all the ancient redwoods that Hurwitz owned and large areas of previously logged forest. "We have a vision that's bigger than Headwaters," said Cecelia Lanman of the Environmental Protection Information Center.

Her vision was definitely more sweeping than that of the Pacific Lumber workers in Scotia, California, a village containing 272 company-owned homes. Because Hurwitz instituted stepped-up logging, which meant more jobs, his employees tended to side with him, not the environmentalists. Workers said that Hurwitz had reinvested more than $100 million in modernizing his mills and had kept up the tradition of paying college scholarships for their children. The environmentalists were the real threat, said one employee. "You've got a group of people who hate Mr. Hurwitz, and they're using the Endangered Species Act and anything they can to hurt him. And we're caught in the middle."

Update In 1999, Hurwitz signed a deal that a federal team led by Senator Dianne Feinstein and Deputy Interior Secretary John Garamendi had begun negotiating with him several years earlier.[102] In exchange for a 7,500-acre tract that includes the Headwaters grove and 2,500 additional acres of old-growth forest, the U.S. government and the state of California agreed to pay Pacific Lumber $480 million. The agreement also bans logging for fifty years on 8,000 other acres of company land in order to safeguard the murrelet, and it sets up buffer zones to protect the river habitats of endangered coho salmon and steelhead trout. A Habitat Protection Plan regulates how and where Pacific Lumber harvests timber on the rest of its land. However, because Hurwitz transferred the $868 million debt that still remains from his original hostile takeover of Pacific Lumber from Maxxam to Pacific Lumber itself, the company needs to log as much as it can to make its interest payments.

Feinstein and Garamendi defended the deal as the best that they could get, and President Clinton and Governor Gray Davis of California called the pact that saved Headwaters "historic." But Darryl Cherney and other activists have criticized the agreement as a sellout. They would like to see Pacific Lumber more closely regulated, claiming that the company still engages in overharvesting, clear-cutting instead of thinning, and various other poor logging practices. They also noted that for 10,000 acres the government paid Hurwitz half of what he originally spent for the entire company with its 220,000 acres of timberland.

Pacific Lumber, for its part, contended that state and federal agencies were so rigidly enforcing the habitat conservation plan that it couldn't cut enough lumber to keeps its mills running, and in late 2001 it closed down Scotia's 104-year-old mill. "We are being strangled by the operating restraints," said Robert Manne, current president of Pacific Lumber, which are "not working to meet the company and its employees' economic needs." To this complaint, conservationists and governmental officials responded that Pacific Lumber, which continued to operate two smaller and much newer mills in neighboring towns, was scapegoating them for problems stemming from falling timber prices and the company's depletion of its old-growth redwood groves by clear-cutting. According to Paul Mason, president of a local environmental organization, "The lumber market is right in the tank, and that takes a bite out of your profit margin. The company has been operating at an unsustainable level for a number of years."

Whatever the exact cause, Pacific Lumber eventually declared bankruptcy and in 2008, as part of a court-supervised reorganization plan, was taken over by the Mendocino Redwood Company, a nine-year-old logging venture owned by Don and Doris Fisher, the founders of Gap. Environmentalists, state officials, and local residents were thrilled at the prospect of Pacific Lumber Company emerging from bankruptcy free of Hurwitz and Maxxam and able to reestablish itself as an environmentally responsible company practicing sustainable forestry. That's because, as U.S. bankruptcy judge Richard Schmidt explained, "MRC [is] an experienced, environmentally responsible operator with a proven track record, and whose experience in operating timberlands and working cooperatively with government regulators was uncontraverted."

Discussion Questions

1. Does an ancient redwood forest have value other than its economic one as potential lumber? If so, what is this value, and how is it to be weighed against the interests of a company like Maxxam? Are redwoods more important than jobs?

2. Is it morally permissible for private owners to do as they wish with the timberland they own? Explain why or why not. What's your assessment of Hurwitz? Is he a robber baron or a socially responsible businessperson, or something in between?

3. Were mainstream environmentalists right to try to thwart Hurwitz, or were they simply trying to impose their values on others? Does a radical group like Earth First! that engages in sabotage go too far, or do its ends justify its means?

4. Do we have a moral obligation to save old redwood forests? Can a forest have either moral or legal rights? Does an old-growth forest have value in and of itself, or is its value only a function of human interests? How valuable is a small but endangered species such as the murrelet?

5. Before its takeover by Hurwitz, did Pacific Lumber neglect its obligations to its stockholders by not logging at a faster rate? What would be a morally responsible policy for a timber company to follow? Do we need a new environmental resource ethic?

6. How would you respond to the argument that there is no need to try to save the Headwaters (or any other private) forest because there are already tens of thousands of acres of old-growth redwood forest in parks and preserves?

7. Was the deal that the U.S. government and the state of California struck with Pacific Lumber a fair and reasonable one? Did the taxpayers end up paying too much, as environmentalists think? Was Pacific Lumber squeezed too hard? What about Scotia and its laid-off workers?

The Organization and the People in It

Jose Luis Pelaez Inc./Jupiter Images

The Organization and the People in It

The Workplace (1): Basic Issues

AP Photo/Ric Feld

Labor Unions

History of the Union Movement
The Plight of Unions Today
Union Ideals
Union Tactics

CASES

AIDS in the Workplace
Web Porn at Work
Speaking Out about Malt
Old Smoke
Have Gun, Will Travel ... to Work

INTRODUCTION

A manufacturer of vinyl replacement windows, Republic Windows and Doors had been in business in Chicago for over forty years. On December 2, 2008, however, it abruptly announced that it was bankrupt. The following day the company told its 260 employees that it would permanently cease operations two days later, at which point their health coverage would end. The company also told the workers that they would not be receiving any severance pay or even their accrued vacation or sick pay.

Republic's workforce is represented by a labor union, the United Electrical, Radio and Machine Workers of America, which immediately filed a complaint charging that the company had violated federal law by failing to give sixty-days' notice of a plant closure and that it owed the workers $1.5 million in severance and vacation pay and an extension of their medical benefits. However, Republic's union workers also took more drastic measures. In a move reminiscent of the famous Flint Sit-Down Strike of 1936–37 that led to the unionization of the U.S. auto industry, they voted to take over the company's plant and sit-in until their grievances were met. The country hadn't seen anything like it for years, and there was an outpouring of support for the workers. People came by the occupied factory to offer food and donations, the Chicago police declined to intervene, and President-elect Barack Obama publicly sided with the workers.[1]

Why the popular support for the workers, who after all were seizing private property? One reason is that Bank of America had halted Republic's line of credit because of a downturn in business and the harsh economic climate, thus making it impossible for the company to stay in business. This infuriated people across the nation because Bank of America had recently received $25 billion from the federal government precisely in order to provide it with the funds to continue making loans to businesses and thus help keep the country out of recession. And yet here was a real American company, one that still made things, and the bank was forcing it to go under. The sit-in became a rallying point for all those who resented bailing out Wall Street and the big banks while ordinary employees were left to fend for themselves. Then the public learned that Republic's owners were not quite the innocent victims they claimed to be. Before declaring bankruptcy, they had begun surreptitiously removing machinery from the factory and shipping it to a plant in Iowa belonging to a company that they had just purchased. Stopping the owners from gutting the factory was what really motivated Republic's workers to take it over.

Widespread media attention, demonstrations in Chicago and other cities, and political pressure resulted in the sit-in at Republic ending after just six days, when Bank of America and JP Morgan Chase agreed to loan Republic sufficient money to cover the workers' severance pay, earned vacation pay, and an extension of their health benefits. Moreover, shortly after reading about the settlement, Kevin Surace, president and CEO of Serious Materials, a Sunnyvale, California, company that specializes in eco-friendly drywall and windows, decided to buy the plant. By March 2009 he had closed the deal and rehired all of Republic's workers.[2]

This story has a happy ending. But employees do not always succeed in having their rights respected, and they are not always treated fairly by their employers. The moral issues are rarely as black-and-white, though, as they were at Republic Windows. Many of the moral dilemmas that arise in the workplace, especially those concerning the civil liberties of employees and the personnel policies and procedures that govern hiring, firing, paying, and promoting them, are complicated and elude easy answer. This chapter looks at some of these issues, in particular:

1. The state of civil liberties in the workplace
2. The efforts of some successful companies to respect the rights and moral dignity of their employees
3. Moral issues that arise with respect to personnel matters—namely, hiring, promotions, discipline and discharge, and wages
4. The role and history of unions in our economic system, their ideals and achievements, and the moral issues they raise

CIVIL LIBERTIES IN THE WORKPLACE

Employees have all sorts of job-related concerns. Generally speaking, they want to do well at their assignments, to get along with their colleagues, and to have their contributions to the organization recognized. Their job tasks, working conditions, and wages and the possibility of promotion are among the many things that occupy their day-to-day thoughts. Aside from the actual work that they are expected to perform, employees, being human, are naturally concerned about the way their organizations treat them. Frequently they find that treatment to be morally deficient and complain that the organizations for which they work violate their moral rights and civil liberties.

Consider Lynne Gobbell, a machine operator who was fired for displaying a John Kerry bumper sticker on her car, or Gonzalo Cotto, who lost his job as an aircraft factory worker for refusing to display an American flag at his workstation during a celebration of the Gulf War. Then there's Louis MacIntire. A chemical engineer at DuPont for sixteen years, he was canned for writing a novel. Several characters in the book inveigh against various management abuses at the novel's fictional Logan Chemical Company and argue for a union for technical employees. Logan Chemical superficially resembles DuPont, and some of MacIntire's supervisors thought his veiled criticisms struck too close to home. Cotto and MacIntire tried suing their employers for violating their constitutional right of free speech, but the courts rejected their claims.[3]

The issue of free speech extends online, where companies have disciplined or discharged employees for the contents of their personal blogs or for comments on a password-protected MySpace.com discussion board. Delta Air Lines, for instance, fired Ellen Simonetti for including mildly provocative photos of herself in a flight attendant's uniform on her blog, even though she wrote under a pseudonym and concealed the identify of her employer. In her blog, Rachel Mosteller, a North Carolina reporter, wrote:

> I really hate my place of employment. Seriously. Okay, first off. They have these stupid little awards that are supposed to boost company morale. So you go and do something "spectacular" (most likely, you're doing your JOB) and then somebody says "Why golly, that was spectacular." Then they sign your name on some paper, they bring you chocolate and some balloons. Okay two people in the newsroom just got it. FOR DOING THEIR JOB.

The next day she was fired—even though in her blog she never identifies herself, her employer, her coworkers, or her location.[4]

Cases like these illustrate what many see as the widespread absence of civil liberties in the workplace. "You should take your passport with you to work because all your rights as an American citizen disappear the second you walk through the office door," contends Lewis Maltby, president of the National Workrights Institute. Employees "think they have the protection of the Bill of Rights; they think they have a right to free speech; they think they have a right to privacy; and they think they have a right to be free of arbitrary punishment," he says. "And they're right—except when they go to work."[5]

David W. Ewing, former editor of *Harvard Business Review,* agrees. He sees the corporate invasion of employees' civil liberties as rampant and attacks it in scathing terms:

> In most ... [corporate] organizations, during working hours, civil liberties are a will-o'-the-wisp. The Constitutional rights that employees have grown accustomed to in family, school, and church life generally must be left outdoors, like cars in the parking lot. As in totalitarian countries, from time to time a benevolent chief executive or department head may encourage speech, conscience, and privacy, but these scarcely can be called rights, for management can take them away at will.... It is fair to say that an enormous corporate archipelago has grown which, in terms of civil liberties, is as different from the rest of America as day is from night. In this archipelago ... the system comes first, the individual second.[6]

The emergence of professional management and personnel engineering promoted workplace authoritarianism.

Two historical factors, in Ewing's view, lie behind the absence of civil liberties and the prevalence of authoritarianism in the workplace. One of these factors is the rise of professional management and personnel engineering at the turn of the twentieth century, following the emergence of large corporations. This shaped the attitudes of companies toward their employees in a way hardly conducive to respecting their rights. As Frederick Winslow Taylor, generally identified as the founder of "scientific management," bluntly put it, "In the past, the man has been first. In the future, the system must be first."

So did the employer's traditional legal right to fire employees for no cause.

The other historical factor is that the law has traditionally given the employer a free hand in hiring and firing employees. In the nineteenth century, a Tennessee court expressed this doctrine in memorable form. Employers, the court held, "may dismiss their employees at will ... for good cause, for no cause, or even for cause morally wrong, without thereby being guilty of legal wrong." Similarly, a California court upheld this traditional rule shortly before World War I, observing that the "arbitrary right of the employer to employ or discharge labor, with or without regard to actuating motives" is a proposition "settled beyond peradventure." The U.S. Supreme Court ratified this common-law principle in 1915, ruling that "an employer may discharge his employee for any reason, or for no reason." This "is an essential element of liberty."[7]

In addition, common law requires that an employee be loyal to an employer, acting solely for the employer's benefit in matters connected to work. The employee is duty-bound not to act or speak disloyally, except when in pursuit of his or her own interests outside work. It's no wonder, then, that traditional employer-employee law has hardly been supportive of the idea of freedom of speech and expression for employees. Against that background, the treatment of employees like Gonzalo Cotto, Louis MacIntire, or Rachel Mosteller and the refusal of the courts to see a First Amendment issue in cases like theirs are not surprising.

According to common law, then, unless there is an explicit contractual provision to the contrary—and only around 10 percent of American workers have such contracts[8]—every employment is **employment "at will,"** and either side is free to terminate it at any time without advance notice or reason.

The common law, however, has been modified in important ways by congressional and state statutory provisions. *The Wagner Act* of 1935 (discussed later in this chapter) was, in this respect, a watershed. It prohibited firing workers because of union membership or union activities. The *Civil Rights Act* of 1964 and subsequent legislation prohibit discrimination on the basis of race, creed, nationality, sex, or age. Equally important, employees in the public sector—that is, in federal, state, and local government—enjoy certain constitutional protections on the job and can be fired only "for cause." And many workers are protected by their union contracts from unjust dismissals.

Thus, today working people have protection against some forms of unjust termination, and many of them enjoy the assurance that they can expect due process and that at least some of their civil liberties and other moral rights will be respected on the job. "But," writes Clyde Summers in *Harvard Business Review,* "random individuals who are unjustly terminated are isolated and without organizational or political voice. For them the harsh common law rule remains."[9] As a result, every year an estimated 200,000 employees are dismissed without cause.[10] Granted, that represents only a small fraction of the total number of discharged employees, but it still means that arbitrary actions by employers seriously disrupt many people's lives and that fear of dismissal is likely to have discouraged or intimidated even more employees from engaging in legitimate conduct.

Current Trends

The law is not static, however, and some courts have been willing in specific cases to break with tradition to protect employees' rights of speech, privacy, and conscience. The U.S. Supreme Court, for instance, has ruled that a state cannot deny unemployment benefits to employees who are fired because they refuse to work on their Sabbath day, even if they aren't members of an organized religion.[11] And in 1987 Montana became the first and so far the only state in the nation to enact legislation saying that workers cannot be fired without "good cause." Even without explicit legislation, wrongfully dismissed employees frequently have legal recourse. Thus, for example, a federal jury held that Mobil Chemical Company had wrongfully dismissed one of its top environmental officials after he refused to perform acts that would have violated federal and state environmental laws. The jury ordered Mobil to pay $375,000 in compensatory damages and $1 million in punitive damages.

But when Daniel Foley, district manager for Interactive Data Corporation, accurately reported to his employer that his new boss was under investigation by the FBI for embezzling funds on a former job, he was dismissed for "inadequate performance" three months later, despite a seven-year record of positive work reviews and a recent $6,700 bonus. Foley sued Interactive Data for wrongful termination, but the California Supreme Court decided that his dismissal did not violate the "public interest" and rejected his suit. And in 2006 the U.S. Supreme Court ruled that the Constitution does not protect public employees from retaliation by their supervisors for things they say in the performance of their work duties. Deputy District Attorney

Summary 8.1
Writers such as David Ewing believe that too many corporations routinely violate the civil liberties of their employees. Historically, this authoritarianism stems from (1) the rise of professional management and personnel engineering and (2) the common-law doctrine that employees can be discharged without cause ("employment at will").

Richard Ceballos had urged his superiors to dismiss a pending criminal case because a police officer had allegedly lied to obtain a search warrant. His advice was rejected, and he was denied a promotion and transferred to a lesser position farther from his home. Writing for the majority in a 5-to-4 decision, Justice Anthony M. Kennedy distinguished between statements public employees make "pursuant to their official duties" and those they make as citizens contributing to the "civic discourse." The First Amendment may sometimes protect the second category but not the first.[12] (This decision concerns only public employees. For other employees, there is no general First Amendment protection at all.)

The law seems to be gradually moving away from employment at will, but our moral obligations are not limited to merely obeying the law.

Thus, although the law seems to be gradually changing, leaving the common-law heritage of employer-employee doctrine behind, recent legal developments are complicated and not entirely consistent. The results not only depend on the details of each case but also vary from jurisdiction to jurisdiction and from court to court. As argued in Chapter 1, however, our moral obligations extend beyond merely keeping within the law.

True, some businesspeople not only support employment at will as a desirable legal policy but also embrace it as a moral doctrine. They reject the normative principle—accepted by most ordinary people—that employees should be fired only for just cause, and they deny that employers have any obligations to their employees beyond those specified by law or by explicit legal contract. Their actions, if not their words, suggest that they view the people who work for them as lacking any meaningful moral rights, seeing them as fungible assets—as means rather than ends in themselves—to be used in whatever way is profitable. But nowadays that is a minority perspective. More and more corporations are coming to acknowledge, and to design institutional procedures that respect, the rights and moral dignity of their employees. Moreover, the firms taking the lead in this regard are often among the most successful companies in the country.

This fact cuts against the old argument that corporate efficiency requires employees to sacrifice their civil liberties and other rights between 9 and 5. Without strict discipline and the firm maintenance of management prerogatives, it has been claimed, our economic system would come apart at the seams. An increasing body of evidence, however, suggests just the opposite. As Ewing writes:

> Civil liberties are far less of a threat to the requirements of effective management than are collective bargaining, labor-management committees, job enrichment, work participation, and a number of other schemes that industry takes for granted. Moreover, the companies that lead in encouraging rights—organizations such as Polaroid, IBM, Donnelly Mirrors, and Delta Air Lines—have healthier-looking bottom lines than the average corporation does.[13]

Companies That Look beyond the Bottom Line

Although under no legal compulsion to do so, a small but growing number of companies encourage employee questions and criticisms about company policies affecting the welfare of employees and the community. Some companies foster open communication through regular, informal exchanges between management and other employees. Others, such as Delta Air Lines, have top officials answer questions submitted anonymously by employees—in the absence of supervisors. Still others, such as General Electric and New England Telephone, have a hotline for questions, worries, and reports of wrongdoing. Finally, some, like Dow Chemical, open the pages of company publications to employee questions and criticisms.

Union contracts frequently require companies to set up grievance procedures and otherwise attempt to see that their members are guaranteed due process on the job. Some enlightened nonunionized companies have done the same. Polaroid, for instance, has a well-institutionalized committee whose job it is to represent an employee with a grievance. The committee members are elected from the ranks, and reportedly a fair number of management decisions are overruled in the hearings. If the decision goes against the aggrieved employee, he or she is entitled by company rules to submit the case to an outside arbitrator.

Some companies—including Johnson Wax, Donnelly, Procter & Gamble, and Aetna Life and Casualty—go further. These companies have long followed no-layoff policies. So do Lincoln Electric and Russell Corporation, the sweatshirt and athletic-wear manufacturer. Another example is Hewlett-Packard. A recession once reduced orders so much that HP management was considering a 10 percent cut in the workforce. Because laying off people was anathema, HP went a different route. It set up a working schedule of nine days out of ten for everybody in the company, from the CEO on down. The program stayed in place for six months, when orders picked up and the full ten-day schedule returned. "The net result of this program," said William Hewlett, "was that effectively all shared the burden of the recession, good people were not turned out on a very tough job market, and, I might observe, the company benefited by having in place a highly qualified work force when business returned."[14]

Companies that respect employee rights and ensure a fair workplace tend to outperform other companies.

Not only, then, is it a moral duty of companies to respect the rights and dignity of their employees, in particular by acknowledging their civil liberties and guaranteeing them due process, but doing so can also work to the company's benefit by enhancing employee morale and, thus, the company's competitive performance. Summarizing volumes of research on human resources management and organizational behavior, Professor Bruce Barry writes that "employees who perceive that workplace procedures are fair are more likely to be satisfied with their jobs, to be committed to the organization, and to make extra contributions over and above job requirements. Evidence also links these justice perceptions with better work performance and with reduced levels of negative behaviors, such as workplace theft."[15] Hence, there is little basis for the widespread belief that efficient management is incompatible with a fair workplace environment. In fact, the publicly traded firms on *Fortune*'s list of the 100 best companies to work for not only outperform the S&P 500, they "wallop it."[16]

"What I absolutely believe is that honoring the people who do the work can produce stunning results for the company," says Sidney Harmon, CEO of Harmon International Industries. "If the people in the factory believe there's a real effort to help improve their skills, provide opportunities for advancement and job security, they can do things that will blow your mind."[17] Some business writers push this point even further. For example, Robert Levering and Milton Moskowitz argue that

> The authoritarian work style—long the standard operating procedure in business—has failed. That failure is at the root of the poor performance of U.S. companies and massive layoffs in the '80s and '90s. When management is disconnected from the people who work in the company, it becomes easy to fire those people. And when workers are disconnected from what they do, it becomes easy not to care about the product or service.[18]

Of course, a company that does not sincerely consider employee rights of inherent moral importance is not likely to reap the benefits of enhanced business performance. Trust, as more and more management theorists are saying, is the key here, and employees can tell the difference between a company that has a genuine regard for their welfare and a company that only pretends to have moral concern.[19]

Summary 8.2
Some very successful companies have taken the lead in respecting employees' rights and human dignity. Corporate profits and efficient management are compatible with a fair workplace environment.

As mentioned in Chapter 1 and elsewhere, whether we are speaking of companies or of individuals, acting morally is generally in one's long-term interest even though there is no guarantee that one will always benefit by doing the right thing. However, people or organizations that worry about whether doing the right thing will profit them or who act fairly and treat people decently only because they believe that doing so will advance their self-interest are unlikely to enjoy the benefits that accrue to those whose lives are genuinely governed by moral principle. People or businesses who act ethically only because they believe it will pay off are likely to act unethically when they think that that will pay off.

So far, this chapter has affirmed that the workplace should provide an environment in which employees are treated fairly and their inherent dignity is respected, and it has argued that doing so can be perfectly compatible with a firm's business goals. Though important, those points are generalities. They do not provide much guidance for dealing with the specific moral issues and dilemmas that arise day in and day out on the job. The remainder of this chapter and the next take a closer look at some of these issues.

HIRING

People make up organizations, and how an organization impinges on the lives of its own members is a morally important matter. One obvious and very important way organizational conduct affects the welfare and rights of employees and potential employees is through personnel policies and procedures—that is, how the organization handles the hiring, firing, paying, and promoting of the people who work for it. These human-resources procedures and policies structure an organization's basic relationship with its employees. This section, on hiring, and the next three sections—on promotions, discipline and discharge, and wages—look at some of the specific, morally relevant concerns to which any organization must be sensitive. Speaking generally, though, if a company's personnel decisions are to be fair, they must reflect policies and

Fair personnel policies and decisions must be based on criteria that are clear, job related, and applied equally.

procedures that are based on criteria that are job related, clear and accessible, and applied equally.

A basic task of the employer or personnel manager is hiring. Employers strive to hire people who will enable the organization to produce the products or services it seeks to provide or to promote its other goals. Furthermore, the courts have used the principle of negligent hiring to broaden the liability of an employer for damage or injury caused by its employees— even after regular hours and away from the job site. For instance, Avis Rent-A-Car was required to pay $800,000 after a male employee raped a female employee; the jury found that the company had been negligent in hiring the man without thoroughly investigating his background.[20] In making hiring decisions, though, employers must be careful to treat job applicants fairly. As one might imagine, determining the fair thing to do is not always easy. One useful way to approach some of the moral aspects of hiring is to examine the principal steps involved in the process: screening, testing, and interviewing.

Screening

When firms recruit employees, they attempt to screen them—that is, to attract applicants who have a good chance of qualifying for the job and to weed out applicants or potential applicants who are unlikely to succeed at the job. When done properly, **job screening** ensures a pool of competent candidates and guarantees that everyone has been dealt with fairly; when done improperly, it undermines effective recruitment and invites injustices into the hiring process.

Screening begins with a job description and a job specification. A **job description** lists all pertinent details about the content of a job, including its duties, responsibilities, working conditions, and physical requirements. A **job specification** describes the qualifications an employee needs, such as skills, background, education, and work experience. Job descriptions and specifications must be complete and accurate. Otherwise, job candidates lack the necessary information for making informed decisions and can waste time and money pursuing jobs they are not suited for. In addition, disappointment and unfairness can result if a position is inaccurately described or wrongly classified.

Summary 8.3
Fairness in personnel matters requires, at least, that policies, standards, and decisions affecting workers be directly job related, based on clear and available criteria, and applied equally.

That sounds simple enough. But in an effort to attract strong job candidates, hiring officers can easily, perhaps even unintentionally, begin to exaggerate what the job offers in regard to opportunities, travel, the ability to work from home, the budget one will control, and so on. And exaggeration can grow into blatant distortion. One recruiter offers this sample lexicon: "Character building" means that the job stinks, "mentoring" translates into babysitting your staff, "expense account" signifies a bagged lunch at your desk, and "work team environment" denotes noisy cubicles.[21] Exaggerations like these may start innocently, but some businesses clearly and intentionally cross the line—for example, by deliberately misclassifying hourly workers as salaried employees to avoid paying them overtime.[22]

Wrongful Discrimination

One of the main moral concerns in screening is to avoid wrongful discrimination. For several decades, the law has forbidden discrimination against individuals on the basis of age, race, national origin, religion, or sex, and these factors should never be alluded to in job specifications or recruitment advertisements. Chapter 11 discusses the moral issues surrounding job discrimination, but it's clear that basing employment decisions on such factors almost always excludes potential employees on non-job-related grounds. Firms must therefore be careful to avoid job specifications that discriminate subtly ("excellent opportunity for college student") or employ gender-linked job terminology (e.g., "salesman" rather than "salesperson" or "waiter" rather than "server") that may discourage qualified candidates from applying.

Bona fide occupational qualifications (**BFOQs**) are job specifications to which the civil rights law does not apply. But BFOQs are very limited in scope. There are no BFOQs for race or color, and in the case of sex, BFOQs exist only to allow for authenticity (a male model) and modesty (a woman for a women's locker room attendant). In line with this, the Equal Employment Opportunity Commission (EEOC) filed a sex discrimination lawsuit against the restaurant chain Hooters, well known for its buxom "Hooter Girl" waitresses, for hiring only women as servers. Hooters resisted the decision, claiming that the job position is legitimately defined as one that makes sex relevant. After some unfavorable publicity (for one thing, no men had complained of discrimination), the EEOC quietly dropped the suit.

In validating job specifications, firms are not permitted to rely on the preferences of their customers as a reason for discriminatory employment practices. For example, the fact that for decades airline passengers were accustomed to being attended to by young female flight attendants and may even have preferred them could not legally justify excluding men from this occupation. Similarly, a court has ruled that the fact that 20 percent of Domino's customers have a negative reaction to pizza deliverymen with beards does not constitute a substantial business justification for the company's no-beards rule. The EEOC holds that such rules discriminate against black men, who sometimes suffer from a genetic skin disorder that makes shaving difficult and painful.

Since Congress passed the **Americans with Disabilities Act** (**ADA**), which became effective for all firms with fifteen or more employees in 1994, employers must be careful not to screen out disabled applicants who have the capacity to carry out the job. The ADA is intended, among other things, to protect the rights of people with disabilities to obtain gainful employment, and it forbids employers from discriminating against employees or job applicants with disabilities when making employment decisions. Employers must also make "reasonable accommodations" for an employee or a job applicant with a disability as long as doing so doesn't inflict "undue hardship" on the business.

Although the general moral imperative here is clear, in practice applying these concepts and making the appropriate determinations can be difficult.

Respect for the rights of people with disabilities may sometimes have to be balanced against expense to the company or inconvenience to other employees, but the expense or inconvenience has to be very great indeed if it is to outweigh the moral injury and financial loss being borne by the person who is denied a job opportunity because of disability. There are other gray areas, too. For example, the ADA doesn't protect employees or job applicants who are addicted to drugs, but is it wrongful discrimination for a company to refuse to hire someone it had forced to resign two years earlier because of substance abuse but who is now rehabilitated?[23]

When screening job applicants, employers should avoid excluding applicants for reasons that may be unfair or ill considered.

When screening potential employees, companies must also be careful to avoid unfairly excluding applicants on the basis of language, physical appearance, or lifestyle. And they should not automatically screen out potential employees because they lack qualifications that aren't really necessary or, contrariwise, are "overqualified," or because they have a gap in their employment history.

Language

Bilingual ability (English-Spanish, English-Vietnamese) may be a justifiable job specification in some areas of the United States, where such skills can be essential for successful job performance. But employers need to be aware of the danger of creating unnecessary specifications for a position, especially if they risk discriminating on the basis of national origin. Although the ability to communicate effectively in English is a common workplace requirement, it can impede the employment prospects of some workers. The EEOC has ruled in several cases that disqualifying a job applicant because the applicant has a pronounced foreign accent is unlawful national-origin bias unless it can be proved that the accent would hinder the job seeker's ability to perform the job. In line with this principle, the U.S. Court of Appeals in San Francisco determined that a heavy Filipino accent was a legitimate basis for rejecting an applicant for a job at a state department of motor vehicles office that required dealing with the public, even though the plaintiff had scored higher than all other candidates on a written examination.[24]

Physical Appearance

After one day, a Georgia employer changed its mind about a new employee because she "was overweight and had large breasts" and hired a smaller woman with less experience instead.[25] Though perfectly legal, the employer's conduct was morally questionable; at the very least, it was offensive and humiliating. In a handful of American cities, however, local ordinances prohibit discrimination against those who are short or overweight. On that basis, Jennifer Portnick brought a case against a San Francisco franchise of Jazzercise, a dance-fitness company. Portnick, who is 5 feet 8 inches tall and weighs 240 pounds, had applied for a job as an aerobics instructor, but Jazzercise rejected her application because it required instructors to have a "fit appearance." After the city of San Francisco sided with Portnick, Jazzercise revised its job criteria and now agrees that "it may be possible for people of varying weights to be fit."[26]

Lifestyle

Some employers wade into morally troubling waters by screening job applicants on the basis of lifestyle. For example, Multi-Developers Inc., a Georgia-based real-estate company, won't hire anyone who engages in recreational activities that are "high risk"—like motorcycling, skydiving, motor racing, mountain climbing, or flying one's own plane. In Indianapolis, Best Lock Corporation won't employ anyone who admits to taking even an occasional alcoholic drink. Other companies, such as Turner Broadcasting System, flatly refuse to hire smokers.[27] More and more companies are following suit.[28] They usually claim that doing so saves them money because employees who smoke have more health problems than nonsmokers. But many smokers resent being discriminated against as individuals on general statistical grounds. They suspect that what really underlies such policies is a holier-than-thou disapproval of smoking.

Educational Requirements

Ill-considered educational requirements are also potentially objectionable. Requiring more formal education than is truly needed for a job is unfair to less-educated candidates who, as a result, aren't even considered for the position. One of them might, in fact, turn out to be the best person for the job, which means that the firm also stands to lose. The other side of the coin is to deny an applicant consideration because he or she seems "overqualified" in education or experience. To avoid hiring someone who may become bored or frustrated by the job or who is likely to jump ship at the first opportunity, firms are justified in raising the issue. But they shouldn't proceed on the basis of assumptions that may be unwarranted. The employment ranks are filled with people successfully doing jobs for which they are technically overqualified.

Gap in Employment History

As traditional gender roles change, more and more men are leaving the work world for personal reasons, such as to help raise children while their wives complete professional training. These men often face obstacles when they return to work. Employers assume that a man who quit work once for personal reasons may do so again. Thus, discontinuity of employment cuts some men off from job consideration, as it has so often done to women.

"The hurdles men face returning to the job market are about three times greater" than those faced by women, says Charles Arons, president and chief executive officer for Casco Industries, a Los Angeles–based employment and recruiting firm. "There isn't a male I know of in an executive position who would accept raising kids as a legitimate excuse for not working for three years." Thomas Schumann, director of selection and placement for Dayton-based Mead Corporation, agrees. "If other qualified candidates are available," he says, "my guess is that a personnel manager would go with somebody who doesn't raise that question."[29]

Certainly, employers in highly technical or rapidly changing fields are warranted in suspecting that an individual's career interruption may have left

---

Summary 8.4
Misleading job descriptions and inaccurate job specifications can injure applicants by denying them information they need to make informed occupational decisions. Ordinarily, questions of sex, age, race, national origin, and religion are not job related and thus should not enter into personnel decisions. Discrimination against the disabled is now expressly forbidden by law. Screening on the basis of language, physical appearance, lifestyle, ill-considered educational requirements, or gaps in employment history may also be unfair.

him (or her) out of touch. But to automatically disqualify a candidate because of that seems arbitrary and unfair.

Testing

Testing is an integral part of the hiring process, especially in large firms. Tests are generally designed to measure the applicant's verbal, quantitative, and logical skills. Aptitude tests help determine an applicant's suitability for a job; skill tests measure the applicant's proficiency in specific areas, such as typing, shorthand, or arithmetic; personality tests help determine the applicant's maturity and sociability. In addition, some firms engaged in the design and assembly of precision equipment administer dexterity tests to determine how nimbly applicants can use their hands and fingers.

To be successful, a test must be valid. **Test validity** refers to whether test scores correlate with performance in some other activity—that is, whether the test measures the skill or ability it is intended to measure. Just as important, tests must be reliable. **Test reliability** refers to whether test results are replicable—that is, whether a subject's scores will remain relatively consistent from test to test (so that a test taker won't score high one day and low the next). Clearly, not all tests are both valid and reliable. Many are not able to measure desired qualities, and others exhibit a woefully low level of forecast accuracy. Some companies use tests that haven't been designed for the company's particular situation. Legitimizing tests can be an expensive and time-consuming project, but if tests are used, the companies using them are obliged to ensure their validity and reliability.

Even tests that are valid and reliable can be unfair if culturally biased or irrelevant to job performance.

Even when tests are valid and reliable, they can be unfair—for example, if the tests are culturally biased or if the skills they measure are irrelevant to job performance. The U.S. Supreme Court took a stand on this issue in 1971 in the case of *Griggs v. Duke Power Company*.[30] The case involved thirteen African-American laborers who were denied promotions because they scored low on a company-sponsored intelligence test involving verbal and mathematical puzzles. In its decision, the Court ruled that the Civil Rights Act prohibits employers from requiring a high school education or the passing of a general intelligence test as a prerequisite for employment or promotion without demonstrating that the associated skills relate directly to job performance. The *Griggs* decision makes it clear that if an employment practice such as testing has an adverse impact (or unequal effect) on minority groups, then the burden of proof is on the employer to show the job-relatedness or business necessity of the test or other procedure. Duke Power Company couldn't do that.

Summary 8.5
A test is valid if it measures precisely what it is designed to determine and reliable when it provides reasonably consistent results. Tests that lack validity or reliability are unfair. Tests may also be unfair if they are culturally biased or if the skills they measure do not relate directly to job performance.

In the aftermath of *Griggs* and other cases, many U.S. firms retreated from administering preemployment tests because of doubts about their legal validity. In recent years, though, testing has made a comeback in both the public and the private sectors. Today, millions of job applicants are putting pencil to paper, or sitting down in front of a computer screen, to take skills tests, leadership tests, personality tests, loyalty tests, and tests to determine accident proneness—even tests to predict what an applicant's coworkers will think of him or her after a year on the job.[31] Management, of course, is seeking through testing to gain a potentially more productive group of workers whose skills match more closely the requirements of the job. The supposed objectivity of tests is often illusory, however. Chapter 9 will have more to say about testing when it discusses privacy, but clearly putting too much faith in tests can lead to arbitrary employment decisions, decisions that are unfair to candidates and not in the best interests of the company. Test results should therefore be treated as, at most, only one measure in an overall evaluative process. Indeed, most experts believe that even the best tests cannot substitute for face-to-face interviews.

Interviewing

When moral issues arise in interviewing, they almost always relate to the manner in which the interview was conducted. Human-resource experts rightly caution against rudeness, coarseness, hostility, and condescension in interviewing job applicants. In guarding against these qualities, personnel managers would do well to focus on the humanity of the individuals who sit across the desk from them, mindful of the very human need that has brought those people into the office. This is especially true when the interviewer might not otherwise identify closely with the person being interviewed because of cultural or other differences. Interviewers must exercise care to avoid thoughtless comments that may hurt or insult the person being interviewed—for instance, a passing remark about a person's physical disability or personal situation (a single parent, for instance). A comment that an unthinking interviewer might consider innocent or even friendly could be experienced as distressing or intrusive by the person across the table. For example, it can be very uncomfortable for candidates when interviewers ask, as a surprising number of them do, about their political affiliation or how they intend to vote.[32]

Roland Wall, a job placement counselor for individuals with disabilities, describes taking a developmentally disabled client, with an IQ of about 70, for a job interview. The personnel manager emerged from the room in which Wall's client was taking an initial test along with several other job applicants. The personnel manager asked Wall where his client was and was amazed to learn that she had gone in along with the others for testing. "Really?" he said. "I didn't see one in there." This personnel manager is probably more sensitive about people with disabilities than many employers, given his willingness to interview Wall's client, yet he assumed that because she was mentally retarded, the applicant would look a certain way—would look like "one."[33]

Even though everyone suffers from conscious and unconscious biases and stereotypes, interviewers should strive to free themselves as much as possible from these "idols of the mind," as the English philosopher Francis Bacon (1561–1626) called them. As Bacon put it: "The human understanding is like a false mirror, which, receiving rays irregularly, distorts and discolors the nature of things by mingling its own nature with it."[34] In short, we view things, people included, through the lens of our own preconceptions. Interviewers need to keep this fact in mind. Panel interviews with a uniform list of questions for all applicants can also help increase objectivity. That technique,

Interviewers should try to free themselves from unconscious biases, stereotypes, and preconceptions.

however, wouldn't have helped the exceptionally well-qualified applicant who was turned down for a vice presidential position at a West Coast sports company because he wore a dark, three-piece suit to the interview. His casually dressed interviewers simply took it for granted that he wouldn't fit into their laid-back operation.[35]

Summary 8.6
Most moral concerns in interviewing relate to how the interview is conducted. Interviewers should focus on the humanity of the candidate and avoid allowing their personal biases to color their evaluations.

Proponents of the new but increasingly popular **situational interview** claim that it predicts future job performance more accurately than a standard interview does and also more accurately than résumé analysis, personality assessments, or pen-and-paper tests.[36] In situational interviews, job candidates have to engage in role playing in a mock office scenario. For example, they might have to face a company manager pretending to be a disgruntled customer. The company's interviewers watch and assess the candidates' performance: how they process the information given by "the customer," how they decide to handle the situation, the words they choose, even their body language. Proponents of the technique believe that job candidates have a harder time putting on a false front during a situational interview than in a standard interview, but there's no escaping the fact that bias and preconceptions can affect the interviewers' assessment of the likely job performance of different candidates based on their role-playing skills.

PROMOTIONS

It's no secret that factors besides job qualifications often determine promotions. How long you've been with a firm, how well you're liked, whom you know, even when you were last promoted—all these influence promotions in the real business world. As with hiring, the key moral ideal here is fairness. Nobody would seriously argue that promoting the unqualified is fair or justifiable. It's a breach of duty to owners, employees, and ultimately the general public. But many reasonable people debate whether promoting by job qualification alone is the fairest thing to do. Are other criteria admissible? If so, when, and how much weight should those criteria carry? These are tough questions with no easy answers. To highlight the problem, we consider seniority, inbreeding, and nepotism, three factors that sometimes serve as bases for promotions.

Are seniority, inbreeding, and nepotism fair and reasonable bases for promotion?

Seniority

Seniority refers to longevity on a job or with a firm. Frequently job transfers or promotions are made strictly on the basis of seniority, but problems can occur with this promotion method. Imagine that personnel manager Manuel Rodriguez needs to fill the job of quality-control supervisor. Carol Balke seems slightly better qualified for the job than Jim Turner, except in one respect: Turner has been on the job for three years longer than Balke. Whom should Rodriguez promote to quality-control supervisor?

The answer isn't easy. Those who'd argue for Carol Balke—opponents of seniority—would undoubtedly claim that the firm has an obligation to fill the job with the most-qualified person. In this way, the firm is best served and the most qualified are rewarded. Those advancing Turner's promotion—proponents of seniority—would contend that the company should be loyal to its senior employees, that it should reward them for faithful service. In this way, employees have an incentive to work hard and to remain with the firm.

When company policies indicate what part seniority should play in promotions and job transfers, the problem abates but does not vanish. We can still wonder about the morality of the policy itself. In cases in which no clear policy exists, the problem begs for an answer.

The difficulty of the question is compounded by the fact that seniority in itself does not necessarily indicate competence or loyalty. Just because Jim Turner has been on the job three years longer than Carol Balke does not necessarily mean he is more competent or more loyal. Of course, in some instances seniority may be a real indicator of job qualifications. A pilot who has logged hundreds of hours of flying time with an airline is more qualified for captaincy than one who hasn't.

Then there's the question of employee expectations. If employees expect seniority to count substantially, management can injure morale and productivity by overlooking it. True, worker morale might suffer equally should seniority alone determine promotions. Ambitious and competent workers might see little point in refining skills and developing talents when positions are doled out strictly on the basis of longevity.

Because work situations vary, specifying what part, if any, seniority ought to play in promotions seems impossible—all the more reason, therefore, for management to consider carefully its seniority policies. Of paramount importance in any decision is that management remember its twin responsibilities: promoting on the basis of qualifications and recognizing prolonged and constructive contributions to the firm. A policy that provides for promotions strictly on the basis of qualifications seems heartless, whereas one that promotes by seniority alone seems mindless. The challenge for management is how to blend these dual responsibilities in a way that is beneficial to the firm and fair to all concerned.

Inbreeding

All the cautions about seniority apply with equal force to **inbreeding**, the practice of promoting exclusively from within the firm. In theory, whenever managers must fill positions, they should look only to competence. The most competent, whether within or outside the firm, should receive the position. In this way responsibilities to owners are best served.

In practice, however, managers must seriously consider the impact of outside recruitment on in-house morale. Years of loyal service, often at great personal expense, invariably create a unique relationship between employer and employee and, with it, unique obligations of gratitude. The eighteen years that Christina Zhuy has worked for National Textile create a relationship between her and the firm that does not exist between the firm and an outsider it may wish to hire for the job Zhuy seeks. Some would argue that management has a moral obligation to remember this loyalty when determining promotions, especially when outside recruitment departs from established policy.

Nepotism

Nepotism is the practice of showing favoritism to relatives and close friends. Suppose a manager promotes a relative strictly because of the relationship between them. Such an action would raise a number of moral concerns, chief among them disregard of managerial responsibilities to the organization and of fairness to other employees.

Not all instances of nepotism raise serious moral concerns. For example, when a firm is strictly a family operation and has as its purpose providing work for family members, nepotistic practices are generally justified. Moreover, many people believe that it is unfair to exclude a person from consideration for a job or for a promotion just because he or she is a relative or friend of someone in the company. In fact, Advest Group, a brokerage firm, traditionally brings sons and daughters into the organization. "Good work ethics seem to run throughout families," says senior vice president Robert Rulevich.[37] But that is probably a minority view. Today, it is more common for companies to prohibit the employment of relatives, or at least to restrict such employment to avoid situations in which one relative is supervising another.

When it comes to senior executives, however, the matter may be different, because there's a long list of well-known, publicly traded companies that employ in lucrative positions the wives, children, and in-laws of their top managers or board members.[38] The companies in question contend that they hire and promote only on the basis of merit, but it's difficult to disagree with Charles Elson of the Center for Corporate Governance, who says, "It just doesn't look right." "It creates the appearance of a conflict of interest," adds Nell Minnow of the Corporate Library, a research firm focusing on corporate governance issues. "The burden of proof is on the company to prove it's an arms-length transaction, and that's hard to do."[39]

Even when a friend, a relative, or a spouse of a manager or some other high-ranking employee is qualified for a position or deserving of promotion, the decision can hurt company morale, breed resentment and jealousy, and create problems with regard to future placement, scheduling, or dismissal of the person. It can make him or her an object of distrust and hostility within the organization and even discourage qualified outsiders from seeking employment with the firm.

> **Summary 8.7**
> Seniority, or longevity on the job, is not necessarily a measure of either competency or loyalty. The challenge for management is to promote the most capable and qualified candidates while also recognizing long-term contributions to the company. Inbreeding, or promoting exclusively from within, presents similar challenges. Nepotism—showing favoritism to relatives or close friends—is not always objectionable, but it may slight managerial responsibilities to the organization and result in unfair treatment of other employees.

DISCIPLINE AND DISCHARGE

For an organization to function in an orderly, efficient, and productive way, managers and personnel departments establish guidelines for employee conduct based on such performance factors as punctuality, dependability, efficiency, cooperativeness, and adherence to the dress code and to other rules. This is not the place to examine the morality of specific rules and regulations; the organization's treatment of employees when infractions occur is our focus here. For example, it's one thing to speak with a person privately about some infraction and quite another to chastise or punish the person publicly. Also, trying to correct someone's behavior on a graduated basis, from oral warning to written reprimand to suspension or other punishment prior to dismissal, is different from firing someone for a first mistake. The point is that although discipline and discharge are inevitable and, indeed, necessary aspects of organizational life, they raise concerns about fairness, noninjury, and respect for persons in the way they're administered.

Two Basic Principles

Just cause and due process are essential to the fair handling of disciplinary issues.

To create an atmosphere of fairness, one in which rules and standards are equally applied, the principles of "just cause" and "due process" must operate. **Just cause** requires that reasons for discipline or discharge deal directly with job performance. AIC Securities in Chicago, for example, lacked just cause for terminating with one day's notice an experienced employee with a good record because he had been diagnosed as having brain cancer.[40] And it's difficult to see why smoking in your car on company property is just cause for dismissal, even though you can be fired for it at two Motorola plants in Illinois.[41] Of course, distinguishing between a job-related and a non-job-related issue is not always easy and can be controversial.

In addition, how a person behaves outside work is often incompatible with the image a company wishes to project. Does the organization have a right to discipline its employees for off-the-job conduct—for example, the doctor who was fired by his HMO for criticizing it on a talk show and at an industry conference?[42] The answer depends largely on the legitimate extent of organizational influence over individual lives—that is, on where precisely the company's legitimate interests stop and one's private life begins. Such concerns raise complex questions about privacy that are explored further in Chapter 9.

The second principle related to fair worker discipline and discharge is **due process**, which refers to the fairness of the procedures an organization uses to impose sanctions on employees. Of particular importance is that the rules be clear and specific, that they be administered consistently and without discrimination or favoritism, and that workers who have violated them be given a fair and impartial hearing. Due process requires both the hearing of grievances and the setting up of a step-by-step procedure by which an employee can appeal a managerial decision.

Dismissing Employees

It is useful to distinguish among four types of discharge. **Firing** is for-cause dismissal—the result of employee theft, gross insubordination, release of proprietary information, and so on. **Termination** results from an employee's poor performance—that is, from his or her failure to fulfill expectations. **Lay-off** usually refers to the temporary unemployment experienced by hourly employees and implies that they are "subject to recall." **Position elimination** designates the permanent elimination of a job as a result of workforce reduction, plant closing, or departmental consolidation.

Before dismissing an employee, management should follow a rational and unbiased decision-making process and analyze carefully the reasons leading to that decision. The organization must ask itself whether its treatment of the employee follows the appropriate procedures for that type of discharge, as those procedures are outlined in the employee handbook, in a collective bargaining agreement, or in a corporate policy statement. In addition, the company must guard against preferential treatment. Have there been employees who behaved in the same way but were not let go?

Even even-handedness and strict compliance with established procedures may not ensure fairness. For example, unless it is stated otherwise in a contract or employees have union representation, a company may not (depending on the type of case and where it occurs) be legally obligated to give reasons for firing an employee or to give advance notice. Employers who terminate someone without notice or cause may have been strictly faithful to contractual agreement or to established practice. But have they been just? Have they acted morally?

Employers have the right to fire employees who perform inadequately, but they should try to do so as painlessly as possible.

In answering those questions, it's helpful to distinguish between two employer responsibilities. Employers bear the responsibility of terminating the employment of workers who fail to fulfill their contractual obligations, but they also are obliged to terminate these workers as painlessly as possible. In other words, although employers have the right to fire, this does not mean they have the right to fire an employee in whatever way they choose. Because firing can be psychologically as well as financially devastating to employees, management should take steps to ease its effects. Moreover, crass firings hurt a company's reputation and impair its ability to attract top-notch employees.[43]

The literature on personnel management provides many suggestions for handling the discharge of employees compassionately and humanely, ranging from the recommendation not to notify employees of termination on Fridays, birthdays, wedding anniversaries, or the day before a holiday, to various steps to respect the terminated employee's privacy and dignity.[44] A company should not notify employees of their dismissal by e-mail,[45] nor should it give a longtime employee a pink slip, as General Dynamics did, on the day he returned to work after burying his six-year-old son.[46] And, certainly, no employer should do what John Patterson, former head of NCR, a computer company, once did. He fired an underperforming executive by taking his desk and chair outside, dousing it with kerosene, and setting it on fire in front of the poor man.[47] Even when an employee is fired for misconduct, the company must be careful not to defame the person.

One obvious thing employers can do to ease the trauma of firing is to provide sufficient notice. Although federal law requires companies to give sixty days' advance notice of plant closings, many companies ignore this legal obligation. Whenever employers have reason to suspect that employees will react to notice of their terminations in a hostile, destructive way, sufficient notice might merely take the form of severance pay. Morally speaking, what constitutes sufficient notice of termination depends primarily on the nature of the job, the availability of similar jobs, and the employee's length of service—not to mention the type of discharge and the reasons for it. Ideally, the length of notice should be spelled out in the work contract as should the firm's policy with regard to severance pay and the maintenance of health insurance and other benefits after the end of employment.

Summary 8.8

Most moral issues in employee discipline and discharge concern how management carries out these unpleasant tasks. Just cause and due process are necessary for fair treatment. Due process requires that there be procedures for workers to appeal discipline and discharge. To ease the trauma associated with discharge, employers should provide sufficient warning, severance pay, and perhaps displacement counseling.

For most people who have to do it, firing a worker is painfully difficult. To help managers with this unpleasant task, some large companies have counselors to help discharged employees deal with their emotions. Other companies seek the services of a displacement firm. For a fee, the firm sends in a specialist to work with the discharged employee to assess personal strengths and weaknesses, analyze the causes of the dismissal, and start planning a job search. Some companies grant laid-off staff continued access to employee-assistance programs that provide hotlines or counseling to deal with stress, depression, marital discord, and money problems.[48] They also try to include former employees in alumni networks, which can help them make new contacts and find jobs.

Companies that provide displacement and other services to discharged employees believe that doing so reduces resentment and possible litigation. Aiding terminated employees can prevent them from damaging a company's reputation with clients or potential future employees, and it can enhance the productivity and morale of employees who remain. Self-serving interests aside, however, companies that assist discharged employees and treat them with dignity deserve recognition for their attempt to ease the anguish of those who must fire and to help those who are terminated salvage both their interrupted careers and their self-respect.

Today, with downsizing, outsourcing, and economic recession combining to eliminate jobs, moral management requires careful study of responsibilities to workers. It's debatable whether Valiant Networks, a consulting company, did that. After laying off nearly one hundred workers, it asked them to return half of the bonuses they'd received six months earlier. Those bonuses were contingent on the employees staying with the company for a year—which the axed employees hadn't done.[49] When weighing their responsibilities to terminated employees, companies need to remember that termination of employment affects not only workers but their families and the larger community as well. It is impossible here to specify further what measures can or should be taken to ease the effects of displacement. Different circumstances suggest different approaches. Whatever the specific situation, though, firms have a moral obligation to terminate workers only for just cause and as a last resort, to follow due process and fair organizational procedures, and to treat dismissed employees as humanely as possible.

WAGES

Every employer faces the problem of setting wage rates and establishing salaries. From the moral point of view, it is very easy to say that firms should pay a fair and just wage, but what constitutes such a wage? So many variables are involved that no one can say with mathematical precision what a person should be paid for a job. The contribution to the firm, the market for labor and products, the competitive position of the company, the bargaining power of the firm and unions, seasonal labor fluctuations, and individual needs all conspire to make a simple answer impossible. The issue is further complicated by the fact that remuneration can also include health care, retirement programs, perquisites like tips or a company car, and bonuses, commissions, and other incentive awards.

Although some writers believe that a fair wage is whatever an employee is willing to accept,[50] the moral issues are more complex than that. In an ethical organization the basis of remuneration should be distributive justice, with a wage and salary system that centers on the employee's value to the business—his or her contribution to the organization—and not on extrinsic, non-job-related considerations such as being a single parent or a relative of the CEO.[51] In addition, salary judgments should be made on criteria that are clear and publicly available and that are impersonally or objectively applied. Consideration of the following seven factors can provide the well-intentioned business manager with some ethical guidelines and help minimize the chances of setting unfair wages and salaries:

Salaries should center on an employee's value to the business and be based on clear, publicly available criteria that are applied objectively. The following seven considerations are important.

1. **What is the law?** Federal law requires that businesses pay at least the minimum wage although the U.S. Department of Labor estimates that half of the nation's garment-sewing shops fail to do so.[52] Since 1938, the federal Fair Labor Standards Act has required employers to pay overtime for every hour worked beyond forty in a week—a law that is violated when companies force employees to work off the clock or skip meal breaks.[53] The Fair Labor Standards Act doesn't apply to executives, professionals, and other white-collar workers, but as more and more office tasks become standardized the old blue-collar/white-collar divide is blurring and a person's job title may not reveal what he or she really does. As a result some companies violate the law by failing to pay required overtime to certain office workers, technical and support personnel, accountants, mortgage brokers, store managers, and even stockbrokers.[54] Other companies violate wage laws when they misclassify workers as independent contractors, deny employees legally mandated benefits, or fail to distribute tips or other gratuities to them.[55]

2. **What is the prevailing wage in the industry?** The salaries given for similar positions in the industry can provide some direction for arriving at a fair wage, but this factor is not a moral barometer, and relying on it can be problematic. For example, when the Jackson, Mississippi, police department raised the pay of junior officers to stop their being poached by better-paying municipalities, the older and more senior officers, whose salaries were higher, charged age discrimination because they were left out.[56]

3. **What is the community wage level?** Some communities have a higher cost of living than others. For example, it is more expensive to live in New York City than in Little Rock. This is one reason many cities or counties and about a dozen states have enacted "living-wage" ordinances that raise the federal minimum wage by up to several dollars an hour. These days the concept of a community wage level includes not only basic maintenance but also medical coverage. In line with this, some states have begun publishing the names of companies with the most employees eligible for public health care programs in an attempt to shame them into improving health benefits.[57]

4. **What is the nature of the job itself?** Some jobs require more training, experience, and education than others. Some are physically or emotionally more demanding. Some jobs are downright dangerous, others socially undesirable. Risky or unskilled jobs often attract the least-educated applicants and the most desperate for work, thus leading to possible worker exploitation. Although it is impossible to draw a precise correlation between the nature of the job and what someone should be paid, a relationship exists that must be taken into account.

5. **Is the job secure? What are its prospects?** Employment that promises little or no security fails to fulfill a basic need of employees. In such cases employers should seek to compensate workers for this deprivation through higher pay, better fringe benefits, or both. A secure job with a guarantee of regular work and excellent retirement benefits (such as a civil service position) may justify a more moderate wage. In addition, a relatively low salary may be acceptable for a job that is understood to be a stepping-stone to better positions inside the organization.

6. **What are the employer's financial capabilities?** What can the organization afford to pay? A start-up company with minimal cash flow and a narrow profit margin may be unable to pay more than a minimum wage. A mature company with a secure market position might easily afford to pay better wages.

7. **What are other employees inside the organization earning for comparable work?** To avoid discrimination and unfairness in setting wage rates, it is important to look at what the organization is already paying its present employees for work of a similar nature. Gross salary disparities that are not warranted by the nature of the work, the experience required, or other objective considerations can also hurt employee morale.

Guidelines 6 and 7 have recently come to the fore as both employees and stockholders have begun scrutinizing the benefits and perks paid to top management. Studies have found that huge salary imbalances between those at the top and their employees create resentment: The greater the differential grows, the more employee loyalty declines and the more turnover increases.[58] That information will come as no surprise to employees of ITT, who saw the company lavish $10.4 million on Chairman Rand Araskog and $5.3 million on President Bob Rowman the very same year that it fired 125 of the 200 workers at company headquarters in order to save $20 million.[59] At the same time, most stockholders are getting tired of seeing company profits go to executives and not to them. Indeed, when one considers the astronomical salaries and bonuses that executives on Wall Street and at the big banks awarded themselves in 2008 after they had run their companies into the ground and left shareholders and taxpayers holding the bag, then their "executive compensation" begins to look like little more than looting.

Two other factors are equally important.

Two final factors are of equal importance with Guidelines 1 through 7. The *first* is job performance. Some people work harder or are more talented, and thus accomplish more for the organization. Most businesses rightly seek to recognize and award achievement. Like an employee's base salary, however, bonuses and other awards must relate to business performance and be

Summary 8.9
The factors that bear on the fairness of wages include the law, the prevailing wage in the industry, the community wage level, the nature of the job, the security of the job, the company's financial capabilities, and the wages the company is paying other employees for comparable work. Also important are job performance and the manner in which the wage is established. Fairness requires a legitimate work contract, one arrived at through free negotiation and informed and mutual consent.

a function of criteria that are measurable and objectively applied. The *second* factor is how the wage agreement was arrived at. A fair wage presupposes a fair work contract, and the fairness of a work contract requires free negotiation and the informed and mutual consent of both employer and employee. Where a surplus exists of workers who are willing and able to perform a given job, the employer enjoys a strong bargaining advantage. In situations where that advantage is great and workers are desperate for employment, the fairness of the work contract may be called into question.

Employees are motivated by many things. One of them is the desire to be fairly treated. Feeling that they have been reasonably rewarded for their efforts is crucial to people's self-esteem. Besides helping management discharge one of its prime moral responsibilities, establishing fair wages can enhance the work environment and remove a potential source of job dissatisfaction. This fact may help explain why economists have found that, year in and year out, firms paying the highest wages are the most profitable.[60] Costco, for example, which pays significantly better wages and provides more generous benefits than does Wal-Mart, is also more profitable, and its employees are more loyal and productive.[61] Likewise, business is booming at the clothing company American Apparel, which, in an industry characterized by sweatshops, pays its workers $13 an hour along with overtime, health insurance, and subsidized lunches. (It even pays its mostly Latino workers while they take English classes on the premises.)[62] But nobody surpasses Semco, the Brazilian company, which lets workers set their own hours and pay. Its revenue increased from $35 million to $212 million in just six years.[63]

A Living Wage

As mentioned earlier, many cities or counties and a handful of states have passed "living-wage" laws that raise the legally mandated minimum wage above federal requirements, sometimes by several dollars an hour. In most cases, these laws apply only to businesses with city contracts, but a few cities have extended them to cover all businesses above a certain size in the city's jurisdiction. In this context, a **living wage** is the amount of money a full-time employee needs to afford the necessities of life, support a family, and live above the poverty line.

Although there are different ways to determine what constitutes a living wage, the concept connects to Guideline 3 above because the amount of money in question will vary from community to community. Still, almost everywhere in the country it is impossible for a person who works full-time but earns only the federally required minimum to pull himself or herself out of poverty, let alone support a family. This fact galvanizes the living-wage movement. Its supporters argue that employers have a moral obligation to pay a living wage, and they ground their case on the utilitarian injunction to promote human welfare, on the Kantian principle of respect for human dignity, or on the commonsense idea that some wages are so low as to be inherently exploitative.

Various moral considerations support the idea that businesses should pay a living wage.

Opponents of a mandated living wage argue that it is bad policy. They say that it is hard on local companies because it raises the cost of doing business. It can also cost taxpayers money because local government must pay more for the goods and services it uses. Moreover, raising the price of anything inevitably lowers the demand for it. Hence, opponents argue, living-wage laws only serve to reduce the number of jobs. They also contend that living-wage advocates exaggerate the number of employees trying to support families on the minimum wage. Many low-wage workers are teenagers, living at home. Raising their wages won't help to reduce poverty. Moreover, they argue, if poverty is the issue, then this problem should be addressed by government programs, not by interfering in the marketplace and setting wages by fiat.

Critics of living-wage laws believe they cost jobs.

Standard economic theory affirms the principle that raising the minimum wage will, other things being equal, lower the demand for minimum-wage labor, thus putting some people at the bottom end of the scale out of work. These people also may be hurt if higher wages attract more skilled people to compete for those jobs. The real world, however, is complicated, and empirical evidence suggests that, in practice, increasing the minimum wage does not necessarily cost jobs or hurt the poor more than it helps them.[64] Living-wage advocates also insist that even if those laws do lead to some job loss, it is still wrong to offer people employment that does not meet this standard. It is worth it for a community to have better-paying jobs even if there are fewer jobs as a result. Moreover, advocates of living-wage laws contend that business really can afford to pay better wages and that in this day of growing economic inequality it is important to pressure them to do so.

LABOR UNIONS

This chapter and Chapter 9 are concerned with a number of moral issues that arise in the workplace between employer and employees, but no discussion of the workplace should overlook one of the basic institutions structuring employer-employee relations, determining the terms and conditions of employment, and shaping the environment in which people work—namely, labor unions. Accordingly, this section briefly examines the history and economic role of unions, the ideals that motivate them, and some of the moral dilemmas they raise.

History of the Union Movement

In a famous remark, Franklin D. Roosevelt said that free and independent labor unions are characteristic of a free and democratic modern nation. Many economists and students of the union movement go on to give it primary credit for raising the standard of living and increasing the security of working people in the United States. They argue that almost all the benefits enjoyed by employees today, whether they happen to be in unions or not, can be traced to union victories or to union-backed legislation. At the same time, the higher wages, paid vacations, health benefits, retirement pensions, and increased job security that unions have brought have, in turn, contributed to social stability in the country and, through enhanced demand, to economic growth itself. Yet as the history of the labor movement reveals, employers have opposed

Employers have opposed unions at almost every step. But unions have increased the security and standard of living of working people and contributed to social stability and economic growth.

unionization and union demands at almost every step of the way—often with violence.

Just as the roots of capitalism can be traced to the handicraft guilds, so the earliest efforts of American unionism can be found in the craft unions of the eighteenth century. At that time, groups of skilled artisans—carpenters, shoemakers, tailors, and the like—formed secret societies for two basic reasons: to equalize their relationship with their employers and to professionalize their crafts. They agreed on acceptable wages and working hours and pledged not to work for any employer who didn't provide them, and they set minimal admission standards for their crafts. They also agreed to keep their allegiance secret—and for good reason. If found out, they would be fired, and if discovered trying to cause a strike, they could be jailed.

Labor historians generally consider the Knights of Labor, established in 1869, to be the first truly national trade union. The Knights endeavored to call together all workers, skilled and unskilled, black and white, male and female, into one mighty association. The Knights were followed by the American Federation of Labor (AFL). Founded in 1886, the AFL united the great national craft unions, such as iron- and steelworkers, boilermakers, tailors, coal miners, and printers, in a closely knit organizational alliance. Appealing to better-paid skilled workers, the AFL soon surpassed the Knights, and the latter eventually faded away. Within seven years, under the astute and temperate leadership of Samuel Gompers, the AFL built a membership of 500,000, which increased to about 2 million by 1917.

The cause of unionism was significantly advanced in 1935 with the passage of the **National Labor Relations Act** (also called the **Wagner Act**). This legislation prohibited employers from interfering with employees trying to organize unions, from attempting to gain control over labor unions, from treating union workers differently from nonunion workers, and from refusing to bargain with union representatives. The act helped increase union membership to almost 12 million by the end of World War II in 1945. Most of these members belonged to the Congress of Industrial Organizations (CIO), an offshoot of the AFL that brought together various workers—auto, sheet metal, steel, and so on—into industry-wide unions. The distinct advantage of the CIO over the AFL was that CIO unions could call a firm's entire workforce out on strike, rather than just its skilled workers.

Increasing union strength raised public suspicions and fears of union power. Many businesspeople and political critics encouraged these worries and quickly pointed to the wave of strikes after World War II as evidence of union abuse of power. In 1947 a newly elected Republican Congress passed the **Taft-Hartley Act**, which amended the National Labor Relations Act. The new law outlawed the *closed shop* (the requirement that a person must be a union member before being hired). Section 14(b) of Taft-Hartley permitted individual states to outlaw the *union shop* (the requirement that a person must join the union within a specified time after being hired). Today, twenty-two states, mostly in the South and West, are so-called **right-to-work states**, with **open-shop laws** on their books. These laws prohibit union contracts requiring all employees on a job site to either join the union or pay the equivalent of union dues, once hired. Taft-Hartley also prohibits various labor practices designated as unfair, such as sympathetic strikes and secondary boycotts (discussed later in this chapter).

Summary 8.10
Working people struggled for decades to form unions and win their legal recognition. Although unions are responsible, directly or indirectly, for many of the benefits employees today enjoy, a changing economy, hostile political environment, and aggressive anti-union policies have weakened them.

The Plight of Unions Today

In 1955, the AFL and the CIO merged to form the **AFL-CIO**. Since then, unions have attempted to increase membership by recruiting outside basic industry—for example, in education, government, white-collar professions, and service jobs. But they have been only moderately successful. For the past twenty years, union membership has been falling, both absolutely and as a percentage of the workforce. Whereas unions represented 36 percent of the private-sector workforce in the 1950s and 20 percent in the early 1980s, today union members constitute only 7.8 percent (or approximately 8.2 million workers plus an additional 8 million government workers). Union membership as a percentage of the workforce is substantially lower in the United States than it is in Japan and most Western nations—for instance, Australia, Belgium, France, Germany, the Netherlands, and the United Kingdom. This fact may explain why hourly compensation for production workers in manufacturing is less in the United States than in those countries; in fact, American workers make only 81 percent of what the average European worker earns and only 69 percent of what their German counterparts make.[65]

In recent years, unions have been on the defensive.

In recent years, unions have been more and more on the defensive, as the industries in which they have been traditionally based have declined. The number of days lost to strikes, for instance, has been at a record low, and many unions have been forced to go along with decreases in wages and benefits. Meanwhile, the general political climate has been unfavorable to labor for the past three decades. President Reagan set the anti-union tone back in the 1980s when he fired nearly twelve thousand striking air traffic controllers and broke their union. The union had been considered powerful, but it was soundly defeated. Pushed by business interests, in recent years the federal government has moved to tighten its regulation of unions and to restrict their ability to organize.[66]

On the legal front, labor unions suffered a major setback when the U.S. Supreme Court ruled that private employers could "replace permanently" striking workers, even though the 1935 Wagner Act makes it illegal for employers to retaliate against workers who go on strike by "firing" them. Whatever the terminology, if workers risk losing their jobs because of a strike, then the balance of power in collective bargaining is dramatically altered. Instead of negotiating in good faith, a company can now provoke a strike, hire new workers to replace the pickets, and cut costs. And management has done exactly that in a number of cases, as many corporations have grown increasingly and aggressively anti-union.

Employers hire anti-union management consultants, hold mandatory anti-union meetings, show anti-union videos at work, have supervisors meet individually with employees to disparage unions, and distribute anti-union leaflets at work or mail them to employees' homes.[67] They try to break existing unions or prevent their formation by harassing and even firing pro-union workers and by waging vigorous, often illegal anti-union campaigns.[68] For example, if a Wal-Mart store thinks its employees may be planning to organize a union, corporate headquarters dispatches a union-busting team by corporate jet to deal with the problem. When, after somehow dodging the corporate police, the meat-cutting department of a Texas Wal-Mart voted to join the Union of Food and Commercial Workers, the company responded a week later by closing the department and firing the offending employees. In 2005 Wal-Mart closed a store in Quebec a few months after it became the only unionized Wal-Mart in North America.[69] It's not surprising, then, that although nearly half of the country's 84 million nonunion workers say they would vote for a union at their company, many are too intimidated to take a pro-union stance.[70]

In the 1980s, Richard Edwards and Michael Podgursky summarized labor's situation in words that still hold true today:

> Bargaining structures built up over many years are crumbling and collapsing.... Rising product market competition, deregulation, and technological changes; adverse labor force dynamics; worsening public policy; and the legacy of the long stagnation have thrust the labor movement into a qualitatively new stage. This new period is characterized ... by: (a) greater corporate mobility, power, and militancy; (b) ineffective labor law and a growing indifference, and in some cases, outright opposition of the government towards organized labor and collective bargaining; and (c) a waning belief in unions as the agents of working class interests. In these hostile circumstances, American unions face a difficult and troubling future.[71]

However, periods of economic crisis and rising unemployment often lead to increased unionization and stronger labor organizations, and that may begin to happen now. Already Americans view unions more positively than they have at any time since the 1970s, and President Obama has spoken of the "need to level the playing field for workers and the unions that represent their interests."[72] Moreover, many economists believe that a lack of bargaining power of ordinary American workers has made the economic recession worse.[73]

Card Check

Under the National Labor Relations Act, there are two main ways for workers to form a union. One is for a majority of the workers at a company to demonstrate their desire for a union by signing up to join it (**card check**). Alternatively, if 30 percent or more of the workers sign a petition requesting union representation, then an election is organized and employees vote by secret ballot whether to have a union. However, employers can refuse to recognize a union chosen by majority signup and can demand an election instead. Recently, Congress has considered legislation that would force employers to recognize unions formed by card check. Proponents of the measure see it as a necessary response to employers' aggressive anti-union campaigns, which too often lead to union-certification elections being a mockery of democracy. They think card check gives workers a fairer chance to unionize by making it possible for them to do so before the company can begin retaliating against them. Among corporate and business leaders, however, there is fervent opposition to the measure, which they describe as an attack on the secret ballot. They contend that with card check individual workers can be pressured to sign up. To this, organized labor's supporters respond that it is companies that do the intimidating, not unions. They argue that what really concerns business, and why it is spending millions of dollars to combat the measure, is not a love of elections, but rather the prospect of increased unionization. Some business leaders admit this. "We like driving the car," says Wal-Mart CEO Lee Scott, "and we're not going to give the steering wheel to anybody but us." Bernie Marcus, co-founder and former CEO of Home Depot agrees: "This is the demise of a civilization." Business leaders who are not actively fighting the measure, he says, "should be shot; should be thrown out of their goddamn jobs."[74]

Union Ideals

From the beginning, unions have fought to protect workers from abuses of power at the hands of employers. Employers have tremendous power over individual workers. They can hire and fire, relocate and reassign, set work hours and wages, create rules and control working conditions. Acting individually, a worker rarely is an employer's equal in negotiating any of these items. The position of most workers acting independently is further weakened by their lack of capital, occupational limitations, and personal and family needs. Furthermore, whereas employers obviously need workers, they rarely need any particular worker. They can, generally speaking, select whomever they want, for whatever reasons they choose.

Interestingly, Adam Smith himself recognized this fundamental imbalance in his classic *The Wealth of Nations*. Regarding the respective bargaining power of workers and their "masters," or employers, he wrote that "upon all ordinary occasions" employers "have the advantage in the dispute, and force the other into a compliance with their terms."

> The masters, being fewer in number, can combine much more easily…. We have no acts of parliament against combining to lower the price of work; but many against combining to raise it. In all such disputes the masters can hold out much longer…. Though they did not employ a single workman, [employers] could generally live a year or two upon the stocks which they have already acquired. Many workmen could not subsist a week, few could subsist a month, and scarce any a year without employment. In the long run the workman may be as necessary to his master as his master is to him, but the necessity is not so immediate.[75]

In an attempt, then, to redress the balance of power in their dealings with employers, workers band together. In acting as a single body, a union, workers in effect make employers dependent on them in a way that no individual worker can. The result is a rough equality or mutual dependence, which serves as the basis for *collective bargaining*—negotiations between the representatives of organized workers and their employers over things such as wages, hours, rules, work conditions, and, increasingly, participation in decisions affecting the workplace. As the World Bank and others have recognized, by giving workers a collective voice, unions do not just push up wages. They also can improve productivity and efficiency, promote stability in the workforce, and make government less likely to meddle in the labor market.[76]

Certainly no one can object to unionism's initial and overriding impulse: to protect workers from abuse and give them a voice in matters that affect their lives. Indeed, those two goals reflect two lofty moral ideals: noninjury and autonomy. Ironically, it is out of respect for these ideals that some individuals criticize modern unions.

The critics argue that union shops infringe on the autonomy and right of association of individual workers. Even if workers are not required to join the union but only to pay some equivalent to union dues, the critics contend, this still infringes on their freedom. In addition, evidence suggests that companies in alliance with unions sometimes treat nonunion personnel less favorably than they treat union members. Some workers have gone to court to argue that favoritism to union members is discriminatory and unlawful. Whether it is or not, it certainly raises a moral question about the right to determine for oneself organizational membership and participation.

Summary 8.11
Unions attempt to protect workers from abuse and give them a voice in matters that affect their lives. Critics charge that forcing workers to join unions infringes on autonomy and the right of association. They allege that union workers receive discriminatory and unlawful favoritism. In response, union sympathizers stress fairness and the importance of solidarity.

Taking the union's viewpoint reveals competing ideals and other consequences that must be considered. *First,* there is organized labor's ideal of solidarity, which is vital to collective bargaining and to winning worker equality. Union proponents point to the fact that workers in unionized workplaces earn more than other workers and that per capita personal income is higher in states with free collective bargaining than in right-to-work states. For instance, of the twenty-two right-to-work states, only Nevada and Virginia have personal incomes above the national average. Practically speaking, if workers receive union benefits without having to belong or pay dues, then they lack an incentive to join the union, which greatly weakens the union's ability to improve wages and strengthen workers' rights.

Second, there is a question of fairness. Is it fair for a nonunion worker to enjoy the benefits won by union members—often at great personal and organizational expense? This question arises most forcefully when unions are attempting to establish an *agency shop,* in which all employees must pay union dues but are not required to join the union. The agency shop is designed to eliminate free riders while respecting the individual worker's freedom of choice. Opponents claim that an agency shop does not so much eliminate free riders as create forced passengers.

Union Tactics

The tactics unions use to try to get management to accept their demands also raise moral issues.

Direct Strikes

The legal right to strike is labor's most potent tool in labor-management negotiations. A strike occurs when an organized body of workers withholds its labor to force the employer to comply with its demands. On libertarian principles, it is clear that employees have a right to agree among themselves to stop working for an employer. However, because strikes can cause financial injuries to both employer and employee, inconvenience and perhaps worse to consumers, and economic dislocations in society, they raise serious moral questions. On the other hand, sometimes workers cannot obtain justice and fair play in the workplace in any other way. Austin Fagothey and Milton A. Gonsalves suggest the following conditions of a justified strike: [77]

1. *Just cause.* "Just cause" refers to job-related matters. Certainly, inadequate pay, excessive hours, and dangerous and unhealthful working conditions are legitimate worker grievances and provide just cause for a strike. Revenge, personal ambition, petty jealousies, and the like do not constitute just cause and thus cannot justify a strike.

2. *Proper authorization.* For a strike to be legitimate, it must be duly authorized. This means, first, that workers themselves must freely reach the decision without coercion and intimidation. Second, if the workers are organized, then the proposed strike must receive union backing (although this condition becomes difficult to apply when the local union chapter and the national organization don't see eye-to-eye).

3. *Last resort.* To be justified, a strike must come as a last resort. This condition acknowledges the serious potential harm of strikes. A basic moral principle is that we should always use the least injurious means available to accomplish the good we desire. Since there is an array of less drastic collective-bargaining tactics that can and usually do achieve worker objectives, all these should be exhausted before a strike is called.

Even when a strike is warranted, however, not every means of implementing it is morally justified. In general, peaceful picketing and an attempt by striking workers to publicize their cause and peacefully persuade others not to cross the picket line are moral means of striking. Physical violence, threats, intimidation, and sabotage are not. More controversially, Fagothey and Gonsalves argue that if workers have the right to withhold their labor and strike, then employers have a right to fill their jobs with other workers but not with professional strikebreakers, whose presence incites violence and whose function extends beyond doing work to denying strikers justice and the right to organize.

The preceding discussion deals with **direct strikes**—that is, cessation of work by employees with the same industrial grievance. There is, however, another kind of strike, far more controversial than the direct strike: the sympathetic strike.

Sympathetic Strikes

A **sympathetic strike** occurs when workers who have no particular grievance of their own and who may or may not have the same employer decide to strike in support of others. The bigger unions become and the more diverse the workers they count among their members, the more likely are sympathetic strikes aimed at different employers. Indeed, the sympathetic strike can take on global proportions, as when American dockside workers refused to unload freighters from the Soviet Union to show support of the Solidarity movement in Poland.

Sometimes the sympathetic strike involves several groups of workers belonging to different unions but employed by the same company. Acting on

Summary 8.12
Direct strikes may be justified when there is just cause and proper authorization and when they are called as a last resort. Because they involve the cessation of work in support of other workers with a grievance, sympathetic strikes raise distinct moral concerns. Primary boycotts seem morally comparable to direct strikes, and secondary boycotts analogous to sympathetic strikes. In corporate campaigns, unions enlist the cooperation of a company's creditors to pressure the company to permit unionization or agree to union demands.

a grievance, one group strikes. But because it is so small, it enlists the aid of the other groups; it asks them to engage in a sympathetic strike. Cases like these do not seem to differ in any morally significant way from direct strikes. Indeed, it could be argued that the affiliated groups have obligations of loyalty and beneficence to join the strike. It is true, of course, that the sympathetic strikers do not have personal grievances, but they do have the same unjust employer, and they are in a unique position to help remedy that injustice by withholding their labor.[78]

Sympathetic strikes involving groups of employees working for different employers differ significantly from direct strikes or sympathetic strikes against the same employer. For one thing, the employers being struck out of sympathy may be perfectly innocent victims whose treatment of workers is beyond reproach. They may have lived up to their end of the work contract, only to have their workers break it.

Sympathetic strikes can be very effective, however. J. P. Stevens & Co., the second-largest company in the U.S. textile industry, fought unionization for decades. The company engaged in a variety of flagrantly unfair labor practices and refused to recognize or bargain collectively with the union, despite various court orders to do so.[79] During a boycott of J. P. Stevens products, United Auto Workers members at a General Motors plant in Canada refused to install J. P. Stevens carpeting in the cars they were producing, thus shutting down the assembly line. In less than half a day, J. P. Stevens carpeting was gone from the plant. Had U.S. workers done something similar, both they and the textile workers union would have been subject to legal action, but J. P. Stevens would not have been able to refuse to bargain as long as it did.

Boycotts and Corporate Campaigns

Like a strike, a boycott tries to strengthen the union's bargaining position. A secondary boycott is analogous to a sympathetic strike.

Besides strikes, unions also use boycotts to support their demands. A **primary boycott** occurs when union members and their supporters refuse to buy products from a company being struck. A **secondary boycott** occurs when people refuse to patronize companies that handle products of struck companies. The Taft-Hartley Act prohibits unions from organizing secondary boycotts. However, because agricultural laborers are not covered by the Wagner Act, Taft-Hartley doesn't apply to them, so the United Farm Workers union was legally able to use this tactic successfully in the 1960s and 70s.

The express purpose of any boycott is the same as that of a strike: to hurt the employer or company financially and thus strengthen the union's bargaining position. In general, a boycott is justifiable when it meets the same conditions as a strike. In the case of the secondary boycott, which is like a sympathetic strike, the damage is extended to those whose only offense may be that they are handling the products of the unjust employer—and perhaps they are handling them out of financial necessity. In such cases, Fagothey and Gonsalves reject secondary boycotts. But this assessment seems too automatic and doesn't allow us to weigh the likely harms and benefits in particular cases.[80]

A relatively new pressure tactic by organized labor is the so-called **corporate campaign**, in which unions enlist the cooperation of a company's creditors to pressure the company to unionize or comply with union demands.

The tactic first gained national recognition after it was successfully used to help the Amalgamated Clothing and Textile Workers Union win contracts with Farah Manufacturing Company, a Texas-based men's garment maker. Union representatives persuaded retailers in Birmingham, Alabama, to stop selling Farah slacks by threatening them with a consumer boycott and then persuaded Farah's major creditors to help mediate the dispute.

In another labor conflict, several unions united to mount a corporate campaign to force Washington Gas Company to settle a dispute with the International Union of Gasworkers. The Teamsters, the Service Employees International Union, the Laborers' International Union, and the Communications Workers of America joined forces with several local unions to pressure Crestar Bank—where Washington Gas has a line of credit—to intervene on the union side. To lean on Crestar, the unions had at their disposal pension funds, payroll accounts, normal operating capital for their organizations, and even the mortgages on their buildings. Crestar complained that it was only caught in the middle. "We are not a party to the dispute," said spokesman Barry Koling. "We are neutral with respect to the issues between them." But union spokesman Jorge Rivera responded, "We judge our business partners by their actions concerning workers."[81]

At the heart of the corporate campaign is the issue of corporate governance. In pressuring financial institutions with mass withdrawals and cancellations of policies, unions and administrators of public-employee pension funds are trying to influence those institutions' policies and business relationships. And when the financial institutions accede to union demands, they in turn pressure the recalcitrant company to change its business policies. The harshest critics of the corporate campaign call it corporate blackmail. Its champions view it as an effective way to get financial institutions and companies to become good corporate citizens. Such tactics, they say, are necessary at a time when wages are stagnating, economic inequality is increasing, and management has been so successful at exploiting labor laws and regulations to undermine unions and thwart their recruitment efforts.

STUDY CORNER

Key Terms and Concepts

AFL-CIO
Americans with
  Disabilities Act
bona fide occupational
  qualifications
card check
corporate campaign
direct strike
due process
employment at will
firing
inbreeding

job description
job screening
job specification
just cause
layoff
living wage
National Labor
  Relations Act
nepotism
open-shop laws
position elimination
primary boycott

right-to-work state
secondary boycott
seniority
situational interview
sympathetic strike
Taft-Hartley Act
termination
test reliability
test validity
Wagner Act

CASE **8.1**

AIDS in the Workplace

Carla Lombard always worked well with people. So when she opened her Better Bagels bagel shop seven years ago, she anticipated that managing her employees would be the easy part. She had worked for enough different bosses that she thought she knew what it took to be a good employer. Whether she was up to the financial side of running a business was her worry. As it turned out, however, Better Bagels flourished. Not only did Carla go on to open three smaller branches of Better Bagels, but her bakery also made daily wholesale deliveries to dozens of coffee shops and restaurants around the city. No, the business was prospering. It was just that the personnel issues turned out to be more difficult than she had ever expected. Take this week, for example.

On Tuesday, Carla was in the main bagel shop when around noon Tom Walters's ex-wife, Frances, came in. Tom oversaw a lot of the early-morning baking at that shop and like most of Carla's employees put in his share of time working the sales counter. He was a good worker, and Carla had been considering

promoting him next month to manager of one of the branch shops. After ordering a bagel, Frances took Carla aside. She beat around the bush for a few minutes before she got to her point, because she was there to tell Carla that Tom had AIDS. Frances said she was telling Carla because she "always liked her and thought she was entitled to know because she was Tom's employer." Carla barely knew Frances, and she was so taken aback that she was at a loss for words. She was shocked and embarrassed and didn't know whether she should even discuss Tom with Frances. While Carla was still trying to recover herself, Frances took her bagel and left.

Carla was still concerned and upset when she saw Tom the next day. Perhaps he had been thinner and looked tired more often the last few months, Carla thought to herself. But she couldn't be sure, and Tom seemed to be his usual upbeat self. Carla wanted to discuss Frances's visit with Tom, but she couldn't bring herself to mention it. She had always liked Tom, but—face it, she thought—he's my employee, not my friend. And it's his business. If I were an employee, I wouldn't want my boss asking me about my health.

Later, however, she began to wonder if it wasn't her business after all. She overheard some customers saying that people were staying away from the local Denny's franchise because one of its cooks was reported to have AIDS. The rumor was that some of his fellow employees had even circulated a petition saying that the cook should go, but a local AIDS support group had intervened, threatening legal action. So the cook was staying, but the customers weren't. Carla knew something about AIDS and thought some of what her customers were saying was bigoted and ill informed. She was pretty sure that you couldn't transmit HIV through food—including bagel—preparation, but she thought that maybe she should double-check her information. But what was really beginning to worry her were the business implications. She didn't want a Denny's-like situation at Better Bagels, but in her customers' comments she could see the possibility of something like that happening once the word got out about Tom, especially if she made him a manager. Carla was running a business, and even if her customers' fears might be irrational or exaggerated, she couldn't force them to visit her shops or eat her bagels.

Carla knew it was illegal to fire Tom for having AIDS, and in any case that's not the kind of person she was. But she couldn't afford to skirt the whole problem, she realized, as some large companies do, by simply sending the employee home at full pay. To be sure, doing that deprives the employee of meaningful work, but it removes any difficulties in the workplace, and the employee has no legal grounds for complaint if he or she is left on the payroll. And then, of course, there was always the question of Tom's future work performance. Putting the question of promotion aside, if he really was ill, as Frances had said, his work performance would probably decline, she thought. Shouldn't she begin developing some plan for dealing with that?

Update   Frances was misinformed. Tom didn't have AIDS. He had developed multiple sclerosis, a degenerative disease of the central nervous system. It's not fatal, but the course of the disease is unpredictable. Attacks can occur at any time and then fade away. A person can feel fine one day, only to have an attack the next day that causes blurred vision, slurred speech, numbness, or even blindness and paralysis. Tom was never worried about losing his job, and he was pretty sure he could continue to perform well at it, maybe even move higher in the business either with Carla or with another employer. But he kept his condition to himself, hiding his symptoms and covering up occasional absences and trips to the doctor, because he was worried that customers and colleagues would perceive him differently. He didn't want looks of pity if he stumbled or constant questions about how he was feeling.

Discussion Questions

1. What are the moral issues in this case? What ideals, obligations, and consequences must Carla Lombard consider? What rights, if any, are at stake? Will it make a difference whether Carla adopts a Kantian approach or a utilitarian approach to this situation?

2. Would it be wrong of Carla to ask Tom Walters about his health? Why or why not? Defend your answer by appeal to moral principle.

3. Suppose Tom had AIDS. What should Carla do? Is an employee's HIV status a job-related issue? In particular, is it a factor Carla should consider in deciding whether to promote Tom? What part, if any, should the attitudes of Tom's coworkers play in Carla's decision?

4. How should companies address the problem of public fear and prejudice when employees with AIDS have direct contact with customers?

5. Should companies develop programs or policies that deal specifically with AIDS? If so, what characteristics should they have? Or should they deal with the problem only on a case-by-case basis? Should large corporations develop AIDS-awareness programs? Or should AIDS be treated no differently than any other disease?

6. Does Tom have a moral obligation to disclose his medical condition to Carla—and, if so, at what point? Suppose a job applicant has a chronic, potentially debilitating medical condition. Should he or she reveal that fact before being hired? Would it be wrong not to mention the disease if the interviewer inquires about the applicant's health?

CASE 8.2

Web Porn at Work

Al Smetana is the founding president of a medium-size, midwestern manufacturing firm, Rayburn Unlimited. He's proud of the way his company has grown, and done so on the basis of an organizational culture committed to honesty, integrity, and the intrinsic value of each individual. But now those values are being put to the test.

It began when Al learned that an employee had tapped into the company's computer system and figured out how to read people's e-mail and to learn what websites they visited. Determining who the culprit was wasn't difficult. When confronted about it, the employee admitted what he had done. Al immediately terminated his employment. But as he left, the employee said angrily, "Just ask Lindley about his computer usage," referring to Craig Lindley, associate vice president for human resources and an old friend of Al's. Although Al didn't trust the discharged employee, he was disturbed by his comment and reluctant to let it go. So he called Craig Lindley into his office and asked him about it.

After a few minutes of gentle questioning, Craig started weeping. When he recovered himself, he explained that for the past year or so he had been hooked on pornography on the web and at the office sometimes spent an hour or so a day looking at it. Al asked him whether his wife knew. Craig said she didn't. He was too ashamed of his habit to talk to her or anybody else about it. Al then told him to take the rest of the day off, to think the matter over, and to return to Al's office the next morning. When Craig left, Al stood and looked out the window, silently asking himself what he should do.[82]

Discussion Questions

1. Is Craig Lindley's behavior a sign of some psychological problem that Rayburn Unlimited should help him overcome, perhaps with personal counseling? Or is dismissal called for? Should Al Smetana fire Craig to send a message to other employees not to misuse company time and resources?

2. Does Al have just cause for dismissing Craig? Does it matter whether or not Rayburn Unlimited has an explicit policy regarding computer use? Suppose it has such a policy and Craig violated it. Does that settle the matter? Would it affect your judgment of the case if Craig had helped draw up that policy?

3. Does the fact that Craig is a valued member of the company with a long record of service make a difference? Or that he is a personal friend of Al's?

4. Was it right for Al to have asked Craig about his computer usage in the first place? Did he violate Craig's privacy or civil liberties?

5. Because Al fired the employee who violated the company's computer system, would it be inconsistent or unfair of him to treat Craig any differently?

6. Al Smetana and Rayburn Unlimited are committed to honesty and integrity (the upholding of which seems to support dismissal) and the intrinsic worth of each individual (which might argue for more lenient treatment). Are these values in conflict? What would you do if you were Al?

CASE 8.3
Speaking Out about Malt

When Mary Davis, associate vice president for plant management at Whitewater Brewing Company, wrote an article for a large metropolitan newspaper in her state, she hadn't realized where it would lead. At first she was thrilled to see her words published. Then she was just worried about keeping her job.

It all started when her husband, Bob, who was working on his MBA, talked her into taking an evening class with him. She did and, to her surprise, really got into the course, spending most of her weekends that semester working on her term project—a study of wine and beer marketing. Among other things her essay discussed those respectable wine companies like E. & J. Gallo (the nation's largest) that market cheap, fortified wines such as Thunderbird and Night Train Express. With an alcohol content 50 percent greater than regular wine and selling for around $1.75 a pint, these screw-top wines are seldom advertised and rarely seen outside poor neighborhoods, but they represent a $125-million-a-year industry. Skid-row winos are their major consumers, a fact that evidently embarrasses Gallo, because it doesn't even put its company name on the label.[83]

Mary's essay went on to raise some moral questions about the marketing of malt liquor, a beer brewed with sugar for an extra punch of alcohol. It has been around for about forty years; what is relatively new is the larger size of the container. A few years ago, the industry introduced malt liquor in 40-ounce bottles that sell for about two dollars. Packing an alcohol content roughly equivalent to six 12-ounce beers or five cocktails, 40s quickly became the favorite high of many inner-city teenagers. Ads for competing brands stress potency—"It's got more" or "The Real Power"—and often use gang slang. Get "your girl in the mood quicker and get your jimmy thicker," raps Ice Cube in a commercial for St. Ides malt liquor. Like baggy pants and baseball caps turned backward, 40s soon moved from the inner city to the suburbs. Teenage drinkers like the quick drunk, and this worries drug counselors. They call 40s "liquid crack" and "date rape brew."[84]

Mary's instructor liked her article and encouraged her to rewrite it for the newspaper. The problem was that Whitewater also brews a malt liquor, called Rafter, that it had recently started offering in a 40-ounce bottle. True, Mary's article mentioned Whitewater's brand only in passing, but top management was distressed by her criticisms of the whole industry, which, they thought, damaged its image and increased the likelihood of further state and federal regulation. The board of directors thought Mary had acted irresponsibly, and Ralph Jenkins, the CEO, had written her a memo on the board's behalf instructing her not to comment publicly about malt liquor without first clearing her remarks with him. Mary was hurt and angry.

"I admit that the way the newspaper edited my essay and played up the malt liquor aspect made it more sensationalistic," Mary explained to her colleague Susan Watts, "but everything I said was true."

"I'm sure it was factual," replied Susan, "but the company thought the slant was negative. I mean, lots of ordinary people drink Rafter."

"I know that. Bob even drinks it sometimes. I don't know why they are so upset about my article. I barely mentioned Rafter. Anyway, it's not like Rafter is a big money-maker. Most of our other beers outsell it."

"Well," continued Susan, "the company is really touchy about the whole issue. They think the product is under political attack these days and that you were disloyal."

"That's not true," Mary replied. "I'm no troublemaker, and I have always worked hard for Whitewater. But I do think they and the other companies are wrong to market malt liquor the way they do. It only makes a bad situation worse."

The next day Mary met with Ralph Jenkins and told him that she felt Whitewater was "invading," as she put it, her rights as a citizen. In fact, she had been invited to speak about wine and beer marketing at a local high school as part of its antidrug campaign. She intended to keep her speaking engagement and would not subject her remarks to company censorship.

Jenkins listened but didn't say much, simply repeating what he had already written in his memo. But two days later Mary received what was, in effect, an ultimatum. She must either conform with his original order or submit her resignation.

Discussion Questions

1. Do you think Mary Davis acted irresponsibly or disloyally? Does Whitewater have a legitimate concern about her speaking out on this issue? Does the company have a right to abridge her freedom of expression?

2. Is your answer to question 1 affected by whether you agree or disagree with the views Mary Davis expressed?

3. Should there be any limits on an employee's freedom of expression? If not, why not? If so, under what circumstances is a company justified in restricting an employee's right to speak out?

4. The case presentation doesn't specify whether the newspaper article identified Mary Davis as an employee of Whitewater. Is that a relevant issue? Does it matter what position in the company Mary Davis holds?

5. What do you think Mary Davis ought to do? What moral considerations should she weigh? Does she have conflicting obligations? If so, what are they?

6. Is the company right to be worried about what Mary Davis writes or says, or is the board of directors exaggerating the potential harm to Whitewater of her discussing these issues?

7. Assume a CEO like Ralph Jenkins is legitimately worried that an employee is making damaging statements about the company. How should the CEO handle the situation? Is discharge or some sort of discipline called for? Should the company adopt a formal policy regarding employee speech? If so, what policy would you recommend?

CASE **8.4**

Old Smoke

The last thing Darlene Lambert felt like doing the first thing Monday morning was inhaling the stench of old cigarette smoke. Darlene wasn't crazy about the smell of cigarettes under the best of circumstances, but today she felt under the weather and the very thought of cigarette fumes made her feel slightly nauseated.

Darlene worked with one other person, a nonsmoker, in a small office of the personnel department at Redwood Associates, but her job sometimes required her to spend extended periods in the main files room, where Frank and Alice worked and smoked. They didn't smoke when Darlene or another nonsmoker had to use their room, and they were always careful to open the windows and air it out ahead of time. But the smell of cigarettes still permeated the room, Darlene thought. Alice and Frank were nice people and sympathetic to her feelings. But Alice had hinted that she thought Darlene was oversensitive to the odor of old smoke, and Frank sometimes joked about smokers being persecuted these days for their habit.

At 9:05 A.M., Darlene marched into the office of her supervisor, Charles Renford, and told him that she couldn't work in the files room that day because of the odor of smoke. Renford was caught off guard and more than a little put out by Darlene's announcement because top management was suddenly requesting a report—"due yesterday"—and he needed Darlene to begin assembling the data in the files room. He reminded her that although the law in their state requires companies to provide a smoke-free work area for employees who desire it, it doesn't force companies to ban smoking altogether. And the law says nothing at all about the smell of stale smoke or other odors that people might dislike but that can't hurt them. Moreover, Charles said, smokers have rights, and making them leave the building to smoke would hurt productivity and morale.

"They should quit smoking," Darlene rejoined. "It would be for their own good."

"Maybe it would," said Charles, "but the company shouldn't force them to quit. Besides, it is easy for you, who's never smoked, to talk about quitting. I know, I used to smoke myself."

Renford brought the conversation back around to the required report and its importance. He pointed out that she had never complained to him before about the smell of Frank and Alice's office, and was now leaving him in the lurch. Darlene simply said, "I'm sorry, Charles, but if writing that report means going into that room—and it does—then I'm simply not going to do it." Then she got up and returned to her office, leaving Charles Renford trying to figure out what he was going to do.

Discussion Questions

1. Would Charles Renford be within his rights to discipline Darlene Lambert for insubordination? Should he order Frank and Alice to stop smoking in their office altogether, or is Darlene oversensitive? How would you handle this situation if you were Charles? Is it possible for employers to find some compromise between smokers and nonsmokers?

2. Do Frank and Alice have a right to smoke in their office if no one is there? Should companies make an effort to accommodate the needs of smokers? What policy on smoking would you recommend to Redwood Associates? If, as in this case, state law doesn't mandate it, are employers morally required to ban smoking altogether inside their facilities? What about smoking outside but on company grounds?

3. Most people these days believe that employees have a right to a smoke-free work area, but do they also have a right to a workplace free of the odor of old smoke—or of any other odors they

dislike? If so, does this right justify Darlene's refusal to do the report? Does it make a difference how important the report is, or how much her refusal inconveniences her employer?

4. Suppose that what bothers Darlene is not old smoke but the smell of Alice's perfume or Frank's body odor? How would this change the case?

5. In 1914 Thomas Edison had a policy of employing "no person who smoked cigarettes." Is such a policy discriminatory? Is it reasonable? Today some companies ban employees even from smoking in their cars in the company parking lot. Is this fair or reasonable?

CASE 8.5

Have Gun, Will Travel... to Work

Organizational theorists and employee advocates frequently emphasize the importance, from both a moral and a practical point of view, of companies' respecting the rights of their employees. Many employees spend long hours at work and remain tethered to the job by phone or computer even when they are off site; not just their careers but also their friendships, social identity, and emotional lives are tied up with their work. All the more reason, it seems, that companies should recognize and respect their moral, political, and legal rights. But enshrined in our Constitution is one right that frequently gets overlooked in discussions of the workplace: the right to bear arms.[85]

In 2002 Weyerhaeuser, the Seattle-based timber-products company, fired several employees at an Oklahoma plant who were discovered to have violated company policy by keeping guns in their vehicles. Their dismissal provoked a response from the National Rife Association (NRA) and other gun-rights advocates, which since then have been lobbying for legislation that would make it illegal for companies to bar employees from leaving guns in their cars in company parking lots. Although no state requires companies to allow workers to carry weapons into the workplace, four states have passed laws guaranteeing them the right to keep guns in their cars, and several other states are weighing whether to follow suit. Gun advocates argue that licensed gun owners should have access to their weapons in case they need them on the trek to and from work. If an employer can ban guns from workers' cars, "it would be a wrecking ball to the Second Amendment" of the U.S. Constitution, says Wayne LaPierre, executive vice president of the NRA.

Brian Siebel, a senior attorney at the Brady Center to Prevent Gun Violence, thinks otherwise. He sees these laws as "a systematic attempt to force guns into every nook and cranny in society and prohibit anyone, whether it's private employers or college campuses ... from barring guns from their premises." But that's not how UCLA law professor Eugene Volokh looks at it. "It's part of the general movement," he says, "to allow people to have guns for self-defense not only at home, but in public places where they're most likely needed." For his part, LaPierre of the NRA contends that the legal right of people to have guns for personal protection is largely nullified if employers can ban guns from the parking lot. "Saying you can protect yourself with a firearm when you get off work late at night," he argues, "is meaningless if you can't keep it in the trunk of your car when you're at work."

Interpreting the somewhat ambiguous language of the Second Amendment is not easy. It only says, "A well-regulated Militia, being necessary to the security of a free State, the right of the people to keep and bear Arms, shall not be infringed." All jurists agree, however, that the Second Amendment does not make all forms of gun control unconstitutional and that, like the rest of the Bill of Rights, it places restrictions only on what government, not private parties, may do.

In particular, the Second Amendment does not give gun owners a constitutionally protected right to carry their weapons onto somebody else's private property against the wishes of the owner. "If I said to somebody, 'You can't bring your gun into my house,' that person's rights would not be violated," explains Mark Tushnet, a Harvard law professor. For this reason, the American Bar Association sides with business owners and endorses "the traditional property rights of private employers and other private property owners to exclude" people with firearms. Steve Halverson, president of a Jacksonville, Florida, construction company agrees that business owners should be allowed to decide whether to allow weapons in their parking lots. "The larger issue is property rights," he says, "and whether you as a homeowner and I as a business owner ought to have the right to say what comes onto our property." However, Tennessee state senator Paul Stanley, a Republican sponsor of legislation requiring that guns be allowed in company parking lots, begs to differ. "I respect property and business rights," he says. "But I also think that some issues need to overshadow this ... We have a right to keep and bear arms." Other gun advocates think that the property-rights argument is a red herring. Corporations are not individuals, they argue, but artificial legal entities, whose "rights" are entirely at the discretion of the state. What's really going on, they think, is that some companies have an anti-gun political agenda.

Property rights, however, aren't the only thing that companies are concerned about. Business and other organizations have a widely acknowledged duty to keep their workplaces—and their employees—as safe as possible, and that means, many of them believe, keeping their campuses free of weapons. There are over five hundred workplace homicides per year; in addition, 1.5 million employees are assaulted at work, many of them by coworkers or former employees. Having guns anywhere in the vicinity, many employers worry, can only make volatile situations more deadly. "There's no need to allow guns [into] parking lots," says the Brady Center's Siebel. "The increased risks are obvious." Steve Halveson drives that point home, too. "I object to anyone telling me that we can't ... take steps necessary to protect our employees." For him it's no different from banning guns from his construction sites or requiring workers to wear hard hats. "The context is worker safety, and that's why it's important."

Discussion Questions

1. Assume that either the Second Amendment or state law gives you a legal right to keep a gun in your car. Do you also have a moral right to do this? Do you have a moral, not only a legal, right to own a gun? Do you have either a moral or a legal right to park a car with a loaded gun in a public parking lot regardless of what the lot's owner wants?

2. In your view, do employees have either a moral or a legal right to park cars with guns in them in the company parking lot? If so, what about the property rights and safety concerns of employers? If employees don't have this right, would it be good policy for companies to allow them to stow guns in their cars anyway? Do companies have good grounds for being concerned about weapons in their parking lots?

3. Do you agree with the NRA that if companies ban guns from their parking lots,

this restriction would take "a wrecking ball to the Second Amendment" or nullify the right of people to have weapons for self-defense? Explain why or why not. In your view, have gun advocates been guilty of politicizing this issue? Do you think state legislatures are right to get involved, or should the matter be left to companies and employees to settle?

4. Because the workplace is the company's private property, the company could choose, if it wished, to allow employees to bring guns not only into the parking lot but also into the workplace itself. Are there ever circumstances in which doing so might be reasonable? Or would the presence of guns automatically violate the rights of other employees to be guaranteed a safe working environment?

5. What would a libertarian say about this issue? What considerations would a utilitarian have to take into account? What conclusion might he or she draw?

6. If you were on a company's board of directors, what policy would you recommend regarding handguns, rifles, or other weapons in employees' cars? In making your recommendation, what factors would you take into account? Would it make a difference how large the company was, the nature of its workforce, or where it was located? If you support banning firearms from the parking lot, what steps, if any, do you think the company should take to enforce that policy?

7. Explain whether (and why) you agree or disagree with the following argument: "If employees have a right to keep guns in the parking lot, then they also have a right to bring them into workplace. After all, we're only talking about licensed, responsible owners, and the same rationale applies: An employee might need a weapon for self-protection. What if a lunatic starts shooting up the company?"

CHAPTER 9

The Workplace (2): Today's Challenges

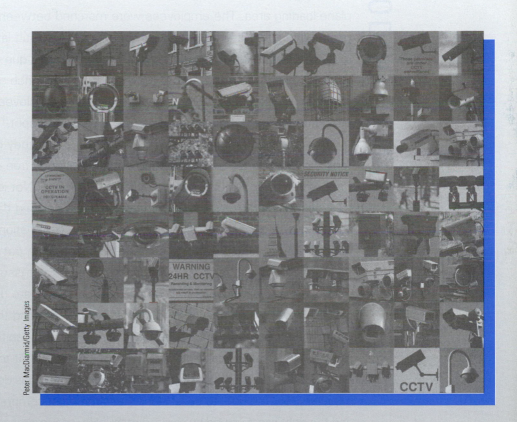

Peter MacDiarmid/Getty Images

Organizational Influence in Private Lives
The Importance of Privacy
Legitimate and Illegitimate Influence

Obtaining Information
Informed Consent
Polygraph Tests
Personality Tests

Monitoring Employees on the Job
Drug Testing

Working Conditions
Health and Safety
Management Styles
Day Care and Maternity Leave

INTRODUCTION

It was a routine business day for Eastern Airlines—until it received an anonymous tip that some of its baggage handlers at Miami International Airport were using drugs. Eastern quickly sprang into action, ordering security guards to round up the ten employees then at work in the airport's plane-loading area. The employees were marched between two rows of guards and into waiting vans—"like terrorists," a lawsuit later claimed—all in full view of other employees and passengers. After questioning the workers, suspicious supervisors put them on a bus, once again in front of onlookers, and took them to a hospital. There the employees were given an ultimatum: Either take a urine test or be fired on the spot.[1]

The baggage handlers were union members, but they caved in and took the test. All ten of them tested negative (that is, free of drugs), but they weren't happy about what they'd been through. Not long afterward, they filed suit against the airline in federal court, seeking damages of $30,000 each on charges of invasion of privacy, defamation, and intentional infliction of emotional distress. Eastern has since gone out of business, but the case represents in dramatic form one of the major issues dividing employers and employees today: privacy. Companies are delving further into employees' personal lives than ever before, claiming the need to monitor their behavior and probe into their health and habits. Workers are resisting ever more adamantly, fighting back for the right to be left alone.

In 1928, U.S. Supreme Court Justice Louis D. Brandeis described the right to privacy, or "the right to be let alone," as "the most comprehensive of rights and the right most valued by civilized men." He was referring to the Fourth Amendment's guarantee that citizens are protected against illegal searches and seizures by government. Today many Americans are resisting invasions of their privacy not just by government agencies or pesky telemarketers but also by intrusive employers. And not without reason: One survey shows that American companies tend to be less respectful of employees' rights to privacy than their counterparts are in Europe and Canada.[2]

It's not only ordinary employees, either, whose privacy companies sometimes fail to respect, as the world learned when the Hewlett-Packard boardroom exploded in controversy in 2006. Concerned about leaks of confidential company information to the *Wall Street Journal* from someone on H-P's board of directors, board chairwoman Patricia Dunn had authorized the company's legal and security personnel to investigate. They did, and at a meeting of the board a few months later, the culprit was disclosed. Board member Jay Keyworth admitted to the group that he was the leaker, but he refused to resign. However, his friend and fellow board member Tom Perkins, a Silicon Valley venture capitalist, was so outraged at H-P's snooping into the phone records of board members that he resigned on the spot and stormed out of the meeting. End of story? Not quite. Perkins managed to get the ear of California's attorney general and other law-enforcement agencies, which launched an investigation into the legality of H-P's spy tactics—in particular, its "pretexting" or use of false pretenses to obtain phone records and other personal information. This eventually led to a congressional hearing, recriminations and denial of responsibility by various H-P executives, and, finally, criminal charges against Dunn and several underlings.[3]

Businesses and other organizations frequently believe, as Eastern Airlines and Hewlett-Packard evidently did, that they have a compelling need to know about the personal lives and conduct of their employees, whether on or off the job—a need that they believe justifies invading their privacy. Employees, however, tend to think otherwise and are responding more and more frequently by firmly asserting their right to a personal sphere not subject to the needs, interests, or curiosity of their employers. "I don't think politicians and corporate executives realize how strongly Americans feel about it," says a San Francisco lawyer who specializes in employee lawsuits. "It's not a liberal or a conservative issue, and the fear of abuse doesn't emanate from personnel policies. It's coming out of the larger, impersonal notion that workers are fungible, expendable items."[4]

Chapter 8 examined personnel policies and procedures, trade unions, the state of civil liberties on the job, and the efforts of some successful companies to respect the rights, dignity, and moral integrity of their workers. This chapter also focuses on moral issues that emerge in the workplace. It looks in detail at one crucial civil liberty—the right to privacy—and at the ethical choices it poses inside the organization. The remainder of the chapter examines several other topics that are stirring up controversy in today's workplace. More specifically, this chapter explores the following:

1. The nature of privacy and the problems of organizational influence over private decisions

2. The moral issues raised by the use of polygraph and personality tests, employee monitoring, and drug testing in the workplace

3. Working conditions—in particular, health and safety, styles of management, and provision of day-care facilities and maternity leave

4. Job satisfaction and dissatisfaction and the prospects for enhancing the quality of work life

---

ORGANIZATIONAL INFLUENCE IN PRIVATE LIVES

Privacy is widely acknowledged to be a fundamental right, yet corporate behavior and policies often threaten privacy, especially in the case of employees. One way this happens is through the release of personal information about employees. The data banks and personnel files of business and nonbusiness organizations contain an immense amount of private information, the disclosure of which can seriously violate employees' rights. Most firms guard their files closely and restrict the type of material that they can contain in the first place, but the potential for abuse is still great. Although a complicated set of laws and court rulings limits access to such information, a wide range of snoops still manage, legitimately or illegitimately, to get their hands on it.

As a related matter, more employees are successfully suing their former bosses for passing on damaging information to prospective employers. The courts have traditionally considered this sort of information exchange between employers to be "privileged," but companies can lose this protection by giving information to too many people or by making false reports. Through fear of defamation suits, in fact, many organizations now refuse to reveal anything about former employees except their dates of employment. Such reticence obviously makes it more difficult for companies to screen job applicants.[5]

More significant are the threats to privacy that can arise on the job itself. For example, some bosses unhesitatingly rummage through the files of their workers, even when they are marked "private." Some companies routinely eavesdrop on their employees' phone calls, and a majority of them read their employees' e-mail and monitor their use of the Internet.[6] Voice mail isn't safe, either, as Michael Huttcut, a manager of a McDonald's outlet in St. Louis, learned the hard way. He was having an affair with a coworker, and the romantic voice-mail messages he sent her were retrieved and played by his boss. When Huttcut complained, he was fired.[7] Other companies secretly quiz managers—or even call in private investigators—to gain knowledge about the personal habits and behavior of workers who call in sick.[8] Meanwhile,

GPS technology lets companies track employees when they are in their company vehicles—often without their knowledge.[9]

Equally important is the way organizations attempt to influence behavior that ought properly to be left to the discretion of their employees—in particular, by trying to impose their own values on their workers. For example, Wal-Mart fired Lauren Allen, who was married but separated from her husband, for dating a coworker, who was single. Wal-Mart says that it "strongly believes in and supports the 'family unit'" and that the conduct of Allen and her coworker violated the company's rules.[10] Or consider the case of Virginia Rulon-Miller, a marketing manager in IBM's office products division. She made the mistake of falling in love. A week after receiving a 13.3 percent pay raise, she was called on the carpet for dating Matt Blum, a former IBM account manager who had gone to work for a competitor. She and Blum had begun dating when Blum was at IBM, and he still played on the IBM softball team. IBM told Rulon-Miller to give up Blum or be demoted. "I was so steeped in IBM culture," she says, "that I was going to break up with Matt." But the next day, before she had a chance to do anything, she was dismissed. Even though IBM's decision was based on written policy governing conflicts of interest, a California jury decided that Rulon-Miller's privacy had been invaded. It awarded her $300,000.

A year later, however, the Oregon Supreme Court upheld JCPenney's firing of a merchandising manager for dating another employee. He claimed that his right to privacy had been violated. Although it may seem harsh to fire an employee on the basis of personal lifestyle, the Oregon court said, private firms aren't barred from discriminating against workers for their choice of mates. And a federal district court permitted the firing of a New Mexico employee with an excellent work record because she was married to a worker at a competing supermarket.[11]

It's not only in affairs of the heart that companies sometimes intrude into the personal sphere of employees by imposing their values on them or telling them what to think or do in matters that bear little relation to their jobs. Some executives, for example, find themselves pressured to contribute cash to their company's political action committee.[12] Other corporations hit up their employees for partisan political contributions. By bundling these together as one gift, companies can circumvent the ban on corporate campaign giving. Or they lean on employees to take a particular political stance, as IBM did a few years back by urging its employees to work to defeat a health care bill then before Congress.[13]

The Importance of Privacy

Our concern for privacy has three aspects.

Both in the workplace and in general, our concern for privacy seems to have at least three dimensions to it. *First*, we want to control intimate or personal information about ourselves and not permit it to be freely available to everyone. We are concerned to restrict who has certain kinds of knowledge about us, the means by which they can acquire it, and those to whom they may disclose it. *Second*, we wish to keep certain thoughts, feelings, and behavior free from the scrutiny, monitoring, or observation of strangers. We don't want our private selves to be on public display. *Third*, we value being able to make certain personal decisions autonomously. We seek to preserve and protect a sphere in which we can choose to think and act for ourselves, free from the illegitimate influence of our employers and others.

There is, however, no consensus among philosophers or lawyers about how precisely to define the concept of privacy, how far the right to privacy extends, or how to balance a concern for privacy against other moral considerations. All of us would agree, nonetheless, that we have a clear right to keep private certain areas of our lives and that we need to have our privacy respected if we are to function as complete, self-governing agents.

Even when a genuine privacy right is identified, the strength of that right depends on circumstances—in particular, on competing rights and interests. Privacy is not an absolute value. Corporations and other organizations often have legitimate interests that may conflict with the privacy concerns of employees. Determining when organizational infringement on a person's private sphere is morally justifiable is, of course, precisely the question at issue.

The burden is on the organization to establish the legitimacy of encroaching on the personal sphere of the individual.

As a general rule, though, whenever an organization infringes on what would normally be considered the personal sphere of an individual, it bears the burden of establishing the legitimacy of that infringement. The fact that a firm thinks an action or policy is justifiable does not, of course, make it so. The firm must show both that it has some legitimate interest at stake and that the steps it is taking to protect that interest are reasonable and morally permissible. But what are the areas of legitimate organizational influence over the individual?

Legitimate and Illegitimate Influence

The work contract; the firm's responsibilities to owners, consumers, and society at large; and the purpose of the firm itself all support the proposition that the firm is legitimately interested in whatever significantly influences work performance. What constitutes a significant influence on work performance, however, eludes precise definition because the connection between an act or policy and the job is often fuzzy.

Summary 9.1
Individuals have a right to privacy, in particular a right to control certain information about themselves, to shelter aspects of their lives from public scrutiny, and to make personal decisions autonomously, free from illegitimate influence. Whenever an organization infringes on an individual's personal sphere, it must justify that infringement.

Take, for example, the area of dress and grooming. A roofing company has a legitimate interest in the type and quality of shoes its workers wear because footwear affects safety and job performance. And perhaps specialty-clothing stores such as Gap, Polo Ralph Lauren, and Abercrombie & Fitch have legitimate grounds for requiring their employees to dress in the store's latest styles. Enterprise Rent-A-Car also puts a high priority on employee grooming and appearance. It lays down thirty dress-code guidelines for female employees (no denim or skirts more than 2 inches above the knee) and twenty-six rules for male employees (no beards; dress shirts with coordinated ties). More debatable is the company's requiring employee Angela Garrett to remove the red tints from her hair because they weren't "appropriate" for her ethnic group (she's African American).[14] Likewise, it's questionable whether American Airlines was legitimately pursuing a genuine corporate interest when it forbade a black employee from wearing her hair in corn rows because the style seemed to clash with the company's corporate image. Or consider the ticket agent who was fired by another airline for refusing to wear makeup. Perhaps that was a legitimate demand in the name of good public relations, but maybe it was arbitrary and narrow-minded.[15]

An employer's concern with dress can interfere with an employee's personal choices in other ways. Consider the case of Margaret Hasselman, who worked as a lobby attendant in a New York City high rise. Wearing the new uniform provided by her employer—a poncho with large openings under the arms, dancer's underpants, and white pumps—she repeatedly ran into sexual harassment. She complained about the outfit to her boss, but to no avail. When she eventually refused to wear it, she was fired. Issues of morality, of course, differ from questions of legality. But it is interesting that when Hasselman filed suit, the court ruled that no employer has the right to force workers to wear revealing or sexually provocative clothing. In contrast, in a subsequent case the Equal Employment Opportunity Commission (EEOC) upheld an employer's firing of several female employees who refused to wear swimsuits as part of a swimsuit promotion. The EEOC agreed that the swimsuits were revealing but found no reason to expect that the women would encounter sexual harassment.[16]

The general proposition that a firm has a legitimate interest only in employee behavior that significantly influences work performance applies equally to **off-the-job conduct**. Bank of America probably fell afoul of this guideline when it fired Michael Thomasson, a legal secretary, for working as a gay stripper during his off-hours. After a coworker read a personal letter Thomasson had written on a company computer that mentioned his job as an exotic dancer, a group of bank employees, including several of Thomasson's supervisors, went to see him perform. Two weeks later he was dismissed—despite a record of positive job evaluations and a recent merit raise.[17]

Years ago, Henry Ford made his autoworkers' wages conditional on their good behavior outside the factory. He had 150 inspectors whose job it was to keep tabs on his employees' hygiene and housekeeping habits. And Milton Hershey, another famous business leader, used to tour Hershey, Pennsylvania, the chocolate-manufacturing town, to make sure his workers were keeping up their lawns, and he even hired private detectives to find out who was throwing trash in Hershey Park.[18] These days it's easy to say that Ford and Hershey crossed the line and were poking their noses into aspects of their employees' lives that had nothing to do with their work performance. In other cases, though, determining when off-the-job conduct bears on job performance can be difficult.

How would you decide the following case? In an off-the-job fight, a plant guard drew a gun on his antagonist. Although no one was injured, the guard's employer viewed the incident as grounds for dismissal. The employer reasoned that such an action indicated a lack of judgment by the guard. Do you think the employer had a right to fire the guard under those circumstances? The courts did. By contrast, consider the employee who sold a small amount of marijuana to an undercover agent, or the employee who made obscene phone calls to the teenage daughter of a client. Their employers fired them, but the employees were reinstated by an arbitrator or the court.

Then there's the amorphous area of company image and the question of whether it can be affected by off-the-job conduct. The political activities of a corporate executive, for example, could affect the image a firm wishes to project, whereas what an obscure worker on the firm's assembly line does politically might have little or no impact on the company's image. Companies and other organizations have an interest in protecting their good names. The off-duty conduct of employees might damage an organization's reputation, but in practice damage is often difficult to establish. For example, two IRS agents were suspended for mooning a group of women after leaving a bar. Would you agree with their suspension? An arbitrator didn't and revoked it. He couldn't see that their conduct damaged the IRS's reputation.[19]

Summary 9.2
A firm is legitimately interested in whatever significantly influences job performance but there is no precise definition of "significant." Organizations may be invading privacy when they interfere with employees' off-the-job-conduct or pressure them to contribute to charities, do volunteer work, or participate in wellness programs.

Obviously we can't spell out exactly when off-duty conduct affects company image in some material way, any more than we can say precisely what constitutes a significant influence on job performance. But that doesn't prevent us from being able to judge that in many cases organizations step beyond legitimate boundaries and interfere with what should properly be personal decisions by their employees. That interference can take many forms, but two are worth looking at more closely.

Involvement in Civic Activities

To enhance their image in the community, businesses and other organizations have long prodded employees to donate to charitable causes during company-led fund-raising drives, or encouraged them to participate in **civic activities** off the job—for example, by running for the local school board or joining community service organizations, such as Kiwanis, Lions, or Rotary. Moreover, since the 1990s there has been a boom in corporate-sponsored employee volunteer programs, with more and more firms encouraging employees to spend off-duty hours helping out at designated charities or donning a company T-shirt and pitching in on Saturdays at some company-run charitable project.[20]

There's no question that the trend toward corporate volunteer programs has been good for society. One in four adults does at least some volunteer work, and corporate programs have probably drawn many of them into doing so. But such programs can collide with accelerating job demands, forcing employees to spend valued off-duty time away from their families and fueling employee resentment and burnout. Moreover, such programs can raise moral questions, especially as the pressure to participate increases. Some employers have "unwritten rules" requiring volunteer work; other companies award employees points for approved volunteer work on their performance evaluations. Employees also have been downgraded, disciplined, or even fired for not contributing the "suggested" amount of money to the United Way or other charitable cause sponsored by the firm. The pressure can be real, too, when the boss solicits donations for his or her favorite charity or goes cubicle to cubicle with a sign-up sheet for Girl Scout cookies.[21]

Employee volunteer programs and other corporate-sponsored civic activities sometimes infringe on the right to privacy.

By striving too hard for a do-gooder image, a company can thus be guilty of attempting to influence the personal choices and off-the-job behavior of employees in ways that constitute an invasion of privacy. By explicitly or implicitly requiring employees to associate themselves with a particular activity, group, or cause, firms are telling workers what to believe, what values to support, and what goals to promote outside work.

Wellness Programs

Sometimes organizations pressure employees in certain directions for "their own good." For example, a group of employers led by Ford, PepsiCo, and

General Mills launched a campaign to get their overweight employees to slim down.[22] Consider also the aggressive **wellness programs** that some companies are mounting to push employees toward healthier lifestyles. These paternalistic programs are aimed at helping employees live longer and improve their health and productivity. The programs teach employees about nutrition, exercise, stress, and heart disease and encourage them to give up smoking, eat more healthfully, moderate their drinking, and work out in the company gym or join a company sports team after work.[23]

Wellness programs try to make fitness part of the corporate culture, and that goal seems innocent enough. But some companies are making employees pay more for their health care benefits if they are overweight, have high blood pressure, or don't exercise.[24] And employees have been fired for smoking or taking a drink at home[25] or for refusing to take a test to prove they're nonsmokers.[26] One organization offers employees a financial incentive for agreeing to undergo a comprehensive health assessment and working with a health coach who telephones periodically to check up on them and who may or may not report back to the boss. Critics charge that this is a kind of "privacy tax." Those with good salaries have enough money to pay it, but what about janitors or other low-wage workers? Can they afford to protect their privacy by refusing to participate?[27] "I think employers are going to get deeper and deeper into the wellness business," says Professor Alan F. Westin of Columbia University. "This is going to throw up a series of profound ethical and legal dilemmas about how they should do it and what we don't want them to do."[28]

OBTAINING INFORMATION

Summary 9.3
Companies often gather highly personal information about employees. The critical issue here is informed consent, which implies deliberation and free choice. Deliberation requires that employees be provided all significant facts concerning the information-gathering procedure and understand its consequences. Free choice entails that the decision to participate must be voluntary and uncoerced.

It's no secret that firms frequently seek, store, and communicate information about employees without their consent. A firm may bug employee lounges, hoping to discover who's responsible for pilfering. Another firm may use a managerial grapevine, with supervisors meeting once a month to exchange anecdotal material about employees, some of it obtained in confidence, all of it gathered with the hope of anticipating potential troublemakers. Still another company may keep detailed files on the personal lives of its employees to ensure compatibility with organizational image and reputation.

Of special interest here are two common practices organizations engage in: subjecting employees to various tests and monitoring employees on the job to discover sundry information. Before beginning the discussion, however, we need to look briefly at the concept of informed consent and how it connects with these topics.

Informed Consent

Certainly no employee is ever compelled to take a lie-detector, personality, or genetic screening test in the sense that someone puts a loaded revolver to the person's head and says, "Take the test or else." But compulsion, like freedom, comes in degrees. Although an employee may not be compelled to take a test in the same way that a prisoner of war, for example, is compelled to cooperate with a captor, enough coercion may be present to significantly diminish the worker's capacity to consent freely to privacy-invading procedures.

Obviously if workers submit to an honesty exam or to a test for genetic disorders, then they agree to do so. But was their consent valid and legitimate? Was it informed consent? That's the issue, and it is an altogether reasonable issue to raise, because information collected on workers is often intimately personal and private and, when used carelessly, can injure them.

The concept of informed consent implies deliberation and free choice.

Informed consent implies deliberation and free choice. Workers must understand what they are agreeing to, including its full ramifications, and must voluntarily choose it. Deliberation requires not only the availability of facts but also a full understanding of them. Workers must be allowed to deliberate on the basis of enough usable information, information that they can understand. But usable information is not of itself enough to guarantee informed consent. Free choice is also important—the *consent* part is as significant as the *informed* part of informed consent.

Everyone agrees that for consent to be legitimate, it must be voluntary. Workers must willingly agree to the privacy-invading procedure. They must also be in a position to act voluntarily. One big factor that affects the voluntariness of consent is the pressures, expressed and implied, exerted on employees to conform to organizational policy. Especially when those pressures to conform are reinforced with implicit reprisals, they can effectively undercut the voluntariness of consent. That is obvious in the case of job applicants asked to undergo some invasion of their privacy. They can either submit or look for work elsewhere.

Polygraph Tests

When an individual is disturbed by a question, certain detectable physiological changes occur. The person's heart may begin to race, blood pressure may rise, respiration may increase. The polygraph simultaneously records changes in these physiological processes and, thus, is often used in lie detection.

Businesses cite several reasons for using **polygraph tests**. *First*, the polygraph is a fast and economical way to verify information provided by a job applicant and to screen candidates for employment. So used, it can help reveal personal philosophy, behavioral patterns, and character traits incompatible with the organization's purpose, function, and image.

Second, the polygraph allows employers to identify dishonest employees or job candidates, at a time when many companies are suffering staggering annual losses through in-house theft. *Third*, companies argue that the use of polygraphs permits business to abolish audits and oppressive controls. They say the use of polygraphs actually increases workers' freedom.

The use of polygraphs rests on three doubtful assumptions.

Those who defend the use of polygraphs rely on three assumptions that are open to question.[29] The *first* assumption is that lying triggers an involuntary, distinctive response that truth telling does not. But this is not necessarily the case. What the polygraph can do is record that the respondent was more disturbed by one question than by another, but it cannot determine why the person was disturbed. Perhaps the question made the person feel guilty or angry or frightened, but deception does not necessarily lurk behind the emotional response.

Second, it is assumed that polygraphs are extraordinarily accurate. Lynn March, president of the American Polygraph Association, says that "when administered correctly by qualified operators, the tests are accurate more than 90 percent of the time."[30] But David T. Lykken, a psychiatry professor, claims that these boasts are not borne out by three scientifically credible studies of the accuracy of polygraphs used on actual criminal suspects. The accuracies obtained by qualified operators in these experiments were 63 percent, 39 percent, and 55 percent.[31] Whether the polygraph is accurate 90 percent of the time or less, the conclusion is the same: It cannot reveal with certainty whether a person is or is not telling the truth.

The *third* major assumption about polygraphs is that they cannot be beaten. Lykken, for one, suggests otherwise. The easiest way to beat the polygraph, the psychiatrist claims, is by augmenting your response to the control question by some form of covert self-stimulation, like biting your tongue. Not everybody believes this. Defenders of the polygraph contend that liars can't fool skilled operators of the machine. But even if the polygraph generally catches the guilty, it will also generate a disturbing number of **false positives**—that is, it will falsely identify as liars people who are telling the truth.

To see this, imagine that the polygraph is 95 percent accurate and suppose, for the sake of illustration, that at a large corporation with an in-house theft problem one out of every fifty employees is stealing from their employer. If the corporation has a thousand employees, then twenty will be crooks and 980 will be honest. If every employee is tested, then the test, being only 95 percent accurate, will identify nineteen of the twenty crooks; one will escape detection. But the test will identify as liars 5 percent of the company's 980 innocent employees; forty-nine people will be falsely accused. By firing all those who fail the polygraph, a company might succeed in weeding out the guilty, but it would also seriously harm many innocent employees.

In addition to these considerations, polygraphs infringe on privacy. As professor of politics Christopher Pyle says, they violate "the privacy of beliefs and associations, the freedom from unreasonable searches, the privilege against self-accusation, and the presumption of innocence."[32] That is not to say employers never have the right to abridge privacy or employees never have an obligation to reveal themselves. In important cases of in-house theft or corporate espionage, employers may be justified in using a polygraph as a last resort. But the threat to privacy remains.

The moral concerns embedded in the use of polygraphs suggest three points—in addition to the question of informed consent—to consider in evaluating their use in the workplace:

1. The information the organization seeks should be clearly and significantly related to the job. This caveat harks back to a determination of the legitimate areas of organizational influence over the individual.

2. Not only should the organization have job-related grounds for using the polygraph, but these must be compelling enough to justify violating the individual's privacy and psychic freedom. At the very least, the organization must have no viable alternative way of getting extremely important information or must have exhausted other legitimate means first.

3. Assuming the grounds for using the polygraph are sufficiently compelling, we must also be concerned about the sort of information being gathered,

who will have access to it, and how it will be disposed of. Normally, not only the results but also the fact that a person is being tested at all should be kept confidential. And it is always important to treat that person respectfully.

Responding to moral concerns about polygraphs as well as to their practical and statistical limitations, in 1988 Congress passed the **Employee Polygraph Protection Act.** It prohibits most private employers from using lie detectors in "preemployment testing." Private security firms are exempted from the law, along with drug companies, contractors with certain government agencies, and selected others. The law permits the use of polygraphs in "ongoing investigations of economic loss or injury," but it provides a number of procedural safeguards. For instance, the employer must explain the test's purpose to the employee and the reason why he or she was selected to take it. The worker also has a right to consult with someone who will explain the workings and limitations of the machine. Ultimately, the worker retains the option not to submit to the test, and no one can be fired on the basis of a lie-detector test "without other supporting evidence."

Scientists, however, are experimenting with new techniques for detecting honesty, such as magnetic-resonance imaging, "cognosensors," and electroencephalography (EEG), all of which look directly at brain activity to see who is lying and who is not.[33] Although these techniques are not yet foolproof, their proponents believe that they promise to prove far more accurate than the antiquated polygraph. Look for them soon at a workplace near you.

Personality Tests

Companies often wish to determine whether prospective employees are emotionally mature, get along well with others, and have a good work ethic, and, more generally, whether they would fit in with the organization, so they sometimes administer **personality tests.** One of the most popular of these tests, the Myers-Briggs Type Indicator, is used by eighty-nine of the *Fortune 100* companies and taken by over two-and-a-half million Americans every year.[34] Personality tests such as the Myers-Briggs can reveal highly personal information, and they often intrude into areas of our lives and thoughts that we normally consider private. Consent is usually less-than-fully voluntary because personality tests are generally part of a battery of tests that job applicants must take if they wish to be considered for a position.

Used properly, personality tests serve two purposes in the workplace. They help screen applicants for jobs by indicating areas of adequacy and inadequacy. And in theory they simplify the complexities of business life by reducing the amount of decision making involved in determining whether an individual has the personal characteristics appropriate for a given job. For example, if a firm knows that Wendy Constantine is an introvert, it would hardly place her in public relations.

But one key premise underlying such tests is questionable. That premise is that all individuals can usefully and validly be placed into a relatively small number of categories of personality types and character traits. In fact, test designers typically believe that one's overall personality is shaped by only five

Summary 9.4
Polygraph tests can infringe employee privacy. Moreover, their accuracy and underlying assumptions are open to question, and they can generate false positives. Their use in employment situations is now legally restricted.

The supposition that individuals fit into a small number of personality types is questionable.

factors and that these factors, which they seek to measure, account for "99 percent of the differences in human behavior."[35] However, people rarely represent pure personality types, such as the classic "introvert" or "extrovert." Nor is the possession of a character trait an all-or-nothing thing. Most of us possess a variety of personality traits in various degrees, and social circumstances often influence the characteristics we display and the talents we develop. When organizations attempt to categorize employees, they oversimplify both human nature and their employees' potential, and they force people into artificial arrangements that may do justice neither to employees nor to the firms they work for.

Personality tests also screen for organizational compatibility, sometimes functioning to eliminate prospective employees whose individuality or creativity may be exactly what the firm needs. Some companies, for example, seek employees who are extremely submissive to authority. Thus, when writer Barbara Ehrenreich submitted to a personality test for a job at Wal-Mart, she was reprimanded for getting the "wrong" answer when she agreed only "strongly" with the proposition "All rules have to be followed to the letter at all times." The correct answer was "totally agree."[36] When used this way, personality tests raise a pressing moral issue in the employer-employee relationship: conformity of the individual to organizational ideals. Organizations by nature represent a danger to individual freedom and independence. When personality tests are used to screen for conformity to organizational values, goals, and philosophy, they can catalyze this natural tendency into a full-blown assault.

Then, of course, there's the intrusive nature of the questions. Questions like "Does driving give you a sense of power?" "Do you like a lot of excitement in your life?" or "If you could, would you work as an entertainer in Las Vegas?" may seem innocuous, but what about a personality test that delves into your love life or that asks men, "Was there ever a time in your life when you liked to play with dolls?" One disgruntled test taker complains about "questions you wouldn't even answer for your own mother, if she asked you."[37] Worse, many of the tests asking these questions have little or no research to back them up or have not been validated for use in preemployment situations. Even those who favor testing admit as much. John Kamp, an industrial psychologist, points out that even intelligent businesspeople can be swayed by a good marketing pitch from companies that peddle invalid or unreliable tests. "That's the unfortunate thing," he says. "A person with a slick pitch and no real research behind their tests can have a good business."[38]

Monitoring Employees on the Job

Many major employers routinely monitor the performance of their employees through the computers and telephones they use. They check the number of keystrokes that word processors enter during the day and record or listen in on calls handled by customer service agents to ensure accuracy and efficiency. The Electronic Communications Privacy Act of 1986 restricts the government or unauthorized parties from eavesdropping on e-mail, fax transmissions, and cell phone conversations. The law applies to employers, but it allows exceptions when the consent of employees has been obtained, when the organization

Summary 9.5
Personality tests help businesses screen candidates and match individuals to appropriate jobs. But their use rests on some questionable psychological premises, and they can invade privacy and reinforce conformity.

owns or maintains the system, or when there is a legitimate business purpose for the surveillance. Workers don't necessarily resent this monitoring, if it is in the open. "I don't think people mind having their work checked," says Morton Bahr, president of the Communications Workers of America. "It's the secretiveness of it" that bothers employees.[39]

According to the American Management Association, three-quarters of employers record employees' voice mail, e-mail, or phone calls; review their computer files; or even videotape them—often without their knowledge.[40] In 2006 an Ohio firm took things a step further when it embedded RDIF (radio frequency identification) chips in the arms of two employees to help control access to secured areas—the first known case of a company's electronically tagging workers.[41] Tightening security and overseeing customer service are not the only reasons companies monitor their employees. Some companies, for example, check employees' computers to see whether they exceed the allotted time for lunch or work breaks; others listen in on phone conversations and examine e-mail messages to catch employees conducting personal business on company time.

"What are they going to think up to do to us next?" wonders one employee. "It's scary. I'll bet no one monitors the phones or e-mail of CEOs and other top executives."[42] Nancy Flynn, executive director of ePolicy Institute, agrees with that sentiment. "In a lot of organizations," she says, "the senior executives are immune from [electronic] monitoring."[43] If so, this raises a basic moral objection. As explained in Chapter 1 and again in Chapter 2's discussion of Kant, if we make a moral judgment, we must be willing to make the same judgment in any similar set of circumstances. These executives, however, are apparently willing to apply to others a policy that they are unwilling to see applied to themselves.

When in-house theft, sabotage, or other threatening conduct occurs, organizations frequently install monitoring devices—mirrors, cameras, and electronic recorders—to apprehend the employees who are responsible. But monitoring suspected trouble spots or private acts can create moral problems. Consider the two male employees of Boston Sheraton Hotel who were secretly videotaped changing clothes in the locker room during a hunt for a drug dealer. They weren't suspects, just bystanders.[44]

Notifying employees of workplace monitoring does not constitute consent.

Like personality and polygraph tests, **monitoring of employees** often gathers personal information about them without their informed consent. Organizations frequently confuse notification of such practices with employee consent, but notification does not constitute consent. When employee restrooms, dressing rooms, locker rooms, and other private places are bugged, an obvious and serious threat to privacy exists—posted notices notwithstanding. It's true that in some cases surveillance devices may be the only way to apprehend the guilty. Nevertheless, they often can do more harm than good by violating the privacy of the vast majority of innocent employees. Obviously, even more serious moral questions arise when monitoring devices are used not exclusively for the purposes intended but also for cajoling, harassing, or snooping on employees (sometimes with the goal of thwarting them from organizing unions[45]).

Drug Testing

Drug testing first became a live issue for some sports fans when the National Collegiate Athletic Association (NCAA) began banning college football players from postseason bowl competition based on the results of steroid testing. But political and legal battles over the drug testing of employees have raged for years. Many companies have warmly embraced testing. A study published in the *Journal of the American Medical Association* supports doing so. It showed that postal workers who tested positive for drug use in a preemployment urine test were at least 50 percent more likely to be fired, injured, disciplined, or absent than those who tested negative.[46] Although many companies remain skeptical of the benefits of testing, 67 percent of large corporations now test either current employees or job applicants for illegal substances.[47]

In principle, testing employees to determine whether they are using illegal drugs raises the same questions that other tests raise: Is there informed consent? How reliable are the tests? Is testing really pertinent to the job in question? Are the interests of the firm significant enough to justify encroaching on the privacy of the individual? But rather than reiterate these issues, all of which are important and relevant, this section limits itself to four additional remarks:

1. The issue of drug testing by corporations and other organizations arises in the broader context of the drug-abuse problem in America today (which includes the abuse not just of illegal street drugs but of alcohol and prescription medicines as well). To discuss this problem intelligently, one needs good information, reliable statistics, and sociological insight, yet these are difficult to come by. Popular newsmagazines run frequent and alarming cover stories on drugs, and hours of television news are given over to sensationalistic drug-related stories. Likewise, many politicians find it advantageous to portray themselves as battling courageously against a rising flood of drugs. Yet most of this media coverage and political hoopla is at best superficial, at worst misleading and even hysterical. This is not to minimize the problems that alcohol and drug abuse can pose for businesses and other oganizations. Such problems are real and serious even though the use of illegal drugs, at least, appears to have dropped significantly among workers since the mid-1980s. Rather, the point is that excessive media attention and political posturing can create a false sense of crisis, leading people perhaps to advocate extreme or unnecessary measures.

2. Drugs differ, so one must carefully consider both what drugs one is testing for and why. Steroids, for instance, are a problem for the NCAA but not for IBM. And it is difficult to believe that Ford Meter Box was warranted in urine testing employees for nicotine in order to root out smokers.[48] To be defensible, drug testing must be pertinent to employee performance and there must be a lot at stake. Testing airline pilots for alcohol consumption is one thing; testing the baggage handlers is something else. To go on a fishing trip in search of possible employee drug abuse, when there is no evidence of a problem or of significant danger, seems unreasonable.

Summary 9.6
Monitoring employees may be necessary, but it can be abused and violate privacy. The same is true of drug testing, which also raises questions of test reliability and job relevance. Companies must consider whether drug testing is really necessary and, if so, design such programs to respect the rights and dignity of employees as much as possible. They must also determine how to respond appropriately to individuals who fail the test.

3. Drug abuse by an individual is a serious problem, generally calling for medical and psychological assistance rather than punitive action. The moral assessment of any program of drug testing must rest in part on the potential consequences for those taking the test: Will they face immediate dismissal and potential criminal proceedings, or therapy and a chance to retain their positions? To put the issue another way, when an organization initiates a testing program, does it approach this as a kind of police function? Or is it responsive to the needs and problems of individual employees? Some business writers argue that voluntary, nonpunitive drug-assistance programs are far more cost-effective for companies, in any case, than testing initiatives.[49]

4. Any drug-testing program, assuming it is warranted, must be careful to respect the dignity and rights of the persons to be tested. Some alternatives to body-fluid testing are less invasive of employee privacy. Due process must also be followed, including advance notification of testing as well as procedures for retesting and appealing test results. All possible steps should be taken to ensure individual privacy.

WORKING CONDITIONS

In a broad sense, the conditions under which people work include personnel policies and procedures, as well as the extent to which an organization is committed to respecting the rights and privacy of its employees. This section, however, examines three other aspects of working conditions: health and safety on the job, styles of management, and the organization's maternity and day-care arrangements.

Health and Safety

In 2008 an explosion at a sugar refinery in Savannah, Georgia, killed six workers and injured forty-two others. This occurred not long after five workers perished from smoke inhalation caused by a fire in a hydroelectric plant in Georgetown, Colorado. About two months before that, six mine workers died when a Utah mine collapsed (a subsequent cave-in also killed three rescuers searching for trapped miners). These dramatic episodes gained newspaper and television coverage across the country. By contrast, the national media ignored altogether the deaths of twenty-one-year-old Dennis Claypool and eighteen-year-old Mark DeMoss, who suffocated working inside a tanker trailer at a trucking company outside Chicago. The two didn't know that the tanker had recently been cleaned with nitrogen, which removes oxygen from the air. A freak accident? Experts say some three hundred workers a year die in such "confined space" incidents.[50]

The scope of occupational hazards remains awesome and generally unrecognized. According to the U.S. Census Bureau, in a given year about five thousand workers are killed on the job.[51] The director of the Occupational Safety and Health Administration (OSHA) puts the figure higher. He says an average of thirty-two workers are killed on the job each day of the year in the United States.[52] Deaths are just part of the problem. Census Bureau statistics reveal that although the rate of industrial injury has been declining since 1960, the absolute number of workers disabled at work every year—approximately 3.7 million men and women—is greater than ever.[53] Job-related injuries and illnesses cost the nation $65 billion a year—$171 billion when indirect costs such as lost wages are included.[54] Researchers believe, however, that government statistics undercount workplace injuries and illnesses.[55] And when we take into account health problems that stem not from specific, identifiable events on the job but rather from years of labor or from long-term exposure to hazardous substances, then the problem escapes reliable measurement.

Employers clearly have a moral obligation not to expose workers to needless risks or to negligently or recklessly endanger their lives or health. In the case of a drilling company that lowered a twenty-three-year-old worker to the bottom of a 33-foot-deep, 18-inch-wide hole, where he then suffocated, a Los Angeles county prosecutor put it this way: "Our opinion is you can't risk somebody's life to save a few bucks. That's the bottom line."[56] Issues of legal liability aside, however, employers are not morally responsible for all workplace accidents. Sometimes coworkers are negligent or act irresponsibly, and sometimes the victims themselves may have behaved stupidly or failed to exercise due care. Sometimes, as people often say, accidents "just happen." Moreover, nothing in life is free of risk, and we often judge the risk worth taking (for example, when we choose to drive a car). And in some circumstances or in certain occupations, an injured worker can reasonably be said to have voluntarily assumed the risk. Although there is some truth in all these points, they are somewhat misleading about the nature of accidents.

To begin with **assumption of risk**, the proposition that Dennis Claypool, Mark DeMoss, or the young Los Angeles man who died at the bottom of the shaft can be inferred to have freely and knowingly decided to gamble with their lives is dubious, to say the least. Voluntary assumption of risk presupposes informed consent. As we have seen, that would require the worker to have been fully informed of the danger and to have freely chosen to assume it, which is rarely true of workers who are just doing what the boss tells them to do. Informed consent entails that employees have a moral right to refuse work when it exposes them to imminent danger and that employers are wrong to reprimand or otherwise retaliate against them for doing so. The U.S. Supreme Court has acknowledged the **right to refuse dangerous work** to be a legal right, too. In a crucial workplace decision, it ruled in favor of two employees of Whirlpool Corporation who had refused to follow their foreman's order to undertake activities they considered unsafe.[57] Of course, what constitutes an "imminent" danger may sometimes be open to debate, and workers should always behave reasonably and, when trying to avoid a perceived danger, take the least disruptive course of action open to them.

Employers, for their part, should inform workers of any life-threatening hazards, and, indeed, a number of states make that a legal requirement. Still, employees are often unaware of the dangers they face, many of which may be long-term, rather than imminent, hazards. Take the electronics industry, for example. It may look safe in comparison with other occupations, but behind its clean, high-tech image lurk health hazards for workers—in particular, the

Voluntary assumption of risk presupposes informed consent. Employees have a right to refuse dangerous work.

Summary 9.7
Employers have a moral obligation not to expose workers to needless risk, and employees have a right to know about and refuse hazardous work. Although industrial accidents sometimes seem to result from employee recklessness or to "just happen," experts believe that they are caused by factors that are under the control of the company.

chemical toxins that are indispensable to the manufacture of computer chips. One workplace toxin causing concern recently is beryllium, a miracle metal—one-third the weight of aluminum yet six times stiffer than steel—which is used in a number of products these days, including computers, cell phones, and golf clubs. More toxic than plutonium, a few millionths of a gram of beryllium can trigger an immune system attack and fatally damage the lungs and other organs. Current legal standards suffice to keep workers handling the stuff from dying after a few days or weeks on the job, but they don't adequately protect them from developing chronic beryllium disease, a risk they may be unaware of.[58]

Putting aside assumption of risk and the right to know about and refuse hazardous work, we turn now to the causes of workplace accidents. As previously stated, it seems that accidents often result not from direct employer malfeasance but rather from employee blunders, coworker negligence, or just plain bad luck with nobody at fault. According to safety experts, though, this way of thinking is inaccurate. Industrial accidents don't just happen. They are caused—by inadequate worker training, sloppy procedures, lack of understanding of the job, improper tools and equipment, hazardous work environments, poor equipment maintenance, and overly tight scheduling.[59] And these are all matters that fall within the purview of the employer. For example, when a worker falls to his death from the tenth floor of a construction site because he wasn't wearing the required safety harness, the accident almost certainly has causes that go beyond poor judgment on his part.[60] Or consider the case of Michael Rodriguez. When some heavy machinery crushed his ankle, he was unable to leave his workplace and get to the hospital for several hours. That's because, until unfavorable publicity forced a policy change, Wal-Mart would lock its employees in at night, and there was no one on duty with a key.[61]

Accidents don't just happen. They result from poor job practices and workplace environments that fail to prioritize safety.

Workplace injuries, most experts believe, are related not to shortcomings in technology but to unsafe human behavior resulting from poor job practices, bad management, and a workplace environment that fails to put safety first. The key to a safer workplace, says risk-management consultant Beth Rogers, is not engineering but changing the company's "hidden culture"—the "unspoken rules that are adhered to"—to a culture that is proactively oriented toward safety.[62] As evidence for what Rogers is saying, consider the cases mentioned at the beginning of this section. The sugar refinery that exploded in Savannah had experienced a blast the year before; the owner of the Utah mine had a history of run-ins with safety officials; and the men who died in Colorado were working for a contractor who had been fined for safety problems ninety times in the preceding twenty years.[63]

OSHA

With the 1970 Occupational Safety and Health Act, the prime responsibility for regulating working conditions passed from the states to the federal government. The thrust of the act is "to ensure so far as possible every working man and woman in the nation safe and healthful working conditions," and it places a duty on employers to provide a workplace "free from recognized hazards that are causing or are likely to cause death or serious injury." In its early years, the **Occupational Safety and Health Administration (OSHA)**, created by the act, added to its own troubles by promulgating some rules that seemed trivial and nitpicking—for example, detailed guidelines regulating toilet seats and the belts to be worn by telephone line workers.[64] Fortunately, most of those rules have been repealed, but controversies have raged over how far OSHA should go in the cause of safety. The organization seeks to require only safeguards that are feasible. It has, for example, never attempted to entirely eliminate toxins in the workplace. But is "feasibility" to be understood in a broad economic and technological sense, or must the gains in safety outweigh the costs that particular companies must bear? And how are those costs and gains to be measured? Sometimes, even when union and industry representatives have agreed on new safety measures, politicians have prevented OSHA from introducing them because of ideological opposition to regulation.[65]

With limited resources and only a few thousand inspectors to monitor millions of workplaces, OSHA has always faced a daunting task, and its performance has been spotty. Worse, the relationship between OSHA and the businesses and industries it regulates has often been too cozy. Consider the case of Stephen Golab, a fifty-nine-year-old immigrant from Poland who worked for a year stirring tanks of sodium cyanide at the Film Recovery Services plant in Elk Grove, Illinois. One day he became dizzy from the cyanide fumes, went into convulsions, and died. OSHA then inspected the plant and fined Film Recovery Services $4,855 for twenty safety violations. OSHA subsequently cut the fine in half. In contrast, the state attorney general for Cook County filed criminal charges. Three company officials were convicted of murder and fourteen counts of reckless conduct. The company itself was also found guilty of manslaughter and reckless conduct and fined $24,000.[66]

Since the Golab case, budget cuts have shrunk OSHA's staff further, and inspections and citations have dropped. For example, an examination of 1,242 cases in which the agency itself concluded that workers had died because of their employer's "willful" safety violations revealed that in 93 percent of those cases OSHA declined to prosecute. At least seventy of those employers willfully violated safety laws again, resulting in more deaths. Yet even those repeat offenders were rarely prosecuted.[67] Why the leniency? "A simple lack of guts and political will," says John T. Phillips, a former regional OSHA administrator.[68] Congress, however, is at least partly responsible. It has pushed the agency from rule making and enforcement to helping businesses comply with federal requirements. As a result, critics call OSHA a "toothless tiger" that has moved from "beat cop to social worker."[69]

New Health Challenges

One problem that both OSHA and business will have to address in the future is the epidemic of occupational injury and illness known as **musculoskeletal disorders**. In offices and factories across the country, millions of workers suffer from aching backs, crippled fingers, sore wrists, and other problems caused or aggravated by their jobs. Carpal tunnel syndrome, low back pain, sciatica, tendinitis, and other musculoskeletal disorders account for one-third of all serious workplace injuries and cause more than 640,000 workers a year to miss time on the job.[70]

Numb fingers, swollen knuckles, and aching wrists from the constant repetition of awkward hand and arm movements may sound like minor complaints, but they are anything but trivial to the many employees who suffer from them. Ask Janie Jue of San Francisco. For seventeen years she keyed in up to forty-eight thousand strokes a day on an automatic letter-sorting machine for the post office. Today, even picking up a book or a coffee pot sends bolts of pain tearing up her hand and arm. "I wish I could work," she says, "but it hurts from my elbow to my fingertips."[71] "For many years," remarks one expert, "it was just considered a cost of doing business. If you did certain jobs, you would end up with hands crippled at the end of your career. That's not acceptable in this country any more."[72]

The breaking up of jobs into smaller and smaller units, so that each worker performs fewer tasks but repeats them thousands of times a day, has contributed to the problem in manufacturing industries. However, musculoskeletal disorders are also rampant among white-collar office workers, especially those who spend all day at a computer. The redesign of jobs, adjustable chairs, training in the proper use of computer terminals, and other preventive measures can often reduce the problem. In the meantime, it is not only the employees who are suffering. Musculoskeletal disorders decrease productivity and dampen morale, and having a skilled worker go out on long-term disability and vocational rehabilitation can cost a company a small fortune. Nevertheless, various employer groups and business lobbies continue to fight vigorously any step toward ergonomic regulation, even thwarting a thirteen-year effort by the National Safety Council to draft voluntary guidelines for preventing repetitive-motion injuries.[73]

An aspect of work life over which OSHA exercises little direct control is the shifts people work. Yet a team of scientists from Harvard and Stanford universities believes that the health and productivity of 25 million Americans whose work hours change regularly could be measurably improved if employers scheduled shift changes to conform with the body's natural and adjustable sleep cycles. This is particularly important given that sleep deprivation and fatigue are prime causes of industrial accidents.[74] According to one expert, they cost Americans $100 billion a year in lost production, illnesses, absences, accidents, and death.[75]

Related to fatigue is an aspect of work we have only recently begun to appreciate fully—the health implications of **job stress**. More than 30 percent of American workers say they are "always" or "often" under stress at work, and a majority of them report increased workloads that leave them "overtired and overwhelmed."[76] One reason is that they put in over 1,800 hours on the job a year; that's 350 more hours, for instance, than their German counterparts do. In addition, four out of ten employees now work "mostly at nonstandard times," according to Harriet Prosser of the University of Maryland. They juggle rotating shifts and work evenings, nights, and weekends to meet the demands of global supply chains and customers in every time zone. Furthermore,

Summary 9.8
The scope of occupational hazards, including musculoskeletal disorders, shift work, fatigue, and stress, and the number of employees harmed by work-related injuries and illness, are greater than many people think. OSHA's enforcement of existing regulations has too often been lax.

technology leashes many employees to the job even when they're at home. As a result, says Donald I. Tepas, a professor of industrial psychology, "the distinction between work and nonwork time is getting fuzzier all the time."

The relation between workplace stress and ill health is now well established. In fact, scientists have even ascertained that stressful job conditions diminish mental health and damage physical functioning as much as smoking does.[77] Workers who report being stressed incur health care costs 46 percent higher than do other employees. It's not surprising, therefore, that workplace stress costs the nation more than $300 billion each year in health costs and missed work. Revamping working environments that produce stress and helping employees learn to cope with it are among the major health challenges facing American business now and in the years to come.

Management Styles

Nothing affects work environment more than the style and quality of management.

How managers conduct themselves on the job—**management styles**—can do more to enhance or diminish the work environment than any other facet of employer-employee relations. Indeed, a poor relationship with their immediate supervisor is the most common reason people give for leaving a job; office politics comes second.[78] "Management creates the conditions in which most adults spend half their waking lives," writes Thomas A. Stewart, editor of *Harvard Business Review*. "Bad management makes lives miserable."[79] In survey after survey, employees rank honest communication, personal recognition, and respectful treatment as more important than good pay. Unfortunately, according to a Columbia University psychologist, millions of workers suffer from bosses who are abusive, dictatorial, devious, dishonest, manipulative, and inhumane.[80]

This workplace reality runs contrary to the teachings of almost all management theorists. For example, in his classic work *The Human Side of Enterprise*, Douglas McGregor described two styles of management, which he called "Theory X" and "Theory Y." Theory X managers believe that workers dislike work and will do everything they can to avoid it.[81] These managers insist that the average person wishes to avoid responsibility, lacks ambition, and values security over everything else. Accordingly, they believe they must coerce and bully workers into conformity with organizational objectives. In contrast, McGregor advocated a Theory Y management style. Theory Y managers assume that employees basically like work and view it as something natural and potentially enjoyable. They believe that workers are motivated as much by pride and a desire for self-fulfillment as by money and job security, and that workers don't dodge responsibility but accept it and even seek it out.

Since the publication of McGregor's book, other management writers have pursued this line of thought and described other management styles—including Theory Z, which touts Japanese-style respect for workers. More recently, some theorists have advocated a management style that eschews a masculine, hierarchical, aggressive, analytic, winner-take-all approach in favor of a more personal, empathetic, and collaborative style, thought to be characteristic of, and more congenial to, women.

Summary 9.9
Management style greatly affects the work environment. Managers who operate with rigid assumptions about human nature or who devote themselves to infighting and political maneuvering damage employees' interests.

This is not the place to discuss different theories of management, but clearly the management styles recommended by different writers, as well as the management styles actually adopted by different bosses, rest on implicit or explicit assumptions about human nature. However, no set of assumptions about human nature is absolutely correct or incorrect, nor is there one perfectly right way to manage. But that's precisely the point. Problems inevitably arise when managers routinize their leadership style, regardless of the needs, abilities, and predilections of their particular employees. When managers ignore individual differences, they risk creating a work atmosphere that's distressing to workers and less productive than it might be. Moreover, implicit assumptions about human nature can easily become self-reinforcing because people tend to behave as they are treated. Thus, managers who treat employees as if they were incapable of taking initiative will probably end up with employees who don't take initiative. As a result managers must carefully examine their preconceptions when determining the most appropriate leadership style to adopt in their workplace. That is easier said than done for many successful managers. "With the success they've achieved," says Michael Feiner of the Columbia Business School, "bosses can come to believe that their way is the right way, the best way—perhaps the only way."[82]

A different problem of management style, which also has moral overtones, stems from the bureaucratic character of many American corporations. The United States has more managers per employee than any other industrial nation,[83] and they make up a bigger share of the workforce than ever before.[84] Corporate bureaucracies often create an environment in which managers and other executive must pay excessive attention to hierarchy—often hoarding information and keeping subordinates in the dark—and in which they are tempted to put personal ambition ahead of other things and spend their energy trying to move up the company ladder. "Corporate infighting," "management power struggles," "maneuvering and politics and power grabbing" and "Machiavellian intrigues" are the phrases one business observer, H. Ross Perot, uses to describe the reality of corporate life today.[85]

Day Care and Maternity Leave

One area often overlooked in discussions of working conditions is the provision of maternity/paternity leave and child-care services for workers with children. The need for both is steadily growing as more and more women enter the paid labor force. Women's participation in the labor force has nearly doubled since 1960; today they constitute nearly half of it. In 1960 only 18.6 percent of married women with children under the age of six were in the paid labor force; today over 60 percent are.[86] Despite these statistics, the United States lags behind many industrialized nations in the provision of child care.[87] Those countries, unlike the United States, view child care as a national responsibility and publicly subsidize it. The situation is even more striking with respect to maternity leave. Only California and Washington require *paid* **maternity leave**, and fewer U.S. companies (about 16 percent) offer it than in 1998.[88] By contrast, 160 countries around the world guarantee women paid maternity leave, and 139 countries require paid sick leave, with

117 of them ensuring at least one week.[89] The United States, however, guarantees only *unpaid* time off for pregnancy or for personal or family illness (and then only if you work for a company with more than fifty employees). Even so, corporate America has recently been campaigning to tighten the rules for unpaid medical absences.[90]

Given that women in our society continue to bear the primary responsibility for child rearing, their increasing participation in the paid workforce represents a growing demand for reasonable maternity-leave policies and affordable child-care services. Nor is that demand likely to diminish. Many families are unable to make satisfactory child-care arrangements, either because the services are unavailable or because the parents cannot afford them. An estimated 5 million children are thus left alone without any supervision while their parents work. The need for child-care services is particularly acute among single-parent families, 91 percent of which are headed by women. Single mothers have a higher rate of participation in the labor force than do married mothers. Nevertheless, many of them are too poor to pay for satisfactory child-care services.

Business and Child Care

Some companies try hard to help with employee child care.[91] Campbell Soup Co., for example, offers on-site **day care**, spending over $200,000 annually to subsidize 50 percent of tuition costs at the child-care center for the children of employees at corporate headquarters. Procter & Gamble holds priority rights for 75 percent of the spaces in two off-site centers near its Cincinnati headquarters. It also provides a day-care resource and referral service for the entire community. IBM provides a free nationwide referral system for its 267,000 employees and has helped develop child-care services where they have been deficient or lacking. Polaroid Corporation provides assistance with child-care costs for permanent employees earning less than $30,000. Because its employees work at all hours, America West Airlines provides 24-hour child care with a sliding-scale subsidy to make it affordable. Goldman, Sachs, and Company, Time Warner, and Chase Manhattan Bank opened child-care centers for employees whose regular child-care arrangements are temporarily disrupted. Unfortunately, these encouraging examples contrast with an overall corporate record on child care that is, to put it mildly, not very impressive.

Employers are in a good position to assist in the provision of child-care services, and the need for it is there, given the paucity of government funding. However, only 4 to 6 percent of employers offer on-site child-care services,[92] primarily because initiating and maintaining such programs cost money. Yet viewed from a broader perspective, day-care arrangements set up by companies themselves or by several companies together in the same area are socially cost-effective. With in-house day-care arrangements, parents need not make special trips to pick up and drop off their children. Because the parents are not far away, they can have more interaction with their children. Depending on the specific organization of work and the firm's flexibility, parents could share in the actual running of the child-care facility at assigned intervals during the course of their working day. Hewlett-Packard took an innovative step in this regard when, in conjunction with the local school district, it set up kindergarten and first-grade classes on company grounds for the children of employees. Some other companies now do the same thing.[93]

Some business writers argue that offering child care as a fringe benefit and dealing as flexibly as possible with employees' family needs can prove advantageous for most employers. Such policies can be cost-effective in the narrower sense by decreasing absenteeism, boosting morale and loyalty to the firm, enhancing productivity, and attracting new recruits. A growing body of empirical research demonstrates the bottom-line benefits for companies that promote their employees' well-being and engage their hearts and minds with family-friendly policies.[94] This is an important consideration.

Three Moral Concerns

Even more important are the underlying moral issues. *First*, women have a right to compete on an equal terrain with men. The legal requirement that large firms provide at least unpaid maternity leave and reinstatement respects that right. Whether companies should also provide paid maternity leave is more controversial, although one might argue that paid leave is necessary to give substance to that right. Or one might defend such a policy on the utilitarian ground that it would enhance total social welfare. As mentioned, many organizations find it in their interest to provide paid leave and flexible work arrangements so they can attract better and more-talented employees, and some are working hard at luring stay-at-home moms back to work.[95] On the other hand, the trend toward tough performance standards and no-fault absence policies can penalize workers for missing work regardless of the reason. That happened to Tanya Frazier, office manager for a payroll company in Burbank, California. After receiving a call from her daughter's elementary school telling her to pick up her flu-stricken nine-year-old, she stayed home from work for a day—and was fired because of it. She claims she had missed work only a handful of days that year, but her boss says he was tired of her taking so much time off.[96] Even when employees aren't sacked, their performance appraisal, year-end raise, or bonus can be affected by their taking a legally protected, unpaid family leave.[97]

Second, from various ethical perspectives, the development of our potential capacities is a moral ideal—perhaps even a human right. For that reason, or from the point of view of promoting human well-being, many theorists would contend that women should not be forced to choose between childbearing and the successful pursuit of their careers. Nor should they be forced to reduce the quality of their commitment either to their children or to their careers. If employment circumstances force them to do so, and if those circumstances could reasonably be changed, then we have not lived up to the ideal of treating those women as persons whose goals are worthy of respect.

Third, although the past two or so decades have seen many criticisms of, and attempts to move beyond, the traditional male-female division of labor within the family, there can be little doubt that the world of work tends to reproduce those patterns. For instance, as mentioned in Chapter 8, men who leave work to help raise children often face enormous hurdles when returning to the job market. It seems clear that many fathers today feel hampered by work arrangements that pit meaningful career advancement against a fully developed family life.[98] Enhanced opportunities for part-time employment and job sharing, along with generous parental-leave arrangements and flexible, affordable, and accessible firm-sponsored child-care facilities, could enable both fathers and mothers to achieve a more personally desirable balance between paid work and family relations.

The moral value here is not to promote any single vision of the good life but rather to permit individuals, couples, and families as much autonomy as possible, given other social goals. They should be able to define the good life for themselves and to seek the arrangement of work and personal relations that makes that life possible. Firm-affiliated child-care services and other institutional arrangements that accommodate parental needs can clearly play a key role in the overall redesigning of work to enhance workers' well-being.

REDESIGNING WORK

Business must confront the fact of widespread job dissatisfaction and consider ways of improving the quality of work life.

Chapter 4 looked at alienation under capitalism and changing attitudes toward work in America. It remains true that many, perhaps even most, employees are dissatisfied with their jobs to some extent. Any investigation of the moral issues arising around the workplace and any discussion of the challenges facing business today must confront this basic problem and consider ways of improving the quality of work life.

Dissatisfaction on the Job

In the early 1970s the federal government conducted a major study of work in America, the basic findings of which remain relevant.[99] The *Work in America* report identified three chief sources of worker dissatisfaction. The first was industry's preoccupation with quantity, not quality; the rigidity of rules and regulations; and the fracturing of work into the smallest possible tasks, together with the monotonous repetition of those tasks. The second source of dissatisfaction was the lack of opportunities to be one's own boss. The third source of dissatisfaction was "bigness": More people work for large corporations now than ever before. Studies since the 1970s have cited workers' feelings of powerlessness, meaninglessness, isolation, and self-estrangement or depersonalization.

The *Work in America* survey reported similar feelings in the managerial ranks. One out of three middle managers at that time was willing to join a union. Moreover, just as industrial workers voiced general complaints about work, so did middle managers. Some resented having so little influence in their organizations; others objected to the organization's goals, policies, and ways of operating. Still other managers complained about the tension, frustration, and infighting that intraorganizational competition can breed. Beyond these complaints, the *Work in America* survey reported that many managers felt like cogs in a machine, like parts that could and would be replaced when a better part came along.

Other studies confirm that workers at all occupational levels express dissatisfaction with employer policies and practices and with the behavior of top management.[100] According to the Conference Board, a business policy organization, only half of American workers are satisfied with their jobs, down from 60 percent in 1995. Only 14 percent said they were "very satisfied," and one-quarter admitted they were simply "showing up to collect a paycheck."[101] Gallup pollster Curt Coffman thinks the situation is even worse. His polls show that 71 percent of all employees are "disengaged"—essentially clock-watchers who can't wait to get home.[102] Whatever the statistics, if industry is to improve productivity, enhance customer satisfaction, and be more competitive, it must seriously confront these attitudes and the sources of employee dissatisfaction. It must devise ways to make work more satisfying and to improve the quality of work life.

Factors Affecting Job Satisfaction

As early as the 1920s, researchers began to realize that workers would be more productive if management met those needs that money cannot buy. Managers at the Hawthorne factory of Western Electric Company were conducting experiments to determine the effect of the work environment on worker productivity. In the literature of work motivation, these studies have become known as the Hawthorne studies. What they discovered has been termed the **Hawthorne effect**.

Researchers at the Hawthorne plant chose a few employees to work in an experimental area, apart from the thousands of employees in the rest of the factory. Every effort was made to improve working conditions, from painting walls a cheerful color to making lights brighter. Worker productivity increased with each improvement. Then the experimenters decided to reverse the process. For example, lights were made dimmer. To everyone's surprise, productivity continued to increase.

Workers respond well to attention and recognition.

The conclusion the researchers drew was that workers were producing more because they were receiving attention. Instead of feeling that they were spokes in an organizational wheel, they felt important and recognized. The attention had the effect of heightening their sense of personal identity and feeling of control over their work environment. Recognition of this effect can help management increase worker motivation and job satisfaction and also increase the organization's productivity.

Subsequent research corroborates and deepens the Hawthorne results.[103] In studying the problem of poor worker motivation, the influential management theorist Frederick Herzberg discovered that factors producing **job satisfaction** differed from those producing job dissatisfaction. Herzberg found that although job dissatisfaction frequently arises from extrinsic problems (such as pay, supervision, working conditions, and leadership styles), resolving those extrinsic problems does not necessarily produce satisfied workers. The reason, Herzberg contends, is that worker satisfaction depends on such intrinsic factors as a sense of accomplishment, responsibility, recognition, self-development, and self-expression.[104] Recent surveys add support to Herzberg's findings. When employees at all occupational levels are asked to rank what is important to them, they list interesting work; sufficient help, support, and information to accomplish the job; enough authority to carry out the work; good pay; the opportunity to develop special skills; job security; and a chance to see the results of their work. Other research shows that what makes people content is being respected by members of groups they respect. In line with this, Roger Martin, dean of the school of management at the University of Toronto, argues that employees are happiest when they are respected members of a team they admire and when the team and company are respected by the outside world.[105]

Importance of Job Satisfaction

Numerous mental-health problems stem from a lack of job satisfaction—low self-esteem, anxiety, impaired interpersonal relations, and psychosomatic ailments such as ulcers and hypertension—especially in low-status, boring, unchallenging jobs that offer little autonomy. Furthermore, such jobs tend to inhibit intellectual growth and the pursuit of richer, more fulfilling activities outside work. Even worse, researchers have found that workers in boring, passive jobs are 33 to 35 percent more likely to die prematurely than workers in active jobs. Stressful work that offers little decision-making opportunity makes an untimely demise even more likely.[106]

One of the most intriguing studies not only suggests a correlation between longevity and job satisfaction but also contends that job satisfaction is the strongest predictor of longevity.[107] The second major factor for longevity is happiness. Both of these factors predict longevity better than either the physical health or the genetic inheritance of individuals.

Because the design of work materially affects the total well-being of workers, work content and job satisfaction are paramount moral concerns. But if we also assume that a happier, more contented worker is generally a more productive one, then it follows that business has an economic reason as well as a moral obligation to devise ways, in concert with labor and perhaps even government, to improve the quality of work life.

Job satisfaction is both a moral concern and an economic one.

Improving Work Life

This book isn't the place for determining precisely what measures firms should take to improve employees' work lives. For some firms it may mean providing workers with less supervision and more autonomy. For others it may mean providing work opportunities to develop and refine skills. Still other firms might try to provide workers with greater participation in the conception, design, and execution of their work—that is, with greater responsibility and a deeper sense of achievement.

Granting workers new responsibilities and respect can benefit the entire organization. Randy Pennington, vice president of Performance Systems Corporation, tells of a friend who showed an ad for a new American car to a Japanese businessperson. The ad said that the car "set a new standard for quality because it was examined by 34 different quality inspectors." "Now, *this*," he said to his Japanese colleague, "is what we need to compete with you. Imagine: 34 quality inspectors!" The Japanese looked at the ad, smiled, and said, "You don't need 34 inspectors to get quality. You just need everyone who works on the car to be proud of the work. Then you'll need only one inspector."[108]

Thawing the antagonistic worker–boss relations that characterize many plants isn't always easy. Some union members are wary, worried about "being co-opted and looking like management flunkies."[109] Investigators believe that the success of workplace reform efforts depends on the ability of the organization to reinforce high levels of trust. To the extent that it does so, organizational performance can improve. But, warns William Cooke, professor at Wayne State University and author of a book on workplace reform, "if [workers] perceive management as doing this without due consideration for the welfare of employees … it will have the potential of destroying the efforts altogether."[110]

After Gerard Arpey took over as CEO of American Airlines in 2003, the company began the arduous but ambitious process of developing better and more stable working relations between managers and employees, something that had long eluded American Airlines. In an apparently successful effort to end adversarial relations with the unions, Arpey created new structures of consultancy across the company, captured in the slogans "Involve before Deciding. Discuss before Implementing. Share before Announcing." "We are trying to make our unions our business partners," Arpey says. "It is not about sitting around the campfire singing Kumbaya."[111]

These days, closer union–management relations also characterize many GM plants. Mike Spitzley, manager of GM's 5,300-worker car-truck plant in Janesville, Wisconsin, for example, says, "Most of the things we talk about, it's 'we.' It's not us versus them. We've pretty much realized that our goals are the same" as the union's. Mike O'Brien, president of the local chapter of the United Auto Workers, agrees. "There's something different going on," he says. "Years ago, it wasn't any of our business what went on in the business." The most striking example is GM's Saturn Corporation, where union and management share all big decisions, from choosing suppliers to picking the company's advertising agency.[112]

At GM and American Airlines, the ideals of improved job atmosphere, employee participation, and employee job security appear to have meshed nicely with the goal of increased productivity. The same is true at BMW, which also gives its creative and motivated workforce a share of the profits—one reason the company receives 200,000 job applications annually.[113] Not only is productivity 5 to 10 percent greater in companies with profit sharing, but productivity is also consistently higher in enterprises with an organized program of worker participation.[114] This is in line with the views of experts who insist that worker-friendly companies outperform traditional command-and-control employers. They argue that new organizational structures and work practices that put a premium on collaboration and cooperation are fundamental to the nation's future economic success.[115]

A range of social and economic research supports that conclusion, but there is no water-tight guarantee that worker participation and an improved quality of work life will always boost productivity. For example, although diversifying tasks may make work more satisfying, Japanese carmakers reduced the number of rejects on their assembly line not by diversifying but by standardizing the cars produced. And Volkswagen found that its productivity and quality were higher when production consisted solely of the standard Rabbit than when other models were introduced. Job-enlargement programs,

Worker participation can increase productivity. Worker-friendly companies tend to outperform traditional command-and-control employers.

Summary 9.11
Studies report extensive job dissatisfaction at all levels. Various factors influence satisfaction and dissatisfaction on the job. Redesigning the work process and increasing employee responsibility and participation can enhance the quality of work life, well-being of workers, and even productivity.

by definition, add to the variety of tasks the worker is assigned; job-enrichment programs add some planning, designing, and scheduling to the operative worker's tasks. Both programs may slow output in some cases. Worker involvement in production management may not fit well, some argue, with the two other ingredients that managers and management consultants see as essential for manufacturing efficiency: a just-in-time approach to eliminating waste and rigorous statistical process control to improve quality.

Employee involvement, however, is essential to work elimination programs—programs that eliminate wasteful and unnecessary tasks, thus enhancing job satisfaction while making the organization leaner and more productive. This is particularly important as competition pressures manufacturers in the car industry and elsewhere to move to smaller, more flexible factories.[116] Still, the possibility of a conflict between the obligation to make work more satisfying and the goal of increasing productivity will likely be at the heart of moral decisions in this area for years to come. To resolve them will require a cooperative effort by labor and management, rooted in the recognition that trade-offs are inevitable.

STUDY CORNER

Key Terms and Concepts

assumption of risk	job satisfaction	personality tests
civic activities	job stress	polygraph tests
day care	management styles	privacy
drug testing	maternity leave	right to refuse dangerous
Employee Polygraph Protection Act	monitoring of employees	work
	musculoskeletal disorders	wellness programs
false positives	Occupational Safety and	
Hawthorne effect	Health Administration	
informed consent	off-the-job conduct	

Points to Review

- examples of business actions that encroach upon privacy
- three dimensions of privacy
- difficulties of determining when companies have a legitimate interest in employee conduct, on and off the job
- privacy issues raised by company-sponsored civic activities and wellness programs
- what informed consent implies
- debatable assumptions behind polygraphs
- problem of false positives
- three points to consider in evaluating workplace use of polygraphs
- one questionable assumption of personality tests
- four points about drug testing

- assumption of risk and the right to refuse hazardous work
- what causes accidents
- the key to workplace safety
- OSHA's spotty record
- new health challenges in the workplace
- management theories and human nature
- corporate record on child care
- three moral reasons to accommodate employees' parental and family needs
- the Hawthorne experiment and the factors affecting job satisfaction
- health effects of job dissatisfaction
- effect of participation and improved quality of work life on productivity

CASE **9.1**

Unprofessional Conduct?

Teaching elementary schoolchildren with intellectual disabilities requires skill, patience, and devotion, and those who undertake this task are among the unsung heroes of our society. Their difficult and challenging work rarely brings the prestige or financial rewards it deserves. Mrs. Pettit was one of those dedicated teachers. Licensed to teach in California, she had been working with mentally challenged children for over thirteen years when her career came to an abrupt end. Throughout that career, her competence was never questioned, and the evaluations of her school principal were always positive.

Teaching was not Pettit's only interest, however. She and her husband viewed with favor various "nonconventional sexual lifestyles," including "wife swapping." Because so-called sexual liberation was a hot topic at the time, the Pettits were invited to discuss their ideas on two local television shows. Although they wore disguises, at least one fellow teacher recognized them and discussed Mrs. Pettit's views with colleagues. A year later Pettit, then forty-eight years old, and her husband joined "The Swingers," a private club in Los Angeles that sponsored parties intended to promote diverse sexual activities among its members. An undercover police officer, Sergeant Berk, visited one of those parties at a private residence. Amid a welter of sexual activity, he observed Mrs. Pettit perform fellatio on three different men in a one-hour period.

Pettit was arrested and charged with oral copulation, which at the time contravened the California Penal Code (although now it does only if one of the parties is under eighteen). After a plea bargain was arranged, she pleaded guilty to the misdemeanor of outraging public decency and paid a fine. The school district renewed her teaching contract the next academic year, but two years later, disciplinary proceedings were initiated against her. The State Board of Education found no reason to complain about her services as a teacher, and it conceded that she was unlikely to repeat her sexual misconduct. But the Board revoked her elementary school life diploma—that is, her license to teach—on the ground that by engaging in immoral and unprofessional conduct at the party, she had demonstrated that she was unfit to teach.

Pettit fought the loss of her license all the way to the California Supreme Court, which upheld the decision of the Board of Education.[117] In an earlier case, the court had reversed the firing of a public school teacher for unspecified homosexual conduct, concluding that a teacher's actions could not constitute "immoral or unprofessional conduct" or "moral turpitude" unless there was clear evidence of unfitness to teach. But Pettit's case was different, the court hastened to explain.

The conduct in the earlier case had not been criminal, oral copulation had not been involved, and the conduct had been private. Further, in that case the Board had acted with insufficient evidence of unfitness to teach; by contrast, three school administrators had testified that in their opinion, Pettit's conduct proved her unfit to teach. These experts worried that she would inject her views of sexual morality into the classroom, and they doubted that she could act as a moral example to the children she taught. Yet teachers, the court reaffirmed, are supposed to serve as exemplars, and the Education Code makes it a statutory duty of teachers to "endeavor to impress upon the minds of the pupils the principles of morality ... and to instruct them in manners and morals."

In a vigorous dissent, Justice Tobringer rejected the opinion of the majority, arguing that no evidence had established that Pettit was not fit to teach. The three experts didn't consider her record; they couldn't point to any past misconduct with students, nor did they suggest any reason to anticipate future problems. They simply assumed that the fact of her sexual acts at the "swingers" party itself demonstrated that she would be unable to set a proper example or to teach her pupils moral principles.

Such an attitude is unrealistic, Tobringer argued, when studies show that 75 to 80 percent of the women of Pettit's educational level and age range engage in oral copulation. The majority opinion "is blind to the reality of sexual behavior" and unrealistically assumes that "teachers in their private lives should exemplify Victorian principles of sexual morality." Pettit's actions were private and could not have affected her teaching ability. Had there not been clandestine surveillance of the party, the whole issue would never have arisen.

Discussion Questions

1. In concerning itself with Pettit's off-the-job conduct, did the Board of Education violate her right to privacy? Or was its concern with her lifestyle legitimate and employment related?
2. Was Pettit's behavior "unprofessional"? Was it "immoral"? Did it show a "lack of

fitness" to teach? Explain how you understand the terms in quotation marks.
3. Was the Board of Education justified in firing Pettit? Explain.
4. Was the court's verdict consistent with its earlier handling of the case of the homosexual teacher?
5. If teachers perform competently in the classroom, should they also be required to be moral exemplars in their private lives? Are employees in other occupations expected to provide a moral example—either on or off the job?
6. Which of the following, in your view, would show unprofessional conduct, immorality, or lack of fitness to teach: drunken driving, smoking marijuana, advocating the use of marijuana, forging a check, resisting arrest for disorderly conduct and assaulting a police officer, being discovered in a compromising position with a student, propositioning a student, cheating on income tax, calling attention to one's openly homosexual lifestyle?
7. Under what conditions do employers have a legitimate interest in their employees' off-the-job conduct?

CASE **9.2**
Testing for Honesty

"Charity begins at home." If you don't think so, ask the Salvation Army. Some years ago, one of the Army's local branches discovered that it had a problem with theft among its kettle workers, the people who collect money for the Army during the Christmas season. Some of the Army's kettlers were helping themselves to the Army's donations before the organization had a chance to dole out the money. To put a stop to the problem, Army officials sought the assistance of Dr. John Jones, director of research for London House Management Consultants.

London House is one of several companies that market honesty tests for prospective employees.[118] Some of these tests, such as London House's Personnel Selection Inventory (PSI), also measure the applicant's tendency toward drug use and violence. All three categories—honesty, drugs, and violence—play a major part in company losses, according to the makers of these tests.

The company losses in question are astronomical. The U.S. Chamber of Commerce estimates that employee theft costs U.S. companies $40 billion annually; some unofficial estimates run three times as high. Moreover, 20 percent of the businesses that fail do so because of employee crime.[119] Compounding the problem is the cost of employee drug use in terms of absenteeism, lost initiative, inattentiveness, accidents, and diminished productivity. Employee violence also costs companies millions of dollars in damage, lost productivity, and lawsuits.

Honesty-test makers say that the only time to deal with these problems is before workers are hired, not after—by subjecting them to a preemployment psychological test that will identify those prospective employees who are likely to steal, who have a history of violence or emotional instability, or who have used illegal drugs on a regular basis.

James Walls, one of the founders of Stanton Corporation, which has offered written honesty tests for twenty-five years, says that dishonest job applicants are clever at hoodwinking potential employers in a job interview. "They have a way of conducting themselves that is probably superior to the low-risk person. They have learned what it takes to be accepted and how to overcome the normal interview strategy," he says. "The high-risk person will get hired unless there is a way to screen him." For this reason, Walls maintains, written, objective tests are needed to weed out the crooks.

Millions of written honesty tests are given annually, thanks to congressional restrictions on polygraph testing. In addition to being legal, honesty tests are also economical because they cost only a fraction of what polygraph tests cost. Furthermore, honesty tests are easily administered at the workplace and can be quickly evaluated by the test maker. The tests also are nondiscriminatory because the race, gender, or ethnicity of applicants has no significant impact on scores.

A typical test begins with some cautionary remarks. Test takers are told to be truthful because dishonesty can be detected, and they are warned that incomplete answers will be considered incorrect, as will any unanswered

questions. Then applicants ordinarily sign a waiver permitting the results to be shown to their prospective employer and authorizing the testing agency to check out their answers. Sometimes, however, prospective employees are not told that they are being tested for honesty, only that they are being asked questions about their background. James Walls justifies this less-than-frank explanation by saying that within a few questions it is obvious that the test deals with attitudes toward honesty. "The test is very transparent, it's not subtle."

Some questions do indeed seem transparent—for example, "If you found $100 that was lost by a bank truck on the street yesterday, would you turn the money over to the bank, even though you knew for sure there was no reward?" But other questions are more controversial: "Have you ever had an argument with someone and later wished you had said something else?" If you were to answer no, you would be on your way to failing. Other questions that may face the test taker are "How strong is your conscience?" "How often do you feel guilty?" "Do you always tell the truth?" "Do you occasionally have thoughts you wouldn't want made public?" "Does everyone steal a little?" "Do you enjoy stories of successful crimes?" "Have you ever been so intrigued by the cleverness of a thief that you hoped the person would escape detection?" Or consider questions like "Is an employee who takes it easy at work cheating his employer?" or "Do you think a person should be fired by a company if it is found that he helped employees cheat the company out of overtime once in a while?" These ask you for your reaction to hypothetical dishonest situations. "If you are a particularly kind-hearted person who isn't sufficiently punitive, you fail," says Lewis Maltby, director of the workplace rights office at the American Civil Liberties Union. "Mother Teresa would never pass some of these tests."

A big part of some tests is a behavioral history of the applicant. Applicants are asked to reveal the nature, frequency, and quantity of specific drug use, if any. They also must indicate if they have ever engaged in drunk driving, illegal gambling, traffic violations, forgery, vandalism, and a host of other unseemly behaviors. They must also state their opinions about the social acceptability of drinking alcohol and using other drugs.

Some testing companies go further in this direction. Instead of honesty exams, they offer tests designed to draw a general psychological profile of the applicant, claiming that this sort of analysis can predict more accurately than either the polygraph or the typical honesty test how the person will perform on the job. Keith M. Halperin, a psychologist with Personnel Decision, Inc. (PDI), a company that offers such tests, complains that most paper-and-pencil honesty tests are simply written equivalents of the polygraph. They ask applicants whether they have stolen from their employers, how much they have taken, and other questions directly related to honesty. "But why," asks Halperin, "would an applicant who is dishonest enough to steal from an employer be honest enough to admit it on a written test?" It is more difficult for applicants to fake their responses to PDI's tests, Halperin contends.

Not everyone is persuaded. Phyllis Bassett, vice president of James Bassett Company of Cincinnati, believes tests developed by psychologists that do not ask directly about the applicant's past honesty are poor predictors of future trustworthiness. This may be because, as some psychologists report, "it is very difficult for dishonest people to fake honesty." One reason is that thieves tend to believe that "everybody does it" and that therefore it would be implausible for them to deny stealing. In general, those who market honesty exams boast of their validity and reliability, as established by field studies. They insist that the tests do make a difference, that they enable employers to ferret out potential trouble-makers—as in the Salvation Army case.

Dr. Jones administered London House's PSI to eighty kettler applicants, which happened to be the number that the particular theft-ridden center needed. The PSIs were not scored, and the eighty applicants were hired with no screening. Throughout the fund-raising month between Thanksgiving and Christmas, the center kept a record of each kettler's daily receipts. After the Christmas season, the tests were scored and divided into "recommended" and "not recommended" for employment. After accounting for the peculiarities of each collection neighborhood, Jones discovered that those kettlers the PSI had not recommended turned in on the average $17 per day less than those the PSI had recommended. Based on this analysis, he estimated the center's loss to employee theft during the fund drive at $20,000.

The list of psychological-test enthusiasts is growing by leaps and bounds, but the tests have plenty of detractors. Many psychologists have voiced concern over the lack of standards governing the tests; the American Psychological Association favors the establishment of federal standards for written honesty exams. But the chief critics of honesty and other psychological exams are the people who have to take them. They complain about having to reveal some of the most intimate details of their lives and opinions.

For example, until an employee filed suit, Rent-A-Center, a Texas corporation, asked both job applicants and employees being considered for promotion true-false questions like these: "I have never indulged in any unusual sex practices," "I am very strongly attracted by members of my own sex," "I go to church almost every week," and "I have difficulty in starting or holding my bowel movements." A manager who was fired for complaining about the test says, "It was ridiculous. The test asked if I loved tall women. How was I supposed to answer that? My wife is 5 feet 3 inches." A spokesman for Rent-A-Center argues that its questionnaire is not unusual and that many other firms use it.

Firms who use tests like Rent-A-Center's believe that no one's privacy is being invaded because employees and job applicants can always refuse to take the test. Critics disagree. "Given the unequal bargaining power," says former ACLU official Kathleen Bailey, "the ability to refuse to take a test is one of theory rather than choice—if one really wants the job."

Discussion Questions

1. Describe how you'd feel if you had to take a psychological test or an honesty test either as an employee or as a precondition for employment. Under what conditions, if any, would you take such a test?

2. How useful do you think such tests are? Assuming that tests like those described are valid and reliable, are they fair? Explain.

3. Do you think tests like these invade privacy and, if so, that this invasion is justified? Explain why or why not.

4. What ideals, obligations, and effects must be considered in using psychological tests as preemployment screens? In your view, which is the most important consideration?

5. If you were an employer, would you require either employees or job applicants to pass an honesty exam? Explain the moral principles that support your position.

6. What do you think a business's reaction would be if the government required its executive officers to submit to an honesty test as a precondition for the company's getting a government contract? If, in your opinion, the business would object, does it have any moral grounds for subjecting workers to comparable tests?

7. Utilitarians would not find anything inherently objectionable about psychological tests as long as the interests of all parties were taken into account and given equal consideration before such tests were made a preemployment screen. Do you think this is generally the case?

8. Should there be a law prohibiting or regulating psychological tests as a preemployment screen? Should a decision to use these tests be made jointly by management and labor, or is testing for employment an exclusive employer right?

CASE 9.3
She Snoops to Conquer

Jean Fanuchi, manager of a moderately large department store, was worried. Shrinkage in the costume jewelry department had continued to rise for the third consecutive month. In fact, this time it had nearly wiped out the department's net profit in sales. Worse, it couldn't be attributed to damage or improper handling of markdowns or even to shoplifting. The only other possibility was in-house theft.

Fanuchi ordered chief of security Matt Katwalski to instruct his security people to keep a special eye on jewelry department employees as they went about their business. She also instructed that packages, purses, and other containers employees carried with them be searched when workers left the store. When these measures failed to turn up any leads, Katwalski suggested they hire a couple of plainclothes officers to observe the store's guards. Fanuchi agreed. But still nothing turned up.

"We're going to have to install a hidden camera at the checkout station in the jewelry department," Katwalski informed the manager.

"I don't know," Fanuchi replied.

"Of course," said Katwalski, "it won't be cheap. But you don't want this problem spreading to other departments, do you?" Fanuchi didn't.

"One other thing," Katwalski said. "I think we should install some microphones in the restroom, stockroom, and employee lounge."

"You mean snoop on our own employees?" Fanuchi asked, surprised.

"We could pick up something that could crack this thing wide open," Katwalski explained.

"But what if our employees found out? How would they feel, being spied on? And then there's the public to consider. Who knows how they'd react? Why, they'd probably think that if we are spying on our own workers, we were surely spying on them. No, Matt," Fanuchi decided. "Frankly, this whole approach troubles me."

"Okay, Ms. Fanuchi, but if it was my store …"

Fanuchi cut in, "No."

"You're the boss," said Katwalski.

When the shrinkage continued, Fanuchi finally gave in. She ordered Katwalski to have the camera and microphones installed. Within ten days the camera had nabbed the culprit.

The microphones contributed nothing to the apprehension of the thief. But because of them Fanuchi and Katwalski learned that at least one store employee was selling marijuana and perhaps hard drugs, that one was planning to quit without notice, that three were getting food stamps fraudulently, and that one buyer was out to discredit Fanuchi. In solving their shrinkage problem, the pair had unwittingly raised another: What should they do with the information they had gathered while catching the thief?[120]

Discussion Questions

1. If you were Jean Fanuchi, how would you feel about your decision to order the installation of the viewing and listening devices? What other options did she have? Did she overlook any moral considerations or possible consequences?

2. Do employees have a right not to be spied on? If you were an employee at Fanuchi's store, would you think your privacy had been wrongly invaded?

3. How would you assess Fanuchi's actions if you were the owner of the store? Whose interests are more important in this case—the employer's or the employees'?

4. Do you think Fanuchi acted immorally? Why or why not? Evaluate her action by appeal to ethical principles.

5. How should Fanuchi and Katwalski handle the information they've gathered about their employees? Explain by appealing to relevant ideals, obligations, and effects.

CASE **9.4**
Protecting the Unborn at Work

The unobtrusive factory sits behind a hillside shopping center in the small college town of Bennington, Vermont. Inside, the men and women make lead automobile batteries for Sears, Good-year, and other companies. However, until the 1990s, none of the women employed there was able to have children. The reason was simple. The company, Johnson Controls, Inc., refused to hire any who could.[121]

Why? Because tiny toxic particles of lead and lead oxide fill the air inside the plant. According to the company, the levels of lead are low enough for adults but too high for children and fetuses. Numerous scientific studies have shown that lead can damage the brain and central nervous system of a fetus. Moreover, lead lingers in the bloodstream, which means that fetuses can be affected by it even if a woman limits her exposure to lead once she learns she is pregnant. Because of this, Johnson Controls decided that it would exclude women at all fourteen of its factories from jobs that entail high exposure to lead—unless they could prove that they couldn't become pregnant. The company made no exceptions for celibate women or women who used contraceptives. The company's position was simple: "The issue is protecting the health of unborn children."

Johnson Controls's stance was in line with the national Centers for Disease Control's recommendation that women of childbearing age be excluded from jobs involving significant lead exposure. Because by law its standards must be "feasible," Occupational Safety and Health Administration (OSHA) regulations permit chemicals in the workplace that are known to cause harm both to fetuses and to some adult employees. But OSHA holds that employers have a general duty to reduce the hazards of the workplace as far as possible. On this basis, employers such as Olin Corporation, American Cyanamid, General Motors, Monsanto, Allied Chemical, Gulf Oil, and B. F. Goodrich also adopted policies excluding women from chemical plant jobs judged to be hazardous to their potential offspring.

Scientific studies of the effect of exposure to toxic manufacturing chemicals on workers' reproductive health are, unfortunately, few. Only a small percentage of the workplace chemicals with a potential for damaging reproduction have been evaluated, and each year many new chemicals are introduced into factories. Although employers are obviously dealing with many unknowns, no one doubts that they have a moral and legal obligation to control and limit these risks as best they can. Lawsuits and even criminal sanctions have battered companies that have managed hazardous chemicals irresponsibly. Monsanto

Chemical Company, for example, agreed to pay $1.5 million to six employees because exposure to a chemical additive used for rubber production allegedly gave them bladder cancer. Fetal protection policies aren't just dictated by management, though. "Women who become pregnant," the *New York Times* reports, "are beginning to demand the right to transfer out of jobs they believe to be hazardous, even when there is only sketchy scientific evidence of any hazard."

But many women were unhappy about the decision of Johnson Controls. They worried that fetal protection policies would be used to exclude women from more and more workplaces on the grounds that different chemical substances or certain tasks such as heavy lifting might be potential causes of miscarriage and fetal injury. In line with this, the United Automobile Workers, which represents many of the Johnson employees, sought to overturn the U.S. Court of Appeals decision that judged Johnson's policy to be "reasonably necessary to the industrial safety-based concern of protecting the unborn child from lead exposure." The union contends, to the contrary, that the policy discriminates against women, jeopardizing their hard-won gains in male-dominated industries.

Many women's advocates see the issue in slightly different terms. They believe policies like that of Johnson Controls challenge a woman's right not only to control her fetus but to control her unfertilized eggs as well. In addition, such policies infringe on privacy: By taking a job at Johnson, a woman was in effect telling the world that she was sterile. And there is also the fundamental question of who knows what is best for a woman.

After bearing two children, Cheryl Chalifoux had a doctor block her fallopian tubes so that she couldn't become pregnant again. Although career advancement wasn't the reason she made her decision, it did enable her to switch from a factory job paying $6.34 an hour to one at Johnson's Bennington plant paying $15 an hour. Still, she says that the policy was unfair and degrading. "It's your body," she complains. "They're implying they're doing it for your own good." Cheryl Cook, also a mother of two who had surgery for the same reason, joined Chalifoux in leaving the other company to work for Johnson Controls. She says, "I work right in the lead. I make the oxide. But you should choose for yourself. Myself, I wouldn't go in there if I could get pregnant. But they don't trust you."

Isabelle Katz Pizler, director of women's rights at the American Civil Liberties Union, agrees. "Since time immemorial," she says, "the excuse for keeping women in their place has been because of their role in producing the next generation. The attitude of Johnson Controls is: 'We know better than you. We can't allow women to make this decision. We have to make it for them.'" And the ACLU has argued in court that "since no activity is risk-free, deference to an employer's analysis of fetal risk could limit women's participation in nearly every area of economic life."

To this the company responded that it has a moral obligation to the parties that cannot participate in the woman's decisions—namely, the unfertilized ovum and the fetus. In addition, the company has an obligation to stockholders, who would bear the brunt of lawsuits brought by employees' children born with retardation, nervous system disorders, or other ailments that lead can cause.

Joseph A. Kinney, executive director of the National Safe Workplace Institute in Chicago, sides with Johnson Controls, but only because he believes that letting women assume the burden of their safety undermines OSHA's responsibility to mandate workplace safety rules. "The discrimination side of the issue needs to be resolved," Kinney says. "But the ideal thing is to regulate lead out of the workplace and any other toxin that poses fetal damage."

However, the U.S. Supreme Court ruled unanimously that the fetal protection policy at Johnson Controls violated the Civil Rights Act of 1964, which prohibits sex discrimination in employment.[122] Pointing to evidence that lead affects sperm and can thus harm the offspring of men exposed to it at the time of conception, the Court stated:

> Respondent does not seek to protect the unconceived children of all its employees. Despite evidence in the record about the debilitating effect of lead exposure on the male reproductive system, Johnson Controls is concerned only with the harms that may befall the unborn offspring of its female employees. ... [The company's policy is] discriminatory because it requires only a female employee to produce proof that she is not capable of reproducing.

The Court was divided over whether fetal protection policies could ever be legally justified. Justice Harry A. Blackmun, writing for a majority of the Court, declared that they could not, that the Civil Rights Act prohibited all such policies:

> Decisions about the welfare of future children must be left to the parents who conceive, bear, support and raise them rather than to the employers who hire those parents. Women as capable of doing their jobs as their male counterparts may not be forced to choose between having a child and having a job.

Referring to the Pregnancy Discrimination Act of 1978, which amended the 1964 Civil Rights Act and prohibits employment discrimination on the basis of pregnancy or potential pregnancy, Blackmun added:

> Employment late in pregnancy often imposes risks on the unborn child, but Congress indicated that the employer may take into account only the woman's ability to get her job done.

A minority of the justices, however, were unwilling to go so far, and in a concurring opinion, Justice Byron R. White wrote that "common sense tells us that it is part of the normal operation of business concerns to avoid causing injury to third parties as well as to employees." But he added that, in his view, a fetal protection policy would not be defensible unless an employer also addressed other known occupational health risks.

Discussion Questions

1. Do you agree that Johnson Controls's fetal protection policy discriminated against women? Do pregnant women have a moral—not just a legal—right to work with lead?

2. Suppose exposure to lead did not affect sperm or the male reproductive system. Would Johnson's policy still have been discriminatory? Would it hamper women's efforts to win equality in the workplace?

3. Can there be a nondiscriminatory fetal protection policy? Is Justice White correct in arguing that companies have an obligation to avoid causing injury to fetuses just as they do to other "third parties"?

4. Suppose a company forbids any employee capable of reproducing from working with lead. Would such a policy wrongly interfere with employees' freedom of choice? Would it be an invasion of their privacy? Would it be fair to employees who are fertile but plan to have no children?

5. Evaluate fetal protection policies from the egoistic, utilitarian, and Kantian perspectives. What rights are involved? What are the likely benefits and harms of such policies?

6. If they are fully informed, do employees with a certain medical condition have a right to work at jobs that can be hazardous to the health of people in their condition? Or can company policy or OSHA regulations justifiably prevent them from doing so for their own good?

7. Would you agree with Joseph Kinney that the real issue is the need to remove toxins from the workplace? Is this a realistic goal?

CASE 9.5
The Mommy Track

"The cost of employing women in management is greater than the cost of employing men. This is a jarring statement, partly because it is true, but mostly because it is something people are reluctant to talk about." So begins a provocative article by Felice N. Schwartz.[123] Schwartz goes on to contend that the rate of turnover in management positions is two-and-a-half times higher among top-performing women than it is among men. Moreover, one-half of the women who take maternity leave return to their jobs late or not at all. "We know that women also have a greater tendency to plateau or to interrupt their careers," she writes. "But we have become so sensitive to charges of sexism and so afraid of confrontation, even litigation, that we rarely say what we know to be true."

Schwartz's article exploded like a bombshell. What really upset her critics was the distinction Schwartz drew between two types of women: the career-primary woman and the career-and-family woman. Those in the first category put their careers first. They remain single or childless, or if they do have children, they are satisfied to have others raise them. The automatic association of all women with babies is unfair to these women, according to Schwartz—after all, some 90 percent of executive men but only 35 percent of executive women have children by age forty. "The secret to dealing with such women," Schwartz writes, "is to recognize them early, accept them, and clear artificial barriers from their path to the top."[124]

The majority of women fall into Schwartz's second category. They want to pursue genuine careers while participating actively in the rearing of their children. Most of them, Schwartz contends, are willing to trade some career growth and compensation for freedom from the constant pressure to work long hours and weekends. By forcing these women to choose between family and career, companies lose a valuable resource and a competitive advantage. Instead, firms must plan for and manage maternity, they must provide the flexibility to help career-and-family women be maximally productive, and they must take an active role in providing family support and in making high-quality, affordable child care available to all women.

Schwartz's various suggestions of ways for organizations to serve the needs of working mothers and benefit from their expertise seem humane and practical. But her feminist critics see her as distinguishing between the strivers and the breeders, between women who should be treated as honorary males and those who should be shunted onto a special lower-paid, low-pressure career track—the now-notorious "mommy track." Former congresswoman Patricia Schroeder of Colorado says that Schwartz actually "reinforces the idea that you can either have a family or a career, but not both, if you're a woman." And other women worry that Schwartz's article will encourage corporations to reduce pay and withhold promotions in exchange for the parental leave, flextime, and child care that they will sooner or later have to provide as they become more and more dependent on female talent.

Barbara Ehrenreich and Deirdre English challenge Schwartz's data and call her article "a tortured muddle of feminist perceptions and sexist assumptions, good intentions and dangerous suggestions—unsupported by any acceptable evidence at all." What they resent is that Schwartz makes no mention of fathers or of shared parental responsibility for child raising. Schwartz is also accused of assuming that mothers don't need top-flight careers and of taking for granted the existing values, structures, and biases of a corporate world that is still male dominated. "Bumping women—or just fertile women, or married women, or whomever—off the fast track may sound smart to cost-conscious CEOs," they write. "But eventually it is the corporate culture itself that needs to slow down to a human pace … [and end] work loads that are incompatible with family life."

"What's so disturbing about Felice Schwartz's article," adds Fran Rodgers, president of Work-Family Directions, a Massachusetts research and referral group, "is that it is devoted to fitting women into the existing culture, instead of finding ways to change that culture." And Rodgers rejects the idea of "dividing women into two groups, but completely ignoring the diversity among men."

Other observers fear that men will simply leave the mommy trackers in the dust. "In most organizations, the mommy track is a millstone around your neck," says Richard Belous, an economist at the National Planning Association. "CEOs and rainmakers don't come out of the mommy track," he warns. "If you go part-time, you're signaling to your employer you're on the B-team." Traditionally, men who make it to the upper ranks have relied on their wives to raise the kids and to take full responsibility at home. A fast-track woman who wants children, however, gets caught in a time and energy squeeze, even if her husband is an equal partner at home. And even though more men today are willing to share child-raising responsibilities, most still seem hesitant about making significant career sacrifices for spouse and family. There's no analogous "daddy track," it seems.

In fact, the evidence points to what's been called a "daddy penalty"—at least for dads in dual-career families. Two recent studies have shown that male managers whose wives stay home to care for their children earn more than their counterparts with working wives. Even when differences in the numbers of hours worked, years of experience, field of employment, and career interruptions are taken into account, men who are the sole breadwinners for their families enjoy incomes at least 20 percent higher than those of married men with children whose wives have careers.[125] Why? No one knows for sure. Some observers suggest that men who are the sole income earners work more, produce more, and push harder for raises and promotions. Others suggest that having a wife at home is a significant career resource, allowing the man to perform more effectively in his job. Yet others speculate that men who are strongly career oriented choose wives who support that choice in the first place, whereas men who want more balance between work and family are more likely to marry women who want to work. And, finally, there are those who believe that the data reflect a corporate prejudice in favor of traditional families.

Discussion Questions

1. Do you think Schwartz is correct to assert that the cost of employing women in management is greater than that of employing men? If you agree, what are the implications for corporate policy?

2. Can working women accurately be divided into Schwartz's two categories? Is it desirable for companies to distinguish the different types of career paths followed by female employees?

3. Do you think there already is such a thing as a mommy track? Is the idea of a mommy track a good one? Is it somehow discriminatory against women? Against men?

4. Should special organizational arrangements be made for workers who wish to combine career and child raising? Identify the steps that companies can take to accommodate parental needs more effectively.

5. Does a firm have an obligation to give employees the flexibility to work out the particular balance of career and family that is right for them? Or does this go beyond the social responsibilities of business?

CHAPTER 10

Moral Choices Facing Employees

Reprinted through the courtesy of the Editors of TIME Magazine © 2008 Time Inc.

THE CASE AGAINST BUCHANAN

SPECIAL INVESTIGATION

BLOWING THE WHISTLE ON NUCLEAR SAFETY

How a showdown at a power plant exposed the federal government's failure to enforce its own rules

George Galatis at Millstone in Connecticut

Obligations to the Firm
Loyalty to the Company
Conflicts of Interest

Abuse of Official Position
Insider Trading
Proprietary Data

Bribes and Kickbacks
The Foreign Corrupt Practices Act
The Case against Overseas Bribery

Gifts and Entertainment

Conflicting Obligations

Whistle-Blowing
The Definition of Whistle-Blowing
What Motivates Whistle-Blowers?
When Is Whistle-Blowing Justified?

Self-Interest and Moral Obligation
Protecting Those Who Do the Right Thing

CASES
Changing Jobs and Changing Loyalties
Two Who Made Waves for the Navy
The Housing Allowance
Ethically Dubious Conduct

INTRODUCTION

When his eldest daughter asked him, "Why don't you just do what they want?" George Betancourt wasn't sure how he should answer. Betancourt was a senior engineer at Northeast Utilities, which operates five nuclear power plants in New England, and all he had done was to speak up and express his professional judgment. Now Northeast wanted him to shut up. First, Northeast's human-resources officer had called him in. After complaining that Betancourt wasn't being a "team player," she described to him the company's termination policies. Three weeks later, Betancourt was informed he was being reassigned. "We'd like to help you, George," Eric DeBarba, vice president of technical services, told him. "But you've got to start thinking company."[1]

George Galatis was the Northeast engineer on whose behalf Betancourt had spoken up. Galatis had discovered what he considered to be a glaring safety problem at Northeast's Millstone No. 1 plant. In an effort to save downtime (and hence money) during the refueling process, the plant's procedures routinely violated federal guidelines and pushed its spent-fuel pool well beyond its design capacity. For eighteen months, Galatis's supervisors denied the problem existed and refused to report it to the Nuclear Regulatory Commission (NRC). Northeast brought in a series of outside experts to prove Galatis wrong, but the consultants ended up agreeing with him. Within the company, Betancourt backed up Galatis's safety concerns. When Northeast finally began to acknowledge a possible problem, it didn't move fast enough to satisfy Galatis. Two years after he first raised his safety concerns, he finally took the case directly to the NRC, only to learn that it had known about the unsafe procedures for years.

He also discovered evidence that suggested collusion between Northeast and NRC officials to subordinate safety to profitability.

As a result of going to the NRC, Galatis experienced "subtle forms of harassment, retaliation, and intimidation." He wasn't being paranoid. Two dozen Millstone No. 1 employees claimed they were fired or demoted for raising safety concerns. Some of his colleagues sided with the company, however, accusing Galatis of aiding anti-nuclear activists and trying to take away their livelihood. But Galatis didn't stop. He hired a lawyer who specializes in representing whistle-blowers and kept after the NRC. With the lawyer's help, the public spotlight was focused on Millstone No. 1. Local politicians began asking questions. Even though the NRC ignored Galatis, it ended up validating his concerns, and Millstone No. 1 was shut down. Citing chronic safety concerns, employee harassment, and a "historic emphasis on cost savings vs. performance," the NRC also put Northeast's other two Millstone plants on its high-scrutiny "watch list." And a new NRC head vowed to shake up the regulatory body itself.

Galatis and Betancourt managed to hang on to their jobs, but their careers are at a standstill. "The two Georges had better watch their backs," says one engineer. "Up at Northeast, they've got long memories." A disillusioned Galatis says, "If I had it to do over again, I wouldn't."

For someone in the shoes of George Galatis or George Betancourt, two general issues come up. *First* is the question of where an employee's overall moral duty lies. For a professional engineer to go public with documented safety concerns may seem to be a more straightforward moral decision than that faced by an employee who suspects irregularities, unsafe procedures, or wrongdoing in an area unrelated to his or her own job. In that case, the employee may possibly have conflicting moral obligations. Furthermore, if an employee reports irregularities to the appropriate authority, the employee must then decide whether he or she is morally obligated to pursue the matter further. Again other moral considerations come into play.

Second, once they have decided that they ought to blow the whistle, employees must face the possible negative consequences. Galatis and Betancourt are skilled, mature, and respected professionals, with established records and good credentials; in terms of employment options, they may have less to risk than do potential whistle-blowers who are just starting their careers or who have limited job options or heavy financial obligations. Nor is this simply a tug-of-war between moral duty and self-interest. Most moral theorists would agree that depending on the circumstances, certain personal sacrifices might be so great that a person cannot reasonably be morally obliged to make them.

These two themes—determining one's moral responsibility amid a welter of conflicting demands and paying the personal costs that can be incurred from living up to one's obligations—recur throughout this chapter. In particular, it looks at the following topics:

1. Employees' obligations to the firm, company loyalty, and the problem of conflicts of interest
2. Illegitimate use of one's official position for private gain, especially through insider trading or access to proprietary data
3. Domestic and foreign bribery and factors to consider in determining the morality of giving and receiving gifts in a business context
4. The obligations employees have to third parties and the considerations they should weigh in cases of conflicting moral duties or divided loyalties
5. What whistle-blowing is and factors relevant to evaluating its morality
6. The problem of how considerations of self-interest are to be weighed by an employee facing a tough moral choice

---

OBLIGATIONS TO THE FIRM

The employment contract governs the employer-employee relationship and provides the framework for understanding the respective obligations of employer and employee.

When you accept employment, you generally agree to perform certain tasks, usually during certain specified hours, in exchange for financial remuneration. Whether oral or written, implicit or explicit, a contract governs your employment relationship and provides the basic framework for understanding the reciprocal obligations between you and your employer. Your employment contract determines what you are supposed to do or accomplish for your employer, and it may cover other matters ranging from parking privileges to your dress and deportment while carrying out your responsibilities. The terms of your employment contract may be specific and detailed or vague and open-ended.

Loyalty to the Company

Because you are hired to work for your employer, you have an obligation, when acting on behalf of the organization, to promote your employer's interests. Insofar as you are acting as an agent of your employer, the traditional law of agency places you under a legal obligation to act loyally and in good faith and to carry out all lawful instructions. But it would be morally benighted to view employees simply as agents of their employers or to expect them to subordinate entirely their autonomy and private lives to the organization. Morality requires neither blind loyalty nor total submission to the organization.

Some writers deny that employees have any obligation of loyalty to the company, even a prima facie obligation, "because companies are not the kind of things that are properly objects of loyalty." Why not? Because a business firm functions to make money, the argument goes, self-interest is all that binds it together, whereas "loyalty depends on ties that demand self-sacrifice with no expectation of reward."[2] From this perspective, then, one can owe loyalty to family, friends, or country but not to a corporation; employees simply work to get paid and are misguided if they see themselves as owing loyalty to the company.

However, the notion of **company loyalty** is commonplace, and most people find it a coherent and legitimate concept. For the many employees who willingly make sacrifices for the organization above and beyond their job descriptions, loyalty is a real and important value. Indeed, it is not clear how well any business or organization could function without employee loyalty, and certainly most companies want more than minimal time and effort from their employees. Loyalty, though, is a two-way street, and most employees believe it's up to the company to earn and retain their loyalty.

Arguably, some obligations of loyalty simply come with the job—for example, the obligation to warn the organization of danger, the obligation to act in a way that protects its legitimate interests, and the obligation to cooperate actively in the furtherance of legitimate corporate goals.[3] To be sure, many businesses demand more than this in the name of loyalty. They may expect employees to defend the company if it is maligned, to work overtime when the company needs it, to accept a transfer if necessary for the good of the organization, or to demonstrate their loyalty in countless other ways. Displaying loyalty in those ways certainly seems morally permissible, even if it is not morally required.[4] In addition, employees, like other individuals, can come to identify with the groups they are part of, accepting group goals and norms as their own. Some moral theorists believe not only that loyalty to the group can become an important value for the individual employee, but also that in the appropriate circumstances the process of group identification can create an additional obligation of loyalty that the employee otherwise would not have.[5]

> Although some writers deny that employees owe loyalty to the company, most people find company loyalty a coherent and legitimate concept.

Conflicts of Interest

Even the most loyal employees can find that their interests collide with those of the organization. You want to dress one way, but the organization requires you to dress another way; you'd prefer to show up for work at noon, but the company expects you to be present at 8 A.M.; you'd like to receive $75,000 for your services, but the organization pays you a fraction of that figure. The reward, autonomy, and self-fulfillment that workers seek aren't always compatible with the demands of the organization. Whatever the matter in question, the perspectives of employee and employer can differ.

Summary 10.1
The employment contract creates various obligations to one's employer. In addition, employees often feel loyalty to the organization. Conflicts of interest arise when employees have a personal interest in a transaction substantial enough that it might reasonably be expected to affect their judgment or lead them to act against the interests of the organization.

Sometimes this clash of goals and desires can take the serious form of a **conflict of interest**. In an organization, a conflict of interest arises when employees at any level have special or private interests that are substantial enough to interfere with their job duties—that is, when their personal interests lead them, or might reasonably be expected to lead them, to make decisions or to act in ways that are detrimental to their employer's interests. That was certainly the case when Enron's chief financial officer, Andrew Fastow, represented the company in negotiations with firms he was a managing partner of (and as a result eventually earned millions of dollars from the deals).

As mentioned, the work contract is the primary source of an organization's right to expect employees to act on its behalf in a way that is unprejudiced by their personal interests. In general, if the contents of the work agreement are legal and if the employee freely consents to them, then he or she is under an obligation to fulfill the terms of the agreement. Implicit in any work contract is the assumption that employees will not sacrifice the interests of the organization for personal advantage. Of course, individuals may seek to benefit from being employed with a certain business or organization, but in discharging their contractual duties, employees should not subordinate the welfare of the organization to their own gain.

When in a certain situation an employee's private interests run counter to the interests of his or her employer in some significant way—or, to put the point differently, when those interests are likely to interfere with the employee's ability to exercise proper judgment on behalf of the organization—a conflict of interest exists. The danger, then, is that those interests will lead the employee to sacrifice the interests of his or her employer. For example, Bart Erdman, sales manager for Leisure Sports World, gives all his firm's promotional work to Impact Advertising because its chief officer is Erdman's brother-in-law. As a result, Leisure Sports World pays about 15 percent more in advertising costs than it would if its work went to another agency. Here Erdman has allowed his decisions as an employee to be influenced by his personal interests, to the detriment of Leisure Sports World. Note that Erdman's interest is not financial; a conflict of interest can take various forms.

Suppose that Erdman does not throw all of his company's promotional work to his brother-in-law; rather, he gives the firm's business to his brother-in-law only when he sincerely believes that doing so is best for Leisure Sports World. Nevertheless, a conflict of interest can still be said to exist. Because of his brother-in-law, Erdman still has a private interest in his business dealings for Leisure Sports World that could possibly lead him to act against the interests of the company. In other words, there is a danger that Bart's judgment may not be as objective as it should be.

Conflicts of interest are morally worrisome not only when an employee acts to the detriment of the organization but also when the employee's private interests are significant enough that they could tempt the person to do so. Indeed, research shows that conflicts of interest can unconsciously distort the decisions of even very honest people.[6] That's why alarm bells went off when *Business Week* disclosed that two members of the audit committee at Qwest

Conflicts of interest are morally worrisome even if the employee doesn't act to the detriment of the employer.

Communications—already under fire for dubious accounting practices—directed companies with million-dollar contracts with Qwest, thus raising questions about their ability to exercise independent judgment.[7] Even the appearance of impropriety can undermine trust and erode the confidence that others are entitled to have in the impartiality and objectivity of one's decisions.

By definition, to have a conflict of interest is to be in a morally risky situation; that is why employees should promptly extricate themselves from such conflicts or avoid them in the first place. But deciding when an employee's private interests are substantial enough for the situation to constitute a conflict of interest can be difficult. Equally difficult can be deciding exactly how the person should deal with a specific conflict. Sometimes people are encouraged simply to disclose the conflict to those relying on their judgment, thus preventing deception and allowing those relying on them to adjust their reliance accordingly. That is often good counsel, but it doesn't end the conflict of interest. Moreover, it's no panacea. Supposedly, if I tell you that I have a financial reason for skewing my advice to you, you'll take that into account and everything will be fine. Unfortunately, however, experimental evidence suggests that even when informed that the advice they're receiving may be biased, people fail to discount it as much as they should.[8]

Financial Investments

Conflicts of interest may exist when employees have financial investments in suppliers, customers, or distributors with whom their organizations do business. For example, Monica Peykova, purchasing agent for Trans-Con Trucking, owns a substantial amount of stock with Timberline Office Works. When ordering office supplies, Peykova buys exclusively from Timberline, even though she could get equivalent supplies cheaper from another supplier. In this case, Peykova has acted against Trans-Con's interests. But even if Peykova never advantages herself this way, a conflict of interest still exists.

During the dot-com boom, executives at high-tech firms often owned stock in other young companies in the same or closely related fields. Those tangled financial relationships sometimes produced conflicts of interest. For example, eight executives at EMC were heavily invested in the start-up StorageNetworks. They recommended it to their clients, and those referrals quickly grew to 40 percent of the younger company's business. But as StorageNetworks got larger and as EMC expanded its own services division, the two companies found themselves competing, leading some at EMC to complain that the other firm was poaching its employees and interfering with its customer relationships. Today EMC says the impact on business was negligible. But a former board member maintains that the eight executives were recommending StorageNetworks when they should have been pushing EMC equipment: "No question, it had an impact on their day-to-day decisions. It was a tremendous financial incentive."[9]

How much of a financial investment does it take to create a conflict of interest? There's no simple answer. Certainly it is acceptable to own stock in large publicly held corporations, such as Coca-Cola or Hewlett-Packard, that

Summary 10.2
When employees have financial investments in suppliers, customers, or distributors with whom their organization does business, conflicts of interest can arise. Company policy usually determines the permissible limits of such financial interests.

are listed on the stock exchange and whose stock price is unlikely to be influenced by your company's buying their products or not. Sometimes companies limit the percentage of outstanding stock their employees may own in a potential supplier, customer, distributor, or competitor (usually up to 10 percent). But in the EMC case, the eight executives owned shares of Storage Networks before the company went public, and with the latter's stock rocketing from 50 cents a share to over $90, adhering to the 10 percent rule wouldn't have prevented the problem. Frequently companies require key officials to make a full disclosure of all outside interests that could cloud their judgment or adversely affect their ability to promote the organization's interests. That's important, but as previously mentioned, full disclosure alone doesn't make the conflict disappear; steps must still be taken. Organizations need a detailed policy, customized to reflect their needs and interests, that spells out the limits of permissible outside financial investments and what employees should do when they have possible conflicts of interest. Because such a policy can affect the financial well-being of those who fall under it, however, it should be open to negotiation just as employee compensation is.

ABUSE OF OFFICIAL POSITION

Using one's official position for personal gain is likely to violate one's obligations to the organization.

The use of one's official position for personal gain always raises moral concerns and questions because of the likelihood that one is violating one's obligations to the firm or organization. Examples of **abuse of official position** range from misusing expense accounts to billing the company for unnecessary travel, from using subordinates for non-organization-related work to exploiting a position of trust within an organization to enhance one's own financial leverage and holdings. Executives who use corporate funds for private purposes like health club memberships, extravagant parties, vacation travel, or remodeling their homes are guilty of abusing their official position, as are CEOs like Bernard J. Ebbers of WorldCom, John Legere of Global Crossing, or L. Dennis Kozlowski of Tyco International, who used their high positions to borrow huge amounts of money at below-market rates—in Ebbers's case over $400 million—from the companies they worked for.[10]

Insider Trading

Insider trading is the buying or selling of stocks on the basis of nonpublic information that is likely to affect their price.

One common way of abusing one's official position is through **insider trading**: the buying or selling of stocks (or other financial securities) by business "insiders" on the basis of information that has not yet been made public and is likely to affect the price of the stock.[11] For example, as soon as he learned that the Food and Drug Administration was not going to approve his company's highly touted cancer drug Erbitux, Dr. Sam Waksal, CEO of ImClone Systems at the time, knew its stock would plummet. Before the FDA's decision was made public, Waksal quickly but quietly sold his stock in the company and told his father and one of his daughters to do so as well. He is also alleged to have passed the word on to his friend Martha Stewart, who dumped her ImClone stock the day before the FDA announced its decision. One doesn't have to profit personally to cross the line, however. For example, the wife of the president and chief executive of Genentech was charged with insider trading for providing confidential information to her brother. Before the biotechnology firm was partly acquired by another company, she told her brother that "some good things were about to happen" to the company and suggested that he buy a few thousand dollars' worth of stock, even if he had to borrow the funds. She also advised him to keep the purchase secret and make it in the name of a "trustworthy" friend.

Inside traders ordinarily defend their actions by claiming that they don't injure anyone. It's true that trading by insiders on the basis of nonpublic information seldom directly harms anyone. But moral concerns arise from indirect injury, as well as from direct. As one author puts it, "What causes injury or loss to outsiders is not what the insiders knew or did; rather it is what [the outsiders] themselves did not know. It is their own lack of knowledge which exposes them to risk of loss or denies them an opportunity to make a profit."[12] Case in point: the famous Texas Gulf Sulphur stock scandal.

When test drilling by Texas Gulf indicated a rich deposit of ore near Timmins, Ontario, some officials at Texas Gulf attempted to play down the potential worth of the Timmins property in a press release by describing it as only a prospect. But four days later a second press release termed the Timmins property a major discovery. In the interim, inside investors made a handsome personal profit through stock purchases. At the same time, stockholders who unloaded stock after the first press release or who sold the stock short, anticipating its price would fall, lost money.

The Securities and Exchange Commission (SEC), which is charged with policing the stock market, subsequently charged that a group of insiders—including Texas Gulf directors, officers, and employees—had violated the disclosure section of the Securities Exchange Act of 1934 by purchasing stock in the company while withholding information about the rich ore strike the company had made. The courts upheld the charge, finding that the first press release was "misleading to the reasonable investor using due care."[13] As a result, the courts not only ordered the insiders to pay into a special court-administered account all the money they had made but also directed them to repay profits made by outsiders whom they had tipped off. The courts then used this account to compensate persons who had lost money by selling their Texas Gulf Sulphur stock on the basis of the first press release.

Insiders and "Misappropriation"

Insider dealings raise intriguing questions. When can employees buy and sell securities in their own companies? How much information must they disclose to stockholders about the firm's plans and prospects? When must this information be disclosed? There's also the question, Who is considered an insider? Corporate executives, directors, officers, and other key employees are certainly insiders. But what about outsiders whom a company temporarily employs, such as accountants, lawyers, and contractors? Or what about those who just happen upon inside information?

In its effort to police the marketplace, the SEC has interpreted "insider" in a broad sense to mean anyone who buys or sells stock based on nonpublic information—whether or not the person is a corporate officer or otherwise linked to the company whose stock is being bought or sold. However, in 1980 the U.S. Supreme Court challenged the SEC's broad conception of insider trading in the case of Vincent Chiarella, a financial printer who traded on information he culled from documents passing through his shop. The Court ruled that Chiarella was not an insider with fiduciary responsibilities and thus had not violated the Securities Exchange Act. The Court reinforced its decision three years later when it reversed the conviction of securities analyst Raymond Dirks, who advised several of his clients to dump their shares in a company that he was about to blow the whistle on for fraud. In so ruling, the Court held that there is nothing improper about an outsider's using information, as long as the information is not obtained from an insider who breaches a legal duty to the corporation's shareholders for personal gain or to show favor to friends.

Since then the SEC has developed a new tactic, arguing that people who trade on confidential information but are not traditional company insiders are guilty of insider trading if they have "misappropriated" sensitive information. Although some appellate courts had rejected the SEC's approach, in 1997 the Supreme Court endorsed the misappropriation theory of insider trading in *U.S. v. O'Hagan*, thus upholding one of the SEC's main legal weapons against insider trading. In this case, James O'Hagan, a lawyer, had reaped a $4.3 million profit after learning that a company represented by his law firm was planning a hostile takeover of another company. O'Hagan had not worked on the case himself, but he had—the Court ruled—misappropriated confidential information belonging to his firm and its client. Writing for the majority, Justice Ruth Bader Ginsburg stressed that the Court's decision reflected the "animating purpose" of the Securities Exchange Act, namely, "to insure honest securities markets and thereby promote investor confidence."

Conflicting Perspectives on Insider Trading

Arthur Levitt, Jr., chairman of the Securities and Exchange Commission at the time, applauds the Court's *O'Hagan* decision, stating that it "reaffirms the SEC's effort to make the stock market fair to all people, whether you're a Wall Street veteran or a Main Street newcomer."[14] Law professor Henry Manne, however, sees nothing inherently wrong with insider trading and thinks the SEC should stay totally out of the insider-trading field. "The use of insider information should be governed by private contractual relationships," he believes, such as those between corporations and their personnel or between a law firm and its members.[15]

Some business theorists dispute the need to outlaw insider trading.

At the core of this disagreement are two opposed perspectives on what makes the market work. Levitt and like-minded analysts contend that the marketplace can work only if it is perceived as being honest and offering equal investment opportunity. Insider trading, they argue, makes that impossible. Those who think like Manne believe that permitting insiders to trade is good for the market because it accelerates the flow of positive or negative information about the stock to other shareholders and investors. As a result, this information is more quickly reflected in the stock's price, which is healthy

Summary 10.3
Insider trading is the buying or selling of stocks on the basis of nonpublic information likely to affect stock prices. Insider trading seems unfair; it can injure other investors and undermine public confidence in the stock market. In practice, determining what counts as insider trading is not always easy, but it typically involves misappropriating sensitive information. Although some writers defend insider trading as performing a necessary and desirable economic function, executives who do it are putting their own interests before those of the company and its shareholders.

for the market. They also believe that permitting insider trading can benefit a company by providing employees an incentive to invent new products, put together deals, or otherwise create new information that will increase the value of a company's stock.

Proving that insider trading harms ordinary investors or that there is something unfair about it isn't easy. Contrary to the view expressed by Manne, however, insider trading doesn't promote market efficiency. That's because insiders profit on the lag between when they start buying or selling and when the rest of the market figures out what's going on. Thus they have every reason to hoard information. In addition, insiders can benefit from negative, not just positive, information about the company they work for; this creates a dangerous incentive. But what's really wrong with insider trading is that executives who do it are putting their own interests before those of their shareholders, thus violating the fiduciary responsibility that is central to business management. All employees, but especially company insiders, have a duty to act in the interests of the firm and its shareholders, but many ways of profiting from insider information do not benefit the company at all—indeed, they may seriously damage its interests.[16]

The information that employees garner within the company is not always the kind that affects stock prices. Sometimes the information concerns highly sensitive data related to company research, technology, product development, and so on. How employees treat such secret or classified data can also raise important moral issues.

Proprietary Data

Companies guard information that can affect their competitive standing with all the zealousness of a bulldog guarding a ham bone. This is especially true of high-tech firms. A typical example is Lexar Media, which sued Toshiba for abusing its business relation with Lexar and passing the latter's confidential flash-memory technology to SanDisk, one of its competitors.[17] But even in the low-tech world, spats over **proprietary data** break out all the time. Procter & Gamble, for example, once sued three rival food chains for allegedly using the patented baking technique in its Duncan Hines brand of chocolate-chip cookies to make "infringing cookies." P&G further claimed that these companies had spied at a sales presentation and at cookie plants. One of the defendants, Frito-Lay, admitted to sending a worker to photograph the outside of a Duncan Hines bakery. But it denied telling the man's college-age son to walk into the plant and ask for some unbaked cookie dough—which the enterprising youth did, and got.[18]

Trade Secrets

When novel information is patented or copyrighted, it is legally protected but not secret. Others may have access to the information, but they are forbidden to use it (without permission) for the life of the patent or copyright. When a company patents a process, as Kleenex did with pop-up tissues, for example, the company has a monopoly on that process. Until the patent expires, no other firm may compete in the production of pop-up facial tissues. Although on the face of it this rule violates the ideal of a free market and would appear to slow the spread of new processes and technology, patents and copyrights are generally defended on the ground that without them technological innovation would be hampered. Individuals and companies would not be willing to invest in the development of a new process if other firms could immediately exploit any new invention without having invested in developing it.

Although patent law is complicated and patents are not easy to acquire, what it means for something to be patented is well defined legally. By contrast, the concept of a trade secret is broad and imprecise. The standard legal definition says that a **trade secret** is "any formula, pattern, device, or compilation of information which is used in one's business and which gives him an opportunity to obtain an advantage over competitors who do not know or use it."[19] Virtually any information that is not generally known (or whose utility is not recognized) is eligible for classification as a trade secret, as long as such information is valuable to its possessor and is treated confidentially. Most states have laws against the theft of trade secrets, and the **Economic Espionage Act** of 1996 makes it a federal crime. By contrast with patents and copyrights, one does not have to declare or register something as a trade secret for it to be protected. Trade secrets, however, do not enjoy the same protection as patented information. The formula for Coca-Cola, for instance, is secret but not patented. No competitor has yet succeeded in figuring it out by "reverse engineering," but if your company managed to do so, then it would be entitled to use the formula itself.

There are at least three arguments for legally protecting trade secrets: (1) Trade secrets are the intellectual property of the company. (2) The theft of trade secrets is unfair competition. (3) Employees who disclose trade secrets violate the confidentiality owed to their employers.[20] In individual cases, what constitutes intellectual property, unfair competition, or a violation of confidentiality is often controversial. But clearly one of the biggest challenges facing an organization can be to prevent its trade secrets and proprietary data from being misused by employees who leave the company.

Employees Who Join a Competitor

Employees who leave the company are often privy to confidential or proprietary information, which their new employer can sometimes take unfair advantage of. For example, Starwood Hotels and Resorts charged that when some of its executives left to take high-profile jobs at Hilton Hotels, they brought with them documents that helped Hilton create a new luxury-hotel brand.[21] And Mattel, maker of the famous Barbie doll, successfully sued MGA Entertainment for having gotten the idea for its popular Bratz doll line from a designer it had hired away from Mattel and who had originally conceived the idea while working there.[22] The problem posed by employees who quit to work for a competitor is especially troublesome for high-tech firms because their employees are so prone to job-hopping (at one point, the job tenure of an executive in the software industry was estimated to be a scant twenty-two months)[23] and because of the difficulty of separating trade secrets from the technical know-how, experience, and skill that are part of the employee's own intellect and talents.

Almost any information that is not generally known can be classified as a trade secret if it is valuable to its possessor and treated confidentially.

Three arguments for legally protecting trade secrets.

A classic case involved Donald Wohlgemuth, who worked in the space-suit department of B. F. Goodrich in Akron, Ohio.[24] Eventually Wohlgemuth became general manager of the spacesuit division and learned Goodrich's highly classified spacesuit technology for the Apollo flights. Shortly thereafter, Wohlgemuth, desiring a higher salary, joined Goodrich's competitor, International Latex Corporation in Dover, Delaware, as manager of engineering for the industrial area that included making spacesuits in competition with Goodrich. Goodrich protested by seeking an order restraining Wohlgemuth from working for Latex or for any other company in the space field. The Court of Appeals of Ohio denied Goodrich's request for an injunction, respecting Wohlgemuth's right to choose his employer, but it did provide an injunction restraining Wohlgemuth from revealing Goodrich's trade secrets.

Proprietary data cases sometimes pit the firm's right to protect its secrets against an employee's right to seek employment wherever he or she chooses.

Cases like Wohlgemuth's pit a firm's right to protect its secrets against an employee's right to seek employment wherever he or she chooses. As a result, the moral dilemmas that arise in proprietary-data cases are not easily resolved. For one thing, the trade secrets that companies seek to protect have often become an integral part of the departing employee's total job skills and capabilities. These may, for instance, manifest themselves simply in a subconscious or intuitive sense of what will or will not work in the laboratory. Wohlgemuth's total intellectual capacity included the information, experience, and technical skills acquired at his former workplace. Goodrich might be justified in claiming much of Wohlgemuth's intellectual capacity as its corporate property, but it is difficult to see how he could divest himself of it.

Summary 10.4
Proprietary data are an organization's classified or secret information. Increasingly, problems arise as employees in high-tech occupations with access to sensitive information and trade secrets quit and take jobs with competitors. Proprietary-data issues pose a conflict between two legitimate rights: the right of employers to keep certain information secret and the right of individuals to work where they choose.

Sometimes companies require employees to sign contracts restricting their ability to get a job with, or start, a competing company within a certain geographical radius or for a certain time. Because they can conflict with freedom of employment, not all such "noncompete" or "nondisclosure" contracts are legally valid, however. But even without one, companies sometimes sue departing employees as Essex Temporary Services did when Frank Cumbo and ten colleagues left the organization to start a competing business. Essex filed a second suit against six other employees who quit a few months later to join the new firm of Lerner, Cumbo, and Associates.[25]

The underlying issue of fairness isn't, of course, just a legal question. Frank Cumbo claims that he didn't take any information from Essex that couldn't be found in a phone book. That's relevant to assessing the morality of his conduct, but one would have to know all the details to determine if he wrongly took advantage of information, connections, or business know-how that he had acquired at Essex. In the Goodrich case, it appears that Donald Wohlegemuth didn't take this moral question very seriously. When asked whether he had acted ethically in leaving Goodrich for a competitor, he replied, "Loyalty and ethics have their price, and International Latex has paid the price."[26]

BRIBES AND KICKBACKS

To **bribe** someone is to pay the person to violate his or her official duties; that is, to perform an action that is inconsistent with the person's work contract or job responsibilities or with the nature of the work the person has been hired to do. Although usually financial, the payment can be anything that is of value to the recipient. Offering a bribe is wrong because it is an inducement to act dishonestly, to disregard one's duties, or to betray a trust—for example, tendering cash to a building inspector to ignore a code violation. For the same reasons, it is wrong to accept a bribe even if one happens to end up not doing what one was bribed to do.[27]

A typical case of bribery was that of Norman Rothberg, an accountant working at ZZZZ Best Carpet Cleaning Company in the Los Angeles area. When he learned that ZZZZ Best had falsified accounts on insurance restoration jobs, he passed on the information to the accounting firm of Ernst & Whinney, which was overseeing ZZZZ Best's planned multimillion-dollar acquisition of another carpet-cleaning chain. When an investigation began, Rothberg accepted $17,000 from ZZZZ Best officials to back off from his initial reports.[28] Rothberg's conduct was wrong because he accepted money in exchange for violating his responsibilities as an accountant. By contrast, a server who accepts a gratuity for providing good service to a restaurant customer is not accepting a bribe, for she is not violating her duties. However, the situation would be different if she took money in exchange for not charging the customer for the drinks he ordered. Of course, bribery can occur in more subtle forms than in the Rothberg case—for example, a contractor who charges a company executive only a nominal fee for building her a home patio on the tacit understanding that the executive will see that her company accepts the contractor's bid for an important project.

Bribery sometimes takes the form of a **kickback**, which is a percentage payment to a person able to influence or control a source of income. Thus, Alicia Rocha, sales representative for Sisyphus Books, offers a textbook-selection committee member a percentage of the handsome commission she stands to make if a Sisyphus civics text is adopted. The money the committee member receives for the preferred consideration is a kickback. A flagrant case of kickbacks involved American executives of the Honda Motor Company. For years they pocketed millions in bribes and kickbacks from local car dealers; in return, the dealers received permission to open lucrative dealerships and had no trouble obtaining models (such as the Acura) that were in scarce supply and could be sold at a large profit.[29]

The Foreign Corrupt Practices Act

In 1977 the FCPA made it illegal for American companies to engage in bribery overseas.

Bribery is generally illegal in the United States, but U.S. companies have a history of paying off foreign officials for business favors. Such acts were declared illegal in the **Foreign Corrupt Practices Act (FCPA)** of 1977, which was passed in the wake of the discovery that nearly four hundred U.S. companies, including Exxon, Gulf Oil, and United Brands, had made such payments. Egregious within this sordid pattern of international bribery were Lockheed Aircraft Corporation's secret payoffs to foreign politicians to get aircraft contracts. Lest one understate the effects of such bribery, it is worth noting that revelations of Lockheed bribes in Japan caused a government crisis there, and that in Holland Prince Bernhard was forced to resign his government duties after admitting that he took a $1 million payoff from Lockheed.

The FCPA provides stiff fines and prison sentences for corporate officials engaging in bribery overseas and requires corporations to establish strict accounting and auditing controls to guard against the creation of slush funds from which bribes can be paid. The FCPA does not, however, prohibit **grease payments** to the employees of foreign governments who have primarily clerical or ministerial responsibilities. These payments are sometimes necessary to ensure that the recipients carry out their normal job duties. On the other hand, the FCPA makes no distinction between bribery and extortion. A company is extorted by a foreign official if, for instance, the official threatens to violate the company's rights, perhaps by closing down a plant on some legal pretext, unless the official is paid off.

One company caught violating the FCPA was Ashland Oil. Under its then-CEO Orin Atkins, Ashland had agreed to pay an entity controlled by an Omani government official approximately $29 million for a majority interest in Midlands Chrome, Inc.—a price far higher than it was worth—for the purpose of obtaining crude oil at a highly favorable price. When Atkins proposed the acquisition of Midlands Chrome to his board of directors, he said that although the acquisition was a high-risk project, it "had the potential for being more than offset by a potential crude oil contract." Midlands Chrome did not in fact prove particularly profitable, but the Omani government awarded Ashland a contract for 20,000 barrels a day for one year at a $3-per-barrel discount from the regular selling price—a discount worth $21.9 million.[30]

The Case against Overseas Bribery

The FCPA has been weakened by amendments that expand the exemption for grease payments and offer corporations more defenses against prosecution. In 1998, however, the law was extended to include bribery by foreign firms on American territory, and, thanks to the Federal Sentencing Guidelines, penalties are now stiffer than those originally specified by the FCPA. Moreover, since 2001 the Justice Department has been pursuing overseas bribery more vigorously than before, launching five or six times as many prosecutions per year.[31] Critics of the FCPA disapprove of this. They insist that the law puts American corporations at a competitive disadvantage in relation to foreign firms whose governments permit them to bribe. For example, in response to a Senate probe into corrupt activities by oil companies in Africa, an oil executive complained that if his company chose to take the moral high road, "Someone [else] will come [in]. The French will, the Russians will, Petronas [of Malaysia] will."[32] Alexandra Wrage of Trace International, a business ethics group based in Washington, D.C., is sympathetic. "The lack of a level playing field is an enormous competitive advantage for non-U.S. companies," she says. "U.S. companies feel like they are in the cross-hairs, which is a good thing for anti-bribery enforcement, but it comes at a pretty high cost."[33]

Such reasoning, however, can be a way of rationalizing conduct that is morally indefensible. For one thing, competition is often not a factor at all. For example, when United Brands paid a Honduran official a $1.25 million bribe, it was to gain a reduction in the country's business export tax, not to

Summary 10.5
A bribe is payment in some form for an act that runs counter to the work contract or the nature of the work one has been hired to perform. The Foreign Corrupt Practices Act prohibits corporations from engaging in bribery overseas. Critics charge that the FCPA puts American firms at a disadvantage and imposes U.S. standards on foreign countries. However, bribery can injure individuals, competitors, and political institutions. It also hurts economic growth and damages the free-market system.

win a contract that might have gone to a foreign competitor. Moreover, when, before passage of the FCPA, U.S. firms did use bribery to beat out competitors, their competitors were usually other U.S. companies.[34] Further, studies show that the FCPA has been at most a minor disincentive to export expansion. Even in nations where the FCPA is alleged to have hurt American business, there has been no statistically discernible effect on U.S. market share. In fact, since passage of the FCPA, U.S. trade with bribe-prone countries has outpaced U.S. trade with other countries.[35]

Thirty-seven countries, including all the world's industrialized nations, have passed domestic legislation implementing the **OECD** (**Organization for Economic Co-operation and Development**) **Anti-Bribery Convention,** a formal treaty concluded in 1997 that outlaws bribing public officials in foreign business transactions and sets up review and monitoring mechanisms. As a result, these days many nations are going after overseas bribery as zealously as the United States does. A Munich court, for example, recently fined Siemens AG, the German giant, nearly $300 million for trying to win contracts by bribing officials in Nigeria, Russia, and Libya.[36] The OECD Convention has been reinforced by separate European anti-corruption conventions, various industry-specific agreements, and by the efforts of the U.N., World Bank, and International Monetary Fund to combat corruption. These developments make it doubtful that the FCPA puts American companies at a competitive disadvantage. But even if the FCPA does handicap U.S. firms and cause them to lose exports, that fact would have to be carefully weighed against the ample documentary evidence of the serious harm done to individuals, companies, and governments as a result of systematic bribery overseas.

The argument that the FCPA wrongly imposes U.S. standards on foreign countries is weak.

A frequently heard argument against the FCPA is that the law imposes U.S. standards on foreign countries and that bribery and payoffs are common business practices in other nations. But that argument is too glib, especially when it comes from those who don't really have a working knowledge of another culture. In some other nations, to be sure, bribery does seem more widespread than it is here, but that doesn't imply that bribery is considered morally acceptable even in those nations. (Drug dealing is not morally acceptable here, even though it is, unfortunately, widespread.) If other countries really did consider bribery and related practices to be morally acceptable, then presumably the people engaging in them would not mind having that fact publicized. But it is difficult to find a real-life example of foreign officials willing to let the public know they accept bribes.

Certainly the FCPA reflects our own moral standards, but those standards are not simply matters of taste (like clothing styles) or completely arbitrary (like our decision to drive on the right, whereas the British drive on the left). Good, objective arguments can be given against bribery and related corrupt practices because they are intended to induce people inside a business or other organization to make a decision that would not be justifiable according to normal business or other criteria. For example, by encouraging on non-market grounds the purchase of inferior goods or the payment of an exorbitant price, bribery can clearly injure a variety of legitimate interests—from stockholders to consumers, from taxpayers to other businesses. It subverts market competition by giving advantage in a way that is not directly or indirectly product related.

There is nothing "relative" about the damage that such corruption can do to a society. Studies show that the more corrupt a nation is, the less it invests and the slower its economic growth.[37] If we were to permit U.S. companies to engage in bribery overseas, we would be encouraging in other countries practices that we consider too harmful to tolerate at home. Moreover, even an occasional corporate bribe overseas can foster bribery and kickbacks at home and lead employees to subordinate the interest of the organization to their own private gain. Corruption is difficult to cordon off; once a company engages in it, corruption can easily spread throughout the organization.

The multiple impacts of bribery can be succinctly drawn out in one final case, which involved Bethlehem Steel Corporation, once the nation's second-largest steel company. Bethlehem was convicted of bribery and other corrupt practices for paying shipowners' representatives, including officers of the Colombian Navy, to steer ships needing repairs to Bethlehem's eight shipyards. Thus, competitive bidding for the contracts was effectively eliminated, various members of the Colombian Navy were corrupted, and the Colombian government presumably ended up paying more for the repair work than it had to. Beyond that, Bethlehem generated the money for the payoffs by padding bills and skimming profits from legitimate shipyard repair work. Thus, unsuspecting clients of Bethlehem were made to pay the bill for Bethlehem's bribery.

> Permitting U.S. companies to engage in foreign bribery would be encouraging something in other countries that we consider too harmful to tolerate at home.

GIFTS AND ENTERTAINMENT

Business gifts and entertainment of clients and business associates are familiar parts of the business world. Normally, giving someone a gift or taking the person out for a nice meal is a gesture of good will or friendship and can help cement a relationship between two people. Unlike a bribe, it involves no quid pro quo or expectation that the recipient will do something specific in return. But gifts do tend to create a sense of gratitude in the recipient, who may feel obligated to reciprocate in some way. For this reason, in a business context gifts can raise conflict-of-interest problems and even border on bribery. Knowing where to draw the line here is not always easy. But one thing is clear: Those who cross that line, wittingly or not, can end up in big trouble. Ask the former General Services Administration (GSA) official who pleaded guilty to a criminal charge of accepting free lunches from a subsidiary of BellSouth Corporation, which was seeking a telephone contract with the GSA.

The federal government provides its procurement officers with two days of lectures and case-study discussions on the ethics of government contracting. Procurement officers, for example, are taught that they may accept an invitation to speak before a trade association consisting of the contractors they buy from, but they must decline the $50 honorarium, whatever the topic of their talk. They also must refuse a ticket for their transportation to the meeting, although they may be permitted to accept lunch as a guest seated at the head of the table, if this is compatible with the policy of their particular agency.

For people in the business world, the rules are not so cut-and-dried, and some of them manage to ignore altogether the conflict of interest issues that gifts create. Consider Colin Dalzell, an executive at MCI Systemhouse. Just before it went public, the e-biz software maker Commerce One offered Dalzell, who had done business with it, a chance to buy its shares. He did, and in one day made a profit of $40,000, which he used to buy a 1965 Cobra racing-car kit. Dalzell says that he had a long, established relationship with Commerce One and that the payment wasn't enough to influence his future dealings with it.[38] But most companies and most businesspeople view behavior like his as morally problematic, to say the least.

Determining the morality of giving and receiving gifts in a business situation is not always easy. But there are several factors a conscientious businessperson should take into account:

1. **What is the value of the gift?** Is the gift of nominal value, or is it substantial enough to influence a business decision? Undoubtedly, definitions of "nominal" and "substantial" are open to interpretation and are often influenced by situational and cultural variables. Nevertheless, many organizations consider a gift worth less than $25 and given infrequently—perhaps once a year—only nominal but view anything larger or more frequent as problematic. Although this standard won't fit all cases, it does indicate that accepting even a rather inexpensive gift might be deemed inappropriate.

2. **What is the purpose of the gift?** Dick Zolezzi, a department store manager, accepts small gifts such as pocket calculators from an electronics firm. He insists that the transactions are harmless and that he doesn't intend to give the firm any preferential treatment in store advertising displays. As long as the gift is not intended or received as a bribe and remains nominal, there doesn't appear to be any problem. But it would be important to ascertain the electronics firm's intention in giving the gift. Is it to influence how Zolezzi lays out displays? Does Zolezzi himself expect it as a palm-greasing device before he'll ensure that the firm receives equal promotional treatment? If so, extortion may be involved. Relevant to the question of purpose is whether the gift is directly tied to an accepted business practice. For example, appointment books, calendars, or pens and pencils with the donor's name clearly imprinted on them serve to advertise a firm. Golf clubs or trips to Hawaii rarely serve this purpose.

3. **What are the circumstances under which the gift was given or received?** A gift given during the holiday season, for a store opening, or to signal other special events is circumstantially different from one unattached to any special event. Whether the gift was given openly or secretly should also be considered. An open gift, say, with the donor's name embossed on it, raises fewer questions than a gift known only to the donor and the recipient.

4. **What are the position and sensitivity to influence of the person receiving the gift?** Is the person in a position to affect materially a business decision on behalf of the gift giver? In other words, could the recipient's opinion, influence, or decision result in preferential treatment for the donor? Another important point is whether the recipient has made it clear to the donor that the gift won't influence his or her action one way or the other.

5. **What is the accepted business practice in the industry?** Is this the customary way of conducting this kind of business? Monetary gifts and tips are standard practice in numerous service industries. Their purpose is not only to reward good service but to ensure it again. But it's not customary to tip the head of the produce department in a supermarket so the person will put aside the best tomatoes for you. When gratuities are an integral part of customary business practice, they are far less likely to pose moral questions.

6. **What is the company's policy?** Many firms explicitly limit or even forbid altogether the giving or receiving of gifts. Wal-Mart, for example, doesn't permit employees to accept anything from companies doing business with it, not even a cup of coffee, and Kmart requires not only its managers but also its vendors, suppliers, and real-estate associates to sign a no-gifts policy.[39] When such a policy exists, the giving or receiving of a gift is usually wrong.

7. **What is the law?** Certain federal, state, or local government employees may be legally forbidden from receiving gifts from firms with which they do business. Sometimes the law also regulates gift giving in specific industries. For example, the Securities and Exchange Commission fined Fidelity Investments, the mutual fund company, because some of its traders had accepted gifts from brokers seeking to do business with it.[40] And several title insurance companies violated Washington state law by lavishing pro-basketball tickets and other goodies on bankers, builders, and representatives of real-estate companies as a way of drumming up referrals.[41] When gift transactions violate the law, they are clearly unacceptable.

Related to gift giving is the practice of entertaining. Some companies distinguish entertainment from gifts as follows: If you can eat it or drink it on the spot, it's entertainment. In general, entertainment should be interpreted more sympathetically than gifts because it usually occurs within the context of doing business in a social situation. Still, the morality of entertainment should be evaluated along the same lines as gifts—that is, with respect to value, purpose, circumstances, position and sensitivity to influence of the recipient, accepted business practice, company policy, and the law. In each case the ultimate moral judgment hinges largely on whether an objective party could reasonably suspect that the gift or entertainment might lead the recipient to sacrifice the interest of the firm for his or her personal gain.

Summary 10.6
The following considerations are relevant in determining the moral acceptability of gift giving and receiving: the value of the gift, its purpose, the circumstances under which it is given, the position and sensitivity to influence of the person receiving the gift, accepted business practice, company policy, and what the law says.

The same seven considerations are also relevant to the moral evaluation of business entertainment.

CONFLICTING OBLIGATIONS

Consider the following situations:

An employee knows that a coworker occasionally sips whiskey on the job. Should she inform the boss?

A dishwasher knows that the restaurant's chef typically reheats three- or four-day-old food and serves it as fresh. When he informs the manager, he is told to forget it. What should the dishwasher do?

A consulting engineer discovers a defect in a structure that is about to be sold. If the owner will not disclose the defect to the potential purchaser, should the engineer do so?

A clerical worker learns that the personnel department has authorized hirings that violate the firm's anti-nepotism rules and neglect its affirmative action commitments. What should she do about it?

On a regular basis, a secretary is asked by her boss to lie to his wife about his whereabouts. "If my wife telephones," he tells her, "don't forget that 'I'm calling on a client.'" In fact, as the secretary well knows, the boss is having an affair with another woman. What should the secretary do?

Such cases are not unusual, but they are different from the ones previously considered in this chapter because they involve workers caught in the crossfire of competing ethical concerns and moral responsibilities. Should the employee ensure the welfare of the organization by reporting the fellow worker who drinks, or should she be loyal to her coworker and say nothing? Should the dishwasher go public with what he knows, or should he simply forget the matter? Should the secretary carry out her boss's instructions, or should she tell his wife the truth? In each case the employee may experience conflicting obligations, diverging ideals, and divided loyalties.

Many of the difficult moral decisions that employees sometimes face involve such conflicts. How are they to be resolved? According to the procedure recommended in Chapter 2, our moral decisions should take into account our specific obligations, any important ideals that our actions would support or undermine, and, finally, the effects or consequences of the different options open to us. To begin with the last consideration, remember that even staunch nonconsequentialists acknowledge that the likely results of our actions are relevant to their moral assessment and that we have some duty to promote human well-being. In general, the fuller our understanding of the possible results of the different actions we might take in the specific situation before us—that is, the better we understand the exact ramifications of the alternatives—the more likely we are to make a sound moral decision. Reflecting on the effects of these different courses of action can help us understand what ideals are at stake and determine the exact strength of the more specific obligations we have.

> Recall from Chapter 2 that our moral decisions should consider the relevant obligations, ideals, and effects.

The impact of our actions on significant moral ideals is the second consideration to be weighed. Any serious moral decision should take into account the various ideals advanced or respected, ignored or hindered, by the alternative courses of conduct open to us. In addition, our moral choices

Summary 10.7
Balancing our obligations to employer or organization, to friends and coworkers, and to third parties outside the organization can create conflicts and divided loyalties. In resolving such moral conflicts, we must identify the relevant obligations, ideals, and effects and decide where the emphasis among them should lie.

are often strongly influenced by the personal weight we place on the different values at stake in a specific situation. Sometimes those values can point in different directions, as when our simultaneous commitment to professional excellence, personal integrity, and loyalty to friends pulls us in different ways.

Finally, any responsible moral decision must, of course, take into account the more specific obligations we have—in particular, those obligations that are a function of the particular relationships, roles, or circumstances we happen to be in. This chapter has already discussed the obligations employees have to the organization based on a freely negotiated work contract, and it is easy to see that employees have moral obligations arising from the business, professional, or organizational roles they have assumed. For example, teachers have an obligation to grade fairly, bartenders to refrain from overserving intoxicated customers, engineers to guarantee the safety of their projects, and accountants to certify that financial statements present data fairly and according to generally accepted accounting principles. Because of his or her role responsibilities, an auditor who suspects some irregularity has an obligation to get to the bottom of the matter, an obligation that is probably lacking when an ordinary employee has a hunch that something is not in order in another department.

Thus, employees have certain general duties to their employers, and because of the specific business, professional, or organizational responsibilities they have assumed, they may have other more precise role-based obligations. In addition, employees are human beings with moral responsibilities to friends, family, and coworkers—to those flesh-and-blood people with whom their lives are intertwined, both inside and outside the workplace. These ongoing relationships are the source of important moral obligations.

What about the obligations of employees to other parties or to society in general? In particular, what obligations do employees have to people with whom they have no relationship and for whom they have no specific professional, organizational, or other role responsibility? Here different moral theories may steer us in slightly different directions, but simply as a matter of ordinary commonsense morality it is clear that employees—like everyone else—have certain elementary duties to other people. Of particular significance are the obligations to avoid injuring others and to be truthful and fair.

When faced with a moral decision, then, employees should follow the two-step procedure set forth in Chapter 2: identifying the relevant obligations, ideals, and effects and then trying to decide where the emphasis should lie among these considerations. There is nothing mechanical about this process, but when we as employees weigh moral decisions, two simple things can help keep our deliberations free from the various rationalizations to which we are all prone. *First*, we can ask ourselves whether we would be willing to read an account of our actions in the newspaper. Is the course of action we are considering one that we would be willing to defend publicly? *Second*, discussing a moral dilemma or ethical problem with a friend can often help us avoid bias and gain a better perspective. People by themselves,

Two simple things can help keep our moral decisions free from rationalization.

and especially when emotionally involved in a situation, sometimes focus unduly on one or two points, ignoring other relevant factors. Input from others can keep us from overlooking pertinent considerations, thus helping us make a better, more objective moral judgment.

As the preceding discussion mentioned, employees sometimes learn about the illegal or immoral actions of a supervisor or firm. When an employee tries to correct the situation within institutional channels and is thwarted, a central moral question emerges: Should the employee go public with the information? Should a worker who is ordered to do something illegal or immoral, or who knows of the illegal or immoral behavior of a supervisor or organization, inform the public?

WHISTLE-BLOWING

Summary 10.8
Employees have duties to their employers, and they may also have more specific obligations based on the business or professional roles and responsibilities they have assumed. In addition, they have the same elementary moral obligations that all human beings have—including the obligation not to injure others and to be truthful and fair.

Morris H. Baslow, a forty-seven-year-old biologist and father of three, won't forget the day he dropped an envelope in the mail to Thomas B. Yost, an administrative law judge with the Environmental Protection Agency (EPA). Later that day, Baslow was fired from his job with Lawler, Matusky & Skelly, an engineering consulting firm hired by Consolidated Edison of New York to help it blunt EPA demands. The EPA was insisting that the power company's generating plants on the Hudson River had to have cooling towers to protect fish from the excessively warm water that it was discharging into the river.

Baslow claimed that the documents he sent showed that Con Ed and Lawler, Matusky & Skelly had knowingly submitted to the EPA invalid and misleading data, giving the false impression that the long-term effects of the utility's effluent on fish were negligible. On the basis of his own research, Baslow believed that the fish could be significantly harmed by the warm-water discharge. He said that for two years he tried to get his employers to listen, but they wouldn't.

Shortly after being fired, Baslow sent seventy-one company documents supporting his allegation to the EPA, the federal Energy Regulatory Commission, and the Justice Department. In the month following those disclosures, Baslow's employers accused him of stealing the documents and sued him for defamation. Baslow countersued, citing the Clean Water Act, which protects consultants from reprisals for reporting findings prejudicial to their employers and clients.

A year later, Lawler, Matusky & Skelly dropped all legal action against Baslow and gave him a cash settlement, reportedly of around $100,000. In return, Baslow wrote to the EPA and other government agencies, withdrawing his charges of wrongdoing and perjury but not recanting his own scientific conclusions. Asked why he finally accepted the cash payment, the unemployed Baslow said, "I've had to bear the brunt of this financially by myself. ... I just wish somebody had listened to me six months ago."[42]

Other whistle-blowers express similar sentiments, even when they have been proved right. Microbiologist David Franklin blew the whistle on Warner-Lambert for promoting its epilepsy drug Neurontin for off-label uses such as migraines, hiccups, and bipolar disorder. Among other things, the company paid doctors to listen to pitches for uses of Neurontin that lacked FDA approval and even treated them to luxury trips to Hawaii and to the Olympics. (Although doctors are free to prescribe drugs for uses not on their FDA-approved label, the agency forbids companies from promoting their drugs for off-label uses.) After a lengthy legal battle, Franklin was completely vindicated when Warner-Lambert pled guilty and agreed to pay more than $430 million to settle the Justice Department's claims against it. As part of the settlement, Franklin even received a multimillion-dollar reward under the False Claims Act, originally passed in 1863 to crack down on Civil War prof-iteering. Still, says Franklin, "This has been the most disruptive thing I can imagine can take place in anyone's life."[43]

Or talk to David Graham, an FDA researcher, who endured rebukes and harassment from superiors for first investigating and then exposing the risk of heart attack that the painkiller Vioxx poses. "I can guarantee you, there are other whistle-blowers at the FDA," says Graham. "Fear has them by the throat. And they struggle with their conscience and they struggle with the wrong they see, and they are paralyzed by their fear. They are looking to see—can that Graham fellow get away with committing the truth? It remains to be seen whether I can." He adds, "Please understand, I am not a hero, and I'm not endowed with extraordinary courage."[44] For his part, David Franklin offers the following advice to potential whistle-blowers: "People who are in the position I was need to think about their own futures and how they feel about themselves and what their kids look up to and why they got into this business in the first place," he says. "That's where the endurance of the thing comes into play."[45]

The Baslow, Franklin, and Graham cases illustrate the ethical issues and personal risks facing employees who blow the whistle on what they perceive as organizational misconduct. We now address three more-specific questions: What exactly is whistle-blowing? What motivates whistle-blowers to do what they do? When is one morally justified in blowing the whistle?

The Definition of Whistle-Blowing

Whistle-blowing refers to an employee's informing the public about the illegal or immoral behavior of an employer or an organization. One expert more fully defines whistle-blowing as

> A practice in which employees who know that their company is engaged in activities that (a) cause unnecessary harm, (b) are in violation of human rights, (c) are illegal, (d) run counter to the defined purpose of the institution, or (e) are otherwise immoral inform the public or some governmental agency of those activities.[46]

Another business ethicist spells out the concept this way:

> Whistle-blowing is the voluntary release of nonpublic information, as a moral protest, by a member or former member of an organization outside the normal channels of communication to an appropriate audience about illegal and/or im-moral conduct in the organization or conduct in the organization that is opposed in some significant way to the public interest.[47]

Summary 10.9
Whistle-blowing refers to an employee's informing the public about the illegal or immoral behavior of an employer or organization. Whistle-blowers frequently act out of a sense of professional responsibility.

These definitions limit the scope of what constitutes whistle-blowing. Whistle-blowing is something that can be done only by a (past or present) member of an organization. An investigative reporter, for example, who exposes corporate malfeasance is not a whistle-blower. Nor is an employee who spreads gossip about in-house gaffes and indiscretions, thus abusing confidentiality and acting disloyally to colleagues and to the organization. By contrast, whistle-blowing involves exposing activities that are harmful, immoral, or contrary to the public interest or to the legitimate goals and purposes of the organization. It does not encompass sabotage or taking retaliatory action against the employer or firm, but it does require going outside normal channels. (This doesn't imply, however, that whistle-blowing must be external. Most writers on the subject hold that there can be internal whistle-blowing, the disclosure of inappropriate conduct to someone inside the organization.)

What Motivates Whistle-Blowers?

Professor of philosophy Norman Bowie correctly points out that today's discussion of whistle-blowing parallels the discussion of **civil disobedience** in the 1960s.[48] Just as civil disobedients of that time felt their duty to obey the law was overridden by other moral obligations, so the whistle-blower believes that the public interest morally outweighs loyalty to colleagues and his or her duties to the organization. Coleen Rowley, for example, was a veteran FBI agent with twenty-one years of experience who had never worked anywhere else—indeed, she had wanted to be an agent ever since she was in fifth grade. When she decided to go public with evidence that her bosses had failed to follow up on information that might have thwarted the terrorist attacks of September 11, 2001, and were now misleading the public about what the FBI had known, her desire to do what was right took precedence over her lifelong love of the Bureau. Although whistle-blowers such as Rowley are often stigmatized as "disloyal," many of them see themselves as acting in the best interests of the organization.

Whistle-blowers believe that the public interest can be more important than loyalty to the organization.

What motivates whistle-blowers? Often, it's simply a sense of professional responsibility. Take F. Barron Stone, for example. He warned his bosses at Duke Power that they were overcharging ratepayers in the Carolinas. When they wouldn't listen, he told state regulators. That triggered an investigation, which led to Duke Power's agreeing to change its accounting procedures and reimburse customers. "I was just doing my job" is all Stone says.[49] Or consider Cynthia Cooper. An internal auditor at WorldCom, she got wind that some of the company's divisions were engaged in crooked accounting practices. She raised the matter with the firm's external auditor, Arthur Andersen, but it assured her there was no problem. When she didn't drop the issue, WorldCom's chief financial officer, Scott Sullivan, told her that everything was fine and she should back off. Troubled and suspicious about what was going on, Cooper ignored Sullivan's order. She and her team began doing what the external auditor was supposed to do. For weeks and weeks they pored over company books, working late at night to avoid detection by management, before eventually exposing the accounting scams Sullivan and others were involved in. "I'm not a hero," she told friends and colleagues. "I'm just doing my job."[50]

In the case of Noreen Harrington, the motivation was a little different. A veteran of the mutual fund industry, she resigned from Stern Asset Management because her in-house complaints about improper transactions were disregarded. But she had no intention of telling authorities. Then a year later, her older sister asked her for advice about her 401(k). She had lost a lot of money and wasn't sure that she would be able to retire. "All of a sudden, I thought about this from a different vantage point," Harrington explains. "I saw one face—my sister's face—and then I saw the faces of everyone whose only asset was a 401(k). At that point I felt the need to try to make the regulators look into [these] abuses." That's when she called the office of Eliot Spitzer, then the New York State attorney general, who was on a crusade to clean up the mutual fund industry.[51]

When Is Whistle-Blowing Justified?

Although the motivations of whistle-blowers such as F. Barron Stone, Cynthia Cooper, and Noreen Harrington are honorable and praiseworthy, whistle-blowing itself is a morally problematic action, as Professor Sissela Bok reminds us.[52] The whistle can be blown in error or malice, privacy invaded, confidentiality violated, and trust undermined. Not least, publicly accusing others of wrongdoing can be very destructive and brings with it an obligation to be fair to the persons accused. In addition, internal prying and mutual suspicion make it difficult for any organization to function. And, finally, one must bear in mind that whistle-blowers are only human beings, not saints, and they sometimes have their own self-serving agenda.[53]

In developing his analogy with civil disobedience, Professor Bowie proposes several conditions that must be met for an act of whistle-blowing to be morally justified. These conditions may not be the last word on this controversial subject, but they do provide a good starting point for further debate over the morality of whistle-blowing. According to Bowie, whistle-blowing is morally justified if and only if

> **It is done from an appropriate moral motive.** For an act of whistle-blowing to be justified, it must be motivated by a desire to expose unnecessary harm, illegal or immoral actions, or conduct counter to the public good or the defined purpose of the organization. Desire for attention or profit or the exercise of one's general tendency toward stirring up trouble is not a justification for whistle-blowing.
>
> Although, as Chapter 2 explained, the question of motive is an important one in Kantian ethics, not all moral theorists would agree with Bowie's first condition. Might not an employee be justified in blowing the whistle on serious wrongdoing by the employer, even if the employee's real motivation was the desire for revenge? Granted that the motivation was ignoble, the action itself might nonetheless have been the morally right one. An action can still be morally justified, say some theorists, even when it is done for the wrong reason. Still, many people were troubled to learn that the whistle-blowing paralegal who provided anti-tobacco

lawyers with crucial documents about a tobacco company's secret studies on the health dangers of cigarettes was paid more than $100,000 by the lawyers.[54]

2. **The whistle-blower, except in special circumstances, has exhausted all internal channels for dissent before going public.** The duty of loyalty to the firm obligates workers to seek an internal remedy before informing the public of a misdeed. This is an important consideration, but in some cases the attempt to exhaust internal channels may result in dangerous delays or expose the would-be whistle-blower to retaliation.

3. **The whistle-blower has compelling evidence that wrongful actions have been ordered or have occurred.** Spelling out what constitutes "compelling evidence" is difficult, but employees can ask themselves whether the evidence is strong enough that any reasonable person in possession of it would be convinced that an illegal or immoral activity has happened or is likely to happen. Although this may not be an unambiguous guideline, the standard of what a reasonable person would believe is commonly invoked in other cases, such as deceptive advertising and negligence lawsuits.

4. **The whistle-blower has acted after careful analysis of the danger: How serious is the moral violation? How immediate is the problem? Can the whistle-blower point to specific misconduct?** These criteria focus on the nature of the wrongdoing. Owing loyalty to employers, employees should blow the whistle only for grave legal or moral matters. The greater the harm or the more serious the wrongdoing, the more likely is the whistle-blowing to be justified. Additionally, employees should consider the time factor. The greater the time before the violation is to occur, the more likely it is that the firm's own internal mechanisms will prevent it, whereas the more imminent a violation, the more justified is the whistle-blowing. Finally, the whistle-blower must be specific. General allegations, such as that a company is "not operating in the best interests of the public" or is "systematically sabotaging the competition," won't do. Concrete examples are needed that can pass the other justificatory tests.

5. **The whistle-blowing has some chance of success.** This criterion recognizes that the chances of remedying an immoral or illegal action are an important consideration. Sometimes the chances are good; other times they're slim. Probably most cases fall somewhere between these extremes. In general, given the potential harmful effects, whistle-blowing that stands no chance of success is less justified than that with some chance of success. Even so, sometimes merely drawing attention to an objectionable practice, although it may fail to improve the specific situation, encourages government and society to be more watchful of certain behavior.

The phrase "morally justified" can be ambiguous, and the preceding discussion does not explicitly distinguish between situations in which whistle-blowing is morally permissible and situations in which it is also morally required (in the sense that one would act wrongly if one failed to blow the whistle). Factors 3, 4, and 5 are particularly relevant to determining this. But

Summary 10.10
An act of whistle-blowing can be presumed to be morally justified if it is done from a moral motive; if the whistle-blower has, if possible, exhausted internal channels before going public; if the whistle-blower has compelling evidence; if the whistle-blower has carefully analyzed the dangers; and if the whistle-blowing has some chance of success.

if the harm in question is great enough and if an employee is well positioned to prevent it by blowing the whistle on the organization, then he or she may well be morally obligated—not just morally justified or morally permitted—to do so.

SELF-INTEREST AND MORAL OBLIGATION

For many employees, protecting themselves or safeguarding their jobs is the primary factor in deciding whether to put third-party interests above those of the firm. Concern with **self-interest** in cases that pit loyalty to the company against other obligations is altogether understandable and even warranted. After all, workers who subordinate the organization's interests to an outside party's expose themselves to charges of disloyalty, disciplinary action, freezes in job status, forced relocations, and even dismissal. Furthermore, even when an employee successfully blows the whistle, he or she can be blacklisted in an industry. Given the potential harm to self and family that employees risk in honoring obligations to third parties, it is perfectly legitimate to inquire about the weight that considerations of self-interest should be given in resolving cases of conflicting obligations.

Sadly, there is no clear, unequivocal answer to this question. Moral theorists and society as a whole do distinguish between **prudential reasons** and moral reasons. "Prudential" (from the word *prudence*) refers here to considerations of self-interest; "moral" refers here to considerations of the interests of others and the demands of morality. Chapter 1 explained that it is possible for prudential and moral considerations to pull us in different directions. One way of looking at their relationship is this: If prudential concerns outweigh moral ones, then employees may do what is in their own best interest. If moral reasons override prudential ones, then workers should honor their obligations to others.

Some theorists believe that prudential concerns sometimes outweigh moral ones.

Consider the case of a cashier at a truck stop who is asked to write up phony chits so truckers can get a larger expense reimbursement from their employers than they really deserve. The cashier doesn't think this is right, so she complains to the manager. The manager explains that the restaurant is largely dependent on trucker business and that this is a good way to ensure it. The cashier is ordered to do the truckers' bidding and is thus being told to violate at least three duties owed to any outside party (in this case, the trucking firms): truth, noninjury, and fairness. Given these moral considerations, the cashier ought to refuse, and perhaps she should even report the conduct to the trucking companies.

But let's suppose that the cashier happens to be a recent divorcée with no formal education. She lacks occupational skills and stands little chance of getting another job in an economy that happens to be depressed—for months she was unemployed before landing her present position. With no other means of support, the consequences of job loss for her would be serious indeed. Now, given this scenario and given that the wrongdoing at issue is relatively minor, prudential concerns would probably take legitimate precedence over moral ones. In other words, the cashier would be justified in "going along," at least on a temporary basis.

Other theorists say that nothing can outweigh morality but that morality itself does not require us to make large sacrifices to right small wrongs.

Some moral theorists would agree with this conclusion but analyze the case somewhat differently. They think it is incorrect to say that in some circumstances we may permit prudential considerations to outweigh moral considerations. There is no neutral perspective outside both morality and self-interest from which one can make such a judgment. Furthermore, they would say that, by definition, nothing can outweigh the demands of morality.

Does that mean the cashier should refuse to do what her manager wants and, thus, lose her job? Not necessarily. Morality does not, these theorists contend, require us to make large sacrifices to right small wrongs. Writing up phony chits does violate some basic moral principles, and the cashier has some moral obligation not to go along with it. But morality does not, all things considered, require her—under the present circumstances—to take a course of action that would spell job loss. She should, however, take less drastic steps to end the practice (like continuing to talk to her boss and the truckers about it) and perhaps eventually find other work. Thus, according to this way of thinking, the cashier is not sacrificing morality to self-interest in "going along" for a while. The idea is that morality does not impose obligations on us without regard to their cost; it does not, under the present circumstances, demand an immediate resignation by the cashier.

Whichever way one looks at it, the question of balancing our moral obligations to others and our own self-interest is particularly relevant to whistle-blowing. On the one hand, in situations in which whistle-blowing threatens one's livelihood and career, prudential concerns may properly be taken into account in deciding what one should do, all things considered. This doesn't mean that if the worker blows the whistle despite compelling prudential reasons not to, he or she is not moral. On the contrary, such an action could be highly moral. (As Chapter 2 explained, ethical theorists term such actions *supererogatory*, meaning that they are, so to speak, above and beyond the call of duty.) On the other hand, when the moral concerns are great (for example, when the lives of others are at stake), elementary morality and personal integrity can require people to make substantial sacrifices.

Two further points are pertinent here. First, an evaluation of prudential reasons obviously is colored by one's temperament and perceptions of self-interest. Each of us has a tendency to magnify potential threats to our livelihood or career. Exaggerating the costs to ourselves of acting otherwise makes it easier to rationalize away the damage we are doing to others. In the business world, for instance, people talk about the survival of the firm as if it were literally a matter of life and death. Going out of business is the worst thing that can happen to a firm, but the people who make it up will live on and get other jobs. Keeping the company alive (let alone competitive or profitable) cannot justify seriously injuring innocent people.

Exaggerating the costs to ourselves allows us to rationalize away the damage we are doing to others.

Not only do we tend to exaggerate the importance of self-interested considerations, but also most of us have been socialized to heed authority. As a result, we are disinclined to question the orders of someone above us, especially when the authority is an employer or supervisor with power to influence our lives for better or worse. It's easy for us to assume that any boat rocking will be very harmful, even self-destructive.

It follows, then, that each of us has an obligation to perform a kind of character or personality audit. Do we follow authority blindly? Do we suffer from moral tunnel vision on the job? Do we mindlessly do what is demanded of us, oblivious to the impact of our cooperation and actions on outside parties? Have we given enough attention to our possible roles as accomplices in the immoral undoing of other individuals, businesses, and social institutions? Do we have a balanced view of our own interests versus those of others? Do we have substantial evidence for believing that our livelihoods are really threatened, or is that belief based more on an exaggeration of the facts? Have we been imaginative in trying to balance prudential and moral concerns? Have we sought to find some middle ground, or have we set up a false self-other dilemma in which our own interests and those of others are erroneously viewed as incompatible? These are just some of the questions that a personal inventory should include if we are to combat the all-too-human tendency to stack the deck in favor of prudential reasons whenever they are pitted against moral ones.

We all have an interest in encouraging people to act in non-self-interested ways.

A second point about the relationship between prudential and moral considerations concerns our collective interest in protecting the welfare of society by encouraging people to act in non-self-interested ways. As we have seen, in some cases considerations of self-interest may mean that one does not have an overriding obligation to blow the whistle. When that is the case, how can society be protected from wrongdoing? Is its welfare to be left to those few heroic souls willing to perform supererogatory actions? And even when employees have a clear duty to blow the whistle, the personal risk involved may, human nature being what it is, keep them from doing the right thing. Who protects society then? The only realistic and reasonable approach, it seems, is to restructure our legal, business, and social institutions so that acting in a morally responsible way no longer brings the severe penalty that it often does. Whether people do what they know to be right—whether they act in a way that respects others and protects their important interests—is not simply a matter of their conscience and the strength of their moral convictions. It is also a function of the environment in which they must act and the incentives and disincentives they face.

Protecting Those Who Do the Right Thing

Although a hodgepodge of legal precedents and state and federal legislation already afforded some assistance to employees who blow the whistle, the **Sarbanes-Oxley Act** of 2002 marked an important advance. The act provides sweeping new legal protection for employees who report possible securities fraud, making it unlawful for companies to "discharge, demote, suspend, threaten, harass, or in any other manner discriminate against" them. Fired workers can sue, and they are guaranteed the right to a jury trial instead of having to endure months or years of administrative hearings. In addition, the Labor Department can order companies to rehire terminated whistle-blowers with no court hearings whatsoever. Moreover, executives who retaliate against employees who report possible violations of *any* federal law now face imprisonment for up to ten years.

Summary 10.11
Prudential considerations based on self-interest can conflict with moral considerations, which take into account the interests of others. Some sacrifices of self-interest would be so great that moral considerations must give way to prudential ones. But employees must avoid the temptation to exaggerate prudential concerns, thereby rationalizing away any individual moral responsibility to third parties. Legislation and changes in corporate culture can reduce the personal sacrifices that whistle-blowers must make.

Companies need to develop explicit, proactive whistle-blower policies.

Unfortunately, Sarbanes-Oxley came too late to help Christine Casey. After a few years working at Mattel, Casey was assigned by the toymaker to develop a system to allocate production among its factories. But she soon discovered that Mattel's official sales forecasts were so high that managers routinely ignored the numbers. "It was a joke around the office," she says. Managers kept two sets of figures and would telephone around to find out what they should really tell their factories to produce. Casey went to a company director with a proposal to fix the numbers and help the company forecast profits more accurately. She then began experiencing hostility from company executives, received her first negative performance review, and was shunted off to a tiny cubicle, stripped of most of her work responsibilities. When Mattel's chief financial officer ignored her concerns, and its human-resources department turned a blind eye to her mistreatment, she telephoned the SEC. Although Mattel later had to pay $122 million to shareholders who sued it for deliberately inflating its sales forecasts, Casey lost her wrongful-termination suit against the company for having harassed her into resigning. She has little chance of getting a job like the one she lost because big companies routinely check job applicants' litigation history.[55]

It is not enough, however, merely to change the law. Corporate attitudes need to change as well. In America, the *Economist* magazine writes, "it is almost always thought cheaper to fire whistle-blowers than to listen to them, despite years of legislation designed to achieve the opposite."[56] Kris Kolesnik, director of the National Whistleblower Center, is equally pessimistic. "No matter how many protections whistleblower laws have created over the years," he says, "the system always seems to defeat them."[57] In the long run, however, organizations benefit more from encouraging employees to come forward with their ethical concerns than they do from ignoring possible wrongdoing and retaliating against those who raise awkward queries. Openness and a receptive attitude toward moral questioning by employees give the organization a chance to take corrective action. This can save it money (by rooting out embezzlement, say, or forestalling litigation) or at least—as recent scandals make clear—help it to head off worse trouble when the problems bothering employees eventually leak out to the public.

To discharge their moral responsibilities and safeguard their own interests, companies need to develop explicit, proactive whistle-blowing policies. At a minimum, these policies should state that employees aware of possible wrongdoing have a responsibility to disclose that information; specific individuals or groups outside the chain of command should be designated to hear those concerns; employees who in good faith disclose perceived wrongdoing should be protected from adverse employment consequences; and there should be a fair and impartial investigative process. Some large companies also hire outside vendors to set up software systems, websites, or toll-free call centers for employees to alert them anonymously to ethical problems.[58] Then, of course, there must be follow-through. In these ways, management can create organizational procedures and a corporate culture that make it less likely that employees will be forced to blow the whistle externally.

STUDY CORNER

Key Terms and Concepts

abuse of official position	Foreign Corrupt Practices	prudential reasons
bribe	Act (FCPA)	Sarbanes-Oxley Act
business gifts and	grease payments	self-interest
entertainment	insider trading	trade secrets
civil disobedience	kickback	*U.S. v. O'Hagan*
company loyalty	OECD Anti-Bribery	whistle-blowing
conflict of interest	Convention	
Economic Espionage Act	proprietary data	

Points to Review

- two issues facing someone like George Galatis or George Betancourt
- importance of the work contract
- why some writers rejects the idea of company loyalty
- why conflicts of interest are a moral problem
- why disclosing a conflict of interest doesn't necessarily solve the problem
- financial investments as possible conflicts of interest
- examples of abuse of official position
- significance of the Chiarella and Dirks cases
- the Supreme Court's position on insider trading in *U.S. v. O'Hagan*
- arguments for and against insider trading
- differences between a patented idea or process and a trade secret
- three arguments for legally protecting trade secrets

- issues raised by the Wohlgemuth/Goodrich case
- FCPA's handling of grease payments and extortion
- pros and cons of the FCPA
- seven factors relevant to determining the morality of business gifts and entertainment
- procedure recommended in Chapter 2 for making moral decisions
- two ways of trying to keep your moral decisions free from rationalization
- the analogy between civil disobedience and whistle-blowing
- why whistle-blowing is morally problematic
- five factors to consider when morally evaluating whistle-blowing
- self-interest and the demands of morality
- how to reduce the personal sacrifices that whistle-blowers must often make

CASE 10.1

Changing Jobs and Changing Loyalties

Cynthia Martinez was thrilled when she first received the job offer from David Newhoff at Crytex Systems. She had long admired Crytex, both as an industry leader and as an ideal employer, and the position the company was offering her was perfect. "It's just what I've always wanted," she told her husband, Tom, as they uncorked a bottle of champagne. But as she and Tom talked, he raised a few questions that began to trouble her.

"What about the big project you're working on at Altrue right now? It'll take three months to see that through," Tom reminded her. "The company has a lot riding on it, and you've always said that you're the driving force behind the project. If you bolt, Altrue is going to be in a real jam."

Cynthia explained that she had mentioned the project to David Newhoff. "He said he could understand that I'd like to see it through, but Crytex needs someone right now. He gave me a couple of days to think it over, but it's my big chance."

Tom looked at her thoughtfully and responded, "But Newhoff doesn't quite get it. It's not just that you'd like to see it through. It's that you'd be letting your whole project team down. They probably couldn't do it without you, at least not the way it needs to be done. Besides, Cyn, remember what you said about that guy who quit the Altrue branch in Baltimore."

"That was different," Cynthia responded. "He took an existing account with him when he went to another firm. It was like ripping Altrue off. I'm not going to rip them off, but I don't figure I owe them anything extra. It's just business. You know perfectly well that if Altrue could save some money by laying me off, the company wouldn't hesitate."

"I think you're rationalizing," Tom said. "You've done well at Altrue, and the company has always treated you fairly. Anyway, the issue is what's right for you to do, not what the company would or wouldn't do. Crytex is Altrue's big competitor. It's like you're switching sides. Besides, it's not just a matter of loyalty to the

company, but to the people you work with. I know we could use the extra money, and it would be a great step for you, but still ..."

They continued to mull things over together, but the champagne no longer tasted quite as good. Fortunately, she and Tom never really argued about things they didn't see eye to eye on, and Tom wasn't the kind of guy who would try to tell her what she should or shouldn't do. But their conversation had started her wondering whether she really should accept that Crytex job she wanted so much.

Discussion Questions

1. What should Cynthia do? What ideals, obligations, and effects should she take into account when making her decision?
2. Would it be unprofessional of Cynthia to drop everything and move to Crytex? Would it show a lack of integrity? Could moving abruptly to Crytex have negative career consequences for her?
3. Is it morally wrong, morally permissible, or morally required for Cynthia to take the new job? Examine Cynthia's choice from a utilitarian point of view. How would Kant and Ross look at her situation?
4. What does loyalty to the company mean, and how important is it, morally? Under what circumstances, if any, do employees owe loyalty to their employers? When, if ever, do they owe loyalty to their coworkers?

CASE **10.2**

Two Who Made Waves for the Navy

Zeke Storms, a fifty-two-year-old retired Navy chief, began his career as a whistle-blower when he wrote Congressman Charles Pashayan to protest proposed cuts in the federal budget.[59] Storms had been employed as a civilian repairing flight simulators at the Lemoore Naval Air Base station near Fresno, California, since his retirement ten years before.

Now he was suggesting that instead of supporting reductions in the civil service pay scale, Pashayan ought to take a closer look at Navy procurement practices. Enclosed in the letter was a list of spare parts showing that defense contractors were charging $435 for ordinary claw hammers and $100 or more for such electronic spare parts as diodes, transistors, and semiconductors, which cost less than $1 each. He also charged that the Navy paid $100 apiece for transistors that it could have obtained through the federal supply system for 5 cents apiece.

Storms's letter prompted Pashayan to query the Defense Department, which in turn kicked off an interservice investigation of military procurement practices. The Defense Department inspector general's office reported that the Navy had indeed failed to determine the most economical manner to acquire the spare parts Zeke Storms had listed. It also suggested that the spare-parts-overcharge problem was more widespread than at first thought. The investigative body left no doubt that the Navy was wasting millions of dollars annually.

In the wake of this report, the Secretary of Defense ordered a tightening of procurement procedures to ensure the lowest price for spare parts. Meanwhile, Navy Secretary John Lehman ordered contractors at Lemoore to refund $160,000 in overcharges. He also gave Storms a $4,000 award.

But Storms wasn't about to lay down his muckrake. He suggested that Defense Department auditors review overpayment for jet-aircraft support equipment in the base shops. The auditors did and discovered overpayment of $482,000, most of it spent on four spectrum analyzers. Had the items been bought through the federal supply system, they would have cost $47,500.

Storms then discovered that the Navy had engaged private contractors to operate its flight simulators for a new aircraft. "I got mad," he says. "[The Navy] had spent $1 million training their own people to do the work, then they just scrapped that and turned the maintenance over to the contractor." The contractor in question apparently was demanding $785,000 to maintain the simulators, which worked out to about $100,000 per person per year. "I showed them that we [a team of Navy and civil service technicians] could do it

for one-fourth that cost, so the contract was dropped to $411,000," says Storms.

That $411,000 was still more than Storms believed the Navy had to pay, especially since the Navy had been maintaining its own simulators for two decades. So he took his case directly to Lehman, arguing that Office of Management and Budget (OMB) regulations required the Navy to do comparative cost studies to ensure the most cost-effective means. Lehman balked at Storms's proposal, saying that such studies would cost $45,000 each. That was too high a price to pay "to indulge Mr. Storms's eccentricities," the Secretary said in a letter to Congressman Pashayan.

Evidently deciding it was time to quiet the querulous Storms, Lehman then sent nine Navy brass to Lemoore. In the two-hour session that ensued, Storms did most of the talking. In the end, a commodore, four captains, two commanders, and two lieutenant commanders could do nothing to divert Storms from his course.

It was shortly thereafter that the ex-Navy chief did the "unpardonable." He accused Secretary Lehman and "his admirals" of lying. He said he had turned over to OMB officials Navy documents showing that Navy admirals willfully ignored requirements to do cost studies for private maintenance work. One of the documents included a message from Vice Admiral Robert F. Schoultz, the commander of naval forces in the Pacific. Addressing Admiral James D. Watkins, then commander of the Pacific Fleet, Schoultz wrote: "It is our intention to contract out all major training device maintenance.... [However] under the [contract] program our objective is hindered with cost studies that would yield inappropriate results." Schoultz's "inappropriate results" apparently was an allusion to the report by the fleet's top training officer, who estimated that the Navy's own people could do for $7 million the same work for which private contractors would charge $28 million.

In response to Storms, N. R. Lessard, officer in charge of the flight training groups for whom the ten-year Lemoore veteran was working, informed him that "your recent comments concerning senior Navy officials … constitute unacceptable employee conduct." To which Storms replied in a way most befitting a tobacco-chewing old salt: "[The Navy is] covering up, goddammit. I've got the facts, and they know it."

By contrast, Aaron Ahearn isn't an old salt, and he doesn't chew tobacco. But when the environmentally conscious, twenty-year-old sailor blew the whistle on the Navy's practice of dumping trash at sea, he made waves almost as big as Storms's.[60] Ahearn was a fireman's apprentice assigned to the scullery aboard the USS *Abraham Lincoln*, the world's largest nuclear-powered aircraft carrier. As part of his duties, Ahearn was supposed to dispose of the ship's garbage by tossing overboard up to two hundred bags of plastic and other trash—some of it alleged to be toxic waste—every day. A surfer who loves the ocean, Ahearn says that his conscience was troubled by what he had to do. He also reports seeing sailors dump broken desks, chairs, and computers into the ocean. When Ahearn's request for a change of assignment was denied, he jumped ship.

Environmentalists contend that plastic trash kills thousands of marine turtles, birds, and mammals annually and that it litters the beaches and wrecks boat propellers. Although private vessels can be fined up to $500,000 for dumping plastic debris, federal law specifically exempts the Navy. For its part, the Navy has always claimed that it can't avoid dumping plastic garbage because its ships house up to 5,500 sailors and spend months at sea.

Meanwhile, Ahearn, who had left the *Abraham Lincoln* on a weekend pass, went into hiding for two months, spending the time living with his girlfriend and surfing in the beach town of Santa Cruz, California. Eventually he decided to turn himself in. Before doing so, he received counseling from the Resource Center for Nonviolence and went to the media, saying his conscience would not allow him to pollute the ocean as ordered. He also announced that he wanted conscientious objector status on environmental grounds. Ahearn's story gained national coverage and focused pressure on the Navy to conform with international law governing plastic and trash disposal at sea. "What he did was commendable and brave," says Jil Zilligen of the Center for Marine Conservation in San Francisco. "I don't think many people realized this was going on at all."

Instead of battening down the hatches in response to the storm that Ahearn's allegations stirred up, the Navy announced that it would stop dumping plastic from all its surface ships and proposed a timetable for full compliance with the relevant international laws. What about Ahearn? Although environmental groups called him a hero, the Navy court-martialed him as a deserter who used his pollution allegations to cover up his unauthorized absence and as an excuse to leave the Navy. The ship's skipper, Navy Captain Ray Archer, contended that Ahearn told friends that he was going to jump ship to visit his girlfriend and would use his environmental concerns to justify it. And the Navy prosecutor, Lieutenant Tony Viera, said that Ahearn simply did not like his duty and needed to "grow up." The scullery is hot and sweaty, Viera remarked, and everybody hates working in it. But instead of sticking it out, Ahearn ran away and went surfing.

Ahearn and his attorney, Robert Rivkin, denied those charges, but the issue was never officially settled. In fact, at the court-martial, there was no mention at all of the environmental issues Ahearn had raised—except for the slogan "Pack Your Trash" tattooed across the back of his neck above the collar of his dress white Navy uniform. Instead, as part of a plea bargain, Ahearn pleaded guilty to unauthorized absence and to missing a ship's movement and was fined $500 and sentenced to thirty-five days in the brig. "Overall," commented his attorney, "it was a pretty good deal. It is a fair and reasonable sentence for what he did." Vicki Nichols, executive director of Save Our Shores, a marine conservation group, added, "I can't imagine that the Navy would ever admit a sailor who went AWOL has had any positive impact. But he did."

Discussion Questions

1. Do you think Storms and Ahearn qualify as whistle-blowers? What do you think their motives were?
2. Examine Storms's and Ahearn's actions from the perspective of Bowie's criteria for justified whistle-blowing. Are those criteria satisfied in both cases? Are Bowie's criteria themselves satisfactory?
3. What specific obligations, ideals, and effects should have been considered before either man became a whistle-blower?
4. Based on the details provided, would you consider Storms morally justified in having gone public with his information? Was Ahearn's conduct justified? Explain.

If you believe Storms's whistle-blowing was permissible, do you also believe that it was morally required of him? What about Ahearn's? Would someone in Storms's position have been justified in subordinating moral reasons to prudential concerns and thus in remaining silent? Explain.

6. What are the advantages and disadvantages of laws protecting whistle-blowers? Are they likely to work? Will they have good results, or will they encourage irresponsible whistle-blowing? If you favor such laws, what should they say?
7. How should corporations address the question of whistle-blowing? How should they deal with whistle-blowers or potential whistle-blowers? How should they handle disgruntled employees who make inaccurate or unfounded allegations? Should companies try to develop explicit policies and procedures or deal with each situation on a case-by-case basis? If the former, what policies and procedures should they put in place?

CASE **10.3**

The Housing Allowance

Wilson Mutambara grew up in the slums outside Stanley, capital of the sub-Saharan African country of Rambia.[61] Through talent, hard work, and luck he made it through secondary school and won a scholarship to study in the United States. He eventually received an MBA and went to work for NewCom, a cellular telephone service. After three years in the company's Atlanta office, Wilson was given an opportunity to return to Rambia, where NewCom was setting up a local cellular service. Eager to be home, Wilson Mutambara couldn't say yes fast enough.

NewCom provides its employees in Rambia with a monthly allowance of up to $2,000 for rent, utilities, and servants. By Western standards, most of the housing in Stanley is poor quality, and many of its neighborhoods are unsafe. By providing the allowance, NewCom's intention is to see that its employees live in areas that are safe and convenient and that they live in a style that is appropriate to the company's image.

To claim their housing allowance, NewCom's employees in Rambia are supposed to turn in receipts, and every month Wilson

Mutambara turned in an itemized statement for $2,000 from his landlord. Nobody at NewCom thought it was unusual that Wilson never entertained his coworkers at home. After all, he worked long hours and traveled frequently on business. However, after Wilson had been in Rambia for about fifteen months, one of his coworkers, Dale Garman, was chatting with a Rambian customer, who referred in passing to Wilson as a person living in Old Town. Garman knew Old Town was one of the slums outside Stanley, but he kept his surprise to himself and decided not to mention this information to anyone else until he could independently confirm it. This wasn't difficult for him to do. Wilson was indeed living in Old Town in the home of some relatives. The house itself couldn't have rented for more than $300, even if Wilson had the whole place to himself, which he clearly didn't. Dale reported what he had learned to Wilson's supervisor, Barbara Weston.

When Weston confronted him about the matter, Wilson admitted that the place did rent for a "little less" than $2,000, but he vigorously defended his action this way: "Every other NewCom employee in Rambia receives $2,000 a month. If I live economically, why should I be penalized? I should receive the same as everyone else." In response, Weston pointed out that NewCom wanted to guarantee that its employees had safe, high-quality housing that was in keeping with the image that the company wanted to project. Wilson's housing arrangements were "unseemly," she said, and not in keeping with his professional standing. Moreover, they reflected poorly on the company. To this, Wilson Mutambara retorted: "I'm not just a NewCom employee; I'm also a Rambian. It's not unsafe for me to live in this neighborhood, and it's insulting to be told that the area I grew up in is 'unseemly' or inappropriate for a company employee."

Barbara Weston pointed out that the monthly receipts he submitted had been falsified. "Yes," he admitted, "but that's common practice in Rambia. Nobody thinks twice about it." However, she pressed the point, arguing that he had a duty to NewCom, which he had violated. As the discussion continued, Mutambara became less confident and more and more distraught. Finally, on the verge of tears, he pleaded, "Barbara, you just don't understand what's expected of me as a Rambian or the pressure I'm under. I save every penny I have to pay school fees for eight nieces and nephews. I owe it to my family to try to give those children the same chance I had. My relatives would never understand my living in a big house instead of helping them. I'm just doing what I have to do."

Discussion Questions

1. Did Wilson Mutambara act wrongly? Explain why or why not. Assess each of the arguments he gives in his own defense. What other courses of action were open to him? What would you have done in his place?

2. Was Dale Garman right to confirm the information he had received and to report the matter? Was it morally required of him to do so?

3. What should Barbara Weston and NewCom do? Should Wilson be ordered to move out of Old Town and into more appropriate housing? Should he be terminated for having falsified his housing receipts? If not, should he be punished in some other way?

4. Is NewCom unfairly imposing its own ethnocentric values on Wilson Mutambara? Is the company's housing policy fair and reasonable? Is it culturally biased?

CASE **10.4**

Ethically Dubious Conduct

Brenda Franklin has worked at Allied Tech for nearly eight years. It's a large company, but she likes it and enjoys the friendly work environment. When she tacked her list onto the bulletin board outside her office, she didn't intend to make things less friendly. In fact, she didn't expect her list to attract much attention at all.

It had all started the week before when she joined a group of coworkers for their weekly lunch get-together, where they always talked about all sorts of things. This time they had gotten into a long political discussion, with several people at the table going on at great length about dishonesty, conflicts of interest, and shady dealings among politicians and corporate leaders. "If this country is going to get on the right track, we need people whose integrity is above reproach," Harry Benton had said to nods of approval around the table, followed by a further round of complaints about corruption and corner-cutting by the powerful.

Brenda hadn't said much at the time, but she thought she sniffed a whiff of hypocrisy. Later that night, after pondering the group's discussion, she typed up her list of "Ethically Dubious Employee Conduct." The next day she posted it outside her door.

Harry Benton was the first one to stick his head in the office. "My, my, aren't we smug?" was all he said before he disappeared. Later that morning, her friend Karen dropped by. "You don't really think it's immoral to take a pad of paper home, do you?" she asked. Brenda said no, but she didn't think one could just take it for granted that it was okay to take company property. She and Karen chatted more about the list. On and off that week, almost everyone she spoke with alluded to the list or commented on some of its items. They didn't object to her posting it, although they seemed to think it was a little strange. One day outside the building, however, an

employee she knew only by sight asked Brenda sarcastically whether she was planning on turning people in for "moral violations." Brenda ignored him.

Now she was anticipating her group's weekly lunch. She had little doubt about what the topic of discussion would be, as she again glanced over her list:

Ethically Dubious Employee Conduct

1. Taking office supplies home for your personal use.
2. Using the telephone for personal, long-distance phone calls.
3. Making personal copies on the office machine.
4. Charging the postage on your personal mail to the company.
5. Making nonbusiness trips in a company car.
6. On a company business trip: staying in the most expensive hotel, taking taxis when you could walk, including wine as food on your expense tab, taking your spouse along at company expense.
7. Using your office computer to shop online, trade stocks, view pornography, or e-mail friends on company time.
8. Calling in sick when you need personal time.
9. Taking half the afternoon off when you're supposedly on business outside the office.
10. Directing company business to vendors who are friends or relatives.
11. Providing preferential service to corporate customers who have taken you out to lunch.

Discussion Questions

1. Review each item on Brenda's list and assess the conduct in question. Do you find it morally acceptable, morally unacceptable, or somewhere in between? Explain.

2. Examine Brenda's list from both the utilitarian and the Kantian perspectives. What arguments can be given for and against the conduct on her list? Is the rightness or wrongness of some items a matter of degree? Can an action (such as taking a pad of paper) be both trivial and wrong?

3. Someone might argue that some of the things listed as ethically dubious are really employee entitlements. Assess this contention.

4. How would you respond to the argument that if the company doesn't do anything to stop the conduct on Brenda's list, then it has only itself to blame? What about the argument that none of the things on the list is wrong unless the company has an explicit rule against it?

5. What obligations do employees have to their employers? Do companies have moral rights that employees can violate? What moral difference, if any, is there between taking something that belongs to an individual and taking something that belongs to a company?

6. What, if anything, can we learn about an employee's character based on whether he or she does or does not do the things on Brenda's list? Would you admire someone who scrupulously avoids doing any of these ethically dubious things, or would you think the person is a prig?

7. What should Brenda do when she finds a fellow employee engaging in what she considers ethically dubious conduct?

CHAPTER 11

Job Discrimination

AP Photo/Michael Conroy

When Notre Dame opened its 2002 football season, its team was led by a new coach, Tyrone Willingham. Nothing surprising about that, one might think; after all, colleges are always hiring and firing coaches. But Coach Willingham's arrival was newsworthy simply because he is African American. He was Notre Dame's first black coach in any sport, and hiring him made the Fighting Irish the only top-flight football team in the nation with a black coach. Indeed, looking at all 120 schools in the NCAA's Football Bowl Subdivision, one finds only seven black head football coaches. That's less than 6 percent of the total, even though half of the players are black.[1]

What explains this imbalance? Experts suggest several answers. At many universities, football is the biggest moneymaking sport, and search committees may fear that boosters and alumni will donate less if the team has a black coach. Another reason is that black men are often passed over for decision-making positions early in their athletic careers. Relatively few blacks play quarterback, for instance, and black assistant coaches may be relegated to recruiting or smoothing out race relations rather than calling plays. In addition, young black athletes may pursue careers in which they have seen their role models succeed—going on to the pros, in particular, instead of becoming a coach.

Finally, most commentators agree that the old-boys' network among athletic directors and coaches is part of the problem. "I don't see the problem as being the same as it was thirty or forty years ago, when people said they didn't want a 'Negro' around," says Allen L. Sach, director of sports management at the University of New Haven. "It's more systemic than it is overt." Athletic directors, naturally enough, tend to look to people they know to fill coaching positions, and only 4 percent of the former are ethnic minorities, according to the Center for the Study of Sport in Society at Northeastern University. "Athletic directors, to the extent that they're white, generally have contacts who are also white, and they use those contacts as they engage in searches at the informal level," says sociologist Jay Oakley of the University of Colorado at Colorado Springs.

It's no secret that Willingham wasn't Notre Dame's first choice. It had initially hired George O'Leary, who resigned five days later when it became known that he had lied on his résumé about his academic and athletic background. In discussing the appointment, Notre Dame athletic director Kevin White explained that he had been charmed by O'Leary's Irish-American background and his rah-rah style. O'Leary was like "something out of central casting," White said. In other words, the flamboyant O'Leary matched White's stereotype about what a Notre Dame coach should be. Sports columnist Mark Purdy writes that White's remark "basically confirms that athletic directors—at Notre Dame and too many other places—really do look for middle-aged white guys as the top choices for the top jobs. And that's depressing." It's to Notre Dame's credit, however, that after the O'Leary debacle, it took a second look at Willingham and, setting aside racial preconceptions and "central casting" stereotypes, went for a coach with a proven track record, one whose integrity, drive, and quiet competence more than made up for any lack of flamboyance.

Unfortunately, the story doesn't end happily there. Three years later, Notre Dame fired Willingham. Football recruitment was solid, the team's morale was strong, and its academic performance had never been better. But that season, the squad had posted only a 6–5 record, and Notre Dame desperately wanted its team to rejoin the elite of college football. A case of job discrimination? It's difficult to say, but some sportswriters and other observers thought so—including the university's outgoing president, Father Edward A. Malloy, who said the decision to fire Willingham was an embarrassment to the university. That's because Willingham's overall record was a respectable 21–15, and Notre Dame, which claims to adhere to higher values than other schools, had never before dismissed a coach after only three years into a five-year contract. In fact, Willingham's record was better than the three-year marks of his two predecessors, who both had kept their jobs.

As it turned out, three years later Willingham's successor, Charlie Weis, had a 22–15 record—almost identical to Willingham's—but Notre Dame made no move to fire him. Looking back, sports writer Jon Wilner says, "I don't think Willingham was treated differently because he was black. I think he was treated differently by Notre Dame because he was different, and being black was not an insignificant part of that difference." As Wilner sees it, Willingham wasn't a Notre Dame guy. He had no ties to South Bend, and his reserved personality "wasn't the type to make boosters and trustees feel comfortable and important—to make them feel like the head coach was one of them." By contrast, "Weiss is one of them. He's a white guy who went to Notre Dame."

Most people oppose racial or sexual bias and reject job discrimination as immoral. But, as the paucity of minority coaches reveals, explicit prejudice and overt discrimination are only part of the problem. Even open-minded people may operate on implicit assumptions that work to the disadvantage of women and minorities, and many who believe themselves to be unprejudiced harbor unconscious racist or sexist attitudes.

No one is more cognizant of the complexities of people's attitudes toward race, their conscious and unconscious assumptions about it, and the many-sided reality of race in American society than is President Barack Obama. "Understanding this reality," he has said,

> requires a reminder of how we arrived at this point. As William Faulkner once wrote, "The past isn't dead and buried. In fact, it isn't even past." We ... need to remind ourselves that so many of the disparities that exist in the African-American community today can be directly traced to inequalities passed on from an earlier generation that suffered under the brutal legacy of slavery and Jim Crow.
>
> Segregated schools were, and are, inferior schools; we still haven't fixed them, fifty years after *Brown v. Board of Education*, and the inferior education they provided, then and now, helps explain the pervasive achievement gap between today's black and white students.
>
> Legalized discrimination—where blacks were prevented, often through violence, from owning property, or loans were not granted to African-American business owners, or black homeowners could not access FHA mortgages, or blacks were excluded from unions, or the police force, or fire departments—meant that black families could not amass any meaningful wealth to bequeath to future generations. That history helps explain the wealth and income gap between black and white, and the concentrated pockets of poverty that persist in so many of today's urban and rural communities.
>
> A lack of economic opportunity among black men, and the shame and frustration that came from not being able to provide for one's family, contributed to the erosion of black families.... And the lack of basic services in so many urban black neighborhoods ... helped create a cycle of violence, blight, and neglect that continue to haunt us.
>
> ...What's remarkable is not how many failed in the face of discrimination, but rather how many men and women overcame the odds.... But for all those who scratched and clawed their way to get a piece of the American Dream, there were many who didn't make it—those who were ultimately defeated, in one way or another, by discrimination. That legacy of defeat was passed on to future generations—those young

men … who we see standing on street corners or languishing in our prisons, without hope or prospects for the future.[2]

We must bear this history in mind as we explore the issue of job discrimination. In particular, this chapter examines the following topics:

1. The meaning of job discrimination and its different forms
2. Statistical and attitudinal evidence of discrimination
3. The historical and legal context of affirmative action
4. Moral arguments for and against affirmative action
5. The doctrine of comparable worth and the controversy over it
6. The problem of sexual harassment in employment—what it is, what forms it takes, what the law says about it, and why it's wrong

THE MEANING OF JOB DISCRIMINATION

To discriminate in employment is to make an adverse decision regarding an employee or a job applicant based on his or her membership in a certain group.[3] More specifically, **job discrimination** occurs when (1) an employment decision in some way harms or disadvantages an employee or a job applicant; (2) the decision is based on the person's membership in a certain group, rather than on individual merit; and (3) the decision rests on prejudice, false stereotypes, or the assumption that the group in question is in some way inferior and thus does not deserve equal treatment. Because historically most discrimination in the American workplace has been aimed at women and at minorities such as African Americans and Hispanics, the following discussion focuses on those groups.

Job discrimination takes different forms.

Job discrimination can take different forms. It can be individual or institutional, and it can be either intentional or unwitting. Individuals, for instance, sometimes intentionally discriminate out of personal prejudice or on the basis of stereotypes. For example, an executive at Rent-A-Center, the nation's largest rent-to-own furniture and home appliance company, purposely disregarded job applications from women because he believed that they "should be home taking care of their husbands and children."[4] Individuals also may discriminate because they unthinkingly or unconsciously accept traditional practices or stereotypes. For example, suppose that the merit-pay recommendations of a Wal-Mart manager are influenced by his implicit assumption that male employees are career oriented and have families to support, whereas female employees are there just to make a little extra money.[5] If the manager is unaware that this bias affects his decisions, his actions would fall into this category.

Institutions discriminate. Sometimes they do so explicitly and intentionally— for example, employment agencies that screen out African Americans, Latinos, older workers, and others at the request of their corporate clients[6] or the Shoney's restaurants that color-coded job applications to separate blacks from whites and that directed blacks, if hired, into kitchen jobs so they would not be seen from the dining room.[7] Sometimes the routine operating procedures of a company reflect stereotypes and prejudiced practices that the company is not fully aware of. That seems to have been the case at Abercrombie & Fitch, which in 2004 paid $50 million to settle a class-action job-discrimination lawsuit. The suit charged that in trying to cultivate its distinctive retail image, the company put minorities in less visible jobs and hired a disproportionately white sales force. Or, to take another example, for years the FBI routinely transferred Hispanic agents around the country on temporary, low-level assignments where a knowledge of Spanish was needed; the agents functioned as little more than assistants to non-Hispanic colleagues. Hispanic agents dubbed this the "taco circuit" and claimed that it adversely affected their opportunities for promotion. A federal court agreed with them that the practice was indeed discriminatory.[8]

In addition, institutional practices that appear neutral and nondiscriminatory may harm members of groups that have been discriminated against in the past. When membership in an all-white craft union, for instance, requires nomination by those who are already members, racial exclusion is likely to result even if the motivation of those who do the nominating is purely nepotistic and results from no racially motivated ill will or stereotyping. Similarly, when USAir had a special backdoor hiring channel for pilots recommended by employees or friends of the company, only white pilots were ever hired this way.[9] Although the policy may look racially neutral, its outcome was biased. Institutional procedures like these may not involve job discrimination in the narrow sense, but they clearly work to the disadvantage of women and minority groups, denying them full equality of opportunity.

There are strong moral arguments against job discrimination on racial or sexual grounds.

From a variety of moral perspectives there are compelling moral arguments against job discrimination on racial or sexual grounds. Since discrimination involves false assumptions about the inferiority of a certain group and harms individual members of that group, utilitarians would reject it because of its ill effects on total human welfare. Kantians would clearly repudiate it as failing to respect people as ends in themselves. Universalizing the maxim underlying discriminatory practices is practically impossible. No people who now discriminate would be willing to accept such treatment themselves. Discrimination on grounds of sex or race also violates people's basic moral rights and mocks the ideal of human moral equality. Furthermore, such discrimination is unjust. To use Rawls's theory as an illustration, parties in the original position would clearly choose for themselves the principle of equal opportunity.

There are no respectable arguments in favor of racial and sexual discrimination. Whatever racist or sexist attitudes people might actually have, no one today is prepared to defend job discrimination publicly, any more than someone would publicly defend slavery or repealing the Nineteenth Amendment (which gave women the right to vote). This attitude toward job discrimination is reflected in legal and political efforts to develop programs to root it out and to ameliorate the results of past discrimination.

Before looking at those programs, however, and at the relevant legal history, we need to examine the relative positions of whites and minorities and of males and females in the American workplace to see what they reveal about ongoing discrimination.

EVIDENCE OF DISCRIMINATION

Summary 11.1
Discrimination in employment occurs when decisions adversely affect employees or job applicants because they are members of a group that is an object of prejudice or false stereotypes or is viewed as inferior and not deserving of equal treatment. Discrimination can be individual or institutional, intentional or unintentional. From various moral perspectives, there are strong arguments against job discrimination.

When investigators sent equally qualified young white and black men—all of them articulate and conventionally dressed—to apply for entry-level jobs in Chicago and Washington, D.C., the results clearly showed racial discrimination against young African-American men.[10] Subsequent studies have confirmed that result.[11] In fact, one of them found that white applicants were more successful than black applicants even when they had criminal records and the otherwise-identical blacks did not.[12] Similarly, Hispanics and African Americans are more likely to be turned down for home mortgages, or to pay higher interest rates, than are whites at the same income level.[13] The same is true for auto loans.[14] And a study has shown that if you work for the federal government, you're more likely to be fired if you're black—regardless of your job status, experience, or education. In fact, race is more important in predicting who gets fired than job-performance ratings or even prior disciplinary history.[15]

Job discrimination certainly exists, but determining how widespread it is isn't easy. However, when statistics indicate that women and minorities play an unequal role in the work world and when endemic attitudes, practices, and policies are biased in ways that seem to account for the skewed statistics, then there is good reason to believe that job discrimination is a pervasive problem.

Statistical Evidence

According to U.N. figures, white Americans have the highest standard of living in the world. African Americans, however, come in only thirty-first, and Hispanics thirty-fifth.[16] Life expectancy for blacks, moreover, is lower than it is for whites, and blacks are twice as likely to die from disease, accident, and homicide.[17] Racial minorities also bear the brunt of poverty in our nation. African Americans are almost three times more likely to be poor than are whites. Whereas one in ten white Americans lives in poverty, one out of every four or five African Americans and Hispanics is poor. Today a black child has one chance in three of being born into poverty.[18]

The median wealth of white households today is more than ten times that of Hispanic or African-American households—$86,370 versus $7,932 for Hispanics and $5,988 for African Americans.[19] In line with this, the rate of home ownership is 50 percent greater for white households than for black or Hispanic households.[20] At the same time, the median income of African-American families is only 62 percent, and that of Hispanic families only 65 percent, the median income of white households.[21] Unemployment also hits racial minorities hard; compared with whites, they are twice as likely to be out of work.

About 40 percent of working African Americans hold white-collar jobs, up from 11 percent in 1960. But black workers with an advanced degree earn 25 percent less than whites with the same education.[22] Moreover, black and other minority workers still tend to be clustered in low-paying, low-prestige, dead-end work. United States government statistics reveal clearly the extent to which the most desirable occupations (in professional and technical jobs, management and administration) are dominated by whites; blacks,

Summary 11.2
Studies reveal the persistence of discrimination in American life, and statistical evidence shows wide economic disparities between whites and racial minorities. It also shows significant occupational and income differences between white males, on the one hand, and women and minorities, on the other.

Hispanics, and other ethnic minorities are relegated to less desirable jobs (in manual labor, service industries, and farmwork). African Americans, for instance, make up 11 percent of the workforce, but they constitute one-fifth to one-third of the nation's barbers, bus and taxi drivers, garbage collectors, and security guards. In contrast, only 4.9 percent of real-estate appraisers, 7 percent of psychologists, 6.4 percent of dentists, 4.4 percent of architects, and 6.3 percent of managers are black.[23]

Women, too, are clustered in poorer-paying jobs—the so-called **pink-collar occupations**. They tend to work as librarians, nurses, elementary school teachers, salesclerks, secretaries, bank tellers, and waitresses—jobs that generally pay less than traditionally male occupations such as electrician, plumber, auto mechanic, shipping clerk, and truck driver. In the real world of work, the top-paying occupations have been, and to a large extent continue to be, almost exclusively male preserves. For example, 99.2 percent of dental hygienists, but only 28 percent of dentists, are women.[24]

In recent years, the across-the-broad wage gap between men and women has shrunk slightly, but only slightly. In 1992 women who worked full-time made 75 percent of what men earned; they now make 79 percent.[25] Today, 45 percent of young women (ages twenty-five to thirty-four) have graduated from college whereas only 36 percent of young men have done so, but young men still earn significantly more.[26] Perhaps this is not so surprising, given that, in general, full-time female workers with a bachelor's degree take home only 75 percent of what their male counterparts make—the same now as in 1992.[27]

Even when women do the same work as men, they make less money. In fact, according to a General Accounting Office report, since 1995 the pay difference between full-time female managers and their male counterparts has increased in seven of the ten industries that collectively employ 71 percent of all female workers.[28] For example, in entertainment and recreation, female managers now earn only 62 cents for each dollar earned by males; in finance, insurance, and real estate, it's 68 cents; in retail trade, 65 cents. In education and in hospital and medical services, women managers have done better. Their earnings have increased to 91 and 85 percent, respectively, of what men make.

Few women and minorities can be found at the very top of the business world.

In recent decades both women and minorities have made considerable inroads into white-collar and professional ranks, but few have made it to the very top of their professions—as a glance at the companies that make up the *Fortune* 500 confirms. At these companies, women account for only 8 percent of those who have reached the level of executive vice president or higher, and they constitute only 5 percent of those who rank among their company's top five earners.[29] The situation for blacks is no better, a fact that is powerfully illuminated by one simple statistic: Until Franklin Raines became CEO of Fannie Mae in 1999, no African American had ever been in charge of a *Fortune* 500 company. And it was only in 2009, when Ursula Burns took the helm at Xerox, that an African-American woman became a *Fortune* 500 CEO.

Attitudinal Evidence

Although some would disagree, statistics alone do not conclusively establish discrimination because one can always argue that other things account for

Statistics by themselves
don't prove discrimina-
tion. One must also con-
sider widespread attitudes
and institutional practices.

the disparities in income and position between men and women and between
whites and other races. The U.S. Supreme Court, in fact, has stated that
"no matter how stark the numerical disparity of the employer's work force,"
statistical evidence by itself does not prove discrimination.[30] But when widespread attitudes and institutional practices and policies are taken into account,
they point to discrimination as a significant cause of the statistical disparities.

Take the case of Bari-Ellen Roberts. She left an $80,000-a-year job at
Chase Manhattan Bank to join Texaco's finance department after a white
friend, whose husband worked for the company, assured her that "Texaco's
changing" and that the company was "looking for blacks." Her new job was
closer to home and held the promise of overseas assignments, but her friend
was mistaken about Texaco's having changed. Soon after she arrived, Roberts
found herself subjected to demeaning racial comments from colleagues and
superiors (for example, one referred to her as a "little colored girl"). They
couldn't understand why Roberts found such remarks offensive. A report on
diversity that she and some other black employees were asked to prepare
was summarily dismissed with the comment "the next thing you know we'll
have Black Panthers running down the halls." And a supervisor downgraded
her performance record because he thought she was "uppity."[31]

Fed up with a "plague of racial insults" and "egregious acts of bigotry,"
she and several other black employees filed a discrimination suit citing "the
poisonous racial atmosphere" at Texaco. Texaco settled the suit for $141 mil-
lion in retroactive raises after the news media got hold of a tape recording
of an executive strategy session at Texaco. In the meeting, one official referred to
black employees as "black jelly beans," saying, "This diversity thing, you know
how all the black jelly beans stick together." To which another responded,
"That's funny. All the black jelly beans seem to be stuck at the bottom of the
bag." One of Roberts's supervisors said, "I can't punch her [Roberts] in the
face, so I play mind games with her." The executives were also heard agreeing
to shred incriminating personnel records.

Consider also the case of Elizabeth Hishon, who went to work for King &
Spaulding, a big Atlanta law firm. Customarily, associates like Hishon are
given a period of time to either make partner or seek another job. So when
Hishon had not attained partner status after seven years, she was terminated.
Hishon, however, claimed that her failure to become a partner was due to the
law firm's sexism, and she filed a suit seeking monetary damages under
Title VII of the Civil Rights Act of 1964, which prohibits sexual and racial discrimination at work. A federal district court held that the rights guaranteed by
Title VII do not apply to the selection of partners in a law firm, but the Supreme
Court overturned that ruling in a unanimous decision that held that women can
bring sex-discrimination suits against law firms that unfairly deny them promotions to partner. In the meantime, however, Elizabeth Hishon had settled out
of court with King & Spaulding, and the case never went to trial.

A few years later, Nancy O'Mara Ezold became the first woman to win a
sex-discrimination case against a law firm in a partnership decision. Shortly
after that, another legal precedent was set when Price Waterhouse, the accounting firm, was ordered to give a partnership and back pay to Ann Hopkins,

against whom it had discriminated. And in 2002 the Equal Employment Opportunity Commission filed its first sex-discrimination lawsuit against a major Wall Street firm, alleging that Morgan Stanley fired Allison Schieffelin, one of its top bond dealers, for complaining about pay discrimination. These cases have had a significant impact on partnerships and professional firms nationwide, causing pay and promotional practices to be reevaluated, not only in law and accounting firms, but also in advertising agencies, brokerage houses, architectural concerns, and engineering firms.

Of particular interest here are the discriminatory attitudes and policies revealed by these cases. In the Ezold case, the judge found that the prominent Philadelphia law firm for which she had worked had applied tougher standards to women seeking partnerships than to men. Ezold said, "It wasn't just that similarly situated men were treated better than me, which is the double-standard idea. Another thing that came out of the trial was that in the year preceding the partnership decision, [the firm] assigned me to less complex cases and to fewer partners than it did men, so that I was denied the exposure that was critical to the partnership decision."[32]

In Ann Hopkins's case, sex stereotyping was at the root of the discrimination. Though she was considered an outstanding worker, Price Waterhouse denied her the position because she was allegedly an abrasive and overbearing manager. Coworkers referred to her as "macho," advised her to go to charm school, and intimated that she was overcompensating for being a woman. One partner in the firm even told her that she should "walk more femininely, talk more femininely, dress more femininely, wear makeup, have her hair styled, and wear jewelry." Hopkins argued, and the court agreed, that comments like these revealed underlying sexism at the firm and that her strident manner and occasional cursing would have been overlooked if she had been a man.[33] The same issue comes up in the case of Schieffelin, who was viewed by her firm as insubordinate, verbally abusive, and "physically threatening."

As for the Hishon decision, the case is noteworthy because the defendants expressed no specific complaints about Hishon's work. They apparently denied her a partnership based on a general feeling that "she just didn't fit in." In the words of another woman who had been an associate at King & Spaulding, "If you can't discuss the Virginia–North Carolina basketball game, you're an outcast."[34] Her pithy comment speaks volumes about how deep-seated attitudes operate against women and minorities in the workplace.

Women and minorities often find themselves measured by a white male value system.

Women entering male turf, or minority workers of either sex going into a predominantly white work environment, can find themselves uncomfortably being measured by a white male value system. At large companies, for instance, 42 percent of female executives and 34 percent of male minority executives report feeling constrained by the white male model, consciously and continually editing themselves to look, sound, and act like their white male counterparts.[35] Here's how Florence Blair, a twenty-five-year-old African American, described working as a civil engineer at Corning Glass Works:

As a minority woman, you are just so different from everyone else you encounter.... I went through a long period of isolation.... When I came here, I didn't have a lot in common with the white males I was working with. I didn't play golf, I didn't drink beer, I didn't hunt. All these things I had no frame of reference to.

You need to do your job on a certain technical level, but a lot of things you do on the job come down to socializing and how well you mesh with people. Sometimes I look at my role as making people feel comfortable with me.[36]

Summary 11.3
Evidence of biased attitudes and sexist or racist assumptions also points to significant job discrimination in the workplace. As they try to fit into a work world dominated by white men, women and minorities can be disadvantaged by stereotypes, false preconceptions, and prejudiced attitudes.

Surveys support the evidence of these cases. Over the years, they have indicated that sex stereotyping and sexist assumptions are widespread in business. Male managers frequently assume that women place family demands above work considerations; that they lack the necessary drive to succeed in business; that they take negative feedback personally rather than professionally; and that they are too emotional to be good managers. Even worse, researchers have found that women internalize many of the stereotypes that men have of them as less-effective leaders despite the well-established fact that there is little difference between the leadership styles of successful male and female bosses.[37] Perhaps it is not surprising, then, that psychological experiments show that, even when they state that it doesn't matter to them, both men and women tend to prefer male bosses.[38]

When it comes to race, the stereotypes can be even more damaging. For example, a survey shows that three out of four whites believe that African Americans and Hispanics are more likely than whites to prefer living on welfare, and a majority of whites also believe that African Americans and Hispanics are more likely to be lazy, unpatriotic, and prone to violence.[39] And many whites, even very well-educated ones, still accept the canard that blacks are less intelligent than whites. Moreover, psychologists at a number of universities have documented that most whites harbor hidden racial biases that they are unaware of and do not consciously agree with.[40]

Myths, stereotypes, false preconceptions, and biased attitudes victimize both women and minorities in the world of work, leading to decisions that disadvantage them in all aspects of their careers. This is especially true when companies give managers too much discretion in hiring, task assignment, promotion, and pay. In such circumstances, writes sociology professor William T. Bielby, all people unknowingly revert to stereotypes in making decisions: "The tendency to invoke gender stereotypes in making judgments about people is rapid and automatic. As a result, people are unaware of how stereotypes affect their perceptions and behavior," including "individuals whose personal beliefs are relatively free of prejudice."[41] Commenting on racial stereotypes, business consultant Edward W. Jones, Jr., writes:

All people possess stereotypes, which act like shorthand to avoid mental overload.... Most of the time stereotypes are mere shadow images rooted in one's history and deep in the subconscious. But they are very powerful. For example, in controlled experiments the mere insertion of the word *black* into a sentence has resulted in people changing their responses to a statement.

One reason for the power of stereotypes is their circularity. People seek to confirm their expectations and resist contradictory evidence, so we cling to beliefs and stereotypes that become self-fulfilling. If, for example, a white administrator makes a mistake, his boss is likely to tell him, "That's OK. Everybody's entitled to one goof." If, however, a black counterpart commits the same error, the boss thinks, "I knew he couldn't do it. The guy is incompetent." The stereotype reinforces itself.[42]

Taken together with the statistics, the attitudes, assumptions and practices reviewed here provide powerful evidence of ongoing discrimination against women and minorities in the American workplace. Recognizing the existence of such discrimination and believing for a variety of reasons that it is wrong, we have as a nation passed laws to provide equality of opportunity to women and minorities. Such laws expressly forbid discrimination in recruitment, screening, promotion, compensation, and firing. But anti-discrimination laws do not address the present-day effects of past discrimination. To remedy the effects of past discrimination and counteract visceral racism and sexism, some companies and institutions have adopted stronger and more controversial affirmative action measures.

Laws guaranteeing equality of opportunity are one response to the problem of discrimination. Another, more controversial response is affirmative action.

AFFIRMATIVE ACTION: THE LEGAL CONTEXT

In 1954, the U.S. Supreme Court decided in the case of ***Brown v. Board of Education*** that racially segregated schooling is unconstitutional. In doing so, the Court conclusively rejected the older doctrine that "separate but equal" facilities are legally permissible. Not only were segregated facilities in the South unequal, the Court found, but also the very idea of separation of the races, based as it was on a belief in black racial inferiority, inherently led to unequal treatment. That decision helped launch the civil rights movement in this country. One fruit of that movement was a series of federal laws and orders that attempt to safeguard the right of each person to equal treatment in employment.

The changes began in 1961, when President John F. Kennedy signed Executive Order 10925, which decreed that federal contractors should "take affirmative action to ensure that applicants are employed without regard to their race, creed, color, or national origin." In 1963, the Equal Pay Act was passed by Congress. Aimed especially at wage discrimination against women, it guaranteed the right to equal pay for equal work. That was followed by the **Civil Rights Act of 1964** (later amended by the Equal Employment Opportunity Act of 1972). It prohibits all forms of discrimination based on race, color, sex, religion, or national origin. Title VII, the most important section of the act, prohibits discrimination in employment. It says:

> It shall be an unlawful employment practice for an employer (1) to fail or refuse to hire or to discharge any individual, or otherwise discriminate against any individual with respect to his compensation, terms, conditions, or privileges of employment, because of such individual's race, color, religion, sex, or national origin; or (2) to limit, segregate, or classify his employees or applicants for employment in any way that would deprive or tend to deprive any individual of employment opportunities or otherwise adversely affect his status as an employee, because of such individual's race, color, religion, sex, or national origin.

The Civil Rights Act of 1964 applies to all employers, both public and private, with fifteen or more employees. In 1967 the Age Discrimination in Employment Act was passed (amended in 1978), and in 1990 the Americans with Disabilities Act extended to people with disabilities the same rights to equal employment opportunities that the Civil Rights Act of 1964 guarantees to women and minorities. In addition, several acts and executive orders regulate government contractors and subcontractors and require equal opportunities for veterans. All of these acts are enforced through the **Equal Employment Opportunity Commission** (**EEOC**).

By the late 1960s and early 1970s, companies contracting with the federal government (first in construction and then generally) were required to develop **affirmative action programs**, designed to correct imbalances in employment that exist directly as a result of past discrimination. These programs reflected the courts' recognition that job discrimination can exist even in the absence of conscious intent to discriminate.[43] Affirmative action riders were added, with various degrees of specificity, to a large number of federal programs. Many state and local bodies adopted comparable requirements.

What do affirmative action programs involve? According to EEOC guidelines, companies and other organizations should issue a written equal employment policy and appoint an official to publicize their commitment to affirmative action and to direct and implement their program. They are expected to survey current female and minority employment by department and job classification. Whenever underrepresentation of these groups is evident, companies are to develop goals and timetables to improve in each area of underrepresentation. They should then develop specific programs to achieve these goals, establish an internal audit system to monitor them, and evaluate progress in each aspect of the program. Finally, companies are encouraged to develop supportive in-house and community programs to combat discrimination.

We saw earlier that Texaco was forced to pay its black employees $141 million, the largest race-discrimination settlement in history, because the company had discriminated against qualified African Americans by refusing to promote them or pay them comparable salaries. Texaco also had retaliated against those who asserted their civil rights. Lawsuits have also exposed discriminatory pay practices at many other companies, including Mitsubishi, Home Depot, Merrill Lynch, American Express, Wal-Mart, and Boeing.[44] Other firms are guilty of ignoring the spirit of equal employment opportunity even if they don't violate the letter of the law. For example, some companies forbid their employees from speaking Spanish among themselves even when their jobs do not require English proficiency or dealing with the public;[45] others have made no effort to expand employment opportunities for women or minorities.

Most large corporations find that diversity benefits the bottom line.

Yet today most large corporations not only accept the necessity of affirmative action but also find that the bottom line benefits when they make themselves more diverse. Because four-fifths of those entering the workforce today are minorities or immigrants,[46] affirmative action expands the pool of talent from which corporations can recruit. It also allows them to reach out to a demographically wider customer base—between now and 2020 most new customers will be minorities—and makes them better able to compete both in the global marketplace

Summary 11.4
The Civil Rights Act of 1964 forbids discrimination in employment on the basis of race, color, sex, religion, and national origin. In the late 1960s and early 1970s, many companies developed affirmative action programs to correct racial imbalances existing as a result of past discrimination. Many companies believe that they benefit from affirmative action by becoming more diverse. Critics charge, however, that in practice affirmative action has often meant preferential treatment of women and minorities and even reverse discrimination against white men.

and in an increasingly multicultural environment at home.[47] United Parcel Service, for example, credits its commitment to diversity for its high customer-satisfaction ratings, and Nicole Barde, a network manager at Intel Corporation, says, "We view diversity as one of our major competitive advantages. It allows us to understand global markets and the needs of our customers."[48] As Christine A. Edwards, chief legal officer at Bank One, puts it, "Diversity is good business."[49]

Empirical evidence supports the proposition that organizations made up of different types of people are more productive than homogeneous organizations.[50] It also shows that companies with a high percentage of women in leadership positions are more efficient and profitable than their rivals.[51] However, despite the strong business case for diversity,[52] genuine equality of opportunity has yet to be achieved in the corporate world. According to a National Urban League survey, only 32 percent of employees believe that their companies do a decent job of hiring and promoting people other than white males. And most executives agree with them; only 47 percent of them think their own diversity efforts are working.[53]

Those sentiments notwithstanding, many Americans oppose affirmative action, and political opposition to it, especially to government affirmative action programs, has grown greater than ever. Critics of affirmative action charge that it means, in practice, illegal quotas, preferential treatment of African Americans and women, and even reverse discrimination against white men. In the 1960s and early 1970s, federal courts dismissed legal challenges to affirmative action, and in 1972 Congress gave it increased legislative validity by passing the Equal Employment Opportunity Act. Eventually, however, the Supreme Court had to address the question. Although its decisions determine the law of the land with regard to affirmative action, the Court's rulings have not always been as simple and straightforward as one might wish.

The Supreme Court's Position

The U.S. Supreme Court's first major ruling on affirmative action was in 1978, in the case of *Bakke v. Regents of the University of California*. Allan Bakke, a white man, applied for admission to the medical school at the University of California at Davis. Only a tiny percentage of doctors are not white. To help remedy this situation, Davis's affirmative action program set aside for minority students 16 out of its 100 entrance places. If qualified minority students could not be found, those places were not to be filled. In addition to the special admissions process, minority students were free to compete through the regular admissions process for the unrestricted 84 positions. When Bakke was refused admission, he sued the University of California, contending that it had discriminated against him in violation of both the 1964 Civil Rights Act and the Constitution. He argued that he would have won admission if those 16 places had not been withdrawn from open competition and reserved for minority students. Bakke's grades, placement-test scores, and so on, were higher than those of several minority students who were admitted. The university did not deny this but defended its program as legally permissible and socially necessary affirmative action.

Bakke won his case, although it was a close, 5-to-4 decision. In announcing the judgment of the Court, Justice Lewis F. Powell's opinion rejected explicit racial criteria setting rigid quotas and excluding nonpreferred groups from competition. At the same time Powell held that the selection process can take race and ethnic origin into account as one factor and pointed to Harvard's admission program as a model. In such a program, "race or ethnic background may be deemed a 'plus' in a particular applicant's file, yet it does not insulate the individual from comparison with all other candidates for the available seats." Powell also granted that numerical goals may be permissible when the institution in question has illegally discriminated in the past.

A year later, in *United Steelworkers of America v. Weber*, the Supreme Court took up the issue again—but in a different situation and with a different verdict. At Kaiser Aluminum's Gramercy, Louisiana, plant, only 5 out of 273 skilled craft workers were black, although the local workforce was 39 percent black. Kaiser therefore entered into an agreement with the United Steelworkers to train employees from its workforce for these craft positions on the basis of seniority, except that 50 percent of the positions would be reserved for African Americans until their percentage in these jobs approximated the percentage of African Americans in the local workforce. The program was challenged in court, and the case eventually reached the Supreme Court, which upheld Kaiser's affirmative action program. In delivering the court's opinion, Justice William Brennan made clear that legal prohibition of racial discrimination does not prevent "private, voluntary, race-conscious affirmative action plans." He wrote:

> We need not today define in detail the line of demarcation between permissible and impermissible affirmative action plans. It suffices to hold that the challenged Kaiser-USWA affirmative action plan falls on the permissible side of the line. The purposes of the plan mirror those of the [Civil Rights] statute. Both were designed to break down old patterns of racial segregation and hierarchy. Both were structured to "open employment opportunities for Negroes in occupations which have been traditionally closed to them."…
>
> At the same time, the plan does not unnecessarily trammel the interest of the white employees…. Moreover, the plan is a temporary measure … simply to eliminate a manifest racial imbalance.

A few years later, though, the Supreme Court upheld seniority over affirmative action in *Memphis Firefighters v. Stotts*. When financial difficulties forced the city to lay off firefighters, it respected the customary practice of "last hired, first to be let go," even though that undermined its recent efforts to increase the number of black firefighters. After reviewing the case, the Supreme Court ruled that seniority systems are racially neutral and that the city may not lay off white workers to save the jobs of black workers with less seniority. However, the court reaffirmed the principle of affirmative action in 1987, this time in a case concerning women. In *Johnson v. Transportation Agency*, it held that considerations of sex were permissible as one factor in promoting Diane Joyce, a female county employee, to the position of road dispatcher over an equally qualified male employee, Paul Johnson. In summing up the Court's position, Justice Brennan stated that the promotion of Joyce "was made pursuant to an affirmative action plan that represents a moderate, flexible, case-by-case approach to effecting a gradual improvement in the representation of minorities and women in the Agency's work force."

Since then, however, the Court has grown more antagonistic to affirmative action programs. For example, in *City of Richmond v. Croson*, the Court invalidated a Richmond, Virginia, law that channeled 30 percent of public-works funds to minority-owned construction companies (see Case 11.1). In *Adarand Constructors v. Pena*, the Supreme Court examined a federal program that provided financial incentives for contractors to hire "socially or economically disadvantaged" subcontractors. In her majority opinion in the 5-to-4 decision, Justice Sandra Day O'Connor affirmed the principle that "federal racial classification, like those of a State, must serve a compelling government interest, and must be narrowly tailored to further that interest." Accordingly, all government action based on race should be subjected to "the strictest judicial scrutiny" to ensure that no individual's right to equal protection has been violated. The Court then sent the case back to a lower court for rehearing.

In addition to O'Connor's majority opinion, however, five other justices wrote opinions in the *Adarand* case, and these reveal a range of perspectives on affirmative action. For instance, Justice David Souter criticized the Court for departing from past practice, reminding his colleagues that it is well established "that constitutional authority to remedy past discrimination is not limited to the power to forbid its continuation, but extends to eliminating those effects that would otherwise persist and skew the operation of public systems even in the absence of current intent to practice any discrimination."

In his dissenting opinion, Justice John Paul Stevens also defended the general principle of affirmative action:

> There is no moral or constitutional equivalence between a policy that is designed to perpetuate a caste system and one that seeks to eradicate racial subordination....
>
> A decision by representatives of the majority to discriminate against the members of a minority race is fundamentally different from those same representatives' decision to impose incidental costs on the majority of their constituents in order to provide a benefit to a disadvantaged minority. Indeed, as I have previously argued, the former is virtually always repugnant to the principles of a free and democratic society, whereas the latter is, in some circumstances, entirely consistent with the ideal of equality.

However, Justice Clarence Thomas explicitly challenged Stevens's position. In an opinion concurring with the majority's judgment, he asserted that

> there is a "moral and constitutional equivalence" between laws designed to subjugate a race and those that distribute benefits on the basis of race in order to foster some current notion of equality. Government cannot make us equal; it can only recognize, respect, and protect us as equal before the law....
>
> In my mind, government-sponsored racial discrimination based on benign prejudice is just as noxious as discrimination inspired by malicious prejudice. In each instance, it is racial discrimination, plain and simple.

Summary 11.5
The Supreme Court has adopted a case-by-case approach to affirmative action. Although the legal situation is complex, in a series of rulings over the years a majority of the Court has upheld the general principle of affirmative action, as long as such programs are moderate and flexible. Race can legitimately be taken into account in employment-related decisions, but only as one among several factors. Affirmative action programs that rely on rigid and unreasonable quotas or that impose excessive hardship on present employees are illegal.

The upshot of recent judicial developments relative to affirmative action is not clear, tangled up as the rulings are in details, legal technicalities, and split opinions. The legal future is difficult to predict. Clearly, the Court is more attuned than ever to what it perceives to be excesses in the cause of affirmative action. Nevertheless, when in 2003 the Supreme Court revisited affirmative action in higher education for the first time in twenty-five years, it reaffirmed the principles it had enunciated in *Bakke*.

In *Grutter v. Bollinger* the Court upheld, by a 5-to-4 majority, the affirmative action program at the University of Michigan's law school. Citing testimony from various business and military leaders, who urged that diversity is essential to the country's economy and security, the Court ruled that the state has a "compelling interest" in promoting educational diversity and that the law school's method of doing so was "narrowly tailored" to meet that interest. Under the law school's "highly individualized" and "holistic" approach, minority race is a "plus factor" in evaluating potential students, but it's also possible for a white student likely to make a particularly interesting contribution to the law school's academic climate to beat out a minority student with better grades and test scores. But in *Gratz v. Bollinger*, a companion case, a different majority of justices ruled, 6 to 3, that Michigan's undergraduate affirmative action program was unconstitutionally rigid and mechanistic because it gave members of underrepresented groups an automatic 20-point bonus on the 150-point scale used to rank applicants.

Despite a division of opinion among the justices, in light of the Michigan cases it appears unlikely that the Supreme Court will reverse itself directly and outlaw moderate and flexible affirmative action programs. However, the Court is clearly impatient. In her majority opinion in *Grutter*, Justice O'Connor stated that "race-conscious admissions policies must be limited in time" and that the Court "expect[s] that 25 years from now, the use of racial preferences will no longer be necessary." That's a hope undoubtedly shared by those on both side of the debate over affirmative action.

AFFIRMATIVE ACTION: THE MORAL ISSUES

Understanding the Supreme Court's evolving position on affirmative action is important, because the Court sets the legal context in which business operates and lets employers know what they are and are not legally permitted to do. But legal decisions by themselves do not exhaust the relevant moral issues. Employers—as well as women, minorities, and white men—want to know whether affirmative action programs are morally right. Indeed, it is a safe bet that the Supreme Court's own decisions are influenced not only by technical legal issues but also by how the justices answer this moral question.

Before evaluating arguments for and against affirmative action, one needs to know what is being debated. *Affirmative action* here means programs taking the race or sex of employees or job candidates into account as part of an effort to correct imbalances in employment that exist as a result of past discrimination, either in the company itself or in the larger society. To keep the discussion relevant, it is limited to affirmative action programs that might reasonably be expected to be upheld by the Supreme Court. Excluded are

programs that establish rigid, permanent quotas or that hire and promote unqualified persons. Included are programs that hire or promote a woman or an
African American who might not otherwise, according to established but fair
criteria, be the best-qualified candidate.

A word about terminology: Critics of affirmative action often label it "reverse discrimination," but this term is misleading. According to the definition
offered earlier, job discrimination involves prejudice, inaccurate stereotypes,
or the assumption that a certain group is inferior and deserves unequal treatment. No such forces are at work in the affirmative action cases already discussed. Those who designed the programs that worked to the disadvantage
of white men like Allan Bakke and Paul Johnson did not do so because they
were biased against white men and believed them inferior and deserving of
less respect than other human beings. Those who designed the programs in
question were themselves white men.

Arguments for Affirmative Action

1. **Compensatory justice demands affirmative action programs.**

   POINT: "As groups, women and minorities have historically been discriminated against, often viciously. As individuals and as a nation, we can't ignore the sins of our fathers and mothers. In fact, we have an obligation
   to do something to help repair the wrongs of the past. Affirmative action
   in employment is one sound way to do this."

   COUNTERPOINT: "People today can't be expected to atone for the sins of
   the past. We're not responsible for them, and in any case, we wouldn't
   be compensating those who rightly deserve it. Young African Americans
   and women coming for their first job have never suffered employment
   discrimination. Their parents and grandparents may deserve compensation,
   but why should today's candidates receive any special consideration? No
   one should discriminate against them, of course, but they should have to
   compete openly and on their merits, just like everybody else."

2. **Affirmative action is necessary to permit fairer competition.**

   POINT: "Even if young blacks and young women today have not themselves suffered job discrimination, blacks in particular have suffered all
   the disadvantages of growing up in families that have been affected by
   discrimination. In our racist society, they have suffered from inferior
   schools and poor environment. In addition, as victims of society's prejudiced attitudes, young blacks and young women have been hampered by
   a lack of self-confidence and self-respect. Taking race and sex into account makes job competition fairer by keeping white men from having a
   competitive edge that they don't really deserve."

   COUNTERPOINT: "Your point is better when applied to blacks than to
   women, it seems to me, but I'm still not persuaded. You overlook the fact
   that there are a lot of disadvantaged whites out there, too. Is an employer
   going to have to investigate everyone's life history to see who had to
   overcome the most obstacles? I think an employer has a right to seek the

best-qualified candidate without trying to make life fair for everybody. And isn't the best-qualified person entitled to get the job or the promotion?"

3. **Affirmative action is necessary to break the cycle that keeps minorities and women locked into low-paying, low-prestige jobs.**

POINT: "You advocate neutral, nondiscriminatory employment practices, as if we could just ignore our whole history of racial and sexual discrimination. Statistics show that African Americans in particular have been trapped in a socioeconomically subordinate position. If we want to break that pattern and eventually heal the racial rifts in our country, we've got to adopt vigorous affirmative action programs that push more African Americans into middle-class jobs. Even assuming racism were dead in our society, with mere nondiscrimination alone it would take a hundred years or more for blacks to equalize their position."

COUNTERPOINT: "You ignore the fact that affirmative action has its costs, too. You talk about healing the racial rifts in our country, but affirmative action programs make everybody more racially conscious. They also cause resentment and frustration among white men. Many African Americans and women also resent being advanced on grounds other than merit. Finally, if you hire and promote people faster and farther than they merit, you're only asking for problems."

Arguments against Affirmative Action

1. **Affirmative action injures white men and infringes their rights.**

POINT: "Even moderate affirmative action programs injure the white men who are made to bear their brunt. Other people design the programs, but it is Allan Bakke, Paul Johnson, and others like them, who find their career opportunities hampered. Moreover, such programs violate the right of white men to be treated as individuals and to have racial or sexual considerations not affect employment decisions."

COUNTERPOINT: "I'm not sure that Bakke and Johnson have the rights you are talking about. Racial and sexual considerations are often relevant to employment decisions. Jobs and medical school slots are scarce resources, and society may distribute these in a way that furthers its legitimate ends—like breaking the cycle of poverty for minorities. I admit that with affirmative action programs white men do not have as many advantages as they did before, and I'm against extreme programs that disregard their interests altogether. But their interests have to be balanced against society's interest in promoting these programs."

2. **Affirmative action itself violates the principle of equality.**

POINT: "Affirmative action programs are intended to enhance racial and sexual equality, but you can't do that by treating people unequally. If equality is the goal, it must be the means, too. With affirmative action programs, you use racial and sexual considerations—but that is the very thing that has caused so much harm in the past and that affirmative action itself is hoping to get rid of."

Summary 11.6
The moral issues surrounding affirmative action are controversial. Its defenders argue that compensatory justice demands affirmative action programs; that affirmative action is needed to permit fairer competition; and that affirmative action is necessary to break the cycle that keeps minorities and women locked into poor-paying, low-prestige jobs.

COUNTERPOINT: "I admit that it is distasteful to have to take racial and sexual considerations into account when dealing with individuals in employment situations. I wish we didn't have to. But the unfortunate reality is that in the real world racial and sexual factors go a long way toward determining what life prospects an individual has. We can't wish that reality away by pretending the world is colorblind when it is not. Formal, colorblind equality has to be infringed now if we are ever to achieve real, meaningful racial and sexual equality."

3. **Nondiscrimination will achieve our social goals; stronger affirmative action is unnecessary.**

POINT: "The 1964 Civil Rights Act unequivocally outlaws job discrimination, and numerous employees and job candidates have won discrimination cases before the EEOC or in court. We need to insist on rigorous enforcement of the law. Also, employers should continue to recruit in a way that attracts minority applicants and to make sure that their screening and review practices do not involve any implicit racist or sexist assumptions. And they should monitor their internal procedures and the behavior of their white male employees to root out any discriminatory behavior. Stronger affirmative action measures, in particular taking race or sex into account in employment matters, are unnecessary. They only bring undesirable results."

COUNTERPOINT: "Without affirmative action, progress often stops. The percentage of minorities and women employed by those subject to federal affirmative action requirements has risen much higher than it has elsewhere. Take the example of Alabama. In the late 1960s, a federal court found that only 27 out of the state's 3,000 clerical and managerial employees were African American. Federal Judge Frank Johnson ordered extensive recruiting of blacks, as well as the hiring of the few specifically identified blacks who could prove they were victims of discrimination. Nothing happened. Another suit was filed, this time just against the state police, and this time a 50 percent hiring quota was imposed, until blacks reached 25 percent of the force. As a result, Alabama's state police quickly became the most thoroughly integrated state police force in the country."[54]

The debate over affirmative action is not the only controversy connected with job discrimination. Two other issues, both primarily concerning women, have been the topic of recent moral, legal, and political discussion: the issue of comparable worth and the problem of sexual harassment on the job.

Summary 11.7

Critics of affirmative action argue that affirmative action injures white men and infringes their rights; that affirmative action itself violates the principle of equality; and that nondiscrimination (without affirmative action) will suffice to achieve our social goals.

COMPARABLE WORTH

Louise Peterson was a licensed practical nurse at Western State Hospital in Tacoma, Washington. For supervising the daily care of sixty men convicted of sex crimes, she was paid $192 a month less than the hospital's groundskeepers and $700 a month less than men doing work similar to hers at Washington state prisons. Convinced of the inequity of the state's pay scale,

Peterson filed a suit claiming that she and other women were being discriminated against because men of similar skills and training and with similar responsibilities were being paid significantly more. A federal judge found Washington guilty of sex discrimination and ordered the state to reimburse its female employees a whopping $838 million in back pay.

Although an appellate court later overturned that ruling, the state of Washington began a program intended to raise the pay for government jobs typically considered "women's work." Even though the program had flaws,[55] it helped raise to national prominence the doctrine of comparable worth and signaled a dramatic escalation in women's fight for equal employment rights.

In essence, the doctrine of **comparable worth** holds that women and men should be paid on the same scale not only for doing the same or equivalent jobs but also for doing different jobs involving equal skill, effort, and responsibility. Advocates of comparable worth point to the substantial statistical evidence demonstrating that women are in more low-paying jobs than men. They also note the consistent relationship between the percentage of women in an occupation and the salary of that occupation: The more women dominate an occupation, the less it pays. Comparable-worth advocates contend that women have been shunted into a small number of pink-collar occupations and that a biased and discriminatory wage system has kept their pay below that of men in occupations involving a comparable degree of skill, education, responsibility, and so on. For example, studies have shown that legal secretaries and instrument-repair technicians hold jobs with the same relative value for a company in terms of accountability, know-how, and problem-solving skill; yet legal secretaries, who are almost all women, earn an average of $9,432 less than instrument-repair technicians, who generally are men.[56]

> Proponents of comparable worth believe that women have been directed into certain occupations and held back by a biased wage system.

As comparable-worth advocates see it, justice demands that women receive equal pay for doing work of comparable value. Jobs should be objectively evaluated in terms of the education, skills, and experience required and in terms of responsibilities, working conditions, and other relevant factors. Equivalent jobs should receive equivalent salaries, even if discriminatory job markets would otherwise put them on different pay scales. Some comparable-worth advocates further argue that when women have not received equivalent pay for jobs of comparable worth, justice requires that employers pay them reparation damages for the money they have lost. That would be expensive. But whether pay adjustments are retroactive or not, all comparable-worth programs envision adjusting the salary schedules of women upward rather than the pay of men downward.

> Opponents insist that women have freely chosen lower-paying occupations.

Opponents of comparable worth insist that women, desiring flexible schedules and less taxing jobs, have freely chosen lower-paying occupations and thus are not entitled to any readjustment in pay scales. Phyllis Schlafly, for one, calls comparable worth "basically a conspiracy theory of jobs.... It asserts that, first, a massive societal male conspiracy has segregated or ghetto-ized women into particular occupations by excluding them from others; and then, second, devalued the women's job by paying them lower wages than other occupations held primarily by men." She adds: "For two decades, at least, women have been free to go into any occupation.... But most women continue

Summary 11.8
Comparable worth is the idea that women and men should be paid on the same scale for doing different jobs if they involve equivalent skill, effort, and responsibility. Advocates of comparable worth say that women have been shunted into low-paying jobs, that they suffer from a discriminatory labor market, and that justice requires that they receive equal pay for doing jobs of equal worth. Some contend further that monetary reparations are due to women who in the past have not received equal pay for work of equal value.

to choose traditional, rather than non-traditional, jobs. This is their own free choice. Nobody makes them do it."[57]

Others who are sympathetic to the concept of comparable worth worry about its implementation. How are different jobs to be evaluated and compared, they wonder. "How do you determine the intrinsic value of one job and then compare it to another?" asks Linda Chavez, former staff director of the Commission on Civil Rights. She points out that "for 200 years, this has been done by the free marketplace. It's as good an alternative as those being suggested by comparable-worth advocates. I'm not sure the legislative bodies or courts can do any better."[58] Job evaluation studies, however, are common in the public sector, and many private companies also utilize them to determine the skill, effort, responsibility, and working conditions that characterize different job categories and, hence, the wages appropriate to them. However, even if reasonably objective judgments of comparability are possible, opponents worry about the price tag: Revising salaries could cost a medium-size company millions of dollars in increased pay and benefits.

Advocates of comparable worth respond to those criticisms by pointing to statistical evidence demonstrating gender-linked pay inequities, as well as to the reality of visceral sexism in the workplace and to the thousands of cases every year involving workplace discrimination against women. They reject the idea that women end up in jobs that pay less than comparable jobs held by men because of their free choice. Rather, discrimination distorts the operation of the labor market and needs to be corrected. Moreover, proponents of comparable worth reject the argument that implementing comparable worth would be prohibitively expensive. They point to Minnesota, which phased in a comparable-worth program over several years so the state incurred an expense of only about 1 percent a year. But the core of their argument remains an appeal to fairness and equity, which, they insist, should not be sacrificed on the altar of economics.

The comparable-worth issue continues to engender controversy because, as one commentator puts it, "The issue pits against each other two cherished American values: the ethics of nondiscrimination versus the free enterprise system."[59] The federal courts have not explicitly accepted the doctrine of comparable worth, even when they've rendered legal decisions that seem to support it. One form of job discrimination against women that the courts agree about, however, is sexual harassment.

SEXUAL HARASSMENT

Many men find the term *sexual harassment* amusing and have a difficult time taking it seriously. "It wouldn't bother me," they feel certain. "In fact," they chuckle, "I wouldn't mind being harassed a little more often." Others shrug it off, saying, "What's the big deal? You know what the world is like. Men and women, love and sex, they make it go 'round. Only uptight women are going to complain about sexual advances." But for millions of working women, the reality of sexual harassment is not something to be shrugged off. For them it is no laughing matter.

Summary 11.9
Opponents of comparable worth claim that women have freely chosen their occupations and are not entitled to compensation. They contend that only the market can and should determine the value of different jobs, and that revising pay scales would be expensive.

The courts agree. Sexual-harassment claims have emerged in the past two decades as a potent force in the effort to eliminate sex discrimination, with over twelve thousand complaints of sexual harassment in the workplace filed annually with the EEOC or state and local authorities.[60] These claims fall primarily under Title VII of the Civil Rights Act, which in certain circumstances imposes liability on employers for the discriminatory acts of their employees—including sexual harassment. The Supreme Court has joined a number of federal district and appeals courts in holding that sexual harassment violates the Civil Rights Act because it is based on the sex of the individual.[61] In short, sexual harassment is illegal.

It is also expensive and—unfortunately—widespread. No large American corporation has escaped the issue, and charges of sexual harassment have cost some of them a small fortune. In the late 1990s, for instance, Ford paid $7.75 million and Mitsubishi $34 million to settle class-action sexual-harassment lawsuits against them. According to the Supreme Court, men as well as women can be victims of sexual harassment.[62] The focus here is on women, however, because they are the ones who suffer most from it. One survey found that 21 percent of women report having been harassed at work and that 54 percent of them believe that supervisors are likely to retaliate if a subordinate rejects their romantic overtures.[63]

Critics may find it odd that sexual harassment is viewed by the courts as a kind of sex discrimination. If an infatuated supervisor harasses only the female employee who is the object of his desire, is his misconduct really best understood as discrimination against women? He does not bother women in general, only this particular individual. In viewing sexual harassment as a violation of the 1964 Civil Rights Act, however, the courts are rightly acknowledging that such behavior, and the larger social patterns that reinforce it, rest on male attitudes and assumptions that work against women.

Accepting this viewpoint still leaves puzzles, however. Assume that the infatuated supervisor is a woman and the employee a man. Are we to interpret this situation as sex discrimination, considering that it does not take place against a social backdrop of exploitation and discrimination against men? Or imagine a bisexual employer who sexually harasses both male and female employees. Because he discriminates against neither sex, is there no sexual harassment?

Legally, sexual harassment is a form of discrimination. But that may not be the worst aspect of it, morally speaking.

These conceptual puzzles have to do with the law's interpretation of sexual harassment as a kind of sex discrimination. Practically speaking, this interpretation has benefited women and brought them better and fairer treatment on the job, but it clearly has its limits. Legally speaking, the most important aspect of sexual harassment may be that it represents discrimination, but it is doubtful that discrimination is morally the worst aspect of sexual harassment. Morally, there is much more to be said about the wrongness of sexual harassment.*

---

*By analogy, compare the fact that often the only grounds on which the federal government can put a murderer on trial is on the charge of having violated the civil rights of his or her victim. The charge of violating the victim's civil rights doesn't get to the heart of the murderer's wrongdoing, even if it is the only legally relevant issue.

The Definition of Sexual Harassment

What exactly is sexual harassment? According to the Equal Employment Opportunity Commission, **sexual harassment** is "unwelcome sexual advances, requests for sexual favors, and other verbal or physical conduct of a sexual nature." Catherine A. MacKinnon, author of *Sexual Harassment of Working Women*, describes sexual harassment as "sexual attention imposed on someone who is not in a position to refuse it." Alan K. Campbell, former director of the Federal Office of Personnel Management, defines it as "deliberate or repeated unsolicited verbal comments, gestures, or physical contact of a sexual nature which are unwelcome."[64] Here is a useful legal definition that reflects the way most courts understand sexual harassment:

> Unwelcome sexual advances, requests for sexual favors, and other verbal or physical conduct of a sexual nature constitute sexual harassment when (1) submission to such conduct is made either explicitly or implicitly a term or condition of an individual's employment, (2) submission to or rejection of such conduct by an individual is used as the basis for employment decisions affecting such individual, or (3) such conduct has the purpose or effect of substantially interfering with an individual's work performance or creating an intimidating, hostile, or offensive working environment.[65]

There are two types of sexual harassment.

Sexual harassment divides into two types: "quid pro quo" and "hostile work environment." The phrase *quid pro quo* refers to giving something in return for something else. **Quid-pro-quo harassment** occurs when a supervisor makes an employee's employment opportunities conditional on the employee's entering into a sexual relationship with, or granting sexual favors to, the supervisor. Sexual threats are an example—in their crudest form, "You'd better agree to sleep with me if you want to keep your job." The immorality of such threats seems clear. In threatening harm, they are coercive and violate the rights of the person being threatened, certainly depriving her or him of equal treatment on the job. Obviously such threats can be seriously damaging, psychologically and otherwise, and hence are morally wrong.

Sexual offers are another species of quid-pro-quo sexual harassment: "If you sleep with me, I'm sure I can help you advance more quickly in the firm." Often such offers harbor an implied threat, and, unlike with genuine offers, the employee may risk something by turning them down. Larry May and John Hughes have argued that such offers by a male employer to a female employee put her in a worse position than she was before and are therefore coercive. Even sexual offers with no hint of retaliation, they contend, change the female employee's working environment in an undesirable way.[66] In the case of both threats and offers, the supervisor is attempting to exploit the power imbalance between him and the employee.

The second kind of sexual harassment—**hostile-work-environment harassment**—is broader, but it may be more important because it is so pervasive. This form of sexual harassment is behavior of a sexual nature that is distressing to women and interferes with their ability to perform on the job, even when the behavior is not an attempt to pressure the woman for sexual favors. Sexual innuendos; sexually explicit e-mails; leering at or ogling a woman;

Summary 11.10
Sexual harassment is widespread. It includes unwelcome sexual advances and other conduct of a sexual nature when either (1) employment decisions are based on submission to it (quid pro quo) or (2) such conduct substantially interferes with an individual's work performance (hostile work environment). Sexual harassment is a kind of discrimination and is illegal.

sexist remarks about women's bodies, clothing, or sexual activities; the posting of pictures of nude women; raunchy office banter; and unnecessary touching, patting, or other physical conduct can all constitute sexual harassment. Such behavior is humiliating and degrading to its victim. It interferes with her peace of mind and undermines her work performance.

Legally, a woman is not required to prove that she was psychologically damaged or unable to work in order to establish sexual harassment. However, an isolated or occasional sexist remark or innuendo does not constitute harassment. To qualify as harassment, the objectionable behavior must be persistent. The same holds for racial slurs and epithets. An ethnic joke by itself does not constitute discriminatory harassment, but a concerted pattern of "excessive and opprobrious" racially derogatory remarks and related abuse does violate the law.[67]

Human beings are sexual creatures, and when men and women work together, there may be sexual undertones to their interactions. Women as well as men can appreciate, with the right persons and at the appropriate times, sexual references, sex-related humor, and physical contact with members of the opposite sex. Flirting, too, is often appreciated by both parties. It is not necessary that a serious and professional work environment be entirely free from sexuality, nor is this an achievable goal.

When, then, is behavior objectionable or offensive enough to constitute harassment? What one person views as innocent fun or a friendly overture may be seen as objectionable and degrading by another. Comments that one woman appreciates or enjoys may be distressing to another. Who can decide what is right? In the case of sexual harassment, who determines what is objectionable or offensive?

To answer that question, the courts ask what the hypothetical "reasonable person" would find offensive if the person were a woman in that situation. What matters morally, however, is to respect each person's choices and wishes. Even if the other women in the office like it when the boss gives them a little hug, it would still be wrong to hug the one woman who is made uncomfortable. If the behavior is unwanted—that is, if the woman doesn't like it—then persisting in it is wrong. The fact that objectionable behavior must be persistent and repeated to be sexual harassment allows for the possibility that people can honestly misread coworkers' signals or misjudge their likely response to a sexual innuendo, a joke, or a friendly pat. That may be excusable; what is not excusable is persisting in the behavior once you know it is unwelcome.

Some lower courts have extended the concept of sexual harassment to include **sexual favoritism**, upholding the claims of women to have been discriminated against because the boss was sleeping not with them but with one or more other employees. That seems to stretch the concept of sexual harassment almost to the breaking point, because the rights of the complaining employee have not been violated. Her employment opportunities have not been made contingent on her acquiescing to her employer's sexual wishes. However, the women who entered into sexual relations with their supervisor may have benefited from doing so, possibly at the expense of the employee who had no

In sexual harassment cases, the courts look to what a reasonable person would find offensive. But what matters morally is to respect each person's choices and wishes.

such relationship with the boss. Moreover, such conduct by a supervisor can create a sexually charged work environment that interferes with the ability of other employees to do their job. It also reinforces beliefs that demean women and perpetuate discrimination against them because, in the words of one judge, "a message is conveyed that managers view women as sexual playthings."[68]

Dealing with Sexual Harassment

Neither the wrongness nor the illegality of sexual harassment requires that the harassing conduct be by the employee's supervisor. This is particularly relevant in hostile-work-environment cases, in which the harassment a woman endures may come from coworkers. Furthermore, companies can be held legally liable for harassing behavior by their employees even if they are unaware of it, especially in cases of quid-pro-quo harassment by supervisors. In hostile-work-environment cases, companies can escape liability if they can show that (1) they took reasonable steps to prevent and promptly correct sexually harassing behavior and (2) the employee unreasonably failed to take advantage of the preventive or corrective procedures established by the company. This fact gives companies an incentive to be proactive, and many have responded by developing comprehensive programs to educate employees about, and to protect them from, sexual harassment. Legal issues aside, companies clearly have a moral obligation to provide a work environment in which employees are free from sexual harassment. They need to be alert to the possibility of sexual harassment, take reasonable steps to prevent it, and deal with it swiftly and fairly should it occur.

Practically speaking, what should a female employee do if she encounters sexual harassment? *First*, she must make it clear that the behavior is unwanted. That may be more difficult to do than it sounds, because most of us like to please others and do not want to be thought to be prudes or to lack a sense of humor. The employee may wish to be tactful and even pleasant in rejecting behavior she finds inappropriate, especially if she thinks the offending party is well intentioned. But in any case, she has to make her feelings known clearly and unequivocally. *Second*, if the behavior persists, she should try to document it by keeping a record of what has occurred, who was involved, and when it happened. If others have witnessed some of the incidents, then that will help her document her case.

Third, the employee should complain to the appropriate supervisor, sticking to the facts and presenting her allegations as objectively as possible. She should do this immediately in the case of sexual threats or offers by supervisors. In the case of inappropriate behavior by coworkers, she should generally wait to see if it persists despite her having told the offending party that she objects. If complaining to her immediate supervisor does not bring quick action, then she must try whatever other channel is available to her in the organization—the grievance committee, for example, or the chief executive's office.

Fourth, if internal complaints do not bring results, then the employee should seriously consider seeing a lawyer and learning in detail what legal options are available. Many women try to ignore sexual harassment, but the evidence suggests that in most cases it continues or grows worse. When sexual threats or offers are involved, a significant number of victims are subject to

What you should do if you encounter sexual harassment.

Summary 11.11
Employees encountering sexually harassing behavior from coworkers should make it clear that the behavior is unwanted. If it persists, harassed employees should document the behavior and report it to the appropriate person or office in the organization. In the case of sexual threats or offers from supervisors, they should do this immediately. If internal channels are ineffective, employees should seek legal advice.

unwarranted reprimands, increased work loads, or other reprisals. The employee must remember, too, that she has both a moral and a legal right to work in an environment free from sexual harassment.

STUDY CORNER

Key Terms and Concepts

affirmative action programs
Bakke case
Brown v. Board of Education
Civil Rights Act of 1964
comparable worth

Equal Employment Opportunity Commission (EEOC)
Grutter and *Gratz* cases
hostile-work-environment harassment

job discrimination
pink-collar occupations
quid-pro-quo harassment
sexual favoritism
sexual harassment

Points to Review

- what the case of Notre Dame and Willingham illustrates
- three defining features of job discrimination
- four different forms of job discrimination
- moral arguments against job discrimination
- statistical evidence of inequality
- attitudes that victimize women like Ezold, Hopkins, and Hishon
- how stereotypes can lead to discrimination
- what was decided in *Brown v. Board of Education*
- what the Civil Rights Act says about discrimination
- EEOC guidelines for affirmative action programs
- why many companies believe in affirmative action
- where the Supreme Court stands on affirmative action

- what's misleading about calling affirmative action "reverse discrimination"
- three arguments for affirmative action
- three arguments against affirmative action
- what the doctrine of comparable worth requires employers to do
- arguments for and against comparable worth
- what's puzzling about viewing sexual harassment as sex discrimination
- two types of sexual harassment
- who decides what is sexual harassment
- sexual favoritism as a possible form of sexual harassment
- how companies can escape legal liability for hostile-work-environment claims
- four things to do when you encounter sexual harassment

CASE 11.1

Minority Set-Asides

Richmond, Virginia, the former capital of the Confederacy, is not the sort of place one would normally associate with controversial efforts at affirmative action. But aware of its legacy of racial discrimination and wanting to do something about it, the Richmond City

Council adopted what it called the Minority Business Utilization Plan—a plan that eventually brought it before the U.S. Supreme Court.

The plan, which the council adopted by a 5-to-2 vote after a public hearing, required contractors to whom the city awarded construction contracts to subcontract at least 30 percent of the dollar amount of their contracts to Minority Business Enterprises (MBEs). A business was defined as an MBE if minority group members controlled at least 51 percent of it, and a minority-owned business from anywhere in the United States could qualify as an MBE subcontractor. (The 30 percent set-aside did not apply to construction contracts awarded to minority contractors in the first place.)

Proponents of the set-aside provision relied on a study that indicated that whereas the general population of Richmond was 50 percent African American, only 0.67 percent of the city's construction contracts had been awarded to minority businesses. Council member Marsh, a proponent of the ordinance, made the following statement:

> I have been practicing law in this community since 1961, and I am familiar with the practices in the construction industry in this area, in the state, and around the nation. And I can say without equivocation, that the general conduct of the construction industry … is one in which race discrimination and exclusion on the basis of race is widespread.

Opponents questioned both the wisdom and the legality of the ordinance. They argued that the disparity between minorities in the population of Richmond and the low number of contracts awarded to MBEs did not prove racial discrimination in the construction industry. They also questioned whether there were enough MBEs in the Richmond area to satisfy the 30 percent requirement.

The city's plan was in effect for five years. During that time, it was challenged in the courts. A federal district court upheld the set-aside ordinance, stating that the city council's "findings [were] sufficient to ensure that, in adopting the Plan, it was remedying the present effects of past discrimination in the construction industry." However, the case was appealed to the Supreme Court, which ruled in *City of Richmond v. Croson* that

the Richmond plan was in violation of the equal protection clause of the Fourteenth Amendment.[69] In delivering the opinion of the majority of the Court, Justice Sandra Day O'Connor argued that Richmond had not supported its plan with sufficient evidence of past discrimination in the city's construction industry:

> A generalized assertion that there has been past discrimination in an entire industry provides no guidance for a legislative body to determine the precise scope of the injury it seeks to remedy. It "has no logical stopping point."… "Relief" for such an ill-defined wrong could extend until the percentage of public contracts awarded to MBEs in Richmond mirrored the percentage of minorities in the population as a whole.
>
> [The City of Richmond] argues that it is attempting to remedy various forms of past discrimination that are alleged to be responsible for the small number of minority businesses in the local contracting industry…. While there is no doubt that the sorry history of both private and public discrimination in this country has contributed to a lack of opportunities for black entrepreneurs, this observation, standing alone, cannot justify a rigid quota in the awarding of public contracts in Richmond, Virginia. Like the claim that discrimination in primary and secondary schooling justifies a rigid racial preference in medical school admissions, an amorphous claim that there has been past discrimination cannot justify the use of an unyielding racial quota.
>
> It is sheer speculation how many minority firms there would be in Richmond absent past societal discrimination, just as it was sheer speculation how many minority medical students would have been admitted to the medical school at Davis absent past discrimination in educational opportunities. Defining these sorts of injuries as "identified discrimination" would give local governments license to create a patchwork of racial preferences based on statistical generalizations about any particular field of endeavor.
>
> These defects are readily apparent in this case. The 30% quota cannot in any realistic

sense be tied to any injury suffered by anyone....

In sum, none of the evidence presented by the city points to any identified discrimination in the Richmond construction industry. We, therefore, hold that the city has failed to demonstrate a compelling interest in apportioning public contracting opportunities on the basis of race. To accept Richmond's claim that past societal discrimination alone can serve as the basis for rigid racial preference would be to open the door to competing claims for "remedial relief" for every disadvantaged group. The dream of a Nation of equal citizens in a society where race is irrelevant to personal opportunity and achievement would be lost in a mosaic of shifting preferences based on inherently unmeasurable claims of past wrongs.... We think such a result would be contrary to both the letter and spirit of a constitutional provision whose central command is equality.

But the Court's decision was not unanimous, and Justice Thurgood Marshall was joined by Justices William Brennan and Harry Blackmun in dissenting vigorously to the opinion of the majority. Justice Marshall wrote:

The essence of the majority's position is that Richmond has failed to ... prove that past discrimination has impeded minorities from joining or participating fully in Richmond's construction contracting industry. I find deep irony in second-guessing Richmond's judgment on this point. As much as any municipality in the United States, Richmond knows what racial discrimination is; a century of decisions by this and other federal courts has richly documented the city's disgraceful history of public and private racial discrimination. In any event, the Richmond City Council has supported its determination that minorities have been wrongly excluded from local construction contracting. Its proof includes statistics showing that minority-owned businesses have received virtually no city contracting dollars; ... testimony by municipal officials that discrimination has been widespread in the local construction industry; and ... federal studies ... which showed that pervasive discrimination in the Nation's tight-knit

construction industry had operated to exclude minorities from public contracting. These are precisely the types of statistical and testimonial evidence which, until today, this Court has credited in cases approving of race-conscious measures designed to remedy past discrimination.

Discussion Questions

1. What was the Richmond City Council trying to accomplish with its Minority Business Utilization Plan? If you had been a member of the council, would you have voted for the plan?
2. What are the pros and cons of a minority set-aside plan like Richmond's? Will it have good consequences? Does it infringe on anyone's rights? What conflicting moral principles, ideals, and values are at stake?
3. Do you believe that there was sufficient evidence of racial discrimination to justify the city's plan? Who is right about this—Justice O'Connor or Justice Marshall?
4. Justice O'Connor and the majority of the Court seem to believe that there must be some specific, identifiable individuals who have been discriminated against before race-conscious measures can be adopted to remedy past discrimination. Do you agree that affirmative action measures must meet this standard?
5. In light of the fact that no federal statute specifically bars racial discrimination in private domestic commercial transactions between two business firms, and given the evidence that racism is an obstacle to African-American business success,[70] what obligation, if any, does state, local, or federal government have to assist minority-owned companies?
6. What measures could Richmond have taken that would have increased opportunities for minority business but would not have involved racial quotas? Would such measures be as effective as the original plan?

CASE **11.2**

Hoop Dreams

In basketball, talent plus hard work equals success. That's an equation that holds true for women as well as men, and in recent years, dedicated female athletes have raised women's basketball to new heights and won the allegiance of many new fans.[71]

But what about their coaches? Do any obstacles stand between them and their dreams? Marianne Stanley didn't think so when she began coaching women's basketball for the University of Southern California, where she earned $64,000 a year—a fair sum, one might think, but less than half that of her counterpart, George Raveling, who coached the men's team. True, Raveling had been coaching for thirty-one years, had been an assistant on the U.S. Olympic team, and was twice named coach of the year. But Stanley was no slouch. She had been a head coach for sixteen years and won three national championships. In her last two years at USC, she had win-loss records of 23–8 and 22–7, which compared favorably with Raveling's 19–10 and 24–6.

So when her initial four-year contract expired, Marianne Stanley sought pay parity with Raveling. Stanley knew that Raveling was also earning tens of thousands of dollars in perks, but she was willing to overlook that and settle for an equal base salary of $135,000. Instead, USC offered Stanley a three-year contract starting at $88,000 and increasing to $100,000. When she rejected that offer, USC countered with a one-year contract for $96,000. Stanley declined the offer and left USC, her hoop dreams diminished, although she later began coaching at UC Berkeley, where her salary was equivalent to that of the men's coach.

For his part, George Raveling didn't mind Stanley's making as much money as he did. But he understood why USC paid him more. He was, after all, a hot property, and if USC was going to prevent his being lured away by some other university trying to boost its basketball program, then it had to pay him a high salary. By contrast, Marianne Stanley didn't have any other job offers.

Too bad, one might say, but that's how the market works in a capitalist society. But what if the market itself is discriminatory? Defenders of comparable worth argue that it is and that coaches like Stanley can't negotiate for comparable salaries because women's basketball isn't valued as highly as men's. And it's college administrators, they argue, who are to blame for that. As one feminist puts it:

> The women didn't get the advertising and marketing dollars. They didn't get the PR. Then when fans weren't showing up, the TV stations weren't carrying the games and other universities weren't fighting over the best coaches, administrators told the women that, because they and their sport didn't draw as much attention as men, they shouldn't be paid as much.

In response, defenders of USC deny that it or any other university is responsible for the fact that men's sports are big revenue earners and women's are not. The higher pay for those who coach men simply reflects that social and cultural reality, which is something college administrators have no control over. If someone like Marianne Stanley wants to enter the big leagues, then she should coach men.

Update Sadly, sometimes even those who have fought against discrimination can discriminate against others. Just a few years after Marianne Stanley assumed her head coaching position at UC Berkeley, one of the assistant coaches, Sharrona Alexander, filed suit against the university, alleging that Stanley told her to get an abortion or lose her job. Stanley denied the abortion allegation, but admitted that she did ask Alexander to resign because of her pregnancy. Either way, a champion of women's rights was guilty of trampling on someone else's hoop dreams. Ironically, Stanley herself played college basketball when she was pregnant (returning to practice eleven days after her daughter was born) and went on, single and with a toddler, to coach Old Dominion University to three national championships. Moreover, some sports commentators believe that, far from being a handicap, motherhood can give a coach an edge in recruiting because the parents of prospective recruits prefer their daughters to be coached by women who, when they say that they treat their teams as family, know what they are talking about. In addition, Arizona State coach Charli Turner Thorne says, because "you're taking young ladies at a very formative time, you have to play the parent role." She adds, "There's absolutely no doubt [motherhood] makes me a better coach."

Discussion Questions

1. The doctrine of comparable worth holds that men and women should be paid the same wage for doing jobs of equal skill, effort, and responsibility. Were Marianne Stanley and George Raveling doing work of comparable value?

2. Was Stanley treated unfairly or in some way discriminated against? Should USC have offered to pay her more?

3. Why do sports played by men tend to be more popular and generate more revenue than sports played by women? Are female athletes—and their coaches—disadvantaged? Are they discriminated against? If so, who is responsible for this discrimination, and do colleges and universities have an obligation to do something about it?

4. Should universities like USC base their coaching salaries entirely on market considerations? Or should they pay the coaches of men's and women's sports comparable salaries based on experience, skill, and performance?

5. Respond to the argument that because men are free to coach women's teams and women to coach men's teams, there is nothing discriminatory in the fact that one job pays more than the other.

6. Was Sharrona Alexander's pregnancy likely to have adversely affected her coaching performance? If so, was Marianne Stanley wrong to ask her to resign? How should Stanley have handled the situation?

CASE **11.3**

Consenting to Sexual Harassment

In the case of *Vinson v. Taylor*, heard before the federal district court for the District of Columbia, Mechelle Vinson alleged that Sidney Taylor, her supervisor at Capital City Federal Savings and Loan, had sexually harassed her.[72] But the facts of the case were contested. In court Vinson testified that about a year after she began working at the bank, Taylor asked her to have sexual relations with him. She claimed that Taylor said she "owed" him because he had obtained the job for her.

Although she turned down Taylor at first, she eventually became involved with him. She and Taylor engaged in sexual relations, both during and after business hours, in the remaining three years she worked at the bank. The encounters included intercourse in a bank vault and in a storage area in the bank basement. Vinson also testified that Taylor often actually "assaulted or raped" her. She contended that she was forced to submit to Taylor or jeopardize her employment.

Taylor, for his part, denied the allegations. He testified that he had never had sex with Vinson. On the contrary, he alleged that Vinson had made advances toward him and that he had declined them. He contended that Vinson had brought the charges against him to "get even" because of a work-related dispute.

In its ruling on the case, the court held that if Vinson and Taylor had engaged in a sexual relationship, that relationship was voluntary on the part of Vinson and was not employment related. The court also held that Capital City Federal Savings and Loan did not have "notice" of the alleged harassment and was therefore not liable. Although Taylor was Vinson's supervisor, the court reasoned that notice to him was not notice to the bank.

Vinson appealed the case, and the Court of Appeals held that the district court had erred in three ways. First, the district court had overlooked the fact that there are two possible kinds of sexual harassment. Writing for the majority, Chief Judge Spottswood Robinson distinguished cases in which the victim's continued employment or promotion is conditioned on giving in to sexual demands and those cases in which the victim must tolerate a "substantially discriminatory work environment." The lower court had failed to consider Vinson's case as possible harassment of the second kind.

Second, the higher court also overruled the district court's finding that because Vinson voluntarily engaged in a sexual relationship with Taylor, she was not a victim of sexual harassment. Voluntariness on Vinson's part had "no bearing," the judge wrote, on "whether Taylor made Vinson's toleration of sexual harassment a condition of her employment." Third, the Court of Appeals held that any discriminatory activity by a supervisor is attributable to the employer, regardless of whether the employer had specific notice.

In his dissent to the decision by the Court of Appeals, Judge Robert Bork rejected the majority's claim that "voluntariness" did not automatically rule out harassment. He argued that this position would have the result of depriving the accused person of any defense, because he could no longer establish that the supposed victim was really "a willing participant." Judge Bork contended further that an employer should not be held vicariously liable for a supervisor's acts that it didn't know about.

Eventually the case arrived at the U.S. Supreme Court, which upheld the majority verdict of the Court of Appeals, stating that:

> [T]he fact that sex-related conduct was "voluntary," in the sense that the complainant was not forced to participate against her will, is not a defense to a sexual harassment suit brought under Title VII. The gravamen of any sexual harassment claim is that the alleged sexual advances were "unwelcome."... The correct inquiry is whether respondent by her conduct indicated that the alleged sexual advances were unwelcome, not whether her actual participation in sexual intercourse was voluntary.

The Court, however, rejected the Court of Appeals's position that employers are strictly liable for the acts of their supervisors, regardless of the particular circumstances.[73]

Discussion Questions

1. According to her own testimony, Vinson acquiesced to Taylor's sexual demands. In this sense her behavior was "voluntary." Does the voluntariness of her behavior mean that she had "consented" to Taylor's advances? Does it mean that they were "welcome"? Do you agree that Vinson's acquiescence shows there was no sexual harassment? Which court was right about this? Defend your position.

2. In your opinion, under what circumstances would acquiescence be a defense to charges of sexual harassment? When would it not be a defense? Can you formulate a general rule for deciding such cases?

3. Assuming the truth of Vinson's version of the case, do you think her employer, Capital City Federal Savings and Loan, should be

held liable for sexual harassment it was not aware of? Should the employer have been aware of it? Does the fact that Taylor was a supervisor make a difference? In general, when should an employer be liable for harassment?

4. What steps do you think Vinson should have taken when Taylor first pressed her for sex? Should she be blamed for having given in to him? Assuming that there was sexual harassment despite her acquiescence, does her going along with Taylor make her partly responsible or mitigate Taylor's wrongdoing?

5. In court, Vinson's allegations were countered by Taylor's version of the facts. Will there always be a "your word against mine" problem in sexual harassment cases? What could Vinson have done to strengthen her case?

CASE 11.4

Facial Discrimination

Scene: A conference room of a branch office of Allied Products, Inc., where Tom, Frank, and Alice have been interviewing college students for summer internships.

Tom: Did you see that last candidate? Jeez, was he sorry looking.

Frank: Too ugly to work here, that's for sure. And those thick glasses didn't help. Still, he wasn't as ugly as that young woman you hired last summer. What was her name… Allison? Boy, she was enormous, and remember that hair of hers. It wasn't surprising we had to let her go.

Alice: Come on, Frank. Don't be so hung up on looks. That last guy seemed to know his stuff, and he certainly was enthusiastic about working for Allied.

Frank: Hey, don't get me wrong, Alice. I know you don't have to be beautiful to work for Allied—after all, look at Tom here. Still, with a face like that guy's, you got to wonder.

Tom: Wisecracks aside, Alice, Frank's got a point. Studies show that it's natural for people to discriminate on the basis of looks. I've read that even babies will look at a pretty face longer than an ugly face.

Alice: I know that. Studies also show that people attribute positive characteristics to people they find attractive and that they treat unattractive people worse than other people in lots of ways. For example, strangers are less likely to do small favors for unattractive people than they are for attractive people, and even parents and teachers have lower expectations for ugly, fat, or odd-looking children. But what this really boils down to is implicit discrimination.

Tom: That's what I'm saying. It's natural. Besides, it's not illegal to discriminate on the basis of appearance.

Frank: That's right. You wouldn't want us to hire somebody with green hair and rings in his nose and put him out at the front desk, would you? This is a business, not a freak show.

Alice: Hey, slow down, guys. First, it may be natural and it may even be legal to favor good-looking people, but that doesn't make it right. And second, I'm not talking about grooming or dress. It's your choice to dye your hair and decorate your face, and if you don't fit in because of that, that's your fault. But the guy we talked to today didn't choose to be ugly, so why hold it against him?

Frank: I suppose next you'll be telling us that we should have kept Allison on last summer just because she was fat.

Alice: No, I'm not saying you have to give preferential treatment to overweight people. But I think that nobody in the office cut her any slack. If she'd been normal size, things would have worked out okay, but people took one look at her and prejudged her to be a loser. You know, Frank, some courts have held that discrimination against the obese violates the Americans with Disabilities Act.

Tom: That's only if it's a medical condition.

Frank: Yeah, Allison's only problem was that she liked to eat.

Alice: You don't know that. You don't know anything about her.

Frank: I suppose her hair was a medical condition, too.

Tom: Okay, you two, take it easy. Seriously, though, Alice, a number of our interns have to interact with the public, and people can be put off by having to deal with ugly people, fat people, or even very short people. So why aren't an employee's looks a job-relevant issue?

Alice: No, I think that as long as the person is clean and well groomed, then the public shouldn't be put off by having to deal with someone who is unattractive or unusual looking. It's unreasonable.

Tom: That's what you say. But what if the public is "unreasonable"? What if they prefer companies with attractive or at least normal-looking employees?

Alice: It's still irrelevant. It's the same as if a company had customers who didn't like dealing with blacks. That's no reason for it not to hire blacks.

Tom: Yeah, I can see that.

Frank: Okay, but what about this ugly guy? Do we have to offer him an internship?

Discussion Questions

1. How frequently are people discriminated against on the basis of their looks? Is it a serious problem in job situations? What about the fact that students give higher instructional rankings to attractive professors?[74]

2. Assess the argument that there is nothing wrong with "facial discrimination"—that it simply reflects the fact that human beings are naturally attracted to, or repelled by, other human beings on the basis of their physical characteristics.

3. Under what circumstances is physical attractiveness a job-related employment criterion? Is it relevant to being a salesperson, a flight attendant, or a receptionist?

4. What arguments can be given for and against a law preventing job discrimination on the basis of immutable aspects of one's appearance?

5. Assess the argument that because fat, ugly, or strange-looking people have it tougher throughout their lives than do attractive people, we should give them preferential treatment whenever we can—for example, in job situations—to make up for the disadvantages they've suffered and to help level the playing field.

6. Are businesses morally obligated to try to prevent or reduce appearance discrimination in the workplace? What steps can they take?

CHAPTER 1

Ethics

David Callahan, *The Cheating Culture* (Orlando, Fla.: Harcourt, 2004), argues that cheating is on the increase throughout American society.

James Rachels and **Stuart Rachels**, *The Elements of Moral Philosophy*, 5th ed. (New York: McGraw-Hill, 2007), and **Louis P. Pojman**, *How Should I Live?* (Belmont, Calif.: Wadsworth, 2005), are excellent, clear introductions.

George Sher, ed., *Moral Philosophy: Selected Readings*, 2nd ed. (Belmont, Calif.: Wadsworth, 2000), and **Louis P. Pojman**, ed., *Ethical Theory: Classical and Contemporary Readings*, 5th ed. (Belmont, Calif.: Wadsworth, 2007), offer more advanced readings on various topics in moral philosophy.

Moral Reasoning

Patrick Hurley, *A Concise Introduction to Logic*, 10th ed. (Belmont, Calif.: Wadsworth, 2008), is a good introduction to all the main areas of logic.

Joel Rudinow and **Vincent Barry**, *Invitation to Critical Thinking*, 6th ed. (Belmont, Calif.: Wadsworth, 2008), provides a guide to argument assessment.

Business and Morality

Both **Richard T. De George**, *Business Ethics*, 6th ed. (New York: Macmillan, 2006) and **Manuel G. Velasquez**, *Business Ethics*, 6th ed. (Upper Saddle River, N.J.: Prentice Hall, 2006) contain useful introductions to moral philosophy in relation to business as does **Robert Audi's** lucid and succinct book, *Business Ethics and Ethical Business* (New York: Oxford University Press, 2009). Two valuable reference works are *The Blackwell Encyclopedia of Management, vol. 2: Business Ethics*, 2nd ed.,

ed. **Patricia Werhane** and **R. Edward Freeman** (Malden, Mass.: Blackwell, 2005) and the five-volume *Encyclopedia of Business Ethics and Society*, ed. **Robert W. Kolb** (Los Angeles: SAGE Publications, 2008). **Robert E. Frederick**, ed., *A Companion to Business Ethics* (Malden, Mass.: Blackwell, 1999) is a collection of essays by different authors on all aspects of business ethics. **William H. Shaw**, ed., *Ethics at Work: Basic Readings in Business Ethics* (New York: Oxford University Press, 2003) is a slim collection of essays on various moral issues that arise in business while **Fritz Allhoff** and **Anand Vaidya's** three-volume *Business Ethics* (London: SAGE, 2005) reprints ninety-six important essays on business and professional ethics. Two pertinent discussions of moral conduct in business are **Glenn Martin**, "Once Again: Why Should Business Be Ethical?" *Business and Professional Ethics Journal* 17 (Winter 1998) and **Kevin Gibson**, "Excuses, Excuses: Moral Slippage in the Workplace," *Business Horizons* 43 (November–December 2000).

Three good sources of advanced work in business ethics are *Business and Professional Ethics Journal*, *Business Ethics Quarterly*, and *Journal of Business Ethics*.

CHAPTER 2

Tom L. Beauchamp, *Philosophical Ethics*, 3rd ed. (New York: McGraw-Hill, 2001), is an introductory text with selected readings covering classical ethical theories, rights, and the nature of morality.

Heimir Geirsson and **Margaret R. Holmgren**, eds., *Ethical Theory: A Concise Anthology* (Peterborough, Ontario: Broadview, 2001); **Judith A. Boss**, ed., *Perspectives on Ethics*, 2nd ed. (New York: McGraw-Hill, 2003); and **Mark Timmons**, ed., *Conduct and Character*, 5th ed. (Belmont, Calif.: Wadsworth, 2006), provide good selections of readings on egoism, relativism, utilitarianism, Kantianism, and other normative theories.

Bernard Gert, *Common Morality: Deciding What to Do* (New York: Oxford University Press, 2004), provides a lucid account of the moral system that implicitly guides thoughtful people's everyday moral decisions.

Hugh LaFollette, ed., *The Blackwell Guide to Ethical Theory* (Oxford: Blackwell, 2000), and **Peter Singer**, ed., *A Companion to Ethics* (Oxford: Blackwell, 1991), are comprehensive reference works with survey essays by many individual authors.

William H. Shaw, *Contemporary Ethics: Taking Account of Utilitarianism* (Oxford: Blackwell, 1999), sympathetically examines the utilitarian approach to ethics.

Jeffrey D. Smith, ed., *Normative Theory and Business Ethics* (Lanham, Md.: Rowman & Littlefield, 2009) is a useful collection probing the normative foundations of business ethics from various theoretical perspectives.

Mark Timmons, *Moral Theory: An Introduction* (Lanham, Md.: Rowman & Littlefield, 2002), provides a clear and accessible survey of all the major moral theories.

CHAPTER 3

John Arthur and **William H. Shaw**, eds., *Justice and Economic Distribution*, 2nd ed. (Englewood Cliffs, N.J.: Prentice Hall, 1991), contains substantial extracts from Rawls's *A Theory of Justice* and Nozick's *Anarchy, State, and Utopia*, contemporary presentations of the utilitarian approach to economic justice, and various other essays on the topic.

Joel Feinberg, *Social Philosophy* (Englewood Cliffs, N.J.: Prentice Hall, 1973), chapter 7, discusses the different types of justice and injustice.

Stephen Holmes and **Cass R. Sunstein**, *The Cost of Rights: Why Liberty Depends on Taxes* (New York: Norton, 1999), argues that because all legally enforceable rights cost money, freedom is not violated by a government that taxes and spends but requires it.

John Isbister, *Capitalism and Justice: Envisioning Social and Economic Fairness* (Bloomfield, Conn.: Kumarian Press, 2001), discusses in a readable but thoughtful way a number of questions of justice in the real world, such as income distribution, taxation, welfare, and foreign aid.

David Cay Johnston, *Perfectly Legal* (New York: Penguin, 2003), argues that our tax system has been corrupted to favor the rich and powerful at the expense of the vast majority.

Will Kymlicka, *Contemporary Political Philosophy*, 2nd ed. (Oxford: Oxford University Press, 2001), covers the major schools of contemporary political thought and their competing views of justice and community.

Jeffrey Moriaty, "Do CEOs Get Paid Too Much?," *Business Ethics Quarterly* 15 (April 2005), argues that they do, according to the leading theories of justice in wages.

Liam Murphy and **Thomas Nagel**, *The Myth of Ownership: Taxes and Justice* (New York: Oxford University Press, 2002), explores the justice of different tax policies in the light of contemporary moral and political philosophy.

David K. Shipler, *The Working Poor: Invisible in America* (New York: Random House, 2004), and **Barbara Ehrenreich**, *Nickel and Dimed: On (Not) Getting By in America* (New York: Henry Holt, 2001), are two vivid accounts of those forgotten Americans who work hard but barely manage to keep their heads above water.

Various authors discuss economic inequality in the United States in special issues of *Social Philosophy and Policy* 19 (Winter 2002): "Should Differences in Income and Wealth Matter?," and *Daedalus* (Winter 2002): "On Inequality." See also **Kevin Phillips**, *Wealth and Democracy* (New York: Broadway, 2002) for a historical perspective. The plight of the middle class today is discussed in **Elizabeth Warren** and **Amelia Warren Tyagi**, "What's Hurting the Middle Class," *Boston Review* (September–October 2005), with critical responses from twelve other experts.

CHAPTER 4

William J. Baumol, Robert E. Litan, and **Carl J. Schramm**, *Good Capitalism, Bad Capitalism, and the Economics of Growth and Prosperity* (New Haven, Conn.: Yale University Press, 2007), distinguishes four different forms of contemporary capitalism, focusing on the essential role of entrepreneurship.

John Douglas Bishop, ed., *Ethics and Capitalism* (Toronto: University of Toronto Press, 2000), is a collection of thought-provoking essays. Bishop's own contribution to the volume, "Ethics and Capitalism: A Guide to the Issues," is a valuable survey of the nature of capitalism and the key ethical issues it gives rise to.

Todd G. Buchholz, *New Ideas from Dead Economists*, rev. ed. (New York: Penguin, 1999), is a balanced and readable guide to modern economic thought applied to today's economy.

John Kenneth Galbraith, *The Economics of Innocent Fraud* (Boston: Houghton Mifflin, 2004), is a brief, masterly critique of our economic system by the famous economist.

Robert L. Heilbroner and **Lester C. Thurow**, *Economics Explained*, rev. ed. (New York: Simon & Schuster, 1998), is two respected economists' analysis of how our economy works, what its current difficulties are, and where it is headed.

Tibor R. Machan, ed., *The Main Debate: Communism versus Capitalism* (New York: Random House, 1986), is a collection of accessible essays that debate the relative merits of capitalism and socialism.

Robert B. Reich, *Supercapitalism: The Transformation of Business, Democracy, and Everyday Life* (New York: Knopf, 2007), is a well-written analysis of contemporary American capitalism, its clash with democracy, and problems our society faces.

David Schweickart, *After Capitalism* (Lanham, Md.: Rowman & Littlefield, 2002), is an argument for worker control socialism.

Joseph E. Stiglitz, *Making Globalization Work* (New York: Norton, 2006), is the Nobel Prize–winning economist's analysis of globalization and his proposals for making it work better for both the developed and the developing worlds.

"A Survey of Globalisation," *Economist*, September 29, 2001; "A Survey of Capitalism and Democracy," *Economist*, June 28, 2003; "A Survey of the World Economy," *Economist*, September 24, 2005; and "A Special Report on Globalization," *Economist*, September 20, 2008, are intelligent, balanced discussions of the capitalist system.

CHAPTER 5

Douglas G. Baird and **M. Todd Henderson**, "Other People's Money," *Stanford Law Review* 60 (March 2008), critically assesses the legal doctrine that directors of a corporation have a fiduciary duty to stockholders.

Joel Bakan, *The Corporation: The Pathological Pursuit of Profit and Power* (New York: Free Press, 2004), is a searing though rather one-sided indictment of the modern corporation (and the basis of a documentary film of the same title).

John R. Danley, "Corporate Moral Agency," in **Robert E. Frederick**, ed., *A Companion to Business Ethics* (Malden, Mass.: Blackwell, 1999), reviews the philosophical literature on this difficult topic with particular attention to the influential views of Peter French.

Thomas Donaldson, *Corporations and Morality* (Englewood Cliffs, N.J.: Prentice Hall, 1982), discusses the moral status of corporations, arguments for and against corporate social responsibility, and the idea of a social contract for business, among other issues.

Peter A. French, *Collective and Corporate Responsibility* (New York: Columbia University Press, 1984), analyzes the philosophical issues involved in assigning moral responsibility to corporations and other collectivities. French's *Corporate Ethics* (Ft. Worth, Tex.: Harcourt Brace, 1996) looks at a wider range of moral issues involving corporations.

"The Good, the Bad, and Their Corporate Codes of Ethics: Enron, Sarbanes-Oxley, and the Problems with Legislating Good Behavior," *Harvard Law Review* 116 (May 2003), discusses the negative impact of recent legislation on corporate codes of conduct.

Thomas M. Jones, Andrew C. Wicks, and **R. Edward Freeman**, "Stakeholder Theory: The State of the Art," in **Norman E. Bowie**, ed., *The Blackwell Guide to Business Ethics* (Malden, Mass.: Blackwell, 2002), discusses one influential way of thinking about the obligations of managers to stockholders and other stakeholders.

Steve May, George Cheney, and **Juliet Roper**, eds., *The Debate over Corporate Social Responsibility* (New York: Oxford University Press, 2007), is an advanced collection of thirty-two essays by business theorists and social scientists.

John Micklethwait and **Adrian Wooldridge**, *The Company: A Short History of a Revolutionary Idea* (New York: Modern Library, 2003), is a readable, well-informed history of the corporation from its earliest beginnings to recent scandals.

David E. Schrader, "The Oddness of Corporate Ownership," *Journal of Social Philosophy* 27 (Fall 1996), argues that stockholders do not own the corporation.

David Vogel, *The Market for Virtue: The Potential and Limits of Corporate Social Responsibility* (Washington, D.C.: Brookings Institution, 2005), provides an insightful analysis and balanced assessment of the growing corporate social responsibility movement.

Thomas I. White, ed., *Business Ethics: A Philosophical Reader* (New York: Macmillan, 1993), contains useful essays on corporate personhood and responsibility in chapter 6 and on the punishing of corporations in chapter 7.

CHAPTER 6

Robert L. Arrington, "Advertising and Behavior Control," *Journal of Business Ethics* 1 (February 1982); **John Waide**, "The Making of Self and World in Advertising," *Journal of Business Ethics* 6 (February 1987); **Roger Crisp**, "Persuasive Advertising, Autonomy, and the Creation of Desire," *Journal of Business Ethics* 6 (July 1987); **Richard L. Lippke**, "Advertising and the Social Conditions of Autonomy," *Business and Professional Ethics Journal* 8 (Winter 1989); and **Andrew Gustafson**, "Advertising's Impact on Morality in Society: Influencing Habits and Desires of Consumers," *Business and Society Review* 106 (Fall 2001), are valuable, philosophical discussions of advertising.

David M. Holley, "A Moral Evaluation of Sales Practices," *Business and Professional Ethics Journal* 5 (Fall 1987), is a seminal discussion of the ethics of sales. Holley revisits the subject in "Information Disclosure in Sales," *Journal of Business Ethics* 17 (April 1998), and replies to Thomas L. Carson in "Alternative Approaches to Applied Ethics: A Response to Carson's Critique," *Business Ethics Quarterly* 12 (January 2002).

Patrick E. Murphy, Gene R. Laczniak, Norman E. Bowie, and **Thomas A. Klein**, *Ethical Marketing* (Upper Saddle River, N.J.: Prentice Hall, 2005), surveys a wide range of issues in marketing ethics, including researching and segmenting markets, product management, distribution and pricing, and sales.

Juliet Schor, *Born to Buy: The Commercialized Child and the New Consumer Culture* (New York: Simon & Schuster, 2005), is a well-researched critique of the ruthless targeting of children by advertisers and of their induction into consumerism.

N. Craig Smith and **John A. Quelch**, eds., *Ethics in Marketing* (Homewood, Ill.: Irwin, 1993), contains informative essays and case studies on all aspects of marketing ethics.

Edward Spence and **Brett Van Heekeren**, *Advertising Ethics* (Upper Saddle River, N.J.: Prentice Hall, 2005), is a succinct and stimulating discussion of, among other issues, truth in advertising, endorsements and testimonials, targeted advertising, and stereotyping.

CHAPTER 7

Robin Attfield, *Environmental Ethics* (Malden, Mass.: Blackwell, 2003); **Joseph R. DesJardins**, *Environmental Ethics*, 4th ed. (Belmont, Calif.: Wadsworth, 2006); and **Holmes Rolston III**, *Philosophy Gone Wild: Environmental Ethics* (Buffalo, N.Y.: Prometheus, 1990), are good introductions to environmental ethics.

Dale Jamieson, ed., *A Companion to Environmental Ethics* (Malden, Mass.: Blackwell, 2001), and **Andrew Light** and **Holmes Rolston III**, eds., *Environmental Ethics: An Anthology* (Oxford: Blackwell, 2003), are valuable, though philosophically advanced, reference works.

Ronald Jeurissen and **Gerard Keijers**, "Future Generations and Business Ethics," *Business Ethics Quarterly* 14 (January 2004), takes a close look at this often neglected issue.

Lisa H. Newton, Catherine K. Dillingham, and **Joanne Cody**, *Watersheds: Classic Cases in Environmental Ethics*, 4th ed. (Belmont, Calif.: Wadsworth, 2006), offers ten detailed and insightful environmental case studies.

Joel Reichart and Patricia H. Werhane, eds., *Environmental Challenges to Business* (Bowling Green, Ohio: Philosophy Documentation Center, 2000), collects new essays on business and the environment by prominent business ethicists.

Mark Sagoff, *Price, Principle, and the Environment* (New York: Cambridge University Press, 2004), is an informed discussion of environmental policy.

Peter Singer, *Animal Liberation*, 3rd ed. (New York: HarperCollins, 2002), is a seminal work advocating a radical change in our treatment of animals. Gary L. Francione, *Introduction to Animal Rights: Your Child or the Dog?* (Philadelphia: Temple University Press, 2000), offers a provocative but very readable critique of our treatment of animals.

"Special Issue: Crossroads for Planet Earth," *Scientific American* (September 2005), contains balanced and informative essays on the environmental challenges facing humanity.

James Sterba, ed., *Earth Ethics: Introductory Readings on Animal Rights and Environmental Ethics*, 3rd ed. (Upper Saddle River, N.J.: Prentice Hall, 2009), is an excellent, wide-ranging collection of essays, representing different environmental and philosophical approaches.

Timothy S. Yoder, "Corporate Responsibility and the Environment," *Business and Society Review* 106 (Fall 2001), takes up the topic of corporate responsibility for environmental malfeasance.

CHAPTER 8

Bruce Barry, *Speechless: The Erosion of Free Speech in the American Workplace* (San Francisco: Berrett-Koehler, 2007), is a balanced, well-written study, rich with examples, that advocates for greater freedom of expression in today's workplace.

Ronald Duska, "Employee Rights," in Robert E. Frederick, ed., *A Companion to Business Ethics* (Malden, Mass.: Blackwell, 1999), discusses the nature of rights in general and the specific rights claimed for employees in recent times.

Gertrude Ezorsky, *Freedom in the Workplace?* (Ithaca, N.Y.: Cornell University Press, 2007), argues that many contemporary philosophers and social scientists hold conceptions of freedom that are too limited to account for the reality of workplace unfreedom.

Thomas Geoghegan, *Which Side Are You On? Trying to Be for Labor When It's Flat on Its Back*, rev. ed. (New York: New Press, 2004), is the insightful and entertaining memoir of a labor lawyer.

Paul Le Blanc, *A Short History of the U.S. Working Class* (Amherst, N.Y.: Prometheus, 1999), is a short, readable, and informative account of working people in America.

Richard L. Lippke, *Radical Business Ethics* (Lanham, Md.: Rowman & Littlefield, 1995), chapter 6, discusses the right to freedom of speech and conscience in the workplace.

David Sirota, Louis A. Mischkind, and Michael Irwin Meltzer, *The Enthusiastic Employee: How Companies Profit by Giving Workers What They Want* (Philadelphia: Wharton School, 2005), presents years of research demonstrating the relationship between high employee morale and strong financial performance.

Alan Strudler, "Confucian Skepticism about Workplace Rights," *Business Ethics Quarterly* 18, no. 1 (January 2008), defends workplace rights while acknowledging the strength of the Confucian critique.

Matt Vidal and David Kusnet, *Organizing Prosperity* (Washington, D.C.: Economic Policy Institute, 2009), use case studies to argue that unions bring wide-spread social and economic benefits.

CHAPTER 9

David Barstow and Lowell Bergman, "Dangerous Business," *New York Times*, January 8, 9, and 10, 2003, is a disturbing, detailed investigative report on the company with the worst safety record in the United States.

Douglas Birsch, "The Universal Drug Testing of Employees," *Business and Professional Ethics Journal* 14 (Fall 1995); Michael Cranford, "Drug Testing and the Right to Privacy," *Journal of Business Ethics* 17 (November 1998); and John R. Rowan, "Limitations on the Moral Permissibility of Employee Drug Testing," *Business and Professional Ethics Journal* 19 (Summer 2000), examine the ethics of drug testing employees.

Gertrude Ezorsky, ed., *Moral Rights in the Workplace* (Albany: State University of New York Press, 1987), is a good collection of articles on the right to meaningful work, occupational health and safety, employee privacy, unions, industrial flight, and related topics.

Ben Hamper, *Rivethead* (New York: Warner Books, 1992), is a riotous look at life on a GM assembly line.

Laura P. Hartman, "Technology and Ethics: Privacy in the Workplace," *Business and Society Review* 106 (Spring 2001), examines employee privacy in light of today's technology, current law, and ethics.

Sylvia Ann Hewlett, "Executive Women and the Myth of Having It All," *Harvard Business Review* 80 (April 2002), discusses the factors that prevent successful career women from having children.

John Kaler, "Understanding Participation," *Journal of Business Ethics* 21 (September 2000), discusses different types of employee participation, and John J. McCall, "Employee Voice in Corporate Governance," *Business Ethics Quarterly* 11 (January 2001), argues for a strong employee right to co-determine corporate policy.

Scott O. Lilienfeld, "Do 'Honesty' Tests Really Measure Honesty?," *Skeptical Inquirer* 18 (Fall 1993), is a critique of honesty exams.

Robert Mayer, "Is There a Right to Workplace Democracy?," *Social Theory and Practice* 26 (Summer 2000), argues on nonlibertarian grounds against such a right.

Adam D. Moore, "Employee Monitoring and Computer Technology," *Business Ethics Quarterly* 10 (July 2000), discusses the tension between privacy and evaluative surveillance.

Social Philosophy and Policy 17 (Summer 2000), special issue on "The Right to Privacy," is an insightful but advanced collection of readings.

CHAPTER 10

Sissela Bok, *Secrets* (New York: Vintage, 1983), includes insightful writing on trade secrets and patents in chapter 10 and on whistle-blowing in chapter 14.

Thomas L. Carson, "Conflicts of Interest," *Journal of Business Ethics* (May 1994), analyzes the concept and discusses the wrongness of conflicts of interest. Also useful is **Michael Davis**, "Conflict of Interest Revisited," *Business and Professional Ethics Journal* 12 (Winter 1993).

Cynthia Cooper, *Extraordinary Circumstances: The Journey of a Corporate Whistleblower* (Hoboken, N.J.: Wiley, 2008), uses her personal story to explain what we can learn from the WorldCom scandal.

Natalie Dandekar, "Can Whistleblowing Be Fully Legitimated? A Theoretical Discussion," *Business and Professional Ethics Journal* 10 (Fall 1990); **Mike W. Martin**, "Whistleblowing: Professionalism, Personal Life, and Shared Responsibility for Safety in Engineering," *Business and Professional Ethics Journal* 11 (Summer 1992), and **C. Fred Alford**, "Whistleblowers and the Narrative of Ethics," *Journal of Social Philosophy* 32 (Fall 2001), are good studies of the moral complexity of whistle-blowing.

Tibor Machan, "What Is Morally Right with Insider Trading," *Public Affairs Quarterly* 10 (April 1996), is a succinct libertarian defense of insider trading.

Brian Schrag, "The Moral Significance of Employee Loyalty," *Business Ethics Quarterly* 11 (January 2001), discusses the meaning of loyalty and whether it is good for either the employee or the employer.

Martin Snoeyenbos, Robert Almeder, and **James Humber**, eds., *Business Ethics*, 3rd ed. (Buffalo: Prometheus, 2001), provides in part 3 essays and cases on conflict of interest, gifts and payoffs, patents, and trade secrets.

CHAPTER 11

Affirmative Action

Steven M. Cahn, ed., *The Affirmative Action Debate*, 2nd ed. (New York: Routledge, 2002); **Francis Beckwith and Todd E. Jones**, eds., *Affirmative Action: Social Justice or Reverse Discrimination?* (Buffalo, N.Y.: Prometheus, 1997); and **George E. Curry**, ed., *The Affirmative Action Debate* (Reading, Mass.: Addison-Wesley, 1996), are good sources of essays both for and against affirmative action.

Gertrude Ezorsky, *Racism and Justice: The Case for Affirmative Action* (Ithaca, N.Y.: Cornell University Press, 1991), provides a succinct, well-informed defense, whereas **Louis P. Pojman**, "The Case against Affirmative Action," in **William H. Shaw**, ed., *Social and Personal Ethics*, 7th ed. (Belmont, Calif.: Wadsworth, 2011), is a robust critique. Philosophers **Carl Cohen** and **James P. Sterba** debate the issue in their valuable book *Affirmative Action and Racial Preference* (New York: Oxford University Press, 2003).

Comparable Worth

Laura Pincus and **Bill Shaw**, "Comparable Worth: An Economic and Ethical Analysis," *Journal of Business Ethics* 17 (April 1998), presents opposing views on pursuing comparable worth as a matter of public policy.

Helen Remick and **Ronnie J. Steinberg**, "Comparable Worth and Wage Discrimination," and **Robert L. Simon**, "Comparable Pay for Comparable Work?" in **Tom L. Beauchamp** and **Norman E. Bowie**, eds., *Ethical Theory and Business*, 4th ed. (Englewood Cliffs, N.J.: Prentice Hall, 1993), provide a clear and thorough introduction to the comparable-worth debate.

Race in America

Glenn Loury, *The Anatomy of Racial Inequality* (Cambridge, Mass.: Harvard University Press, 2002), examines the complex reality of "racial stigma" and the self-replicating patterns of racial stereotypes that rationalize and sustain discrimination.

How Race Is Lived in America (New York: Henry Holt, 2001), a collection of personal narratives and conversations produced by the *New York Times*, probes race relations today from various individual perspectives.

Sexual Harassment

Karen A. Crain and **Kenneth A. Heischmidt**, "Implementing Business Ethics: Sexual Harassment," *Journal of Business Ethics* 14 (April 1995), is a useful essay that discusses what actions companies should take.

Augustus B. Cochran III, *Sexual Harassment and the Law: The Mechelle Vinson Case* (Lawrence: University of Kansas Press, 2004), examines the origin, context, and impact of this landmark case.

Linda LeMoncheck and **Mane Hajdin**, *Sexual Harassment: A Debate* (Totowa, N.J.: Rowman & Littlefield, 1997), probes the philosophical and ethical issues. Also relevant are **M. J. Booker**, "Can Sexual Harassment Be Salvaged?," *Journal of Business Ethics* 17 (August 1998); **Vrinda Dalmiya**, "Why Is Sexual Harassment Wrong?," *Journal of Social Philosophy* 30 (Spring 1999); and **Linda L. Peterson**, "The Reasonableness of the Reasonable Woman Standard," *Public Affairs Quarterly* 13 (April 1999).

Workplace Discrimination

John Chandler, "Mandatory Retirement and Justice," *Social Theory and Practice* 22 (Spring 1996), argues against viewing mandatory retirement as unjust age discrimination.

D. W. Haslett, "Workplace Discrimination, Good Cause, and Color Blindness," *Journal of Value Inquiry* 36 (March 2002), provides a helpful theory of what constitutes unethical discrimination in the workplace.

Elizabeth Kristen, "Addressing the Problem of Weight Discrimination in Employment," *California Law Review* 90 (January 2002), argues that job discrimination against the overweight is a serious problem that the law should address.

NOTES

CHAPTER 1

1. For more on the Enron scandal, see Bethany McLean and Peter Elkind, *The Smartest Guys in the Room: The Amazing Rise and Scandalous Fall of Enron* (New York: Penguin, 2003), which is the basis of the fine 2005 documentary film *Enron: The Smartest Guys in the Room.* See also Kurt Eichenwald, *Conspiracy of Fools: A True Story* (New York: Broadway, 2005).

2. Cicero, *Selected Works* (London: Penguin, 1971), 177–80.

3. On characteristics of moral standards, see Manuel G. Velasquez, *Business Ethics*, 6th ed. (Upper Saddle River, N.J.: Prentice Hall, 2006), 9–10.

4. Martin Luther King, Jr., "Letter from Birmingham Jail," in *Why We Can't Wait* (New York: Harper & Row, 1963), 85.

5. *Newsweek*, May 26, 1997, 54.

6. "Supererogation Stops Here," *Economist*, October 27, 2007, 70.

7. Albert Z. Carr, "Is Business Bluffing Ethical?," *Harvard Business Review* 46 (January–February 1968): 143–153.

8. Ibid., 145.

9. Richard B. Brandt, *A Theory of the Good and the Right* (New York: Oxford University Press, 1979), 165–170.

10. James E. Post, Anne T. Lawrence, and James Weber, *Business and Society: Corporate Strategy, Public Policy, and Ethics*, 10th ed. (New York: McGraw-Hill, 2002), 104–105; Marjorie Kelly, "Holy Grail Found," *Business Ethics* (Winter 2004); "Shares of Corporate Nice Guys Can Finish First," *New York Times*, April 27, 2005 (online); Thomas Donaldson, "Defining the Value of Doing Good Business," *Financial Times* (supplement on "Mastering Corporate Governance"), June 3, 2005, 2; Bruce Barry, *Speechless: The Erosion of Free Speech in the American Workplace* (San Francisco: Berrett-Koehler, 2007), 194–195; Linda K. Treviño and Katherine A. Nelson, *Managing Business Ethics: Straight Talk about How to Do It Right,* 4th ed. (Hoboken, N.J.: Wiley, 2007), 40–42; and O. C. Ferrell, John Fraedrich, and Linda Ferrell, *Business Ethics: Ethical Decision Making and Cases*, 7th ed. (Boston: Houghton Mifflin, 2008), 17–22. For more theoretical reflections, see Robert H. Frank, *What Price the Moral High Ground? Ethical Dilemmas in Competitive Environments* (Princeton, N.J.: Princeton University Press, 2004), esp. chapter 4, "Can Socially Responsible Firms Survive in Competitive Environments?"

11. American Management Association, *The Ethical Enterprise*, p. 55 (available at www.amanet.org/research).

12. Joseph L. Badaracco, Jr., and Allen P. Webb, "Business Ethics: A View from the Trenches," *California Management Review* 37 (Winter 1995): 8.

13. See Milton Snoeyenbos, Robert Almeder, and James Humber, eds., *Business Ethics*, 3rd ed. (Buffalo, N.Y.: Prometheus, 2001), 136. See also the 2007 "National Business Ethics Survey" by the Ethics Resource Center, available at www.ethics.org.

14. Badaracco and Webb, "Business Ethics," 10.

15. See Solomon E. Asch, "Opinion and Social Pressure," *Scientific American* (November 1955): 31–35.

16. See Malcolm Gladwell, *The Tipping Point* (Boston: Little, Brown, 2000), 27–28; John M. Doris, *Lack of Character* (Cambridge: Cambridge University Press, 2002), 28–29, 32–33; and A. M. Rosenthal, *Thirty-Eight Witnesses: The Kitty Genovese Case* (New York: Melville House, 2008).

17. Lynn Sharp Paine, "Managing for Organizational Integrity," *Harvard Business Review* 72 (March–April 1994): 108.

18. Barton G. Malkiel, "The Great Wall Street?," *Wall Street Journal*, October 14, 2002, A16.

19. Tom Regan, *Defending Animal Rights* (Urbana: University of Illinois Press, 2001), 45.
20. The facts and quotations reported in this case are based on Mark Dowie's essays in *Mother Jones* (November 1979) and on Russell Mokhiber, *Corporate Crime and Violence* (San Francisco: Sierra Club Books, 1988), 181–195. See also "Global Dumping of U.S. Toxics Is Big Business," *San Francisco Examiner*, September 23, 1990, A2; and "Danger for Sale," *San Jose Mercury News*, May 19, 1991, 9A, and May 20, 1991, 3A.
21. Bernard Gavzer, "We Can Make Our Food Safer," *Parade*, October 19, 1997, 5–6.
22. The material for this case has been drawn from Kermit Vandivier, "Why Should My Conscience Bother Me?," in Robert Heilbroner, ed., *In the Name of Profit* (New York: Doubleday, 1972). For a discussion skeptical of Vandivier's version of these events, see John H. Fielder, "Give Goodrich a Break," *Business and Professional Ethics Journal* 7 (Spring 1988). John M. Darley discusses the Goodrich case in his informative essay "How Organizations Socialize Individuals into Evildoing," in David M. Messick and Ann E. Tenbrunsel, eds., *Codes of Conduct: Behavioral Research into Business Ethics* (New York: Sage, 1996).

CHAPTER 2

1. T. M. Scanlon, *What We Owe to Each Other* (Cambridge, Mass.: Harvard University Press, 1998), 197–198.
2. Bernard Williams, *Ethics and the Limits of Philosophy* (Cambridge, Mass.: Harvard University Press, 1985), 16.
3. Richard B. Brandt, "Toward a Credible Form of Utilitarianism," in Hector-Neri Castañeda and George Nakhnikian, eds., *Morality and the Language of Conduct* (Detroit: Wayne State University Press, 1963), 109–110.
4. A. C. Ewing, *Ethics* (New York: Free Press, 1965), 40.
5. Molly Moore, "Did the Experts Really Approve the 'Brown Lung' Experiment?," *Washington Post National Weekly Edition*, June 4, 1984, 31.
6. Adam Smith, *The Wealth of Nations* (New York: Modern Library, 1985), 223–225.
7. Immanuel Kant, *Grounding for the Metaphysics of Morals* (Indianapolis: Hackett, 1988), 30–31 (translation modified).
8. Kurt Eichenwald, "Commissions Are Many, Profits Few," *New York Times*, May 24, 1993, C1.
9. See, in particular, W. D. Ross, *The Right and the Good* (London: Oxford University Press, 1930).
10. Immanuel Kant, *Practical Philosophy*, ed. M. J. Gregor (Cambridge: Cambridge University Press, 1996), 611–615.
11. Ross, *The Right and the Good*, 21.
12. Ibid., 30.
13. Ibid., 31.
14. Richard B. Brandt, "The Real and Alleged Problems of Utilitarianism," *Hastings Center Report* (April 1983): 38.
15. Ibid., 42.
16. Ibid.
17. John Austin, *The Province of Jurisprudence Determined*, ed. W. E. Rumble (Cambridge: Cambridge University Press, 1995), 49.
18. Vincent Ryan Ruggiero, *The Moral Imperative* (Port Washington, N.Y.: Alfred, 1973).
19. This case study is based on "Hacker Hits Top Business Schools" and "Schools Boot Snoopy Grad Students," *CBS News*, March 4 and April 15, 2005 (online); "Harvard Rejects 119 Accused of Hacking" and "MIT Says It Won't Admit Hackers," *Boston Globe,* March 8 and 9, 2005 (online); Dan Carnevale, "Business-School Applicants, under Cover of Anonymity, Dispute 'Hacker' Label," *Chronicle of Higher Education*, March 11, 2005 (online); and "A Lesson in Moral Leadership," *Financial Times*, April 25, 2005, 11.
20. This case study is based on Douglas Birsch and John H. Fielder, eds., *The Ford Pinto Case* (Albany, N.Y.: SUNY Press, 1994). For a recent discussion, see John R. Danley, "Polishing Up the Pinto: Legal Liability, Moral Blame, and Risk," *Business Ethics Quarterly* 15, no. 2 (April 2005): 205–236. On SUV safety, see "Ford to Pay $369 Million in Rollover Accident," *New York Times*, June 4, 2004 (online); "Safety Data Give SUVs Poor Grade in Rollover Tests," *Wall Street Journal*, August 10, 2004, A1; "Stability Shouldn't Be Optional," *Business Week*, August 30, 2004, 50; and "Gains Seen in Redesign of S.U.V.'s," *Wall Street Journal*, February 3, 2006, C1.
21. This and following three paragraphs are based on a case created by T. W. Zimmerer and P. L. Preston in R. D. Hay, E. R. Gray, and J. E. Gates, eds., *Business and Society* (Cincinnati: South-Western, 1976). The remainder of the case draws on Peter Singer, "Rights and the Market," in John Arthur and William H. Shaw, eds., *Justice and Economic Distribution*, 2nd ed. (Englewood Cliffs, N.J.: Prentice-Hall, 1991), and Richard M. Titmuss, *The Gift Relationship* (London: Allen & Unwin, 1972).
22. Singer, "Rights and the Market." Reprinted by permission of the author. See also "Blood Donation—Altruism or Profit?," *British Medical Journal*, May 4, 1996, 1114, and "Economics Focus: Looking Good by Doing Good," *Economist*, January 17, 2009, 76.
23. "Kidney Shortage Inspires a Radical Idea: Organ Sales," *Wall Street Journal*, November 13, 2007, A1. See also "Why We Need a Market for Human Organs," *Wall Street Journal*, May 16, 2008, A11, and "Unique Model," *Wilson Quarterly*, Winter 2007, 89.

CHAPTER 3

1. "The Loophole Factory," *Wall Street Journal*, April 15, 2008, A18.
2. "Richest Are Leaving Even the Rich Far Behind," *New York Times*, June 5, 2005, sec. 1, 17; Paul Krugman, "Weapons of Math Destruction," *New York Times*, April 14, 2006, A23; and "Taxes: Who Pays and How Much?" *Wall Street Journal*, April 15–16, 2006, A5.
3. Matthew Miller, "Me and My Secretary," *Forbes*, November 26, 2007, 42.
4. David Wessel, "Budget Reality Means Obama Can't Deliver It All," *Wall Street Journal*, April 9, 2009, A2. See also "Income-Inequality Gap Widens," *Wall Street Journal*, October 12, 2007, A3; "Mind the Gap," *Financial Times*, April 8, 2008, 7; and "Richest See Income Share Rise," *New York Times*, July 23, 2008, A3.

5. "The Rich under Attack," *Economist*, April 4, 2009, 15. See also "Plain Truth about Taxes and Cuts," *New York Times*, October 31, 2007, C1; "The Rich, the Poor, and the Growing Gap between Them," *Economist*, June 17, 2006, 30; Andrew Hacker, "The Rich and Everyone Else," *New York Review of Books*, May 25, 2006, 17–18; and "Stuck in the Middle," *Financial Times*, October 29, 2008, 9.

6. U.S. Census Bureau, *Statistical Abstract of the United States: 2009* (Washington, D.C.: U.S. Government Printing Office, 2008), Table 675, and U.S. Census Bureau, *Current Population Reports*, series P60–204, "The Changing Shape of the Nation's Income Distribution, 1974–1998," Table 2, p. 4 (June 2000).

7. Gerald F. Seib, "Taming Populist Anger is Big Test," *Wall Street Journal*, April 3, 2009, A2.

8. "One Pay Gap Shrinks, Another Grows," *Wall Street Journal*, November 1, 2007, A2; Lester C. Thurow, "The Boom That Wasn't," *New York Times*, January 18, 1999, 17; Edward N. Wolff, "The Stagnating Fortunes of the Middle Class," *Social Philosophy and Policy* 19 (Winter 2002): 55, 58; and Hacker, "The Rich," 17–18.

9. Robert Reich, "America's Middle Classes Are No Longer Coping," *Financial Times*, January 28, 2008, 9.

10. "A Payday for Performance," *Business Week*, April 18, 2005, 78, and "The Boss's Pay," *Wall Street Journal*, April 10, 2006, R7. See also "Motorola Co-CEO Tops Pay Survey," *Wall Street Journal*, April 3, 2009, B1.

11. Lynn Brenner, "How Does Your Salary Stack Up?," *Parade*, April 13, 2008 (online).

12. "American Pay Rattles Foreign Partners," *New York Times*, January 17, 1999, sec. 4, 1.

13. "Learning How to Talk about Salary in Japan," *New York Times*, April 7, 2002, sec. 3, 12.

14. "Behind Soaring Executive Pay, Decades of Failed Restraints," *Wall Street Journal*, October 12, 2006, A1; "Off the Leash: What Will Bring Executive Pay under Control?," *Financial Times*, August 24, 2004, 11. See also Albert Hunt, "Greed, Grasso, and a Gilded Age," *Wall Street Journal*, September 18, 2003, A17, and Andrew Tobias, "How Much Is Fair?," *Parade*, March 2, 2003, 5.

15. "Suite Deals," *U.S. News and World Report*, April 29, 2002, 33.

16. "The Return of Larry Summers," *New York Times*, November 26, 2008, B4. See also "For Many, a Boom That Wasn't," *New York Times*, April 9, 2008, B1, and "Stuck in the Middle," *Financial Times*, October 29, 2008, 9.

17. Andrew Hacker, "The Underworld of Work," *New York Review of Books*, February 12, 2004, 38, and "Out on a Limb," *Financial Times*, May 3, 2006, 11.

18. "Margin for Error: How Stocks Could Be Hit by Falling Profits," *Wall Street Journal*, October 3, 2007, D1; "Breaking Records," *Economist*, February 12, 2005, 12; Michael Lind, "Are We Still a Middle-Class Nation?," *Atlantic Monthly* (January–February 2004): 125; "Special Report: China and the World Economy," *Economist*, July 30, 2005, 62; "Dividing the Pie," *Economist*, February 4, 2006, 70; and "Real Wages Fail to Match a Rise in Productivity," *New York Times*, August 28, 2006, A1. See also Martin Wolf, "The Rich Rewards and Poor Prospects of a New Gilded Age," *Financial Times*, April 26, 2006, 15.

19. Robert B. Reich, *Supercapitalism: The Transformation of Business, Democracy, and Everyday Life* (New York: Knopf, 2007), 103.

20. Simon Head, "They're Micromanaging Your Every Move," *New York Review of Books*, August 16, 2007, 42.

21. Reich, "America's Middle Classes," 9.

22. Hacker, "Underworld of Work," 38, and "The Squeeze on the American Worker," *Business Week*, June 23, 2008, 82.

23. David Brooks, "How to Reinvent the G.O.P.," *New York Times Magazine*, August 29, 2004, 37, and "Back in Business," *Financial Times*, October 16, 2008, 9. See also "America's Bitterness Quotient," *Business Week*, June 16, 2008, 19.

24. "One in 5 Jobs Pays Poverty Wages," *San Jose Mercury News*, October 12, 2004, 5A. See also "Working and Poor," *Business Week*, May 31, 2004, 58–68.

25. Robert Solow, "Trapped in the New 'You're on Your Own' World," *New York Review of Books*, November 20, 2008, 80.

26. Reich, *Supercapitalism*, 113–114, and Edward N. Wolff, *Top Heavy: The Increasing Inequality of Wealth in America and What Can Be Done about It,* rev. ed. (New York: New Press, 2002), 8, 27. See also "Would You Like Your Class War Shaken or Stirred, Sir?," *Economist*, September 6, 2003, 28, and (for slightly different figures) "Richest of American Families Add to Their Share of U.S. Net Worth," *New York Times*, April 6, 2006, A4.

27. Ray Boshara, "The $6,000 Solution," *Atlantic Monthly* (January–February 2003): 92.

28. "Class in America: Shadowy Lines That Still Divide," *New York Times*, May 15, 2005, sec. 1, 17. See also "Special Report: Meritocracy in America," *Economist*, January 1, 2005, 22–24; "Out on a Limb," 11; and "The Rich, the Poor, and the Growing Gap between Them," *Economist*, June 17, 2006, 30.

29. See "As Rich–Poor Gap Widens in U.S., Class Mobility Stalls," *Wall Street Journal*, May 13, 2005, A1; "Promotion Track Fades for Those on Bottom," *Wall Street Journal*, June 6, 2005, A1; and "Back in Business," *Financial Times*. For a more upbeat assessment, see Michael J. Mandel, "The End of Upward Mobility?," *Business Week*, June 20, 2005, 132.

30. "Is America Becoming More of a Class Society?," *Business Week*, February 26, 1996, 86. See also "Land of Less Opportunity," *Business Week*, June 30, 2003, 28, and "Waking Up from the American Dream," *Business Week*, December 1, 2003, 54.

31. "Rich–Poor Gap Widens in U.S.," A7.

32. "Meritocracy in America," 24, and "Minding the Gap," *Economist*, June 11, 2005, 32. See also "Does Meritocracy Work?" *Atlantic Monthly* (November 2005): 120; "The New College Try," *New York Times*, September 24, 2007, A27; and Andrew Delbanco, "Scandals of Higher Education," *New York Review of Books*, March 29, 2007, 40.

33. "College Education? Gumption Won't Cover It," *Business Week*, May 31, 2004, 68. See also "Higher Education Gap May Slow Economic Mobility," *New York Times*, February 20, 2008 (online).

34. Tony Judt, "Europe vs. America," *New York Review of Books*, February 10, 2005, 38.

35. "Taxing the Poor to Pay the Poor," *Economist*, April 3, 2004, 80, and Nathan Glazer, "On Americans and Inequality," *Daedalus* (Summer 2003): 111.

36. Andrew Hacker, "They'd Rather Be Rich," *New York Review of Books*, October 11, 2007, 31. For an international comparison of child welfare, see "The Best Places to Breed," *Economist*, December 13, 2008, 70.

37. "Would You Like Your Class War Shaken?," 28. See also Andrew Hacker, *Money: Who Has How Much and Why* (New York: Simon & Schuster, 1997), 54, and John Isbister, *Capitalism and Justice: Envisioning Social and Economic Fairness* (Bloomfield, Conn.: Kumarian Press, 2001), 55.

38. John Stuart Mill, *Utilitarianism* (Indianapolis: Bobbs-Merrill, 1957), 71.

39. Michael Walzer, *Spheres of Justice* (New York: Basic Books, 1983). See also Jon Elster, *Local Justice: How Institutions Allocate Scarce Goods and Necessary Burdens* (New York: Sage, 1992).

40. Walzer, *Spheres of Justice*, 6.

41. Ibid., 10.

42. Mill, *Utilitarianism*, 66.

43. Ibid., 73.

44. Ibid., 71.

45. Ibid.

46. Smith's ideas are discussed further in Chapter 4.

47. John Stuart Mill, *Principles of Political Economy*, ed. Donald Winch (Harmondsworth, Middlesex: Penguin, 1970), 129.

48. Ibid., 128.

49. Ibid., 129.

50. Ibid., 133.

51. Ibid., 139–140.

52. Ibid., 140–141.

53. Richard B. Brandt, *A Theory of the Good and the Right* (New York: Oxford University Press, 1979), 312–313.

54. Ibid., 310.

55. F. A. Hayek, *The Constitution of Liberty* (Chicago: University of Chicago Press, 1960), 11.

56. John Hospers, *Libertarianism* (Los Angeles: Nash, 1971), 5.

57. Robert Nozick, *Anarchy, State, and Utopia* (New York: Basic Books, 1974).

58. John Locke, *Second Treatise of Government* (Indianapolis: Hackett, 1980), 23–24.

59. Nozick, *Anarchy, State, and Utopia*, 161.

60. Ibid., 163.

61. Amartya Sen, *Development as Freedom* (New Delhi: Oxford University Press, 1999), ch. 7. See also Amartya Sen, *Poverty and Famines* (New York: Oxford University Press, 1981), and Jean Drèze and Amartya Sen, *Hunger and Public Action* (Oxford: Oxford University Press, 1989).

62. Sen, *Development as Freedom*, 167, 170–171.

63. Lawrence C. Becker and Kenneth Kipnis, eds., *Property: Cases, Concepts, Critiques* (Englewood Cliffs, N.J.: Prentice Hall, 1984), 3–5.

64. John Rawls, *A Theory of Justice*, rev. ed. (Cambridge, Mass.: Harvard University Press, 1999). For subsequent developments in Rawls's thinking, see John Rawls, *Political Liberalism* (New York: Columbia University Press, 1993), and *Justice as Fairness: A Restatement* (Cambridge, Mass.: Harvard University Press, 2001).

65. Rawls, *A Theory of Justice*, 266; cf. *Political Liberalism*, 291.

66. Rawls, *Political Liberalism*, 6; cf. *A Theory of Justice*, 53, 72, 266.

67. John Rawls, "Justice as Fairness," *Philosophical Review* 67 (April 1958): 167.

68. Arthur MacEwan, "Ask Mr. Dollar," *Dollars and Sense* (November–December 1997): 39; and Michelle Cottle, "The Real Class War," *Washington Monthly* (July–August 1997): 12.

69. Rawls, *A Theory of Justice*, 3–4.

70. Rawls, "Justice as Fairness," 168.

71. *Political Liberalism*, 265–266.

72. Ibid., 269.

73. Rawls, "A Kantian Conception of Equality," *Cambridge Review* 96 (February 1975): 95.

74. *A Theory of Justice*, 89.

75. Ibid., 87.

76. This case study is based on "Government Says It's Too Nice for Them to Call Home," *New York Times*, January 30, 2005, sec. 1, 25; "Case for the Public Good Collides with Private Rights," *Financial Times*, February 14, 2005, 14; "Clear the Way, Fellows,"*New York Times*, May 8, 2005, sec. 1, 25; and "Justices Uphold Taking Property for Developing," *New York Times*, June 24, 2005, A1.

77. "Eminent Domain: Is It Only Hope for Inner Cities?," *Wall Street Journal*, October 5, 2005, B1, and "Eminent Domain Revisited: A Minnesota Case," *New York Times*, October 5, 2005, C10.

78. This case study is based on "Where They're Boiling over Water," *Business Week*, May 27, 2002; "Fight over Bottled Water," *Detroit Free Press*, May 4, 2003; "No New Bottled Water Operations for Now," *Detroit Free Press*, May 27, 2005 (online); "Ice Mountain Hopes Court Will Increase Flow, *Grand Rapids Press*, June 12, 2005 (online); and "The Conversation" at www.jennifergranham.com (July 9, 2008). See also "A Town Torn Apart by Nestlé," *Business Week*, April 14, 2008, 42.

79. *Statistical Abstract of the United States: 2009*, Table 687.

80. Mark R. Rank and Thomas A. Hirschl, "The Likelihood of Poverty across the American Adult Life Span," *Social Work* 44 (May 1999): 205.

81. "Poverty Mars Formation of Infant Brain," *Financial Times*, February 16–17, 2008, 2.

82. Nicholas D. Kristoff, "Health Care? Ask Cuba," *New York Times*, January 12, 2005 (online).

83. "Household Food Security in the United States, 2007" (November 2008) by the Economic Research Service of the U.S. Department of Agriculture (available online).

84. "Not Always What They Seem," *Economist*, October 20, 2007, 46, and "Gimme a Roof over My Head," *Economist*, August 23, 2003, 19. See also "Homeless Facts and Figures" at www.pbs.org/now (February 2, 2007).

85. "One in Five Jobs," 5A, and "Working and Poor," 61.

86. "Working Full Time Is No Longer Enough," *Wall Street Journal*, June 29, 2000, A2; and "Exploding Myths about the Poor," *Fortune*, September 29, 2003, 54.

87. *Wall Street Journal*, December 21, 2004, A1.

88. Christopher Jencks, "What Happened to Welfare?" *New York Review of Books*, December 15, 2005, 76.

89. Robert Pear, "Welfare Buying Power Wanes, Report Says," *San Francisco Chronicle*, November 19, 1996, A9.

90. U.S. Census Bureau, *Statistical Abstract of the United States: 1998* (Washington, D.C.: U.S. Government Printing Office, 1997), 390.

91. See Jencks, "Welfare," 76, and Isbister, *Capitalism and Justice*, 118.

92. "Welfare System Failing to Grow as Economy Lags," *New York Times*, February 2, 2009, A1.

93. *Statistical Abstract of the United States: 2009*, Table 676.

94. "Single Women Face Financial Challenges," *AARP Bulletin*, January–February 2009, 47.

95. *Statistical Abstract of the United States: 2009*, Tables 674 and 689.

96. Glazer, "On Americans and Inequality," 113. See also "A Nation Apart: A Survey of America," *Economist*, November 8, 2003, 8.

97. "U.S. Election 2004: A Special Briefing," *Economist*, October 9, 2004, 13.

98. William Julius Wilson, *When Work Disappears* (New York: Random House, 1996), 159–160, 179–181; "A Nation Apart," 8; and "Back in Business," *Financial Times*, October 16, 2008, 9.

99. Glazer, "On Americans and Inequality," 113.

100. Ibid., 114.

101. Donatella Gatti and Andrew Glyn, "Welfare States in Hard Times," *Oxford Review of Economic Policy* 22, no. 3 (Autumn 2006): 307–308.

CHAPTER 4

1. For a succinct treatment of the rise of the Fugger dynasty, see Ned M. Cross, Robert C. Lamm, and Rudy H. Turk, *The Search for Personal Freedom* (Dubuque, Iowa: W. C. Brown, 1972), 12. For a curious legacy of the Fuggers, see "In this Picturesque Village, the Rent Hasn't Been Raised Since 1520," *Wall Street Journal*, December 26, 2008, A1.

2. John Micklethwait and Adrian Wooldridge, *The Company: A Short History of a Revolutionary Idea* (New York: Modern Library, 2003), xv.

3. Robert Heilbroner, *The Worldly Philosophers*, 5th ed. (New York: Simon & Schuster, 1980), 22–23.

4. Adam Smith, *The Wealth of Nations* (New York: Modern Library, 1985), 16.

5. Ibid., 223–225.

6. John Stuart Mill, *Principles of Political Economy, Part II (Collected Works of John Stuart Mill*, vol. 3), ed. J. Robson (Toronto: University of Toronto Press, 1965), 766n.

7. As quoted by G. A. Cohen, *History, Labour, and Freedom* (Oxford: Oxford University Press, 1988), 265.

8. Quoted by Joseph E. Stiglitz, "A Fair Deal for the World," *New York Review of Books*, May 23, 2002, 28.

9. Robert Heilbroner, *The Economic Problem* (Englewood Cliffs, N.J.: Prentice Hall, 1972), 725.

10. Ed Diener et al., "Subjective Well-Being: Three Decades of Progress," *Psychological Bulletin* 125, no. 2 (1999): 228; Richard A. Easterlin, "The Economics of Happiness," *Daedalus* (Spring 2004): 31; and Robert H. Frank, "How Not to Buy Happiness," *Daedalus* (Spring 2004): 70. For a different perspective, see "Money Doesn't Buy Happiness. Well, on Second Thought …," *New York Times*, April 16, 2008, C1.

11. "The Next Society: A Survey of the Near Future," *Economist*, November 3, 2001, 16.

12. "Pumped Up," *New Yorker*, June 12, 2006, 56.

13. Joseph E. Stiglitz, *Making Globalization Work* (New York: Norton, 2006), 187–188.

14. Sarah Anderson and John Cavanagh, "The Top 200: The Rise of Corporate Global Power," Institute for Policy Studies (December 2000), available at www.ips-dc.org.

15. "Hear, Hear? Why '07 Should Be Toasted," *Wall Street Journal*, December 24, 2007, C3; "The Year That Made Deal Makers Giddy," *Wall Street Journal*, January 5, 2007, C6.

16. Carson, *Business Issues Today*, 29.

17. "Competition by Proxy," *Forbes*, October 29, 2007, 34. See also "Firms Keep Lobbying as They Get TARP Cash," *Wall Street Journal*, January 23, 2009, A4.

18. Robert B. Reich, *Supercapitalism: The Transformation of Business, Democracy, and Everyday Life* (New York: Knopf, 2007), 135; see also 143–156.

19. Stiglitz, *Making Globalization Work*, 191.

20. David E. Sanger, "Bush Puts Tariffs of as Much as 30% on Steel Imports," *New York Times*, March 6, 2002, A1, and "Rust Never Sleeps," *Economist*, March 9, 2002, 61.

21. "U.S. Steelmakers Draw Fire," *Wall Street Journal*, November 12, 2007, A10.

22. Daniel W. Drezner, "The Outsourcing Bogeyman," *Foreign Affairs* 83, no. 2 (May–June 2004): 33–34.

23. Ibid., 33; Dennis Byrne, "A Bitter Lesson about Sugar," *Chicago Tribune*, January 26, 2004, sec. 1, 11; and George F. Will, "Lethal Quotas," *San Francisco Chronicle*, February 13, 2004, A31.

24. Nicolas Heidorn, "The Enduring Political Illusion of Farm Subsidies," *San Francisco Chronicle*, August 18, 2004, B9.

25. Matthew Miller, "Campaign Rhetoric," *Forbes*, September 6, 2004, 65.

26. "The Cotton Club," *Wall Street Journal*, October 15, 2007, A22. See also "The WTO Whacks the U.S.," *Business Week*, June 16, 2008, 10, which puts the annual subsidy for cotton growers at $3 billion.

27. "Briefing: Food Prices," *Economist*, December 8, 2007, 82; and "Big Oil's Big Stall on Ethanol," *Business Week*, October 1, 2007, 42.

28. Thomas A. Hemphill, "Confronting Corporate Welfare," *Business Horizons* 40 (November–December 1997): 5.

29. Timothy Taylor, "Corporate 'Welfare' Is Tricky," *San Jose Mercury News*, September 21, 1995, 7F.

30. Stephen Moore, "Corporate Welfare Queens," *National Review*, May 19, 1997, 27–28. See also Ralph Nader, "Investments in Corporate Welfare Pay Off," *San Jose Mercury News*, January 7, 1996, 7C.

31. "Public Money in the Pipeline," *Mother Jones* (January–February 2003): 15–16.

32. See Donald L. Barlett and James B. Steele, "How the Little Guy Gets Crunched," *Time*, February 7, 2000, 34–38; Timothy W. Maier, "Business Fares Well with Welfare," *Insight on the News*, December 29, 1997, 12; Hemphill, "Confronting Corporate Welfare"; Moore, "Corporate Welfare Queens"; and "Wish List," *Wall Street Journal*, October 2, 2008, A4.

33. Paulette Olson and Dell Champlin, "Ending Corporate Welfare As We Know It," *Journal of Economic Issues* 32 (September 1998): 759; Donald L. Barlett and James B. Steele, "Corporate Welfare," *Time*, November 9, 1998, 38; and Hemphill, "Confronting Corporate Welfare," 2.

34. "The Unequal Tax Burden on Companies," *Business Week*, May 4, 2009, 50. See also "A Special Report on Offshore Finance," *Economist*, February 24, 2007, 10; "Many Companies Avoided Taxes Even As Profits Soared in Boom," *Wall Street Journal*, April 6, 2004, A1. See also "The Taxman Barely Cometh," *Business Week*, December 3, 2007, 56–58.

35. Howell Raines, "Crude Reporting," *Condé Nast Portfolio*, August 2008, 33.

36. W. Michael Cox, "What Would Adam Smith Say?," *Wall Street Journal*, October 21, 2003, A26.

37. Greg LeRoy, *The Great American Job Scam: Corporate Tax Dodging and the Myth of Job Creation* (San Francisco: Berrett-Koehler, 2005), 2–3.

38. Quoted in "Economic Focus: Competition Is All," *Economist*, December 6, 2003, 70.

39. Alfie Kohn, *No Contest: The Case against Competition* (Boston: Houghton Mifflin, 1986), 46–55. This paragraph and the next are based on chapter 3, "Is Competition More Productive?" Empirical evidence also suggests that promising people large rewards for a task diminishes their performance. See Dan Ariely, "What's the Value of a Big Bonus?," *New York Times*, November 20, 2008, A33.

40. Kohn, *No Contest*, 55.

41. This extract is from *Karl Marx: Early Writings*, translated by T. B. Bottomore, 1963. Used with permission of McGraw-Hill Book Company.

42. Studs Terkel, "How I Am a Worker," in Leonard Silk, ed., *Capitalism: The Moving Target* (New York: Quadrangle, 1974), 68–69. Reprinted by permission of the *New York Times*.

43. "America's Savings Shortfall Is Hurting Its Workers," *Financial Times*, October 21, 2004, 15. See also Gerald F. Seib, "Obama Walks a Fine Line," *Wall Street Journal*, March 31, 2009, A4.

44. "Industrial Metamorphosis," *Economist*, October 1, 2005, 69.

45. For informative discussions, see "How to Tap the Opportunities for Outsourcing," *Financial Times*, August 25, 2004, 7; "A World of Work: A Survey of Outsourcing," *Economist*, November 13, 2004; and "The Future of Outsourcing," *Business Week*, January 30, 2006, 50.

46. Quoted in "The Hollow Corporation," *Business Week*, March 3, 1986.

47. David Friedman, "One-Dimensional Growth," *Atlantic Monthly* (January–February 2003): 110, and "Manufacturers Find Themselves Increasingly in Service Sector," *Wall Street Journal*, February 10, 2003, A2.

48. "America's Savings Shortfall," 15.

49. "Laid-Off Factory Workers Find Jobs Are Drying Up for Good," *Wall Street Journal*, July 21, 2003, A1.

50. "The Tale of Barbie and Li Mei," *Economist*, May 5, 2007, 94.

51. See "Is Your Job Next?," *Business Week*, February 2, 2003, 50–60, and "Where Your Job Is Going," *Fortune*, November 24, 2003, 84–94.

52. "Shaking Up Trade Theory," *Business Week*, December 6, 2004, 118.

53. See ibid.; Paul Craig Roberts, "The Harsh Truth about Outsourcing," *Business Week*, March 22, 2004, 48; Paul Krugman, "Trouble with Trade," *New York Times*, December 28, 2007, A23; and "Economists Rethink Free Trade," *Business Week*, February 11, 2008, 32.

54. Quoted in "Shaking Up Trade Theory," 118. For an advanced discussion, see Paul A. Samuelson, "Where Ricardo and Mill Rebut and Confirm Arguments of Mainstream Economists Supporting Globalization," *Journal of Economic Perspectives* 18, no. 3 (Summer 2004): 135–146. See also William J. Baumol, "Errors in Economics and Their Consequences," *Social Research* 2, no. 1 (Spring 2005): 183–184, 186–192.

55. Sherle R. Schwenninger, "America's 'Suez Moment,'" *Atlantic Monthly* (January–February 2004): 129; "More Tough Questions for Candidates," *Business Week*, October 11, 2004, 40; "Behind Big Drop in Currency: Imbalance in Global Economy," *Wall Street Journal*, December 2, 2004, A1; "Our Faith Based Future," *Atlantic Monthly* (December 2005): 37–38; "Mind the Gap," *Condé Nast Portfolio* (November 2007): 64; "America for Sale," *Fortune*, February 18, 2008, 58; and "Dollar Shift: Chinese Pockets Fill as Americans Emptied Theirs," *New York Times*, December 26, 2008, A1.

56. "Inside the Banks," *Economist*, January 24, 2009, 13, and "When a Flow Becomes a Flood," *Economist*, January 24, 2009, 74–76. On the financial crisis of 2008–9, see John Cassidy, "He Foresaw the End of an Era," *New York Review of Books*, October 23, 2008, 10–16, and Jeff Madrick, "How We Were Ruined and What We Can Do," *New York Review of Books*, February 12, 2009, 15–18.

57. See, for example, Robert Z. Aliber, "The Dollar's Day of Reckoning," *Wilson Quarterly* (Winter 2005); Martin Wolf, "America Is Now on the Comfortable Path to Ruin," *Financial Times*, August 18, 2004, 11; and Nail Ferguson, "Reasons to Worry," *New York Times Magazine*, June 6, 2006.

58. See "America for Sale," 58, and Warren Buffett, "America's Growing Trade Deficit Is Selling the Nation out from under Us," *Fortune*, November 10, 2002, 106–115.

59. "Corporations to the Rescue? Not So Fast," *Wall Street Journal*, July 14, 2004, C1; "Tired of Playing Quarters," *Wall Street Journal*, September 14, 2004, B2; and "Call to End Quarterly Guidance 'Obsession,'" *Financial Times*, July 24, 2006, 1.

60. See "China Steps Up Pressure on Western Rivals," *Financial Times*, October 13, 2004, 5; Adam Segal, "Is America Losing Its Edge?" *Foreign Affairs* (November–December 2004); Thomas Bleha, "Down to the Wire," *Foreign Affairs* (May–June 2005); and "Can America Keep Up?" *Business Week*, March 27, 2006, 48–56.

61. Adrian Slywotsky and Richard Wise, "Resist the Urge to Merge," *Wall Street Journal*, July 16, 2002, B2.

62. Francesco Guerra, "A Need to Reconnect," *Financial Times*, March 13, 2009, 9. See also "Shareholder Value Re-Evaluated," *Financial Times*, March 16, 2009, 8.

63. "Greenspan Issues Hopeful Outlook as Stocks Sink," *Wall Street Journal*, July 17, 2002, A1.

64. "Excerpts from President's Speech," *Wall Street Journal*, July 10, 2002, A8, and Bill Staub, "A Matter of Greed," *Rocky Mountain News*, July 5, 2002, 3B.

65. Majorie Kelly, "Waving Goodbye to the Invisible Hand," *Business Ethics* (March–April 2002): 5.

66. "U.S. Wealth Tied More to Work than Productivity, Report Says," *Wall Street Journal*, July 8, 2004, A2, and "Lazy Ways for Corporate Days," *Financial Times*, August 14–15, 2005, W5.

67. A. Alvarez, "Learning from Las Vegas," *New York Review of Books*, January 11, 1996, 16. See also "America's Bitterness Quotient," *Business Week*, June 16, 2008, 19.

68. Sherwood Ross, "Workers Fearful of Being Laid Off," *San Jose Mercury News*, December 17, 1995, 2PC.

69. *New York Times*, May 14, 1989, sec. 3, 1.

70. *Chicago Tribune*, October 29, 1995, sec. 1, 17.

71. Paul Bernstein, "The Work Ethic That Never Was," *Wharton Magazine* 4 (Spring 1980): 19–25.

72. "Memo from the Editor," *Medical Economics*, November 7, 1988.

73. For more examples and further discussion of occupational licensure, see "Informer," *Forbes*, April 26, 2004, and "The New Unions," *Forbes*, February 25, 2008, 100.

74. See the chapter entitled "Occupational Licensure" in Milton Friedman, *Capitalism and Freedom* (Chicago: University of Chicago Press, 1962), in particular, 149.

75. Atul Gawarde, "Piecework," *New Yorker*, April 4, 2005, 44.

76. "Competition and Cutbacks Hurt Foreign Doctors in U.S.," *New York Times*, November 7, 1995, B15.

77. Ibid.

78. The United Kingdom has about the same number, but Poland has fewer. U.S. Census Bureau, *Statistical Abstract of the United States: 2009* (Washington, D.C.: U.S. Government Printing Office, 2008), Table 1300.

79. Jay Greene, "Now Forecast Is for Shortage of Physicians," *amednews.com*, January 21, 2002; Myrle Croasdale, "Physician Shortage? Push Is on for More Medical Students," *amednews.com*, March 14, 2005. See also Myrle Croasdale, "Study Confirms Shortage of Critical Care Doctors," *amednews.com*, June 19, 2006.

80. Bernard Gert, "Licensing Professions," *Business and Professional Ethics Journal* 1 (Summer 1982): 52; and Donald Weinert, "Commentary," *Business and Professional Ethics Journal* 1 (Summer 1982): 62.

81. This case study is based on Lee Gomes's *Boomtown* column "In Attacking 'Parasite,' Publishers' Lawsuit May Hurt Your Rights," *Wall Street Journal*, July 15, 2002, B1, and "New Battleground over Web Privacy: Ads That Snoop," *Wall Street Journal*, August 27, 2003, A1. See also "Google Toolbar Inserts Links in Others' Sites," *Wall Street Journal*, March 10, 2005, B1; "Why Microsoft May Wade into 'Adware,'" *Wall Street Journal*, July 1, 2005, B1; and "The Plot to Hijack Your Computer," *Business Week*, July 17, 2006, 41–48.

82. This case study is based on "Is Wal-Mart Too Powerful?" *Business Week*, October 6, 2003, 102–110; Simon Head, "Inside the Leviathan," *New York Review of Books*, December 16, 2004, 80–89; Jeffrey Useem, "Should We Admire Wal-Mart?" *Fortune*, March 8, 2004, 118–120; "Wal-Mart Memo Suggests Ways to Cut Employee Benefit Costs," *New York Times*, October 26, 2005, C1; "Wal-Mart Era Wanes among Big Shifts in Retail," *Wall Street Journal*, October 3, 2007, A1; and "Wal-Mart: The New Washington," *New York Times*, February 3, 2008 (online). See also Wal-Mart Watch at www.walmartwatch.com.

83. James W. Sheehy, "New Work Ethic Is Frightening, "*Personnel Journal* (June 1990), is the source of this case.

84. Adam Geller, "Amid the Recession More Employees Are Stealing from Work," *Santa Cruz Sentinel*, March 24, 2002, D1.

CHAPTER 5

1. John McDermott, *Corporate Society: Class, Property, and Contemporary Capitalism* (Boulder, Colo.: Westview, 1991), 4.

2. Anthony J. Parisi, "How Exxon Rules Its Great Empire," *San Francisco Chronicle*, August 5, 1980, 27. See also "Inside the Empire of Exxon the Unloved," *Economist*, March 15, 1994.

3. Quoted in Larry D. Soderquist, Linda O. Smiddy, A. A. Sommer, Jr., and Pat K. Chew, *Corporate Law and Practice*, 2nd ed. (New York: Practicing Law Institute, 1999), 11.

4. Thomas Donaldson, *Corporations and Morality* (Englewood Cliffs, N.J.: Prentice Hall, 1982), 4.

5. David E. Schrader, "The Oddness of Corporate Ownership," *Journal of Social Philosophy* 27 (Fall 1996): 106.

6. Donaldson, *Corporations and Morality*, 5.

7. Ibid., 3.

8. 435 U.S. 765 (1978).

9. "Prosecutor's Dilemma," *Economist*, June 15, 2002, 76.

10. Parisi, "How Exxon Rules," 38.

11. See Kenneth Goodpaster and John B. Matthews, Jr., "Can a Corporation Have a Conscience?" *Harvard Business Review* 60 (January–February 1982): 132–141.

12. Donaldson, *Corporations and Morality*, 10.

13. See Peter A. French, "The Corporation as a Moral Person," *American Philosophical Quarterly* 16 (July 1979): 207–215, and French, "Corporate Moral Agency," in *The Blackwell Encyclopedia of Management*, Vol. 2: *Business Ethics*, 2nd ed., ed. P. H. Werhane and R. E. Freeman (Malden, Mass.: Blackwell, 2005).

14. See Manuel G. Velasquez, "Why Corporations Are Not Morally Responsible for Anything They Do," *Business and Professional Ethics Journal* 2 (Spring 1983), and Velasquez, "Debunking Corporate Moral Responsibility," *Business Ethics Quarterly* 13 (October 2003).

15. Quoted in Goodpaster and Matthews, "Can a Corporation Have a Conscience?" 141.

16. Jeffrey L. Seglin, "A Safer World for Mea Culpas," *New York Times*, March 21, 1999, sec. 3, 4. See also "Mattel Seeks to Placate China with Apology on Toys," *Wall Street Journal*, September 22–23, 2007, A1.

17. Quoted in Clarence C. Walton, *Corporate Social Responsibilities* (Belmont, Calif.: Wadsworth, 1967), 169–170.

18. Quoted in Bernard D. Nossiter, *The Mythmakers: An Essay on Power and Wealth* (Boston: Houghton Mifflin, 1964), 100.

19. Milton Friedman, *Capitalism and Freedom* (Chicago: University of Chicago Press, 1962), 133.

20. Theodore Levitt, "The Dangers of Social Responsibility," *Harvard Business Review* 36 (September–October 1958).

21. Milton Friedman, "The Social Responsibility of Business Is to Increase Its Profits," *New York Times Magazine*, September 13, 1970, 33, 126. For a recent endorsement of Friedman's position, see Henry G. Manne, "Milton Friedman Was Right," *Wall Street Journal*, November 24, 2006, A12.

22. Friedman, "Social Responsibility," 124.

23. Quoted in Robert B. Reich, *Supercapitalism: The Transformation of Business, Democracy, and Everyday Life* (New York: Knopf; 2007), 45.

24. Reprinted from Keith Davis, "Five Propositions for Social Responsibility," *Business Horizons* 18 (June 1975): 20. Copyright © 1975 by the Foundation for the School of Business at Indiana University. Used with permission.

25. John Kay, "Business Leaders Have No Natural Authority," *Financial Times*, April 5, 2005, 17.

26. Robert Kuttner, "The Great American Pension-Fund Robbery," *Business Week*, September 8, 2003, 24.

27. "The Corporate Tax Game," *Business Week*, March 31, 2003, 79–83.

28. Kay, "Business Leaders," 17.

29. Melvin Anshen, "Changing the Social Contract: A Role for Business," *Columbia Journal of World Business* 5, no. 6 (November–December 1970), and Melvin Anshen, *Corporate Strategies for Social Performance* (New York: Free Press, 1980). See also James E. Post, Anne T. Lawrence, and James Weber, *Business and Society: Corporate Strategy, Public Policy, Ethics*, 10th ed. (New York: McGraw-Hill, 2002), 16–17.

30. Anshen, "Changing the Social Contract," 10.

31. Davis, "Five Propositions for Social Responsibility," 22.

32. "Work Week," *Wall Street Journal*, May 21, 1996, A1.

33. Thomas Donaldson, "Defining the Value of Doing Good Business," *Financial Times* (supplement on "Mastering Corporate Governance"), June 3, 2005, 2. See also the Goldman Sachs report (July 2007), "Shaping the New Rules of Competition," prepared for the U.N. Global Compact, available at www.unglobalcompact.org.

34. Friedman, "The Social Responsibility of Business," 122.

35. Ibid.

36. "When Companies Put Shareholders Second," *Financial Times*, February 28, 2005, 10.

37. Adolf A. Berle, Jr., and Gardiner C. Means, *The Modern Corporation and Private Property* (New York: Macmillan, 1932).

38. Quoted in "Design by Committee," *Economist*, June 15, 2002, 71. See also Alan Murray, "Political Capital," *Wall Street Journal*, July 16, 2002, A4, and July 13, 2004, A4; James Surowiecki, "The Financial Page: Board Stiff," *New Yorker*, June 1, 2009 (online); and the references in note 42 below.

39. "Lavish Pay Puts a Bite on Profit," *Wall Street Journal*, January 11, 2006, C1.

40. "Fat Merger Payouts for CEOs," *Business Week*, December 12, 2005, 34; "Lavishly Rewarded Trio Faces an Embarrassing Day," *Wall Street Journal*, February 23–24, 2008, A2; and "A Brighter Spotlight, Yet the Pay Rises," *New York Times*, April 6, 2008, Sunday Business Section, 1.

41. Joann S. Lublin, "How CEOs Retire in Style," *Wall Street Journal*, September 13, 2002, B1. See also Arthur Levitt, Jr., "Money, Money, Money," *Wall Street Journal*, November 22, 2004, A14; "Terminated? Who Cares?," *Wall Street Journal*, April 14, 2008, R4; and "How Some Firms Boost the Boss's Pension," *Wall Street Journal*, January 23, 2009, A1.

42. Louis Lavelle, "How Shareholder Votes Are Legally Rigged," *Business Week*, May 20, 2002, 48; "CEO Elections out of Shareholders' Control," *Financial Times*, August 17, 2004, 8; "No Democracy Please, We're Shareholders," *Economist*, May 1, 2004, 13; "Keeping Shareholders in Their Place," *Economist*, October 13, 2007, 69; "Shareholder Rights and Wrongs," *Economist*, December 1, 2007, 80; and "Rewarding Failure," *Fortune*, April 28, 2008, 22.

43. "Revising a Boardroom Legacy," *New York Times*, September 28, 2007, C5. On the difficulty of firing CEOs, see John Cassidy, "The CEO's New Armor," *Condé Nast Portfolio* (June 2008): 56–59.

44. Quoted in Reich, *Supercapitalism, 75.*

45. "As California Starved for Energy, U.S. Business Had a Feast," *Wall Street Journal,* September 16, 2002, A1, and "How Energy Traders Turned Bonanza into an Epic Bust," *Wall Street Journal,* December 31, 2002, A1. See also "California Restarts Daily Electricity Auction," *Wall Street Journal*, March 30, 2009, A2.

46. "The Corporate Givers," *Business Week,* November 29, 2004, 102–103. See also "Luxury Brands Fail to Make Ethical Grade," *Financial Times,* November 7, 2007, 2; Linda K. Treviño and Katherine A. Nelson, *Managing Business Ethics: Straight Talk about How to Do it Right,* 4th ed. (Hoboken, N.J.: Wiley, 2007), 31; and "Does Being Ethical Pay?," *Wall Street Journal,* May 12, 2008, R4.

47. See Post, Lawrence, and Weber, *Business and Society,* 104–105; "Shares of Corporate Nice Guys Can Finish First," *New York Times, April 27, 2005* (online); Marjorie Kelly, "Holy Grail Found," *Business Ethics* (Winter 2004); and Thomas Donaldson, "Defining the Value of Doing Good Business," *Financial Times* (supplement on "Mastering Corporate Governance"), June 3, 2005, 2. For an accessible theoretical discussion, see Robert K. Frank, "Can Socially Responsible Firms Survive in a Competitive Environment?," in David M. Messick and Ann E. Tenbrunsel, eds., *Codes of Conduct: Behavioral Research into Business Ethics* (New York: Sage, 1996), 86–103.

48. Quoted by John Micklethwait and Adrian Wooldridge, *The Company* (New York: Modern Library, 2003), 182.

49. Robert B. Reich, "How to Avoid These Layoffs," *New York Times*, January 4, 1996, A13. See also Robert B. Reich, "No Obligations," *Condé Nast Portfolio* (January 2008): 39, and Reich, *Supercapitalism*, ch. 5.

50. Reich, *Supercapitalism*, 197–199.

51. "From a Handout to a Hand Up," *Financial Times,* February 3, 2005, 3. For a different example, see "Goldman Launches '10,000 Women' Drive," *Financial Times,* March 6, 2008, 6, and "Goldman's Conspicuous Compassion," *Condé Nast Portfolio* (November 2008): 54–61.

52. Levitt, "The Dangers of Social Responsibility," 44. See also George G. Brenkert, "Private Corporations and

Public Welfare," *Public Affairs Quarterly* 6 (April 1992): 155–168.

53. Davis, "Five Propositions for Social Responsibility," 20.

54. Paul F. Camenisch, "Business Ethics: On Getting to the Heart of the Matter," *Business and Professional Ethics Journal* 1 (Fall 1981).

55. "The Cecil Rhodes of Chocolate-Chip Cookies," *Economist,* May 25, 1996, 74.

56. "Good Citizens of the Community," *Business Ethics* (March–April 2002): 9. See also "The Corporate Donors," *Business Week,* December 1, 2003, 92, and "How Companies Dig Deep," *Business Week,* November 26, 2007, 52.

57. Camenisch, "Business Ethics."

58. See Christopher D. Stone, *Where the Law Ends* (New York: Harper & Row, 1975), ch. 11. For other problems of overreliance on legal rules, see Michael L. Michael, "Business Ethics: The Law of Rules," *Business Ethics Quarterly* 16 (October 2006): 475–504.

59. See note 10 in Chapter 1.

60. Kenneth J. Arrow, "Social Responsibility and Economic Efficiency," *Public Policy* 21 (Summer 1973).

61. Milton Snoeyenbos and Barbara Caley, "Managing Ethics," in Milton Snoeyenbos, Robert Almeder, and James Humber, eds., *Business Ethics,* 3rd ed. (Buffalo, N.Y.: Prometheus, 2001), 143. See also Betsy Stevens, "Corporate Ethical Codes: Effective Instruments for Influencing Behavior," *Journal of Business Ethics* 78, no. 4 (April 2008): 601–609.

62. Snoeyenbos and Caley, "Managing Ethics," 141.

63. Gillian Flynn, "Make Employee Ethics Your Business," *Personnel Journal* (June 1995).

64. "Organisations, Too, Can Be Put on the Couch," *Financial Times,* June 20, 2003, 12.

65. Donald P. Robin and R. Eric Reidenbach, *Business Ethics: Where Profits Meet Value Systems* (Englewood Cliffs, N.J.: Prentice Hall, 1989), 59.

66. Ibid., 59. Robert Audi distinguishes between a company's *ethos,* which he defines as its standards of acceptable behavior, and its *culture,* which includes its ethos, but also its workplace atmosphere, managerial style, and nature of governance. See Robert Audi, *Business Ethics and Ethical Business* (New York: Oxford University Press, 2009), 98–101.

67. "When Something Is Rotten," *Economist,* July 27, 2002, 53.

68. "Donaldson Laments U.S. Chiefs' Lack of Ethical Leadership," *Financial Times,* September 20, 2004, 1.

69. Lynn Sharp Paine, "Managing for Organizational Integrity," *Harvard Business Review* 72 (March–April 1994): 107–108.

70. "Culture at Fannie Mae Led to Fraud," *Financial Times,* February 24, 2006, 17.

71. "Businesses Are Signing Up for Ethics 101," *Business Week,* February 15, 1988, 56. See also "Adding Ethics to the Core Curriculum," *CRO: Corporate Responsibility Officer* (September–October 2007): 43.

72. Sandra Waddock and Neil Smith, "Corporate Responsibility Audits: Doing Well by Doing Good," *Sloan Management Review* 41 (Winter 2000): 75–83.

73. Scot J. Paltrow, "Brokers Who Break the Rules," *Los Angeles Times,* July 1, 1992, A1.

74. "GE to Release Audit of Ethical Violations," *Financial Times,* May 19, 2005, 19.

75. "Businesses Are Signing Up," 56.

76. "Lessons Thomas Still Could Learn," *New York Times,* October 24, 2007, C1.

77. *Economist,* April 8, 1995, 57, and August 19, 1995, 56.

78. This case is based on new stories and commentary in the *Financial Times,* September 8 and 12, 2005, February 23, 2006, and November 7, 2007; in the *New York Times,* September 8 and October 24, 2005, and January 6 and February 9, 2006; in the *Wall Street Journal,* November 7, 2007; and in Reich, *Supercapitalism,* 199. See also "Microsoft in China," *Fortune,* July 23, 2007, 84. For further discussion and analysis, see G. Elijah Dunn and Neil Haddow, "Just Doing Business or Doing Just Business: Google, Microsoft, Yahoo! and the Business of Censoring China's Internet," *Journal of Business Ethics* 79, no. 3 (May 2008): 219–234.

79. The first section of this case study is based on Jeannie Kever, "What Price Layoffs?," *San Francisco Examiner,* November 18, 1990, D1. The second section is based on G. Pascal Zachary, "Exporting Rights," *Wall Street Journal,* July 28, 1994, A1; William Beaver, "Levi's Is Leaving China," *Business Horizon* 38 (March–April 1995): 35–40; Kevin Donaher, "Niketown–Just Don't Do It," *San Francisco Chronicle,* February 20, 1997, A23; Bob Herbert, "Nike's Bad Neighborhood," *New York Times,* June 14, 1996, A29; "Mr. Young Gets It Wrong," *New York Times,* June 27, 1997, A21; and Steven Greenhouse, "Nike Shoe Plant in Vietnam Is Called Unsafe for Workers," *New York Times,* November 8, 1997, A1. The third and fourth sections are based on reports in the *San Francisco Chronicle,* November 12, 1997, April 9, 1998, February 29, 1999, and September 26, 2003; *New York Times,* April 9 and May 13, 1998; and *San Jose Mercury News,* April 9, 2002, and September 26, 2003.

80. For more on this case, see "Just How Far Does First Amendment Protection Go?," *Wall Street Journal,* January 10, 2003, B1; "Suit against Nike Raises Free Speech Questions," *San Jose Mercury News,* April 21, 2003, 1A; "Free Speech or False Advertising?," *Business Week,* April 28, 2003, 69; and Robert J. Samuelson, "The Tax on Free Speech," *Newsweek,* July 24, 2003, 41.

81. Fernando Quintero, "B of A Will Now Fund Boy Scouts," *San Jose Mercury News,* August 19, 1992, B3.

CHAPTER 6

1. Helen Epstein, "Getting Away with Murder," *New York Review of Books,* July 19, 2008, 38, quoting the American Cancer Society.

2. See the Centers for Disease Control and Prevention website, www.cdc.gov/tobacco/issue.htm.

3. "Low-Tar Duplicity," *New York Times,* December 3, 2001, A22. See also "Altria Case Deals Blow to Efforts Reining in Lawsuits," *New York Times,* December 16, 2008, A17.

4. "Philip Morris Readies Global Tobacco Blitz," *Wall Street Journal,* January 29, 2008, A1; "Philip Morris Unbound," *Business Week,* May 4, 2009, 39–42. Cancer will soon be the world's top killer, thanks mostly to smoking in developing countries; see "What's News," *Wall Street Journal,* December 10, 2008, A1.

5. U.S. Census Bureau, *Statistical Abstract of the United States: 2009* (Washington, D.C.: U.S. Government Printing Office, 2008), Table 193. See the Consumer Product Safety Commission's regular reports on toy-related deaths and injuries, at www.cpsc.gov.

6. The Consumer Product Safety Commission reports regularly on electrocutions associated with consumer products. See www.cpsc.gov.

7. "Teenage Shooting Opens a Window on Safety Regulation," *Wall Street Journal,* April 29, 2004, A6. For an interesting example, see "U.S. Probes Off-Road Vehicles after a String of Accidents," *Wall Street Journal,* November 4, 2008, A1.

8. "Worlds Apart on Product Safety," *Wall Street Journal,* September 15, 2004, A19.

9. Ira Sager, "Upfront," *Business Week,* September 15, 2003, 12.

10. "One in Twelve Cars Recalled Last Year," *Wall Street Journal,* March 4, 2004, D1; "Auto Recalls at Annual Record," *San Jose Mercury News,* November 6, 2004, 1C.

11. "Tough New Standards for State's Raw Milk," *San Francisco Chronicle,* October 26, 2007, A1.

12. "Why Blaming Canada Isn't Enough; U.S. Mad Cow Inspections Lack Teeth," *Wall Street Journal,* December 30, 2003, D1; "Varying Standards," *Wall Street Journal,* January 2, 2004, B1; and "Remedy for an Insane Policy— Test All Beef for Mad Cow," *San Francisco Chronicle,* May 14, 2004, B11. See also "U.S. Falls Behind in Tracking Cattle to Control Disease," *Wall Street Journal,* June 21, 2006, A1.

13. "Many Red Flags Preceded a Recall," *New York Times,* October 23, 2007, C1; "Food Safety Officials to Review Procedures after Lapses in Recall of Tainted Beef," *New York Times,* October 5, 2007, A18; "Agency Orders Largest Recall of Ground Beef," *New York Times,* February 18, 2008, A1.

14. "Unapproved Drugs Linger on the Market," *Wall Street Journal,* March 20, 2003, A4. See also "What's Behind an F.D.A. Stamp?," *New York Times,* September 30, 2008, D3.

15. "Grooming Products' Contents Untested," *San Francisco Chronicle,* June 8, 2004, A1.

16. See Michael Specter, "Miracle in a Bottle," *New Yorker,* February 2, 2004; Nathan Vardi, "Poison Pills," *Forbes,* April 19, 2004; and "Study Urges More Oversight of Dietary Items," *New York Times,* March 4, 2009, B3.

17. "Teenage Shooting," A1.

18. "FDA Restricts 'Morning After' Pill," *Wall Street Journal,* May 7, 2004, A3. See also "Drugs, Politics, and the F.D.A.," *New York Times,* August 28, 2005, 1.

19. "Reefer Madness," *Economist,* April 29, 2006, 83.

20. "What's Behind an F.D.A. Stamp?"

21. "FDA Faulted for Scrutiny of Medical-Device Makers," *Wall Street Journal,* January 29, 2008, A2; "Report Criticizes F.D.A. on Device Testing," *New York Times,* January 16, 2009, A15.

22. "Where's the Food Safety Net?," *Business Week,* June 23, 2008, 34. See also "Good Enough to Eat?," *Financial Times,* April 16, 2009, 7.

23. "Behind Flu-Vaccine Shortage: Struggle to Police Drugs Globally," *Wall Street Journal,* November 5, 2004, A1; "U.S. Orders New China Toy Recall," *Wall Street Journal,* November 8, 2007, A3; "Salmonella Outbreak Exposes Food-Safety Flaws," *Wall Street Journal,* July 23, 2008, A2.

24. "Dangerous Sealer Stayed on Shelves after Recall," *New York Times,* October 8, 2007 (online); "Tire Recalls Show Flaws in the System," *Wall Street Journal,* November 7, 2007, D1; "Safety Agency Faces Scrutiny amid Changes," *New York Times,* September 2, 2007 (online).

25. "The Financial Page: Parsing Paulson," *New Yorker,* April 28, 2008, 26.

26. "Where's the Food Safety Net?"

27. "No Limit for Waits on Runways," *New York Times,* September 26, 2007, C1; "From Paradise to Perdition on the Tarmac," *Wall Street Journal,* April 28, 2009, D1.

28. "Toy Makers Seek Standards for U.S. Safety," *New York Times,* September 7, 2007, C1.

29. "In Turnaround, Industries Seek U.S. Regulation," *New York Times,* September 16, 2007 (online); "Retailers Face the Test of Testing," *Wall Street Journal,* November 26, 2007, A6.

30. Dan Oldenburg, "Chrysler's Reversal in Airbag Debate," *San Francisco Chronicle,* August 23, 1989, in "Business Briefing," 9.

31. Quoted by N. Craig Smith, "Arguments for and against Corporate Social Responsibility," in Fritz Allhoff and Anand Vaidya, eds., *Business Ethics, Vol. 1: Ethical Theory, Distributive Justice, and Corporate Social Responsibility* (London: Sage, 2005), 305.

32. "Gains Seen in Redesign of S.U.V.'s," *New York Times,* February 3, 2006, C1.

33. "Dangerous Candies," *San Jose Mercury News,* June 13, 2002, 1A.

34. "Witness Says Police-Vest Maker Ignored Safety Concerns," *Wall Street Journal,* November 15, 2004, C1.

35. "Gun Dealer Is Held Liable in Accident for Not Teaching Customer Safe Use," *Wall Street Journal,* June 6, 1989, B10.

36. Marisa Manley, "Products Liability: You're More Exposed Than You Think," *Harvard Business Review* 65 (September–October 1987): 28–29; "High Court Eases Way to Liability Lawsuits," *Wall Street Journal,* March 5, 2009, A1.

37. "As ATVs Take Off in Sales, Deaths and Injuries Mount," *Wall Street Journal,* February 10, 2004, A1; "Too Close to Nature," *Economist,* August 18, 2007, 27; "Safety Agency Faces Scrutiny."

38. Melvyn A. J. Menezes, "Ethical Issues in Product Policy," in N. Craig Smith and John A. Quelch, eds., *Ethics in Marketing* (Homewood, Ill.: Irwin, 1993), 286.

39. "Child Contracts Reye's Syndrome," *ACLU News* (San Francisco), (July–August 1993): 1.

40. "Safety Agency, Mattel Clash over Disclosures," *Wall Street Journal,* September 4, 2007, A1.

41. Terry Ann Halbert, "The Fire-Safe Cigarette: The Other Tobacco War," *Business and Society Review* 102–103 (1998): 25–26; J. Jennings Moss, "Smoke, but No Fire," at www.abcnews.go.com (January 11, 2000); "State Ponders 'Fire-Safe' Push for Cigarettes," *Denver Post,* July 18, 2004, 1C; and "States Target Cigarette Fire Risks," *USA Today,* May 9, 2006 (online).

42. "Expiration Dates Sought for Tires," *Wall Street Journal,* September 22, 2003, A8, and "Tires Get an Expiration Date," *Wall Street Journal,* May 31, 2005, D1.

43. These are taken from Tad Tuleja, *Beyond the Bottom Line* (New York: Penguin, 1987), 77–78.

44. *New York Times*, March 31, 1999, A16, and *San Francisco Chronicle*, March 31, 1999, A1. See also "A Little Secret about Bottled Water," *Wall Street Journal*, February 11, 2004, D1; "Bottled Water Isn't Always Pure," *Wall Street Journal*, November 2, 2004, D7; and "Some Bottled Water Toxicity Shown to Exceed Law," *San Francisco Chronicle*, October 15, 2008 (online).

45. Smith and Quelch, *Ethics in Marketing*, 337–339.

46. "For First Time, Justices Reject Punitive Awards," *New York Times*, May 21, 1996, C1.

47. Jeffrey H. Birnbaum, "Pricing of Product Is Still an Art, Often Having Little Link to Costs," *Wall Street Journal*, November 25, 1981, sec. 2, 29.

48. Ibid.

49. Ibid. See also Matthew Miller, "Absolute Chaos," *Forbes*, December 13, 2004.

50. "The Discount Cards That Don't Save You Money," *Wall Street Journal*, January 21, 2003, D1.

51. "Markdown Lowdown," *Fortune*, January 12, 2004, 40.

52. Smith and Quelch, *Ethics in Marketing*, 407.

53. "The Great Rebate Runaround," *Business Week*, December 5, 2005, 34–37.

54. "How a Drug Maker Tries to Outwit Generics," *Wall Street Journal*, November 8, 2008, B1.

55. "U.S. Will Not Pursue Price-Fixing Case against Mercedes Dealers," *New York Times*, December 25, 2003 (online).

56. *San Francisco Chronicle*, October 1, 1997, A3.

57. "Supreme Court Lifts Ban on Minimum Retail Pricing," *New York Times*, June 29, 2007, C1.

58. "Discounters, Monitors Face Battle on Minimum Pricing," *Wall Street Journal*, December 4, 2008, A1. See also "State Law Targets 'Minimum Pricing,'" *Wall Street Journal*, April 28, 2009, D1.

59. "Price-Fixing Probe Nets Dairy Giants," *San Jose Mercury News*, May 23, 1993, 8A.

60. *San Francisco Chronicle*, May 9, 1997, A1.

61. "Why Do We Pay More?," *Business Week*, August 11, 2003, 26–27. See also Donald L. Barlett and James B. Steele, "Why We Pay So Much for Drugs," *Time*, February 2, 2004.

62. "What Is Organic?," *New York Times*, November 1, 2005, C1.

63. Melinda Beck, "The Fine Print: What's Really in a Lot of 'Healthy' Foods," *Wall Street Journal*, May 5, 2009, D1.

64. Scot Case, "Not Paint-by-Numbers," *CRO: Corporate Responsibility Officer* (November–December 2007): 52; TerraChoice Environmental Marketing, "The Six Sins of Greenwashing" (November 2007), available at http://www.terrachoice.com; and "'Greenwash' Hype Fails to Sway Sceptical Consumers," *Financial Times*, May 1, 2009, 18.

65. "Let Them Eat Carbs," *Wall Street Journal*, July 26, 2004, B1.

66. Kevin Helliker, "In Natural Foods, a Big Name's No Big Help," *Wall Street Journal*, June 6, 2002, B1. See also "The Organic Myth," *Business Week*, October 16, 2006, 51.

67. "Steakhouse Confidential," *Wall Street Journal*, October 8–9, 2005, P4.

68. Michael J. McCarthy, "Taking the Value out of Value-Sized," *Wall Street Journal*, August 14, 2002, D1.

See also Omprakash K. Gupta and Anna S. Rominger, "Blind Man's Bluff: The Ethics of Quantity Surcharges," *Journal of Business Ethics* 15 (1996):1299–1312.

69. Gupta and Rominger, "Blind Man's Bluff."

70. "L'Occitane Leading the Blind," *Fortune*, November 13, 2006, 55.

71. *New York Times 2008 Almanac* (New York: Penguin, 2007), 357, 358.

72. Roger Draper, "The Faithless Shepherd," *New York Review of Books*, June 26, 1986, 17.

73. Paul Stevens, "Weasel Words: God's Little Helpers," in Paul A. Eschhol, Alfred A. Rosa, and Virginia P. Clark, eds., *Language Awareness* (New York: St. Martin's Press, 1974), 156.

74. Samm Sinclair Baker, *The Permissible Lie* (New York: World, 1968), 16.

75. "FDA's Crackdown Adds a Wrinkle to Marketing of Antiaging Skin Treatments," *Wall Street Journal*, March 14, 2004, B1.

76. For a discussion of puffery and deception in the case of failing banks' having described themselves as "high quality" or "conservative," see "Fury Builds Over Crisis at Banks," *New York Times*, December 12, 2008, B1.

77. Ivan L. Preston, *The Great American Blow-Up: Puffery in Advertising and Selling*, rev. ed. (Madison: University of Wisconsin Press, 1996), 181.

78. Ibid., 24.

79. Wilson Bryan Key, *Subliminal Seduction* (New York: New American Library, 1973), 11. See also Martin Lindstrom, *Buyology: Truth and Lies about Why We Buy* (New York: Doubleday, 2008), especially chapter 4.

80. Preston, *Great American Blow-Up*, 113–123.

81. 302 U.S. 112 (1937).

82. Preston, *Great American Blow-Up*, 122–123.

83. "Reclaiming Childhood," *San Francisco Chronicle*, March 11, 2003, D4, and the National Institute on Media and the Family's "fact sheet," available at www.mediafamily.org.

84. "Hey Kid, Buy This," *Business Week*, June 30, 1997, 63. Except as otherwise noted, the following four paragraphs are based on this article.

85. Lisa J. Moore, "The Littlest Consumers," *San Francisco Chronicle*, January 13, 1991, in "This World," 8.

86. Joel Bakan, *The Corporation* (New York: Free Press, 2004), 119–120.

87. "Hey Kid, Buy This"; "This Is the Car We Want, Mommy," *Wall Street Journal*, November 6, 2007, D1.

88. Wallace S. Snyder, "Ethics in Advertising: The Players, the Rules, the Scorecard," *Business and Professional Ethics Journal* 22 (Spring 2003): 41.

89. "Panel Faults Food Packaging for Kid Obesity," *New York Times*, December 7, 2005, B1.

90. "Kellogg and Viacom to Face Suit over Ads for Children," *New York Times*, January 19, 2006, C3.

91. "Why Kraft Decided to Ban Some Food Ads to Children," *Wall Street Journal*, October 31, 2005, A1. See also "Limiting Ads of Junk Food to Children," *Wall Street Journal*, July 18, 2007, C1.

92. Randall Rothenberg, "Executives Defending Their Craft," *New York Times*, May 22, 1989, C7.

93. Theodore Levitt, "The Morality (?) of Advertising," *Harvard Business Review* 48 (July–August 1970): 84–92.

94. John Kenneth Galbraith, *The Affluent Society*, 3rd ed. (New York: Houghton Mifflin, 1976), 131.

95. John Kenneth Galbraith, *The New Industrial State* (New York: Signet, 1967), 219.

96. John Kenneth Galbraith, *The Economics of Innocent Fraud* (Boston: Houghton Mifflin, 2004), 12.

97. Marcia Angell, "Drug Companies and Doctors: A Story of Corruption," *New York Review of Books*, January 15, 2009, 10–12.

98. See A1 Gini, "Work, Identity, and Self: How We Are Formed by the Work We Do," *Journal of Business Ethics* 17 (May 1998): 711.

99. This case study is based on the *Frontline* program "Breast Implants on Trial," aired on PBS, February 27, 1996. For background details, see Anne T. Lawrence, "Dow Corning and the Silicone Breast Implant Controversy," in John R. Boatright, ed., *Cases in Ethics and the Conduct of Business* (Englewood Cliffs, N.J.: Prentice Hall, 1995).

100. See "Talk of the Town," *New Yorker*, January 11, 1999, 23–24, and *New York Times*, July 11 and November 10, 1998, and June 2, June 29, and December 2, 1999.

101. This case study is based on one in Joseph R. DesJardins and John J. McCall, eds., *Contemporary Issues in Business Ethics*, 4th ed. (Belmont, Calif.: Wadsworth, 2000), 345–346.

102. This case study is based on Diana B. Henriques, "Black Mark for a 'Good Citizen,'" *New York Times*, November 26, 1995, sec. 3, 1.

103. This case study is based on Marcia Angell, "The Truth about the Drug Companies," *New York Review of Books*, July 15, 2004; Gina Kolata, "Companies Facing Ethical Issues as Drugs Are Tested Overseas," *New York Times*, March 5, 2004 (online); and Angell, "The Body Hunters," *New York Review of Books*, October 6, 2005. See also "Drug Testing Goes Overseas," *Fortune*, August 8, 2005; "Drug Company Ethics on Trial in Developing World," *Financial Times*, June 8, 2009, 12; and Angell, "Drug Companies and Doctors."

CHAPTER 7

1. "Hundreds of Coal Ash Dumps Lack Significant Regulation," *New York Times*, January 7, 2009, A1.

2. Martin Rees, "Science: The Coming Century," *New York Review of Books*, November 20, 2008, 42. See also "The Illusion of Clean Coal," *Economist*, March 7, 3009, 20; Scott Martelle, "Killing King Coal," *Sierra* (March–April 2009): 30–37; and "The Dirtiest Fuel," *Sierra* (May–June 2009): 42–42.

3. Silas House, "The Dirt on Coal," *Sierra* (January–February 2009): 40–45.

4. See *Millennium Ecosystem Assessment Synthesis Report* (March 2005), available at www.millenniumassessment. org, and *Global Environment Outlook 4* (September 2007), published by the United Nations Environment Program and available at www.unep.org/publications. See also Eugene Linden, "Critical Condition," *Time* (Special Edition), (April–May 2000): 19, 20. On water shortages in particular, see "Sin Qua Non," *Economist*, April 11, 2009, 59–61.

5. "Flying Blind," *Economist*, February 21, 2009, 10; "A Cosmic Question: How to Get Rid of That Orbiting Space Junk?," *Wall Street Journal*, March 11, 2009, A1.

6. Tom Regan, ed., *Earthbound: Introductory Essays in Environmental Ethics* (New York: Random House, 1984), 3.

7. John Wargo, *Our Children's Toxic Legacy: How Science and Law Fail to Protect Us from Pesticides* (New Haven, Conn.: Yale University Press, 1996). See also "Group Names Most Contaminated Produce," *New York Times*, October 21, 2003, A18, and "Unsafe Food Additives across Asia Feed Fears," *Wall Street Journal*, May 10, 2007, 10.

8. "From *Silent Spring* to Barren Spring?," *Business Week*, March 18, 1996, 42. On endocrine disrupters, see Chris Wood, "NAFTA and the Unmanning of North America," *Miller-McCune* (March–April 2009), 20–23.

9. "Kids Need More Protection from Chemicals," *Los Angeles Times*, January 28, 1999, B9, and "Does It Pay to Buy Organic?," *Business Week*, September 6, 2004, 102.

10. For details, consult "Toxic America," *San Francisco Chronicle*, March 28, 2004, E1. See also Florence Williams, "Toxic Breast Milk?," *New York Times Magazine*, January 9, 2005, 21.

11. *San Jose Mercury News*, October 2, 2005, 2P.

12. "Private Lands," *Sierra* (March–April 2004): 33; *New York Times 2008 Almanac* (New York: Penguin, 2007), 788.

13. "Study Reveals How Much Industry Pollutes the Air," *San Francisco Chronicle*, March 23, 1989, A1; "Toxic Release Increased in 2002, Study Says," *Wall Street Journal*, June 23, 2004.

14. "Major Study Links Smoggy Days to More Deaths in 95 Urban Areas," *San Jose Mercury News*, November 17, 2004, 10A, and "Every Breath You Take," *Sierra* (July–August 2006): 56.

15. "Heavy Smog Cuts Teens' Lung Capacity," *San Francisco Chronicle*, September 9, 2004, A6.

16. "Study Links Soot to Heart Disease," *Wall Street Journal*, December 16, 2003, D7; "Air Pollution a Risk in Heart Disease," *San Francisco Chronicle*, June 2, 2004, A4; and "Study Links Air Pollution, Heart Defects in Newborns," *San Jose Mercury News*, December 31, 2002, 17A.

17. American Lung Association, "State of the Air 2008," available at www.stateoftheair.org.

18. "Report Questions EPA's Progress on Reducing Smog," *Wall Street Journal*, October 24, 2004, A4, and "EPA Says 224 Counties Fail to Meet Soot Levels," *Wall Street Journal*, December 20, 2004, A4.

19. On the 2007 report of the Intergovernmental Panel on Climate Change, see Bill McKibben, "Warning on Warming," *New York Review of Books*, March 15, 2007, 44–45. For further discussion, see Bill McKibben, "Can Anyone Stop It?," *New York Review of Books*, October 11, 2007, 38–40; Freeman Dyson, "The Question of Global Warming," *New York Review of Books*, June 12, 2008, 43–46; "Arctic Melt Unnerves the Experts," *New York Times*, October 2, 2007, D1; "Special Report: Global Warming," *Business Week*, August 16, 2004, 60–69; "The Pentagon's Weather Nightmare," *Fortune*, February 9, 2004, 101–107; and "Cloudy with a Chance of Chaos," *Fortune*, January 23, 2006, 135–145.

On the efforts of industries with profits tied to fossil fuels to debunk the idea of global warming, see "On Climate Issue, Industry Ignored Its Scientists," *New York Times*, April 24, 2009, A1.

20. McKibben, "Warning on Warming," 44; "Carbon Dioxide Hits Record Level in Atmosphere," *San Francisco Chronicle*, March 21, 2004, 84; "Carbon Dioxide Levels Spike," *San Jose Mercury News*, October 23, 2007, 4A; and "Geochemists Chart Carbon-Dioxide Levels at 650,000-Year High," *Wall Street Journal*, December 14, 2007, B1.

21. On disease, see "Feverish Analysis," *Economist*, November 5, 2005, 89. On species extinction, consult J. Alan Pounds and Robert Puschendorf, "Ecology: Clouded Futures," *Nature* 427 (January 8, 2004): 107–109, and Chris D. Thomas et al., "Extinction Risk from Climate Change," *Nature* 427 (January 8, 2004): 145–148. See also "Fewer Creatures Great and Small," *Economist*, October 18, 2008, 68–69.

22. Ken Silverstein, "Meat Factories," *Sierra* (January–February 1999). See also "Group's Surprising Beef with Meat Industry," *San Francisco Chronicle*, April 27, 1999, A1; "Big Farms Making a Mess of U.S. Waters, Cities Say," *New York Times*, February 10, 2002, sec. 1, 20; and "Hogging the Air," *Mother Jones* (July–August 2004): 20.

23. "U.S. Response to Air Pollution at Animal Farms Is Criticized," *Wall Street Journal*, December 18, 2002, B4; "Huge Farm Cesspools Blamed for Noxious Clouds," *San Jose Mercury News*, May 11, 2003, 9A. See also "The Hunt for the Odourless Pig," *Economist*, November 24, 2007, 36.

24. See the report by the OECD's Nuclear Energy Agency, "Chernobyl: Assessment of Radiological and Health Impact 2002," 81–98, available at www.nea.fr.

25. This paragraph is based on "Hunting Habits of Yellowstone Wolves Change Ecological Balance in Park," *New York Times*, October 18, 2005, D3. For a discussion of the effect of global warming on the ecology of Yellowstone, see "In a Warmer Yellowstone Park, a Shifting Environmental Balance," *New York Times*, March 18, 2008, D3.

26. "The Dead Zone," *Economist*, August 24, 2002, 26. See also "Dead Water," *Economist*, May 17, 2008, 97.

27. "*Playboy* Interview: Dr. Paul Ehrlich," *Playboy* (August 1970): 56.

28. John Steinbeck, *America and Americans* (New York: Viking Press, 1966), 127.

29. Garrett Hardin, "The Tragedy of the Commons," *Science* 162 (December 13, 1968): 1243–1248.

30. "Heading for the Final Filet," *Economist*, October 2, 2004, 83. See also "Scientists Warn Fewer Kinds of Fish Are Swimming the Oceans," *New York Times*, July 29, 2005, A6; "Managed to Death," *Economist*, November 1, 2008, 93; and "Troubled Waters: A Special Report on the Sea," *Economist*, January 3, 2009, 10–13.

31. Jonathan Rowe, "Accounting for the Commons," *Business Ethics* (Winter 2003): 4. See also "Yet Another 'Footprint' to Worry about: Water," *Wall Street Journal*, February 17, 2009, A11.

32. William T. Blackstone, "Ethics and Ecology," in William T. Blackstone, ed., *Philosophy and Environmental Crisis* (Athens: University of Georgia Press, 1974).

33. Sharon Begley, "Furry Math? Market Has Failed to Capture the True Value of Nature," *Wall Street Journal*, August 9, 2002, B1. See also "Are You Being Served?," *Economist*, April 23, 2005, 76–78, and Art Jenkins, "Mother Nature's Sum," *Miller-McCune* (October 2008): 44–53. For a critical assessment of ecological economics, see Mark Sagoff, "Locke Was Right: Nature Has Little Economic Value," *Philosophy and Public Policy Quarterly* 25, no. 3 (Summer 2005), 2–11.

34. Begley, "Furry Math?," B1.

35. "Would You Pay More to Let Nature Thrive?," *San Jose Mercury News,* October 4, 1994, 1A. For the doubts of an economist, see Amartya Sen, "The Discipline of Cost-Benefit Analysis," *Journal of Legal Studies* 29 (June 2000): 946–950.

36. On windmills, see "Debate over Wind Power Creates Environmental Rift," *New York Times*, June 6, 2006, A14. On solar power, see "Environmentalists in a Clash of Goals," *New York Times*, March 24, 2009, A17.

37. On windmills, see "In Vermont, a Mine Pits 2 Green Goals against Each Other," *Wall Street Journal,* October 7, 2003, A1.

38. "A Real Energy Boom," *Sierra* (March–April 2006): 13.

39. "Clean-Air Rules Worth It, Says White House Study," *San Jose Mercury News*, September 27, 2003, 7A.

40. "Cleaner Air Has Boosted Life Spans," *Wall Street Journal*, January 22, 2009, A14.

41. Mark Hertsgaard, "A Global Green Deal," *Time* (Special Edition), (April–May 2000): 82–83. See also "Handicapping the Environmental Gold Rush," *Wall Street Journal,* October 29, 2007, R1, and "Rural Renewal," *Mother Jones* (May–June 2008): 54–55.

42. As quoted in Joanna B. Ciulla, Clancy Martin, and Robert C. Solomon, eds., *Honest Work: A Business Ethics Reader* (New York: Oxford University Press, 2007), 483.

43. "Why China Could Blame Its CO2 on West," *Wall Street Journal*, November 12, 2007, A3. See also "Chinese Polluters Point to Western Demand," *Business Week*, April 6, 2009, 76.

44. *Business Horizons* 39 (January–February 1996): 67; *Time* (Special Edition), 87; "Waste Not," *San Francisco Chronicle,* July 9, 2000, "Sunday," 1; and "A Load of Rubbish," *Economist*, February 28, 2009, 16.

45. "The Oil Factor Wanes," *Los Angeles Times*, June 27, 2004, C1; see also "Good News, Bad News on Fuel-Economy Trends," *Wall Street Journal*, October 2, 2007, B12.

46. See David Villano, "A Future of Less," *Miller-McCune* (September 2008): 61, 65.

47. "Would You Pay More?," 1A.

48. Harry Hurt III, "The Toxic Ten," *Condé Nast Portfolio* (March 2008): 144.

49. "U.S. Fines Mine Owner $20 Million for Pollution," *New York Times*, January 18, 2008, A14.

50. "Grime and Punishment," *New Republic*, February 20, 1989, 7.

51. Ibid.

52. Ibid., 8.

53. "Environmental Enemy No. 1," *Economist*, July 6, 2002, 11. See also "Dirty Secret: Coal Plants Could Be Much Cleaner," *New York Times*, May 22, 2005, sec. 3, 1.

54. James Lis and Kenneth Chilton, "Limits of Pollution Prevention," *Society* 30 (March–April 1993): 53.

55. "Political Pressure Keeps Cash Flowing into Ethanol's Tanks," *Financial Times*, October 12, 2008, 6, and Elizabeth Chiles Shelburne, "The Great Disruption," *Atlantic Monthly* (September 2008): 28–29.

56. "How Many Planets? A Survey of the Global Environment," *Economist*, July 6, 2002, 16.

57. "Efforts to Curtail Emissions Gain," *Wall Street Journal*, September 22, 2008, A13.

58. "A Green Future," *Economist*, September 11, 2004, 69, and "Welcome to Kyoto-Land," *Economist*, October 9, 2004, 57. See also Kevin Drum, "Trading Up," *Mother Jones* (March–April 2009): 49–51.

59. Paul Krugman, "The Mercury Scandal," *New York Times*, April 6, 2004 (online). See also "On the Air," *New Yorker*, May 3, 2004, 33, and "Mapping Mercury," *Scientific American* (September 2005): 20–21.

60. Michael J. Sandel, "It's Immoral to Buy the Right to Pollute," *New York Times*, December 15, 1997, A19.

61. Michael E. Porter and Claas van der Linde, "Green and Competitive: Ending the Stalemate," *Harvard Business Review* 73 (September–October 1995): 120, 122, 125; and Hertsgaard, "Global Green Deal."

62. Porter and van der Linde, "Green and Competitive," 125–126, 128–129.

63. See the special supplement "The Business of Green," *New York Times*, May 17, 2006; Amory B. Loving, "More Profit with Less Carbon," *Scientific American* (September 2005): 74–83; "How Going Green Draws Talent, Cuts Costs," *Wall Street Journal*, November 12, 2007, B10; "Where Ecological and Economical Meet," *Wall Street Journal*, November 21, 2007, A2; and "Green and Greed: Can They Get Along?," *Sierra* (January–February 2008): 26–33.

64. "Yes, Global Warming," *International Herald Tribune*, February 2, 1997, 8, and Hertsgaard, "Global Green Deal," 82–83. See also "Eight Great Green Ideas," *Fortune*, April 28, 2008, 116.

65. "How to Kick the Oil Habit," *Fortune*, August 23, 2004, 104; and "The Oil Uproar That Isn't," *New York Times*, July 12, 2005, C7.

66. John Cassidy, "Pump Dreams," *New Yorker*, October 11, 2004, 42.

67. U.S. Census Bureau, *Statistical Abstract of the United States: 2009* (Washington, D.C.: U.S. Government Printing Office, 2008), Table 1336.

68. Joseph E. Stiglitz, *Making Globalization Work* (New York: Norton, 2006), 171. See also "New Lifestyle Option for the Eco-Minded: 'Carbon-Neutral,'" *Wall Street Journal*, May 14, 2004, B1; S. Julio Friedmann and Thomas Homer-Dixon, "Out of the Energy Box," *Foreign Affairs* (November–December 2004): 74; "The Greener Guys," *New York Times*, May 30, 2006, C1; and "8 lbs, 21 Inches, 3,800 Diapers, and 1,525 Tons of Carbon," *Mother Jones* (May–June 2008): 24.

69. "Poor Nations Are Littered with Old PC's, Report Says," *New York Times*, October 24, 2005, C5; "High-Tech Trash," *National Geographic* (January 2008) (online).

70. Mathis Wackernagel et al., "Tracking the Ecological Overshoot of the Human Economy," *Proceedings of the National Academy of Sciences* 99 (June 27, 2002): 9266. See also "UN Warns of Rapid Decay of Environment," *New York Times*, October 26, 2007, A8, and "Study Warns of Gloomy Future for Resources," *Financial Times*, October 26, 2007, 3.

71. Joel Feinberg, "The Rights of Animals and Unborn Generations," in Tom L. Beauchamp and Norman E. Bowie, eds., *Ethical Theory and Business*, 2nd ed. (Englewood Cliffs, N.J.: Prentice Hall, 1983), 435.

72. Derek Parfit, *Reasons and Persons* (New York: Oxford University Press, 1986), 365.

73. Annette Baier, "The Rights of Past and Future Persons," in Joseph R. DesJardins and John J. McCall, eds., *Contemporary Issues in Business Ethics* (Belmont, Calif.: Wadsworth, 1985), 501; and Robert Elliot, "The Rights of Future People," *Journal of Applied Philosophy* 6 (1989).

74. See John Rawls, *A Theory of Justice,* rev. ed. (Cambridge, Mass.: Harvard University Press, 1999), 251–258.

75. William F. Baxter, *People or Penguins: The Case for Optimal Pollution* (New York: Columbia University Press, 1974), ch. 1.

76. Homes Rolston III, "Just Environmental Business," in Tom Regan, ed., *Just Business: New Introductory Essays in Business Ethics* (New York: Random House, 1984), 325.

77. "Switzerland's Green Power Revolution," *Wall Street Journal*, October 10, 2008, A1.

78. Steven M. Meyer, "End of the Wild," *Boston Review* (April–May 2004): 20. See also "Watching the Numbers and Charting the Losses—of Species," *New York Times*, October 15, 2008, A30, and "A Conversation with Stuart L. Pimm," *New York Times*, November 4, 2008, D2.

79. See W. Wayt Gibbs, "On the Termination of Species," *Scientific American* (November 2001).

80. Jeremy Bentham, *An Introduction to the Principles of Morals and Legislation* (1789), ch. 17, sec. 2.

81. Peter Singer, "Animal Liberation," *New York Review of Books,* April 5, 1973.

82. Quoted by Rolston, "Just Environmental Business," 340.

83. Peter Singer, "Animal Liberation at 30," *New York Review of Books*, May 15, 2003, 25.

84. Tom L. Beauchamp, *Case Studies in Business, Society, and Ethics* (Englewood Cliffs, N.J.: Prentice Hall, 1983), 118–119.

85. Bradley S. Miller, "The Dangers of Factory Farming," *Business and Society Review* 65 (Spring 1988): 44; "What Humans Owe to Animals," *Economist*, August 19, 1995, 11.

86. Miller, "Dangers of Factory Farming," 43, 44.

87. Tom Regan, "Ethical Vegetarianism and Commercial Animal Farming," in Richard A. Wasserstrom, ed., *Today's Moral Problems*, 3rd ed. (New York: Macmillan, 1985), 463–464. See also "Also a Part of Creation," *Economist*, August 19, 1995, 19.

88. Jeremy Rifkin, "Hold Your Nose at the Steak House," *International Herald Tribune,* March 25, 1992, 4.

89. Singer, "Animal Liberation at 30," 26. See also Nicholas D. Kristof, "Humanity Even for Nonhumans," *New York Times*, April 9, 2009, A23.

90. "Animal Liberation at 30," 26.

91. "Animal Attraction," *Economist,* February 15, 2003, 75.

92. This case study is based on "At War with a Lead-Smelter," *Economist*, April 6, 2002, 30; "Lead Dust Still Places Herculaneum at Risk," *Columbia Tribune*

(Missouri), February 8, 2007 (online); "EPA Gets Tough on Lead Emissions," *St. Louis Post-Dispatch,* May 2, 2008 (online); "E.P.A. Toughens Standard on Lead Emissions; Change Is the First in 3 Decades," *New York Times,* October 14, 2008, A14; front-page reports on Superfund in the *San Francisco Chronicle,* May 29 and May 30, 1991; Michael Wines, "Waste Dumps Untouched, Survey Says," *Los Angeles Times,* September 7, 1984, I5. See also "www.epa.gov/superfund.

93. See Noel Grove, "Air: An Atmosphere of Uncertainty," *National Geographic* (April 1987).

94. Ibid.

95. The following paragraphs are based on "Let Them Eat Pollution," *Economist,* February 8, 1992, 66; "Pollution and the Poor," *Economist,* February 15, 1992, 18; "Economics Brief: A Greener Bank," *Economist,* May 23, 1992, 79; and "A Great Leap Forward," *Economist,* May 11, 2002. See also "How Green Is Their Growth," *Economist,* January 28, 2008, 57.

96. "U.N. Warns of Climate-Related Setbacks," *New York Times,* November 28, 2007, A6. See also "Where Climate Change Hurts Most," *U.S. News & World Report,* April 2009, 52–53.

97. David R. Wheeler, *Greening Industry* (New York: Oxford University Press, 1999), ch. 5.

98. This case study is based on Donald W. Nauss, "Ford about to Unveil 4 Tons of Controversy," *Los Angeles Times,* March 11, 1999, A1.

99. Margot Roosevelt, "How Green Was My SUV," *Time* (overseas edition), August 14, 2000, 34; "Getting to Green" and "Better Mileage? Lower Emissions? You Can Do It, Detroit," *New York Times,* October 24, 2007 (in "Cars: A Special Supplement"), 1, 14.

100. On Bill Ford, see "Bill Ford on Tipping Points and Thinking Small," *Business Week,* August 11, 2008, 18–20, and Fara Warner, "Losing Focus," *Mother Jones* (November–December 2008): 56–60. On the Cadillac Escalade Hybrid, see "Cadillac's Not-So-Green Golaith," *Wall Street Journal,* December 6–7, 2008, W9. Bill Lutz's remark is quoted by Thomas L. Friedman, "How to Fix a Flat," *New York Times,* November 12, 2008, A27, and by Peter J. Boyer, "The Road Ahead," *New Yorker,* April 27, 2009, 56.

101. The primary source for this case study is Elliot Diringer, "Cutting a Deal on Redwoods," *San Francisco Chronicle,* September 4, 1996, A1. See also "Timber!," *Fortune,* December 12, 2005, 102–106.

102. This update is based on news stories in *San Francisco Chronicle,* March 3, 1999, A1; *New York Times,* March 3, 1999, A1, and March 6, 1999, A7; *Economist,* March 6, 1999, 30; *San Jose Mercury News,* December 8, 2001, 21A; *Wall Street Journal,* June 6, 2008; and *San Francisco Chronicle,* June 7, 2008; and Josh Harrison, "Out of the Woods," *Mother Jones* (November–December 2008): 62–64, 99.

CHAPTER 8

1. "In Factory Sit-In, an Anger Spread Wide," *New York Times,* December 7, 2009 (online).

2. Mike Cassidy, "Serious Materials' Purchase of Chicago Window Factory a Bright Spot in Dismal Economy,"

MercuryNews.com, February 27, 2009 (online); "New Owners Will Reopen Plant in Sit-In," *New York Times,* February 27, 2009, A15.

3. Bruce Barry, "The Cringing and the Craven: Freedom of Expression in, around, and beyond the Workplace," *Business Ethics Quarterly* 17, no. 1 (April 2007): 263 (Gobbell and Cotto cases); David W. Ewing, "Civil Liberties in the Corporation," in Tom L. Beauchamp and Norman E. Bowie, eds., *Ethical Theory and Business,* 2nd ed. (Englewood Cliffs, N.J.: Prentice Hall, 1983), 141 (MacIntire case).

4. Bruce Barry, *Speechless: The Erosion of Free Speech in the American Workplace* (San Francisco: Berrett-Koehler, 2007), 169, 189 (Simonetti and Mosteller cases); "Employers Watching Workers Online Spurs Privacy Debate," *Wall Street Journal,* April 23, 2009, A11 (password-protected websites).

5. Jared Sanberg, "Cubicle Culture," *Wall Street Journal,* May 18, 2005, B1.

6. Ewing, "Civil Liberties," 139–140.

7. *Coppage v. State of Kansas,* 236 U.S. 1 (1915), 1.

8. "Women in Suits," *Economist,* March 2, 2002, 61.

9. Clyde W. Summers, "Protecting All Employees against Unjust Dismissal," *Harvard Business Review* 58 (January–February 1980): 136.

10. Barry, *Speechless,* 57.

11. Stephen Wermiel, "High Court Backs Refusal to Work on Sabbath Day," *Wall Street Journal,* March 30, 1989, B8.

12. "Some Whistle-Blowers Lose Free Speech Protections," *New York Times,* May 31, 2006, A14.

13. Ewing, "Civil Liberties," 148.

14. See Tad Tuleja, *Beyond the Bottom Line* (New York: Penguin, 1987), ch. 5. More recently, Hewlett-Packard implemented tiered pay cuts in order to avoid layoffs. See "Pay Cuts Made Palatable," *Business Week,* May 4, 2009, 87.

15. Barry, *Speechless,* 194–195.

16. "The 100 Best Companies to Work For," *Fortune,* January 23, 2006, 100. See also Jeffrey Pfeffer, "Practices of Successful Organizations: Employment Security," in Joseph R. DesJardins and John J. McCall, eds., *Contemporary Issues in Business Ethics,* 5th ed. (Belmont, Calif.: Wadsworth, 2005); "Happy Workers Are the Best Workers," *Wall Street Journal,* September 6, 2005, A21; and "Rules of Engagement," *Wall Street Journal,* October 1, 2007, R3.

17. Richard W. Stevenson, "Do People and Profits Go Hand in Hand?," *New York Times,* May 9, 1996, C1.

18. "The Work Place 100," *USA Weekend,* January 22–24, 1993, 4.

19. See "Trust in Me," *Economist,* December 16, 1995, 61, and Sue Shellenbarger, "Workers Leave If Firms Don't Stick to Values," *San Francisco Sunday Examiner and Chronicle,* June 27, 1999, CL31.

20. See Marian M. Extejt and William N. Bockanic, "Issues Surrounding the Theories of Negligent Hiring and Failure to Fire," *Business and Professional Ethics Journal* 8 (Winter 1989).

21. "Short Hours, Big Pay and Other Little Lies," *Wall Street Journal,* October 22, 2003, B1.

22. "The Big Squeeze on Workers," *Business Week,* May 13, 2002, 96–97.

23. "High Court Issues Narrow Ruling on ADA's Scope," *Wall Street Journal,* December 3, 2003, A3.

24. Eric Matusewitch, "Language Rules Can Violate Title VII," *Personnel Journal* (October 1990): 100. See also "Firms Can Insist on English," *San Jose Mercury News,* July 17, 1993, 9D, and "English Required Near Slots," *Reno Gazette-Journal,* August 11, 2008 (online).

25. "Why Weight-Discrimination Cases Pose Thorny Legal Tests," *Wall Street Journal,* October 2, 2007, B4.

26. "Instructor Wins Weight-Bias Case," *San Jose Mercury News,* May 7, 2002, 1B.

27. "If You Light Up on Sunday, Don't Come In on Monday," *Business Week,* August 26, 1991, 68–70; "Fight over Hiring Bans Reaches Law Makers," *San Jose Mercury News,* April 28, 1994, 1E; "One Whiff of Smoke and You're Out," *San Francisco Chronicle,* January 25, 1997, D2; and "At Risk from Smoking: Your Job," *Business Week,* April 15, 2002, 12.

28. "Smoke? Then You Can't Be a Deputy," *San Francisco Chronicle,* March 5, 2004, A1; "Companies Get Tough with Smokers, Obese to Trim Costs," *Wall Street Journal,* October 14, 2004, B1.

29. Dean Rotbart, "Father Quit His Job for the Family's Sake; Now Hirers Shun Him," *Wall Street Journal,* April 13, 1981, 1. See also Martha Groves, "Letting Down Their Corporate Shields," *Los Angeles Times,* August 12, 1996, "Business," Part II, 7.

30. 401 U.S. 424 (1971).

31. "Employers Score New Hires," *USA Today,* July 9, 1997, 1B; "Put Applicants' Skills to the Test," *HR Magazine* (January 2000): 75–80; "Job Applicants' First Screener Is … Screen," *San Francisco Chronicle,* May 31, 2004, D3; and "Applicants' Personalities Put to the Test," *Wall Street Journal,* August 26, 2008, D4.

32. Kris Maher, "The Jungle," *Wall Street Journal,* September 28, 2004, B10.

33. Roland Wall, "Discovering Prejudice against the Disabled," *ETC* 44 (Fall 1987): 236.

34. Francis Bacon, *The New Organon* (New York: Bobbs-Merrill, 1960), 48.

35. Kris Maher, "The Jungle," *Wall Street Journal,* December 9, 2003, D6.

36. "Improv at the Interview," *Business Week,* February 3, 2003, 63.

37. "Work Week," *Wall Street Journal,* May 21, 1996, A1. See also Adam Bellow, *In Praise of Nepotism* (New York: Doubleday, 2003), 12.

38. "Family Ties," *San Francisco Chronicle,* April 4, 2004, J1.

39. Ibid.

40. "Disability Act's First Lawsuit," *San Jose Mercury News,* November 8, 1992, 3C.

41. *San Francisco Chronicle,* July 3, 1996, B5.

42. *Santa Cruz Sentinel,* December 27, 1995, B5.

43. "An Alternative to Cocker Spaniels," *Economist,* August 25, 2001, 49.

44. See, for example, "Termination with Dignity," *Business Horizons* 43 (September–October 2000): 4–10, and Jathan W. Janove, "Don't Add Insult to Injury," *HR Magazine* (May 2002): 113–120.

45. John Challenger, "Downsize with Dignity," *Executive Excellence* (March 2002): 17.

46. "Waging War in the Workplace," *Newsweek,* July 19, 1993.

47. "Special Report: Corporate Governance," *Economist,* June 15, 2002, 70.

48. "Employers See Value in Helping Those Laid Off," *Wall Street Journal,* September 24, 2007, B3; "The Three-Minute Manager," *Fortune,* May 26, 2008, 30. See also "You're Fired—But Stay in Touch," *Business Week,* May 4, 2009, 54–55.

49. "Axed Workers Asked to Return Bonuses," *San Jose Mercury News,* November 6, 2001, 1C.

50. For example, Tibor R. Machan and James E. Chester, *A Primer on Business Ethics* (Lanham, Md.: Rowman & Littlefield, 2002), 88.

51. Elizabeth Vallance, *Business Ethics at Work* (Cambridge: Cambridge University Press, 1995), 71.

52. "Garment Industry Turns to Self-Policing," *San Jose Mercury News,* May 6, 1996, 8E. See also "Dress Code," *Economist,* April 19, 1997, 28.

53. "Wal-Mart to Pay $54 Million to Settle Suit over Wages," *New York Times,* December 10, 2008, B7.

54. "Wage Wars," *Business Week,* October 1, 2007, 52–60.

55. For examples, see "Big Labor's Big Chance," *Business Week,* September 8, 2008, 26; "Spa Employees to Share Millions in Gratuity Settlement," *New York Times,* October 24, 2008 A13; and "Economy Complicates Labor Dispute," *New York Times,* December 11, 2008, A24.

56. "Accidental Ageism: Can Innocence Be Any Defense?" *Financial Times,* November 29, 2004, 8.

57. "Shaming Companies into Action?," *USA Today,* June 23, 2005, 3B.

58. "High CEO Pay Can Damage Workers' Morale, Report Says," *San Francisco Examiner,* May 4, 1997, CL11.

59. "Zapping the Little Folks," *Newsweek,* May 26, 1997, 54. More generally, see "Who Profits If the Boss Is Overfed?," *New York Times,* June 20, 1999, sec. 3, 9, and "The CEO's New Armor," *Condé Nast Portfolio* (June 2008): 56–59.

60. Robert H. Frank, "Why Is Cost-Benefit Analysis So Controversial?" *Journal of Legal Studies* 29 (June 2000): 920. See also page 50 of the Goldman Sachs report (July 2007) "Shaping the New Rules of Competition," prepared for the U.N. Global Compact, available at www.unglobalcompact.org.

61. "The Costco Way," *Business Week,* April 12, 2004, 76–77; "How Costco Became the Anti-Wal-Mart," *New York Times,* July 17, 2005, sec. 3, 1; and Wayne F. Cascio, "Decency Means More than 'Always Low Prices': A Comparison of Costco to Wal-Mart's Sam's Club," *Academy of Management Perspectives* 20, no. 3 (August 2006): 26–37. For a related example, see "The Secret Sauce at In-N-Out Burger," *Business Week,* April 20, 2009, 68–69.

62. "Living on the Edge at American Apparel," *Business Week,* June 27, 2005, 88–90.

63. Dave Murphy, "Set Your Own Pay and Hours," *San Francisco Chronicle,* May 15, 2004, C1.

64. See "Voters Weigh Plentiful Jobs vs. Scant Pay," *New York Times,* October 25, 2006, C1, and "For $7.93 an Hour, Crossing the State Line Is Worth It," *New York Times,* January 11, 2007, A1.

65. U.S. Census Bureau, *Statistical Abstract of the United States 2009* (Washington, D.C.: U.S. Government Printing Office, 2008), Table 1343.

66. "Critics Claim Union Clampdown Is Latest Washington Concession to Big Business," *Financial Times,* April 4, 2005, 1. See also "The Rush to Squash a Promising Union Tactic," *Business Week,* August 2, 2004, 87, and "Brothers at Arms," *Economist,* May 14, 2005, 32.

67. "Can This Man Save Labor?," *Business Week,* September 24, 2004, 84.

68. Robert Kuttner, "Labor and Management—Will They Ever Wise Up?," *Business Week,* May 9, 1994, 16.

69. Simon Head, "Inside the Leviathan," *New York Review of Books,* December 16, 2004, 88, and Anthony Bianco, "No Union, Please, We're Wal-Mart," *Business Week,* February 13, 2006, 78–81. See also "How Wal-Mart Keeps Unions at Bay," *Business Week,* October 28, 2002, 96; Karen Olsson, "Up against Wal-Mart," *Mother Jones* (March–April 2003): 54–59; and the Human Rights Watch report "Discounting Rights: Wal-Mart's Violation of U.S. Workers' Right to Freedom of Association" (May 2007), available at http://hrw.org.

70. "Can This Man Save Labor?," 84.

71. "Labor Unions: Context and Crisis," in R. C. Edwards, M. Reich, and T. E. Weisskopf, eds., *The Capitalist System,* 3rd ed. (Englewood Cliffs, N.J.: Prentice Hall, 1986), 165.

72. "In from the Cold?" *Economist,* March 14, 2009, 65–67.

73. Ibid., 66.

74. Thomas Frank, "It's Time to Give Voters the Liberalism They Want," *Wall Street Journal,* November 19, 2008, A19. See also Thomas Frank, "Card Check is Dead," *Wall Street Journal,* April 22, 2009, A13; "One Struggle for a Nurse's Union Awaits the Vote on a Labor Bill," *New York Times,* April 21, 2009, B1; and "A Deal to Organize," *Financial Times,* April 24, 2009, 7.

75. Adam Smith, *An Inquiry into the Nature and Causes of the Wealth of Nations* (New York: Modern Library, 1985), 68.

76. See "The Future of Unions" and "Unions for the Poor," *Economist,* July 1, 1995, 16, 56.

77. Austin Fagothey and Milton A. Gonsalves, *Right and Reason: Ethics in Theory and Practice* (St. Louis: Mosby, 1981), 428–429.

78. Ibid., 429.

79. See chapter 4 of Mary Gibson, *Workers' Rights* (Totowa, N.J.: Rowman & Allanheld, 1983). The film *Norma Rae* portrays the dogged resistance of a company like J. P. Stevens to unionization.

80. Fagothey and Gonsalves, *Right and Reason,* 428–429.

81. "Unions Threaten Huge Bank Withdrawal," *San Jose Mercury News,* April 10, 1996, 1C.

82. This case is based on Willard P. Green, "Pornography at Work," *Business Ethics* (Summer 2003): 19.

83. David Dietz, "The Bottom of the Barrel," *San Francisco Chronicle,* July 7, 1996, in "Sunday," 1.

84. "The Drink of Choice," *Santa Cruz Sentinel,* May 26, 1996, D1.

85. This case is based on "States Mull Gun-Access Laws," *USA Today,* February 8, 2008, 3A. See also "Showdown," *Economist,* July 5, 2008, 38.

CHAPTER 9

1. The facts reported here are from "Privacy," *Newsweek,* March 28, 1988, 61–68.

2. "Don't Pry," *Economist,* October 6, 1990, 18.

3. "How Not to Fix a Leak," *San Jose Mercury News,* October 15, 2006, 1A.

4. Quoted in "Privacy."

5. See Jeffrey L. Seglin, "Too Much Ado about Giving References," *New York Times,* February 21, 1999, sec. 3, 4. See also David W. Arnesen, C. Patrick Fleenor, and Martin Blizinsky, "Name, Rank, and Serial Number? The Dilemma of Reference Checks," *Business Horizons* 41 (July–August 1998): 71–78.

6. "Snooping E-mail by Software Is Now a Workplace Norm," *Wall Street Journal,* March 9, 2005, B1. See also Eilene Zimmerman, "HR Must Know When Employee Surveillance Crosses the Line," *Workforce* (February 2002): 38, and Chauncey M. DePree, Jr., and Rebecca K. Jude, "Who's Reading Your Office E-mail? Is That Legal?," *Strategic Finance* (April 2006): 45–47.

7. "Is Office Voice Mail Private?," *Wall Street Journal,* February 28, 1995, B1.

8. "As Abuse of Sick Leave Continues, Crackdown Raises Issues of Privacy," *New York Times,* November 30, 1992, A1. See also "Shirking Working: The War on Hooky," *Business Week,* November 12, 2007, 72.

9. "On the Road Again, but Now the Boss Is Sitting beside You," *Wall Street Journal,* May 14, 2004, A1.

10. Charles Reich, "The Corporate Control of Big Government," *Business and Society Review* 95 (1996): 61.

11. "Firms Find It Tougher to Dismiss Employees for Off-Duty Conduct," *Wall Street Journal,* March 29, 1988, 31.

12. "Up Front," *Business Week,* August 16, 2004, 10.

13. "How Would You Have Reacted to IBM's E-mail Health Care Plea?" *San Jose Mercury News,* August 27, 1994, 10D.

14. "Enterprise Takes Idea of Dressed for Success to a New Extreme," *Wall Street Journal,* November 20, 2002, B1.

15. *Dollars and Sense* (April 1989): 4; and *San Francisco Examiner,* May 12, 1994, A14.

16. *Dollars and Sense,* 4.

17. "Legal Secretary Fired over Gay Stripper Job," *Santa Cruz Sentinel,* June 7, 1992, A10.

18. Laura P. Hartman, "Technology and Ethics," in Laura P. Hartman, ed., *Perspectives in Business Ethics,* 3rd ed. (New York: McGraw-Hill, 2005), 730–731.

19. Terry L. Leap, "When Can You Fire for Off-Duty Conduct?" *Harvard Business Review* 66 (January–February 1988): 36.

20. See Sue Shellenbarger, "Unpaid Overtime: Coping with Pressure to Volunteer for Company Causes," *Wall Street Journal,* November 20, 2003, D1, which is also the source of the next paragraph.

21. Jared Sandberg, "Your Boss's Obsession Too Often Becomes Your Job Obligation," *Wall Street Journal,* December 11, 2007, B1.

22. "Firms Aim to Trim Fat, Literally," *International Herald Tribune,* June 19, 2003, 12; "Cutting the Fat at Work," *Monterey County Herald,* January 18, 2004, A2; and "Trimming the Fat," *American Way,* January 15, 2004, 80–81.

23. See Scott Campbell, "Better than the Company Gym," *HR Magazine* (June 1995); "Wellness Becomes an Issue in the Workplace," *Santa Cruz Sentinel,* April 28, 2002, D1; and "Seeking Savings, Employers Help Smokers Quit," *New York Times,* October 27, 2007, A1.

24. Greg Jaffe, "Weighty Matters," *San Francisco Examiner,* February 22, 1998, J1; "Companies Get Tough with Smokers, Obese to Trim Costs," *Wall Street Journal,* October 12, 2004, B1; and "Wellness Programs May Face Legal Tests," *Wall Street Journal,* January 16, 2008, D9.

25. "Shape Up—Or Else," *Newsweek,* July 1, 1991, 42; "If You Light Up on Sunday, Don't Come In on Monday," *Business Week,* August 26, 1991, 68–70.

26. "Why Wellness Is Making Employees Feel Sick," *Financial Times,* February 17, 2005, 9.

27. Ibid.

28. "Privacy," 68.

29. See David T. Lykken, "Three Big Lies about the Polygraph," *USA Today,* February 17, 1983, 10A. See also William A. Nowlin and Robert Barbato, "The Truth about Lie Detectors," *Business and Society Review* 66 (Summer 1988); "Scientists Say Lie Detector Doesn't Always Tell Truth," *Wall Street Journal,* October 9, 2002, B1; and "The Polygraph Paradox," *Wall Street Journal,* March 22–23, 2008, A1.

30. Lynn March, "Lie Detectors Are Accurate and Useful," *USA Today,* February 17, 1983, 10A. See also "Polygraph Paradox," A8, and "Ministry of Truth," *Economist,* April 14, 2007, 34.

31. Lykken, "Three Big Lies."

32. Christopher H. Pyle, "These Tests Are Meant to Scare People," *USA Today,* February 17, 1983, 10A.

33. "Making Windows in Men's Souls," *Economist,* July 10, 2004, 71–72.

34. Malcolm Gladwell, "Personality Plus," *New Yorker,* September 20, 2004, 43. See also "Applicants' Personalities Put to the Test," *Wall Street Journal,* August 26, 2008, D4.

35. "Personality Counts," *HR Magazine,* February 2, 2002, 30–31. See also Gladwell, "Personality Plus"; Graham Lawton, "Let's Get Personal," *New Scientist,* September 13, 2003; and Annie Murphy Paul, *The Cult of Personality* (New York: Free Press, 2004).

36. Barbara Ehrenreich, "Two-Tiered Morality," *New York Times,* June 30, 2002, sec. 4, 15.

37. "Trying to Get a Job? Check Yes or No," *New York Times,* November 28, 1997, B1.

38. Ibid.

39. "Privacy," 68. See also Barry A. Friedman and Lisa J. Reed, "Workplace Privacy: Employee Relations and Legal Implications of Monitoring Employee E-mail Use," *Employee Responsibilities and Rights Journal* 19, no. 2 (June 2007): 75–83.

40. See the 2005 and the 2007 "Electronic Monitoring and Surveillance Survey," produced by the American Management Association and the ePolicy Institute, available at www.amanet.org.

41. "US Group Implants Electronic Tags in Workers," *Financial Times,* February 13, 2006, 1.

42. "The Boss May Be Listening," *San Jose Mercury News,* February 25, 1996, 1PC.

43. Jared Sandberg, "Monitoring of Workers Is Boss's Right but Why Not Include the Top Brass?," *Wall Street Journal,* May 18, 2005, B1.

44. "What the Boss Knows about You," *Fortune,* August 9, 1993.

45. See the Human Rights Watch report "Discounting Rights: Wal-Mart's Violation of U.S. Workers' Right to Freedom of Association" (May 2007): 152, 156–158, available at http://hrw.org.

46. "Study May Spur Job-Applicant Drug Screening," *Wall Street Journal,* November 28, 1990, B1.

47. Kris Maher, "The Jungle," *Wall Street Journal,* April 13, 2004, B4.

48. "If You Light Up on Sunday," 68.

49. James T. Wrich, "Beyond Testing: Coping with Drugs at Work," *Harvard Business Review* 66 (January–February 1988); "Drug Testing in the Workplace: Report of the Independent Inquiry into Drug Testing at Work," Joseph Roundtree Foundation (June 2004), available at http://www.jrf.org.uk.

50. William Serrin, "The Wages of Work," *Nation,* January 28, 1991, 80–82.

51. U.S. Census Bureau, *Statistical Abstract of the United States 2009* (Washington, D.C.: U.S. Government Printing Office, 2008), Tables 635, 636, and 639.

52. "OSHA Vows to Make Workplace Safer," *San Jose Mercury News,* April 3, 1994, 1PC.

53. *Statistical Abstract,* Table 635. For a historical perspective, see Cynthia Crossen, "It Was 'Safety First,' but Critics Worried Folks Were Going Soft," *Wall Street Journal,* September 17, 2007, B1.

54. "Job Injuries, Illnesses Cost the U.S. as Much as Heart Disease, Study Says," *San Francisco Chronicle,* July 28, 1997, A5; Paul Leigh, Steven Markowitz, Marianne Fahs, and Phillip J. Landrigan, *Costs of Occupational Injuries and Illnesses* (Ann Arbor: University of Michigan Press, 2000).

55. "Study Finds That U.S. Undercounts Workplace Injuries, Illnesses," *Wall Street Journal,* May 1, 2006, A2; "Injuries May Be Undercounted," *Wall Street Journal,* June 19, 2008, A4.

56. Quoted in John R. Boatright, *Ethics and the Conduct of Business,* 4th ed. (Upper Saddle River, N.J.: Prentice Hall, 2003), 316.

57. *Whirlpool Corporation v. Marshall,* 445 U.S. 1 (1980).

58. "The 'Unrecognized Epidemic,'" *Business Week,* May 2, 2005, 40.

59. Myron I. Peskin and Francis J. McGrath, "Industrial Safety: Who Is Responsible and Who Benefits?," *Business Horizons* 35 (May–June 1992). See also Alan Tidwell, "Ethics, Safety, and Managers," *Business and Professional Ethics Journal* 19 (Fall–Winter 2000).

60. "Worker Dies in a Fall at a Construction Site," *New York Times,* March 19, 2009, A25. For another example of an accident cause by "management decisions and human error," see "Safety Panel Cites Errors in Blast at Chemical Plant," *New York Times,* April 24, 2009, A14.

61. Steven Greenhouse, "Workers Assail Night Lock-ins by Wal-Mart," *New York Times,* January 18, 2004 (online).

62. Beth Rogers, "Creating a Culture of Safety," *HR Magazine* (February 1995): 85. See also James Reason, "Achieving a Safe Culture: Theory and Practice," *Work and Stress* 12 (July–September 1998): 293–306.

63. "Sugar Refinery Suffered Previous Blast," *New York Times,* February 18, 2008, A10; "Mine Owner Has History of Run-Ins on Work Issues," *New York Times,* August 24, 2007, A14; and "Smoke Inhalation Cited in Colorado Deaths," *New York Times,* October 15, 2007, A18.

64. Archie B. Carroll and Ann K. Buchholtz, *Business and Society: Ethics and Stakeholder Management,* 6th ed. (Mason, Ohio: Thomson South-Western, 2006), 552.

65. Susan Podzila, "Safety Starts at the Top," *New York Times,* June 12, 2008, A31.

66. For a discussion of the Golab case, see James F. Brummer, "Excuses and Vindications: An Analysis of the Film Recovery Systems Case," *Business and Professional Ethics Journal* 18 (Spring 1999): 21–46.

67. David Barstow, "U.S. Rarely Seeks Charges for Deaths in Workplace," *New York Times,* December 22, 2003, A1.

68. Ibid.

69. Dana Wilkie, "The Uphill Struggle for Workplace Health," *State Legislatures* 23 (June 2, 1997): 27–32. See also "A Dangerous Business," *Frontline,* January 9, 2003, interview with Charles Jeffress (available at www.pbs.org), and "OSHA Leaves Worker Safety in Hands of Industry," *New York Times,* April 25, 2007 (online).

70. "U.S. Acts to Cut Aches on the Job," *New York Times,* February 20, 1999, A1; Jennifer Powell, "A New Pain in the Neck," *PC/Computing* (April 2000): 44; and "New Ballgame for Repetitive-Stress Ailments," *Wall Street Journal,* April 28, 2002, D-6.

71. David Tuller, "The '90s 'Occupational Epidemic,'" *San Francisco Chronicle,* June 12, 1989, C1.

72. "U.S. Acts to Cut Aches," A8.

73. "Employers Win Ergonomics Duel by Achieving Delay in Guidelines," *Wall Street Journal,* November 3, 2003, A3.

74. See "Fatigue: The Hidden Culprit," *USA Weekend,* January 29–31, 1993, and "Worker Fatigue Can Be Deadly," *San Jose Mercury News,* March 3, 1996. On pilot fatigue and air safety, see "Some Airlines Fight Proposals on Crew Rest," *Wall Street Journal,* January 5, 2009, B1.

75. Dorothy Foltz-Gray, "Sheepless Nights," *American Way,* May 1, 1999, 72.

76. John Schwartz, "Always at Work and Anxious: Employees' Health Is Suffering," *New York Times,* September 5, 2004, sec. 1, 1. Except where noted, this article is the basis also of the next paragraph. For a contrary perspective, see Dan Seligman, "New Crisis—Junk Statistics," *Forbes,* October 18, 2004, 118.

77. Yawen Cheng et al., "Association between Psychosocial Work Characteristics and Health Functioning in American Women," *British Medical Journal* 30 (May 27, 2000): 1432–1436. For an overview of the physical toll that stress can take on many body systems, see Melinda Beck, "Stress So Bad It Hurts—Really," *Wall Street Journal,* March 17, 2009, D1.

78. Thomas Stewart, "Managers Look for the Moral Dimension," *Financial Times,* August 27, 2004, 7.

79. Ibid.

80. Harvey Hornstein, *Brutal Bosses and Their Prey* (New York: Putnam, 1996). See also Jack and Suzy Welch, "An Employee Bill of Rights," *Business Week,* March 16, 2009, 72.

81. Douglas McGregor, *The Human Side of Enterprise* (New York: McGraw-Hill, 1960).

82. "How to Influence Your Boss and Keep Your Friends," *Financial Times,* February 26, 2005, 8.

83. David M. Gordon, *Fat and Mean: The Corporate Squeeze of Working Americans and the Myth of Managerial "Downsizing"* (New York: Free Press, 1996), 43, and

"The Glut of Managers," *Business Week,* March 25, 2002, 26.

84. "The Real Reasons You're Working So Hard," *Business Week,* October 3, 2005, 62.

85. "For Ross Perot, GM Ouster Still Rankles," *International Herald Tribune,* November 19, 1987.

86. *Statistical Abstract of the United States 2009,* Table 580; U.S. Census Bureau, *Statistical Abstract of the United States 2004–5* (Washington, D.C.: U.S. Government Printing Office, 2004), Table 579.

87. For a discussion of the relevant issues, see also Debbie Kaminer, "The Child-Care Crisis and Work-Family Conflict: A Policy Rationale for Federal Legislation," *Berkeley Journal of Employment and Labor Law* 8, no. 2 (2007): 331–373.

88. Michael Skapinger, "Paid Maternity Leave is a Win-Win Formula," *Financial Times,* March 13, 2009, 11.

89. "U.S. Family Leave Trails Other Nations," *Honolulu Star-Bulletin,* June 21, 2004, C1.

90. "The Fight over Family Leave," *Business Week,* June 13, 2005, 62.

91. See Bonnie Harris, "Child Care Comes to Work," *Los Angeles Times,* November 19, 2000, W1, and Sue Shellenberger, "Rules of Engagement," *Wall Street Journal,* October 1, 2007, R3.

92. Sue Shellenberger, "What Makes a Company a Great Place to Work Today," *Wall Street Journal,* October 4, 2007, D1.

93. "Kids Go to School at H-P Work Site," *San Jose Mercury News,* February 10, 1993, 1A; "Companies Providing Schools for Workers' Children," *San Jose Mercury News,* July 28, 1996, 1PC.

94. "Rules of Engagement," R3. See also Sue Shellenbarger, "Perking Up: Some Companies Offer Surprising New Benefits," *Wall Street Journal,* March 18, 2009, D1.

95. "Employers Step Up Efforts to Lure Stay-at-Home Mothers back to Work," *Wall Street Journal,* February 9, 2006, D1.

96. "As Demands on Workers Grow, Groups Push for Paid Family and Sick Leave," *New York Times,* March 6, 2005, sec. 1, 15.

97. Sue Shellenbarger, "A Downside of Taking Family Leave: Getting Fired While You're Gone," *Wall Street Journal,* January 23, 2003, D1. See also "Shirking Working: The War on Hooky," *Business Week,* November 12, 2007, 72–73.

98. See, for example, "Hopping aboard the Daddy Track," *Business Week,* November 8, 2004, 100–101; Hilary Stout, "Fathers Speak Out about Balancing Work and Family," *Wall Street Journal,* May 12, 2005, D4; and "The Next Frontier: Paternity Leave," *Wall Street Journal,* July 8–9, 2006, B1.

99. *Work in America: Report of a Special Task Force to the Secretary of Health, Education, and Welfare* (Cambridge, Mass.: MIT Press, 1972).

100. See "Work Week," *Wall Street Journal,* August 21, 2002, B2; "Poll Gives Workers Morale Boost," *Wall Street Journal,* January 29, 2003, D2; and "Hate Your Job? Join the Club," *Business Week,* October 6, 2003, 40.

101. Michael Skapinker, "Workplace Misery Spells Trouble for Employers Too," *Financial Times,* March 9, 2005, 8.

102. Jared Sandberg, "Cubicle Culture," *Wall Street Journal,* January 28, 2004, B1.

103. But for a critical discussion of the original study, see "Light Work," *Economist*, June 6, 2009, 74.

104. For an accessible discussion of Herzberg's ideas, see J. Michael Syptak, David M. Marsland, and Deborah Ulmer, "Job Satisfaction: Putting Theory into Practice," *Family Practice Management* (October 1999): 26.

105. Michael Skapinker, "Money Can't Make You Happy but Being in a Trusted Team Can," *Financial Times*, June 1, 2005, 8.

106. "Bored to Death at Work—Literally," *Business Week*, July 1, 2002, 16.

107. E. Palmore, "Predicting Longevity: A Follow-Up Controlling for Age," *Gerontologist* 9 (1960): 247–250.

108. Randy Pennington, "Collaborative Labor Relations: The First Line Is the Bottom Line," *Personnel* (March 1989): 78.

109. "A Top-Flight Employee Strategy," *Financial Times*, April 4, 2005, 8.

110. Sharon Cohen, "Management, Unions Join Forces," *San Francisco Examiner*, December 9, 1990, D3.

111. "A Top-Flight Employee Strategy," 8.

112. Cohen, "Management, Unions." See also "Japanese Plants in the U.S. Lose Edge to the Big Three," *International Herald Tribune*, June 17–18, 2000, 14, and "The NUMMI Road to Japan," *San Jose Mercury News*, May 18, 2002, 1C.

113. "BMW's Dream Factory," *Business Week*, October 16, 2006, 70–80.

114. Alan S. Blinder, "Want to Boost Productivity? Try Giving Workers a Say," *Business Week*, April 17, 1989, 10; and "A Firm of Their Own," *Economist*, June 11, 1994, 59. See also "Workers Who Run the Show," *Financial Times*, August 24, 2005, 7.

115. See Roger E. Alcaly, "Reinventing the Corporation," *New York Review of Books*, April 10, 1997, and "Happy Workers Are the Best Workers," *Wall Street Journal*, September 6, 2005, A21.

116. "Special Report: Car Manufacturing," *Economist*, February 23, 2002, 72.

117. 109 *Cal. Rptr.* 665 (1973).

118. Except where noted, this case study is based on "More Employers Attempt to Catch a Thief by Giving Job Applicants 'Honesty' Exams," *Wall Street Journal*, August 3, 1981, 15; "Honest Answers—Postpolygraph," *Personnel* (April 1988): 8; "Job Applicants Would Disappoint Diogenes," *San Francisco Examiner*, December 18, 1988, D15; "Searching for Integrity," *Fortune*, March 8, 1993, 140; "Trying to Get a Job? Check Yes or No," *New York Times*, November 28, 1997, B1; and "Texas Company Settles over Nosy Questions to Employees," *San Francisco Chronicle*, July 8, 2000, A3.

119. Samuel Greengard, "Theft Control Starts with HR Strategies," *Personnel Journal* (April 1993): 81–88; "The Thief on the Payroll," *San Jose Mercury News*, April 14, 1996, 1PC. See also "Taking at the Office Reaches New Heights," *New York Times*, July 12, 2000, C8; "To Catch a Corporate Thief," *Business Week*, February 16, 2009, 52; "Small Businesses Face More Fraud in Downturn," *Wall Street Journal*, February 19, 2009, B5; and "In-House Fraud Cases Surge," *Financial Times*, May 11, 2009, 1.

120. This case study is based on a case reported in Thomas Garrett et al., *Cases in Business Ethics* (Englewood Cliffs, N.J.: Prentice Hall, 1968), 9–10.

121. Peter T. Kilborn, "Who Decides Who Works at Jobs Imperiling Fetuses?" *New York Times*, September 2, 1990, 1, is the main source for this case study.

122. *New York Times*, March 21, 1991, A1. Excerpts from *Automobile Workers v. Johnson Controls* quoted in the following paragraphs are from page A14.

123. Felice N. Schwartz, "Management Women and the New Facts of Life," *Harvard Business Review* 67 (January–February 1989): 65.

124. Ibid., 69. The other quotations in the case study are from Tamar Lewin, "New Look at Working Moms," *San Francisco Chronicle*, March 8, 1989, A1; Barbara Ehrenreich and Deirdre English, "Blowing the Whistle on the 'Mommy Track,'" *Ms.* (July–August 1989): 56 and 58; and "The Mommy Track," *Newsweek*, March 20, 1989, 132.

125. "Primary Sources," *Atlantic Monthly* (November 2004): 58. See also "Men Whose Wives Work Earn Less, Studies Show," *New York Times*, October 11, 1994, A1; and "Marriage's 'Unique Effect,'" *Business Week*, May 13, 2002, 32.

CHAPTER 10

1. See "Nuclear Warriors," *Time*, March 4, 1996, 47–54, from which the details that follow are taken.

2. Ronald Duska, "Whistleblowing and Employee Loyalty," in Tom L. Beauchamp, Norman E. Bowie, and Denis G. Arnold, eds., *Ethical Theory and Business*, 8th ed. (Upper Saddle River, N.J.: Prentice Hall, 2009), 158. For a critical assessment of Duska's argument, see John Corvino, "Loyalty in Business?," *Journal of Business Ethics* 41, nos. 1–2 (November–December 2002): 179–185.

3. John H. Fielder, "Organizational Loyalty," *Business and Professional Ethics Journal* 11 (Spring 1992): 87.

4. Richard T. De George, *Business Ethics*, 6th ed. (Upper Saddle River, N.J.: Prentice Hall, 2006), 412.

5. Fielder, "Organizational Loyalty," 80–84. For further discussion of loyalty to the firm, see the essays by Daniel R. Gilbert, Domènec Mele, George D. Randels, and Brian Schrag in *Business Ethics Quarterly* 11, no. 1 (January 2001): 1–66.

6. Mahzarin R. Banaji et al., "How (Un)Ethical Are You?," *Harvard Business Review* (December 2003): 61.

7. "A Case of Conflicts at Qwest," *Business Week*, April 22, 2002, 37.

8. "Conflict-of-Interest Disclosures May Not Protect the Unsophisticated," *Wall Street Journal*, January 13, 2005, A2, and "Simply Disclosing Funds behind Studies May Not Erase Bias," *Wall Street Journal*, August 4, 2006, A11.

9. "Tech's Kickback Culture," *Business Week*, February 10, 2003, 76.

10. "Loans to Corporate Officers Unlikely to Cease Soon," *Wall Street Journal*, July 2, 2002, A8.

11. Some business analysts use the term *insider trading* in a broad way to refer to any buying or selling of corporate stock or securities by high-ranking members of the

company. If it is not based on material, nonpublic information, such buying or selling does not constitute insider trading as defined in the text and may be perfectly legal.

12. John A. C. Hetherington, "Corporate Social Responsibility, Stockholders, and the Law," *Journal of Contemporary Business* (Winter 1973): 51.

13. "Texas Gulf Ruled to Lack Diligence in Minerals Case," *Wall Street Journal* (Midwest Edition), February 9, 1970, 1.

14. "Supreme Court Upholds S.E.C.'s Theory of Insider Trading," *New York Times,* June 26, 1997, C1.

15. "SEC, Professor Split on Insider Trades," *Wall Street Journal,* March 2, 1984, 8. See also Henry G. Manne, "The Case for Insider Trading," *Wall Street Journal,* March 17, 2003, A14, and Manne, "The Welfare of American Investors," *Wall Street Journal,* June 13, 2006, A14 (with replies to Manne on June 21, A13).

16. See Jennifer Moore, "What Is Really Unethical about Insider Trading?," *Journal of Business Ethics* 9 (March 1990), 171–182.

17. "Lexar Wins Millions in Damages," *San Francisco Chronicle,* March 23, 2005, C1.

18. See "Cookie Cloak and Dagger," *Time,* September 10, 1984, 44.

19. Sissela Bok, *Secrets* (New York: Vintage, 1983), 136.

20. John R. Boatright, *Ethics and the Conduct of Business,* 6th ed. (Upper Saddle River, N.J.: Prentice Hall, 2009), 111–119.

21. "U.S. Probes Hilton over Theft Claims," *Wall Street Journal,* April 22, 2009, B1.

22. "Mattel Wins Ban on MGA over Rights to Bratz Line," *Wall Street Journal,* December 4, 2008, B1.

23. Rory J. O'Connor, "Trade-Secrets Case Casts Chill," *San Jose Mercury News,* March 7, 1993, 1A.

24. See Michael S. Baram, "Trade Secrets: What Price Loyalty?," *Harvard Business Review* 46 (November–December 1968): 66–74.

25. Kris Mahler, "The Jungle," *Wall Street Journal,* June 8, 2004, B4. See also "Watch for Legal Traps When You Quit a Job to Work for a Rival," *Wall Street Journal,* November 6, 2007, B1.

26. Baram, "Trade Secrets."

27. See Robert Audi, *Business Ethics and Ethical Business* (New York: Oxford University Press, 2009), 113–115.

28. Kim Murphy, "Accountant for ZZZZ Best Convicted of Fraud," *Los Angeles Times,* December 20, 1988, II-1.

29. "Prosecutors Link Honda Fraud Cases to U.S. Executives," *New York Times,* March 15, 1994, A1.

30. Bill Shaw, "Foreign Corrupt Practices Act: A Legal and Moral Analysis," *Journal of Business Ethics* 7 (October 1988): 789–790.

31. "Cost of Turning a Blind Eye to Graft," *Financial Times,* April 10, 2008, 12; "Special Report: Bribery and Business," *Economist,* March 2, 2002, 64; and "U.S. Cracks Down on Corporate Bribes," *Wall Street Journal,* May 23, 2009, A1.

32. "Spotlight Lands on Multinationals' Links with Oil-Rich African Nations," *Financial Times,* September 24, 2004, 3.

33. "Decline and Fall of the Freebie," *Financial Times,* April 20, 2005, 8.

34. Norman C. Miller, "U.S. Business Overseas: Back to Bribery?," *Wall Street Journal,* April 30, 1981, 22.

35. Bartley A. Brennan, "The Foreign Corrupt Practices Act Amendments of 1988: 'Death' of a Law," *North Carolina Journal of International Law and Commerce Regulation* 15 (1990): 229–247, and Wesley Cragg and William Woof, "The U.S. Foreign Corrupt Practices Act: A Study of Its Effectiveness," *Business and Society Review* 107 (Spring 2002): 99.

36. "Siemens Ruling Suggests Bribery Spanned Globe," *Wall Street Journal,* November 16, 2007, A1. See also "Bribery Inquiry at Manufacturer MAN," *New York Times,* May 13, 2009, B8.

37. "A Global War against Bribery," *Economist,* January 16, 1999, 22–23, and "The Worm That Never Dies," *Economist,* March 2, 2002, 12.

38. "Tech's Kickback Culture," 75, 77.

39. "Wal-Mart's Lesson for Wall Street," *Wall Street Journal,* December 6, 2006, A2; "New Kmart Code Bans Gifts, Bribes," *San Jose Mercury News,* April 12, 1996, 6C.

40. "8 Former Fidelity Traders to Pay Finds," *New York Times,* December 12, 2008, B4.

41. "Title Insurers Paid Thousands for Lavish Gifts for Referrals," *New York Times,* October 17, 2006, C3.

42. "Speaking Up Gets Biologist into Big Fight," *Wall Street Journal,* November 26, 1980, sec. 2, 25.

43. "A Question of Conscience," *San Francisco Chronicle,* May 14, 2004, C3.

44. "Behind the Vioxx Headlines," *Business Ethics* (Winter 2004): 7.

45. "Question of Conscience," C3.

46. Ronald F. Duska, "Whistleblowing," in R. Edward Freeman and Patricia H. Werhane, eds., *The Blackwell Encyclopedic Dictionary of Business Ethics* (Oxford: Blackwell, 1998), 654.

47. Boatright, *Ethics and the Conduct of Business,* 92.

48. Norman Bowie, *Business Ethics* (Englewood Cliffs, N.J.: Prentice Hall, 1982), 142.

49. "The Whistle-Blowers," *Business Week,* January 13, 2003, 90.

50. "The Night Detective," *Time,* December 30, 2002–January 6, 2003, 45–50. See also "How Three Unlikely Sleuths Discovered Fraud at WorldCom," *Wall Street Journal,* October 30, 2002, A1.

51. Jean Chatzky, "Meet the Whistle-Blower," *Money* (February 2004): 156.

52. Bok, *Secrets,* ch. 14.

53. See Dan Seligman, "Blowing Whistles, Blowing Smoke," *Forbes,* September 6, 1999, and "Whistle-Blower Finds a Finger Pointing Back," *New York Times,* October 25, 2007, A1.

54. "Tobacco Whistle-Blower Acknowledges He's Paid," *New York Times,* May 1, 1996, A12.

55. "Christine Casey: Whistleblower," *Economist,* January 18, 2003, 66.

56. "Peep and Weep," *Economist,* January 12, 2002, 56. See also "Getting More Workers to Whistle," *Business Week,* January 28, 2008, 18.

57. "Peep and Weep," 56. See also, Michael Skapinker, "What Would-Be Whistleblowers Should Know," *Financial Times,* February 17, 2009, 13.

58. "Learning to Love Whistleblowers," *Inc.* (March 2006): 21–23.

59. The facts and quotations about Storms come from Ronald B. Taylor, "Making Waves: Whistle Blower

Keeps Heat on Navy in Revealing Waste of Millions of Dollars," *Los Angeles Times,* June 26, 1984.
60. The discussion that follows is based on news stories in the *Santa Cruz Sentinel,* August 14 and 17, 1993, and the *San Jose Mercury News,* August 17, 1993.
61. This case study was inspired by one in *Across the Board* 36 (January 1999): 45.

CHAPTER 11

1. This and the following five paragraphs are based on Edward Wong, "The Mystery of the Missing Minority Coaches," *New York Times,* January 6, 2002, sec. 4, 5; Mark Purdy, "Riley Seems Right for Stanford, and That's Just the Problem," *San Jose Mercury News,* January 6, 2002, 1D; Ann Killion, "Willingham Kept Dreams Quiet, Then Played His Hand Wisely," *San Jose Mercury News,* January 3, 2002, 1D; "Notre Dame Fires Willingham," http://msn.foxsports.com (November 30, 2004); Jon Wilner, "Why Does Weis Get a Golden Pass?," *San Jose Mercury News,* January 15, 2007, 1D; and "Diversity Everywhere but the Sidelines," *New York Times,* February 20, 2009, A23.
2. "Barack Obama's Speech on Race" (transcript), *New York Times,* March 18, 2009 (online).
3. Manuel G. Velasquez, *Business Ethics,* 6th ed. (Upper Saddle River, N.J.: Prentice Hall, 2006), 307.
4. "A Texas-Size Case of Discrimination?," *Business Week,* March 18, 2002, 14.
5. "Wal-Mart Facing Possibly Huge Suit," *San Jose Mercury News,* September 24, 2003, 3C.
6. "Screening Out Minority Workers," *San Francisco Chronicle,* December 5, 1990, A1.
7. "Restaurant Chain Must Pay $105 Million for Racial Bias," *San Jose Mercury News,* February 5, 1993, 14A.
8. Philip Shenon, "Judge Finds F.B.I. Is Discriminatory," *New York Times,* October 1, 1988, 1.
9. Tom L. Beauchamp and Norman E. Bowie, *Ethical Theory and Business,* 4th ed. (Englewood Cliffs, N.J.: Prentice Hall, 1993), 437.
10. Richard Rothstein, "Must Schools Fail?," *New York Review of Books,* December 2, 2004, 29; "Nearer to Overcoming," *Economist,* May 10, 2008, 34.
11. "Must Schools Fail?," 29; "Race and Red Tape," *Economist,* November 15, 2008, 92.
12. "Must Schools Fail?," 29. See also Dawn D. Bennett-Alexander, "Such Stuff as Dreams Are Made On," in Laura P. Hartman, ed., *Perspectives in Business Ethics,* 3rd ed. (New York: McGraw-Hill, 2005), 385.
13. "Lending Patterns Remain Unequal," *Wall Street Journal,* December 10, 2003, A2; "The Thick Red Line," *Atlantic Monthly* (April 2004): 44; "Black and Hispanic Home Buyers Pay Higher Interest on Mortgages, Study Finds," *New York Times,* June 1, 2006, A20; and "Study Finds Disparities in Mortgages by Race," *New York Times,* October 15, 2007, A20.
14. "Banks Are in Talks about Bias Suits over Auto Loans," *Wall Street Journal,* January 17, 2005, A3, and "GM's Finance Arm Is Close to Settling Racial-Bias Lawsuit," *Wall Street Journal,* January 30, 2004, A1.
15. "Black Staff Fired More, Study Finds," *San Jose Mercury News,* October 20, 1994, C1.
16. "90% of World Lacks Full Rights, U.N. Says," *San Jose Mercury News,* May 16, 1993, 14A.
17. "Disparities Still Abound between Blacks, Whites," *Santa Cruz Sentinel,* March 24, 2004, C1; "Nearer to Overcoming," 33; *New York Times Almanac 2008* (New York: Penguin, 2007), 386, 388.
18. U.S. Census Bureau, *Statistical Abstract of the United States 2009* (Washington, D.C.: U.S. Government Printing Office, 2008), Tables 689, 690.
19. "Wealth Gap Widens in U.S. between Minorities, Whites," *Wall Street Journal,* October 18, 2004, A2. See also "Nearer to Overcoming," 34.
20. "Wealth Gap Widens."
21. *Statistical Abstract,* Table 674. See also "Study Shows Blacks Trail in Income Growth," *New York Times,* November 13, 2007, A2.
22. "Progress without Parity," *Business Week,* July 14, 2003, 102. See also "On Diversity, America Isn't Putting Its Money Where Its Mouth Is," *Wall Street Journal,* February 25, 2008, B1.
23. *Statistical Abstract,* Table 596; *New York Times Almanac,* 339.
24. *Statistical Abstract,* Table 596.
25. "A Diploma's Worth? Ask Her," *New York Times,* May 21, 2008, C1. For slightly different figures, see "On Diversity."
26. "The 'Sex' Effect: Empowering to Some, Trashy to Others," *Wall Street Journal,* May 29, 2008, D1.
27. "A Diploma's Worth."
28. "Women Losing Ground on Pay," *San Jose Mercury News,* January 24, 2002, 1C; and Toddi Gutner, "How to Shrink the Pay Gap," *Business Week,* June 24, 2002, 151. See also "How Corporate America Is Betraying Women," *Fortune,* January 10, 2005, 70.
29. "How Corporate America Is Betraying Women," 69. See also "Sexism," *Condé Nast Portfolio* (April 2008): 92–97, and Judith M. Havemann, "Great Expectations," *Wilson Quarterly* (Summer 2007): 49.
30. *Wards Cove Packing Co., Inc. v. Atonio,* 109 S. Ct. 2115 (1989).
31. This paragraph and the next are based on Andrew Hacker, "Grand Illusion," *New York Review of Books,* June 11, 1998, 28–29.
32. Tamar Lewin, "Sex Bias Found in Awarding of Partnerships at Law Firm," *New York Times,* November 30, 1990, B14.
33. "Judge Orders Partnership in a Bias Case," *Wall Street Journal,* December 5, 1990, B6, and *Price Waterhouse v. Hopkins,* 109 S. Ct. 1775 (1989).
34. Ellen Goodman, "Women Gain a Better Shot at the Top Rungs," *Los Angeles Times,* May 29, 1984, II-45.
35. "How Subtle Bias Keeps Minorities out of the Boardroom," *Financial Times,* October 26, 2005, 13. See also "The Conundrum of the Glass Ceiling," *Economist,* July 23, 2005, 63–65.
36. "Science: Still Few Chances for Women," *Los Angeles Times,* March 7, 1984, 1. See also "An Outsider's View of the Corporate World," *San Francisco Chronicle,* October 27, 1997, B2.
37. "Too Many Women Fall for Stereotypes of Selves, Study Says," *Wall Street Journal,* October 24, 2005, B1.
38. "The Price of Prejudice," *Economist,* January 27, 2009, 77.

39. "Racial Stereotypes Still Persist among Whites, Survey Finds," *San Francisco Chronicle,* January 9, 1991, A10.

40. See Charles M. Blow, "A Nation of Cowards?," *New York Times,* February 21, 2009, A17, and "The Price of Prejudice," 77–78. See also Phillip Atiba Goff, Jennifer L. Eberhardt, Melissa J. Williams, and Matthew Christian Jackson, "Not Yet Human: Implicit Knowledge, Historical Dehumanization, and Contemporary Consequences," *Journal of Personality and Social Psychology* 94, no. 2 (2008): 292–306. For a more skeptical view of bias tests, see John Tierney, "In Bias Test, Shades of Gray," *New York Times,* November 18, 2008, D1.

41. "White Men Can't Help It," *Business Week,* May 15, 2006, 54. See also "The War over Unconscious Bias," *Fortune,* October 15, 2007, 90–102.

42. Edward W. Jones, Jr., "Black Managers: The Dream Deferred," *Harvard Business Review* 64 (May–June 1986): 88.

43. See *Griggs v. Duke Power Co.,* 401 U.S. 424 (1971), and *Wards Cove Packing Co., Inc. v. Atonio,* 109 S. Ct. 2115 (1989) at 2115, in which the Court reiterates that Title VII can be violated by "not only overt discrimination but also practices that are fair in form but discriminatory in practice."

44. "How Corporate America," 70.

45. "Language Rights," *ACLU News* (San Francisco), (March–April 1994): 7, and "But Some Entry-Level Workers Still Face Difficulties," *San Francisco Chronicle,* April 7, 1997, B1.

46. "Diversity Is About to Get More Elusive, Not Less," *Business Week,* July 7, 2003, 31.

47. Ibid.

48. "Business Affirmative on Diversity," *San Jose Mercury News,* August 24, 1995, 3B.

49. "Memo to the Supreme Court: 'Diversity Is Good Business,'" *Business Week,* January 27, 2003, 96.

50. "In Professor's Model, Diversity = Productivity," *New York Times,* January 8, 2008, D2.

51. "Gender Equality: A Solid Business Case at Last," *Financial Times,* October 27, 2007, 11; Roy Douglas Adler, "Profit, Thy Name is … Woman?," *Miller-McCune* (March–April 2009): 32–35.

52. "Casting a Wider Net," *Wall Street Journal,* June 21, 2004, R6; "An Issue That Is Not Black and White," *Financial Times,* February 21, 2005, 7; and "The New Diversity," *Wall Street Journal,* November 14, 2005, R1.

53. Anne Fisher, "How Can You Do Better on Diversity?," *Fortune,* November 15, 2004, 60.

54. Herman Schwartz, "Affirmative Action," in Gertrude Ezorsky, ed., *Moral Rights in the Workplace* (Albany: State University of New York Press, 1987), 276.

55. Peter Kilborn, "Comparable-Worth Pay Plan Creates Unseen Woe for State," *Denver Post,* June 3, 1990, 3A.

56. Velasquez, *Business Ethics,* 338.

57. Caroline E. Mayer, "The Comparable Pay Debate," *Washington Post National Weekly Edition,* August 6, 1984, 9.

58. Ibid.

59. Nina Totenberg, "Why Women Earn Less," *Parade,* June 10, 1984, 5.

60. http://www.eeoc.gov/stats/harass.html; cf. "Women in Suits," *Economist,* March 2, 2002, 60–61.

61. *Meritor Savings Bank v. Vinson,* 477 U.S. 57 (1986); *Harris v. Forklift Systems,* 510 U.S. 17 (1993).

62. *Oncale v. Sundowner Offshore Service,* 523 U.S. 75 (1998).

63. "One-Fifth of Women Are Harassed Sexually," *HR Focus* (April 2002): 2.

64. Mary Jo Shaney, "Perceptions of Harm: The Consent Defense in Sexual Harassment Cases," *Iowa Law Review* 71 (May 1986): 1109.

65. Ibid.

66. Larry May and John C. Hughes, "Sexual Harassment," in Ezorsky, ed., *Moral Rights.*

67. Terry L. Leap and Larry R. Smeltzer, "Racial Remarks in the Workplace: Humor or Harassment?," *Harvard Business Review* 62 (November–December 1984).

68. "Discrimination Has Been Defeated," *Financial Times,* July 25, 2005, 9.

69. *City of Richmond v. J. A. Croson Co.,* 109 S. Ct. 706 (1989).

70. Robert E. Suggs, "Rethinking Minority Business Development Strategies," *Harvard Civil Rights–Civil Liberties Law Review* 25 (Winter 1990); Brent Bowers, "Black Owners Fight Obstacles to Get Orders," *Wall Street Journal,* November 16, 1990, B1.

71. This case study is based on Joan Ryan, "Playing Field Is Still Not Level," *San Francisco Chronicle,* June 13, 1999, "Sunday," 1, and Ann Killion, "Belief That Coach Can't Be Pregnant Outdated," *San Jose Mercury News,* September 17, 2002, 1A.

72. See Shaney, "Perceptions of Harm," for the relevant legal citations and a presentation of the facts of this case.

73. *Meritor Savings Bank v. Vinson,* 106 S. Ct. 2399 (1986).

74. "Gender Diffs," *Wilson Quarterly* (Summer 2004): 10. The impact of good looks is greater for male instructors than for female.

INDEX